# ENCYCLOPEDIA OF FILM NOIR

# ENCYCLOPEDIA OF FILM NOIR

Geoff Mayer and Brian McDonnell

GP

GREENWOOD PRESS
Westport, Connecticut • London

**Library of Congress Cataloging-in-Publication Data**

Mayer, Geoff.
   Encyclopedia of film noir / by Geoff Mayer and Brian McDonnell.
      p. cm.
   Includes bibliographical references and index.
   ISBN-13: 978–0–313–33306–4 (alk. paper)
   ISBN-10: 0–313–33306–8 (alk. paper)
  1. Film noir—Encyclopedias. I. McDonnell, Brian. II. Title.
   PN1995.9.F54M39 2007
   791.43'655–dc22        2007003659

British Library Cataloguing in Publication Data is available.

Library of Congress Catalog Card Number: 2007003659
ISBN-13: 978–0–313–33306–4
ISBN-10: 0–313–33306–8

First published in 2007

Greenwood Press, 88 Post Road West, Westport, CT 06881
An imprint of Greenwood Publishing Group, Inc.
www.greenwood.com

Printed in the United States of America

The paper used in this book complies with the
Permanent Paper Standard issued by the National
Information Standards Organization (Z39.48–1984).

10  9  8  7  6  5  4  3  2  1

# Contents

# List of Films, Actors, and Directors

# Preface: The Problem of Film Noir

Consider the following statements:
From Linda Williams:

> Melodrama is the fundamental mode of popular American moving pictures. It is . . .
> a peculiarly democratic and American form that seeks dramatic revelation of moral
> and emotional truths through a dialectic of pathos and action. It is the foundation of
> the classical Hollywood cinema.[1]

And Steve Neale:

> As a single phenomenon, *noir*, in my view, never existed. That is why no one has
> been able to define it, and why the contours of the larger *noir* canon in particular are
> so imprecise.[2]

Or Alain Silver:

> Questions of phenomenology aside, film history is as clear now about *film noir* as
> ever: it finds its existence as obvious as Borde and Chaumeton did forty years ago. If
> observers of *film noir* agree on anything, it is on the boundaries of the classic period
> which began in 1941 with *The Maltese Falcon* and ends less than a score of years later
> with *Touch of Evil*.[3]

Again, Alain Silver and Elizabeth Ward:

> With the Western, film noir shares the distinction of being an indigenous American form. It is a self-contained reflection of American cultural preoccupations in film form. In short, it is the unique example of a wholly American film style.[4]

Finally, James Naremore:

> If we abandoned the word *noir*, we would have to find another, no less problematic means of organizing what we see.[5]

These statements, each from a respected scholar, highlight the difficulties in discussing film noir. Williams, for example is correct: melodrama, as a form that seeks the dramatic revelation of moral and emotional truths, is the fundamental dramatic mode of Hollywood cinema. The narrative trajectory of mainstream American cinema, as she points out, is ultimately concerned with the "retrieval and staging of virtue through adversity and suffering."[6] However, while most non-noir films produced in the 1940s and 1950s conform to this pattern, film noir does not and its most representative examples refuse to unequivocally endorse the prevailing moral norms. For example, *Criss Cross*, Robert Siodmak's 1949 film for Universal Studios starring Burt Lancaster as Steve Thompson: Thompson is virtuous and innocent. He is also selfish, obsessive, morally weak, covetous of another man's wife, and vulnerable; his demise at the end of the film is humiliating. Yet, like most Hollywood films, he is the audience's entry point into the film as the director is careful to bind the viewer into Thompson's experience through a protracted series of point of view shots. Thompson is, in effect, both good and bad and the film's moral stance is compromised as a result. This pattern is evident in many noir films.

A more compelling problem, as seen in the conflicting views offered above by Steve Neale and Alain Silver, involves the intrinsic questions of what film noir is and what its historical parameters are. Containing film noir to one or two neat periods—such as 1939 to 1958, or 1981 to the present—and to assume that films produced during these periods share a rigid set of common characteristics is difficult. It is a much more volatile mode than this. Similarly, this volume shows that film noir is not a unique American form and that other film cultures, such as the British, have a strong legacy of noir films.[7] *The Encyclopedia of Film Noir* celebrates the vitality and depth of British film noir through an extensive selection of representative films.

Furthermore, *The Encyclopedia of Film Noir* does not limit itself to the large budget films produced by major studios, such as Paramount and Warner Brothers; we have tried to include a representative selection of low budget films produced by so-called Poverty Row studios, such as Republic, Monogram, PRC, and Film Classics. While the significance of seminal noir films is emphasized throughout the book, we also acknowledge the importance of many low budget films to the experiences of filmgoers. Many low-budget noir films have disappeared from film history. Large films like *Double Indemnity*, for example, benefited from Paramount's extensive financial resources and its large network of theatres situated in prime locations throughout the United States, as well as efficient distribution overseas. The availability of films such as this, and the frequent scholarly analysis of them for the past forty years, has resulted in a biased history of film noir. Low budget films, on the other hand, often had to fend for themselves with little promotion and sporadic distribution. This meant that films such as *Decoy* (Monogram, 1946), *Blonde Ice* (Film Classics, 1948), and *The Great Flamarion* (Republic, 1945), disappeared under the critical radar and are absent from many studies of film noir. Hence, this volume not only provides an entry on *Double Indemnity* but also PRC's *Apology for Murder* (1945), starring Ann Savage, Hugh Beaumont, and Charles D. Hicks, in the roles played by Barbara Stanwyck, Fred MacMurray, and Edward G. Robinson in Billy Wilder's film. Both films were based on the same real-life incident—the 1927 murder of Albert Gray by his wife and her lover—which, in turn, inspired James M. Cain's novella. Similarly, less obscure low budget films, such as *Detour* (1945), which was filmed in days (as opposed to weeks or months) on a miniscule budget, and *Gun Crazy* (1950), which had a slightly higher budget but extensive distribution problems, are included alongside films produced by the major studios, as these Poverty Row productions are as important, if not more so, in providing an authentic representation of film noir in the 1940s and 1950s.

*The Encyclopedia of Film Noir* is designed to provide an accessible yet scholarly, user-friendly but research-informed, comprehensive account of the phenomenon of film noir—both the *classical* film noir cycle (approximately 1939–1959) as well the modern, or *neo-noir*, period, which constitutes films produced after 1959. The encyclopedia presents this survey of film noir in two main ways. First, it offers five substantial overview essays in which the authors investigate significant aspects of film noir and the various contexts within which it developed. These essays explore the contested nature of noir, as evidenced above in the radically different position taken by Neale and Silver; in the vexed question of whether it can considered a film genre; in its relationship to hard-boiled crime fiction; in its iconic presentation of the American city; in political and cultural influences associated with the post-war and Cold War periods (including the activities of the House Committee on Un-American Activities); and in film noir's distinctive visual style.

Thereafter, the encyclopedia presents an alphabetically organized set of detailed entries on the films together with significant American and British directors and actors associated with film noir. Each actor or director entry contains a selected filmography that is designed to be inclusive, rather than exclusive, and many so-called borderline noir films are listed alongside more familiar ones. Similarly, each film entry provides details on cast, characters, and filmmakers together with a contextual overview and critique of its themes, narrative structure, and relevance.

The selected bibliography has been compiled as a guide to help the reader find specific books on specialized aspects of film noir. We tried to cater to both the novice reader—who requires an introduction to film noir—as well as to the more experienced noir devotee seeking to extend his or her knowledge of this fascinating period in film history. Each reader, we assume, is interested in the anarchic spirit of film noir and this volume is designed to satisfy this demand.

## NOTES

1. Linda Williams, "Melodrama Revised" in Nick Browne (ed.), *Refiguring American Film Genres*. Los Angeles, University of California Press, 1998, p. 42.

2. Steve Neale, *Genre and Hollywood*. London, Routledge, 2000, pp. 173–174.

3. Alain Silver and James Ursini (eds.), *Film Noir Reader*. New York, Limelight Edition, p. 11.

4. Alain Silver and Elizabeth Ward, *Film Noir: An Encyclopedic Reference to the American Style*. New York, The Overlook Press, 1992, p. 1.

5. James Naremore, *More Than Night: Film Noir in its Contexts*. Los Angeles, University of California Press, 1998, p. 276.

6. See Linda Williams, *Playing the Race Card: Melodramas of Black and White From Uncle Tom to O.J. Simpson*. Princeton, Princeton University Press, 2001, p. 15.

7. See, for example with regard to the British cinema, Robert Murphy, *Realism and Tinsel: Cinema and Society in Britain 1939–1949*. London, Routledge, 1989; Andrew Spicer, *Film Noir*. Harlow, Pearson Education Limited, 2002; Geoff Mayer, *Roy Ward Baker*. Manchester, Manchester University Press, 2004.

# PART I

# ESSAYS

# Introduction:
# Readings on Film Noir

Geoff Mayer

## THE FILM NOIR MYTH

Film noir is more than just 1940s and 1950s crime films infused with a higher quotient of sex and violence than their 1930s counterparts. There is, however, as Andrew Spicer (2002, vii) argues, a prevailing noir myth that "film noir is quintessentially those black and white 1940s films, bathed in deep shadows, which offered a 'dark mirror' to American society and questioned the fundamental optimism of the American dream." There is, of course, some truth contained in this so-called mythology, although it is more complex than this. Film noir is both a discursive construction created retrospectively by critics and scholars in the period after the first wave of noir films (1940–1959) had finished, and also a cultural phenomenon that challenged, to varying degrees, the dominant values and formal patterns of pre-1940 cinema.

Within this mythology, there is generally agreement as to the influences that shaped film noir and provided its parameters. For example, most studies followed the lead of the French critics in the 1940s and pointed to the importance of the pulp stories and hard-boiled fiction of writers such as Dashiell Hammett, Raymond Chandler, James M. Cain, and Cornell Woolrich. Later, other writers, such as W. R. Burnett and David Goodis, were added to this list. Often this took place because the novels and short stories from these writers were used as bases for a number of key noir films in the 1940s—notably Hammett's *The Maltese Falcon* (1941) and *The Glass Key* (1942); Woolrich's *The Black Curtain* (1941, which was filmed as *Street of Chance* in 1942), *Phantom Lady* (1944), and *The Black Angel*

(1946); Cain's *Double Indemnity* (1944), *Mildred Pierce* (1945), and *The Postman Always Rings Twice* (1946); Burnett's *High Sierra* (1941); and Goodis's *Dark Passage* (1947). However, it was not as simple as this, and it is not entirely correct, as discussed later, to assume that the dark, nihilistic vision expressed by many of these novelists was merely replicated in the film versions.

A significant aspect of the film noir myth is its formal style, especially the chiaroscuro lighting with its low key and frontal lighting setups that produced dark areas interspersed by extreme brightness. This style, which was largely the result of restricting the use of fill lights, thereby accentuating the harsh effect of the key light, was often associated with the influence of German expressionism on film noir. This visual style, reinforced by the fragmentation of space through set design and camera compositions that produced unstable lines and surfaces, was perceived as suggesting a dislocated world permeated by alienation and human despair.

These tendencies found in German expressionism were, it was argued, imported into Hollywood by German émigrés who had fled Germany after Hitler assumed power in 1933. This included directors such as Fritz Lang (*The Woman in the Window*, 1945), Otto Preminger (*Fallen Angel*, 1946), Billy Wilder (*Double Indemnity*, 1944), and Robert Siodmak (*Criss Cross*, 1949) as well as German-born cinematographers such as Karl Freund, Rudolph Maté, John Alton, and Theodore Sparkuhl. Again, the significance of film noir style and the role of the German émigrés is not as simple as some studies suggest. German expressionism peaked almost 20 years before the proliferation of film noir in Hollywood, and these German émigrés worked on many Hollywood films that had no relevance to film noir. Also, there were many noir films produced in Hollywood in the 1940s that did not have German filmmakers working on them.

## WHAT IS FILM NOIR?

Prolific American writers Alain Silver and James Ursini ask in their book *Film Noir*, What is noir? Their answer includes a familiar list of themes, archetypes, and influences. They cite, for example, Dashiell Hammett and the "hard-boiled school of detective fiction" as well as "existentialism and Freudian psychology" because "these theories helped promote a worldview that stressed the absurdity of existence along with the importance of an individual's past in determining his or her actions. . . . Two of the most important themes of the noir movement, 'the haunted past' and 'the fatalistic nightmare,' draw directly from these two sources" (Silver and Ursini 2004, 15).

They also argue that the 1941 version of *The Maltese Falcon* was the "first noir adaptation of writer Dashiell Hammett's work, starring Humphrey Bogart, and the 'official' beginning of the noir movement or classic period" (p. 187). The aim of their book is to condense and catalogue accepted explanations and evaluations in the development of film noir. It is often assumed, for example, that because Hammett's novels were the basis for the 1941 version of *The Maltese Falcon* and the

1942 version of *The Glass Key*, his cynical view of the world provided, at least in part, the philosophical basis for noir in general and for these two films in particular. Second, it is also assumed that his so-called noir sensibility is not found in the 1931 version of *The Maltese Falcon* or the 1935 version of *The Glass Key*.

Does this mean that film noir did not begin until 1941? No, but there are significant differences between the 1930s and 1940s versions in terms of style, motivation, and the intensity of the despair and psychological turmoil experienced by protagonists in the 1940s. This delineation between the 1930s and 1940s brings us back to the question, What is film noir? Silver and Ursini (2004) address this issue by dividing noir into separate formal, thematic, and philosophical elements. Out of this, they argue, a movement called "film noir" emerged with the 1941 version of *The Maltese Falcon*, as discussed previously. However, as Steve Neale (2000, 173) argues, as "a single phenomenon, noir . . . never existed." Many of its so-called characteristic features, such as the use of voice-over and flashback, the use of high-contrast lighting and other expressionist elements, the downbeat endings, and the culture of distrust between men and women, which often manifested itself in the figure of the femme fatale, are "separable features belonging to separable tendencies and trends that traversed a wide variety of genres and cycles in the 1940s and early 1950s" (p. 174). Neale (2000, 174) concludes that

> [any] attempt to treat these tendencies and trends as a single phenomenon, to homogenise them under a single heading, "*film noir*," is therefore bound to lead to incoherence, imprecision, and inconsistency—in the provision of the criteria, in the construction of a corpus, or in almost any interpretation of their contemporary sociocultural significance.

Film noir, as we know, is unlike other studies of Hollywood genres or cycles as it was not formed out of the usual sources such as contemporary studio documents. It is, in essence, a discursive critical construction that has evolved over time. However, despite its imprecise parameters and poorly defined sources, it is, as James Naremore (1998, 176) points out, a necessary intellectual category, for if "we abandoned the word *noir* we would need to find another, no less problematic, means of organizing what we see." The contemporary term used by reviewers to describe films now classified as noir was *melodrama*—as Steve Neale (1993) points out in his intensive survey of American trade journals from 1938 to 1960, nearly every film noir was labeled or described in the trade press as some kind of melodrama. This included key films such as *The Maltese Falcon* (1941), *This Gun for Hire*, *Phantom Lady*, *The Postman Always Rings Twice*, *The Killers*, *Scarlet Street*, *Detour*, *Gilda*, *Raw Deal*, *Out of the Past*, and many other detective, gothic, gangster, or horror films enveloped by the noir label.

The reviewers, in an attempt to signify that these films were somehow different from other Hollywood melodramas, often attached the terms *psychological*, *psychiatric*, or even *neurotic* to the *melodrama*—this included films as diverse as

*White Heat*, *This Gun for Hire*, *My Name Is Julia Ross*, *The Gangster*, *High Wall*, *Secret Beyond the Door*, and *On Dangerous Ground*. These labels indicated a shift in dramatic emphasis. No longer was the focus only on external obstacles confronting the hero or heroine, a characteristic of simple melodrama, but also the internal conflict *within* the protagonist. Thus film noir went beyond presenting the drama as a simple or unequivocal conflict between good and evil. Instead, they shifted the dramatic focus to the "psychological" conflict that emanated from an ambivalent presentation of moral norms.

This tendency was recognized by French writers Raymond Borde and Etienne Chaumeton (1966) in the first book-length study of film noir. Courage and heroism were often superseded by doubt, despair, and vulnerability. While this did not render the traditional melodramatic quest for moral legibility irrelevant, and it did not mean, as some have suggested, its replacement by an ethically irrational universe, it did represent a shift in (some) Hollywood films in the 1940s. Unlike novelists such as Dashiell Hammett and Cornell Woolrich, the films were ultimately reluctant to abandon all hope of a moral world and rational universe.

A change in the Hollywood crime film was noted by French critics such as Nino Frank and Jean-Pierre Chartier, who, in the summer of 1946, were exposed to a sudden influx of Hollywood films that were not available in France during the German occupation. Frank (1999), who coined the term *film noir*, or more precisely, "*films, 'noirs,'*" argued that films such as *The Maltese Falcon, Murder My Sweet, Laura*, and *Double Indemnity* presented a different moral sensibility than so-called museum pieces such as *The Letter* (1940) and *How Green Was My Valley* (1941). In a similar, if less spectacular, manner, Hammett scholar and professor of English and comparative literature at Columbia University Steven Marcus (1975, 12) described the effect that John Huston's 1941 version of *The Maltese Falcon* had on him when he first viewed it as a 12-year-old:

> What was striking about the event was that it was one of the first encounters I can consciously recall with the experience of moral ambiguity. Here was this detective you were supposed to like—and did like—behaving and speaking in peculiar and un-expected ways. He acted up to the cops, partly for real, partly as a ruse. He connived with crooks, for his own ends and perhaps even for some of theirs. He slept with his partner's wife, fell in love with a lady crook, and then refused to save her from the police, even though he could have. Which side was he on? Was he on any side apart from his own? And which or what side was that? The experience was not only mor-ally ambiguous; it was morally complex and enigmatic as well.

*Double Indemnity* also had a similar effect on Jean-Pierre Chartier in Paris in 1946, although he was much less complimentary than Marcus when he wrote that "it's hard to imagine story lines with a more pessimistic or disgusted point of view regarding human behaviour" (Chartier 1999, 21).

## NOIR IN LITERATURE AND FILM:
## THREE CASE STUDIES

Film noir is difficult to describe, let alone define. Most studies cite the 1941 version of *The Maltese Falcon* as the first major film noir, although there is some support for RKO's low-budget *Stranger on the Third Floor*, which was released in 1940. However, *The Maltese Falcon* occupies a key place in the canon of film noir. The fact that it was based on Dashiell Hammett's novel, a point emphasized by Nino Frank in 1946, established an early association between film noir and American hard-boiled fiction. The 1941 film, however, was not the first version of Hammett's 1930 novel. In 1931, Warner Bros. released a version that was closely based on Hammett's story and starred Ricardo Cortez as Sam Spade, with Bebe Daniels as Ruth Wonderly and direction by Roy Del Ruth. This version is often overlooked, and few writers consider it a film noir. A second version of Hammett's novel, *Satan Met a Lady*, was released in 1936, and it was directed by William Dieterle and starred Bette Davis as Valerie Purvis and Warren William as private detective Ted Shane. This film tried, unsuccessfully, to transform Hammett's novel into a broad comedy, and it has little relevance to film noir.

The fact that there are two very similar versions of the same novel, 10 years apart, provides an opportunity to distil, or at least discuss, those qualities that are traditionally emphasized as noir in the cinema and those that are not. It is also useful to distinguish between the noir elements in Hammett's fiction and the film adaptations of his novels as the first critical analysis of film noir came from the French in the mid-1940s, and they readily linked Hammett's fiction with the noir elements in the Hollywood cinema.

This comparison is assisted by the fact that in 1931, Hammett's next novel, *The Glass Key*, was published, and two film versions, produced by Paramount, followed. A 1935 version starring George Raft and Edward Arnold closely followed Hammett's novel, and in 1942, Paramount released another version starring Alan Ladd and Brian Donlevy. Most studies of film noir include the 1942 version but reject the 1935 film as an early example of film noir. Again, this pattern of inclusion and rejection assists in at least isolating the noir qualities of the 1940s films. A third case study, of the 1946 Columbia film *Night Editor*, is also included as this film, one of many variations that followed the success of *Double Indemnity*, clearly shows the way dramatic emphasis in the 1940s was internalized as films focused less on the external problems confronting the male protagonist and more on the psychological turmoil and guilt raging within.

### The Maltese Falcon (1941)

Warner Bros.'s third production of Dashiell Hammett's novel *The Maltese Falcon* began on Monday, June 9, 1941. The studio, which purchased the rights for $8,500 in 1930 just five months after the publication of the last installment in *Black Mask*, allotted a budget of $381,000 and 36 days to the film. This was a tight schedule for a first-time director. John Huston's preparation, however, was meticulous, and he sketched out the shooting angles for each scene weeks before the start of filming. He also shot the script in sequence, and so over three days and a long Saturday night in the middle of July, Huston filmed the final confrontation between Sam Spade (Humphrey Bogart) and Brigid O'Shaughnessy (Mary Astor). On July 18, following the burning of the studio "ship" the *La Paloma* on the back lot and a brief scene between Bogart and Sydney Greenstreet on Stage 19, the picture officially closed two days ahead of schedule and $54,000 under budget.

There was, however, one more scene in Huston's script to shoot. This was the epilogue in Spade's office where the detective tries to explain to his secretary Effie Perine (Lee Patrick) why he handed Brigid over to the police. Huston's script ends with him preparing to greet his mistress, Iva Archer (Gladys George), the widow of his dead partner. Effie stands by the window, mouth twisted, eyes reproachful:

Effie    You did that, Sam, to her?
Sam     She *did* kill Miles, Angel. . . .
Effie    Don't, please—don't touch me.

A doorknob rattles in the corridor. Effie goes out to see, comes back, and announces Iva Archer. The story ends on a note of defeat and self-recognition as Spade, with a shiver, accepts Iva, whose seedy amorality matches his own: "Send her in."

This scene was never shot as Huston and producer Henry Blanke decided to end the film outside Spade's apartment. Jack Warner, vice president and head of production, agreed with this decision, and a week later, Huston restaged Brigid's arrest. The reshot sequence begins with Lieutenant Detective Dundy (Barton MacLane) escorting Brigid O'Shaughnessy out of the apartment while Spade remains behind with Detective Tom Polhaus (Ward Bond). As Polhaus gathers up the evidence, the Maltese Falcon, he asks Spade, "What is it?" The detective replies, "The stuff that dreams are made of." Spade walks into the corridor and then pauses to watch Brigid enter the elevator. She, however, stares straight ahead as the shadows formed by the bars of the elevator grate stretch across her face and body. The film ends with Spade, holding the worthless statue, walking down the stairs as the elevator begins its descent.

Warner Bros. released 51 films in 1941. *The Maltese Falcon* was not regarded by the studio as a so-called prestige production in the same category as Frank Capra's *Meet John Doe* or Howard Hawks's *Sergeant York*. A week before the release of the film, executive producer Hal Wallis changed the title to *The Gent from Frisco*. However, after one of the film's previews, Jack Warner changed it back to *The Maltese Falcon*. While Huston and Jack Warner were pleased with the film, and it was one of the 10 nominees for best picture in 1941, box office receipts were only average as the studio never spent much money on promotion of the film.

Roy Del Ruth's 1931 version of *The Maltese Falcon* follows Hammett's novel closely and, due to a more liberal censorship policy in Hollywood in the early 1930s, included two key scenes not found in the 1941 film: after Spade has sex with Wonderly, he searches her apartment while she is sleeping in his bed. In the second scene, Spade forces Wonderly to take off all her clothes in Gutman's hotel room to find out whether she has stolen a $1,000 note given to Spade by Gutman; Wonderly resents Spade's lack of trust. Yet most studies of film noir ignore or dismiss the 1931 version. Andrew Spicer (2002, 8), for example, asserts that Huston's film is the first adaptation of Hammett true to the spirit of the original as it "began to close the gulf between the hard-boiled tradition and its screen equivalent." "Huston's adaptation," Spicer (2002, 50) maintains, "was much closer than previous versions to the cynical tone of Hammett's hard-boiled novel, retaining as much of Hammett's dialogue as possible." He rejects the 1931 version, which he groups with *Satan Met a Lady*, as they "significantly modified Hammett's style, softening the characterization of the detective so that he became the much more respectable figure of the gentleman amateur" (p. 8). On the other hand, James Naremore (1998, 61), while not quite so dismissive of the 1931 film, praises Huston's ability to make the 1941 film both romantic and humorous as the "wit is just sly enough to humanize the action without destroying its power as melodrama."

Frank Krutnik (1991) insists that of all the Hammett adaptations, only two are recognizably hard-boiled—John Huston's 1941 version of *The Maltese Falcon* and the 1942 version of *The Glass Key*. He attributes the dearth of hard-boiled films in the 1930s to the "strengthening of the Hays Code self-regulatory form of censorship in 1933 and 1934 which required the studios to 'play it safe' in matters of sexual content and violence" (pp. 35–36). While this may offer a possible explanation for the shortage of hard-boiled films in the second half of the 1930s, it does not affect the 1931 version of *The Maltese Falcon* as it was produced in a more liberal censorship environment than the 1941 version, and it does not explain the noir qualities in the 1935 version of *The Glass Key*.

William Luhr (1995, 7–8), in his book-length celebration of Huston's film, approaches this aspect in a slightly different way. He concludes that

> when sound came to dominate Hollywood around 1930, however, detective films flourished, but they employed thematic norms quite different from the "hard-boiled" fiction popular at the time, even when they used that fiction as their source. . . .
>
> This pattern is evident in the first two versions of *The Maltese Falcon*. In each, the detective . . . is a happy-go-lucky, wise-cracking two-fisted ladies man. The films give as much attention to comedy and seduction as to the mystery and, in many ways, the mystery is really an excuse for comedy and seduction.
>
> Huston's film is altogether different in tone and points to a major trend for detective films to follow. . . . Spade [in the 1941 film] does not happily juggle a plethora of women but is bitterly involved with only two. . . . For him, sexuality is not carefree but dangerous and guilt-ridden. The mystery and the evil world it reveals dominate

the mood of the movie, and this sinister atmosphere does not entirely disappear at the end.

Such an atmosphere presages *film noir*.

Seriousness and a guilt-ridden protagonist, it would seem, are essential attributes of film noir, and many studies find these qualities in Huston's film—and not in the 1931 version. Seriousness, in turn, is often associated with Spade's emotional state, the vulnerability he displays in his final confrontation with Brigid. Here the external conflict between the "good detective" and the "evil woman" is superseded by Spade's torment and his inner battle between his love for Brigid, his fear that he will be just another fall guy to her, and, perhaps, his social conscience regarding his partner's murder. The inner battle taking place within Spade is perceived as a crucial factor in isolating this version as a film noir.

Yet this should not be confused with Hammett's view of the world as essentially irrational and devoid of moral meaning. The film, for example, deletes the novel's most transparent expression of Hammett's worldview—the Flitcraft parable.

### The Flitcraft Parable in The Maltese Falcon

In the novel Spade tells a story to Brigid concerning a case involving Mr. Flitcraft, a happily married and successful real estate dealer in Tacoma. One day in 1922, Flitcraft went out to lunch and never returned to his home, leaving his job and wife and two young boys. Five years later, his wife visits Spade's detective agency after seeing a man in Spokane who resembled her husband. Spade investigates and confirms that the man is Flitcraft and that he is living in Spokane under the name of Charles Pierce. What is even more surprising is that Pierce has assumed a lifestyle identical to the one he left behind in Tacoma. He owns a successful automobile business; he has a wife, a baby, and a suburban home; and he plays golf after work, just as he did in Tacoma. When Spade confronts Flitcraft, he tells the detective that he does not have any feelings of guilt regarding his first family as he left them well provided for and "what he had done seemed to him to be perfectly reasonable" (Hammett 1975b, 58).

Flitcraft tells Spade that on his way to lunch in 1922, a beam from a nearby building site narrowly missed him after falling 8 or 10 stories onto the sidewalk. Up to this point in his life he had been a "good citizen and a good husband and father" (Hammett 1975b, 59) who believed that life "was a clean, orderly, sane, responsible affair. Now a falling beam had shown him that life was fundamentally none of those things" (Hammett 1975b, 59). He suddenly realized that this "good citizen-husband-father" could be wiped out just walking between his office and a restaurant and that people "died at haphazard like that, and lived only while blind chance spared them" (Hammett 1975b, 59). This incident, Flitcraft explained, left him more shocked than frightened as he "felt like somebody had taken the lid off life and let him look at the works" (Hammett 1975b, 59). Consequently, he decided to "change his life at random by simply going away" (Hammett 1975b, 60). After drifting around for a couple of years, he eventually settled in Spokane and remarried, and as Spade tells Brigid, Flitcraft was probably unaware that he had resumed the same kind of life: "That's the part of it I always liked. He adjusted to beams falling, and then no more of them fell, and he adjusted himself to them not falling" (Hammett 1975b, 60).

This parable is Spade's warning to Brigid in the novel that the world does not function in a rational way and that unless she changes her behavior, a "beam" will eventually fall on her. Brigid, along with her fellow villains Casper Gutman and Joel Cairo, assumes that life is orderly and that its random elements can be controlled. She fails. Spade, on the other hand, understands the ethical irrationality of existence and is able to adjust—and survive. After handing his lover (Brigid) over to the police, he returns to his office and prepares to greet his ex-mistress, Iva Archer. As Ilsa Bick (1995, 182) points out, "Hammett has Spade re-encountering his own Flitcraftian fate." For Hammett, Bick argues, "the only sure release from such repetition is death" (p. 182). Bogart's biographers Ann Sperber and Eric Lax (1997, 163) put it differently but reach the same point when they argue that while Huston's ending "showed off the stars to optimum effect . . . it also altered the nature of the story and of Hammett's hero. In place of an unsavory poetic justice, there were romantic closing images."

Robert Porfirio (1996, 89) argues that film noir shares the same "sense of meaninglessness" as existentialism and that films such as *The Maltese Falcon* reflect "existentialism's emphasis on individual consciousness with their denial of any sort of cosmic design or moral purpose." Yet this is not accurate as both the 1931 and 1941 film versions delete the Flitcraft parable and end with Spade leaving Brigid in jail (1931) or under arrest (1941). Neither film ends by replicating the novel's nihilism, whereby Hammett concludes his story by suggesting that Spade is about to resume his affair with Iva Archer, the wife of his dead partner. On the other hand, both films conclude with Spade's torment at having to hand the woman he loves over to the police.

These differences—between the 1931 film and the 1941 version on the one hand, and between the films and the novel on the other—are clarified when the final confrontation between Spade and Brigid is compared in each version. The most obvious difference is the degree of Spade's inner torment and emotional vulnerability that is most evident in the 1941 film compared to the novel or the 1931 version. While the novel emphasizes Spade's self-interest, his desire to survive, as the prime reason for handing Brigid over to the police, Huston's film depicts a tormented detective trying to stay within the bounds of conventional morality by rejecting the temptations offered by an attractive, but ruthless, woman.

Hammett, on the other hand, emphasizes Spade's determination to survive when he writes, "One of us has got to take it, after the talking those birds [Cairo and Gutman] will do. They'd hang me for sure. You're likely to get a better break"

(Hammett 1975b, 196). Huston omits this passage from the film, as he does Spade's equivocation as to whether he really loves Brigid. After Brigid tells him that he should know whether he loves her, Hammett's Spade replies,

> "I don't. It's easy enough to be nuts about you." He looked hungrily from her hair to her feet and up to her eyes again. "But I don't know what that amounts to. Does anybody ever? But suppose I do? What of it? Maybe next month I won't. I've been through it before—when it lasted that long. Then what?" (Hammett 1975b, 199)

Huston replaces Hammett's cynicism with a more romantic gesture from Spade as he tells Brigid, "Maybe I do [love you]."

While Ricardo Cortez's Spade in 1931 is more or less resigned to handing Wonderly over to the police, Huston extends this sequence by accentuating the psychological disturbance within the detective. His torment is palpable, especially when he shouts into her face that "I won't [fall for you] because all of me wants to, regardless of the consequences." While this is not an existential moment, as some claim, it does represent a significant moment in the development of film noir. Unlike the novel, where survival is all that matters to the detective, Spade's torment in the 1941 film nearly destroys him.

### The Glass Key (1942)

The 1942 version of *The Glass Key* stars Alan Ladd as Ed Beaumont, Brian Donlevy as Paul Madvig, and Veronica Lake as Janet Henry and is directed by Stuart Heisler. An earlier version of the film appeared in 1935 starring George Raft as Ed Beaumont, Edward Arnold as Paul Madvig, and Claire Dodd as Janet Henry and directed by Frank Tuttle. This latter version has been almost totally ignored by most studies of film noir.

The story is set in an unnamed city, probably Baltimore, where Ned (Ed in the films) is a political fixer for the real boss of the city, construction owner Paul Madvig. Paul, because of his obsession with Janet Henry, supports the reelection of her father, Senator Henry, and his reform ticket. This brings Paul into conflict with Shad O'Rory and his gambling interests. When Ned finds the body of Senator Henry's son Taylor, suspicion falls on Paul as Taylor was conducting a passionate affair with Paul's daughter Opal. A series of anonymous notes sent to District Attorney Farr accuse Paul of the murder. Ned, in an attempt to protect Paul, destroys an incriminating affidavit. However, he suffers a terrible beating at the hands of Jeff and Rusty, an "apish dark man and . . . [a] rosy-cheeked boy with sandy hair" (Hammett 1975a, 94). When Opal accuses her father of Taylor's murder, Ned, to prevent the publication of her accusations, provokes the suicide of the editor of the local newspaper by seducing his wife.

Despite Ned's efforts to protect Paul, the friendship between the two men falters after Paul tells Ned that he killed Taylor. The bitterness between them escalates when Ned tells Paul that Janet was only using him to get her father reelected and that she is responsible for the anonymous notes. In an effort to save his friend, Ned tries to get information from Jeff. Jeff, however, strangles his boss (O'Rory) while Ned looks on. Ned finally forces Senator Henry to confess that he killed his son. The novel ends on a bleak note, with Ned and Paul totally estranged after Ned tells Paul that he is leaving the city with Janet:

> Madvig's lips parted. He looked dumbly at Ned Beaumont and as he looked the blood went out of his face again. When his face was quite bloodless he mumbled something of which only the word "luck" could be understood, turned clumsily around, went to the door, opened it, and went out, leaving it open behind him. Janet Henry looked at Ned Beaumont. He stared fixedly at the door. (Hammett 1975a, 220)

Both films replace the novel's utterly bleak ending with upbeat closures. The 1935 film reunites Paul with Ed and suddenly converts Opal, Paul's daughter, into a romantic partner for Ed. Similarly, the 1942 film eliminates the hostility between Ed and Janet Henry, and in a last-minute gesture of his friendship, Paul gives his blessing to Ed's union with Janet, his ex-fiancée.

More important, both films omit Janet Henry's dream in the novel, which provides the meaning to the title of the book (and the films), *The Glass Key*. It also performs the same ideological function as the Flitcraft parable did in *The Maltese Falcon* as it reaffirms Hammett's vision of a world predicated on moral chaos. It occurs near the end of the novel, when Ned tells Janet that he had a dream about her the previous night that "I don't much like" (Hammett 1975a, 184). Janet smiles and asks him, "Surely you don't believe in dreams." Ned replies, "I don't believe in anything, but I'm too much of a gambler not to be affected by a lot of things" (Hammett 1975a, 184). Intrigued, Janet demands to know what "was this dream that makes you mistrust me?" (Hammett 1975a, 184). He tells her a story involving a large rainbow trout that she throws back into the river. Janet reciprocates by telling him about her dream that they were lost in the forest, and after walking some distance, they came to a little house. When they peered through the window, they saw a large table piled high with food. After knocking on the door of the house and receiving no answer, they found a key under the doormat. However, when they opened the door, they discovered hundreds and hundreds of snakes "sliding and slithering" toward them (Hammett 1975a, 184). So they climbed onto the roof, where Ned leaned down and opened the front door. The snakes poured out of the house and slithered off into the forest, allowing Janet and Ned to use the key, lock the door, and eat the food: "I woke sitting up in bed clapping my hands and laughing" (Hammett 1975a, 184).

Later, however, Janet admits to Ned that she lied about her dream and that it was really a nightmare as the key was made of glass and it shattered after they opened the front door:

We couldn't lock the snakes in and they came out all over us and I woke up screaming. (Hammett 1975a, 217)

The nihilistic significance of Janet's dream about a glass key was too confronting for the films, and so they strip away the ideological significance of the glass key and replace it with a personal rebuke from Ed Beaumont to Paul Madvig. Ed warns Paul that he is being used by Janet Henry and her father and that when they have no more use for him after the election, he will find that their hospitality, the "key" to their house, is a "glass key."

The pattern is the same in film versions of *The Glass Key* as in *The Maltese Falcon*. Both pull back from the existential significance of Hammett's novel while retaining the significant changes in the characterization of his protagonist by accentuating his moral dilemma and his emotional vulnerability. Again, these qualities emerge more strongly in the 1940s adaptations than in the versions produced in the 1930s. For example, only the 1942 version of *The Glass Key* includes Ed's callous seduction of Eloise Matthews that leads to her husband's suicide. On the other hand, both films retain Hammett's suggestion that Ned's protection of Paul is not just a reflection of his friendship but involves a perverse masochistic desire on Ned's part to experience the "pleasures" of brutal beatings by Jeff. Hammett is unusually explicit with regard to the underlying sexual manifestations Jeff's relationship with Ned:

Jeff knocked aside Ned Beaumont's upraised hand and pushed him down on the bed. "I got something to try." He scooped up Ned Beaumont's legs and tumbled them on the bed. He leaned over Ned Beaumont, his hands busy on Ned Beaumont's body. (Hammett 1975a, 97)

Later, when Ned submits to the possibility of another beating, Jeff tells the men around him that Ned "likes it" as he is a "God-damned massacrist [*sic*]" (Hammett 1975a, 191), a line censored by the Production Code Authority. Nevertheless, both films include sufficient cues to replicate the intentions of the novel in this regard—especially Jeff's references to Ed as "baby" and "sweetheart" while he is hitting him. On one occasion, when Ed shows up unexpectedly, Jeff greets Ed with a broad smile: "Look Rusty, little rubber ball is back. I told you he likes the way we bounced him around."

Both films also include a disconcerting incident from the novel that foregrounds a significant change in the depiction of the screen detective. It occurs when Ed, desperate to save Paul, seeks information from Jeff in a dingy bar. Exposing himself to the possibility of another beating, Ed allows Jeff to put his hands around him as he greets him. When Jeff invites Ed upstairs "for a drink," the sexual basis of their liaison is suggested by Jeff as he excuses himself from his drinking companions: "Excuse us gents. We've got to go up and play handball, me and cuddles." Upstairs, Ed tries to get information out of the inebriated thug, but he is interrupted by the arrival of Jeff's boss—O'Rory in 1935 and Vanna in 1942. When Jeff takes offense at O'Rory's/Vanna's desire to curb his drinking, he lunges at him, accidentally knocking the single overhead light. O'Rory/Vanna, in an attempt to protect himself, pulls out a gun from his pocket, but Ed takes it away and then calmly watches Jeff murder the defenseless man. The 1935 film, in an almost textbook example of noir imagery, depicts the killing with a chiaroscuro lighting effect as Ed's face alternates between darkness and light. Even more startling is the way director Frank Tuttle suggestively implicates Ed in the murder by cutting between Ed's impassive gaze and Jeff slowly strangling O'Rory. Director Stuart Heisler achieves a similar effect in 1942.

## Night Editor (1946)

Film noir, according to James Naremore (1998, 220), occupies "a liminal space somewhere between Europe and America, between 'high modernism' and 'blood melodrama.'" The former, he argues, was reflected in "Hollywood thrillers of the 1940s," which are "characterised by urban landscapes, subjective narration, non-linear plots, hard-boiled poetry, and misogynistic eroticism" (p. 45). Naremore's positioning of film noir within the context of melodrama is significant, although it is dependent on understanding that melodrama is not necessarily a simplistic, sentimental form or a narrow genre based on family or romantic films produced in Hollywood in the 1950s. Instead, as Steve Neale, Christine Gledhill, and Linda Williams argue, it is the dominant mode underpinning the popular cinema. Thus film noir should be perceived as one of melodrama's dramatic inflections in the 1940s, a view consistent with Christine Gledhill's (2000, 227) that melodrama traditionally operated as a "genre producing machine" for the "mass production of popular genres capable of summoning up and putting into place different kinds of audience." Film noir was one of melodrama's many inflections in the 1940s and represented melodrama's constant ability, as Linda Williams (2001, 23) points out, to "shed its 'old-fashioned' values, ideologies and mise-en-scene and assume an 'imprimatur of realism.'"

*Night Editor*, a low-budget film produced by Columbia to meet the demands of the double bill, was based on a popular radio program. It was also a melodrama fashioned on the pattern established by *Double Indemnity* two years earlier. It fulfilled the same need as Billy Wilder's film, as described by Richard Schickel (1992, 20) in his monograph on *Double Indemnity:* "What was needed now [the 1940s], especially in its melodramas, was an enlivening dose of the down and dirty—a note of 'devilishness.'" A weak man, a police detective, jeopardizes his career and his family through his sexual infatuation with a cold, scheming woman. The film was notable for its explicit association between sexual arousal and violence, an aspect evident in James M. Cain's *Double Indemnity* and, in a more subdued way, Wilder's film. It is this aspect that has attracted the most interest in *Night Editor*.

The film involves a long flashback that functions as a framing device in explaining the moral basis of the story. The night editor of *The New York Star* tells a young reporter, who arrived late after a prolonged drinking binge following an argument with his wife, the story of detective Tony Cochrane (William Gargan). The flashback begins with Tony promising his wife (played by Jeff Donnell) and his young son that he will never leave them. However, a low-angle shot of the legs of wealthy, married socialite Jill Merrill (Janis Carter) waiting for Tony to pick her up in his car indicates the basis of Tony's inability to keep his promise. Tony takes Merrill to an isolated road by the beach, where he tries to end the affair: "You're worse than blood poison . . . there's an illness inside of you that has to hurt or be hurt." However, Jill, who is attracted to him because he is married, tells him "you'll never get away from me" before lying on top of him in the car.

Their lovemaking is interrupted by the screams of a young woman in a nearby car who is being attacked by a man wielding a tire iron. Tony runs to assist her, but when he has a clear shot at the assailant, Jill's warning that there will be a scandal if they are involved stops him from firing his gun. After the killer runs away, Merrill, in a heightened state of sexual excitement, screams at Tony that she wants to see the battered body of the dead girl.

When Tony is assigned to investigate the murder, he eliminates all evidence of his presence at the killing. His turmoil intensifies after the police arrest a local handyman for the murder. In an attempt to clear the innocent man, Tony builds a circumstantial case against the killer, Douglas Loring (Frank Wilcox), a local banker. However, his case is destroyed when Jill testifies that she was with Loring on the night of the murder. Finally, only hours before the execution, Tony destroys his career and jeopardizes his marriage by confessing that he witnessed the crime and that he was with Merrill at the beach. As the police move in to arrest Loring, Tony confronts Jill, who stabs him in the back with an ice pick. The flashback ends with the young reporter vowing that he will return home to his wife. However, before he leaves the newspaper building, he realizes that Tony is the elderly man who operates the cigarette franchise in the lobby and that Tony's son is a decorated policeman.

Carl Macek's (Silver and Ward 1992, 202) review of *Night Editor* in *Film Noir: An Encyclopedic Reference to the American Style* emphasizes the film's "sadistic brutality and violence" and the fact that there is "little pity in the film, which uses every opportunity to describe people as 'rotten through and through.'" The fact that it is a melodrama of redemption involving a femme fatale who seduces a "good" man to deceive his family and neglect his vocation is ignored in Macek's review. Tony's moral and judicial transgressions are punished, and the flashback ends with him lying seriously wounded in the street. While the superficial noir aspects are obvious—involving a dangerous woman and a "respectable" man—this external plot strand only functions to establish the film's main dramatic element involving the internal conflict within Tony.

## FILM NOIR, REALISM, AND VULNERABLE INTERIORITY

If John Huston's 1941 version of *The Maltese Falcon* and the 1942 version of *The Glass Key* are film noir, and the 1930s versions are not, it is primarily because the 1940s films expressed more explicitly the shift, or shifts, within the melodramatic mode that underpins all Hollywood dramatic films produced during this period. While it is impossible to define film noir by pointing to the introduction of a single technique, such as the intensive use of high-contrast lighting, first-person narration, convoluted flashbacks, bleak or downbeat endings, or even iconic characters such as the femme fatale, it is possible that these techniques and characters were symptomatic of the specific nature of the shift within melodrama in the 1940s as its characters lost their moral purpose and experienced self-doubt and a sense of vulnerability. There was, in effect, a marked degree of "vulnerable interiority" in these films as the dramatic emphasis shifted from the traditional source found in simple or elementary melodrama, notably externalized problems such as villainous characters, to a more complex mode that embroiled the protagonist in his or her guilt.

French critic Jean-Pierre Chartier (1999, 23) detected this shift in 1946 when he noted that the action in *Double Indemnity* does not necessarily "spring from exterior causes" as in most American films. Instead of a "formal mystery," the film employs a "psychological mechanism" that "unwinds before our eyes." Other critics responded to the first wave of noir films, such as *The Maltese Falcon*, *Phantom Lady*, *The Postman Always Rings Twice*, *Gilda*, and *The Locket*, by emphasizing their moral ambiguity and the degree of psychological conflict with the characterization. Thus most film noir protagonists expressed varying degrees of vulnerable interiority as they battled not only a hostile world, but also their own doubts and anxieties. Most critics in the 1940s regarded this as a shift away from the predictable generic patterns, and sentimental basis, favored by Hollywood films in the 1930s toward a greater degree of realism. For example, novelist James M. Cain wrote in 1946 that films such as *Double Indemnity* seemed more real and that this change had "nothing to do with the war" or any "of that bunk" (Shearer 1999, 12):

> It's just that producers have got hep to the fact that plenty of real crime takes place every day and that makes it a good movie. The public is fed up with the old-fashioned melodramatic type of hokum. You know, the whodunit at which the audience after the second reel starts shouting, "We know the murderer. It's the butler. It's the butler. It's the butler." (p. 13)

## REFERENCES

Bick, Ilsa J. 1995. "The Beams That Fell and Other Crises in *The Maltese Falcon*." In *The Maltese Falcon. John Huston, Director*, ed. William Luhr, 181–202. New Brunswick, NJ: Rutgers University Press.

Borde, Raymond, and Etienne Chaumeton. 1966. *Panorama du Film Noir Américain (1941–1953)*. Paris: Éditions de Minuit.

Chartier, Jean-Pierre. 1999. "Americans Also Make *Noir* Films." In *Film Noir Reader 2*, ed. Alain Silver and James Ursini, 21–73. New York: Limelight Editions.

Frank, Nino. 1999. "A New Kind of Police Drama: The Criminal Adventure." In *Film Noir Reader 2*, ed. Alain Silver and James Ursini, 15–19. New York: Limelight Editions.

Gledhill, Christine. 2000. "Rethinking Genre." In *Reinventing Film Studies*, ed. Christine Gledhill and Linda Williams, 221–243. London: Arnold.

Hammett, Dashiell. 1975a. *The Glass Key*. London: Pan Books.

Hammett, Dashiell. 1975b. *The Maltese Falcon*. London: Pan Books.

Krutnik, Frank. 1991. *In a Lonely Street: Film Noir, Genre, Masculinity*. London: Routledge.

Luhr, William, ed. 1995. *The Maltese Falcon. John Huston, Director*. New Brunswick, NJ: Rutgers University Press.

Marcus, Steven. 1975. "Introduction." In *The Continental Op*, ed. Dashiell Hammett, 7–23. London: Pan Books.

Naremore, James. 1998. *More Than Night: Film Noir in Its Contexts*. Berkeley: University of California Press.

Neale, Steve. 1993. "Melo-Talk: On the Meaning and Use of the Term 'Melodrama' in the American Trade Press." *The Velvet Light Trap* 32 (Fall): pp. 66–89.

Neale, Steve. 2000. *Genre and Hollywood*. London: Routledge.

Porfirio, Robert. 1996. "No Way Out: Existential Motifs in the Film Noir." In *Film Noir Reader*, ed. Alain Silver and James Ursini, 77–93. New York: Limelight Editions.

Schickel, Richard. 1992. *Double Indemnity*. London: British Film Institute.

Shearer, Lloyd Shearer. 1999. "Crime Certainly Pays on the Screen." In *Film Noir Reader 2*, ed. Alain Silver and James Ursini, 9–13. New York: Limelight Editions.

Silver, Alain, and Elizabeth Ward. 1992. *Film Noir: An Encyclopedic Reference to the American Style*. New York: Overlook Press.

Silver, Alain, and James Ursini. 2004. *Film Noir*. Cologne, Germany: Taschen.

Sperber, Ann M., and Eric Lax. 1997. *Bogart*. New York: William Morrow.

Spicer, Andrew. 2002. *Film Noir*. Harlow, UK: Longman.

Williams, Linda. 2001. *Playing the Race Card: Melodramas of Black and White from Uncle Tom to O. J. Simpson*. Princeton, NJ: Princeton University Press.

# The Hard-Boiled Influence

## Geoff Mayer

I don't know what the game was. I'm not sure how it should be played. No one ever tells you. I only know we must have played it wrong, somewhere along the way. I don't even know what the stakes are. I only know they're not for us.

We've lost. That's all I know. We've lost. And now the game is through.

The End

—Cornell Woolrich, *I Married a Dead Man* (1948)

Many of the ingredients that formed film noir in Hollywood in the 1940s were developed a decade or more earlier in the hard-boiled fiction that reached the American public via pulp magazines and, to a lesser extent, the crime novel. The critical and commercial success of *Double Indemnity* (1944), based on James M. Cain's 1936 novel and coscripted by Raymond Chandler; *Murder, My Sweet* (1945), based on Chandler's 1945 novel; *The Big Sleep* (1946), based on Chandler's 1939 novel; and *The Postman Always Rings Twice* (1946), based on Cain's 1934 novel, consolidated the growing interest in Hollywood in the adaptation of hard-boiled novels.

Although Dashiell Hammett, James M. Cain, Raymond Chandler, Cornell Woolrich, and others are frequently grouped together as a kind of "hard-boiled" school of writing, there are substantial differences between these writers, and all of them would refute any kind of grouping. Yet Hammett, followed by Cain and the others, did change the basis of American crime fiction. The dominant crime genre prior to Hammett was the classical, or English, detective story. In the 1920s, and especially the 1930s, this type of crime fiction lost its preeminence in America and was replaced by a much tougher, less cerebral form of crime writing.

Whereas hard-boiled crime fiction assumes that the world is inherently corrupt, classical writers present a more optimistic view of the world—once the guilty person is exposed, the assumption is that innocence will return as the moral equilibrium is restored. This view is represented in the fiction of European and American writers such as Arthur Conan Doyle, Agatha Christie, Dorothy L. Sayers, Ellery Queen, John Dickson Carr, S. S. Van Dine, Earl Derr Biggers, and Rex Stout. They, in turn, structured their stories on the model created by Edgar Allan Poe. In 1841 Poe wrote "The Murders in the Rue Morgue" and introduced the first fictional private detective, Chevalier C. Auguste Dupin. Dupin's characteristics, intellectually gifted, eccentric, arrogant, superior, and overbearing, provided a prototype for subsequent classical detectives who took on cases out of interest, not economic necessity. Dupin is not part of ordinary society—he is above it.

The most well-known example of this kind of crime fiction is Conan Doyle's Sherlock Holmes, who first appeared in 1887. When this formula developed in America with Nick Carter in 1886, there were a few changes as Carter was more of an adventurer than Holmes. He, unlike the British detective, was more physical and less removed from everyday society. While Carter also utilized the classical detective's ratiocinative skill in solving crimes, the stories also emphasized action and violence.

The first Nick Carter story appeared in the September 18, 1886, edition of Street and Smith's *New York Weekly*. He appeared in pulp magazines, dime novels, comics, film and radio series, and in 1964, he was reformulated into a secret agent fighting Cold War spies. Carter's most popular period, however, was prior to World War I, and he was part of the spectacular success of so-called sensational literature, which found its greatest outlet in America in pulp magazines, which began in the early 1880s. This medium also became a prime outlet for hard-boiled fiction. Between 1915 and 1955, there were nearly 200 mystery-detective magazines.

Hard-boiled fiction developed out of the melodramatic patterns formulated by the penny dreadfuls in Britain and the dime novels in the United States in the second half of the nineteenth century. This rapid spread of crime stories, which were part of sensational literature, was largely due to an increase in literacy together with the invention of the rotary steam press and other techniques that facilitated the cheap production of newspapers and weekly magazines. The first pulp magazine, a term given to magazines printed on pulpwood paper, was published in 1882. The first crime pulp, based on the exploits of detective Nick Carter in *Nick Carter Weekly*, appeared in 1891.

This was followed by a host of similar magazines, including *Detective Story Magazine*, that began in 1915. From the point of view of hard-boiled fiction, the most important pulp magazine was *Black Mask,* which was established in 1920 by H. L. Mencken, who described his magazine as a "louse," and George Jean Nathan to offset losses incurred by their more "sophisticated" magazine, *Smart Set. Black Mask* was an immediate success, and circulation rose to 250,000 within the first year, although Mencken and Nathan sold it for a substantial profit within six months for $100,000; their initial investment was only $500.

The hard-boiled crime story, as opposed to the classical model, first appeared in 1922–1923 with the publication of two short stories in *Black Mask* from men with totally different backgrounds: Carroll John Daly and Dashiell Hammett. While Hammett was well read and self-taught, with firsthand experience of the criminal world through his employment as a Pinkerton detective, Daly was a former usher and owner of a movie theater in Atlantic City, New Jersey. Daly's hard-boiled story "The False Burton Combs" appeared in the December 1922 issue of *Black Mask,* three months before Hammett's crime story.

Although Daly lacked Hammett's writing skills, he created the hard-boiled protagonist who resided somewhere between law-abiding society and the criminal underworld:

> I ain't a crook; just a gentleman adventurer and make my living working against the law breakers. Not that I work with police—no, not me. I'm no knight errant either. (Daly 1977, 3)

Daly initially described his protagonist as an "adventurer":

> Not the kind the name generally means; those that sit around waiting for a sucker or spend their time helping governments out of trouble. . . . There ain't nothing in governments unless you're a politician. . . . I'm a kind of a fellow in the center—not a crook and not a policeman. Both of them look on me with suspicion, though the crooks don't often know I'm out after their hides. And the police—well they run me pretty close at times but I got to take the chances. (Daly 1977, 4)

Even more important than "The False Burton Combs" was Daly's second story for *Black Mask* in May 1923, where he introduced private investigator Terry Mack in "Three-Gun Terry." Soon after, in the June 1, 1923, issue of *Black Mask,* he introduced readers to private detective Race Williams, his most popular series figure, in "Knights of the Open Palm." In this short story, Williams fights the Ku Klux Klan, and the ensuing violence became a recurring feature of hard-boiled fiction. Williams, in this story, functioned as a vigilante not interested in working with law officers, as Daly, who showed no interest in the intellectual puzzles used by classical fiction, tried to capture the speech patterns of the everyday world.

Hammett, Cain, Chandler, Woolrich, and others retained Daly's emphasis on the individuality, and even alienation, of Daly's protagonist while extending his assumption that the world is irredeemably corrupt. As Raymond Chandler explained,

It was the smell of fear which these stories managed to generate. Their characters lived in a world gone wrong, a world in which, long before the atom bomb, civilization had created the machinery for its own destruction and was learning to use it with all the moronic delight of a gangster trying out his first machine-gun. The law was something to be manipulated for profit and power. The streets were dark with something more than the night. (Chandler 1950, 7)

This evocative passage, which was first published in the *Saturday Review* on April 15, 1950, captures the essential difference between American hard-boiled fiction and the classical form. It also reveals the essence of the relationship between film noir and hard-boiled fiction, with its assumption that corruption permeates every layer of society, thereby generating a cynical attitude that, in the best example, exposes the underlying nihilism shared between both media.

Frank Krutnik (1991) estimates that almost 20 percent of noir films produced between 1941 and 1948 were adaptations of hard-boiled novels and short stories, although its influence went well beyond just literal adaptations as hard-boiled conventions infiltrated many American genres and many different types of production, from the expensive "A" films from the major studios to the "poverty row" programmer released for a preinterval screening from studios such as Republic, Monogram, and PRC. For example, in 1945, one year after the release of *Double Indemnity,* PRC released *Apology for Murder*. The film starred Ann Savage as the mercenary wife of an older man who encourages a newspaper reporter to kill her husband. After the murder, the love affair between the wife and her lover turns sour. She dies, and he writes his confession while mortally wounded. The film's producer, Leon Fromkess, was even tempted to call the film *Single Indemnity*. However, Paramount was not impressed and forced PRC to withdraw their film two days after its release. While other scriptwriters were more creative in adapting the characters and situations in *Double Indemnity* and *The Postman Always Rings Twice,* James M. Cain became so annoyed with these thinly disguised copies, and the fact that he was not receiving any money from them, that he left Hollywood for Maryland.

Hammett's first *Black Mask* story appeared a few months after Daly's debut, and his detective, the Continental Op, was also willing to play both sides against each other. Unlike Daly, Hammett had firsthand experience of the underworld as an operative for the Pinkerton National Detective Service. When "Captain" Joseph T. Shaw took over the editorship of *Black Mask* in 1926, he recognized Hammett's talent and encouraged Raymond Chandler, and other writers, to emulate Hammett's sparse, tough writing style.

Shaw's period as editor of *Black Mask,* which ended in 1936, was significant as the magazine maintained a high standard of crime fiction with regular stories from Erle Stanley Gardner (Perry Mason), Raymond Chandler, Raoul Whitfield, Brett Halliday (Michael Shayne), Cornell Woolrich, Louis L'Amour, George Harmon Coxe, Frederick Nebel, Horace McCoy, Max Brand, Steve Fisher, Frank Gruber,

W. T. Ballard, Bruno Fischer, and John D. MacDonald. Many years later, Shaw outlined his approach to hard-boiled crime fiction:

> The formula or pattern emphasizes character and the problems inherent in human behaviour over crime solution. In other words, in this new pattern, character conflict is the main theme; the ensuing crime, or its threat, is incidental. . . . Such distinctive treatment comprises a hard, brittle style. (Wilt 1991, 2)

Shaw also encouraged Hammett to adapt some of his short stories into novels, and his first four novels, *Red Harvest* (1929), *The Dain Curse* (1929), *The Maltese Falcon* (1930), and *The Glass Key* (1931) were all published in *Black Mask* prior to their publication by New York publisher A. A. Knopf. Other pulp writers soon followed Hammett's example with novels such as Paul Cain's *The Fast One* (1932), Erle Stanley Gardner's *The Case of the Velvet Claw* (1933), Raymond Chandler's *The Big Sleep* (1939), and Cornell Woolrich's *The Bride Wore Black* (1940).

The film studios in Hollywood in the 1930s mostly ignored hard-boiled fiction and preferred the classical mode of detective fiction. Even though the first screen appearance of Hammett's *The Maltese Falcon* was released by Warner Bros. in 1931, it was Hammett's final novel, *The Thin Man*, published in 1934, that attracted MGM's attention—the studio quickly rushed a film version into production.

*The Thin Man* differs from Hammett's earlier short stories and novels. Although it retains Hammett's clever prose and carefully detailed characters, it does not present the nihilistic view of the world that characterized novels such as *The Maltese Falcon* and *The Glass Key*. The story concerns a former detective (Nick Charles), now living the life of a socialite, who is drawn back into the world of crime when an old friend asks him to investigate the disappearance of a relative. However, the section of the story that most appealed to MGM was the relationship between the often inebriated former detective, Nick Charles, and his wife, Nora. This element, which had some of the qualities of the screwball comedy, was further developed by MGM so that Nick, who is living off the wealth of his wife, only helps those people he cares for. Unlike the hard-boiled detective, Nick does not have to work. The success of the first film, starring William Powell and Myrna Loy as the battling Charleses, resulted in five sequels.

The same year that MGM bought the rights to *The Thin Man*, they also purchased James M. Cain's *The Postman Always Rings Twice*. However, unlike the quick success enjoyed by *The Thin Man*, censorship objections from Joseph Breen and his Production Code Administration delayed the adaptation of Cain's novel until 1945. When Paramount showed interest in purchasing the rights to Cain's *Double Indemnity*, the Production Code Administration also opposed a screen version, and it did not reach the screen until 1944.

Aside from objections from the Production Code Administration, Frank Krutnik (1991) suggests that the delay in film adaptations of hard-boiled stories published in the 1930s was primarily due to government policies in the period following America's entry into World War II on December 7, 1941. Krutnik argues that the studios were "warned off" these stories as they violated the "wartime projects of 'cultural mobilisation'" (p. 36). Consequently, John Huston's *The Maltese Falcon* and Alfred Hitchcock's *Shadow of a Doubt* (1943) did not immediately initiate a cycle of similar films in the early 1940s because the Office of War Information rejected such films as suitable entertainment. These films did not, Krutnik maintains, endorse the "general wartime ideology of commitment and community" (p. 36).

While there is some truth in this argument, there were also notable film noirs released prior to *Double Indemnity*. Paramount, for example, produced two noir films in 1942: *This Gun for Hire,* based on Graham Greene's novel, in May and *The Street of Chance,* an excellent adaptation of Cornell Woolrich's *The Black Curtain,* in November. Both films provided wartime audiences with an alternative to combat, espionage, and other war-related films that proliferated during this period. Hence the studios, in late 1942 and early 1943, began planning a shift to detective films and suspense thrillers—the term *film noir* was unknown at this time. As a consequence of this shift, they began employing pulp writers such as Frank Gruber, Steve Fisher, and Raymond Chandler.

In 1943 Paramount purchased the rights to James M. Cain's novella *Double Indemnity* after it was published, with two other stories, in a hardcover novel by Knopf as *Three of a Kind.* By the time filming began in September 1943, Universal was also shooting their adaptation of Cornell Woolrich's *Phantom Lady*. The success of these two films encouraged other studios to begin purchasing the rights to hard-boiled novels and short stories for their own productions.

It is also significant that *Double Indemnity* and *Phantom Lady* were budgeted as "A" films by their studios. Detective films in the 1930s, with the exception of *The Thin Man* series and a few other films, were mostly low-budget films with little critical prestige. When Columbia purchased the rights to Cornell Woolrich's 1937 short story "Face Work" and released it as *Convicted* in 1938, it continued this trend of low-budget crime films. Similarly, the first two adaptations of Raymond Chandlers' fiction in the early 1940s were low-budget films. His second novel, *Farewell, My Lovely,* which was published in 1940, was purchased by RKO in July 1941 and reworked into their Falcon series, starring George Sanders as the debonair detective. It was released as the third film in the series, *The Falcon Takes Over* (1942).

After Chandler's agent, Sydney Sanders, sold the rights to *Farewell, My Lovely* to RKO for $2,000, he sold the film rights to Chandler's third novel, *The High Window,* to Twentieth Century Fox for $3,500. Fox did the same thing as RKO and adapted the novel to its low-budget detective series starring Lloyd Nolan as Michael Shayne. It was released as *Time to Kill* in 1942, the seventh film in the series. Although both films have their merits, especially *Time to Kill,* their hard-boiled attributes were compromised by the series format, which had to delete Chandler's detective, Philip Marlowe, and insert either the Falcon or Mike

Shayne, who had little in common with Marlowe, especially the night-clubbing Falcon.

## HARD-BOILED WRITERS

### W. R. Burnett (1899–1982)

Burnett wrote 33 novels, 18 of which were thrillers, 27 screenplays, and received 60 screen credits. His importance to the gangster genre and, to a lesser extent, film noir cannot be overestimated. Two of his novels changed film history (*Little Caesar* and *The Asphalt Jungle*), and a third, *High Sierra*, marked a change in the gangster genre that prefigured the influence of noir a few years later. Each film adaptation was 10 years apart—*Little Caesar* in 1930, *High Sierra* in 1941, and *The Asphalt Jungle* in 1950—and each represented a substantial, and influential, reworking of the genre he established in 1930. *Little Caesar* influenced Horace McCoy to write as well as encouraging William Faulkner's *Sanctuary* and Graham Greene's *Brighton Rock*.

Born in Springfield, Ohio, Burnett's career as a novelist only developed after he left a secure job as a statistician in Ohio in 1927 for the uncertainty of life in Chicago. Working as a night clerk at the Northmere Hotel, Burnett listened to the gangsters that populated the hotel. This not only provided material, but also taught Burnett how to incorporate their distinctive slang in his stories. This was evident in his first novel, *Little Caesar*, which was published in 1929. Building on the stories from the local gangsters, Burnett used Machiavelli's story of power, betrayal, and corruption in *The Prince* to give structure to his novel, which traced the rise and fall of a gangster, Cesare Bandello ("Rico"). After the novel was an immediate success, Warner Bros. purchased the rights and adapted it into a highly successful film starring Edward G. Robinson as Rico. *Little Caesar* also created a prototype for subsequent gangster films such as *The Public Enemy* (1931).

After the success of his first novel, Burnett was offered employment as a screenwriter, and he continued in this role until 1972 while also continuing to write novels in a range of genres, including *Iron Man* (1930), a tough boxing novel; *Saint Johnson* (1930), a revisionist version of the gunfight at the O.K. Corral; *Dark Command: A Kansas Iliad* (1938), which was purchased by Republic for their big-budget 1940 western starring John Wayne; and *Nobody Lives Forever* (1943), a hard-boiled crime novel concerning a small-time grifter, which Burnett adapted into the 1946 Warner Bros. film starring John Garfield, and in 1950, MGM released John Huston's film version of Burnett's 1949 novel *The Asphalt Jungle*. This was also the source of two direct remakes: Delmer Dave's 1959 western *The Badlanders* starring Alan Ladd and Ernest Borgnine and the inferior 1972 version *Cool Breeze*.

Burnett's major contribution to film noir was his 1940 novel *High Sierra*. In this novel he changed the characterization of the gangster story from the aggressive, ambitious figure characteristic of the 1930s to the aging Roy Earle, a gangster well past his prime. A sense of fatalism pervades the story, and Burnett and John Huston scripted a film version for Warner Bros. which was released in 1941 with Humphrey Bogart as Earle. Ten years later, Burnett's *The Asphalt Jungle* assimilated the conventions of film noir and the gangster genre, and the result was the prototypical caper film, coscripted and directed by John Huston.

## James M. Cain (1892–1977)

James M. Cain always argued that he did not belong to a hard-boiled school of crime fiction. In fact, he denied that such a school of writing ever existed. But the first line of his most famous novel, *The Postman Always Rings Twice*, encapsulated the tough attitude to life that epitomized this style of writing: "They threw me off the hay truck about noon" (1955, 5). Cain, unlike Hammett, Chandler, and Woolrich, did not develop his crime writing craft in the pulp magazines, nor, unlike Hammett or Chandler, did he utilize a recurring private detective such as Sam Spade or Philip Marlowe. Instead of these tough, self-assured men, Cain favored marginal characters that gravitated to Los Angeles from the Midwest seeking fame, fortune, and excitement. Instead, they found disillusionment and death.

Although Cain's contribution as a screenwriter to noir films was minimal, his influence was profound because of the structure he developed with *The Postman Always Rings Twice* and *Double Indemnity*. These novels served as a template for many screenwriters in the 1940s and 1950s. His tough, lurid tales of murder and lust involving everyday people were narrated in direct, simple speech patterns that were reminiscent of the naturalism of Theodore Dreiser. This style, however, was used for melodramatic stories told from the point of view of disenfranchised souls eager to taste the fruits of American capitalism.

What Cain brought to crime fiction was his understanding of the dark side of human psychology and a pervasive sense of fatalism as his protagonists rush toward their own destruction. As Geoffrey O'Brien (1997, 69) notes, "Cain was another chronicler of the gratuitousness of fate, in the sexual rather than the criminal sphere—but for Cain the two spheres are rarely far apart." In the typical Cain story, O'Brien argues, "someone opens a door at random (and in the first paragraph) and his destiny is sealed then and there. Generally it is not long before he realizes what has happened, but, as if hypnotized, he does nothing to alter the course of events" (p. 69). His best novels, according to O'Brien, "are in full gear from the first word and drive forward without a pause for breath until the final inevitable moment—the point where they click off neatly, leaving you with the void" (p. 69).

The son of a college professor and an opera singer, Cain was born in Annapolis, Maryland, and he studied at Washington College in Chesterton. After serving in World War I, he worked for *The Baltimore American* and *The Baltimore Sun*.

A short stint teaching journalism at St. John's College in Annapolis preceded his appointment as editorial writer for *The New York World* after moving to New York in 1924. In 1928 H. L. Mencken published Cain's first story, "Pastorale," in *American Mercury*. Cain was then appointed managing editor of a new magazine, *The New Yorker*, but he became disillusioned with journalism, and after he failed to establish himself as a playwright, he moved to Hollywood in 1931 and secured a screenwriting job with Paramount.

Although he never succeeded as a screenwriter, Cain relished the West Coast, and it rejuvenated his imagination. During this period he developed what was to become his archetypal noir story of a murderous triangle involving two men and a sensual woman. The genesis of this story came from two sources. First, the specific setting for the story came to Cain when he observed a young woman who worked at a gas station he regularly frequented. He combined this with details from the well-publicized 1927–1928 trial and execution of Ruth Snyder and her lover, Judd Gray, for the murder of Snyder's husband, Albert. *The New York Daily News* even carried a photo of Snyder's execution.

*The Postman Always Rings Twice*, which was tentatively titled *Bar-B-Que*, was the result, and in this novel Cain introduced the dramatic technique that shaped his fiction, a technique he borrowed from screenwriter Vincent Lawrence. It involved the notion of the "love rack" as Cain was especially interested in the fact that once Ruth Snyder and Judd Gray had killed Albert, their affair lost its passion, and they soon turned on each other. Lawrence also provided the title for the book after the publisher, Knopf, rejected *Bar-B-Que*. When Lawrence told Cain that he always knew when his postman was at the door because the "son of a bitch always rang twice," Cain knew he had his title as it conveyed the notion that punishment, even if delayed, was inevitable.

Published in 1934 by Knopf, *The Postman Always Rings Twice* was an immediate best seller, and sales remained strong for many years, especially after the book invoked an obscenity trial and banning in Canada and Boston. Cain's career, after failing as a playwright and screenwriter, received a great boost from the book. In 1936 he wrote "Double Indemnity" as an eight-part serial for *Liberty* magazine, and it was also published, with other stories, as *Three of a Kind* in 1943. He followed this in 1937 with *Serenade*, his most bizarre novel, featuring a bisexual opera singer and a Mexican prostitute, and he continued writing until his death in 1977. However, his last major hard-boiled novels were *Mildred Pierce* in 1941 and *Love's Lovely Counterfeit* in 1942.

Cain had little time for Hollywood, although he welcomed the money he received. He established the American Author's Society in an attempt to get a better deal for authors from the studios. Cain had little success as a screenwriter, even after *The Postman Always Rings Twice*. Despite relatively long periods employed by the studios, only five screenplays were credited to him, and none were noir films. His influence on film noir came from adaptations of his novels by other screenwriters. After the failure of his third marriage to Aileen Pringle, he married Florence

McBeth in 1947 and left Hollywood for Hyattsville, Maryland, where he lived until his death.

### Raymond Chandler (1888–1959)

The names of Raymond Chandler and Dashiell Hammett are synonymous with film noir and hard-boiled fiction. However, Chandler's style and view of the world was different from Hammett's. Whereas Hammett's protagonist, whether the Continental Op, Sam Spade (*The Maltese Falcon*), or Ned, the political fixer in *The Glass Key,* was essentially a nihilist determined just to survive a corrupt world, Chandler's detective, whether he was called Dalmas, Mallory, Carmady, or Marlowe, was a more traditional hero figure who tried to make a difference—even if institutional corruption was endemic. Chandler's hero was, as he pointed out in *The Simple Art of Murder,* "a man of honor" and "the best man in his world and a good enough man for any world" (Chandler 1973, 198). His search for a hidden truth might ultimately be futile, but it must proceed.

Chandler began writing crime fiction relatively late in life, and his fiction contains a persistent strain of melancholia and a longing for an earlier age. His rich similes and rhythmic dialogue express contempt for most aspects of modern life, a characteristic that culminated in *The Long Goodbye.* Yet this aspect was also evident in his 1930s short stories published in the pulp magazines, where the detective's investigation was often punctuated by his caustic descriptions of Los Angeles, mixed with more than a hint of sadness at his alienation from mainstream society. Thus, in the final moments in the 1938 short story "Red Wind,"

> I went out of the bar without looking back at her, got into my car and drove west on Sunset and down all the way to the Coast Highway. Everywhere along the way gardens were full of withered and blackened leaves and flowers which the hot wind had burned. (Chandler 1978, 125)

Born in Chicago on July 23, 1888, Chandler's father, a hard-drinking railroad engineer of British descent, deserted his family when Raymond was seven. His mother took him with her to live with relatives in London, and in 1907 he became naturalized. He was a first-class scholar, with a strong grounding in Latin and the classics, and after graduating from Dulwich Preparatory School in 1904, he struggled to establish a literary career with his poems, book reviews, and essays in small specialist publications. He returned to Los Angeles in 1912 but found it difficult to secure a job. After service with the Canadian Army during World War I, where he developed a taste for alcohol, Chandler found employment in the Californian oil boom with the Dabney Oil Syndicate.

In 1924, aged 36, he married Cecilia "Cissy" Pascal, who was 18 years older than her husband. Chandler was promoted to the position of vice president at Dabney, but his drinking, womanizing, and absenteeism forced the company to terminate his services in 1932, one of the worst years of the 1930s Depression. Aged 44, without a job, this was a hard period for Chandler and Cissy. He enrolled in a correspondence school and became interested in writing for the pulp magazines. After five months of rewrites, his first story, "Blackmailers Don't Shoot," was published in *Black Mask* in December 1933. Chandler received $180 and, six months later, followed with "Smart Aleck Kill." Both stories featured Mallory, a private detective who was a precursor for Philip Marlowe.

When Joseph Shaw left *Black Mask* in 1936, Chandler, out of loyalty to his editor, also left the magazine and began publishing his stories in *Dime Detective*. However, his income in the 1930s, relative to his salary as an oil executive, was small, and after 21 short stories between 1933 and 1938, Chandler realized that he must start earning money by publishing a novel. Mallory became Carmady and then Philip Marlowe, the detective in his first novel, *The Big Sleep*. This story was cannibalized from two short stories, "Killer in the Rain" and "The Curtain." After the publication of *The Big Sleep* in 1939, he never returned to the pulps.

Chandler's next novel, *Farewell, My Lovely*, appeared in 1940, and although initial sales were disappointing, as was his next novel, *The High Window*, which appeared in 1942, it is now considered one of his best. When James M. Cain was unavailable as screenwriter for the adaptation of *Double Indemnity*, Chandler was hired. Chandler disliked Cain's novel with its mixture of sex with violence, but the film was a success and enhanced his reputation in Hollywood.

He joined Paramount, without success, as a screenwriter, and his drinking and womanizing returned with a vengeance. His most notable screenplay was produced following a bizarre arrangement with the studio. Paramount wanted another film from Alan Ladd before he returned to the army in 1945, and when producer John Houseman learned that Chandler had a partial script, *The Blue Dahlia*, he told the studio. *The Blue Dahlia* was, in fact, a failed novel, and Chandler's treatment was submitted on January 18, 1945. He was then assigned to write a complete screenplay, which, because of Ladd's imminent departure for the army, had to be completed very quickly. After the first half of the script was delivered in the first three weeks, Paramount scheduled shooting to begin in three weeks. However, the filming soon caught up with Chandler's writing, which had slowed down due to his drinking. Also, he had a problem with the ending as the Department of the Navy refused to sanction the film as Chandler's killer is revealed to be a disturbed navy veteran.

When the head of production, Henry Ginsberg, offered Chandler a $5,000 "bonus" if he completed the script by the deadline, Chandler threatened to resign as he considered the money a bribe. However, out of loyalty to Houseman, a fellow graduate of the English public school system, Chandler agreed to complete the script—with one proviso: he argued that as he could not meet the deadline if he remained sober, he needed to drink steadily if he was to finish it. Hence he requested the services of two limousines to take pages of the script back and forth to the studio plus two teams of three secretaries to take dictation and typing, together with a doctor for glucose injections. Chandler met the deadline, but the film's ending remained a problem as a minor character had to be suddenly worked into the story to replace the navy veteran as the killer.

Chandler, like Cain, disliked Hollywood, although he enjoyed its money. His bitterness toward the film industry motivated his next novel, *The Little Sister*, which was published in 1948. In 1951 he returned to Hollywood to work with Alfred Hitchcock on *Strangers on a Train*. However, the two men did not get on, and Hitchcock eliminated large sections of Chandler's script, which was reworked by Czenzi Ormonde. After Chandler's most ambitious novel, *The Long Goodbye*, was published in 1953, his career went into a decline, especially after the death of Cissy in December 1954. After five years of traveling back and forth between England and the United States, and one more novel (*Playback*), Chandler died in La Jolla on March 26, 1959.

## Steve Fisher (1912–1980)

As a hard-boiled novelist, Steve Fisher was not as talented as Dashiell Hammett, James M. Cain, David Goodis, or Raymond Chandler. But as a screenwriter, and later television writer, he was more successful, with a long career stretching from the late 1930s to the 1970s. Unlike these other writers, Fisher relished the demands of writing for film and television and was, unlike Cain or Chandler, able to adapt his writing skills to meet the specific demands of writing for the screen in a wide range of genres.

After attending a military academy in California, Fisher joined the navy and began writing short stories while serving on a submarine in the early 1930s. After leaving the service, he went to New York in 1933 and began publishing a series of lurid novels for second-rate publishers, including *Spend a Night* (1935), *Satan's Angel* (1935), and *Forever Glory* (1936). When Fanny Ellsworth replaced Joseph Shaw as the editor of *Black Mask* magazine, she encouraged Fisher, who, in 1937, published his first story for the magazine, "Murder at Eight." Thereafter he was a regular contributor for the next few years.

Fisher's one noncrime novel during this period, *Destroyer*, was published in 1941, and it depicted Americans fighting German and Japanese forces before the United States had entered World War II. However, it was his other 1941 novel, *I Wake Up Screaming*, that gave his career a major boost. Twentieth Century Fox immediately purchased the film rights, and filming began in August 1941, starring Victor Mature as a promoter accused of murdering his protégée. This early noir film starred Betty Grable in her first nonmusical role as the sister of the murdered woman. It is a significant film noir due to the fact that it focused on the psychological and sexual obsession of a disturbed cop (Laird Cregar) aptly named "Cornell." This was an oblique reference by Fisher to the tormented novelist Cornell Woolrich, who was an acquaintance at the time.

Although Fisher began writing scripts in 1938, beginning with low-budget films for Universal, his status in Hollywood improved markedly after the success of *I Wake Up Screaming,* even though he did not contribute to the film adaptation. In the next few years he wrote screenplays in a number of genres, including *To the Shores of Tripoli* (1942); *Berlin Correspondent* (1942); *Destination Tokyo* (1943), starring Cary Grant; *The Song of the Thin Man* (1947), the final entry in MGM's Thin Man series; and *Tokyo Joe* (1949), starring Humphrey Bogart.

Fisher also wrote noir films such as *Johnny Angel* (1945), starring Claire Trevor and George Raft; *Lady in the Lake* (1947), which became director Robert Montgomery's failed attempt to replicate Raymond Chandler's first-person narration by filming (almost) the entire film with a subjective camera; and *Roadblock* (1951), a tough, low-budget film starring Charles McGraw as an insurance investigator who destroys his career by trying to satisfy the mercenary demands of his wife. Fisher continued working throughout the 1950s, 1960s, and 1970s with films such as *City That Never Sleeps* (1953) and *36 Hours* (1953). From the mid-1950s he was also active in television, working on westerns such as *Have Gun—Will Travel,* crime programs such as *Peter Gunn,* as well as *Kolchak,* a strange hybrid of pulp fiction and horror. Fisher's last series was *Fantasy Island,* and he died on March 27, 1980.

## David Goodis (1917–1967)

If Dashiell Hammett was the father of the hard-boiled detective, David Goodis was the poet of its victims. His novels do not merely chronicle their fall but the period after the fall, their descent into oblivion—his first novel was called *Retreat from Oblivion* (1939). Even in his relatively more optimistic novels, such as *Dark Passage* (1946), the sense that there is little hope for a happy future is evident in the opening passage:

> It was a tough break. Parry was innocent. On top of that he was a decent sort of guy who never bothered people and wanted to lead a quiet life. But there was too much on the other side and on his side of it there was practically nothing. The jury decided he was guilty. The judge handed him a life sentence and he was taken to San Quentin. (p. 249)

His protagonists were usually passive, sometimes frightened men facing a bleak future. Death was ever-present, and an unrelenting sense of fatalism pervades his stories. His career followed the same trajectory, for after briefly enjoying mainstream success as a serious novelist and screenwriter in the late 1940s, he spent the last 17 years of his life working at the lowest level of the industry, churning out paperback originals for publishers such as Fawcett Gold Medal Books and Lion Books.

Goodis was born in Philadelphia and graduated from Temple University after majoring in journalism. In 1938, while writing copy for an advertising agency, he completed his first novel, *Retreat from Oblivion*. When it did not bring the critical and commercial success Goodis hoped for, he left Philadelphia for New York and quickly established himself as a prolific pulp writer. He averaged more than five million words in five and a half years, sometimes writing as much as 10,000 words per day. Goodis contributed to most of the popular genres, although he became a specialist in World War II air force stories. He also wrote scripts for many of the popular 1940s radio programs such as *Superman* as well as for the air force adventure serial *Hop Harrigan*.

During this period Goodis also worked on more mainstream literary endeavors, and after a number of rejections, the *Saturday Evening Post* serialized, in 1946, what was to become his most famous novel, *Dark Passage*. Its original title was *The Dark Road*, and after reading the galleys, Humphrey Bogart sent them to producer Jerry Wald with a note urging Warner Bros. to adapt them into a film for him and his wife, Lauren Bacall. The studio, however, was reluctant to commit, and it took considerable pressure from Bogart, who was Warner's number one star at that time, to get the film into production.

Warner Bros. offered Goodis a three-year contract as a screenwriter that also allowed him six months each year to work on his novels. This was a successful period, and one of his best novels, *Nightfall*, was published in 1947. Ten years later, it was adapted into an excellent film noir directed by Jacques Tourneur and starring Aldo Ray, Brian Keith, and Anne Bancroft.

Goodis was an eccentric character who, with his shabby clothes and colorful lifestyle, which occasionally involved sado-masochistic activities with prostitutes, was soon disenchanted with his Hollywood career. He objected to the studio imposing a happy ending on *Dark Passage*, with the final scene showing Bogart's romantic reunion with Bacall in a coastal town in Peru. Also, his screenwriting at Warner Bros. produced little of real substance as his only substantial credit was on Vincent Sherman's *The Unfaithful* (1947), starring Ann Sheridan.

After the publication of *Behold This Woman* in 1947 and *Of Missing Persons* in 1950, Goodis left Los Angeles and Warner Bros. and returned to Philadelphia. He also lost his prestigious publishing contract and began publishing paperback originals. His first paperback novel, *Cassidy's Girl*, published by Gold Medal Books in 1951, was a great success, selling more than one million copies. It also established a dramatic prototype that would dominate much of his fiction for the rest of his life: in *Cassidy's Girl* the male is a disgraced airline pilot involved in a bizarre relationship with two women—one a vulnerable woman and the other, a recurring figure in Goodis's fiction, an obese, callous woman willing to do anything to keep the pilot under her control.

Most of his novels placed his protagonists in a bleak context and focused on their suffering, and survival, due to past mistakes. Only the occupations changed—from the artist forced to work for a gang of burglars in *Black Friday* to the crooner reduced to poverty on the street in *Street of No Return*. In 1956 Columbia Studios commissioned Goodis to adapt one of his best novels, *The Burglar* (1953), to the screen. Released in 1957, this low-budget film was filmed in Philadelphia by Paul Wendkos and starred Dan Duryea as a thief in a strange relationship with his guardian, Jayne Mansfield. Both become involved in a jewel robbery, and although the film deletes the novel's conclusion, when they commit suicide in the sea near Atlantic City, the film retains the novel's "incestuous" obsession between a middle-aged thief and his young protégé.

The most prestigious adaptation of a Goodis paperback original was Francois Truffaut's second film as a director, *Shoot the Piano Player* (1960), based on Goodis's 1956 novel *Down There*. Aside from changing the setting from Philadelphia to Paris, Truffaut's film is faithful to the novel, and its success should have revitalized Goodis's career. Instead, there were only two more routine novels, *Night Squad* (1961) and *Somebody's Done For* (1967), before his death at the age of 49. With most of his fiction out of print throughout the 1960s, his death was largely anonymous. Perhaps that is what he wanted.

## Dashiell Hammett (1894–1961)

The term *film noir* was not an industry term—it originated with Nino Frank, and other French critics, in Paris in 1945. In attempting to explain the meaning of this term, they stressed the impact Hammett's fiction had on the detective story. Although he published only five crime novels in his lifetime, of which three were filmed in the 1930s and 1940s, Hammett's influence on film noir was profound. Hammett, along with Race Williams and a small number of other hard-boiled writers in the 1920s and early 1930s, changed the formal and ideological basis of the crime/suspense story and provided the basis for film noir in the 1940s.

Born Samuel Dashiell Hammett in Maryland on May 27, 1894, he was an inveterate reader of fiction and nonfiction in his youth and qualified for the Baltimore Polytechnic Institute. However, the family was poor, and he was forced to leave school after his father became ill. Hammett worked a variety of jobs until, at the age of 20, he joined the Pinkerton Detective Agency. Although his employment as a Pinkerton detective was interrupted by military service in World War I, his detective work was varied, from trailing suspects and finding husbands to assisting strikebreakers. Diagnosed with tuberculosis during the war, Hammett spent long periods in military hospitals as the disease never left him. After the war he returned to the Pinkertons and, based in Spokane in Washington, worked throughout the Northwest. When his tuberculosis returned in 1920, he was forced into part-time detective work in San Francisco, but even this was too much for his frail body, and he left the Pinkertons and began writing advertising copy for Albert Samuels, a jeweler.

Hammett's early stories for magazines such as *Smart Set* failed to attract interest in his fiction, and it was not until he published "Arson Plus," featuring an unnamed detective who came to be known as the Continental Op, in *Black Mask* in October 1923 that Hammett found his niche and, in the process, altered the nature of detective fiction with his understated style, devoid of sentiment and deeply ironic.

Although hampered by tuberculosis, Hammet was relatively prolific in 1924 and 1925, and he decided to live apart from his wife and daughter. In July 1926, after the birth of his second daughter, he was found unconscious in one of Samuel's jewelry shops, and his output declined. Nevertheless, his 1920s stories for *Black Mask* formed the basis for his novels. For example, "The Cleansing of Poisonville," which was serialized in *Black Mask* in 1927, became *Red Harvest*. The same was true for *The Dain Curse* (1929), *The Maltese Falcon* (1930), and *The Glass Key* (1929).

After the publication of *The Maltese Falcon* in early 1930, there was considerable interest in Hammett in Hollywood as well as in literary circles in New York. The gray-haired writer attracted many female admirers, and eventually, he established a long, volatile relationship with a young playwright and scriptwriter named Lillian Hellman. When MGM purchased the film rights to *The Thin Man* after its publication in 1934, he was able to live off the royalties for many years as MGM produced five sequels. In the 1940s Sam Spade, Hammett's detective in *The Maltese Falcon*, was also adapted to the radio and the comics.

Hammett, however, did not write another novel after *The Thin Man*. He spent some time as a scriptwriter and writing stories for a comic book as well as assisting Hellman with her own work. While his drinking intensified, he gradually became more involved in left-wing causes that caused problems for him after World War II. In 1951 he was imprisoned for nearly six months for refusing to testify to a federal court. Despite his age (47 years old), tuberculosis, and other health problems, Hammett enlisted in the army during World War II and served in the Aleutian Islands.

His health deteriorated in the 1950s, and Lillian Hellman looked after him for much of the period leading up to his death in 1961. Under pressure from anti-Communist forces in the late 1940s and 1950s, his publications were not reprinted, and the radio adaptations were terminated, leaving Hammett without money. Tax problems with the Internal Revenue Service meant that his final years were difficult, and he failed to complete a semiautobiographical novel titled *Tulip*. Nevertheless, his name remains synonymous with American detective fiction, and his tough view of the world influenced the numerous noir films of the 1940s.

### Jonathan Latimer (1906–1983)

As a screenwriter of hard-boiled films, Jonathan Latimer was one of its most prolific practitioners. Born in Chicago in 1906, Latimer worked as a police reporter for *The Chicago Tribune* and *The Chicago Herald-Examiner* in the 1930s, and this brought him into contact with criminals such as Al Capone. Latimer described his first five novels, which were based on the exploits of hard-drinking detective Bill Crane, as "booze, babes, and bullets" (Latimer, 1981). Latimer, like Hammett with *The Thin Man*, mixed comedy with murder, and his first novel, *Murder in the Madhouse*, was published in 1935. Three of his Crane stories were adapted to the cinema by Universal and starred Preston Foster as Crane: *The Westland Case*, based on *Headed for a Hearse*, was released in 1937; *Lady in the Morgue* in 1938; and *The Last Warning*, based on *The Dead Don't Care*, in 1939.

After five Crane novels, Latimer became tired of the character and replaced the light tone of this series with a more somber, hard-edged style. However, when Latimer completed *Solomon's Vineyard* he could not find an American publisher for the book, although it was released in Britain in 1941. A censored version eventually appeared in the United States by *Mystery Book Magazine*, where the editor changed the title to *The Fifth Grave*. A complete version did not appear in the United States until a small publisher, Blackmask, published it in 2004. Latimer's inspiration for the novel came when *The Chicago Herald-Examiner* sent him to Benton Harbor in Michigan to cover a trial and he encountered a religious colony a few miles out of town. The novel, which is similar to Hammett's *The Dain Curse*, combined murder with sado-masochism and political corruption, and much of the novel was set inside a bizarre religious cult.

At this time Latimer also began writing screenplays, beginning with two low-budget films: *The Lone Wolf Spy Hunt* in 1939, starring Warren William as Michael Lanyard's jewel thief, followed by *Phantom Raiders* in 1940, which was part of MGM's short-lived Nick Carter series, starring Walter Pidgeon. After coscripting the last of the Topper series, *Topper Returns* (1941), Latimer adapted Hammett's *The Glass Key* in 1942 for Paramount's remake of its 1935 film.

After serving in the U.S. Navy during World War II, Latimer moved to La Jolla, California, where he became a close friend of Raymond Chandler and his wife, Cissy. For the next three years Latimer wrote a number of noir films for RKO and Paramount, including *Nocturne* (1946), starring George Raft; *The Big Clock* (1948), based on Kenneth Fearing's novel; and *The Night Has a Thousand Eyes* (1948), based on Cornell Woolrich's novel. His best noir script during this period was the RKO film *They Won't Believe Me*. Produced by Joan Harrison, who had worked with Alfred Hitchcock and Robert Siodmak, Latimer's script skillfully assimilated many of the central attributes of film noir such as the morally flawed male dominated by his wealthy wife. The film concludes with a stunning court-room sequence, with the man jumping to his death just prior to the jury's verdict of not guilty for killing his wife.

His last film noir, *The Unholy Wife* (1957), was an uneven melodrama involving a wife's (Diana Dors) attempt to eliminate her husband (Rod Steiger). After a 15-year absence, Latimer returned to mystery novels (such as *Sinners and Shrouds*) in the mid 1950s and 1960s while also scripting many episodes of television series such as *Perry Mason*, *Markham*, and *Hong Kong*. He retired in 1973 and died in La Jolla in 1983.

## Horace McCoy (1897–1955)

W. R. Burnett claimed that Horace McCoy's decision to become a novelist was made after McCoy read Burnett's *Little Caesar*. Both men labored for the Hollywood studios in the 1930s, 1940s, and 1950s on genre films while working on their novels. However, while McCoy published two great novels, *They Shoot Horses, Don't They?* and *Kiss Tomorrow Goodbye*, as well as a few significant scripts, he did not have the same impact as Burnett. While Burnett was working with directors such as John Ford, Howard Hawks, and John Huston, McCoy spent many years writing for low-budget and poor-quality films.

Born in Pegram, near Nashville, in April 1927, McCoy left school when he was 16 and worked in a variety of jobs, including cab driving in New Orleans and Dallas. During World War I he was sent to France as an aerial observer and was awarded the Croix de Guerre for flying his plane back to the base, despite being wounded, after the pilot was killed. After the war, he returned to Dallas and worked for *The Dallas Journal* from 1920 to 1929 as a sports reporter and columnist while also dabbling as an actor in the Dallas Little Theater. Beginning with "The Devil Man" in the December 1927 issue of *Black Mask*, he followed this South Seas adventure with stories based on the adventures of pilot Jerry Frost, a Texas Ranger. While he also wrote for other pulp magazines, Jerry Frost remained his most popular magazine character.

In September 1929 McCoy was appointed editor of *The Dallasite*, but after the magazine collapsed in April 1930, he left Dallas in May 1931 for Los Angeles, hoping to get a Hollywood acting job. For the next 18 months he worked periodically as an extra and in the theatre while writing for magazines such as *Black Mask*, *Action Aces*, *Detective Dragnet Magazine*, *Battle Aces*, *Man Stories*, and *Western Trails*. He also began his most famous story, *They Shoot Horses, Don't They?*, as a short story. This bleak story, one of the best American pieces of fiction, was based on his experiences as a bouncer at a marathon dance contest on the Santa Monica pier.

At the end of 1932 McCoy was employed as a screenwriter, and his first screen credit was for *Her Resale Value*, an independent film for Mayfair Pictures. He joined, and left, RKO in 1932 and then began a two-year contract with Columbia in 1933, where he scripted five low-budget films. He also spent part of this period completing *They Shoot Horses, Don't They?*, which was expanded from short story to a (short) novel, which was published in 1935. This powerful novel of corruption and despair did not sell well in the United States, and it was not until French critics in the 1940s praised its terse, hard-boiled style and bleak, unsentimental view of life that it received recognition in the United States. In France, as Geoffrey O'Brien (1997, 80) points out, the

> post war *philosophes* were inclined to see what no American critic of the time would have noticed—that McCoy had penetrated deeper than anyone into the zero state at the heart of the hardboiled novel. He had produced a sharp, dry, arbitrary kind of book, a book poised so precisely on the edge of the real that it seems to cancel itself out.

McCoy's novel is, in some ways, the finest manifestation of hard-boiled fiction. Its story of a failed actress (Gloria) who enters a marathon dance contest with Robert, ostensibly to be discovered by Hollywood and win money, but in reality, to die, as she lacks the courage to kill herself. Sydney Pollack's 1969 film, starring Jane Fonda as Gloria, softened McCoy's novel by focusing more on the role of the crooked dance organizers as the motivation for her fatalism, weakens the social criticism inherent in the novel. Screenwriting contracts with Paramount and then Universal followed in the mid-1930s before McCoy left Hollywood for two years so that he could complete two novels. The first, *No Pockets in a Shroud,* was published in Britain in 1937 after McCoy's American publisher refused to publish the book. In 1948 the New American Library published an abridged version of the book after altering what they described as its "left-wing" attitudes and changing the heroine from a Communist to a "sexual pervert." In the novel McCoy drew on his experiences as a sport journalist in Dallas to attack corruption in sports and politics as well as racial injustice.

His next novel, *I Should Have Stayed at Home,* was published in 1938. It was an attack on the shady and superficial aspects of the Hollywood studio system. However, a lack of income soon forced McCoy back to the lucrative but unrewarding task of working for formulaic films. This included 10 crime films for Paramount between 1937 and 1940 as his career as a novelist was put on hold for nearly a decade.

In 1940 McCoy, weary of studio contracts and low-budget films, decided to work as a freelance scriptwriter. However, the quality of the assignments offered to him did not improve until he signed on with Warner Bros. in February 1942 for *Gentleman Jim,* a semifictional biography of boxer Jim Corbett, starring Errol Flynn and directed by Raoul Walsh. Another semifactual film followed for RKO, *Flight for Freedom* (1943), starring Rosalind Russell, partly based on McCoy's screen story "Stand to Die," which was inspired by the exploits of aviator Amelia Earhart.

McCoy cut back on his screenwriting from 1944 to 1947, and he spent most of 1947 writing his next novel, *Kiss Tomorrow Goodbye,* which was published in 1948. The novel attracted considerable critical attention in France, and Warner Bros. bought the rights so that James Cagney could portray another psychologically disturbed gangster after his success in *White Heat* (1949).

A heart attack in 1948 slowed McCoy down for a period, but the last six years of his life, until his death in 1955, were busy. In 1951 he spent part of the year on the rodeo circuit while he was working on his script for *The Lusty Men.* This atmospheric tale has some of the bleak, haunting qualities that distinguishes *They Shoot Horses, Don't They?* However, instead of a dance marathon, McCoy's script for *The Lusty Men* concentrated on the complex relationship between a former rodeo rider (Robert Mitchum) and a married couple (Susan Hayward and Arthur Kennedy). It was McCoy's best screenplay, and he worked on the film between October and December 1951 at the rate of $1,000 per week.

In 1951 McCoy sold a story treatment to Hal Wallis at Paramount that was filmed as *Bad for Each Other* (1953). He then transformed this script into a novel, *Scalpel,* which was published in 1954. This medical melodrama was set in a Pennsylvania mining town and starred Charlton Heston and Elizabeth Scott. He followed with a crime film, *Dangerous Mission* (1954), for RKO that brought McCoy and W. R. Burnett together on the screenplay. Unfortunately, this routine film did not live up to the talents of its writers.

In 1950 McCoy sold another story treatment, "This Is Dynamite," which was filmed by Paramount in 1952 as *The Turning Point,* starring William Holden as investigative reporter Jerry McKibbon. Although the film weakened McCoy's focus on the endemic corruption in a midwestern city, it remains one of McCoy's best noir stories. His film treatment was published as a novel, *Corruption City,* three years after his death.

## Cornell Woolrich (1903–1968)

Cornell Woolrich, writes Francis Nevins (1982, vii), "was the Poe of the 20th century and the poet of its shadows, the Hitchcock of the written word." While novels by Dashiell Hammett, James M. Cain, and Raymond Chandler have remained in print since their publication more than 60 years ago and are known by every aficionado of film noir, Woolrich's novels and short stories have been out of print for most of this period. Yet Woolrich was, at least in the 1940s, a significant influence on forming the themes and characters as well as the despairing world-view that were characteristic of film noir. Most of Woolrich's post-1934 fiction dramatizes a key noir question: why me?

A sense of doom and personal impotence pervades much of Woolrich's fiction. While it is sometimes reductive to rely heavily on biographical details, there is ample evidence, thanks mainly to the efforts of Francis Nevins over the past 35 years, to argue that Woolrich's lifestyle was an important determinant in his work—particularly in the way he generated an overwhelming sense of paranoia in his fiction—whatever the setting and whatever the period. Woolrich lived with his mother, Claire Attalie Tarler, in an apartment in the Hotel Marseilles in New York from the early 1930s until her death in 1957. Devoid of close personal friends, he did little except write, and from 1934 until 1948, he published more than 200 stories, and from 1940 to 1948, 11 novels.

Unlike Hammett's sparse fiction, Woolrich's florid style anticipated the high contrast lighting and visual touches that were seen as characteristic of film noir. For example, in his 1944 novel *The Black Path of Fear,* which was filmed as *The Chase* in 1946, his protagonist is fleeing from the police in Cuba when he approaches an opium den:

> We went down a new alley . . . ribbons of light spoked across this one, glimmering through the interstices of an unfurled bamboo blind stretched across an entryway.

The bars of light made cicatrices across us. He reached in at the side and slated up one edge of the pliable blind, made a little tent-shaped gap. For a second I stood alone, livid weals striping me from head to foot. (Woolrich 1982, 113)

Most of his novels, and many of his short stories, were adapted to the cinema and the radio. Between the low-budget Columbia film *Convicted* in 1938 and Paramount's *No Man of His Own* in 1950, there were 15 films based on his fiction. There were also more than 20 radio plays based on his novels and short stories during this period.

Cornell Woolrich was born in New York in 1903, and after his parents separated in 1907, he remained with his father in Mexico until, as a teenager, he joined his mother in New York. This was a turbulent period in Mexican history, and as a hobby, Woolrich collected the spent rifle cartridges that littered the streets. Whether the violence associated with this period affected his fiction, and his view of the world, cannot be reasonably gauged, but after his death, the following fragment was found among his papers: "one night when I was eleven and, huddling over my knees, looked up at the low hanging stars of the Valley of Anahuac, and I knew I would surely die finally, or something worse." This, he continues, marked the beginning of "the sense of personal, private doom" that pervaded his entire life: "I had that trapped feeling, like some sort of poor insect that you've put inside a downturned glass, and it tries to climb up the sides, and it can't, and it can't, and it can't" (Nevins 2004, xix).

In 1921 Woolrich enrolled at Columbia University, but he abandoned his studies after the success of his first novel, *Cover Charge* (1926). When his second novel, *Children of the Ritz* (1927), was purchased by First National Pictures, Woolrich, who always had a strong interest in the movies, went to Hollywood to work on its adaptation. He remained with First National as a staff writer for a few years, although he never received a screen credit. During the late 1920s and early 1930s he continued to publish novels and short stories and, in 1930, married Gloria Blackton, the daughter of pioneer film producer J. Stuart Blackton. The marriage, however, was never consummated, and after leaving his wife a diary detailing his homosexual affairs during their marriage, he returned to his mother in New York.

In the early 1930s he abandoned mainstream fiction after his inability to complete his seventh novel, *I Love You, Paris*. Desperate for money during the Depression, Woolrich turned to the pulp magazines, and his first crime/suspense story, "Death Sits in the Dentist's Chair," was published in *Detective Fiction Weekly* in August 1934. This bizarre story of a man who discovers that his brother's fingers have been removed, along with his tongue, and tracks down the perpetrator, an insane abortionist, indicated that Woolrich's fiction was not compatible with the classical detective mode of writing.

This marked the beginning of an amazing transformation in his career, and over the next 15 years, he wrote for magazines such as *Ace-High Fiction, All-American*

*Fiction, Argosy, Baffling Detective Mysteries, Black Mask, Dime Detective,* and *The Shadow*.

Although Woolrich published 10 crime stories in 1935, he was even more prolific in the years between 1936 and 1939, with two book-length magazine serials and at least 105 stories. He frequently returned to the same settings—the cheap dance hall, the precinct station backroom, the rundown movie theater, and the seedy hotel room—where he dramatized the same motifs over and over: a race against the clock, the destructive power of love and trust, and the innocent trapped by powers beyond their control.

Woolrich had as much effect on crime fiction in the middle and late 1930s as Hammett had a decade earlier. He brought a psychological dimension and paranoid intensity to the genre that was, up to that time, largely unknown. The economic and social dislocation of the Depression years informed much of his fiction, resulting in a kind of masochistic hysteria coupled with a pervasive sense of futility and doom. Often, as in his first suspense novel, *The Bride Wore Black*, which was published in 1940 and filmed by Francois Truffaut in 1968 as *La Mariée était*, his idealization and fear of women produced a strange hybrid—the punishing woman who was also shown to be both maternal and fanatically protective of her true love. In *The Bride Wore Black* the distraught heroine tracks down and murders the five men she believes were responsible for the death of her husband on their wedding day. In a customary twist Woolrich's novel concludes with the revelation that the men were innocent of the crime and that another man killed her husband. Truffaut's film, however, concludes without Woolrich's twist as the heroine kills the fifth man.

The success of *The Bride Wore Black* initiated a series of novels in the 1940s by Woolrich that were dubbed the Black series and appeared in France as part of the *Série Noire*. Woolrich received $2,225 from Paramount for the rights to his next novel, *The Black Curtain* (1941), which was released in November 1942 as *Street of Chance*. Although it is sometimes cited as the first film adaptation of Woolrich's fiction, at least one of his presuspense novels, *Children of the Ritz*, was filmed in 1929 by First National, and in 1938 Columbia paid Woolrich $448.75 for the rights to his short story "Face Work," which was published in *Black Mask* in October 1937. The resultant film, *Convicted*, starring Rita Hayworth as a dancer trying to prevent the execution of her younger brother after he is found guilty of murder, was a low-budget film that had little impact. *Street of Chance*, on the other hand, starring Burgess Meredith as Frank Thompson, a man trying to discover whether he committed murder while suffering from amnesia, was one of the best film adaptations of Woolrich's fiction. It was also adapted for radio in the 1940s, starring Cary Grant as Frank Thompson.

RKO bought the rights to Woolrich's next novel, *Black Alibi* (1942), for $5,175 and gave it to producer Val Lewton, who had just completed two memorable low-budget horror films, *Cat People* (1942) and *I Walked with a Zombie* (1943). Lewton, working with screenwriter Ardel Wray, proceeded to change the setting of Woolrich's novel from Latin America to New Mexico. They also altered the story line and the title of Woolrich's book was changed to *The Leopard Man* (1943). Woolrich's five sequences involving different women who are stalked by a killer jaguar and, subsequently, a man, were changed to two deaths, with only the first one caused by a black leopard, instead of a jaguar. However, the first killing, a young girl sent by her mother into the night to buy bread for the family, remains one of the most frightening moments in the cinema as Tourneur blends silence, natural sounds, and stylized lighting with images that capture the terror of the young girl as she moves through the darkness toward her house, only to discover that her mother has locked the door. Her death is presented mainly by the use of sound and lighting.

Up to this point, Woolrich's stories had only been adapted for low-budget films. *Phantom Lady*, produced by Joan Harrison and directed by Robert Siodmak, changed that. Filming began in October 1943, and it was released in February 1944 by Universal. The film's credits, however, did not mention Woolrich as he wrote the novel under one of his pseudonyms, William Irish. In fact, Woolrich was so prolific in the 1940s that he created two pseudonyms, William Irish and George Hopley, so that he could supply publishers other than Simon and Schuster, who had exclusive rights to his name, with manuscripts. *Phantom Lady* utilizes the same motif as *Convicted*, four years earlier, the race against time to save an innocent man from execution after he has been found guilty of a killing he did not do. This time, however, Universal made sure that the atmosphere and paranoia in Woolrich's story reached the screen, and the first half of the film stands out as an exemplary example of film noir. The consistent noir mise-en-scène involving a young woman, played by Ella Raines, stalking a bartender late at night through the dark streets of New York, culminating on the Third Avenue elevated platform, followed by her visit to a seedy nightclub cellar, where drug-addicted musicians provide the setting for an outrageous sexual metaphor involving Raines and Elisha Cook. In this notorious sequence, as Raines teases Cook, a drummer, his stroking of his drums intensifies as his sexual desire escalates and director Robert Siodmak leaves little to the imagination with his compositions and editing. However, the second half of the film, involving an insane killer, is less successful as the film deviates from the novel into a more conventional murder mystery involving an insane killer.

"Dormant Account," published in *Black Mask* in May 1942, was bought by Columbia for its Whistler series of eight films between 1944 and 1948. The second film in the series, *The Mark of the Whistler*, was released in 1944 and starred Richard Dix, who appeared in all the Whistler films, except one, as a hobo who claims the bank account of a missing man who shares the same name. However, this brings him into conflict with two men determined to kill the owner of the bank account.

While *The Mark of the Whistler* had no ambitions beyond that of a series film, RKO's *Deadline at Dawn*, based on Woolrich's 1944 novel (under his pseudonym William Irish), which was expanded from his 1941 short story "Of Time and Murder" (published in *Detective Fiction Weekly*), had ambitions well beyond the conventional mystery thriller. Scripted by Clifford Odets and directed by Harold Clurman, who were major figures in New York's Group Theater in the 1930s, most of Woolrich's story was jettisoned, except the basic premise of a young couple trying to escape the dark canyons of Manhattan and clear themselves of a murder charge. The entire action of the novel, and the film, occupies a single night. The film utilizes Woolrich's characteristic race against time as the couple believes that they will be trapped unless they escape the city by dawn. Unfortunately, the film's script tries to inject overt social meaning, and Woolrich's clever plot is pushed aside by Odets's pretentious dialogue.

Universal's production of *Black Angel*, based on Woolrich's 1943 novel, was more successful. Roy Chanslor's screenplay reduced the number of characters and eliminated the episodic basis of the novel to create a more coherent and linear story line. The basic premise is similar to *Phantom Lady*, with a woman, Catherine Bennett, desperate to save a man, her adulterous husband, from execution after he has been found guilt of murdering his mistress. Bennett, in the film but not in the novel, receives assistance in her hunt for the killer from an alcoholic pianist, Martin Blair, who is a composite of two characters in Woolrich's story.

Released in 1946, *Black Angel* was a success. Another 1946 release, *The Chase*, based on Woolrich's 1944 novel *The Black Path of Fear*, was more problematic. Similar to Fritz Lang's 1944 film *The Woman in the Window* and Robert Siodmak's 1945 film *The Strange Affair of Uncle Harry*, Phillip Yordan's script for *The Chase* ultimately reveals that the bulk of the story is a nightmare. As the film's protagonist, Chuck Scott (Robert Cummings), is shot to death, he emerges from a nightmare brought on by a bout of malaria. Based on the short story "Havana Night," which was published in *Flynn's Detective Weekly* in December 1942, Woolrich's novel focused on the doomed love affair between Scott and Eve Roman, the wife of a vicious gangster. Scott and Eve escape from Miami to Havana, where she is killed by agents of her husband. Scott is framed for Eve's murder, and most of the novel concerns his desperate attempts to escape from Havana while being pursued by both the law and Roman's agents. While the film's dream ending produces a happy ending for Scott and Eve, the novel concludes on a more bittersweet note, with Scott alone in Havana longing for his dead lover.

Three low-budget films based on Woolrich's short stories were released in 1947. *Fall Guy* was based on the 1940 *Black Mask* story "C-Jag," *The Guilty* was based on the 1941 *Detective Fiction Weekly* story "He Looked Like Murder," and *Fear in the Night* was based on the 1941 *Argosy* story "And So to Death." The first two films were cheaply produced by Monogram Studio, and both have poor production values in the form of sparse sets, unimaginative compositions and lighting, and perfunctory performances. *Fall Guy* dramatizes another hapless Woolrich protagonist who, after ingesting a drug-laced drink, wakes up with a blood-splattered knife nearby and the feeling that he has killed a woman. *The Guilty* reworks another recurring Woolrich technique whereby the apparently innocent central character turns out to be the killer.

*Fear in the Night*, a low-budget Paramount film, shares a similar plot to *Fall Guy* whereby a young man wakes up from a nightmare believing he has committed murder. This film, unlike *Fall Guy* and *The Guilty*, benefits from a larger budget; stronger performances, especially from DeForest Kelley as the tormented man and Paul Kelly as his policeman brother-in-law; and fine direction from Maxwell Shane, who captures the vulnerability and paranoia in Woolrich's tale. Nine years after the release of *Fear in the Night*, Maxwell Shane wrote and directed a remake, titled *Nightmare*, starring Edward G. Robinson as the policeman and Kevin McCarthy as the tormented man with the recurring nightmare.

Three films based on Woolrich's fiction were released in 1948. His 1940 *Argosy* story "All at Once, No Alice" was bought by Columbia and used in their Whistler series as *Return of the Whistler*. This was the only Whistler film not to star Richard Dix, and his absence hurt the film, the last one in the series. The story line, another familiar Woolrich plot, involves a woman who mysteriously disappears the night before her wedding, and her fiancé sets out to find out what happened to her.

*I Wouldn't Be in Your Shoes*, another low-budget Monogram production based on the short story of the same name published in *Detective Fiction Weekly* in 1938, was a variation of the familiar Woolrich story line involving a wife forced to prove that her husband is innocent of killing another woman. Again, as in *Black Angel*, she is assisted by a man who is in love with her, and again, he is revealed to be the killer. The third Woolrich-based film released in 1948, *Night Has a Thousand Eyes*, had a more lavish budget, but it was a disappointing adaptation. Writing under another one of his pseudonyms, George Hopley (Woolrich's two middle names), *Night Has a Thousand Eyes* was published as a novel in 1945, although it was based on his 1937 short story "Speak to Me of Death." The adaptation of the novel to the screen by hard-boiled writer Jonathan Latimer was a disappointment as the film lacked the fine balance between the rational and the supernatural world evident in the novel. Instead, the John Farrow–directed film strips away Woolrich's sense of fatalism and doom in this story of a recluse who predicts the death of a millionaire by the jaws of a lion at midnight in three weeks. This sets up another race against time as the millionaire's daughter and a detective try to avert the man's death.

RKO's 1949 production of *The Window*, based on Woolrich's 1947 short story "The Boy Cried Murder," was one of the best screen adaptations of his fiction. This low-budget film, without much publicity, became a major commercial success for RKO, who borrowed Bobby Driscoll from Disney to star as the young boy who witnesses a murder in a nearby apartment. However, as he has a history of telling tall stories, nobody, except the killers, believe him. At the film's climax his parents lock him in their apartment as the killers move in. The premise of this story is similar to another Woolrich short story, "It Had to Be Murder," published in *Dime Detective* magazine in 1942 and extended by Alfred Hitchcock into his 1954 film *Rear Window*.

Woolrich's creative period was over by the late 1940s, and he only published a few new short stories and novels in the 1950s and 1960s, while also trying to rework earlier stories and pass them off as new. Toward the end of the 1940s, however, he published two of his best novels. As William Irish, he wrote *Waltz into Darkness* in 1947, and in 1948, an even better novel appeared: *I Married a Dead Man*.

The beginning of this story is pure Woolrich—a typical, vulnerable person trapped within a hostile universe with little hope of salvation. Although the specific nature of the trap varies from novel to novel, its function is always the same—to dramatize Woolrich's paranoid view of existence whereupon the individual is shown to be impotent and unable to understand, let alone control, his or her world. Woolrich rarely drew on the traditional mystery or detective story and never used series characters. He rejected the processes of ratiocination that underpinned the traditional detective story as he was not interested in the restoration of a social or moral equilibrium. Instead, his work detailed its disintegration as he explored the absurdities and inequities of life. This often produced strange twists and unresolved endings and provoked criticism of his fiction as implausible and unrealistic. Woolrich did not care—he was only interested in generating a sense of despair and emotional chaos. Nowhere is this more evident than in the conclusion to *I Married a Dead Man*, where he refuses to resolve the dilemma facing the two main characters. Unlike in the film, the identity of who killed Helen's husband is not revealed, and the novel ends with Helen's quiet cry, "We've lost. That's all I know. We've lost. And now the game is through." His view of the world was an arbitrary and incomprehensible place, where, as Francis Nevins (2004, xix) points out, "Beams happen to fall, and are predestined to fall, and are toppled over by malevolent powers; a world ruled by chance, fate and God the malign thug."

Paramount bought the rights to the novel, and in 1950 it was released as *No Man of Her Own*, starring Barbara Stanwyck as the hapless heroine. The film version, however, rejected Woolrich's nihilistic ending and replaced it with the happy ending found in the novella *They Call Me Patrice*, which was published in 1946 in the woman's magazine *Today's Woman*. Two years later, Woolrich reworked the basis story line of the novella into his novel *I Married a Dead Man*, although he also changed the ending from the happy closure in *They Call Me Patrice* to one of his bleakest endings in *I Married a Dead Man*. This novel was filmed in France as *J'ai épousé une ombre*, was released in the United States as *I Married a Dead Man*, and, in 1996, was reworked again into *Mrs. Winterbourne*, starring talk show hostess Ricki Lake as the young heroine and Shirley MacLaine as her benefactor.

By the early 1950s, most of Woolrich's novels hade been filmed in Hollywood, most interest in his fiction came from television, and a number of his short stories were adapted for anthology series such as *Pepsi Cola Playhouse*, *Lux Video Theater*, *Ford Theater*, *Thriller*, *Suspicion*, and *Alfred Hitchcock Presents*. In 1973, one of his most suspenseful short stories, "You'll Never See Me Again," which was first published in 1939 in the pulp magazine *Detective Story*, appeared on ABC television in the United States in February 1973 as a made-for-television film.

After 1950, the French, especially director Francois Truffaut, became interested in Woolrich's fiction. When American producer-director Hall Bartlett was unable to raise sufficient money to film Woolrich's first novel, *The Bride Wore Black*, he sold the rights to Truffaut's production company, and it was released as *La Mariée était en noir* in 1968, starring Jeanne Moreau as the woman who destroys the lives of five men after her husband is shot outside the church on her wedding day. Released in the United States as *The Bride Wore Black*, this was a critical and commercial success for Truffaut, and he followed this film with an adaptation of *Waltz into Darkness*. This was released in France in 1969 as *La Siréne du Mississippi* and in the United States as *Mississippi Mermaid*, and it starred Jean-Paul Belmondo as the man prepared to forgive his lover (Catherine Deneuve) virtually everything, including theft and attempted murder. Truffaut, who also scripted the film, transformed Woolrich's grim, masochistic tale into a more positive story where love eventually overcomes betrayal and loneliness. The film was remade as an American-French coproduction in 2001 as *Original Sin*, starring Angelina Jolie and Antonio Banderas and directed by Michael Christofer.

A diabetic, Woolrich was a lonely alcoholic in his final years. When he developed gangrene in his leg in late 1967, he neglected the injury for so long that the doctors had little alternative but to remove the leg when he finally sought treatment. He died of a stroke on September 25, 1968, and left an estate of nearly $1 million to Columbia University for a scholarship fund to encourage budding writers.

Woolrich's fiction returned time and again to the same theme—personal impotence in a hostile world. Although many of his plots are riddled with implausible events and coincidences, he was able to draw the reader into his bizarre stories. His excessive, sometimes hysterical style often intensified his sense of paranoia and fatalism. After his death in 1968, the following fragment was found in Woolrich's papers:

> I was only trying to cheat death.... I was only trying to surmount for a while the darkness that all my life I surely knew was going to come rolling in on me one day and obliterate me. I was only trying to stay alive a little brief while longer, after I was already gone. To stay in the light, to be with the living, a little while past my time. (Nevins 2004, xix)

## REFERENCES

Cain, James. 1953. *The Postman Always Rings Twice*. Melbourne: Penguin Books.

Chandler, Raymond. 1978. "Red Wind." In *The Great American Detective*, ed. William Kittredge and Steven M. Krauzer. New York: New American Library

Chandler, Raymond. 1973. "The Simple Art of Murder." Reprinted in *Pearls are a Nuisance*, Raymond Chandler, 198. Harmondsworth, England: Penguin Books.

Daly, Carroll John. 1977. "The False Burton Combs." In *The Hard-Boiled Detective. Stories From Black Mask Magazine (1920 – 1951)*, ed. Herbert Ruhm, 3–30. New York: Vintage Books.

Goodis, David. 1983. "Dark Passage." In David Goodis, *4 Novels by David Goodis*. London: Zomba Books.

Krutnik, Frank. 1991. *In a Lonely Street: Film Noir, Genre, Masculinity*. London: Routledge.

Latimer, Jonathan. Interview with Maurice Neville and James Pepper, November 15, 1981. *Black Mask Magazine.com* (reprint). Available at http://www.blackmaskmagazine.com/bm_06.html.

Nevins, Francis M. 2004. "Introduction." In Cornell Woolrich, *Night and Fear: A Centenary Collection of Stories by Cornell Woolrich*. New York: Carroll and Graf.

Nevins, Francis M. 2005. "Tonight, Somewhere in New York." *The Last Stories and an Unfinished Novel by Cornell Woolrich*. New York: Carroll and Graf.

Nevins, Francis M., Jr. 1971. "Introduction." In Cornell Woolrich, *Nightwebs*, v–xxxii. New York: Equinox Books.

Nevins, Francis M., Jr. 1982. "Introduction." In Cornell Woolrich, *Black Path of Fear*. New York: Ballentine Books.

O'Brien, Geoffrey. 1997. *Hardboiled America: Lurid Paperbacks and the Masters of Noir*. New York: Da Capo Press.

Wilt, David. 1991. *Hardboiled in Hollywood*. Bowling Green, OH: Bowling Green State University Popular Press.

Woolrich, Cornell. 1982. *Black Path of Fear*. New York: Ballentine Books.

# Film Noir and the City

Brian McDonnell

## INTRODUCTION

Although a tiny proportion of the films do have small-town or rural settings, classical film noir is quintessentially an urban cycle. A list of selected titles from the classical period of film noir clearly emphasizes this city focus, either by the use of the word *city* in the title (e.g. *Dark City*, *The Naked City*, *City of Shadows*, *City for Conquest*, *Cry of the City*, *Night and the City*, *The Sleeping City*, *While the City Sleeps*, *The City That Never Sleeps*, *Edge of the City*), or by naming actual cities in the title (e.g. *The Phenix City Story*, *New York Confidential*, *Port of New York*, *The Killer That Stalked New York*, *Chicago Deadline*, *Chicago Confidential*, *Kansas City Confidential*), or by employing the term or the notion of the *street* (e.g. *The Naked Street*, *Scarlet Street*, *Mystery Street*, *Street of Chance*, *The Street with No Name*, *One Way Street*, *Panic in the Streets*, *Side Street*, *Pickup on South Street*, *Where the Sidewalk Ends*, *711 Ocean Drive*, *99 River Street*, *Sunset Blvd*, *The House on 92nd Street*), or sometimes even by a metaphorical reference to the brutal savagery inherent in urban life (e.g. *The Asphalt Jungle*, *The Human Jungle*, *The Steel Jungle*).

The centrality of a city setting as a key genre characteristic has been stressed ever since the first influential discussions in English of the phenomenon of film noir occurred in Higham and Greenberg's (1968) *Hollywood in the Forties*. This can clearly be seen in the famous opening sentences from their chapter "Black Cinema," a passage inspired in general terms by any number of film noirs but specifically by a notable early scene in *The Unsuspected* (1947): "A dark street in the early morning hours, splashed with a sudden downpour. Lamps form haloes in the murk. In a walk-up room, filled with the intermittent flashing of a neon sign from across the street, a man is waiting to murder or be murdered . . . the specific ambience of *film noir*, a world of darkness and violence" (p. 19).

Most general texts written on the genre have continued to stress this city link. Andrew Spicer (2002), for example, in his recent book *Film Noir*, reiterates the elements that make up such an ambience, writing that film noir's "iconography (repeated visual patterning) consists of images of the dark, night-time city, its streets damp with rain which reflects the flashing neon signs. Its sleazy milieu of claustrophobic alleyways and deserted docklands alternates with gaudy nightclubs and swank apartments" (p. 4). Eddie Muller (1998) even structures his popular, entertaining, nonacademic account of film noir *Dark City: The Lost World of Film Noir* as a series of chapters whose titles describe city thoroughfares and neighborhoods: "Blind Alley," "Hate Street," "Vixenville," "Loser's Lane," and so on. Of course, the nature of urban life had been treated in film cycles before, such as the so-called city films produced in Germany and France in the 1920s and 1930s. In the classical film noir, however, it is the modern American city rather than the European city that becomes the central setting of a substantial genre.

## SEMIDOCUMENTARIES AND LOCATION SHOOTING

For some viewers the most obvious expression of the urban world of noir is to be found in the subgenre of the semidocumentary film made popular in postwar years by commercially successful movies such as *The Naked City* (1948). These films were shot on actual locations rather than on studio back-lots, and there is no doubt that they had a more authentic city feel than earlier studio-bound examples of noir. Semidocumentary film noirs tended to portray (rather than any furtive private transgressions) cities riven by public crimes, especially by political corruption, as in *The Captive City* (1952), *The Phenix City Story* (1955), *The Big Heat* (1953), *The Racket* (1951), or *Street with No Name* (1948).

Their protagonists are frequently members of various law enforcement bodies, a feature which has led some critics to consider them as being different ideologically from the radicalism of much film noir portraying "heroes" who are, in the main, downtrodden victims. Instead of lonely tenement rooms, these semidocumentaries feature locations appropriate for gangsters and organized crime, such as nightclubs, gambling joints, boxing rings, and arenas, along with other metonyms of city life such as boarding houses. *The Killing* and *The Harder They Fall* (both 1956) are late classical noirs that share with these semidocumentaries a setting in the urban worlds of sport and gambling. Racetracks, for example, feature in many noir films because (with their large deposits of cash) they obviously link in well with crime stories and heist plots.

## EXISTENTIALISM/ALIENATION

Far more representative, however, than the semidocumentary treatment of the noir city is a distorted, expressionistic portrayal of it as an existential site of alienation. This aspect of the nature of the city, pessimistic in tone, is reflected in its often solitary inhabitants. The typical city dwellers of such stories are existential heroes, loners alienated in and by the city, which is impersonal and isolating. They are observed scurrying furtively beneath the street lights and along the alleyways and wet streets. They are revealed sitting alone in a darkened room, fearful and lonely. These protagonists seem so different from the heroes of more traditional Hollywood films, who occupy sunny urban landscapes, but there are sometimes hints that the shadowy city of sin and crime is present all along, lying below the shiny surface of those movies, if only the protagonists could see it. Even in Frank Capra's *It's a Wonderful Life* (1946), for instance, the noirish Pottersville exists as a nightmare town below the surface of Bedford Falls.

Symptomatic of the view within film criticism of the city as inhospitable and alienating is Michael Walker's introduction to *The Movie Book of Film Noir* (1992), where he characterizes the noir city as dangerous, bleak, and isolating: "The hero tends to take to the streets uneasily, aware of himself as an outsider" (p. 30). Specific city settings (which may initially look glamorous) are mediated by the protagonist's voice-over narration, especially in adaptations of Raymond Chandler's detective novels, and such soundtrack adjuncts to the film's visuals can color the viewer's interpretation of the city observed. This emphasis on alienation in the big city suggests to some an influence on visual tone from prior American works of art, including, for instance, those of the painter Edward Hopper. Nicholas Christopher (1997), in his book *Somewhere in the Night*, has discussed the influence of Hopper's paintings on *Force of Evil* (1948). He describes, for instance, how director Abraham Polonsky took his cinematographer George Barnes along to a Hopper exhibition in Greenwich Village to show the man exactly how he wanted the film to look.

Another writer who makes a similar point about alienating spaces is Paula Rabinowitz (2002) when discussing rooming houses in her book *Black and White and Noir: America's Black Modernism*. The following citation she gives from Cornell Woolrich's *I Married a Dead Man* (which was adapted into the Barbara Stanwyck film noir *No Man of Her Own* [1950]) vividly evokes the subjectivity of the isolated urban dweller:

> She climbed the rooming-house stairs like a puppet dangling from slack strings. A light bracketed against the wall, drooping upside down like a withered tulip in its bell-shaped shade of scalloped glass, cast a smoky yellow glow. A carpet-strip ground to the semblance of decayed vegetable-matter, all pattern, all color, long erased, adhered to the middle of the stairs, like a form of pollen or fungus encrustation. (p. 32)

The overall city experience of alienation for its citizens is here exemplified in the isolated lives of the sole occupants of tenement rooms.

In fact, the mise-en-scène of many of the films in the classical noir cycle presents a world of nightmarish distortion similar to that found in Woolrich's prose portrait, a good example being the haunted epilogue of Fritz Lang's *Scarlet Street* (1945). That film begins more or less with protagonist Christopher Cross (Edward G. Robinson), seen after a testimonial dinner wandering the nighttime city, lost (and a little drunk) in the bewilderingly tangled narrow roads of Greenwich Village. He is disoriented as he traverses the rainy and confusing streets, caught out of his normal world. *Scarlet Street* ends, after all the intricacies of its plot and the duplicity of its characters Johnny and Kitty, with Cross becoming obsessed by guilt. In a shabby room where a neon light blinks on and off as he hears the disembodied voices of Kitty (murdered by him) and Johnny (wrongly executed for Chris's crime due to Chris's silence), Cross exists anguished and distraught inside a waking nightmare. A newspaperman (in a nod to the Production Code) preaches sententiously about how a man's conscience sentences him worse than a judge could do. Cross tries to hang himself, but they cut him down. The epilogue concludes some years later with him sleeping in the snow in a park where patrolling cops disbelieve his rambling confessions. He is condemned to walk the streets as if in purgatory expiating his sins.

The mise-en-scène of Robert Siodmak's *Phantom Lady* (1944) provides another salutary example: what starts early in that film as a normal cityscape becomes more nightmarish as the predicament and plight of its wrongly convicted hero worsen. When his secretary (transformed into a bejeweled dame) goes out to investigate the crime for which he has been unjustly imprisoned, she enters a grim, expressionistic cityscape. Following a man to an elevated rail station across wet nighttime streets with the disturbing noise of footsteps on metal and the click of a barrier arm, she stands alone and in jeopardy on the El platform. When she enters a cramped cellar to witness a frenzied jam session among musicians, the camerawork and editing create a hellish atmosphere. Stylization has made the city an almost malignant force.

Another metaphorical move away from the documentary treatment of the city can be found in Polonsky's *Force of Evil*, which has a well-known poetic closing sequence set by the river, in which the protagonist, Joe (John Garfield), finds the body of his brother Leo. At the end of a story containing lots of claustrophobic, tightly framed studio-shot interiors reflecting the fated lives of its characters, this film, for its concluding scene, in which Garfield attempts to cleanse himself of guilt, goes on location to a real New York bridge (the George Washington). Joe says it is "like going down to the bottom of the world" as he descends the steps beside the bridge's abutments. The tone is sinister yet lyrical, with the location work emphasizing the bridge's stone towers, its steel span, and the jumble of rocks below. Like Orpheus and Eurydice heading up from the underworld, Joe and his female companion, Doris, then slowly climb back up from the rocks and the body, symbolizing his return to integrity and his intention to help clean up city crime and corruption.

Indeed, the city itself can actually be personified in film noir. In *City That Never Sleeps* (1953), with Gig Young as policeman Johnny Kelly, the "spirit" of the city of Chicago itself is the film's spectral narrator. The credits pan across buildings while a ghostly voice-over says, "I am the city, hub and heart of America." In a fantasy plot element, this mysterious figure (played by Chill Wills with seeming preternatural powers and called Joe Chicago) becomes a temporary police partner for Young. The film's climactic chase is reminiscent of street scenes in *The Third Man*, and the elevated electric rail track where the chase culminates leads to a violent electrocution of the villain. The fight on the tracks in *City That Never Sleeps* is, by the way, similar also to the climax of the 1984 Clint Eastwood neo-noir *Tightrope*. Young's character eventually finds redemption and gets his badge back, and *City That Never Sleeps* ends with the cop finding his missing brother in a Catholic church. His mysterious partner disappears, and Young reunites with his wife in a moralistic conclusion. The ghostly voice-over intones the ponderous closing lines: "Johnny Kelly is home, home to stay . . . people are working, laughing and dying, and some like Johnny Kelly are being born again in a city that never sleeps."

## THE LABYRINTH

Perhaps the critical work that contains the most elaborate and detailed examination of the urban setting of film noir is *Somewhere in the Night* by Nicholas Christopher (1997). Christopher defines the relationship of the film noir genre with the city most emphatically in the following:

> However one tries to define or explain noir, the common denominator must always be the city. The two are inseparable. The great, sprawling American city, endlessly in flux, both spectacular and sordid, with all its amazing permutations of human and topographical growths, with its deeply textured nocturnal life that can be a seductive, almost otherworldly *labyrinth* of dreams or a tawdry bazaar of lost souls: the city is the seedbed of noir. (p. 39; emphasis mine)

This image of the noir city as a labyrinth dominates the conceptualization of Christopher's book, and he defines his use of the word (Christopher 1997, 17), first by saying that the term *labyrinth* includes the actual physical maze of the city, with its streets, tunnels, and docks, its warrens of offices, apartments, and tenements; second, by evoking with the word a human condition in which the films' characters intersect and interact with complex plot twists and stratagems, bound by enmeshments of time, space, and chance; and third, by examining the hero's inner workings, which are imaged as a corollary of the city's own inner workings: its politics, languages, cultural crosscurrents, sewers, and other networks and infrastructures. A classic example would be Orson Welles's use of the baroque alleys and sleazy interiors of his border town setting in *Touch of Evil*.

Another helpful instancing of this labyrinth image is Christopher's account of a maze-like building seen in an early scene in *Johnny Eager* (1941) that shows the transformation of the eponymous protagonist (played by Robert Taylor) from a cabbie to a gangster. Johnny walks confidently through several front offices and through a number of ordinary doors in a new office building at a dog racetrack, then moves through a big steel door that leads to a luxury apartment, where he changes into very expensive clothes. The audience now realizes that this secret back area is the hub of his criminal empire and learns a strong lesson about the typical deceptiveness of surface appearances in this genre.

One salient aspect of labyrinths is that people become hopelessly lost in them, and hence they may be thought of as traps. Rob White's (2003) book on the British film noir *The Third Man* talks in detail about this notion of the city as a trap:

> Cities are among the most fundamental of the cinema's subjects—cities not 'the city.' A city has no meaningful reality. The same street or building exists differently, depending on the point of view. It is not the same for the shopper, the lost child, the man on the run, the pickpocket, the immigrant, the policeman, the beggar, the tourist, the terrorist or the bomber pilot thousands of feet above. Carol Reed [director of *The Third Man*] was one of the great directors of city-experience, and what he emphasised was disorientation and alarm. His heroes are purposeful in the city but hunted. There are traps all about and ambush is always expected. Often it comes, if the purposefulness is forgotten or made impossible by injury, delirium, grief or obsession. In film after film, characters stumble along a street, their minds disintegrating. (p. 46)

In a metaphor drawn from geometry, White contrasts the two-dimensional view of the city taken by pursuers such as Calloway in *The Third Man* with the three-dimensional view of the city experienced by those fleeing their pursuers:

> He [the fugitive] can move unpredictably, he can remain hidden, and he can move vertically as well as at ground level, on the look out for hiding places and eyries above. *Odd Man Out*, *The Third Man* and *The Man Between* all insist on this advantage, showing their protagonists clambering up scaffolds, on window ledges, down winding stairs and mounds of debris—or, of course, moving and sheltering below ground, in the sewers . . . but always their advantage is lost and they die, gunned down. (p. 48)

From these numerous examples, it could be claimed that the notion of the city in film noir is, in the final analysis, a complicated one. Spicer (2002) is one film historian who insists on the complexity of film noir representations of the city:

> The noir city has a fundamental ambivalence, dangerous, violent, squalid and corrupt but also exciting and sophisticated, the place of opportunity and conspicuous consumption. . . . Noir protagonists may occupy dingy rooming-houses, grimy diners and run-down smoke-filled bars, but they are drawn to the world of smart money—to bright garish nightclubs, spacious, over-decorated luxury apartments and imposing mansions—like moths to a flame. (p. 67)

To adequately illustrate this complexity in richer detail, it is necessary to canvass the wide variety of city settings in American film noir by looking systematically at the actual major cities that feature in the majority of examples of the genre.

## LOS ANGELES

First and foremost as a locus classicus of the genre is the very city in which Hollywood is located and where the studios that produced film noir operated: Los Angeles. There is no doubt that the stringent minimizing of production expenses imposed by the comparatively low budgets of most films today categorized as noir had an influence in this regard. Plainly, the films' stories were usually set in Los Angeles to save money on travel to plot locations (a policy practiced even more stringently during World War II because of government restrictions). They tended to emphasize the darker and seamier side of a city that was otherwise stereotyped by boosters of its development as sunny and prosperous. In its early years, Los Angeles was dubbed "Los Diablos" (i.e., a devilish rather than an angelic city) by more cynical newspaper writers throughout the United States, and the city certainly seems more diabolic than angelic, as it is generally portrayed in film noir.

Perhaps predictably, the film adaptations of Raymond Chandler's detective novels show this tendency very clearly. *Murder, My Sweet* (1944) is a classic example of the way a detective such as Philip Marlowe is able to lead viewers into a wide variety of urban milieux, ranging from a huge millionaire's estate to a seedy gambling dive. A similar range of Los Angeles locations features in *The Brasher Doubloon* (1947), from its Pasadena mansion buffeted by the warm Santa Ana winds to Marlowe's rundown firetrap of an office. In this film, the old Victorian streets and buildings of Bunker Hill are panned by the camera while Marlowe's voice-over narration describes them as once being the choice place to live in Los Angeles but concedes that presently, they are places where people live because they do not have any choice. Interestingly, *The Brasher Doubloon* also employs newsreel footage of an actual Tournament of Roses parade in Pasadena to explore different viewpoints on a murder (compare the famous Zapruder film of the John Kennedy assassination). Chandler's Los Angeles can also be glimpsed from its articulation in his reworking as scriptwriter of James M. Cain's novel *Double Indemnity*. That 1944 film version directed by Billy Wilder also proffers a classic suburban noirscape, seemingly wholesome on the surface but evil underneath. Protagonist Walter Neff's voice-over descriptions of setting, which provide an important statement on how subjectivity governs people's responses to places, are understandably very similar in tone to the narration of Chandler's own Philip Marlowe novels (e.g., in their use of metaphors).

The steep Bunker Hill streets of *The Brasher Doubloon* with their old Gothic wooden villas also are a notable feature too of *Criss Cross* (1949), which has impressive location work around the industrial areas of Los Angeles in its payroll holdup sequence. Incidentally, *Criss Cross* starts with an aerial helicopter shot of downtown Los Angeles, one of the first such shots ever seen in a feature film. The steep downtown cable car line known as the Angel's Flight, which leads up from downtown Los Angeles into Bunker Hill (and which more resembles San Francisco than Los Angeles), features in *Criss Cross* and is seen, too, in *Hollow Triumph* (1948) and *Kiss Me Deadly* (1955). In each film the cable car's precipitous route emphasizes the off-kilter and bewildering atmosphere of the plot.

*Cry Danger* (1951) uses as a key setting the type of temporary housing seen in many American cities in the postwar years. The Clover Trailer Park, where the main characters live in a form of transit housing, is in sight of the towering Los Angeles City Hall, the bold civic statement of the tower contrasting with the shabby and makeshift character of the trailer park. *Somewhere in the Night* (1946) is another film noir that highlights a range of particular postwar Los Angeles settings—a field hospital, Camp Pendleton, public baths, a bar frequented by demobilized soldiers, and squalid hotel rooms—that accentuate the absence of comfortable domestic spaces for the film's characters.

*Armored Car Robbery* (1950) is a B movie that uses particularly unusual locations for its criminal plot. Its heist at a ballpark employs location shooting at Wrigley Field (the Los Angeles one, not the more famous Chicago park). Its cameras also roam into the downtown district with its old bridges, the Long Beach oil fields, and the oil terminal shipyard. Even a San Fernando Valley motor court adds to the authenticity of the location work. Another B movie, *Roadblock* (1951), belies its small budget with the elaborate location shooting of its climactic police chase along the strangely concrete-lined bed of the Los Angeles River, a topographical oddity that was later made famous in John Boorman's neo-noir *Point Blank* (1967).

Another film noir with intriguing Los Angeles locations is *He Walked by Night* (1948), which has a sequence filmed in the sewers under Los Angeles, a setting also used effectively in the science fiction film *Them!* (1954). Some noir films, such as *The Clay Pigeon* (1949) and *The Devil Thumbs a Ride* (1947), also stray beyond the Los Angeles city limits to include locations on the southern coastal highway toward San Diego. Perhaps most intriguingly, Nicholas Ray's moody *In a Lonely Place* (1950) is set in the filmmaking world of Hollywood. Its locations range from a typical suburban West Hollywood low-rise courtyard block of apartments to the Beverly Hills retail district, Hollywood streets and nightspots, Pacific Palisades, and Malibu Beach.

## NEW YORK

For most people both within and outside the United States, New York is the apotheosis of the American city, with its Manhattan skyline being the most iconic image of that urban landscape. Unsurprisingly, it is (apart from Los Angeles) the most common setting for noir movie stories. New York is frequently shown in generalized terms: skyscrapers and so on, often employing stock footage, with the actors only seen recognizably on sound sets in their Los Angeles studios. It was rare for budgets to allow for production in actual New York locations until the creation of a fashion for authenticity first engendered by the popularity of *The Naked City*.

Director Jules Dassin was determined to make *The Naked City* the first film to be shot entirely on location. His hankering for complete geographical authenticity is clear from the film's opening scene: an aerial camera aboard a helicopter or plane approaches the tip of Manhattan in a shot anticipating the famous credit sequence of *West Side Story* (1961). Producer Mark Hellinger introduces the film *The Naked City* in voice-over, emphasizing that it is not a studio-bound movie but that all its scenes will be played out on real streets and in the buildings of the actual city. This (he says) is "the city as it is . . . [at] one o'clock in the morning on a hot summer night." The "pulse" of the city, which never stops beating, is then shown by a montage of night workers doing their graveyard shifts: cleaners, newspaper printers, and so on. After the film's climax high on the superstructure of a bridge, his closing voice-over famously explains that "there are eight million stories in the naked city: this has been one of them."

It is the forbidding facades of Wall Street seen in close-ups that emphasize the impersonality of central New York in *Force of Evil* and also in Anthony Mann's *Side Street* (1949). In the opening shots of the latter film, an aerial view of the Empire State Building and other Manhattan skyscrapers is accompanied by a voice-over describing New York as an "architectural jungle" and characterizing it as the "busiest, loneliest, kindest, cruelest of cities." While repeated montages of its police at work create a more reassuring image of social control, in the film's climactic cab ride/chase (which is filmed from high above as well as at street level), the city more resembles a confusing maze.

Highly emblematic of the harsh but romantic view of New York as a tough but glamorous city is *The Sweet Smell of Success* (1957), in which the busy pavements of Manhattan at night are memorably photographed by James Wong Howe. The neon signs of Times Square and the newspaper delivery trucks, filmed as if they were moving versions of Weegee photographs, are given extra edge by Elmer Bernstein's brassy, driving music. The busy street life full of diners, theatergoers, and dazzling neon signs introduces the world of which lead actors Burt Lancaster and Tony Curtis are denizens. A superficially similar film noir *Deadline at Dawn* (1946) moves away from this hyperrealism to present a clearly symbolic city, depicting in a more stylized manner its rooming houses, newsstands, night workers, and dance halls, where one can buy a fleeting dance with a partner who nonetheless remains a stranger.

## SAN FRANCISCO

With its harbor edged by busy piers, its hills and its tightly packed downtown streets, San Francisco more resembles in appearance New York than it does its fellow Californian city Los Angeles. Its picturesquely precipitous streets, its congested downtown neighborhoods, and the exoticism of its Chinatown have all encouraged noir filmmakers to use the city as a symbol of mystery, duplicity, and confusion. This can be seen in the most bewildering section of *Out of the Past* (1947), where the Robert Mitchum character feels framed in a convoluted trap in which he is the fall guy, or even more dramatically in the kaleidoscopic concluding scenes of *The Lady from Shanghai* (1948). Most elaborately of all, San Francisco is used as a hypnotically ensnaring environment in Alfred Hitchcock's *Vertigo* (1958).

In the pioneering serial killer film *The Sniper* (1952), San Francisco's tumbled topography emphasizes the isolation and alienation of its protagonist, a disturbed young man brooding in his room with a gun. A sex criminal, his "enemy is womankind." A delivery man for dry cleaning, the film follows him at work, with the San Francisco harbor repeatedly seen through his vehicle's windows and with giddy views down the many steep streets his van goes along. Significantly, he sees the city's people not in face-to-face interactions but instead through the crosshairs of his rifle's telescopic sights. There are rooftop chases that exploit the dramatic extremes of the city's contours, and at one point he shoots a steeplejack working on a high chimney. As the inhabitant of an urban landscape he finds literally sickening, he is rather like an early version of Travis Bickle in Martin Scorsese's *Taxi Driver* (1976). Other notable San Francisco film noirs include *Dark Passage* (1947), *Born to Kill* (1947, after an early section in Reno), *The Maltese Falcon* (1941), *Raw Deal* (1948), *Sudden Fear* (1952, after a prelude in New York and a transcontinental train trip), *Where Danger Lives* (1950), *The Lineup* (1958), and *Impact* (1949).

## OVERSEAS CITIES

A few American film noirs are actually set outside the United States, although the budget constraints mentioned earlier meant that Hollywood soundstages were almost invariably used to depict foreign places instead of real overseas location shooting. An exception is *Night and the City* (1950), set in London and directed by Jules Dassin when he was virtually exiled from Hollywood by McCarthy-era blacklisting. London is filmed in much the same way that New York City, Los Angeles, and San Francisco are in other noir movies. As in many of them, a voice-over introduces both setting and theme. In the film's opening moments (and in the climax) a man is pursued and is seen as tiny and powerless. St. Paul's dome looms over the action, and cobblestoned alleyways form a labyrinthine trap. Raucous music provides impulsion for the character's flight through the inescapable maze of the city. Trapped in headlights like a doomed animal, he is cornered in a wasteland of debris from the Blitz of World War II and summarily killed and dumped in the river.

Another film that, like *Night and the City*, uses the actual ruins of war in a European city is Carol Reed's British film noir *The Third Man* (1949), which is set in Vienna. Unlike American cities, London and Vienna both suffered major damage from wartime bombing, and the debris and rubble create apt settings for a story of moral turpitude. In *The Third Man*, the Occupied Zones of Vienna, each supervised by a different occupying power (France, Russia, Britain, and the United States), are linked by the city's underground sewers. It is in those sewers that the villain of the film, Harry Lime, is pursued to his death (a demise very like that of the villain of *He Walked by Night*) in the famous chase sequence that climaxes *The Third Man*.

One other very exotic overseas location that features in several classical film noirs (all, incidentally, made entirely in Hollywood) is South America. Particularly popular were the Brazilian capital of that time, Rio de Janeiro, the setting for Alfred Hitchcock's *Notorious* (1946), and the Argentine capital, Buenos Aires, where the stories of *Cornered* (1945) and *Gilda* (1946) are located. South America loomed much larger in American consciousness in the 1940s than in more recent decades, largely through Franklin Roosevelt's economic and strategic initiatives there, and Hollywood's temporary interest in the continent reflects that historical relationship.

## OLD CITY VERSUS NEW CITY

The city in film noir is not just specific in a geographical sense but is also historically specific. It is primarily the postwar American city of the late 1940s and early 1950s, a city not destroyed physically like those of Europe or Asia, but somehow morally ruined. This metaphor of damage or wounding is evident in the epigraph of *Kiss the Blood Off My Hands* (1948): "The aftermath of war is rubble—the rubble of cities and of men. They are the casualties of a pitiless destruction. The cities can be rebuilt, but the wounds of men, whether of the mind or of the body, heal slowly." Setting, character, and theme are thus tightly bound together at the film's outset. Nevertheless, many films contrasted this idea of ruin and decay with a concentration on the bright and the new. The shiny modernity of the urban world of America is especially prominent in films such as *The Big Clock* (1948), with its swanky apartments; its slick, technologically advanced office building; and its rapid elevators and automated cafeteria.

Since the classical noir cycle lasted well over a decade, the city it presents in the films of that period does develop and change—at least on the surface. *Kiss Me Deadly* (1955), for example, stands at the cusp of a shift in Los Angeles from an older noir landscape to a newer, shinier 1960s style. Some scenes are definitely placed in this new world, for example, the apartment of detective Mike Hammer, but at times he travels to older, darker areas of the city such as Bunker Hill. In style he is a *Playboy* magazine type, looking ahead to the 1960s with his clothes, sports cars, and gadgets such as a telephone answering machine. Adapted from a Mickey Spillane novel originally set in New York, *Kiss Me Deadly* shows the viewer two versions of Los Angeles: an old and a new. Hammer moves from modern apartment either to the old, dark Los Angeles of wooden Bunker Hill boarding houses or to a garishly modern art gallery.

Nicholas Christopher (1997), in his book *Somewhere in the Night*, highlights *Kiss Me Deadly* as an exemplar of this old/new contrast, but he makes the difference in city settings not an historical one, but a diurnal one:

> The Los Angeles of *Kiss Me Deadly* is by day a city of broad, sun-blanked boulevards, of tree-lined streets with antiseptic lawns and boxy cars parked in pools of shade, of dusty vacuous office buildings with black windows . . . by night, the city's downtown is a tableau of slashing white light, steep jet shadows, and richly luminous surfaces punctuated by the flashes of chrome and glass on parked cars, the mirrors on vending machines, and even the stainless steel cart of an all-night popcorn vendor. . . . When we are permitted a look into some building's interior, we inevitably see dappled Gothic hallways, jagged stairwells, galleries out of a de Chirico painting, or obliquely lit, repressive rooms. (p. 29)

## A TALE OF TWO CITIES: CITY VERSUS SUBURBS

The noir city can be defined by another kind of antithesis in setting: that between the more traditionally urban central downtown area and the suburban havens that adjoin it, either directly or more distantly. Such juxtapositions can be seen, for instance, in *Act of Violence* (1949), *Pitfall* (1948), and *The Reckless Moment* (1949). In these films, the contrast is not just a literal one between different landscapes but a metaphorical contrast between security and fear, between safety and jeopardy. The world outside one's house and one's familiar, reassuring neighborhood tends (especially for middle-class characters) to be the locus and source of danger, offering adventure and an attractive but destructive otherness.

Few film noirs set their stories even partially in traditional domestic spaces, but an exception is *Kiss of Death* (1947), which has a rare noir depiction of a family home. Even here, though the sinister criminal world of the city intrudes, the plot of *Kiss of Death* brings the threat of violent crime into the home. Idyllic scenes are presented in a nice New York neighborhood, where Victor Mature lives with his two sweet little roller-skating girls and his doting wife. However, his mood of vulnerable security can be undercut by something as simple as a newspaper headline, a phone call, or a car passing his house at night. He lies awake worrying, paranoid about a home invasion by gangsters from his past, then sends his family away before meeting his own death. The suburbs have provided no real escape.

There is a similar sense of a dark city world sullying the moral nature of the suburban American home in Fred Zinnemann's *Act of Violence*. This film has Van Heflin living with wife Janet Leigh in affluent suburban Glendale until Robert Ryan limps in from the city, bringing with him memories of Van Heflin's dark past during World War II. The interaction between dark city and sunny suburb is here a two-way thing: Van Heflin also travels to the more traditionally noir milieu of the city center to attend a business conference. There he enters a demimonde that is populated by kindly whores drinking in skid row bars and in which he is pursued through confusingly dark and tangled streetscapes. Tellingly, his suburban home becomes literally more shadowy and darker as the film's plot becomes increasingly bleak and tragic.

*Pitfall*, which opens with a scene in a bright kitchen that could come from a television sitcom, also features a domestic milieu threatened by darker urban figures. Driven by his wife to work in central Los Angeles, bored protagonist Dick Powell feels that he's "a wheel within a wheel within a wheel." An encounter with an attractive woman promises to lift him out of this rut. But the noir world penetrates the safety of his home when a jealous rival provokes the woman's ex-convict boyfriend to come calling for Powell with a gun. Once again, the film's mise-en-scène of shadows and silhouettes emphasizes the tarnishing of the family home's sanctity by unwholesome urban forces. One more clear example of this theme is found in *The Reckless Moment*, which also has the noir city world infesting the suburban home in its story of blackmailers who come to a seaside community and threaten scandal for a mother trying to cope with her daughter's foolish fling with a criminal and with the absence overseas of her husband.

## URBAN VERSUS RURAL AMERICA

In addition to the instances discussed previously, which contrast city and suburban settings, there are a few film noirs offering a direct contrast of the crowded city with the small towns and empty rural landscapes of pastoral America. In their story lines they juxtapose the metropolitan city with small settlements or farming and ranching districts. Three examples will clarify the picture of urban life that emerges in such situations.

Nicholas Ray's *On Dangerous Ground* (1952) is very much a film of two unlike halves. The first is a typically noir portrayal of a bustling city where a brutal cop chases baddies along the darkened streets of downtown. The second half is a fable of a man's redemption set in a snowy mountainous region virtually devoid of people. What unites the two sections is Robert Ryan as Jim Wilson, the violent cop who finds his humanity by befriending a blind woman during his pursuit of her brother. The early segments of the story carry viewers along on a roller-coaster ride following detective Wilson and his less excitable team tooling around the nighttime city streets in a Ford Single-Spinner rounding up sleazy miscreants, beating up masochistic suspects, interrogating scrofulous informants, and sidestepping seductive teenagers. To get him out of circulation after a particularly savage beating, Wilson's boss sends the burnt-out case up country to help the locals solve the brutal murder of a young girl. From that point the film is dominated visually by images of pristine snowy uplands and pine-forested mountain vistas. The new setting has thematic implications, and the film becomes a stark morality play, rather like a western in which the characters play out their destiny against an almost empty landscape. The hero's only chance for a happy, nonviolent life is to eschew the city altogether.

A different set of oppositions are at work in Robert Wise's *Odds Against Tomorrow* (1959). Three New York residents, played by Ed Begley, Harry Belafonte, and Robert Ryan, plan a bank heist in Melton, a small town 100 miles up the Hudson. The plans of their little gang are undone by petty bigotry and distrust, and the rural world becomes not a solution to their problems in the big city, but the setting for their schemes to unravel and for their lives to be forfeited. Manhattan is filmed as bleak, draughty, wintry, and inhospitable in the film's first half, while Melton and its environs fare little better, with infrared filters burnishing its skies with harsh contrasts and the modest town center being cloaked in an alienating twilight gloom. The frosty tone of most of the settings of *Odds Against Tomorrow* is encapsulated in the cold riverscapes that Wise films in the scenes showing the trio of robbers waiting for nightfall, motionless in a moody wasteland where their futility is imaged by an abandoned doll floating in stagnant water.

John Huston's *The Asphalt Jungle* (1950) combines within its overall story line both a grittily realist depiction of the noir city and a hyperrealist portrayal of the countryside in its almost hallucinatory conclusion. The film's credit sequence is made up of atmospheric nocturnal urban landscapes photographed with alienating effect by Harold Rosson. At the end of the credits a patrol car cruises the empty streets at dawn. The cityscape thus revealed looks like a de Chirico painting: old buildings, a solitary man walking past columns, overhead wires, a dingy diner, the arrest of a fatalistic suspect that leads to a lineup. Yet another heist film in which a gang disintegrates into a rabble of atomized fugitives, *The Asphalt Jungle* sends its chief protagonist, played by Sterling Hayden, on a doomed road trip to his boyhood home in Kentucky. Huston contrasts the constrictive urban world shown for most of the film's length with the dream-like rural landscape that the Hayden figure tries to escape into. Once more, the rural heartland of America is revealed to be no refuge, and in the film's last shots he dies a pointless death in a beautiful field nuzzled by curious horses.

## NOIR CITY AND POSTERS

Since Hollywood film genres are, to a large extent, tied into audience expectations, one might expect that the city setting of film noir would visually dominate such secondary marketing texts as posters. However, with their emphasis on stars and their recognizable faces, these posters do not actually show much of the city at all. Among the rare exceptions are a nighttime street scene on the poster for *Cry of the City* (1948) and the tag line for *The Asphalt Jungle* (1950)—"The city under the city"—in this instance meaning the criminal underworld. Sometimes there are visual metonyms of the city such as the street lamp prominent on the posters for both *Scarlet Street* and *Side Street*. Perhaps the image most evocative of urban danger in all the classical cycle is the vertiginous external light well of an apartment building seen in the poster of *Manhandled*, its fire escape foregrounded along with a dramatic depiction of a woman being thrown down it.

## REFERENCES

Christopher, Nicholas. 1997. *Somewhere in the Night: Film Noir and the American City*. New York: Free Press.

Higham, Charles, and Joel Greenberg. 1968. *Hollywood in the Forties*. New York: A. Zwemmer and A. S. Barnes.

Muller, Eddie. 1998. *Dark City: The Lost World of Film Noir*. New York: St. Martin's Griffin.

Rabinowitz, Paula. 2002. *Black and White and Noir: America's Pulp Modernism*. New York: Columbia University Press.

Spicer, Andrew. 2002. *Film Noir*. London: Pearson.

Walker, Michael. 1992. "Film Noir: Introduction." In *The Movie Book of Film Noir*, ed. Ian Cameron, 8–38. London: Studio Vista.

White, Rob. 2003. *The Third Man*. London: British Film Institute.

# McCarthyism, the House Committee on Un-American Activities, and the Caper Film

Geoff Mayer

I think I am a crook at heart.

—Jules Dassin

After World War II ended in 1945, the United States experienced intense political turmoil. The dominant concern was the spread of Communism, and after the Communist victory in China in 1949 and the beginning of the Korean War, this fear intensified and affected all levels of American life, including the Hollywood film industry. There were also interrelated issues such as the opposition to the development of an industry-wide union in Hollywood and the determination of conservative and right-wing groups to dismantle many of the liberal programs developed during Roosevelt's presidency. This change in American politics affected film noir.

Beginning in 1947, the left-liberal elements in Hollywood were under severe pressure, and many were forced to leave the industry, while others suffered the humiliation of denouncing their beliefs and providing the House Committee on Un-American Activities (HUAC) with the names of friends and colleagues. Some were also required to work on anti-Communist films such as Howard Hughes's notorious *I Married a Communist* (1949), which was rereleased as *Woman on Pier 13*. There were others, however, like Jules Dassin, who left the United States and found work in Europe.

The change in the political climate after 1947 meant that films such as *Crossfire* (1947) and *Gentleman's Agreement* (1947), with their criticism of anti-Semitism in the United States, were no longer possible. In fact, it was virtually impossible to produce films with overt, or literal, liberal sentiments after 1947–1948. Such films were replaced by a cycle of so-called caper films, which, in some cases, continued film noir's ability to critique various aspects of capitalism—even if this critique was heavily camouflaged by generic conventions. The first major film in this cycle, and the one that established its key attributes, was John Huston's *The Asphalt Jungle*.

## THE ASPHALT JUNGLE AND RIFIFI

In 1949 Darryl F. Zanuck, the head of production at Twentieth Century Fox, went to Jules Dassin's home in Los Angeles, gave him a book by Gerald Kersh, and told him to get out of town immediately and go to London. Zanuck also told Dassin to get a screenplay completed as fast as he could and then begin shooting the most expensive scenes in the script so that it will be costly to remove him from the film. Dassin, who was a member of the Communist Party, took Zanuck's advice and filmed *Night and the City*, one of the best noir films ever made. Just prior to shooting, Zanuck told Dassin that he owed him a favor and wanted a part for Gene Tierney, who was going through a bad emotional period. He complied with Zanuck's request, and while the film was a success, Dassin's career at Twentieth Century Fox, and in Hollywood, was finished due to the blacklist.

It was five years before Dassin made another film, *Du Rififi chez les hommes*, which was released in the United States, Britain, and Australia as *Rififi*. This film, based loosely on Auguste Le Breton's novel, initially had little appeal to Dassin. However, attracted to the possibilities of the robbery sequence that he transformed into a 28-minute tour de force, Dassin's motivation for reworking Breton's novel had more to do with his experiences over the past five years than merely aesthetic considerations.

Dassin was part of a culture that was repressed and marginalized in the period after the death of Franklin D. Roosevelt in 1945. This community, who played a prominent part in the development of film noir throughout the 1940s, was under attack as the simmering bitterness that was held in check by the demands of war broke down as soon as the war was over. This community included Communists, socialists, liberals, and other left-wing factions of actors, writers, directors, and producers such as Dassin, Edward Dmytryk, Robert Rossen, Abraham Polonsky, Dalton Trumbo, Elia Kazan, Clifford Odets, Nicholas Ray, Cy Endfield, John Garfield, Lee J. Cobb, Howard Da Silva, Karen Morley, Sterling Hayden, John Huston, Humphrey Bogart, and Robert Ryan.

James Naremore (1998, 124) argues in *More Than Night* that some of these people "responded to the threat of political repression by creating what amounted to a subgenre." This included John Huston and Jules Dassin, who utilized many of the conventions of film noir while intensifying the level of social realism and, sometimes, psychological depth. By 1949, many members of this community realized that their dream of a tolerant liberal democracy in the United States was not feasible. As actress Karen Morley remarked years later, the "right wing rolled over us like a tank over wildflowers" (qtd. in Naremore 1998, 107). Some acquiesced before the HUAC; others left the country or the film industry.

For members of this group this realization was bitter as many, such as Dassin, Edward Dmytryk, John Huston, Elia Kazan, Joseph Losey, Abraham Polonsky, Nicholas Ray, and Robert Rossen, began their careers in the 1930s in the social and radical theaters of New York. This included the Group Theater and the Yiddish Artef (Arbeter Theatre Farband or Workers Theater Organization), which was founded as an agitprop theater based on the Soviet model. Born in Middletown, Connecticut, in 1911 of Russian immigrant parents, Dassin began in the Artef as an unpaid actor and director while working in a paid occupation during the day. During this period he worked with Elia Kazan on a Federal Theater Production of the Marxist children's play *The Revolt of the Beavers*, which was terminated after three weeks by the New York police commissioner.

When the radical theaters collapsed in the late 1930s, Dassin went to Hollywood and RKO, and in 1941 MGM offered him his first film as director, *Nazi Agent*, starring Conrad Veidt. Dassin hated his period at MGM, and it was not until 1947, when he began working with producer Mark Hellinger at Universal on the prison film *Brute Force*, that he felt comfortable in Hollywood. He followed this with *Naked City* (1948), with Hellinger and Universal, and then directed another film noir, *Thieves Highway* (1949), at Twentieth Century Fox.

While Dassin felt dissatisfied with these films, each blended the conventions of film noir with a left-wing ethos as well as mixing social realism with, especially in the case of *Naked City* and *Thieves Highway*, documentary techniques. *Brute Force* perpetuated the wartime theme of collective action against Fascist tyranny. However, instead of a combat unit, this theme is developed within a prison setting that, unlike the propaganda films of World War II, yields a kind of fatalistic melodrama. In the film the sadistic Captain Munsey (Hume Cronyn) runs his prison as a fascist state, and because the liberal authorities are powerless to stop him, death provides the only relief for the prisoners. After most of them die trying to escape, the film concludes with the humane prison doctor (Art Smith) facing the camera and telling the audience that "nobody escapes, nobody ever really escapes."

The social message in *Naked City* and *Thieves Highway* was less obvious, although the latter film, scripted by proletarian writer A. I. Bezzerides, emphasizes the corrupt side of capitalism through the exploitation of farm workers by mercenary wholesalers. However, these films, along with other films with a relatively strong social-realist inflection, such as *Crossfire* (1947) and *Force of Evil* (1948), created severe problems for those involved in the production after 1947 as the political climate moved rapidly to the Right.

In 1946 the Republicans gained control of both houses of Congress, and President Harry S. Truman, a Democrat, ordered that government employees must take a loyalty oath. In 1947 the Taft-Hartley Act forbade communists in labor unions, and the so-called Waldorf Declaration, following a meeting of prominent studio executives at the Waldorf Hotel in New York, initiated the blacklisting of many left-wing and "troublesome" filmmakers. This was accompanied by a sustained congressional attack, orchestrated by the Republican-controlled Congress, on the Left in Hollywood, and in 1947 and 1951 the HUAC, which was formed in 1938, conducted public hearings in Washington, D.C.

Dassin had just left Rome for Cannes, after investigating the possibility of directing a film about a Communist and a priest, *Le Petit monde de Don Camillo*, when he heard that he had been publicly named as a Communist. As he was eager to be questioned, he returned to the United States, and while waiting to receive a summons to appear before the HUAC, he directed a revue starring Bette Davis. The subpoena never eventuated, and he was forced to leave the United States in search of work.

Dassin was offered the direction of *L' Ennemi public no 1*, starring Fernandel, in France. However, just before the start of filming, Roy Brewer, a highly influential Hollywood union official, told the film's producer that this film, and any other film he produced, would never be released in the United States if Dassin was involved in the production. Brewer also threatened the career of one of the film's stars, Zsa Zsa Gabor. After he was ejected from the film, the French press took up Dassin's case, but this did not help his career. His career was also damaged when his American passport was revoked, which meant travel in Europe was difficult. However, friends enabled him to get to Italy to work with Italian writer Vitaliano Brancati on developing a script based on the classic Italian novel *Mastro Don Gesualdo*. Again, he was removed from this project when the American ambassador to Italy, Clare Boothe Luce, intervened, and Dassin was forced to leave the country.

He returned to France and the close-knit community of exiled Hollywood filmmakers living in Paris. This was a painful, difficult period for Dassin. Not only was he broke and dependent on others, but the news came through of close friends in Hollywood who were appearing before the HUAC as "friendly" witnesses and who were supplying the committee with the names of left-wing and Communist actors and filmmakers in Hollywood. Dassin wept and suffered every time one of his "champions" caved in, and he considered the testimony of friends such as Lee J. Cobb, Elia Kazan, and the "poet of the working class" Clifford Odets a betrayal of their ideals.

*Rififi* rescued Dassin from five years of unemployment. Ironically, his political exile from Hollywood was a significant factor in receiving the offer to script and direct the film. First, the film's producers knew that Dassin was unemployed and consequently that they could get him for little money. Second, they were worried that the North African nationality of the villains in Auguste Le Breton's story would cause problems for the film as relations between France and Algeria were very volatile at the time. Hence the producers wanted the villains to be Americans, and they thought that Dassin would be an ideal director. Dassin, however, convinced them to change their nationality to French.

Dassin had one weekend to read the novel and give his answer. However, he could not understand the dense argot in the book, and only after he forced his agent to forgo an amorous weekend and read the book to him could Dassin make any sense of it. He still did not like it as he considered it cruel and perverse. One incident, however, intrigued him—the robbery. Nevertheless, he decided to reject the project. But broke and desperate to work, he heard himself say yes.

*Rififi* was influenced by *The Asphalt Jungle*. Huston's film established many of the key narrative conventions and characterizations that would shape the caper film for many years. Based on W. R. Burnett's novel, Huston reworked Ben Maddow's script by shifting the emphasis toward the criminals and away from the activities of a reformist police commissioner determined to eradicate corruption in a Midwestern town. The film's sympathies are obvious—especially when corrupt lawyer Alonzo D. Emmerich (Louis Calhern) tells his wife that "crime is only the left-handed form of human endeavor."

Huston, like Dassin in *Rififi*, gives each of the criminals his own story. The hooligan, the petty crook Dix Handley (Sterling Hayden), desires to go back to his childhood farm in Kentucky, the mastermind "Doc" Riedenschneider (Sam Jaffe) wants money to retire to Mexico, and the boxman, safecracker Louis Ciavelli (Anthony Caruso), needs money for his sick child.

Both *The Asphalt Jungle* and *Rififi* emerged from the gangster genre. Here W. R. Burnett is a crucial figure. His 1930 novel *Little Caesar* established the basis of the 1930s gangster film, while his 1940 novel *High Sierra*, filmed by Warner Bros. in 1941 (and scripted by John Huston), replaced the energy and arrogance of the 1930s gangster with an aging gangster, Roy Earle. Earle, a sad figure, prefigured the change in the gangster genre in the 1940s as the genre became increasingly inflected by the fatalism and despair associated with film noir.

Many 1940s films, such as *The Killers* (1946), *Criss Cross* (1949), and *Gun Crazy* (1950), contain robbery sequences. *The Asphalt Jungle*, however, changed the formula by introducing a three-part narrative structure—the recruitment of the criminals; the rehearsal and robbery; and the aftermath resulting in the deaths of the criminals, often due to the combined action of fate and human weakness. However, it is the point of view of these films that makes this cycle interesting. As James Naremore (1998, 128) argues, "after 1947, many leftist filmmakers were treated as outlaws, and it is not surprising that they made some of their best pictures from the point of view of criminals." This is certainly true of *The Asphalt Jungle*, which shows institutional corruption permeating every level of American life. This theme is conveyed in the film's schematic style whereby each scene is intensely claustrophobic, with horizontal and vertical lines fracturing each frame. The only visual relief comes at the end, with Dix dying in a field in the Kentucky bluegrass country. Catharsis comes only with death.

Dassin, like Huston, also uses this genre as a response to the subjugation of the Left in the late 1940s and 1950s. However, Dassin adds betrayal to this mixture, and he is explicit as to his motivation in reworking Le Breton's novel and shifting the film's sympathy toward the criminals and away from the police. As he stated later, his script reflects his view of himself as being a "crook at heart."

Years later he said, "I like authority being conquered so I always want my guys to succeed, and since I am on their side I try to find good things for them to do" (Dassin 2005).

Betrayal of the code that binds these criminals together is a central motif in the film. This appears early when the consumptive criminal Tony le Stéphanois (Jean Servais) learns from Jo le Suedois (Carl Möhner) that Mado (Marie Sabouret), Tony's ex-girlfriend, is living with Pierre Grutter (Marcel Lupovici), the owner of L'Age–D'Or. Tony, who has recently been released from jail after serving five years, goes to Grutter's club and takes Mado back to his dingy apartment, telling her, "I got busted in May. In June you were on the Riviera with a gigolo." He forces her to remove her expensive fur and jewelry before taking her into his bedroom, where she has to take off her clothes. Tony then hits her violently with a belt seven times before throwing her, half-dressed, out of his apartment. Mado accepts her punishment but refuses to forgive him until late in the film.

After throwing Mado out of his apartment, Tony changes his mind and tells Jo and Mario that he will participate in their plan to rob a large jewelry store—providing they drop their idea of a smash and grab and rob the store's safe. The motivation for this change is not clear as Tony appears to have no plans as to what he will do with his share of the money from the robbery.

As the men need a safecracker, they recruit Cesar (Jules Dassin as Perlo Vita), who forms a close bond with the men, especially Tony. However, Tony is aware of Cesar's weakness for women, and he warns the Italian after the robbery, "You sleep here at Mario's. No hotel registers. And no runnin' around Montmartre." Cesar gives Tony his word, but he really intends visiting L'Age–D'Or, where he has formed a relationship with singer Vivienne (Magali Nöel). This action is indicated during the robbery when, unknown to the other men, he takes a valuable ring.

Cesar's weakness brings disaster, just as Doc's penchant for young women leads to his capture in *The Asphalt Jungle*. Grutter traces the ring back to the robbery, and as a result, Mario and his wife, Ida, are murdered. When Tony discovers their bodies, he confronts the Italian, who is tied to a pole in the backroom of Grutter's nightclub:

CESAR: Forgive me.
TONY: It was you. You ratted on him.
CESAR: Forgive me.
TONY: I liked you. I really liked you, Macaroni.
But you know the rules.

Cesar, like Mado, accepts his punishment and gently nods: "The rules." Tony walks backward as the camera shifts to a point-of-view shot of the Italian looking at Tony, who fires three shots into Cesar's body. Later, Dassin, who was forced to play Cesar when another actor pulled out because of a dispute over his contract, said that this scene was directly motivated by his reaction to the HUAC hearings, where his friends betrayed him and other members of the Left in Hollywood: "There I was just thinking of all my friends who, in a bad moment during the McCarthy era, betrayed other friends and that was what I was writing and thinking about." Pointedly, Dassin contrasts Cesar's betrayal of the group with the heroic actions of Mario and Ida, who accept death rather than inform on Tony to Grutter. After Remi Grutter (Robert Hossein) cuts their throats, Mario and Ida receive a lavish funeral.

In terms of the genre, *Rififi* is structurally similar to *The Asphalt Jungle*. There are, however, significant differences due to the different cultural context in each country in the 1950s. For example, the censorship strictures underpinning each film are different. In France, there was greater tolerance of nudity and deviate behavior compared with the United States. In *The Asphalt Jungle* the corrupt lawyer, Alonzo D. Emmerich, participates in the heist because he requires money to finance the needs of his young mistress, Angela Phinlay (Marilyn Monroe). However, although the sexual basis of this relationship is clear, the Production Code prohibited any literal representation of this relationship—the closest the film comes is Emmerich lovingly holding up Angela's stiletto shoe after she kisses him before going off to her bedroom. Huston, however, bypasses the restrictions of the code by emphasizing Monroe's inherent animal sexuality and her references to Emmerich as "Uncle Lon."

Dassin in *Rififi* has more freedom. Tony's whipping of the naked Mado with his belt is still shocking, even though the director pans away to a photo of the couple in happier times as he is hitting her. Yet the noise the belt makes on her body has a powerful impact, and this scene provoked a negative review from Pauline Kael. Similarly, when the men return from the robbery to Mario's apartment, Ida greets them in a negligee that exposes her nipples. This follows an earlier scene with Ida, in a brief costume, washing Mario in the bath. These and other scenes show the healthy sex life that Mario shares with his wife—which only makes their sacrifice more poignant.

The other major distinction between the two films emerges as Dassin emphasizes a sense of community and shared values among his thieves—not only the four men and Ida, but also in a wider sense. After Jo's young son is kidnapped by Grutter, there is outrage in the Parisian criminal community, and they band together to assist Jo and Tony. It is this action that brings Mado back into the fold, and she provides the vital piece of information that leads Tony to the boy. Consequently, as Andrew Dickos (2002, 78) argues in *Street with No Name*, "*Rififi* literally defines the phrase 'honor among thieves' as only a Gallic noir could render understandable." Whereas *The Asphalt Jungle* and subsequent Hollywood caper films, such as Stanley Kubrick's *The Killing* (1956), reiterate a nihilistic view of the world, motivated only by self-interest, Dassin gives Tony's death a heroic dimension as he is not motivated by his own survival. While Dix in *The Asphalt Jungle* dies alone in his Kentucky pasture, Tony dies amid the local community after delivering the boy to his mother.

# REFERENCES

Dassin, Jules. 2005. "Interview." *Rififi*. DVD, directed by Jules Dassin. Australia: Madman Films.

Dickos, Andrew. 2002. *Street with No Name: A History of the Classic American Film Noir*. Lexington: University Press of Kentucky.

Naremore, James. 1998. *More Than Night: Film Noir in Its Contexts*. Los Angeles: University of California Press.

# Film Noir Style

Brian McDonnell

## INTRODUCTION

Does the term *film noir* denote a genre or a style? Should film noir be defined by its look or by its content? And exactly what is noir style? These are questions that film scholars, historians, and critics have asked ever since the notion of film noir began to be written about in English. The following essay will survey some of the opinions proffered on these topics over the years and will lend support to current cautions about generalizing too readily on this subject. In recent books on noir, there has been a general move away from the early 1970s pattern of foregrounding style as a key defining element of the genre, and that aspect is afforded less emphasis now. Despite this shift, the agenda of writers in the 1970s remains commendable in that it represented an attempt to make up for the regrettable lack of writing on visual style up to that point. Previously, writers on film had concentrated more on literary features such as theme and characterization.

One obvious reason why some academics turned to visual style and iconography in order to distinguish noir as a genre is simply that the films of the classical noir cycle often looked so different, both from their contemporaries (1940s and 1950s westerns, musicals, costume epics, and so on) and from the average Hollywood releases of the late 1960s and early 1970s that were the standard cinema diet of the authors of the first writings on film noir. Classical film noir was a clear reminder of the black-and-white years in the studio system. By the 1970s, people had started to lose their familiarity with black-and-white cinematography since color was by then so prevalent, so that any black-and-white film stood out, one that was artfully photographed even more so. An important adjunct to this was the practice of screening black-and-white films as late-night shows on American television that began in the mid 1960s. The networks had bought up massive libraries of old studio films, and TV became the first and only place where many film buffs as well as scholars could view older films. The advent of the *Late Show* also coincided with the first cinema classes being taught in American universities and marked the first time that someone from the general public could become, in effect, a film historian.

Among the early writers on noir to foreground visual style was Raymond Durgnat (1970), who wrote that any attempt to characterize noir "takes us into the realm of classification by motif and tone" (p. 48). He wished to distinguish noir from other film genres based on subject matter, setting, stock characters, and so on. About the same time, Paul Schrader (1972, 53), in his influential essay "Notes on Film Noir," also took up this new interest in style by claiming something similar to Durgnat's (1970) assertion when he stated that "[film noir] is not defined, as are the western and gangster genres, by conventions of setting and conflict, but rather by the more subtle qualities of tone and mood." Place and Peterson (1996) elaborated on these general claims in their essay "Some Visual Motifs in Film Noir" (originally published in 1974). As has been well recorded, this approach itself later became unfashionable and was taken over (if not swamped) by the dominance of political and ideological concerns emanating from the field of identity politics and from the dispersion of theories based on semiotics, structuralism, Marxism, and psychoanalysis.

More recently, several writers, such as Frank Krutnik (1991) and Alain Silver and Elizabeth Ward (1980), have discussed the complexities of definition that are involved in trying to delimit the phenomenon of noir. Other commentators have written that the most important unifying criterion of noir is actually not its look at all, but instead something to do with theme and narrative, or else they argue that the essence of noir grows out of the interaction of a number of different aspects. It is also axiomatic to some academics that notions of style should not be artificially separated out from other aspects of noir, but instead should be understood in conjunction with them. Many agree that there is, in any formulation of the central characteristics of noir, a need to account for the heterogeneity of films included in most film noir genre lists. Other film historians interested in neo-noir movies made since the 1970s have pointed out that this group of films at least can be said to have a self-conscious style, as seen in films such as *Body Heat* (1981), *Kill Me Again* (1989), and *Sin City* (2005). In many cases the creators of these films learned about film noir at film school, and often what they borrowed from earlier films was their attractive and distinctive visual style. Even keeping all these cautions in mind, several aspects of film noir style can nonetheless be examined.

## INFLUENCES ON NOIR STYLE

Scholars have posited a number of major influences leading to the formation and development of the particular visual style associated with classical film noir.

These include both domestic influences within the Hollywood studio system and also influences from European film industries that were brought to Hollywood by émigré directors and other craft workers settling in the United States, especially during the period of the rise to power of Hitler and the Nazis in Germany. Many of these migrants had worked in the German industry in the 1920s at a time when the cycle of films most associated with the movement of German expressionism was in production in that country. Others had worked in France in the 1930s, being either French themselves or else being Germans who were stopping over in France before traveling on to America. Several of these figures also played a role in the production of those French films of the 1930s which came to be known collectively as French poetic realism. Among the noir directors who migrated from Germany were Fritz Lang, Robert Siodmak, Curtis Bernhardt, Max Ophuls, William Dieterle, Billy Wilder, Edgar G. Ulmer, and Otto Preminger. Some of these, such as Ophuls, also worked in France, as, understandably, did Jacques Tourneur.

The term *expressionism* in the arts is usually taken to denote works that attempt somehow to depict the inner emotional life of a person rather than merely showing the reality of the external environment. Indeed, in such works the visual lineaments of the outer world may be distorted in order to better express the anxious (even tormented) inner world of the characters. In terms of cinema, the label *German expressionism* is commonly applied to a group of silent films made after World War I such as *The Cabinet of Dr Caligari* (1919) and *Nosferatu* (1922), among others. As Foster Hirsh (1983) puts it in his book *The Dark Side of the Screen: Film Noir*, expressionism was an

> angular, hallucinatory, violently emotional style, one that sought images of chaos and despair, and that seemed to celebrate the artist's own instability. The Expressionist artist embraced his madness, converting inner demons into images of tumult and breakdown which radiated a terminal bleakness. Painting as if he felt faithful only to his own inner vision, he created phantasmagoric transformations of reality. (p. 54)

As deployed in the German films of the 1920s, this style featured such techniques (later to be associated with film noir) as the following: deep focus; a particularly mobile camera, often used to convey an air of subjectivity; a plethora of oddly angled shots; an emphasis on chiaroscuro lighting with angular wedges of light; and an atmospheric use of shadowy mazes, vehicle headlights, and a patina of fog or mist. Screen space was frequently fractured by zigzag lines. It should be noted though that recently, some scholars have problematized any easy link between classical noir and German expressionism through revelations garnered by deeper historical research. An example is Marc Vernet (1993), who argues in his essay "Film Noir on the Edge of Doom" for an earlier American usage of noir techniques, that is, during the first decades of the twentieth century, even before German expressionism. In support of this claim, Vernet emphasizes that many of the notable noir cinematographers had begun working in the teens of the twentieth century or in the 1920s.

A number of the German émigrés had also worked on films regarded as examples of French poetic realism, especially Ophuls and Siodmak and, of course, the Frenchman Tourneur. In terms of subject matter, these films (e.g., *Quai des brumes* [1938], *Le jour se lève* [1939], *Hôtel du Nord* [1938]) were about the troubled lives of members of either the Parisian proletariat or the lower middle class, and they had pessimistic romantic/criminal narratives emphasizing doom and despair. The films in this French cycle of the 1930s also exhibited a mixture of the artificiality and stylization associated with German expressionism, along with some location shooting (especially in Paris), which brought in elements of realism. Nonetheless, in these movies an ironical poetry was found in the everyday: hence the term *poetic realism*. The iconography of the cycle included the shiny cobblestones of nighttime Parisian streets (the faubourgs), the shadowy interiors of neon-lit night-clubs, and the moody, haunted, doom-laden faces of actors such as Jean Gabin. As well as inspiring Hollywood filmmakers, who viewed them admiringly, some of these French films were actually remade as American noirs, for example, *Le Chienne* (1931) was remade as *Scarlet Street* (1945), *La bête humaine* (1938) as *Human Desire* (1954), *Pépé Le Moko* (1937) as *Algiers* (1938), *Le Jour se lève* as *The Long Night* (1947), and *Le Corbeau* (1943) as *The Thirteenth Letter* (1951).

In terms of influences from Hollywood's own domestic tradition as opposed to foreign models, there is, in classical noir, definitely some continuity of visual style from the 1930s horror films made at Universal, such as *Frankenstein* (1931) and *Dracula* (1931), and the 1930s gangster films made at Warner Bros., such as *Little Caesar* (1930), *Scarface* (1932), and *Twentieth Century* (1934), along with aspects of the house style of directors such as von Sternberg at Paramount and the economical, atmospheric visuals created by RKO's B units under the leadership of Val Lewton (e.g., *The Seventh Victim* [1943]). Most descriptions of these local influences concentrate either on examples such as those described previously, or else they point to the high estimation in which many Hollywood figures held the work of Orson Welles and cinematographer Gregg Toland in *Citizen Kane* (1941). *Citizen Kane* emerged as something of a creative "textbook" for many directors and cinematographers because of its innovative use of unusual angles, idiosyncratic framing, high-contrast lighting, brilliant mise-en-scène, elaborate camera movement, sustained duration of shots, ingenious optical effects, and associative montage. All of these features can be discerned in many of the canonical works of the classical film noir cycle.

## THE CHARACTERISTICS OF NOIR STYLE

Standard accounts of what renders film noir style distinctive stress those aspects that mark it out in contrast to the so-called invisible style most often associated with the storytelling mode of classical Hollywood cinema. Typical instances of such differences include these oppositions: classical cinema has low-contrast lighting, while noir has high contrast; classical cinema most commonly uses a balanced mix of three-point lighting (key light, backlight, fill light), whereas noir often employs imbalanced lighting, with a marked lack of fill light (this high-contrast style gives much blacker shadows); the classical method shoots day-for-night (i.e., scenes set at night are filmed in daylight, with filters and narrow aperture settings used to simulate darkness), while noir prefers night-for-night shooting. Other stylistic contrasts between the two modes include classical Hollywood's use of shallow focus versus noir's deep focus; "normal" focal lengths versus wide-angle focus lengths; a symmetrical mise-en-scène versus dissymmetrical mise-en-scène; eye-level camera versus extreme low and high angles; and an open, unobstructed view of subject matter, especially people, versus people being filmed through foreground obstructions or obscured by shadows. As Paul Schrader's (1972, 57) essay claims, "no character can speak authoritatively from a space which is being continually cut into ribbons of light."

This catalogue of commonly encountered noir photographic techniques can be extended to include mirror reflections, "choker" (very tight) close-ups, and visual distortion to simulate subjectivity. The many mirror shots in film noir (especially of the femme fatale) can indicate both narcissism and a duplicitous nature. Significantly, this characteristic style was integral to a film's theme rather than merely decorative. It helped create iconic noir images: sultry femmes fatales, a panorama of city bars, nightclubs, hotel rooms, and precinct stations. These were often bleak, isolating images: people as casualties of capitalism, casino gamblers, an archetypal man alone at night in an unfurnished office with the room's spaces fractured by the stripes of Venetian blinds. As Raymond Chandler (qtd. in Naremore, 1998, epigraph) put it in his nonfiction piece *The Simple Art of Murder,* "the streets were dark with something more than night." Furthermore, such technological advances as faster film stocks, coated lenses, and more powerful lights, and the model of realism provided by photojournalistic magazines such as *Life* and *Look,* all helped noir cinematography push the boundaries and stretch the artistic envelope.

It must be borne in mind that such an emphatic noir visual style is not necessarily evident throughout the length of any individual film. In many instances, there are particular times in a film's narrative when style is foregrounded and emphasized to a greater degree than usual, and these scenes are called by Foster Hirsch (1983, 86) "italicized moments." A salutary example of this is the famous sequence showing a guilt-ridden killer in *The Unsuspected* (1947). Director Michael Curtiz's visual strategy here is to move from his use of standard classical lighting in glamorous party and nightclub scenes and in the upmarket milieu of a radio station's studio to the deployment of something more expressionistic as the narrative ventures out into the nighttime world of crime. While viewers hear the syrupy voice of mystery show announcer Victor Grandison (Claude Rains) describing a murderer's mental processes, the visuals shift first to show a nervous passenger on a train, then segue through a complex lap dissolve between traveling shots to reveal a city street and a hotel's neon sign flashing the name

HOTEL PEEKSKILL. Inside one of its darkened rooms, a sinister man reclines smoking as Grandison's voice-over talks of "conscience," of "murder," and of an "unsuspected" killer. The man on the bed looks pensively at a neon sign outside, where only the sign's letters KILL are visible to him (and to us through an over-the-shoulder shot).

Noir cinematographers were frequently given more artistic freedom than was common in the classical house styles of the major studios. This was because many film noirs were cheaper B pictures, where lower budgets meant less financial risk and thus less constraining supervision for creative personnel from studio executives. The very low budgets of many noir B features also encouraged low-key lighting for purely pragmatic reasons: to hide or flatter the tawdry look of cheap sets. Furthermore, the practice of eschewing traditional three-point lighting saved labor costs by not requiring crews to work long hours setting up the lights. With most noir films using low-key lighting, some interesting effects have resulted. The black-and-white, high-contrast photography has a chiaroscuro effect, like the old paintings of figures such as Carravaggio. This lighting and shadowing also has an effect on tone and mood. It can be virtually religious, hinting at a Manichaean world in which the forces of good and evil contend. Venetian blinds crisscross the faces of the morally ambivalent heroes, making visible their state of entrapment. Light sources in film noir became part of the narrative content of shots, for example, bare bulbs glow in police interrogation rooms (e.g., in *I Wake Up Screaming* [1941] or *Laura* [1944]). In Robert Siodmak's *Cry of the City* (1948), there is a particularly striking use of high-contrast source lighting in a single shot where a series of house lights are shown being successively turned on by the gargantuan and butch masseuse (Hope Emerson) walking toward the Richard Conte character, who is waiting at her front door. She opens an interior door and switches on the lights in three different spaces as she walks forward through them, creating a three-dimensional effect. When the last light is turned on, all the spaces behind her become eerily invisible.

There was some German influence in the craft personnel involved in this look, as well as by émigré directors mentioned earlier (Fritz Lang, Otto Preminger, Robert Siodmak, Billy Wilder, and so on) who came from the German expressionistic tradition. While they had only B picture budgets to work with, some directors, such as Edward Dmytryk, wanted to impress studio executives so that they could move up to make A pictures. An early example of the influence of people trained in German expressionism can be seen in *Murder My Sweet* (1944), especially in its nightmare sequence, when Marlowe is drugged by the villains. That sequence displays tropes of distortion that simulate Marlowe's disturbed mental state. Another example of a flashy, out-to-impress style is the very long take of the bank robbery in Joseph H. Lewis's *Gun Crazy* (1949), a shot lasting several minutes and so realistic that people on the street location where it was filmed actually yelled, "They're robbing the bank!" In another caper film, *The Killers* (1946), the central robbery is also filmed in a long, unedited take.

Occasionally, in even quite dark films, there are isolated, more brightly lit scenes set in city nightspots and country roadhouses. These sequences often include songs or dances, performed in fashionable nightclubs. In such scenes the film's story/narrative virtually stops for the viewer's greater appreciation of the spectacle. Lighting, too, can reflect character and psychology. For instance, a sense of imprisonment is often shown by the camera looking at characters through a set of vertical bars or their shadows.

Much of the early writing on the noir genre emphasized the aspect of iconography, a topic popular in genre studies in the 1960s and 1970s. Indeed, genres were commonly defined in books of the period by their visual style and their iconography. It was believed, for example, that the themes and characterizations of film noir could be revealed through elaborate systems of visual coding, which could be analyzed by semiotic means. One project of iconographic studies therefore was the assembly and analysis of lists of the most striking images and visual items associated with a particular genre (e.g., the western film). Among the sign systems of classic film noir were visual symbols, motifs, and an iconography composed of such items as nighttime streets, echoing sewers, pool halls, people dwarfed by décor, bars, diners, hotel rooms littered with empty spirits bottles and cigarette butts, tenements, parking lots—in fact, every kind of urban wasteland. The very settings used thus carried connotations of decay, moral turpitude, and despair. Considered especially iconic was the image of a sultry female holding a gun (perhaps derived from the motifs of pulpy paperback book covers) that often made its way onto film noir posters. Janey Place (1998), in her essay (originally written in 1975) "Women in Film Noir" (in the book of the same name), writes of the iconography and visual motifs associated with the so-called spider woman: her long hair, overt makeup, flashy jewelry, cigarettes, phallic gun, and long legs. These women frequently dominate the screen composition and have a freedom of movement, their independence from men shown by their narcissism, for example, by their constant looking at themselves in mirrors.

The fact that the characteristics catalogued here remain problematic for some critics can be discerned in two starkly contrasting lists from two different texts on the noir genre. In their book *The Noir Style*, Alain Silver and James Ursini (1999, 4) cite a "random" group of film noirs released over a period of 18 months in the late 1940s: *The Big Clock* (1948), *Brute Force* (1947), *Cry of the City* (1948), *Force of Evil* (1948), *Framed* (1947), *Out of the Past* (1947), *Pitfall* (1948), and *The Unsuspected* (1947). These films had eight different directors, eight different cinematographers, eight different screenwriters adapting eight different original stories, eight different stars, and eight different studios, but despite the disparate casts and crews, they share, according to Silver and Ursini, one cohesive style. In contrast, James Naremore (1998, 168) claims that noir is a "more stylistically heterogeneous category than critics have recognised." To illustrate this point, he sets up a list of noir films with similar names (*The Big Sleep* [1946], *The Big Clock* [1948], *The Big Steal* [1949], *The Big Heat* [1953], *The Big Combo* [1955]) in apparent opposition to

Silver and Ursini's (1999) to assert that the eight have quite disparate visual styles, at least at the level of photography.

## THE HISTORICAL EVOLUTION OF NOIR STYLE

It is important to emphasize that the general characteristics of classical film noir visual style as described previously definitely did not remain static during the years from 1940 to 1959. There are discernible developments that mark stages in the stylistic evolution of the genre, a topic well surveyed by Spicer (2002). A good starting point might be Boris Ingster's curious little 1940 film *Stranger on the Third Floor*, which precedes *Citizen Kane* and is noted for its impressive central nightmare sequence photographed by Nicholas Musuraca (best known as the cinematographer of *Out of the Past*). The art director of *Stranger on the Third Floor* (Van Nest Polglase, who was also the set designer on *Citizen Kane*) designed the expressionistic sets in the nightmare sequence, which featured stylized, distorted, and starkly lit renditions of courtrooms, prison cells, and places of execution. The whole design contrasted with the more conventional flat lighting of most of the other scenes in the film and was planned to give an insight into the tortured and anxious mind of the protagonist. This was to be the first of many such sequences in classical noir. Indeed, so many film noirs contain dream and nightmare sequences that the term *oneiric* (dreamlike) is sometimes applied to their overall tone. Two other early films with similarly interesting visual distortions were 1941's *Street of Chance* and *Among the Living*.

Early classical noir was limited largely to shooting on studio sets rather than using real locations, as can be seen in such films as *Scarlet Street*, *The Maltese Falcon* (1941), *The Big Clock*, *The Big Sleep*, or (one of the very best examples) *The Blue Dahlia* (1946). These films dramatized what in essence was a closed world, characterized visually by the tight framing of a trapped, claustrophobic milieu often viewed through high-angle shots. *Murder My Sweet* (1944) and *Out of the Past* (1947) show variations on this pattern, the former with its subjective camerawork attempting to reproduce Chandler's first-person prose, the latter with its romantic, nonexpressionistic camerawork by Musuraca, sometimes employing real locations such as California's Sierra Nevada mountains. The memorably surreal opening scene of *Murder My Sweet* with Marlowe "blindfolded" as he talks to police resembles a Magritte painting. The low-budget noir *Detour* (1945) opens its flashback narrative in a similarly disturbing manner by throwing distorting shadows onto Tom Neal's face (shot in close-up with intense lighting) during his opening voice-over.

*Double Indemnity* (1944) is often considered the first complete or thoroughgoing film noir. Its cinematographer, John Seitz, working for the first time with Billy Wilder as director (Seitz also shot *Sunset Boulevard* with Wilder in 1950), was at the time considered the number one director of photography at Paramount. *Double Indemnity*, as realized by the vision of both men, features an almost revolutionary amount of darkness on the screen. This is well exemplified in the scenes where protagonist Walter Neff paces his own living room, or in the last sequence in Phyllis Dietrichson's darkened home, or in shots of the strikingly lit rear deck of a train's club car slatted by the shadows of Venetian blinds, or by Neff's clandestine entrance into a nighttime office building in the film's opening. Seitz included a great range of contrasts in texture and shading within his black-and-white photography. Also worthy of note is the film's deliberate avoidance of thriller genre lighting clichés (comparable to Hitchcock's own policies in this matter) when the two murder conspirators talk of their plans for death in a brightly lit supermarket rather than in a murky bar or dark alley. Unlike many of the other early studio-bound film noirs, though, *Double Indemnity* included a considerable amount of effective location shooting.

In 1942, the U.S. War Production Board imposed on the studios a $5,000 ceiling on new set construction, and by dint of necessity, lighting design had subsequently to disguise the limitations this restriction created. Much of the low-key noir style of this period may then have had at least partly a pragmatic motivation. The war, with its overall emphasis on accelerating technological development, had also brought faster film stocks, more mobile and flexible crab dollies, and smaller, lightweight cameras into the arsenal of the Hollywood filmmakers. All these innovations facilitated the cheap, quick lighting setups necessary for the production of money-strapped B films, and night-for-night shooting meant that crew members employed on more standard studio fare during the day could moonlight cheaply on B noirs. Low budgets also discouraged the standard policy of multiple successive camera setups shooting individual pieces of story action in order to facilitate later editing decisions so that in many noir films, conversations were instead shot as continuous two-shots: one character talking, while a second looked toward (or talked to) the back of the first character's head.

Among the best of the italicized moments of noir style in this early period are Mildred watching her daughter kissing her husband in a darkened room in *Mildred Pierce* (1945); the opening sequence in a diner in *The Killers* (1946), inspired by Edward Hopper's 1942 painting *Nighthawks*; the fight between Jeff Markham and Fisher in the cabin in *Out of the Past*, as Kathie watches enthralled; the extremely darkly lit office struggle in *Force of Evil*; and the outstanding location photography by John Alton throughout *Hollow Triumph* (1948). In fact, instances of John Alton's brilliant work as director of photography for Anthony Mann could be singled out as a highlight of this period: the chiaroscuro in *T-Men* (Charles McGraw's granite-like face, the steam bath murder), Pat's visage reflected in a clock face in *Raw Deal* (1948), or the super-rich shades of black prevalent in both films. In *T-Men* (1947) a criminal's face emerges out of blackness like that of a hunting snake or some other reptile. John Alton also later photographed *The Big Combo*, with its indelible shots of a beautiful woman running through the echoing spaces of a sports stadium and its famous ending, where a searchlight picks out a couple moving through the fog as silhouettes accompanied by stark, abstract jazz music.

Another effect of wartime social developments was to encourage a general move toward greater realism in film and in particular to foster the use of documentary techniques in fictional feature films. Americans had become used, during the war, to watching extended newsreels and documentaries made in support of the war effort. They were accustomed to the strident voice-overs of these nonfiction films and had become more inured to the brutality of war violence. All these influences led to what has been labeled the semidocumentary subgenre of classical noir. These semidocumentary stories, often shot completely on location, began at Twentieth Century Fox with producer Louis de Rochemont, who had worked on the *March of Time* newsreels. He brought to his fictional crime films voice-over narration, uplifting music, and a sense of factually based true cases being filmed in the actual places where they had occurred. The trend started with the FBI spy film *The House on 92nd Street* in 1945 and culminated with such titles as *Panic in the Streets* (1950) and *The Naked City* (1948), the latter based on hyperrealist photographer Weegee's 1945 book *The Naked City*.

Some films of the late 1940s, such as *Kiss of Death* or *T-Men*, were mixtures of this style and more expressionistic sequences, and this mix of two styles (in varying relative proportions) was to prevail as the classical film noir cycle gradually faded from prominence in the mid 1950s. There were, though, a handful of exceptional films from that period that looked back to the experimentation seen earlier in the cycle. Charles Laughton's 1955 film *The Night of the Hunter*, for instance, is a good late example of expressionistic lighting in noir. *Kiss Me Deadly* presents its idiosyncratic take on a transitional Los Angeles half in the high-contrast lighting of the 1940s and half in the blander lighting typical of its release year of 1955. Orson Welles's baroque 1958 B picture *Touch of Evil* can perhaps be viewed as a culmination of these tendencies. This status is evidenced by the many varied visual flourishes Welles displays through the story: the handheld camera work used in the scene of Uncle Joe Grandi being killed by Hank Quinlan, the deep focus used in the many investigative scenes, the flashlight shining voyeuristically on Susan Vargas in her hotel room, the high-contrast lighting of the street scenes shot in Venice, California. In a very real way, this film brings the evolution of film noir style full circle right back to 1941, and to *Citizen Kane* itself, through the common presence of director Orson Welles.

## CONCLUSION

Perhaps the best way to conclude this examination of film noir style is to note in detail the very useful analysis of the issues involved made by Steve Neale (2000), one of the leading contemporary writers in film genre studies. In his book *Genre and Hollywood*, Neale comments on the wide range of views concerning the nature of film noir style that have been expressed from the 1940s onward. Neale points out that the original French definers of noir (Nino Frank, Jean-Pierre Chartier, and so on) did not write about visual style at all. The kind of approach that highlights style instead came much later in the pioneering English-language work of writers such as Schrader (1972) and Durgnat (1970). As an example of the way the 1970s writers linked style and content, Neale (2000) quotes Place and Peterson (1996, 68) on their definition of the archetypal noir composition: "the extreme high-angle long shot, an oppressive and fatalistic angle that looks down on its helpless victim to make it look like a rat in a maze." Neale (2000) says that in their seminal essay on the general field of visual style, Place and Peterson (1996) pay most attention to lighting, which they characterize as "low key" and for which they claim "connotations of the mysterious and the unknown." Neale (2000) says that this formulation became the dominant conception of noir visual style but notes that it was somewhat modified by Hirsch (1983) and Krutnik (1991), the latter stating that there is a "disparate set of stylistic markings which can be seen as noir when they occur in conjunction with sets of narrative and thematic conventions" (p. 19). Furthermore, Krutnik avers that such markings are not actually specific to film noir, to crime film, or even to 1940s cinema.

Neale (2000) continues this line of thought by considering just how prevalent these features are in the classical noir canon and then goes on to discuss whether, in his view, they are "exclusive" to noir. While allowing that the canon is imprecise, he lists films, such as *Laura*, *The Maltese Falcon*, and *The Woman in the Window*, that are exceptions to the general rules of noir style, all of them adhering to a more classically Hollywood visual strategy, rather than employing expressionistic lighting. Neale cites director Edward Dmytryk, who said that the term *high contrast* was a more accurate term than *low key* for the lighting style he practiced in the 1940s. Both Dmytryk and John Alton, according to Neale, insisted that this kind of lighting had become quite "traditional" in most Hollywood stories of mystery and suspense, whether or not they might subsequently have been considered noir. In summary, then, Steve Neale (2000) concludes his analysis by counseling any sincere student of the noir phenomenon against the temptation to concoct an overly simplistic account of a noir style or look. That is surely good advice for anyone investigating this topic.

## REFERENCES

Durgnat, R. 1970. "Paint It Black: The Family Tree of Film Noir." *Cinema* 6/7: 48–56.

Hirsch, F. 1983. *The Dark Side of the Screen: Film Noir*. New York: Da Capo Press.

Krutnik, F. 1991. *In a Lonely Street: Film Noir, Genre, Masculinity*. London: Routledge.

Naremore, J. 1998. *More Than Night: Film Noir in Its Contexts*. Berkeley: University of California Press.

Neale, S. 2000. *Genre and Hollywood*. London: Routledge.

Place, J. 1998. "Women in Film Noir." In *Women in Film Noir*, ed. E. Ann Kaplan, 47–68. London: British Film Institute.

Place, J. A., and L. S. Peterson. 1996. "Some Visual Motifs in Film Noir." In *Film Noir Reader*, ed. A. Silver and J. Ursini, 65–76. New York: Limelight Editions.

Schrader, P. 1996. "Notes on Film Noir." In *Film Noir Reader*, ed. A. Silver and J. Ursini, 53–63. New York: Limelight Editions.

Silver, A., and J. Ursini. 1999. *The Noir Style*. London: Aurum Press.

Silver, A., and E. Ward, eds. 1980. *Film Noir: An Encyclopedic Reference to the American Style*. New York: Overlook Press.

Spicer, Andrew. 2002. *Film Noir*. Harlow, UK: Longman.

Vernet, M. 1993. "Film Noir on the Edge of Doom." In *Shades of Noir: A Reader*, ed. J. Copjec, 1–31. London: Verso.

PART II

# ENTRIES ON FILMS, ACTORS, AND DIRECTORS

# A

**ACT OF VIOLENCE** (MGM, 1949). *Director:* Fred Zinnemann. *Producer:* William H. Wright. *Script:* Robert L. Richards. *Cinematography:* Robert Surtees. *Music:* Bronislau Kaper. *Cast:* Van Heflin (Frank Enley), Robert Ryan (Joe Parkson), Janet Leigh (Edith Enley), Mary Astor (Pat), Phyllis Thaxter (Ann), Berry Kroeger (Johnny).

One of the most impressive of those film noirs that uncover the darkness and violence hidden behind the curtains of the brightly lit streets of American suburbia, *Act of Violence* explores, through the characteristic noir themes of revenge and guilt, the lasting effects of wartime experience on people. Protagonist Frank Enley harbors a dark secret about his war service that the arrival of a wounded comrade in his idyllic suburban home threatens to expose. Joe Parkson, the damaged man seen limping into Frank's small Californian town in the film's credit sequence, is a symbol of the psychic wounds of war. Similarly, the darkness that comes to envelop the home Frank shares with his wife, Edith, is an image of the persisting shadow cast by the war over postwar American life.

What Joe is seeking throughout the film's highly compressed plotline of just two days and nights is revenge. His purpose is indicated in the multiple meanings of the title of *Act of Violence:* alluding to the atrocity that occurred during the war, to what Joe has planned for Frank, and to what happens in the film's climax. The opening scenes show Joe's sense of mission, his goal. He tells Edith that her husband, with whom he had suffered the privations of a German prison camp, had been a stool pigeon for the Nazis, betraying a group of escapers to the guards so that all but Joe were killed. Behaving almost like an automaton and bearing both

*Act of Violence* (1948). Directed by Fred Zinnemann. Shown from left: Janet Leigh (as Edith Enley), Van Heflin (as Frank Enley). MGM/Photofest.

the mental and physical scars of war, Joe is ready to take Frank's life as vengeance. Only his noble girlfriend, Ann, newly arrived from New York, tries to dissuade him from this course using her compensating moral values of forgiveness and mercy.

Once he hears of Joe's visit, Frank begins to feel that he does not deserve the happiness and prosperity he is experiencing. Frank is firstly jumpy, then passive and accepting, questioning his motives in the war. Fearing scandal, he tells Edith his side of the story: that he had informed on the escapers for their own sakes and was shocked at the Nazi response of bayonets, dogs, and men left to die. But he acknowledges that perhaps he did it only to be able to eat some decent food. Self-preservation is offered to Frank a second time as he thinks of ways to deflect Joe's revenge. Edith, his sexy younger wife (Van Heflin was 17 years older than Janet Leigh), is braver than him. She dutifully accepts his faults (a trait representative of American women acknowledging the effects of war on their men). Stressing their strength and unity as a couple, Edith tells Frank that you cannot suffer all your life for one mistake.

*Act of Violence* is thus typical of the noir genre in that it depicts a man whose life is disrupted by weakness and ill fortune. As well as dramatizing a loss of trust between husband and wife, it also embodies the noir phenomenon of the reversal of goodies and baddies. This is most clearly delineated in the sequence of Frank's flight through the nighttime city. Leaving a drunken convention in downtown Los Angeles in flight from Joe, Frank descends to a stylized demimonde under the Angel's Flight cableway and into a bewildering landscape, which becomes symbolic of the shift in this suburban man's life. At a low-rent bar he meets Pat, a hooker, and uses her to try to buy off Joe by handing over his business to him. When that does not work, she suggests employing a hit man. Once this course of action is in train, Frank staggers outside and, in a highly subjective scene, comes close to committing suicide under a train after hearing echoing accusatory inner voices in the Bunker Hill tunnel. The following day, Frank wakes to the realization of what he has set in motion , suffering the agonies of conscience and feeling that his morals have been compromised by drink and desperation. With an air of doom, he tries to prevent the death of Joe. Still trying to protect Edith, Frank sneaks out of the house to intercept the hired killer and the main characters gather at the hometown's train station for the climax. It is a dark, windy location, an existential no-man's-land. In a sequence edited like a western gunfight, Frank is shot by the hit man instead of Joe as he jumps in the way in an act of atonement. A bewildered Joe kneels over him, as Ann looks on with a heavy heart.

In its visual style, *Act of Violence* efficiently evokes the contradictions of postwar America. Pride in war service is symbolized by a military parade of veterans in progress on the day Joe arrives in town, but its positivity is undercut by the sight of him limping counter to the rhythm of their healthy march. A housing project opening, which salutes Frank's dynamism, represents postwar promise. However, Frank's own house becomes visibly darker after Joe calls in. Thereafter Frank and Edith are seen in shadows, and his face is harshly lit when he behaves out of character. The bright music at the builders' convention ("Happy Days Are Here Again") is ironic, and his running through the dark city tunnel revives memories of the war's terrors. In their book *Film Noir: An Encyclopedic Reference to the American Style*, Alain Silver and Elizabeth Ward say that the film is typical of Zinnemann's detached, dispassionate tone (p. 10) but that it is still very subjective in such scenes, drawing the audience inside the mind of Frank.

Brian McDonnell

**ALDRICH, ROBERT** (1918–1983). As a director, Aldrich worked in many different film genres, and his reputation rests with his achievements in a wide variety of projects such as *Attack, Whatever Happened to Baby Jane?*, and *The Dirty Dozen*, all of which demonstrate his exhilarating visual style. Often depicting excessive characters in highly emotional stories, he made only one great film noir (*Kiss Me Deadly*), but that was enough as it is an absolutely crucial title from the classical period. Robert Aldrich was born in Cranston, Rhode Island, into a prominent political and business family. He started his film career at the RKO studio in the 1940s and was an assistant director to luminaries such as Jean Renoir,

Charlie Chaplin, Lewis Milestone, Robert Rossen, Abraham Polonsky, and Joseph Losey. An example of his exposure to the emerging genre of film noir during this period was the creative freedom he was given as assistant director by Milestone on *The Strange Love of Martha Ivers* in 1946. Aldrich also briefly worked in television during the 1950s. His work in classical noir occurred at the start of his directing career, and he went on to make films of other genres subsequently. His first noir film was *World for Ransom* (1954), starring Dan Duryea, which was set in Asia and had a particularly convoluted story line.

The film noir he directed the following year, *Kiss Me Deadly*, was perhaps Aldrich's finest film. In it he and writer A. I. Bezzerides subverted the swaggering persona of protagonist Mike Hammer, novelist Mickey Spillane's macho private eye figure. Aldrich elicited great performances, not just from Ralph Meeker in the central role, but also from the rest of the principal cast of *Kiss Me Deadly*. The violence inherent in the film's story line is certainly exploited, but at the same time it is lampooned, and a subplot about atomic warfare is added to the sadistic concerns of the Spillane novel. In effect, Bezzerides and Aldrich give their own view on what a 1950s private eye should be, rather than trying to accurately show Spillane's vision. *The Big Knife* (1955) is a very different piece, a dark exposé of Hollywood infighting adapted from a Clifford Odets play and retaining some of the staginess of the original. In the middle of the 1970s, at a time when the first modernist examples of the neo-noir genre (such as *Chinatown*, *Night Moves*, and *Hickey and Boggs*) were being released, Aldrich directed the bleak, pessimistic *Hustle*, starring Burt Reynolds as a fated detective.

**Selected Noir Films:** *World for Ransom* (1954), *Kiss Me Deadly* (1955), *The Big Knife* (1955), *Hustle* (1975).

Brian McDonnell

**AMONG THE LIVING** (Paramount, 1941). *Director:* Stuart Heisler. *Producer:* Sol C. Siegel. *Script:* Lester Cole and Garrett Fort, from the unpublished story by Brian Marlow and Lester Cole. *Cinematography:* Theodor Sparkuhl. *Music:* Gerard Carbonara. *Cast:* Albert Dekker (John Raden/Paul Raden), Susan Hayward (Millie Pickens), Harry Carey (Dr. Ben Saunders), Frances Farmer (Elaine Raden), Gordon Jones (Bill Oakley), Jean Phillips (Peggy Nolan), Ernest Whitman (Pompey), Maude Eburne (Mrs. Pickens).

*Among the Living* was released in September 1941, 12 months after *Stranger on the Third Floor* and a month before *The Maltese Falcon*. This film is another example of the significance of the horror genre in the development of film noir. In a pattern similar to *Stranger on the Third Floor*, *Among the Living* was promoted as a horror film, and it does include many aspects of the traditional Gothic story with its story of twin brothers—one insane, Paul Raden, and the other, John Raden, a successful businessman. Both brothers are played by Albert Dekker.

When John returns to his small southern hometown for his father's funeral, the family doctor, Ben Saunders, tells him that Paul, who supposedly died 25 years ago, was living in the family mansion under the care of Pompey, a family servant. Paul kills Pompey during a frenzied attack, which is brought on by the sound of a woman screaming. Paul escapes from the family mansion and tries to assimilate himself into the local community while the police search for Pompey's murderer. He befriends the flirtatious, and mercenary, Millie, daughter of the proprietor of the local boarding house, when he seeks a room. Sexually excited by Millie, who shows him a new dress she purchased with his money, Paul visits a sleazy bar late that night, where he is picked up by Peggy Nolan, a crude facsimile of young Millie. However, when he tells Peggy that he prefers Millie, she humiliates him. Later, in the early hours of the morning, Paul follows her from the bar, and after a long chase through the empty streets, he kills her when she screams.

The final section of the film is less successful as the film's short running time of 67 minutes inhibits the full development of the characters and situations. After John offers a reward for the killer, Millie persuades Paul to take her to the Raden mansion. However, when she screams, Paul attacks her and then runs away. Just at this moment, John enters the house and is arrested for the murders committed by Paul as the townspeople believe that only one Raden is still alive—John. The film's use of coincidence as well as the last-minute change of heart by Dr. Saunders that Paul is not dead, clearly reveals the melodramatic basis of the film. John, saved from a lynching by Saunder's confession that he falsified the death certificate 25 years ago in exchange for money for a medical center, warns the townspeople that Paul is still alive. However, consistent with melodrama's reliance on pathos, they find Paul's body draped over his mother's grave, a reminder that his insanity was caused by the violence inflicted on his mother by his father as her screams triggered Paul's violence.

Despite its meager budget, this is an impressive film due largely to Theodor Sparkuhl's evocative cinematography, which captures the repressive desolation in the Raden mansion that fostered Paul's insanity. This visual correlation culminates in the film's set piece, Peggy Nolan's desperate attempt to flee from the monster pursuing her as she runs through the streets in the early hours of the morning. Her murder in an alley, filmed by Sparkuhl and director Heisler in a deep-focus long shot, is an archetypal noir image that combines terror, pathos, and alienation. Sparkuhl's career extended from German expressionism in the 1920s, to French poetic realism in the 1930s, including *La Chienne,* to key Hollywood productions in the 1940s, such as Paramount's remake of Dashiell Hammett's *The Glass Key* in 1942, also directed by Heisler. *Among the Living* also gave Susan Hayward her best role to date as Millie, the sexually aware young woman eager to exploit Paul's interest in her, as it did Albert Dekker, who, due to typecasting and political obstacles, rarely had such a chance to display his acting range.

Geoff Mayer

**ANDREWS, DANA** (1909–1992). Though not nearly as famous as figures such as Humphrey Bogart or Robert Mitchum, the phlegmatic Dana Andrews was very effective in the leading roles he played in more than half a dozen key film noirs. He generally played the part of a man of integrity and decency who was tough and stoical on the outside but vulnerable on the inside, a man with weaknesses who could slip over the edge of respectability. Undervalued by some critics because he tended to underplay his roles, Andrews became very much the American Everyman. Born Carver Dana Andrews, he was the son of a Baptist minister who moved the family around several parts of the South. Andrews studied accountancy before traveling to Hollywood to try his hand at acting. A small part in *The Westerner* (1940) by chance garnered him much exposure because studio publicists mistook his first name for a female one and mistakenly billed him as Gary Cooper's costar on the film's posters. Andrews's first significant role was as one of the men condemned to hang in *The Ox-Bow Incident* (1943), an allegorical western that is included on some film noir lists because of its dark, pessimistic tone. However, he became forever an iconic part of the genre when he memorably played the determined, unflappable, philistine, and eventually obsessed police detective Mark McPherson in *Laura* (1944). This was one of the earliest A budget noirs, and, along with Gene Tierney, Clifton Webb, and Vincent Price, Andrews helped make the film a popular hit.

The next year he went on to play a rather more morally ambiguous figure in *Fallen Angel*, as the drifter Eric Stanton. Stanton is at first happy to bilk the naïve June Mills (Alice Faye) out of her money and for a while is suspected of killing sultry waitress Stella (Linda Darnell), but in the pat and unsatisfactory ending of the film, he turns out to be righteous. Andrews had one of his most complex roles as the somewhat sadistic cop Mark Dixon in *Where the Sidewalk Ends*, in which he was reteamed with Tierney and director Otto Preminger from *Laura*. He is again excellent here in a truly noir role as the man caught up in frightening moral compromises and having to face up to weakness and a criminal heritage. Andrews' essential integrity shone through in his role as caring priest Father Roth in *Edge of Doom*, a part that was expanded from the original plot to make Roth a more central figure. Andrews made two late noirs in the mid-1950s for director Fritz Lang: *While the City Sleeps* and *Beyond a Reasonable Doubt*. In the first he is a rather unlikable and ruthless television newsman, while in the latter he is a calculating killer caught up in a bewilderingly tortuous narrative whose guilt is discovered only through chance. In these two films Andrews's handsome features had begun to coarsen a little, and drinking problems plagued his later career, with rumors that he was even sometimes under the influence while working on set in the studio.

**Selected Noir Films:** *The Ox-Bow Incident* (1943), *Laura* (1944), *Fallen Angel* (1945), *Boomerang!* (1947), *Where the Sidewalk Ends* (1950), *Edge of Doom* (1950), *While the City Sleeps* (1956), *Beyond a Reasonable Doubt* (1956), *Brainstorm* (1965).

Brian McDonnell

**ANGEL FACE** (RKO, 1953). *Director:* Otto Preminger. *Producer:* Otto Preminger. *Script:* Frank Miller and Oscar Milliard, from an unpublished story by Chester

Erskine. *Cinematography:* Harry Stradling. *Music:* Dimitri Tiomkin. *Cast:* Robert Mitchum (Frank Jessup), Jean Simmons (Diane Tremayne), Mona Freeman (Mary), Herbert Marshall (Mr. Tremayne), Leon Ames (Fred Barrett), Barbara O'Neill (Mrs. Tremayne), Kenneth Tobey (Bill).

From 1947 to 1953, Robert Mitchum perfected his screen persona as the laconic, detached, slightly amoral drifter/victim in a series of film noirs for RKO, beginning with *Out of the Past* (1947) and culminating with *Angel Face*. *Angel Face*, adapted from an unpublished story by Chester Erskine titled "Murder Story," was written in 18 days as Howard Hughes, the owner of RKO, wanted one last film from Jean Simmons before her contract expired. Simmons, who was cast against type as the femme fatale in *Angel Face*, was assigned to the film by Hughes as a punishment for her refusal to "socialize" with him. In a further attempt to antagonize Simmons, Hughes ordered that her long black hair be severely cut before the start of filming.

Hughes borrowed the autocratic director Otto Preminger from Twentieth Century Fox and told him to shoot the film quickly—which he did, in 19 days. There was, however, considerable tension on the set, especially after an incident early in the film when the script required Mitchum to slap Simmons. When Preminger called for retake after retake, Mitchum, worried about his costar's face, finally hit the director across the face and then asked him if he would like another slap. This incident brought Simmons and Mitchum closer together.

Mitchum is ambulance driver Frank Jessup, who is called out to the Tremayne house in Beverly Hills after Mrs. Tremayne is nearly asphyxiated due to gas poisoning. Jessup is intrigued by Tremayne's stepdaughter Diane, especially after he finds her playing the piano while her stepmother suffers upstairs. His interest intensifies when Diane becomes hysterical after learning that her stepmother did not die. The young woman's reaction provokes Frank into slapping her face in an attempt to calm her down. Diane reacts to his slap by slapping him back, and from this moment Diane and Frank are locked into a perverse relationship involving lust, denial, and murder. Frank immediately deceives his long-time girlfriend, Mary. Diane then exploits this indiscretion by telling Mary that Frank has betrayed her and invites Frank to work as the chauffeur in the Tremayne household.

Frank is initially fascinated by Diane's childlike beauty and her promise to convince her stepmother to provide financial assistance so that he can open his own garage business. However, his lust dissipates when he realizes that Diane intends killing her stepmother, and he tries to leave. But, in an action that is repeated in the final moments of the film, Diane subverts his desire to leave by tampering with the brakes of the family car, sending her stepmother to her death over the cliff at the back of the property. However, Diane also kills the only man she really loves, her father, when he enters the car just prior to its backward plunge over the cliff.

Diane is sent to the prison hospital pending trial for the murder of stepmother and father. However, Frank, who played no part in the murder, is also charged, and only the intervention of an unscrupulous lawyer, Fred Barrett, saves Diane and Frank from being executed. Barrett devises a clever plan to win the jury's sympathy by marrying the young couple. However, after their acquittal, Frank tells Diane that he does not want to remain married to her and wants to return to Mary. Mary, however, prefers a more reliable boyfriend, Frank's coworker Bill, and refuses to take Frank back.

Dejected, Frank returns to the Tremayne house to pack his belongings and leave California for Mexico. After calling a cab, he accepts Diane's offer to drive him to the bus depot. However, just as he enters her car, with a cold bottle of champagne and a couple of glasses, Diane puts the car into reverse, sending it over the same cliff where her father and stepmother died. This strange film ends by emphasizing the sense of futility that permeates the film, with a taxi waiting outside the front entrance of the house for passengers that will not appear as they are all dead.

Stylistically, *Angel Face* demonstrates that not all noir films are characterized by striking imagery based on high-contrast lighting. Preminger, faced with the need to shoot the film quickly, employs few scenes with low-key lighting. Instead, he reserves his most effective imagery for the end of the film, when Diane walks slowly from room to room in a bizarre mixture of pathos and madness as she revisits the pleasures of her close relationship with her father and her bittersweet feelings toward Frank. The haunting basis of her meanderings from room to room is intensified by Dimitri Tiomkin's score, which evokes both the underlying sadness and the pervasive insanity of this troubled woman.

What *Angel Face* does share, and extends, with other examples of film noir is the strangeness, the masochistic basis, of the relations between men and women. Unlike earlier femmes fatales, such as Kathie in *Out of the Past* and Phyllis in *Double Indemnity*, Diane is not motivated by money or the need to survive in a predominantly masculine world. She is psychologically disturbed—she wants both her father and Frank—and totally amoral. Yet her ruthlessness is tempered by a sense of melancholy—a quality assisted by the casting of Jean Simmons.

*Angel Face* is also notable by reversing the conventional stereotype concerning sex. Mary, the "good" girl, is shown to have an active sexual life, a trait emphasized by Preminger, who shows Mary dressed only in a slip in her bedroom as she maintains a casual conversation with Frank. On the other hand, Diane, who is 12 years younger than Frank, appears childlike and sexually immature, and he tires of her games of invitation and denial. When she comes to his room above the garage at 2:40 A.M. one night and tells him that she fears her stepmother is trying to kill her, Frank expresses only disinterest. However, his indifference extends to his responsibility to warn Mrs. Tremayne of her stepdaughter's murderous intentions. Instead, he tells Diane, "I'm not getting involved—how stupid do you think I am?"—a statement that encapsulates the Mitchum screen persona of the past six years, and although he would eventually return to film noir in the latter part of his career, in films such as *The Friends of Eddie Coyle* (1973) and *Farewell, My Lovely* (1975), Frank Jessup in *Angle Face* represents the most extreme example of the amoral, detached protagonist that characterized Mitchum's tenure at RKO from 1947 to 1953.

Geoff Mayer

**APOLOGY FOR MURDER** (PRC, 1945). *Director:* Sam Newfield. *Producer:* Sigmund Neufeld. *Script:* Fred Myton. *Cinematography:* Jack Greenhalgh. *Music:* Leo Erdody. *Cast:* Ann Savage (Toni Kirkland), Hugh Beaumont (Kenny Blake), Russell Hicks (Harvey Kirkland), Charles D. Brown (Ward McGee), Pierre Watkin (Craig Jordan), Sarah Padden (Maggie), Norman Willis (Allen Webb), Eva Novak (Maid).

This low-budget film, with a short shooting schedule and poor production values, reduces James M. Cain's formula, involving a materialistic, sexual woman wishing to rid herself of a wealthy husband, to its essence. Cain developed this premise in his most famous stories, *Double Indemnity* and *The Postman Always Rings Twice*. PRC almost acknowledged a debt to Cain when they were tempted to call the film *Single Indemnity*. However, when Paramount realized what PRC was up to, they threatened legal action, and the film was withdrawn from circulation two days after its Los Angeles release.

Walter Neff's insurance salesman in *Double Indemnity* is replaced in *Apology for Murder* by journalist Kenny Blake. He meets femme fatale Toni Kirkland during an interview with her wealthy husband regarding a new business venture. However, at the interview, Blake appears more interested in Kirkland's legs than the businessman. Although he rejects her initial invitation to murder her husband, Blake's resolve collapses when Toni intensifies her seduction of the hapless journalist.

There are many similarities between *Apology for Murder* and *Double Indemnity*. Both films share the bond between the protagonist and his more mature mentor. In *Apology for Murder* this takes place between Blake and his editor Ward McGee, and the film replicates the recurring motif of the younger man's inability to light his cigarettes, an action regularly completed by McGee (the reverse takes place in *Double Indemnity*). Similarly, director Sam Newfield follows Billy Wilder's lead by showing the actual murder through the reaction of the woman—in this case, Kirkland's face. Again, the film replicates the famous scene in *Double Indemnity* when Keyes unexpectedly visits Neff's apartment just before the arrival of the woman. In *Apology for Murder* Blake is forced to duck for cover as McGee leaves Kirkland's house.

More important, *Apology for Murder* reprises the main theme in *Double Indemnity* with regard to Cain's notion of the so-called love rack—that the initial passion between the lovers will turn sour after the murder. While Blake turns to alcohol to deal with his guilt when another man is convicted for their crime, Toni Kirkland loses interest in the reporter and begins an affair with her lawyer. All die in the film's climax.

Hugh Beaumont, who was a popular television figure in the 1950s as the caring father in *Leave It to Beaver*, is effective as the reporter unable to resist the femme fatale, while Ann Savage reprises her role from *Detour*, released a few months before *Apology for Murder*, as the deadly woman, and her performance matches the intensity, if not the subtle nuances, of Barbara Stanwyck in *Double Indemnity*.

Geoff Mayer

**THE ASPHALT JUNGLE** (MGM, 1950). *Director:* John Huston. *Producer:* Arthur Hornblow Jr. *Script:* Ben Maddow and John Huston, from the novel by W. R. Burnett. *Cinematography:* Harold Rosson. *Music:* Miklos Rozsa. *Cast:* Sterling Hayden (Dix Handley), Louis Calhern (Alonzo Emmerich), Jean Hagen (Doll Conovan), James Whitmore (Gus Minissi), Sam Jaffe (Doc Riedenschneider), Marilyn Monroe (Angela Phinlay), Marc Lawrence (Cobby), Anthony Caruso (Ciavelli), John McIntire (Commissioner Hardy), Brad Dexter (Bob Brannon).

After helping kick off the classical film noir cycle by helming *The Maltese Falcon* in 1941 and contributing the marginal noir *Key Largo* in 1948, director John Huston returned to the dark world of city crime with the heist film *The Asphalt Jungle* in 1950. This film is a highlight of the subgenre of noir caper films and blazed a path for such later examples as *The Killing* (1956) and *Odds against Tomorrow* (1959). *The Asphalt Jungle* definitely has the most typical noir look of any of Huston's films with its high contrast and source lighting. Furthermore, its thematic preoccupation with temptation, loss, failure, and marginalized lives is a central issue in the genre. Because of these very features, it was quite an unusual film for the MGM studio, which was usually associated with Technicolor, glamour, and high production values. Significantly, *The Asphalt Jungle* was made by their B unit, then under the supervision of Dore Schary, who had gained experience with this style of film during his time at RKO.

While the film's surface story line depicts the preparation, execution, and aftermath of a jewelry store robbery, its narrative features a complex web of relationships among the participants. A number of sequences showing the assembly of the team under the leadership of mastermind Doc Riedenschneider make up the opening third of the plot, and these scenes provide succinct portraits of the characters, including tough guy Dix and his on/off girlfriend Doll; lawyer Emmerich and his wife and mistress; safecracker Ciavelli; hunchbacked, cat-loving diner proprietor Gus; and bookie/financier Cobby. The caper itself begins 45 minutes in and lasts just 15 minutes or so. The philosophical Doc complains of "blind accident" when things inevitably go wrong with the plan, such as alarms going off unexpectedly and the freakish wounding of the safecracker with a guard's dropped pistol. Conflicts also arise when the financially strapped Emmerich suggests to a venal employee that they double-cross his fellow conspirators.

Out of these twisted, lawless behaviors emerge such common noir themes as isolation, existential angst, corruption, betrayal, and cupidity. To balance out the general tone of immorality, the details of the caper are overlain with the moralizing statements of police commissioner Hardy, who hectors members of the press about the "jungle" of city life and the need for vigorous law enforcement. Huston does not appear overly interested in integrating this material with the rest of the narrative and instead concentrates on creating a particularly rich and vivid collection of characters. At the center is the hooligan Dix Handley, with his dream of making it big and escaping the city. He is from a Kentucky farming family which once had 160 acres but which had fallen on hard times. In one scene, Doll wakes Dix, who says he has dreamed of a colt called Corn Cracker that he loved as a child. She sympathizes with his loss. By film's end, Dix's dream of a return to reclaim the lost family farm has turned into a nightmare as he drives badly wounded back into Kentucky. Talking incoherently and bleeding to death, Dix stops at a stud farm and staggers toward a group of beautiful horses. He falls and dies while the horses graze up to him and around him; Dix is close enough to touch his dream but is unable to grasp it.

*The Asphalt Jungle* displays many other damaged and flawed people, such as Gus, fiercely loyal to Dix, who bears his mark of difference on the outside of his body. Another example is the urbanely dissolute lawyer Emmerich, who claims that "crime is just a left-handed form of human endeavor." His mistress, Angela, is played by a sexy young Marilyn Monroe, to whom he refers as a "sweet kid," while she calls him "uncle." Even as he prepares to commit suicide, Emmerich assures her that there will always be older men to support her luxurious lifestyle. The film's complex litany of character flaws includes Doc's predilection for nubile young girls. In an early scene he looks at a girlie calendar, and later he risks capture to enjoy watching as a teenage girl dances in a diner. In contrast to these self-centered people is the Italian safecracker Ciavelli, whose poignant death leaves a grieving family who appear close to the breadline.

Throughout, Huston and cinematographer Harold Rossen give *The Asphalt Jungle* a distinctive look. The credit sequence is especially striking, with its De Chirico–like spaces with columns and empty streets supposedly part of an anonymous Midwestern city. Through this stark cityscape the tiny lone figure of Dix moves, stealthily dodging a prowling cop car. *The Asphalt Jungle* bears some similarity to the 1956 caper film *The Killing,* and not only because of the shared presence of Sterling Hayden. As much as any film in the heist subgenre, *The Asphalt Jungle* conveys a convincing sense of a network of crooks who can be drawn on by a planner for the execution of a particular crime. What makes it distinctive is its powerful exposure of corruption across the divides of class and wealth. Emmerich's mansion conceals an innate venality just as ruthless as that found in the low-rent dives that Gus and Dix occupy. It is this panoramic dramatization of urban crime that makes the title's image of an asphalt jungle more persuasive than the police commissioner's Production Code Authority–inspired tirades on the subject.

Brian McDonnell

**B**

---

**BEAUMONT, HUGH** (1909–1982). For most people, Hugh Beaumont will be remembered as the calm, wise urbane father Ward Cleaver in more than 200 episodes of *Leave It to Beaver*, an immensely popular television sit-com that was in production between 1957 and 1963. However, in films such as *Money Madness*, Beaumont displayed another side as a ruthless killer, and he had an extensive career prior to *Leave It to Beaver* in low-budget noir films.

Beaumont was born in Lawrence, Kansas, and studied for the clergy before entering show business in 1931, and he continued as a lay preacher for most of his life. After performing in nightclubs, theaters, and on radio, Beaumont went to Hollywood in 1940 and gradually worked his way up from uncredited parts to leading roles in B films in the mid-1940s. Along the way, he played the sinister German agent Otto Skaas, who terrorized John Garfield in Richard Wallace's noir film *The Fallen Sparrow* (1943), and the hapless husband of Jean Brooks who commits suicide at the end of Val Lewton's nihilistic noir film *The Seventh Victim* (1943). However, it was in the period from 1945 to 1948, until the collapse of small Poverty Row studios such as PRC, Eagle-Lion, and Film Classics, that Beaumont's film career really blossomed in roles that were the antithesis of his television persona of Ward Cleaver. Beaumont's first starring role was in *The Lady Confesses* (1945), a low-budget noir film produced by PRC. In this film he plays Larry Craig, the film's nominal hero, who discovers that his wife, who had been missing for seven years, is still alive. When she dies, the police suspect a nightclub owner. However, Craig, who has been romancing Mary Beth Hughes throughout the film, is exposed as the killer, and the police shoot him as he is about to murder

Hughes. This film established a character that Beaumont would return to regularly in the next four years as the seemingly likeable leading man with a character flaw that leads to murder. He followed *The Lady Confesses* with another film noir from PRC, a fascinating rip-off of *Double Indemnity* called *Apology for Murder* (1945), with another luminary of low-budget noir films, Ann Savage. She costars with Beaumont in the roles played by Barbara Stanwyck and Fred MacMurray in Billy Wilder's 1944 film. With poor production values, *Apology for Murder* is no match for *Double Indemnity*, although Beaumont and Savage are effective as the murderous duo that kill Savage's husband.

When PRC reprised the Michael Shayne character after Twentieth Century Fox had made seven movies based on Brett Halliday's detective hero between 1941 and 1942, starring Lloyd Nolan as Shayne, they cast Beaumont as the detective. Four films were produced between 1946 and 1947, but due to the limited budgets, the films did not match the quality of the Fox series. After this series concluded, Beaumont costarred with John Ireland in Anthony Mann's tough noir film *Railroaded* (1947). Beaumont, as Police Sergeant Mickey Ferguson, kills the sadistic gangster Duke Martin (Ireland) at the climax of the film.

In his next two noir films, *Bury Me Dead* (1947) and *Money Madness* (1948), Beaumont was the killer. In *Bury Me Dead*, made by PRC, he is the family lawyer who murders out of greed, while a similar desire motivates his character in *Money Madness*. *Money Madness*, produced at Film Classics, gave Beaumont his best role in feature films. He plays Steve Clark, a good-looking psychotic killer who ingratiates himself into a young woman's life so that he can hide stolen money in her aunt's house. However, this leads to murder and the downfall of the young woman, played by Frances Rafferty.

As the small Poverty Row studios closed in the late 1940s, so did Beaumont's film career as a leading man. Until *Leave It to Beaver,* he was cast in supporting roles in a wide range of genre films. When *Leave It to Beaver* finished production, he worked in many television programs throughout the 1960s such as *Wagon Train*, *Lassie*, *Petticoat Junction*, *The Virginian*, and *Mannix*

**Selected Noir Films:** *The Fallen Sparrow* (1943), *The Seventh Victim* (1943), *The Lady Confesses* (1945), *Apology for Murder* (1945), *Murder Is My Business* (1946), *The Blue Dahlia* (1946), *Larceny in Her Heart* (1946), *Blonde for a Day* (1946), *The Guilt of Janet Ames* (1947), *Three on a Ticket* (1947), *Too Many Winners* (1947), *Railroaded* (1947), *Bury Me Dead* (1947), *Money Madness* (1948), *Night without Sleep* (1952).

Geoff Mayer

**BENNETT, JOAN** (1910–1990). Bennett was an excellent actress with a very wide range, someone who could play a brassy, self-serving tramp just as easily as she could embody a woman of class, virtue, and substance. She was a central player in a number of noir's best-known films, and many of her portrayals have become definitive and memorable. Joan Bennett was the youngest of three acting sisters from a New Jersey theatrical family. Producer Walter Wanger became her third husband and introduced her to director Fritz Lang, with whom she soon became good friends. The three of them founded Diana Productions, named for Bennett's daughter, and made several significant film noirs together. Noir-like personal events even penetrated into their real lives: in 1951 Wanger shot Bennett's press agent, with whom she was having an affair, and was imprisoned for the crime. This scandal affected Bennett's career for several years. She was first able to show the self-possession, sexual confidence, and pragmatic attitude of a classic femme fatale in Lang's film *The Woman in the Window* (1944), where she played opposite Edward G. Robinson and Dan Duryea. Bennett was again united with these three in *Scarlet Street* (1945). The character of Kitty March that she plays in *Scarlet Street* shows Bennett in her most dissembling role. Kitty is a slovenly woman with a blatant sexual tie to her boyfriend Johnny, and Bennett does exceedingly well in a nasty role that requires her to act as a woman who is herself putting on an act. This time, her character suffers the fate of being murdered with an ice pick. She played deceitful and seductive wives (rather than paramours) in *The Macomber Affair*, *The Woman on the Beach*, and *Secret Beyond the Door*. Bennett went on to do very well in *Hollow Triumph* (1948), where she was able to develop subtle shadings in a rather underwritten role, playing a woman who starts out as brassy and hard-headed but who develops a softer side and a clearer set of moral convictions. Perhaps her most accomplished role in the classical noir cycle was a rare instance of an interesting good woman in Max Ophul's *The Reckless Moment* (1949). Here, as Lucia Harper, she is a tower of strength who will only allow herself tears when she is alone. She is a respectable bourgeois woman who is prepared to skirt the criminal world or even break the law in order to protect her family.

**Selected Noir Films:** *The Woman in the Window* (1944), *Scarlet Street* (1945), *The Macomber Affair* (1947), *The Woman on the Beach* (1947), *Secret Beyond the Door* (1948), *Hollow Triumph* (a.k.a. *The Scar*, 1948), *The Reckless Moment* (1949), *Highway Dragnet* (1954).

Brian McDonnell

**THE BIG CLOCK** (Paramount, 1948). *Director:* John Farrow. *Producer:* Richard Maibaum. *Script:* Jonathan Latimer, based on the novel by Kenneth Fearing. *Cinematography:* John F. Seitz. *Music:* Victor Young. *Cast:* Ray Milland (George Stroud), Charles Laughton (Earl Janoth), Maureen O'Sullivan (Georgette Stroud), George Macready (Steve Hagen), Rita Johnson (Pauline York), Elsa Lancaster (Louise Patterson), Harold Vermilyea (Don Klausmeyer), Dan Tobin (Ray Cordette), Harry Morgan (Bill Womack), Richard Webb (Nat Sperling).

In Kenneth Fearing's 1946 novel *The Big Clock*, reporter and editor George Stroud meets a blonde woman, Pauline Delos, and spends the night in a hotel with her. Two months later, when his wife and daughter are out of town, he takes her out again—only this time, they are seen by Earl Janoth, Delos's boyfriend and

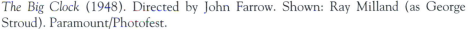

*The Big Clock* (1948). Directed by John Farrow. Shown: Ray Milland (as George Stroud). Paramount/Photofest.

Stroud's boss at *Crimeways Magazine*. Janoth kills Delos, although he does not know the identity of the man she is sleeping with. Janoth then assigns Stroud to find this man.

Paramount's 1948 film version follows the novel's basic plot, with a few notable deviations. The first is the film's opening, which is pure film noir as the camera begins with an image of a dark city before moving in on one man, George Stroud, who is hiding in the darkness of the large building that houses Janoth's publishing empire. Then Stroud's voice-over begins recounting the events of the past 24 hours leading up to the predicament where both the police and Janoth's hit man are searching for him. The second deviation concerns his indiscretion with Pauline Delos, renamed Pauline York. Here Stroud appears guilty of little more than innocent flirtation and a few drinks. While the novel clearly, and more logically, presents the relationship as a sexual affair, the film shows George as a victim of circumstance.

The novel also presents Stroud as relatively unconcerned that Janoth killed Pauline Delos, and only an accident, described in the final line of the novel, records Janoth's death. The film, on the other hand, shows that George, once he has deduced that Janoth killed Delos, is determined to bring him to justice, and the final section of the film, unlike the novel, relies on tension and suspense. However, what both forms share is a depiction of escalating corporate power in America, particularly media conglomerates such as Janoth's empire. This fear of centralization and large business units is superbly realized in the film in Janoth's obsession with the huge clock in the Janoth Publications Building, an overpowering art deco building that synchronizes and controls all of the clocks in Janoth's publishing houses. Late in the film, as the investigation into Pauline's death leads the police and the reporters closer to Stroud, he hides in the room housing the clock's mechanism, and when he accidentally disturbs its operations, the clock suddenly stops, thereby disrupting all the other clocks in Janoth's domain. This moment, coupled with Janoth's rage and sense of impotence, provides a powerful metaphor of the centralization of financial power in America.

This presentation of the destructive effects of corporate power is assimilated into a familiar noir story concerning a married man's dalliance with an attractive woman. This leads to murder and establishes the noir credentials of *The Big Clock*. Otherwise, the film, aside from its opening sequence, shares little of the visual expressionism and fractured characters that characterize most noir films in the 1940s. Mostly, the tone is light, and some of it is played for comedy.

Geoff Mayer

**THE BIG COMBO** (Allied Artists, 1955). *Director:* Joseph H. Lewis. *Producer:* Sidney Harmon. *Script:* Philip Yordan. *Cinematography:* John Alton. *Music:* David Raksin. *Cast:* Cornel Wilde (Lieutenant Leonard Diamond), Richard Conte (Mr. Brown), Brian Donlevy (Joe McClure), Jean Wallace (Susan Lowell), Robert Middleton (Police Captain Peterson), Lee Van Cleef (Fante), Earl Holliman (Mingo), Helen Walker (Alica Brown), Jay Adler (Sam Hill), John Hoyt (Nils Dreyer), Ted De Corsia (Bettini), Helene Stanton (Rita).

The credits for *The Big Combo* are shown over footage of a large American city. Thereafter the film is a totally closed, self-contained universe expressed visually through the lighting, unbalanced compositions, and stylized dialogue. It begins with socialite Susan running along the dark alleys of a boxing stadium pursued by Fante and Mingo, two gangsters employed by Mr. Brown. This visual transformation from the flat documentary footage of the city streets behind the credits to the stylized noir lighting of the dark alleyway in the first scene is sudden and illuminating.

John Alton's expressive, low-key cinematography; David Raksin's jazz score; Philip Yordan's deliberately stylized dialogue; and Joseph Lewis's interesting direction, pushing both the conventions of the 1950s crime film and the censorship restrictions imposed by the Production Code, make *The Big Combo* one of the most memorable noir films of the 1950s, and the film rivals his earlier masterpiece, *Gun Crazy* (1950). However, while *Gun Crazy* utilized location shooting to enhance its story, *The Big Combo* allows virtually no outside reality to intrude— there is little sunlight or brightness and virtually no happiness. These aspects are

*The Big Combo* (1955). Directed by Joseph H. Lewis. Shown: Richard Conte (as Mr. Brown), Brian Donlevy (as Joe McClure), Cornel Wilde (as Lieutenant Leonard Diamond). Allied Artists/Photofest.

replaced by a neurotic battle between police lieutenant Leonard Diamond and his alter ego, the gangster Mr. Brown. The overt theme of the film is expressed by Brown when he tells a hapless boxer that "number one is somebody and number two is nobody."

The narrative framework of *The Big Combo* is familiar—the desire of a cop to bring a mobster to justice—and within this structure, screenwriter Philip Yordan's desire to break out of its restrictions is evident in the excessive, stylized dialogue and in his characterizations, which subvert some of the expectations associated with this formulaic setup. Hence Diamond's motivation to bring down Brown is not based solely on his vocation but emanates from a mixture of repressed sexual desire for Susan, a self-righteous belief in his authority, and a sense of jealousy that Brown articulates throughout the film. Diamond does not just want to bring Brown to justice—he wants Brown's power, both sexual and financial, and he wants Brown's mistress, the blonde socialite Susan Lowell. Lowell, on the other hand, wants to be saved from herself and her own aberrant desire for Brown.

The film begins when this battle is well under way, at a point where both men are beginning to psychologically unravel. The catalyst comes when Susan attempts to kill herself by taking an overdose of pills. During her delirium she murmurs the name *Alicia*, and this appears to be the circuit breaker that Diamond has been waiting for. While it eventually leads to Brown's arrest, it causes pain to a number of people along the way. Nevertheless, Alicia turns out to be Brown's estranged wife, and her testimony incriminates her husband.

The plot is less important than the film's litany of sad characters that are destroyed, psychologically or physically, by either Brown or Diamond. For example, Alicia, Brown's wife, feigns insanity to stay alive, while an informer, Bettini, waits to die in a squalid room. On the other side, Diamond periodically visits a stripper, Rita, for sex and psychological comfort. In return, her association with Diamond leads to her brutal death when she is murdered by Fante and Mingo. Fante and Mingo, a thinly veiled homosexual couple, remain loyal to Brown, and he repays their trust by planting an explosive device in a box that should contain sufficient money for them to escape the police by leaving the country.

*The Big Combo* refuses to polarize between good and evil as it is a film that espouses relative moral values. It is also a film permeated, for a 1950s film, with a strong sense of sadism and sexual perversity. Director Lewis appears determined that the audience should experience, as far as possible, the moments of psychological and physical violence. For example, when Diamond is captured and tortured by Brown, Fante, and Mingo, they place a hearing aid worn by displaced mob boss Joe McClure in Diamond's ear while music is played loudly through the earpiece. Similarly, when it is McClure's time to die, he is shot by Fante and Mingo, but he, like the audience, cannot hear it as Brown removes his earpiece in a prolonged point-of-view shot of McClure's death.

The film also contains an infamous scene involving oral sex. Susan Lowell, although suffering regular bouts of self-disgust, cannot resist Brown's touch, especially when he satisfies her orally. This scene, which Lewis spoke about in recent years, directly challenged the censorship strictures of the Production Code Authority. Lewis, however, avoided censorship by keeping the camera on Susan's rapturous face as Brown slowly disappears from view as he moves down her body. This scene, however, also disturbed actor Cornel Wilde, who played Diamond, as his wife, Jean Wallace, was cast as Susan Lowell. Wallace only agreed to shoot the scene while Wilde was absent from the set, and he was not pleased with Lewis when he finally saw the scene.

Geoff Mayer

**THE BIG HEAT** (Columbia, 1953). *Director:* Fritz Lang. *Producer:* Robert Arthur. *Script:* Sydney Boehm, from the *Saturday Evening Post* serial by William P. McGivern. *Cinematography:* Charles Lang. *Music:* Mischa Bakaleinikoff. *Cast:* Glenn Ford (Dave Bannion), Gloria Grahame (Debby Marsh), Lee Marvin (Vince Stone), Jocelyn Brando (Kate Bannion), Alexander Scourby (Mike Lagana).

Fritz Lang is one the most significant directors associated with classical film noir, and *The Big Heat* is perhaps the finest example of his work in the genre.

*The Big Heat* (1953). Directed by Fritz Lang. Shown in foreground from left: Lee Marvin (as Vince Stone), Glenn Ford (as Det. Sgt. Dave Bannion). Background center: Gloria Grahame (as Debby Marsh). Columbia Pictures/Photofest.

One of many films of the early 1950s that examine civic corruption and the links between organized crime and city officialdom, it nonetheless still retains as its central character the sort of marginal victim hero fighting against malevolent fate who was more commonly seen in films of the 1940s. However, Dave Bannion, as played by Glenn Ford, emerges as an incorruptible upright cop, and some critics have described him as an almost fascistic figure whose relentless pursuit of criminals draws him away from the antiauthoritarian noir tradition. In his book *Film Noir*, Andrew Spicer, for instance, claims that Bannion becomes an "existential Golem, beyond rational control or appeal and yet acting with an implacable logic" (p. 127).

The ethical world of *The Big Heat* is efficiently sketched in during the opening scenes. A corrupt police officer named Duncan commits suicide, leaving a disturbingly unemotional widow behind. Mrs. Duncan soon uses a letter left by her husband to blackmail Mike Lagana, a leading criminal in the city. Dave Bannion is also introduced as a conscientious detective with a rewarding and happy domestic life. He lacks respect for his superiors at work, calling one of his bosses a "leaning tower of jelly," but he finds both support and solace from his wife, Kate, at their suburban home. Lang sets up the home as blissful: a brightly lit kitchen with meals cooking, an adoring apron-clad spouse, an angelic child, a baby carriage. In an early scene his toddler is building a police station with blocks, but Bannion accidentally knocks it over. This is a portent of his future purging of corruption within the real police station.

Lang contrasts the moral haven of Bannion's home with the sleazy world of gangster Lagana, who pulls the strings of politicians while enforcing his will through a violent pack of underlings led by sadistic Vince Stone. Lee Marvin plays Vince to the hilt in a memorable performance, but he is matched by Gloria Grahame as his girlfriend Debby. She is a mixture of goodness and vanity, her moral ambiguity symbolized in the film's many mirror shots, which reveal her mild narcissism, but her duality is most shockingly visualized after Vince scalds her face with hot coffee and she survives with one side scarred and the other unmarked. Dave's decision to accost Lagana in his mansion in order to pithily express his contempt for the gangster's veneer of respectability has a devastating consequence, which produces one of the most shocking scenes in all of film noir. Lagana's hoods plant a bomb in Bannion's car, but by mischance, it explodes when his wife abruptly drives to pick up a babysitter, and she is killed. This leaves Dave bereft but also implacably determined to gain revenge. His professional quest for justice thus becomes a personal drive for vengeance and satisfaction.

The procedural aspects of his investigation are skillfully dramatized in the film's second half through a succession of deftly drawn minor characters. These include a limping woman who works in a car wrecker's yard, her crippled leg linked metaphorically to the damaged car bodies. It is she who provides Dave with valuable clues about the provenance of the fatal car bomb. There are as well the ex-army buddies of Dave's brother-in-law, who rally around against the thugs when there is a threat of abduction to his little girl. Of most significance is the development of Debby as an unlikely ally for Dave. She, too, seeks revenge for her scarring, and she is prepared to kill to bring down Lagana's and Vince's operation. She shoots Mrs. Duncan to free up the incriminating letter and even manages to scald Vince's face before he guns her down. Bannion is present at this latter scene but foregoes his chance to kill Vince. Instead, he ministers to the dying Debby. After his long period of being on the out with his police bosses, the rebellious Bannion is reintegrated in the epilogue of *The Big Heat*. Having brought down the city's most corrupt figures with Debby's help, and having fostered renewed fortitude among his colleagues, Dave is seen once again as part of a virtuous team in the film's closing moments. As one of his pals had remarked earlier, "No man is an island," a motto that summarizes the filmmakers' social values.

Brian McDonnell

**THE BIG SLEEP** (Warner Bros., 1946). *Director/Producer:* Howard Hawks. *Script:* William Faulkner, Leigh Brackett, and Jules Furthman, from the novel by Raymond Chandler. *Cinematography:* Sid Hickox. *Music:* Max Steiner. *Cast:* Humphrey

Bogart (Philip Marlowe), Lauren Bacall (Vivian Sternwood), John Ridgeley (Eddie Mars), Martha Vickers (Carmen Sternwood), Charles Waldron (General Sternwood), Dorothy Malone (Bookstore Proprietress), Peggy Knudsen Mona Mars), Regis Toomey (Chief Inspector Bernie Ohls), Elisha Cook Jr. (Harry Jones).

After RKO so successfully adapted Raymond Chandler's novel *Farewell, My Lovely* into the 1944 film *Murder My Sweet,* it was only a matter of time before more of Chandler's Philip Marlowe stories would be given film treatment. Versions of his first novel, *The Big Sleep* (Warner Bros.), and *The High Window* (retitled *The Brasher Doubloon* by Twentieth Century Fox) were soon to follow. Warner Bros. wanted to reteam the popular pairing of Humphrey Bogart and Lauren Bacall that had proved such a hit in *To Have and Have Not* in 1944. In fact, an early version of *The Big Sleep* previewed to overseas troops in 1945 was modified before the official 1946 release to accentuate the screen chemistry between the real-life lovers. The resulting film is definitely a classic murder mystery, but its status as film noir is slightly less straightforward. This is because Bogart as Marlowe maintains an air of invulnerability throughout the story so that a sense of possible damage to the hero is much less evident than in other noirs that are thematically more central to the genre. Under Howard Hawks's expert direction, this is definitely one of the best of the private eye subgenre of film noir, but the wise-cracking and poised Marlowe always seems in control, letting the audience remain relaxed more than film noir usually allows them to.

The plot of *The Big Sleep* is very convoluted, indeed so labyrinthine in parts that even Chandler was alleged to be unable to name the perpetrator of one of the murders. The sense of bewilderment and intrigue is heightened by the absence of a voice-over narration that might have helped audience understanding. Unlike *Murder My Sweet,* there is no attempt here to have Marlowe tell his own story. However, this narrative confusion is not too damaging because in *The Big Sleep,* story line is not as important as setting, character, witty dialogue, and visualization. The pace is so fast that only seldom do characters pause to try to explain what is going on. Nevertheless, the basic narrative setup is a standard one. Marlowe is hired by wealthy General Sternwood to stop his younger daughter, Carmen, from being blackmailed, while older daughter, Vivian, seems anxious that Marlowe may have been hired to find a missing man named Sean Regan. Naturally these two quests eventually coalesce into one enigma, but along the way, a heady mix of gambling, possible pornography, nymphomania, cold-blooded murder, seduction, and dope-taking keep Marlowe on his toes. A succession of beautiful women offer themselves to the detective with varying degrees of success, and he has what was for 1946 a very daring and detailed discussion of sexual practices with Vivian (Bacall) using the terminology of horse racing. Marlowe is able to knit together all the frayed strands of the plot, to outwit those who scheme and those who mean him harm, and to engineer some poetic justice, in which the guilty die and the fragile are cocooned from harm.

Certain contrasts with the Marlowe figure as played by Dick Powell in *Murder My Sweet* are significant in generic terms. Apart from the lack of voice-over already mentioned, which means that the narration of *The Big Sleep* is less subjective and closer to the classical Hollywood model, Marlowe, as played by Bogart, faces a lower level of physical threat than did Dick Powell's version of Marlowe. Instead of being drugged and slugged, Bogart always seems to have the best of his enemies and to never lose his aplomb or sangfroid, even in tricky situations. The film's baddies, such as Joe Brody and Eddie Mars, are much more charming and agreeable than they are frightening or sadistic, and even the cops are more genial. Everyone, in spite of the circumstances, seems entertaining, and Bogart is able to best them without too many bruises or scratches or without rumpling either his suit or his toupee. Most significantly, there is in *The Big Sleep* no femme fatale to rival Velma in *Murder My Sweet*. There is no spider woman to trap the hero or to have her secret felonies and plots subjected to scrutiny. Vivian comes closest with her sexual allure and her failure to disclose to Marlowe her knowledge of Sean Regan's death, but Vivian is loyal to the detective rather than treacherous, and her minor deception is altruistic in that she is only trying to protect her younger sister. Carmen may literally have killed someone (Regan), but she is seen infrequently and is portrayed as helplessly compromised mentally. None of her bad actions are dramatized, and every time she appears, she is either drugged or is fluttering her eyes simperingly, calling Marlowe "cute" or trying to sit in his lap when he is standing up.

*The Big Sleep* is even more studio-bound than *Murder My Sweet*, with no location work at all. Despite this, it conveys wonderfully the flavor of Chandler's Los Angeles in its Hollywood renditions of humid hothouses; swanky nightspots; rare-book shops; foggy or rainy streets; deserted office buildings; campy, overdecorated Laurel Canyon bungalows; semirural hideouts; and piers where dripping limousines are fished out of the sea. Bogart's Marlowe may not be as easily damaged as other noir seeker heroes, but he still leads the viewer on a compelling journey through the noir universe.

Brian McDonnell

**BLACK ANGEL** (Universal, 1946). *Director:* Roy William Neill. *Producers:* Tom McKnight and Roy William Neill. *Script:* Roy Chanslor, based on the novel by Cornel Woolrich. *Cinematography:* Paul Ivano. *Music:* Frank Skinner. *Cast:* Dan Duryea (Martin Blair), June Vincent (Catherine Bennett), Peter Lorre (Marko), Broderick Crawford (Captain Flood), Constance Dowling (Mavis Marlowe), Wallace Ford (Joe), Hobart Cavanaugh (Jake), Freddie Steele (Lucky), John Phillips (Kirk Bennett), Ben Bard (Bartender), Archie Twitchell (George Mitchell).

Cornell Woolrich, and other hard-boiled writers such as Raymond Chandler, often reworked their short stories into full-length novels. Woolrich's *The Black Angel*, published in 1943, was no exception. "Murder in Wax," published in the pulp magazine *Dime Detective* in March 1935, reworked elements of Woolrich's

1932 novel *Manhattan Love Song*. In "Murder in Wax" a man is about to leave his wife with another woman when she, the other woman, is murdered. After he is arrested and sentenced to death, the story is narrated by the condemned man's wife as she searches for the killer. The twist in this story is that after she has seemingly cornered the murderer, she is revealed to be the killer. Two years later, Woolrich reworked this story again in "Face Work," published in *Black Mask* in October 1937, although the story was later reissued under the title "Angel Face." "Face Work," which was sold to Columbia Pictures soon after publication and transformed into the B film *Convicted* (1938), changed the characters from husband and wife to brother and sister as a New York stripper, Jerry Wheeler, tries to save her younger brother from being executed after he is found guilty of killing singer Ruby Rose. To achieve this, Wheeler has to insinuate herself into the life and affections of a sadistic nightclub owner.

Woolrich extended this premise in *The Black Angel*, an episodic novel that shares the race-against-the-clock motif of *Phantom Lady*, both the novel and film (1944). The essence of each story is similar—a young woman is forced to ingratiate herself into the underbelly of society, and in each case, her morality is compromised during her investigation. In Universal's film adaptation of *The Black Angel*, screenwriter Roy Chanslor and veteran director Roy William Neill tightened Woolrich's narrative structure by eliminating the episodic structure whereby four stories were reduced to one. Hence the alcoholic pianist in the film, Marty Blair, is a composite of two characters in the novel. Similarly, the M-monogrammed matchbook in the film leads to only one man, Marko, the sinister nightclub owner, while in the novel, it leads to four men.

When Cathy Bennett's husband is convicted of the murder of singer Mavis Marlowe, she sets out to find the real killer, even though Marlowe was, at one time, her husband's mistress and was blackmailing him. Cathy is assisted by Marlowe's husband, Marty Blair, and a monogrammed matchbook leads them to nightclub owner Marko. So that they can gain access to the nightclub, Marty and Cathy develop a musical act—he writes the music and plays the piano, and she sings. When Marko appears to leave the club with gossip columnist George Mitchell one night, Cathy sneaks into his office and opens his safe. However, Marko's departure was only a ruse so that he could catch her and, possibly, torture and molest her. This is prevented by the arrival of policeman Captain Flood.

This plot element turns out to be a red herring. The killer is Marty Blair, although he only becomes aware of this fact late in the film as the murder was carried out during a drunken binge. Similar to his counterpart in the novel, Ladd Mason, Blair sacrifices himself for Cathy (Alberta in the novel) and saves her philandering husband from death. The film's inherent irony is that Blair is the most virtuous male character as he genuinely loves Cathy.

Cornell Woolrich disliked the film version of his novel, and while Cathy is not forced to compromise her morality to the same extent that Alberta Murray is forced to do in the novel, *Black Angel* is a stylish film noir that benefits from the casting and performance of Dan Duryea as Marty Blair. After attracting attention with strong performances as villainous or compromised characters in a number of noir films, especially the blackmailer in *The Woman in the Window* (1944) and the weak husband in *The Great Flamarion* (1945), Duryea's performance as the hero in *Black Angel* provides a problematic basis to the story, especially after he redeems himself in the latter part of the film.

There is a bizarre footnote to the production of *Black Angel*. The film's British born director, Roy William Neill, had labored in Hollywood for nearly two decades, mostly on low-budget films, including Universal's popular series of Sherlock Holmes films, starring Basil Rathbone as Sherlock Holmes and Nigel Bruce as Dr. Watson. Neill directed 11 of the 12 films in this series between 1942 and 1946. However, *Black Angel* was his final film, and having accumulated sufficient money, he retired to Maidenhead-on-Thames in England. However, just after arriving home, he died of a heart attack.

Geoff Mayer

**BLONDE ICE** (Film Classics, 1948). *Director:* Jack Bernhard. *Producers:* Martin Mooney and Robert E. Callaghan (associate). *Script:* Kenneth Gamet and Raymond Schrock, based on the novel *Once Too Often* by Whitman Chambers. *Cinematography:* George Robinson. *Music:* Irving Getz. *Cast:* Robert Paige (Les Burns), Leslie Brooks (Claire Cummings), Russ Vincent (Blackie Talon), Michael Whalen (Stanley Mason), James Griffith (Al Herrick), Emory Parnell (Captain Bill Murdock), Walter Sande (Hack Doyle), John Holland (Carl Hanneman), Mildred Coles (June Taylor), David Leonard (Dr. Geoffrey Kippinger), Selmer Jackson (District Attorney Ed Chalmers), Rory Mallinson (Sergeant Benson).

*Blonde Ice* was produced by Film Classics, a small production company that released a dozen films in the late 1940s before going out of business. Executive producer Martin Mooney had the good sense to obtain veteran cinematographer George Robinson from Universal, where he had photographed some of the most visually striking horror films, such as *Dracula's Daughter* (1936) and *Son of Dracula* (1943), in the 1930s and 1940s. Robinson's expert compositions and lighting ensure that *Blonde Ice* is a superior film noir compared to the average low-budget quickie produced by Poverty Row studios in the 1940s, such as Monogram and PRC. The visual quality is matched by the performances, especially Leslie Brooks as Claire Cummings, a sociopath who kills three men, and Robert Paige as Les Burns, the masochistic newspaper reporter unable to end his association with Cummings, even after she marries, and murders, two men.

Because their budgets were so small, and the corresponding financial risk was not high, the writers and directors of many 1940s B films faced little interference from studio executives compared with their high-budget counterparts. This allowed films such as *Blonde Ice* to be more adventurous with their characterizations and themes. Thus, although *Blonde Ice* was similar, at least thematically, to films such as *Double Indemnity* (1944) and *Murder, My Sweet* (1944), it extends its presentation beyond such films. Claire Cummings in *Blonde Ice*, for example, is similar to Phyllis Dietrichson in *Double Indemnity*—she is motivated primarily by greed and a desire to elevate her status in society, and she uses sex to seduce her male associates, or victims, while seemingly taking little pleasure in the sex act itself. It is the power she craves and the pleasure she displays in inflicting pain. Thus, while Phyllis is calculating and deceitful in *Double Indemnity*, Claire is a more extreme sociopath who revels in her transgressive behavior, and her evident pleasure when Les Burns is blamed for her third killing goes way beyond Phyllis's cool demeanor in *Double Indemnity*. This aspect is reinforced by the posters promoting *Blonde Ice*, which show Leslie Brooks dressed in a backless evening gown and about to fire her gun. This is accompanied by the words *Blonde Svengali, Beautiful . . . Evil . . . Be Deviling . . . Daring.*

The film begins with the marriage between society columnist Claire Cummings and wealthy businessman Carl Hanneman. Attending the wedding are Claire's fellow reporters, and lovers, Les Burns and Al Herrick. During the reception Claire slips away from Carl to tell Les that she does not love her husband and really loves him. Later, while on his honeymoon in Los Angeles, Hanneman discovers that Claire is still writing love letters to Burns, and he flies home alone to San Francisco. Claire, however, devises an ingenious plan to kill her husband by hiring a pilot to fly her to San Francisco, where she murders Hanneman, and back to Los Angeles all in one night. She then flies back to San Francisco, where, in the company of Burns, she finds the body.

Claire keeps her affair with Burns simmering while romancing another wealthy man, lawyer and prospective politician Stanley Mason. A similar pattern follows, with Claire killing Mason when he discovers that she is still involved with Burns. In between, she also murders the pilot who flew her from Los Angeles to San Francisco when he tries to blackmail her. Only with a perfunctory ending, when psychiatrist Dr. Geoffrey Kippinger pressures Claire into a confession, does the film falter by weakening its presentation of this seductive, heartless woman. *Blonde Ice* prefigured similar post-1980 noir films such as *Black Widow* (1987) and *The Last Seduction* (1994), although the Production Code Administration in 1948 would never have given filmmakers the freedom four decades later in allowing the fatal woman to escape death. Yet as Claire Cummings lies dead on the floor of the newspaper office, she still dominates the men circled around her body.

Geoff Mayer

**BLOOD SIMPLE** (River Road Productions, 1984). *Director:* Joel Coen. *Producer:* Ethan Coen. *Script:* Joel Coen and Ethan Coen. *Cinematography:* Barry Sonnenfeld. *Music:* Carter Burwell. *Cast:* John Getz (Ray), Frances McDormand (Abby),

*Blood Simple* (1984). Directed by Joel Coen. Shown: Frances McDormand (as Abby). USA Films/Photofest.

Dan Hedaya (Julian Marty), M. Emmet Walsh (Loren Visser), Samm-Art Williams (Meurice).

Despite their having separate official producing, directing, and writing credits, it is widely known that Coen brothers Ethan and Joel codirect (as well as cowrite) their quirky seriocomic movies. *Blood Simple* was their debut movie and was the founding film of that subgenre of neo-noir sometimes termed *tumbleweed noir*. Movies in this category are crime films generally set in desert areas of the American Southwest but deploying the plot, character, and thematic conventions of traditional urban film noir. They include *After Dark My Sweet* (1990), *Clay Pigeons* (1998), *The Dark Wind* (1994), *Delusion* (1990), *The Hot Spot* (1990), *Kalifornia* (1993), *Kill Me Again* (1989), *Red Rock West* (1993), *The Salton Sea* (2002), and *U-Turn* (1997). In the case of *Blood Simple*, the central characters include an adulterous couple, the woman's husband, and the venal private eye the husband hires to obtain evidence of the wife's unfaithfulness. The plot involves betrayal, double-crossing, and murder, and the themes embrace determinism, fatal misunderstandings through ignorance and sheer lack of intelligence, and the fickle workings of fate. The terse narrative style is an effective updating of the hard-boiled tradition of crime literature, and the Coens' visual style helps produce a minor classic of neo-noir.

The story line of *Blood Simple* belongs to the lineage of romantic triangle/crime-of-passion films that originated with the classical 1940s adaptations of James M. Cain novels such as *Double Indemnity* and *The Postman Always Rings Twice*. A young couple, Ray and Abby, conduct an affair in a remote rural area of southern Texas. Abby is keen for them to run away and begin a future together, but Ray is less enthusiastic about throwing away his current mode of living. Abby's jealous and vengeful husband (called by his surname of Marty) hires a private eye named Loren to gather proof of the infidelity. When this is produced, Marty confronts Ray and fires him. Marty then asks the private eye (whose laconic voice-over narration has opened the film's narrative) to kill the pair while he himself is away fishing and establishing an alibi in Corpus Christi. When Marty returns, the private eye tells him the job is done and passes over photos of the bodies. It transpires, though, that he has merely photographed Abby and Ray asleep in bed and then doctored the prints by adding bloodstains. A major shock twist occurs when Loren shoots Marty with Abby's own pistol after the money has been handed over. Oblivious to what has just happened, Ray arrives to collect his termination pay, finds the dying Marty, and assumes that Abby has shot him. In a long, suspenseful, and macabre sequence that might have come from a Hitchcock film such as *Psycho* or *Frenzy*, Ray takes the body out into the countryside and begins to bury it in the middle of the night in a plowed field. The horror is intensified when Marty, not quite dead, begins to flail about, groaning and gurgling, as he is covered up with dirt.

There follows a series of fateful misapprehensions as the central characters start leaping to the wrong conclusions and making decisions based on insufficient information. Ray begins to suspect that Abby is already betraying him with another man, namely Meurice, the black bartender from Marty's drinking establishment. Meurice then picks up a phone message left by Marty before he died. In it Marty mentions a robbery at the bar, but this is merely a fiction designed to cover the removal of the large sum of money that he was to pay to the private eye. Loren discovers Marty's body missing and hunts in his office safe for the incriminating photo. Abby later happens by, sees the ransacked safe, and assumes that Ray has killed Marty. However, Meurice tells her that Marty cannot be dead as he had rung him after the robbery. Confused, Abby now believes that Marty must still be alive. Ray finds the key photo and goes to Abby's new apartment to confront her. As he does so, a sniper (Loren) shoots him dead from an adjacent building. The terrified Abby grabs a gun and hides in the bathroom. When Loren comes to kill her as well, neither can see the other, and she mistakenly believes it is actually Marty coming for revenge. The ensuing climax of *Blood Simple* is masterfully designed, shot, and edited and is exciting and suspenseful. Abby gains time by impaling Loren's hand on a window sill with a knife as he reaches around to gain access to her hiding place. Then, as she shoots him through the partition wall, she calls him "Marty," and the detective sees the ironic humor in this misidentification before he dies.

*Blood Simple* is thus a tightly structured, small-scale story of rather stupid people (the word *simple* in the title implies stupidity) in an isolated environment where the forces of law and order seem entirely absent. It has the starkness of an allegory and at its heart is a morality tale about the way in which even the best-laid plans can go terribly astray. Joel Coen's wife, Frances McDormand, has one of her best early roles as the plucky but unimaginative Abby, and M. Emmet Walsh is gloriously seedy as the hefty and unkempt private eye who is full of inappropriate hilarity and, at times, is reminiscent of Orson Welles as Hank Quinlan in *Touch of Evil*. Above all, as well as initiating a new, arid, and windswept milieu for the noir genre, *Blood Simple* introduced the filmgoing public to the pleasures associated with the idiosyncratic style of the Coen brothers: inanimate objects, such as ceiling fans, being photographed as if they had a life of their own, odd camera angles (e.g., vertically down through the fan) that become utterly pertinent to the story, and music tracks (here the Four Tops' *It's the Same Old Song*) blended in to powerful effect.

Brian McDonnell

**BODY HEAT** (Warner Bros./The Ladd Company, 1981). *Director:* Lawrence Kasdan. *Producer:* Fred T. Gallo. *Script:* Lawrence Kasdan. *Cinematography:* Richard H. Kline. *Music:* John Barry. *Cast:* William Hurt (Ned Racine), Kathleen Turner (Matty Walker), Richard Crenna (Edmund Walker), J. A. Preston (Oscar Grace), Ted Danson (Peter Lowenstein), Mickey Rourke (Teddy Lewis).

*Body Heat* (1981). Directed by Lawrence Kasden. Shown from left: Kathleen Turner (as Matty Walker), William Hurt (as Ned Racine). Warner Bros./Photofest.

The highly laudatory review of *Body Heat* in *TIME Magazine* began with the sentence "It is 1946; it is 1981." This clever summation stresses the elements that link this neo-noir film to the classical tradition of such steamy 1940s thrillers as *The Postman Always Rings Twice* and *Double Indemnity*. *Body Heat* reinvents the James Cain–style sexual triangle of the earlier films, ditching the deterministic flashback structure and utilizing all the freedoms that were not available in the repressed era of the Production Code Administration. The impact of the film is greatly aided by the strong performances of Kathleen Turner and William Hurt (who were then at the beginning of their careers) as protagonists Matty Walker and Ned Racine. In Matty, *Body Heat* has a femme fatale similar to Cora Smith and Phyllis Dietrichson in *Postman* and *Double Indemnity* cited previously but here she is allowed to win at the end; Matty survives and prospers, while both Cora and Phyllis die for their sins. *Body Heat* also features much more graphic and explicit sex and violence than was allowed in the heavily censored classical films of the 1940s and 1950s. Director and scriptwriter Lawrence Kasdan claimed he wanted in his first film to explore a wide stylistic range of things, such as camerawork, and because of this, he consciously chose the genre of film noir in order to help enable that to occur.

Kasdan also claims that he wrote what was largely a standard noir story. South Florida lawyer Ned Racine is a listless and relatively discontented bachelor in his thirties. By chance (so he believes) he meets the wealthy, beautiful, and sensual Matty Walker at an outdoor concert, and they begin a torrid affair that is aided by her husband Edmund's routine of being out of town, except on weekends. As the film's title hints, she permanently has an above-average body temperature, and she is certainly more passionate and exciting than the other women with whom he has casual sex. His two friends, prosecutor Lowenstein and cop Oscar, feel that this new anonymous woman is just another of his flings. However, Matty and Ned's talk soon turns to the advantages of having Edmund off the scene altogether, and they conceive a plan to kill him. A prenuptial agreement means that Matty will inherit only half her husband's estate, with the other portion going to his young niece. Ned plans to kill Edmund at his home but then stage an accidental death in a derelict shoreline nightspot called the Breakers, where Edmund will appear to have expired in an attempted arson gone wrong. Edmund's criminal connections will make this more plausible to investigators, and before the killing occurs, Ned recruits an ex-client named Teddy to construct an incendiary bomb for him. He also encounters briefly Matty's friend Maryann, whose resemblance to Matty is so striking that he initially confuses one woman with the other.

The lovers' plot seems to proceed well, despite Edmund's surprisingly spry defense of his own life, but soon after, things start to unravel in the noir tradition of perfect crimes going awry and of thieves falling out. Ned has constructed an alibi for the night of the murder by traveling to Miami and then sneaking back, but he discovers that someone has deliberately kept ringing his Miami hotel room through the switchboard operator in order to undermine his alibi. Edmund's glasses are also missing, and this may be incriminating for Ned. In a major plot twist he also discovers that Matty, in a greedy attempt to inherit all her husband's money, has changed his will, even pretending that Ned, acting as her lawyer, made the alteration. In a move that is ingenious in its apparent clumsiness, she engineers a disqualification of the new will, which thus renders Edmund's death intestate, sending all the money her way instead of giving half to the niece. The bewildered Ned is chided severely by a judge for his incompetence.

Matty wins over the angry Ned with sex, but his suspicion that she is setting him up as a fall guy is confirmed when another lawyer reveals that he had once recommended Ned as a possible attorney to Matty, despite his past failings in estate cases. Teddy tells Ned that Matty has enquired about bomb making, so Ned wisely declines her telephoned instruction to retrieve the missing glasses from a boathouse. As the police close in on him as a suspect, he confronts Matty, and she declares that she will fetch the glasses. An explosion rips apart the boathouse, and Ned is arrested for the deaths of both husband and wife. Later, in jail, he realizes that Matty is still alive, having faked her death by using the body of her friend Maryann. The film closes with him attempting to convince the police of this explanation (using an old high school yearbook as evidence), and the final shots are of a tropical beach, where Matty is seen sunbathing. The ending is an open one with two questions left hanging: Will Ned be exonerated? Is Matty actually unhappy and remorseful about her treatment of Ned?

*Body Heat* remains one of the most crucial films in the neo-noir genre, with its innovative reinvigoration of noir style and preoccupations strengthening its historical significance. Its themes of betrayal, lust, the falling out of conspirators, a man trapped, and double-crossing all link it firmly with the noir tradition, as does the 1940s style saxophone music and the lurid, neon colors of its early scenes, which become the equivalent of classical noir's chiaroscuro, high-contrast, black-and-white cinematography. Kasdan's first film creates both a look and a mood that have been widely imitated by other practitioners of neo-noir.

Brian McDonnell

**BOGART, HUMPHREY** (1899–1957). Easily the best known male face associated with classical noir, Bogart represented in the 1940s and 50s a new and particular kind of masculinity in Hollywood film. He gained slowly mounting popularity, even an eventual posthumous cult status, by adding a layer of humor to his image of essential decency and toughness. Born into a high-status New York family, Humphrey Bogart was the son of an eminent surgeon and was educated at prestigious private schools. He served in the U.S. Navy in World War I but did not begin his stage career until the late 1920s. The course of Bogart's acting path changed crucially when he moved from fresh-faced ingénue roles to become the tough Duke Mantee in the 1935 stage play *The Petrified Forest*. He was asked to repeat the role in a film version the next year, being given the break through the insistence of the film's star, Leslie Howard, that he be cast. This was to prove, for the 37-year-old Bogart, a decisive turning point in what had been an unpromising career. There were still many roles in B films to come, but he broke his gangster stereotype in 1940's *They Drive by Night* with a more sympathetic characterization. Critics and audiences noticed in his performance previously unseen qualities of stillness and presence.

Bogart may not have been handsome in a matinee-idol sense, but he had an agreeably lived-in look. His characters were never gullible, and they had a sense of incorruptibility, a moral center. Even the plastic surgeon working on his face in *Dark Passage* describes his look as intelligent and approachable. The onset of the classical film noir cycle initiated Bogart's development from his tough-guy, vicious persona in the 1930s gangster films. In this particular evolution, the turning point was his portrayal of the alienated Roy Earle in *High Sierra* (1941), where at last he could show a degree of humanity and where he conveyed a palpable sense of the weight of Earle's past history. Bogart received widespread praise for his work in *High Sierra,* and humor was added to the mix with *The Maltese Falcon* that same year. That film's central role, Sam Spade, fit him like a glove, and he was on his way to establishing the tough/romantic persona most often associated with him. Nonetheless, he was still happy to play both heroes and villains, a good example of the latter being the wife killer in *Conflict* (1945). It was, though, as a private detective, such as Spade or Philip Marlowe, that he was able to finesse his depiction of the worldly wise, quick-witted gumshoe who lived according to his own code. The private eye was a kind of protagonist well suited to America's mood in the 1940s: Bogart created a highlight of this type in *The Big Sleep*. Philip Marlowe had a mix of romantic streak and hardheadedness. In the middle to late 1940s Bogart made several films with eventual wife Lauren Bacall, not all of them authentically noir at their core because he seems effortlessly on top of things and even indestructible. Some critics wonder if such films are truly noir since the protagonist always seems so capable and lacking in that central noir characteristic of vulnerability.

A more unequivocally noir part for Bogart was his leading role in *Dead Reckoning* (1947) as Rip Murdock, where he is much more vulnerable. He also had a quite unusual role in *Dark Passage* (1947), where for plot reasons, his face is unseen until 40 minutes into the story, and he has had plastic surgery that renders him into the familiar visage of Humphrey Bogart. *Knock on Any Door* (1949) has a rather cumbersome flashback structure with an extraordinarily long address by District Attorney Bogart to the court. In 1950, in the part of Dixon Steele in Nicholas Ray's *In a Lonely Place* (made for Bogart's company Santana Productions), he played his most complex role and perhaps the one that was most like him in real life. Bogart's character here has none of the romantic air he displays in *Casablanca* or *The Big Sleep*. Instead, Dix is a borderline psychotic screenwriter, an alcoholic with a bad temper. Surrounded by phonies and bullies and a suspect in a homicide, he is shown to certainly have the potential to murder. He is self-destructive, volatile, and vulnerable. Like many other Hollywood figures, Bogart was involved in the HUAC anti-communist hearings, first as a protester, then recanting his earlier statements. The ravages of the cancer that would eventually kill him were becoming evident by the mid-1950s. Bogart's many fans found it sad to seem him appear so aged and ill in his last film, *The Harder They Fall* (1956), but he is nonetheless good in the role of a morally indecisive sportswriter. The story was based on the pathetic career of boxer Primo Carnera, who was reputedly unhappy with his fictional depiction.

**Selected Noir Films:** *They Drive by Night* (1940), *High Sierra* (1941), *The Maltese Falcon* (1941), *Casablanca* (1942), *Conflict* (1945), *The Big Sleep* (1946), *Dead Reckoning* (1947), *The Two Mrs. Carrolls* (1947), *Dark Passage* (1947), *The Treasure of the Sierra Madre* (1948), *Key Largo* (1948), *Knock on Any Door* (1949), *In a Lonely Place* (1950), *The Enforcer* (1951), *Beat the Devil* (1953; and producer uncredited), *The Desperate Hours* (1955), *The Harder They Fall* (1956).

Brian McDonnell

**BORN TO KILL** (RKO, 1947). *Director:* Robert Wise. *Executive Producer:* Sid Rogell. *Producer:* Herman Schlom. *Screenplay:* Eve Greene and Richard Macaulay,

*Born to Kill* (1947). Directed by Robert Wise. Shown: Isabel Jewell (as Laury Palmer), Lawrence Tierney (as Sam Wild). RKO Radio Pictures/Photofest.

from the novel *Deadlier Than the Male* by James Gunn. *Cinematography:* Robert de Grasse. *Music:* Paul Sawtell. *Cast:* Claire Trevor (Helen Trent), Lawrence Tierney (Sam Wild), Walter Slezak (Arnold Arnett), Philip Terry (Fred Grover), Audrey Long (Georgia Staples), Elisha Cook Jr. (Marty Waterman), Isabel Jewell (Laury Palmer), Esther Howard (Mrs. Kraft).

The film begins in Reno with Helen Trent living in a boarding house run by Mrs. Kraft, finalizing her divorce. After completing the formalities, Trent returns to the boarding house to pay her rent and pack. However, as she prepares to leave, she listens to another boarder, Laury Palmer, entertain Mrs. Kraft with a description of her new love interest ("big with broad shoulders") as she tells Kraft why she is so smitten with him: "He's a quiet sort and you get the feeling if you stepped out of line, he'd kick your teeth down your throat." Kraft is similarly impressed and tells Laury, "Ain't that wonderful." Trent is also intrigued by Palmer's emphasis on his ruthlessness and sadism and agrees when they compare these qualities with the spinelessness of most men, who behave like "turnips."

This scene establishes the film's dominant motif —Trent's perverse attraction to Sam Wild's brutality and power. After Laury makes the mistake of inciting Wild's jealousy, he kills both Palmer and her boyfriend. Trent, who noticed Wild in a casino, becomes involved when she returns to the boarding house and finds the bodies. However, she does not contact the police and catches a train back to her home in San Francisco. This is a crucial decision that affects the rest of the film as it establishes her as a morally flawed character. When Wild enters her life by joining her on the train, she is vulnerable, although she rejects his initial advances due to her social position—she is the adopted sister of newspaper heiress Georgia Staples—and the fact that she is engaged to Fred Grover, a cultivated and wealthy young man.

The second half of the film becomes a cat-and-mouse game between Trent and Wild. When he learns that Georgia is wealthy, he marries her and lives in the same house as Trent. Eventually, Trent succumbs when Wild corners her in the kitchen pantry. Racked by guilt and the fear that her privileged social position will be damaged, Trent tries to explain to Wild why she must marry Grover as he can give her the financial independence she craves: "Without him I'm afraid of the things I'll do, afraid of what I might become. Fred is goodness and safety." Wild, however, is undeterred and mockingly tells her, "And what am I? Your strength and excitement—and depravity." This hits the right chord with Trent, and her masochism overpowers her need for respectability and security as she tells Wild, "There's a kind of corruption inside you, Sam." And it appeals to her.

There are many examples of masochistic males exploited by ruthless women in the 1940s and 1950s. *Born to Kill* reverses this pattern. Wild, like Kathie Moffat in *Out of the Past* and Phyllis Dietrichson in *Double Indemnity,* is amoral, sexual, and utterly ruthless. He not only kills Laury Palmer and her beau but also his best friend, Marty Waterman, because he spotted Waterman leaving Trent's room late at night ("nobody cuts in on me"). Trent, on the other hand, is the vulnerable noir protagonist who has everything to lose if she cannot control her lust. Like Jeff Bailey in *Out of the Past* and Walter Neff in *Double Indemnity*, Trent jettisons her morality and abandons herself to her desires by submitting to Wild. This leads to her death as the police kill Wild in the film's brutal conclusion.

*Born to Kill* was Laurence Tierney's best role as the film exploits his smooth good looks, which, in 1947, had not yet deteriorated by alcohol and off-screen brawling—in 1946 he was jailed for drunken behavior, and in 1948 he served three months for assault, a pattern that continued throughout the 1950s. His off-screen behavior gave the film a perverse sense of authenticity. Claire Trevor is equally effective as the morally problematic Trent, and Trevor is a key figure in the film noir of the 1940s. She was able to convincingly convey perversity with sensuality as the femme fatale in *Murder, My Sweet* while expressing vulnerability (and murder) in *Street of Chance* (1942) and masochistic perversity in *Born to Kill*. The following year, she refined these traits in two iconic noir films—the sad protagonist in love with a man who desires another woman in Anthony Mann's *Raw Deal* (1948) and the alcoholic mistress of a brutal gangster in John Huston's *Key Largo* (1948).

Geoff Mayer

**THE BREAKING POINT** (Warner Bros., 1950). *Director:* Michael Curtiz. *Producer:* Jerry Wald. *Script:* Ranald MacDougall, based on the novel *To Have and Have Not* by Ernest Hemingway. *Cinematography:* Ted McCord. *Music:* Ray Heindorf. *Cast:* John Garfield (Harry Morgan), Patricia Neal (Leona Charles), Phyliss Thaxter (Lucy Morgan), Juano Hernandez (Wesley Park), Wallace Ford (Duncan), Edmon Ryan (Rogers), William Campbell (Concho), Guy Thomajan (Danny).

*The Breaking Point* is the second, and by far the best, of three adaptations of Ernest Hemingway's *To Have and Have Not*. The most famous version, Howard Hawk's 1944 film *To Have and Have Not*, which starred Humphrey Bogart as Harry Morgan, used only selected portions of Hemingway's story, while Don Siegel's low-budget 1958 film *The Gun Runners*, starring Audie Murphy as Morgan, was a lackluster version. *The Breaking Point* with John Garfield as Morgan, on the other hand, was much closer to the spirit of Hemingway's novel, although screenwriter Ranald MacDougall borrowed aspects of the three Hemingway stories based on the exploits of Harry Morgan to complete his screenplay. This is most evident in the film's ending. In Hemingway's *To Have and Have Not* Morgan is killed by Cuban revolutionaries. *The Breaking Point*, however, ends with Morgan badly wounded after killing the bandits on his charter boat the *Sea Queen*. MacDougall also changed the setting from Florida and Cuba to California and Mexico and brought the story forward from the 1930s to the postwar period. He also created a new character, the call girl Leona Charles, who invites Morgan to join her in a sexual relationship.

*The Breaking Point* is a highlight in John Garfield's illustrious film career that began at Warner Bros. with *Four Daughters*, directed by Michael Curtiz, in 1938.

*The Breaking Point* (1950). Directed by Michael Curtiz. Shown from left: Patricia Neal (as Leona Charles), John Garfield (as Harry Morgan). Warner Bros./Photofest.

*The Breaking Point*, which was also directed by Curtiz, proves a nice symmetry to Garfield's career, although his final years, when he was hounded by anti-Communist zealots in America, and specifically by the HUAC, contributed to his death at the age of 40 and were an indictment of the hysteria that controlled much of America at that time. This climate also meant that the film failed at the box office in the United States as Warner Bros. had no faith in it and spent little money on advertising; this wonderful film has remained virtually unnoticed since its release.

While Garfield, Curtiz, and MacDougall were eager to work on *The Breaking Point*, they knew that this resolutely downbeat story would be a difficult proposition. Specifically, they were interested in Hemingway's theme that "a man alone ain't got no chance," and this motif is dramatized in a variety of ways. Throughout the film Morgan continually fights to maintain his independence in the form of his charter boat against almost insurmountable odds. Only his wife recognizes that his fight is futile and gently pushes him toward alternative employment with her father's flourishing lettuce-growing business in Salinas.

The film begins when a wealthy businessman, Hannagan, and his mistress, Leona Charles, charter Harry's boat for a fishing trip to Mexico. However, Hannagan flies out of Mexico without paying Morgan's fee, leaving Leona behind without any money to get back to the United States. Harry, also without any money for the docking fee, reluctantly accepts an offer from Duncan, a crooked lawyer, to smuggle Chinese migrants into the United States. When the Chinese organizer withholds Harry's money, he is killed in a fight with Morgan. On return to California, Harry's boat is seized by the Coast Guard, and he is reliant on Duncan for a court order to release it. Without any money, and with the likelihood that his boat will be taken away from him due to his failure to keep up his repayments, Harry agrees to accept Duncan's offer of another charter—this time transporting gangsters to Catalina Island after they have robbed the local racetrack. When the hoodlums kill Morgan's first mate and best friend, Wesley Parks, Harry kills each gangster. Seriously wounded and drifting helplessly in the sea, Morgan finally realizes that his obsessive determination to maintain his independence is futile—not only has it caused him to break the law and endangered his life, it is also destroying his family. Harry's change is signaled in the film when he is forced to rely on somebody else—in this case, a doctor, who amputates his left arm.

*The Breaking Point* has a dual, interrelated narrative structure. The action sequences involving Harry on his boat are paralleled by the domestic triangle involving Morgan, his hard-working wife, Lucy, and Leona Charles, the seductress attracted to Morgan. Initially, during the boat trip to Mexico, he attempts to deflect her offer by telling her to "be nice." However, his resistance only intensifies her determination to have him, and she tells Harry, "Nice, there's no future in it."

Leona keeps reappearing in Harry's life, which shows him to be a loving family man with two daughters. However, as events conspire to threaten his ability to retain his boat, his resistance to Leona weakens, and he finally succumbs and tells her that "a man can love his wife and still want something exciting to happen." However, when Harry begins making love to Leona, he finds that he cannot muster the energy for a sexual response, and this scene, in Leona's affluent apartment, reinforces Harry's downward spiral—as he explains to Leona after his lackluster attempt to kiss her, "Once I wouldn't have walked out on this. Once everything went just the way I wanted." Now his sex life, like his vocation, is diminished.

This is a film dominated by a pervasive sense of personal failure tinged with a strong sense of melancholy. This is particularly evident when Morgan's wife Lucy tries to retain her husband's affection by copying Leona's hairstyle and color. However, her transformation from a mousy, nondescript brunette to a striking blonde only provokes ridicule from her young daughters ("Really mother, we'll be the laughing stock") and astonishment from her husband, who manages to disguise his shock by hiding his mouth behind an apple.

This is also a sad film that cleverly uses the sound track to reinforce its melancholy tone in a number of ways—from the mournful sound of the accordion played by a neighbor's son as Harry walks home to the final image in the film of a little boy, Wesley Park's son, waiting in vain on the pier for his father to return. After the crowd disperses following Morgan's departure, a high-angle shot of the young boy waiting for a father who will never return provides a haunting image and an effective closing shot to this wonderful film.

Geoff Mayer

**BRIGHTON ROCK** (Associated British, 1947). *Director:* John Boulting. *Producer:* Roy Boulting. *Script:* Graham Greene and Terence Rattigan. *Photography:* Harry Waxman. *Music:* Hans May. *Cast:* Richard Attenborough (Pinkie Brown), Hermione Baddeley (Ida Arnold), William Hartnell (Dallow), Harcourt Williams (Prewitt), Wylie Watson (Spicer), Nigel Stock (Cubitt), Alan Wheatley (Fred Hale), Carol Marsh (Rose Brown).

*Brighton Rock,* along with films such as *Pink String and Sealing Wax* (1945), *They Made Me a Fugitive* (1947), *Mine Own Executioner* (1947), and, of course, *The Third Man* (1949), was a strong indication that the postwar British cinema had changed and could produce what we now term noir films that equaled the best that Hollywood could offer. *Brighton Rock* is a striking adaptation of Graham Greene's novel, and although it does not duplicate its bleak ending, the film reworks Greene's ending and closes on a moment of intense humiliation and deep irony. The nature of this shift in the tone of British films is evident in the film's first image of young Richard Attenborough, the amoral, mentally disturbed Pinkie Brown. He is filmed not as an innocent youth, but as a tormented figure, consistent with the film's bleak, oppressive view of human nature.

Seventeen-year-old Pinkie Brown assumes control of a group of small-time gangsters in pre–World War II Brighton when its leader is killed by a rival gang. Brown blames the killing on activities of a newspaper journalist, Fred Hale, who is visiting Brighton as part of a promotional stunt to increase circulation of his newspaper. After Brown kills Hale on the ghost train in the local amusement park, the film shifts its focus to the psychology of the young gangster. Brown, reluctantly, is forced to court and marry 17-year-old waitress Rose because her evidence could destroy his alibi. However, his plan to force his young bride to suicide is disrupted by blowsy entertainer Ida Arnold. Arnold takes an interest because she believes that the journalist was murdered and not, as the police maintain, that he committed suicide.

When the film was released in the United States, it was retitled *Young Scarface* as both a way of exploiting public awareness of Howard Hawks's 1932 gangster film *Scarface,* but also hinting at the twisted sexuality of Pinkie Brown, a trait he shares with the gangster in the 1932 film. Baby-faced Brown hates virtually everybody, especially women, and his only source of pleasure comes from inflicting pain. After killing an elderly gang member, Spicer, Brown's treatment of Rose on their wedding night is truly warped. He records his contempt for her on a gramophone record as a wedding present, and instead of the expected declaration of his love, he records, "You asked me to make a record of my voice. Well here it is. What you want me to say is I love you. Here is the truth. I hate you, you little slut. You make me sick.

Why don't you get back to Nelson Place and leave me alone." The perverseness of this scene is emphasized by the way the scene is set up, with Brown in the foreground, while Rose, unable to hear him, looks adoringly at her husband as the camera slowly shifts toward her face. Rose does not hear this recording until the final scene in the film, after Pinkie's death. However, the record has become warped, and all she hears is the first part: "You asked me to make a record of my voice. Well here it is. What you want me to say is I love you." At this point the record sticks on the repetition of "I love you, I love you . . ." This ending was criticized by some critics as a sentimental gesture that betrays the tragic ending in Greene's novel. However, this is a misinterpretation as it is anything but sentimental. It is deeply ironic, bleak, and totally consistent with the overall tone of the film.

A superb film, *Brighton Rock* was popular with British audiences but enjoyed less success in the United States. Young, cherubic-faced Richard Attenborough, who had played the part of Pinkie Brown at the Garrick theater in 1943, brilliantly conveyed the appropriate mixture of psychological disturbance and repressed violence, and the film marked a significant change in the development of the British gangster film. It clearly reflected the assimilation of noir influences into this popular British genre.

Geoff Mayer

**BRODIE, STEVE** (1919–1992). Steve Brodie, in more than 140 film and television appearances between 1944 and 1988, played the lead actor only once—in Anthony Mann's film noir *Desperate* (1947). He rarely played a heroic part. In *Crossfire* he plays Floyd Bowers, a bigoted soldier who watches Robert Ryan beat a Jewish man to death, and in *Out of the Past* (1947) he is a shady private detective who jeopardizes Robert Mitchum's life. These roles were typical of Brodie's overall career. Born in Kansas, Brodie, who was born John Stevenson, choose the name of a man who jumped off the Brooklyn Bridge in the 1880s for his film career. His first film was an uncredited role in Universal's 1944 propaganda film *Ladies Courageous*, starring Loretta Young as an executive officer of the Women's Auxiliary Ferrying Squadron. His first substantial role was in Lewis Milestone's combat film *A Walk in the Sun* (1945) as Private Judson, a squad member of a small unit ordered to capture a farmhouse in Italy from the Germans.

From the mid-1940s Brodie was typecast in crime melodramas and westerns as a villain, including a cycle of Tim Holt westerns in 1948 and 1949—most notably as Quirt Butler in *The Arizona Ranger* (1948), whose sadistic behavior drives his wife into the arms of Holt. *Desperate* was the exception, and this film gave Brodie the chance to play an average guy, Steve Randall, a truck driver who is threatened by gangster Raymond Burr. When Randall fails to participate in a robbery, which leads to the capture of Raymond Burr's brother, Randall has to flee with his young wife. This excellent Anthony Mann–directed film did not elevate Brodie into more lead roles. He was hoodlum Al Mapes in Richard

Fleischer's excellent crime film *Armored Car Robbery* (1950) and Jinx Raynor, James Cagney's fellow escapee, in Gordon Douglas's tough film version of Horace McCoy's hard-boiled novel *Kiss Tomorrow Goodbye* (1950).

Throughout the 1950s and 1960s Brodie was one of the screen's most dependable villains, and the only change in this pattern was the violent 1976 exploitation film *Bobby Jo and the Outlaw*, where Brodie did not appear on screen but coproduced this Mark Lester–directed road movie featuring Lynda Carter as the bored woman who joins up with Marjoe Gortner in a murderous rampage. Ironically, Brodie's last screen appearance was in Mike Jittlov's gentle, low-budget comedy *The Wizard of Speed and Time* (1988) about a group of youngsters who try to bypass the Hollywood system and make their own films.

**Selected Noir Films:** *Criminal Court* (1946), *Crossfire* (1947), *Desperate* (1947), *Out of the Past* (1947), *Bodyguard* (1948), *I Cheated the Law* (1949), *Tough Assignment* (1949), *Armored Car Robbery* (1950), *Kiss Tomorrow Goodbye* (1950), *M.* (1951).

Geoff Mayer

**THE BROTHERS** (Gainsborough, 1947). *Director:* David Macdonald. *Producer:* Sidney Box. *Script:* Muriel Box and Sidney Box, adaptation by David Macdonald, L.A.G. Strong, Paul Vincent Carroll, based on the novella by L.A.G. Strong. *Cinematography:* Stephen Dade. *Music:* Cedric Thorpe Davie. *Cast:* Patricia Roc (Mary Lawson), Will Fyffe (Aeneas McGrath), Maxwell Reed (Fergus Macrae), Finlay Currie (Hector Macrae), Duncan Macrae (John Macrae), John Laurie (Dugald), Andrew MacDonald (Willie McFarish), James Woodburn (Priest), Megs Jenkin (Angusina).

Strikingly photographed by Stephen Dade, this nihilistic pastoral film is set on the Isle of Skye in 1900. *The Brothers* is also a clear example of why film noir cannot be contained within one genre, such as the crime film. The tone of the film is noir, its plot motivation comes from sexual tensions and frustrated desires, and it concerns the effect a beautiful woman has on a repressed patriarchal community. The film shows the inability of this community to deal with these tensions—the fault is not due to the woman, but to the pathological male society depicted in the film.

Mary Lawson is sent to the island to live with, and serve, the all-male household of the Macraes, who are her distant relatives. The arrival of this young, pretty woman, however, triggers sexual hostility and tension, particularly from the eldest son, John, a puritanical figure in the film. This situation is aggravated by the feud between the Macraes and the McFarishes. When Willie McFarish attempts to rape Mary, the two clans confront each other in a rowing race, leading to the demise of Hector, the head of the Macrea family. On his death bed Hector tells John to let Fergus, his other son, marry Mary. However, John ignores this advice as he covets her himself.

Mary loves Fergus, and his neglect prompts her into accepting a sexual invitation from Willie McFarish while rejecting similar advances from John Macrae. Although John marries another woman, Angusina, he cannot get Mary out of his mind. After further rejection, he convinces Fergus to kill Mary. Fergus, however, commits suicide, and the film ends with Willie McFarish demanding that John Macrae be tied up and lashed to a cork in the ocean with a fish attached to his head as live bait for the skull-crushing sea eagles.

*The Brothers* is a bleak film that presents a dark view of Hebridean life at the turn of the 20th century. Despite the location shooting and strong, naturalistic performances from Scottish character actors Will Fyffe, Duncan Macrae, Andrew Crawford, Finlay Currie, and John Laurie, the film was criticized for its sadism and "morbidity." While the film includes scenes of violence, such as Fergus cutting off his own thumb when it is trapped by a conger eel and the death of an informer with a fish attached to his head, its harsh depiction of repressed male desire shows how the violence is a product of such a warped community.

Geoff Mayer

**THE BROTHERS RICO** (Columbia, 1957). *Director:* Phil Karlson. *Producer:* Lewis J. Rachmill. *Script:* Lewis Meltzer and Ben Perry, with an uncredited contribution by Dalton Trumbo, based on Georges Simenon's short novel *Les Frères Rico*. *Cinematographer:* Burnett Guffey. *Music:* George Duning. *Cast:* Richard Conte (Eddie Rico), Diane Foster (Alice Rico), Kathryn Grant (Norah Malaks Rico), Larry Grant (Sid Kubrik), James Darren (Johnny Rico), Argentina Brunetti (Mrs. Rico), Harry Bellaver (Mike Lamotta), Paul Picerni (Gino Rico), Paul Dubov (Phil), Rudy Bond (Charlie Gonzales), Richard Bakalyan (Vic Tucci), William Phipps (Joe Wesson).

*The Brothers Rico* represents a stylistic and thematic consolidation of the dominant trend in film noir in the 1950s. Stylistically, this film, like most 1950s films, rarely utilized the striking expressionist devices, especially with regard to lighting, favored by many 1940s films. In *The Brothers Rico* Phil Karlson employs functional camera setups, and visually, the film differs little from the average late 1950s television series. Thematically, the film draws more on the social context of the 1950s, especially an awareness that nationwide crime syndicates operated in America, and less on the personal torment that underpinned many 1940s films.

Eddie Rico, a former accountant for the syndicate, is forced to leave his successful laundry business in Bay Shore, Florida, when his brother Gino asks for his help after participating, with younger brother Johnny Rico, in a killing. Eddie contacts the syndicate's boss, Sid Kubik, who assures him that he owes the Rico family a debt as Mrs. Rico saved his life many years ago. Kubik tells Eddie that he has to find Johnny and get him to leave the country. However, Kubik really wants Johnny Rico dead and uses his brother to locate him.

Eddie, with the help of his mother, finds Johnny living with his pregnant wife, Norah, in California. This leads to Johnny's death, setting up the most powerful scene in the film, which records Eddie's torment when he learns that Johnny is about to be executed due to the fact that he led the mobsters to him. Eddie's prolonged suffering shifts the film away from melodrama, the usual dramatic basis of film noir, and toward tragedy. Richard Conte, as the tormented brother, gives his finest screen performance, and his suffering is palpable; it is this sense of personal impotence in the face of pervasive corporate corruption that makes this film a key film noir. Only a perfunctory ending, which differs from its source, a novella by Georges Simenon, showing Kubik's death in a shootout in Mrs. Rico's New York house, weakens the film.

While *The Brothers Rico* shares the thematic concern of other 1950s films with national crime syndicates, such as Karlson's *The Phenix City Story* (1955), it is a restrained film with little of Karlson's usual physical violence. Even Johnny's execution by the mob is carried out off-screen, with Karlson preferring to show the impact of the killing on Eddie. The film also spends, for a gangster film, an inordinate amount of time in the opening section detailing Eddie's wife, Alice, and her need to adopt a child. These domestic scenes between husband and wife provide an unusual insight, for a film noir, on the film's positive message regarding family unity. Also, Larry Gates as Sid Kubik, a "friend" of the Rico family, continues the shift in the depiction of the Hollywood gangster from a working-class thug to a smooth, seemingly benign corporate manager.

Geoff Mayer

**BURR, RAYMOND** (1917–1993). Despite being an actor who later in life was predominantly associated with the right side of the law as a courtroom attorney and as a senior detective, Raymond Burr, in his many appearances in classical film noir, was almost always a villain and always impressive and powerful. He was in his height and bulk of frame a natural heavy who could convey menace very well. Born in Canada's British Columbia to an American mother, Burr trained as an actor in a local stock company in Vancouver. He moved with his family to Los Angeles at the age of six and later began his lengthy screen career. He had an enigmatic and contradictory war record, an early example of the discrepancies between publicity claims about him and the eventual historical record. In his first film noir, Anthony Mann's *Desperate* (1947), he is a vengeful gangster named Walt Radak who pursues Steve Randall (Steve Brodie) and meets with a memorable death in a darkened stairwell in the film's climax. The following year, in Mann's *Raw Deal*, Burr played a vicious sadist who, in one of several brutal scenes, throws a hot dish of food at his girlfriend. In *Pitfall* he is the sinister ex-cop McDonald, obsessed with heroine Mona Stevens. Burr conveys cleverly the creepy persistence of McDonald as well as his smarmy manipulation of people. His later noir performances sometimes ended with death scenes as spectacular as that in *Desperate*. Burr was, for example, spectacularly electrocuted in *Red Light* (1949), and he falls to his death from a window escaping flames in *Raw Deal*. He was perhaps most widely known to people unfamiliar with details of the film noir genre as the wife murderer in Hitchcock's *Rear Window* (1954). A late and little known highlight of the later noir period was his performance opposite Barbara Stanwyck in *Crime of Passion* (1957), where (as police inspector Tony Pope) he is inveigled by her into an affair and ultimately murdered by her. After his film career petered out, he gained huge fame on television with leading roles in the long-running series *Perry Mason* in the 1960s and *Ironside* in the 1970s. Burr worked all his adult life as a philanthropist in several countries but also worked hard to suppress knowledge of his gay sexual orientation until his death.

**Selected Noir Films:** *Desperate* (1947), *Sleep, My Love* (1948), *Ruthless* (1948), *Raw Deal* (1948), *Pitfall* (1948), *Walk a Crooked Mile* (1948), *Criss Cross* (1949, uncredited bit part), *Red Light* (1949), *Abandoned* (1949), *Unmasked* (1950), *Borderline* (1950), *M.* (1951), *A Place in the Sun* (1951), *His Kind of Woman* (1951), *The Whip Hand* (1951), *The Blue Gardenia* (1953), *Rear Window* (1954), *A Cry in the Night* (1956), *Crime of Passion* (1957), *Affair in Havana* (1957).

Brian McDonnell

**CARNIVAL** (Twin Cities, 1946). *Director:* Stanley Haynes. *Producers:* John Sutro and William Sassoon. *Script:* Stanley Haynes, Guy Green, and Eric Maschwitz, with additional dialogue by Peter Ustinov, based on a novel by Compton McKenzie. *Cinematography:* Guy Green. *Music:* Nicholas Brodszky. *Cast:* Sally Gray (Jenny Pearl), Michael Wilding (Maurice Avery), Stanley Holloway (Charlie Raeburn), Bernard Miles (Trewhella), Jean Kent (Irene Dale), Catherine Lacey (Florrie Raeburn), Nancy Price (Mrs. Trewhella), Hazel Court (May Raeburn), Michael Clarke (Fuzz).

*Carnival* assimilates a noir attitude, primarily a strong sense of fatalism, into the narrative conventions of the British romantic melodrama. Although it had been filmed before in 1931 (as *Dance Pretty Lady*), the 1946 version presents a different, much darker perception of human existence. This is signaled by the film's opening images showing the dark, wet streets of London as a carriage brings three elderly women to take away a newborn child from its mother. When Florence Raeburn rejects an offer from three aunts to raise her child in a more "respectable" environment, the elderly women stand at the end of the nursing mother's bed and predict dire consequences for the child (Jenny). They want her removed from her "immoral" surroundings—Florence's husband is an alcoholic involved with the theater.

This prediction permeates the film, which becomes a battle between temptation and repression. Jenny, a ballet dancer, attracts numerous men to her stage door because of her beauty. She falls in love with Maurice Avery, a young artist determined to maintain his artistic independence by not marrying. Jenny's mother dies soon after Avery leaves for Spain, and Jenny's younger sister, the crippled May, is left in her care. This double blow leaves Jenny financially and emotional vulnerable, and she reluctantly accepts a marriage proposal from the puritanical Trewhella, who also offers to care for May on his farm in Cornwall.

After Jenny marries Trewhella, she discovers the extent of his bigotry and hatred for the immorality of "city folk." Encouraged by his mother, who urges her son to berate and punish his wife, Trewhella torments Jenny and May for their "loose" behavior and permissive attitudes. When Maurice comes to Cornwall and offers to take Jenny back to London, Trewhella kills her, and the prediction made at the start of the film is realized.

Sally Gray, as Jenny, is presented as a symbol of persecuted innocence and the victim of her father's sins, Trewhella's bigotry, and Avery's selfishness. She is sacrificed because of her working-class background and the effect beauty has on a repressed, patriarchal society. The film demonstrates the unequal balance of power in Victorian society. While Trewhella, his mother, and Jenny's aunts represent extreme sexual repression, Avery, a more moderate figure, cannot save her. Jenny's attempt to live according to her own moral standards results in her refusal to travel with him to Spain unless he marries her. Her defiance of Trewhella's moral authority results in her death. She is trapped, and ultimately sacrificed, when she attempts to struggle against the twin forces of sexual repression and patriarchal tyranny.

Geoff Mayer

**CASH ON DEMAND** (Hammer, 1961). *Director:* Quentin Lawrence. *Producer:* Michael Carreras. *Script:* David T. Chantler and Lewis Greiffer, based on the play by Jacques Gillies. *Cinematography:* Arthur Grant. *Music:* Wilfred Josephs. *Cast:* Peter Cushing (Fordyce), André Morell (Hepburn), Richard Vernon (Pearson), Norman Bird (Sanderson), Barry Lowe (Harvill), Edith Sharpe (Miss Pringle), Lois Daine (Sally), Kevin Stoney (Detective Inspector Mason), Vera Cook (Mrs. Fordyce).

Except for four exterior scenes, showing the (studio) street outside a bank in Haversham on Christmas Eve, *Cash on Demand* confines its action to the rooms of the bank. The dramatic pretext of the film is a robbery attempt, but the film is more concerned with the regeneration of a miserly bank manager, Mr. Fordyce. Fordyce, who treats his employees with cruelty and derision, is subjected to the scrutiny of "Colonel" Hepburn, a gentleman robber. Circumstances finally force Fordyce to turn to his employees for their help in this clever reworking of Dickens's *A Christmas Carol.* Morell is excellent as the persuasive robber who not only wants to steal the bank's money, but is also determined to subject Fordyce to the kind of persecution that he inflicts on his employees.

The film begins with Sanderson, Harvill, Sally, Pearson, and Miss Pringle arriving for work on the day before Christmas. Their mood is jovial as they look forward to the Christmas party, but Fordyce's arrival signals the end of their happiness—beginning with his humiliation of Pearson over a faulty pen. The inquisition continues with Fordyce berating Harvill over a minor irregularity in the bank's accounts, although it is soon obvious that Pearson, the chief clerk, is the real target of Fordyce's hostility. The arrival of a bank robber, Hepburn, disguised as security expert transfers power from Fordyce to Hepburn after he convinces the bank manager that his wife and child are being held prisoner. The rest of the film expertly weaves together Hepburn's robbery attempt with a scrutiny of Fordyce's class-based attitudes and behavior. At the film's climax Hepburn convinces Fordyce that if the police are notified in the hour after his escape, the manager's wife and child will die. When Pearson warns the police about Hepburn, Fordyce is forced to rely on his employees to convince the police that there has not been a robbery at the bank.

*Cash on Demand*, a low-budget genre film released during the height of the British new wave, was virtually ignored by critics. However, it is expertly photographed by veteran Arthur Grant and effectively directed by Quentin Lawrence, known mainly for his television work, and Peter Cushing and André Morell head a professional cast. *Cash on Demand* is an intelligent crime melodrama, and this tale of regeneration was produced by Hammer Films, a company better known for its horror films. With *Cash on Demand* the studio returned to its origins in the late 1940s and early 1950s as a producer of low-budget crime films.

Geoff Mayer

**THE CHASE** (United Artists, 1946). *Director:* Arthur D. Ripley. *Producers:* Seymour Nebenzal and Eugene Frenke (associate). *Script:* Philip Yordan, based on the Cornell Woolrich novel *The Black Path of Fear*. *Cinematography:* Frank (Franz) F. Planer. *Music:* Michel Michelet. *Cast:* Robert Cummings (Chuck Scott), Michéle Morgan (Lorna Roman), Steve Cochran (Eddie Roman), Peter Lorre (Gino), Jack Holt (Commander Davidson), Lloyd Corrigan (Emmerick Johnson), Alex Minotis (Lieutenant Acosta), James Westerfield (Job), Yolanda Lacca (Midnight), Nina Koshetz (Madame Chin).

This is the most controversial adaptation of a Woolrich story among Woolrich aficionados. *The Chase* was based on his 1944 novel *The Black Path of Fear*, which, in turn, was expanded from his 1942 short story "Havana Night." The film version was scripted by Philip Yordan, who had a penchant for subverting, or violating, genre stories (see, e.g., his female-centered Cold War western *Johnny Guitar* [1954]), and directed by Arthur Ripley. Ripley was a strange choice as he worked only sporadically on the fringe of the Hollywood system, and he never had a mainstream hit, although his last film, *Thunder Road* in 1958, remains a cult favorite.

It was not surprising that this combination of two eccentric talents, Yordan and Ripley, would produce a bizarre film, and they did not disappoint. First, they eliminated most of Woolrich's story, keeping only a portion of the first section of the book, which describes Bill Scott (Chuck in the film) fleeing Miami with Eve (Lorna in the film) Roman, the wife of a vicious gangster. In Havana, Eddie

Roman's agents kill Eve/Lorna and frame Scott for her murder. Thereafter the bulk of the novel, unlike the film, is concerned with Scott's fight for survival in an alien environment of dope dens, dark alleys, and exotic characters. *The Black Path of Fear* is not one of Woolrich's best stories as it is highly repetitive, with Scott repeatedly escaping the police or gangsters as they are about to capture or kill him. Yordan and Ripley virtually eliminate this section by condensing it into a relatively short sequence that presents Havana as a nightmarish labyrinth. Chuck only escapes capture with the assistance of a local prostitute (Midnight), but this merely prolongs his fate as his flight ends in his death when Roman's chief henchman, Gino, kills him and then dumps his body into the sea.

At this point Ripley and Yordan make the radical decision to show Chuck's death in Havana as only a dream, and they completely abandon Woolrich's story. This produces a complex series of narrative reversals in the film. On the day that he planned to flee Miami with Lorna, Chuck apparently suffered a relapse of the malaria he contracted in the Pacific while serving in the navy during World War II. Ripley and Yordan then push the credibility of their film even further by linking Scott's malaria relapse with amnesia so that when he awakens from his fever-induced blackout, he cannot remember that Lorna is still waiting for him at Roman's house. Only when he goes to a bar with his former navy commander does it come back to him, and he collects Lorna and boards a boat bound for Havana. Then, in an even more bizarre touch, Roman and Gino die when their uniquely automated car crashes into a train. Finally, to top all of this, Scott and Lorna are taken by the same coachman to the same nightclub in Havana where, in Scott's dream, Lorna was murdered. This means that the line between reality and Chuck's dream is virtually eliminated in the final moments of the film.

While Ripley and Yordan do away with most of the plot details in the film, *The Chase* captures the sense of paranoia and fear that is the essence of Woolrich's novel. They also reiterate a familiar Woolrich motif concerning the futility of love just as it is about to flower. The problem with *The Chase*, however, is that audiences may not tolerate this convoluted reworking as the film strains credibility with its contrived narrative detailing Chuck's malaria-induced nightmare and his subsequent amnesia.

Geoff Mayer

**CHINATOWN** (Paramount, 1974). *Director:* Roman Polanski. *Producer:* Robert Evans. *Script:* Robert Towne. *Cinematography:* John A. Alonzo. *Music:* Jerry Goldsmith. *Cast:* Jack Nicholson (Jake Gittes), Faye Dunaway (Evelyn Mulwray), John Huston (Noah Cross), John Hillerman (Yelburton), Perry Lopez (Escobar), Darrell Zwerling (Hollis Mulwray), Burt Young (Curly), Diane Ladd (Ida Sessions), Roman Polanski (Man with Knife).

Released at the height of the Watergate scandal and in the wake of American combat withdrawal from Vietnam, *Chinatown* was inevitably read at the time as a

*Chinatown* (1974). Directed by Roman Polanski. Shown: Jack Nicholson (as Jake "J.J." Gittes), Faye Dunaway (as Evelyn Mulwray). Paramount Pictures/Photofest.

comment on the public and political corruption of the early 1970s in the United States and was seen as part of the emerging interest in the revival of the film noir spirit and of the private eye genre in those years of malaise. Since the film's story line involves events of the late 1930s, it might best be labeled as retro noir, that subgroup of neo-noir where the narrative settings are of the 1930s, 1940s, or 1950s, but the frankness and explicitness of theme are very much of the post–Production Code era. Furthermore, director Roman Polanski and script writer Robert Towne introduce fresh variations into the old form. With the passage of more than 30 years since its release, it is possible now to view *Chinatown* as transcending the limits of story type and indeed as being one of the most accomplished films of the late twentieth century of any genre.

*Chinatown* nonetheless belongs firmly to the tradition of film noir and exhibits many of the special features of the genre—a seedy urban landscape, stock characters and situations, a mood of existential angst, complications and convolutions of plot—and turns them into its greatest strengths. The sheer complexity of the film's plot can overwhelm at first, but close examination of the twists, turns, and shocks can be rewarding. The film traces the investigations of private detective and divorce specialist Jake Gittes, who discovers that one of his clients, the aggrieved wife of the Los Angeles water commissioner, is an impostor. Jake has been tricked into uncovering an apparent affair between the man and a much younger woman. Soon afterward, the commissioner Hollis Mulwray is found dead under suspicious circumstances. His real wife, Evelyn, appears to be hiding something, and her powerful father, Noah Cross, seems intent on realizing his own dark ambitions. It eventually turns out that Cross is both at the center of a scheme by a wealthy group of developers to pull off a lucrative land grab and also that he has fathered incestuously with his daughter a child whose existence Evelyn is desperate to conceal. In trying to penetrate these political machinations and dark family secrets, Gittes goes through a disorienting series of misadventures. Despite all his resources of skill, insight, and sheer audacity, he is unable to prevent the eventual tragedy of Evelyn's death.

Three stock characters from classical noir (and from the fiction of Raymond Chandler) are the decadent rich man, the dissembling woman, and the sardonic detective, types represented in *Chinatown* by Noah Cross, Evelyn Mulwray, and Gittes himself. Evelyn is always convincing, shifting sideways with crab-like agility, ever ready with a plausible variation of her story that can send Gittes and the audience off on fresh speculatory tangents. Noah Cross is a man out to "buy the future," the deceptively genial focus of civic and personal corruption. Gittes is brash and overconfident, caught up in events and forces over which he has little control. Nonetheless, he does share three characteristics with the heroes of classical film noir: continual questing, an easy command of the tricks of his trade, and a wise-cracking brand of humor. Jake is seen constantly knocking at doors, spying from rooftops, climbing fences, sifting the contents of ponds, rifling desks, or searching through the Hall of Records. He is an inveterate voyeur and inquirer who at one point has his nose sliced open because criminals object to his "sniffing around." The film's settings recall those of classical noir: Gittes's own office with its vintage racing prints, the mysterious Mar Vista rest home, the Spanish-style mansions of Noah Cross and Hollis Mulwray. Through these and other locales (a morgue, a barber shop, the Macondo Apartments) the film is able to convey a palpable sense of Los Angeles's sinister languor in the 1930s.

Cinematographer John Alonzo joined the attempt to reproduce stylistically the look of classical Hollywood films by reviving old-fashioned lighting techniques that had languished unused for decades. The photographic model throughout for both Alonzo and Polanski was James Wong Howe, who had shot several classical noirs, including *City for Conquest, Out of the Fog, Danger Signal, Body and Soul,* and *Sweet Smell of Success.* The Technicolor laboratory even cooperated in the creation of a period feel for the film's visuals by adjusting their dye transfer matrices to give release prints a suitably "toasty" look. The impressively managed tone and atmosphere of *Chinatown* is further enhanced by the romantic Jerry Goldsmith musical score. At intervals throughout the story, a snippet of its haunting and disturbing trumpet solo can instantly propel the viewer into a vertiginous mood of mystery.

*Chinatown* is beautifully structured in plot terms (Robert Towne won its only Oscar for his original screenplay). Its narrative tapestry has been finely designed, and a pattern of echoes and intimations of varying degrees of subtlety is woven through the film. Perhaps the most felicitous of these intimations occurs midway through the story when Gittes is questioning Evelyn as they sit in her car. Seeming to slump under the pressure of his insistent queries, her head drops forward onto the steering wheel. This sets off the car's horn, which momentarily startles her. At the end of the film, when the police fire shots after her fleeing car, we do not see her hit but merely hear the car horn blaring. Because of the earlier scene, even if we do not consciously know why, we are sure she has been shot in the head.

In 1990 a much delayed sequel to *Chinatown* entitled *The Two Jakes* and directed by Jack Nicholson was released, but it received indifferent reviews and is generally considered a disappointing follow-up to the 1974 classic.

Brian McDonnell

**COLLATERAL** (Paramount/Dreamworks, 2004). *Director:* Michael Mann. *Producers:* Michael Mann and Julie Richardson. *Script:* Stuart Beattie. *Cinematography:* Dion Beebe and Paul Cameron. *Music:* James Newton Howard. *Cast:* Tom Cruise (Vincent), Jamie Foxx (Max), Jada Pinkett Smith (Annie Farrell), Mark Ruffalo (Fanning), Peter Berg (Richard Weidner).

Director Michael Mann made a fine crime procedural with *Heat* in 1995 and in 2006 released a dark-toned film version of his 1980s hit television show *Miami Vice*. Perhaps his finest achievement, though, in the neo-noir genre is 2004's *Collateral*, a two-hander with tight dramatic unities and technical experimentation that pits a trained criminal professional against an honest but bumbling Everyman, matching an assassin named Vincent against Max, the cab driver who reluctantly ferries him from target to target. The film's events are crowded into one busy night in Los Angeles as the meticulous plans of Vincent begin to unravel and as Max finds that his low-profile personality has to evolve into assertiveness and heroic decisiveness. Noir themes involving existential anguish, a man wrongly accused, and the uneasy friction between virtue and vice come to the fore. Mann elicits powerful performances from Tom Cruise and Jamie Foxx in the leads and mounts the film with his usual virtuosity, particularly in his use of digital video to gain unprecedented depth of field in his night photography. Los Angeles has been the classical setting for film noir since the 1940s, but Mann is able to show a novel side of the city in a manner that indicates that the noir genre is still surviving healthily using the new cinematic language of the early twenty-first century.

Max, who is introduced plying his trade as a methodical taxi driver, is a thoughtful and intelligent black man who gets on with people of all colors and who has ambitions to eventually own his own limousine business. He drives a pretty young black woman across the city and flirts with her in a mild way as they debate the most efficient route. She turns out to be a state prosecutor named Annie Farrell. At her destination (a downtown office tower) she alights and is replaced by Vincent wearing a snappy gray suit, which matches his hair and beard. He wants to hire

Max's cab for several hours, but when Max is parked outside Vincent's first stop, a dead body topples down onto the taxi's roof from the apartment building Vincent has entered. Thus the film's narrative moves into its main series of conflicts and complications. Vincent quickly admits he has shot the man, puts the body in the trunk, and then informs Max that he is now being dragooned into driving him around all night to the locations of the various people he has been paid to murder. He next kills a lawyer (off-screen), and then guns down a group of muggers attempting to rob Max, who has been tied to the steering wheel. Police officers Fanning and Weidner are called to the first killing, and when witnesses mention the cab, they recall a previous case in San Francisco where a taxi driver had apparently killed three people before shooting himself. Fanning feels that the earlier assumption was wrong and that a professional hit man may have killed all four. Nevertheless, Max is now a prime suspect. Meanwhile, Vincent has had time to shoot a jazz bar proprietor, take Max to see his hospitalized mother, be charming and polite to her, and unburden himself to Max about his unhappy childhood.

Events take a new turn after Max tosses onto the freeway Vincent's laptop containing his instructions for the remaining hits. The assassin then forces Max to go to a Hispanic country-and-western bar posing as Vincent to get the details of the final two victims. The Hispanic gangster who provides the data decides to have his henchmen follow Max. The bar is also under FBI surveillance, which adds yet another contingent to the multiple pursuit of Vincent. A large-scale action scene (a standard set piece in most Michael Mann films) ensues at the crowded Fever club, where the next target, an Asian mobster, is partying. There is confusing mayhem as the FBI agents fight the gangster's bodyguards and Vincent kills at least six people, including his official target, and then shoots to death the Los Angeles Police Department detective Fanning, who has only just come to believe in Max's innocence. As Max and Vincent flee the scene, Max accuses him of lacking any empathy for his fellow humans, and Vincent complains that instead of a cabbie, he has been stuck with Sigmund Freud and Dr. Ruth. Spouting a sarcastic pastiche of existential philosophy, Max speeds up and deliberately crashes the cab. Vincent flees, and to his horror, Max discovers on the computer that the final target is Annie, the young prosecutor he had earlier driven to her office. In the film's extended climactic sequence he pursues Vincent to the tower and wounds him before Vincent can shoot Annie. The two flee into the city's subway system chased by Vincent, who manages to follow them on board. As their train hurtles along the tracks, they are unable to escape. Both men fire at each other through the glass doors of the car, and Vincent is killed.

Much of *Collateral* is straight action, and in many scenes Vincent displays the type of silent self-possession shown by the laconic heroes of the French noir films of Jean-Pierre Melville. At other times he waxes philosophical, and his conversations with Max express an existential concern with the insignificance of small people and the random nature of life and death. *Collateral* is also concerned with the ways in which the fates of people can become intertwined and the changes caused in an honest man by an encounter with criminal or psychopathic behavior. As much as anything else, though, the film is an exercise in style. The nighttime city becomes one of the stars, with its character laid out in the many aerial shots. The high-definition digital camerawork that Mann employs so skillfully is able to make the night sky lighter than it ever was in more conventionally photographed films. In *Collateral*, for once, noir characters can move and act in an after-dark space that is truly three-dimensional.

Brian McDonnell

**CONTE, RICHARD** (1910–1975). A key actor in noir films in Hollywood, Richard Conte was invaluable because he could play tough heroes, such as the ex-GI trucker Nick Garcos in Jules Dassin's *Thieves Highway* (1949), as well as conniving villains, such as Bert Galvin in Ted Tetzlaff's underrated prison film *Under the Gun* (1951). The son of an Italian-American barber, Conte was born in Jersey City, New Jersey, and after working as a singing waiter in a Connecticut resort, he went to New York. In 1935 Elia Kazan and John Garfield assisted Conte in obtaining a scholarship to study acting. His first Broadway play, *Moon over Mulberry Street* (1939), was a financial and critical failure, and he made his film debut the same year, as Nicholas Conte, in *Heaven with a Barbed Wire Fence*, a Twentieth Century Fox film which also gave Glenn Ford his first screen role. He then returned to the theater for the next three years.

Conte's big break came in 1942 when Twentieth Century Fox signed him as a contract player and promoted him as the "new John Garfield." He was cast in a succession of prestigious, large-budget films at Fox, beginning with *Guadalcanal Diary* (1943), based on reporter Richard Tregaskis's best-selling book detailing the conflict between Japanese and American marines in the Solomon Islands. Other military roles followed, most notably his performance as the smart-talking Private Rivera in one of the finest combat films produced in Hollywood during World War II, Lewis Milestone's elegiac *A Walk in the Sun* (1945).

Conte was at his peak from 1945 to 1948, during which time, at Twentieth Century Fox, he alternated between sympathetic roles, from Fred Wiecek in *Calling Northside 777* (1948) as a man wrongfully sentenced to life imprisonment for killing a policeman during a grocery store robbery to his intense performance as Martin Rome, a tough, amoral thug relentlessly pursued through New York by Victor Mature in Robert Siodmak's *Cry of the City* (1948).

When Conte left Twentieth Century Fox at the end of the 1940s, his career as a major star faltered, although he continued in medium- to low-budget crime films throughout the 1950s—sometimes as the problematic hero, sometimes as the chief villain. While in the best of these films, such as *The Sleeping City* (1950), *Under the Gun*, Fritz Lang's *The Blue Gardenia* (1953), and, especially, Joseph H. Lewis's masterly noir film *The Big Combo* (1955), with Conte as the sadistic crime boss Mr. Brown, he was allowed sufficient space to invest his characters with a mixture of charm and less desirable qualities, while films such as *Slaves of Babylon* (1953) and *Highway Dragnet* (1954) were merely formulaic.

Conte's last great performance in the 1950s was in Phil Karlson's noir film *The Brothers Rico* (1957) as Eddie Rico, who unwittingly leads gangsters to his younger brother Johnny and has to passively await news of Johnny's fate while trapped in a hotel room. Throughout the late 1950s and much of the 1960s Conte worked in American television series, even starring in one series in 1959—*The Four Just Men*. His film career received a boost when Frank Sinatra cast Conte as Detective Santini in the Tony Rome detective films *Tony Rome* (1967) and *Lady in Cement* (1968). However, his last major role in Hollywood was as Emilio Barzini, Don Corleone's rival in Francis Ford Coppola's masterpiece *The Godfather* (1972). Conte also worked as an actor in Europe in the 1960s and 1970s, where he directed a war film, *Operation Cross Eagles* (1968), in Yugoslavia starring Rory Calhoun.

**Selected Noir Films:** *The Spider* (1945), *Somewhere in the Night* (1946), *13 Rue Madeleine* (1947), *Calling Northside 777* (1948), *Cry of the City* (1948), *House of Strangers* (1949), *Thieves Highway* (1949), *Whirlpool* (1949), *The Sleeping City* (1950), *Under the Gun* (1951), *Hollywood Story* (1951), *The Blue Gardenia* (1953), *Highway Dragnet* (1954), *The Big Combo* (1955), *New York Confidential* (1955), *The Big Tip Off* (1955), *Little Red Monkey* (1955), *The Brothers Rico* (1957), *Tony Rome* (1967), *Lady in Cement* (1968), *The Godfather* (1972).

Geoff Mayer

**COOK, ELISHA, JR.** (1903–1995). Cook was an excellent character actor who played a multitude of minor roles but was never a leading man. Audiences became familiar with him in dozens of brief appearances, and the vividness of his portrayals often made him more memorable than some of the bigger stars with whom he shared the screen. Cook was a short, wiry man who could readily look craven or sniveling. Small-time hoods and petty criminals were his specialties: he was never the protagonist of a story but was part of the fabric of the noir genre. Cook is best remembered by many for his part in the western *Shane* as a pathetic victim of Jack Palance's gunslinger than for most of his film noir roles, except perhaps for his appearances with Bogart in *The Maltese Falcon* and *The Big Sleep*. Elisha Cook Jr. was born in San Francisco and worked as a stage actor before signing with Paramount in 1935. They immediately pigeonholed the small and insignificant-looking actor with his pop eyes and nervous look as a natural victim, one of life's losers. In 1940 he had a crucial role in the proto-noir *Stranger on the Third Floor*, where he played the innocent man condemned to death in that low-budget film of paranoia, nightmare, and murder. Cook's next noir appearance was his defining role as the weasel-like gunsel Wilmer in *The Maltese Falcon*, a performance that impressed many critics. His characterization was daring for the time as it hinted that Wilmer might be the sexual plaything of Sydney Greenstreet's Gutman. Cook played another nervy isolated character later in 1941 in *I Wake Up Screaming*, where he indeed does turn out to be the killer. One of his most memorable cameos was as the lecherous jazz drummer in Robert Siodmak's *Phantom Lady* (1944), who indulges in an onanistic jam session to impress the inquisitive secretary Kansas, played by Ella Raines. He reunited with Humphrey Bogart as a pathetic fall guy in Howard Hawk's *The Big Sleep* (1946), where a helpless Bogart (playing detective Philip Marlowe) hears him being poisoned in an adjacent office. Unlike most of these passive and impotent individuals, Cook's character got the chance to shoot back and kill the people who pester him when he played the cuckolded husband of Marie Windsor in *The Killing*. Long after the classical noir cycle was complete, Cook made spasmodic appearances in Hollywood films, most effectively as the agent who shows Mia Farrow and John Cassavettes through their new sinister apartment building in Roman Polanski's *Rosemary's Baby* in 1968.

**Selected Noir Films:** *Stranger on the Third Floor* (1940), *The Maltese Falcon* (1941), *I Wake Up Screaming* (1941), *Phantom Lady* (1944), *Dark Waters* (1944), *Dillinger* (1945), *Blonde Alibi* (1946), *Two Smart People* (1946), *The Big Sleep* (1946), *Fall Guy* (1947), *Born to Kill* (1947), *The Long Night* (1947), *The Gangster* (1947), *Don't Bother to Knock* (1952), *I, the Jury* (1953, uncredited), *The Killing* (1956), *The Wrong Man* (1957), *Chicago Confidential* (1957), *Plunder Road* (1957), *Baby Face Nelson* (1957), *The Outfit* (1973).

Brian McDonnell

**CORRIDOR OF MIRRORS** (Apollo Films, 1948). *Director:* Terence Young. *Producer:* Rudolph Cartier. *Script:* Rudolph Cartier and Edana Romney, based on the novel by Christopher Massie. *Cinematography:* Andre Thomas. *Music:* Georges Auric. *Cast:* Eric Portman (Paul Mangin), Edana Romney (Mifanwy Conway), Barbara Mullen (Veronica), Hugh Sinclair (Owen Rhys), Alan Wheatley (Edgar Orsen), Joan Maude (Caroline Hart), Bruce Belfrage (Sir David Conway), Leslie Weston (Mortimer), Thora Hird (Old Woman), Christopher Lee (Charles).

*Corridor of Mirrors* is similar to *Laura* (1944) in the tension it creates between a fantasy of romance and sexual freedom tempered by the inhibitions imposed by daily life. Ultimately, the film presents such desires as futile and dangerous. Directed by Terence Young and produced by Rudolph Cartier, who was trained at the German studio UFA, *Corridor of Mirrors* expertly and adventurously blends English gothic with the low-key photographic attributes of German expressionism to enhance its story of male desire thwarted by the restriction and norms imposed by contemporary society.

This neglected film focuses on an artist, Paul Mangin, who believes in reincarnation and wants to live not in 1938 England, but in 1486 Italy. He hopes to recapture love lost during a previous life in Mifanwy Conway, a beautiful young woman who attracts Paul because she is similar to a young woman depicted in a 400-year-old Italian painting. Initially, Conway is fascinated by his dream, and they rapturously dance in his corridor of mirrors as she abandons her comfortable existence to embrace his dark, perverse fantasy. However, as the extent of his obsession becomes apparent, she retreats to the less threatening world of a conventional boyfriend (Owen Rhys). Mangin refuses to let go of his dream and invites Conway to a lavish Venetian ball. Intrigued, she agrees to attend the festivities but later refuses to participate in his fantasy. When a woman, Caroline Hart, is murdered in one of Mangin's bedrooms, he takes the blame rather than have his fantasy subjected to public scrutiny. Some years later, Conway returns to view Mangin at Madame Tussaud's wax museum, where she learns the identity of the real killer, a demented woman living with Mangin. Mifanwy returns to the rural security of north Wales and her husband (Rhys) and their three children.

Although *Corridor of Mirrors* was possibly influenced by Jean Cocteau's *Beauty and the Beast* (1946), its low-key photography and story of a tragic protagonist born out of his time was consistent with themes found in a number of postwar British films. Mangin's perverse desire to transform Conway into a fantasy woman that exists only in a fifteenth-century Italian painting predates a similar theme in Alfred Hitchcock's *Vertigo* by more than a decade. The film was coscripted by the leading lady, Edana Romney.

Geoff Mayer

**COSH BOY** (Romulus, 1953). *Director:* Lewis Gilbert. *Producer:* Daniel M. Angel. *Script:* Lewis Gilbert and Vernon Gilbert Harris, based on the play *Master Crook* by Bruce Walker. *Cinematography:* Jack Asher. *Music:* Lambert Williamson. *Cast:* James Kenney (Roy Walsh), Joan Collins (Rene Collins), Robert Ayres (Bob Stevens), Hermione Baddeley (Mrs. Collins), Hermione Gingold (Queenie), Betsy Ann Davies (Elsie Walsh), Laurence Naismith (Inspector Donaldson), Frederick Piper (Mr. Easter), Walter Hudd (Magistrate), Sid James (Sergeant), Ian Whittaker (Alfie Collins).

*Cosh Boy*, the first British film to receive an X-certificate, dramatized the growing fear of juvenile delinquency as an emerging social problem in Britain. The film's release coincided with the murder trial of teenager Christopher Craig and his older companion Derek Bentley. The solution provided in the film was a plea for the restoration of strict family discipline. This theme is dramatized in the film's presentation of a soft parent (Elsie Walsh), combined with the absence of a strong father figure (Roy's father died in World War II), which resulted in a young criminal such as Roy Walsh.

Roy Walsh rules over a gang of teenage criminals who rob women at night by hitting them with coshes or blackjacks while stealing their handbags. After Roy and one of his companions, Alfie Collins, are arrested and ordered to undertake community service, he develops the local youth center into a base for his criminal activities. At the center Roy meets, terrorizes, and seduces Rene Collins. After impregnating her, he rejects her plea to get married, preferring instead to encourage her to suicide. While the suicide attempt fails, Rene loses her baby.

Roy organizes the robbery of the local sports stadium and shoots one of the workers. Cornered by Bob Stevens, the manager of the stadium, who also happens to be his mother's new husband, Roy hopes that the police will save him from a thrashing from his stepfather. However, the police disappear so that Stevens can punish the boy, and the film ends with the sound of his screams. *Cosh Boy* was criticized by most of the daily papers, although James Kenney, who repeated his stage role, gives a strong performance as the amoral thug.

Geoff Mayer

**CRACK-UP** (RKO, 1946). *Director:* Irving Reis. *Producer:* Jack J. Gross. *Script:* John Paxton, Ben Bengal, and Ray Spencer, based on Frederic Brown's short story "Madman's Holiday." *Cinematography:* Robert de Grasse. *Music:* Leigh Harline. *Cast:* Pat O'Brien (George Steele), Claire Trevor (Terry Cordeau), Herbert Marshall (Traybin), Ray Collins (Dr. Lowell), Wallace Ford (Cochrane), Dean Harens (Reynolds), Damien O'Flynn (Stevenson), Erskine Sanford (Barton), Mary Ware (Mary).

John Paxton, who wrote the scripts for *Murder, My Sweet* (1944) and *Crossfire* (1947), also cowrote *Crack-Up*. Paxton's scripts often imbued his criminal stories with a liberal humanist edge. *Crack-Up* is no exception, and while the film does not have the same impact as *Murder, My Sweet*, or, especially, his powerful attack on anti-Semitism in *Crossfire*, his script for *Crack-Up* establishes a link between the aesthetic pretensions and obsessions of wealthy art patrons as similar to the fascist ideology practiced by the Nazis in Germany in the 1930s and 1940s. This association was not totally surprising considering Paxton's views and the fact that the film was produced just months after the end of World War II.

*Crack-Up*, which suffers to some extent from an unduly convoluted script, opens with a strong first act. It begins with art expert George Steele behaving in an irrational manner when he attempts to break into the New York Metropolitan Museum late at night. Steele, who is employed as a lecturer at the museum, justifies his behavior by claiming that he has just been involved in a train wreck. However, when the police discover that there was no train accident, Steele's credibility is questioned. This is the whole point as, earlier that night, Steele had delivered a controversial lecture that attacked the behavior of the art community, especially the supporters of surrealism, who, he claims, are elitist. Steele, on the other hand, proposes a democratic sensibility where art should be accessible to the general public. Steele is a populist who believes in art for the masses, a view considered subversive by the museum supervisor, Mr. Barton, and the museum's wealthy patrons.

Following his erratic behavior, Steele's position at the museum is undermined and his lecture series terminated. Determined to find the truth, Steele, with the assistance of journalist Terry Cordeau, uncovers a complicated plan to substitute forgeries for some of the museum's most prestigious paintings. His delusions regarding the train wreck were engineered by a wealthy art collector, Dr. Lowell, who injected him with sodium pentothal so as to induce a state of narcosynthesis. Under the effects of the drug, Steele was convinced that he was involved in a train wreck, and this was part of Lowell's plan to undermine Steele's credibility and prevent him from detecting the forgeries.

The opening section in the film is superb and provides a classic example of the role of noir imagery in presenting a fractured world. In this regard, the noir cinematography from Robert de Grasse seamlessly combines with Leigh Harline's evocative score and director Irving Reis's determination to present a world that is chaotic and threatening—as presented in Steele's irrational behavior. Unfortunately, the rest of the film does not match the opening section—primarily as a result of the need for narrative coherence in this situation. Although he ultimately solves the mystery, he is dependent on a female reporter, Cordeau, and a Scotland Yard detective, Traybin, to rescue him after he has been injected, again, with sodium pentothal. In a nice touch he leaves the film as it started—utterly confused.

Geoff Mayer

**THE CRIMINAL** (Anglo-Amalgamated, 1960). *Director:* Joseph Losey. *Producer:* Jack Greenwood. *Script:* Alun Owen and Jimmy Sangster; *Cinematography:* Robert Krasker. *Music:* John Dankworth. *Cast:* Stanley Baker (Johnny Bannion), Sam Wanamaker (Mike Carter), Margit Saad (Suzanne), Gregoire Aslan (Frank Saffron), Patrick Magee (Chief Warden Barrows), Jill Bennett (Maggie), Rupert Davies (Mr. Edwards), Laurence Naismith (Mr. Town), Noel Willman (Prison Governor), Tom Bell (Flynn).

The roles played by Stanley Baker in the second half of the 1950s, from his villains in *Checkpoint* (1956) and *Campbell's Kingdom* (1957) and working-class victim in *The Good Die Young* (1954) to the heroic truck driver in *Hell Drivers* (1957), were symptomatic of the shift in the British crime film during this period. In *The Criminal*, script writer Alun Owen, assisted by director Joseph Losey, moved the genre even further in their desire to present prison life as a metaphor for a materialistic, oppressive society. Baker's character, Johnny Bannion, was based on real-life racetrack criminal Alfred Dimes, and the film dramatizes the transformation of crime from the realm of the individual criminal to the operations of large-scale organizations. Inside prison, Bannion is efficient and can easily cope. Outside, he is hopelessly trapped within a greedy, materialistic society.

The film begins with Bannion as the master of his cell block, although another convict, Frank Saffron, controls the prison with Chief Warden Barrows. After Bannion is released, he resumes his criminal activities by robbing a racetrack, but Maggie, a jealous ex-girlfriend, betrays him to the police, and he is sent back to prison for 15 years—after burying the money in a field. Former colleague Mike Carter kidnaps Suzanne, Bannion's new girlfriend, and pressures him into making a deal with Saffron whereby Bannion will be allowed to escape providing he gives up the money. Outside prison, Bannion is shown to be out of his depth, and a sense of alienation, which pervades the film, is beautifully captured by cinematographer Robert Krasker in the film's final moments with Bannion's death in a bleak, snow-covered field. *The Criminal* parallels the shift in the American crime film in the 1950s, especially Phil Karlson's *The Brothers Rico* (1957), with its theme that aligns the power of corporations with the growth of large-scale criminal activities. Bannion represents the small-time individual criminal who fails to survive this shift. Mike Carter, on the other hand, epitomizes the new breed of corporate criminals, totally devoid of feelings. In the film's final scene Carter cradles the dying Bannion in an attempt to find out where he has buried the money. When he fails, he callously throws Bannion's body aside.

Geoff Mayer

**CRISS CROSS** (Universal, 1949). *Director:* Robert Siodmak. *Producer:* Michael Kraike. *Script:* Daniel Fuchs, based on the novel by Don Tracy. *Cinematography:* Franz Planer. *Music:* Miklos Rozsa. *Cast:* Burt Lancaster (Steve Thompson), Yvonne De Carlo (Anna), Dan Duryea (Sim Dundee), Stephen McNally (Pete

*Criss Cross* (1949). Directed by Robert Siodmak. Shown from left during production: Robert Siodmak, Yvonne De Carlo (as Anna), Burt Lancaster (as Steve Thompson). Universal Pictures/Photofest.

*Criss Cross* (1949). Directed by Robert Siodmak. Shown: Yvonne De Carlo (as Anna), Burt Lancaster (as Steve Thompson). MCA/Universal/Photofest.

Ramirez), Richard Long (Slade Thompson), Percy Helton (Frank), Alan Napier (Finchley), Esy Morales (Orchestra Leader).

Based on Don Tracy's 1934 novel, which was much tougher than the 1949 film adaptation, director Robert Siodmak tightened Tracy's episodic plot into a coherent Hollywood narrative that builds steadily toward its inevitable ending. While the novel concludes with Thompson surviving the attempts on his life and then discovering that his kid brother Slade is sleeping with Anna, the film opts for a clear-cut ending, with both Thompson and Anna murdered by Dundee just before the police arrive. The novel's ending was not, of course, possible under the censorship requirements involving so-called aberrant sexual behavior as well as the need to clearly punish legal and moral transgressions, and it has the effect of reinforcing the film's presentation of Thompson as a gullible innocent sacrificing his life for an unworthy woman (Anna), while the novel is a good deal more cynical and presents him as an amoral survivor—only when he witnesses Slade with Anna does his hard exterior falter.

*Criss Cross* resembles Siodmak's 1946 noir film *The Killers*, also starring Burt Lancaster as a man unable to resist a deadly woman, and he dies in both films. Both films display a sense of lassitude, a loss of energy and moral purpose. In *The*

*Killers* Lancaster's "the Swede" waits in a darkened room in a small town for hired killers to murder him. Although he is warned that they are coming, he passively waits to be killed. Similarly, in *Criss Cross* Steve Thompson is unable to get on with his life after Anna divorces him. Early in the film, in a revealing sequence that combines music and images, but no dialogue, Thompson passively watches Anna dance sensually with a handsome young man (Tony Curtis). Thompson's longing is palpable, and life has little meaning for him—despite the best efforts of his mother and colleagues.

He starts seeing Anna again, although she is now married to the gangster-gambler Slim Dundee. Eventually, they are caught together in Dundee's house, and to prevent the gangster from killing him and Anna, Thompson tells him that they were meeting to discuss his plan to rob the company he works for, an armored car company that carries the payrolls for many local companies. Anna persuades Thompson to go through with the robbery with Dundee and promises to leave her husband once they have the money. However, Thompson's plan to steal the payroll while it is being transported is disrupted by Dundee's desire to kill Thompson and take all the money. After Dundee's men kill Pop, Thompson's elderly colleague, Thompson kills two gangsters and saves the payroll. Hailed as a hero by the local media, he is hospitalized because of injuries suffered in the shoot-out.

The last section in the film begins with a prolonged, almost silent, bravura sequence whereby Siodmak again reveals his mastery of the medium with his selection of images and sounds. Incapacitated in a hospital bed, Thompson is aware that Dundee will send a hit man to kill him. In a brilliant series of point-of-view shots, which alternate from Thompson in bed with images, and sounds, of the hospital corridor, Siodmak generates tremendous tension. His combination of subjective and objective shots, as Thompson's only view is a tilted mirror in his hospital room, rivals the very best of Hitchcock's work. Finally, a seemingly benign stranger starts up a conversation with Thompson before kidnapping him. Thompson bribes the kidnapper and is taken to Anna's hideout. Anna, however, quickly realizes that Thompson has been tricked and that Dundee will soon arrive to kill them both. She tries to abandon Thompson, but Dundee walks in and kills both of them—just as the police arrive.

*Criss Cross*, together with *Cry of the City* (1948), are among Siodmak's most powerful noir films, both of which are imbued with a sense of melancholy and futility. Both are predicated on the belief that the innocent cannot survive this sordid world and depict this cruel universe expressively with a lighting pattern that is now seen as an iconic aspect of 1940s film noir. The high-contrast lighting and dramatic camera angles convey an unrelenting sense of entrapment and psychic pain. In *Criss Cross* he even transforms a conventional sequence, such as the robbery of the armored car, into a confused, chaotic event, with masked figures struggling through the smoke and where the instigator of the crime is ultimately celebrated as a hero and savior figure.

The main story line of *Criss Cross* was remade in 1995 as *The Underneath*, directed by Steven Soderbergh and starring Peter Gallagher in Burt Lancaster's former role.

Geoff Mayer

**THE CROOKED WAY** (United Artists, 1949). *Director:* Robert Florey. *Producer:* Benedict Bogeaus. *Script:* Richard H. Landau, based on the radio play *No Blade Too Sharp* by Robert Monroe. *Cinematography:* John Alton. *Music:* Louis Forbes. *Cast:* John Payne (Eddie Rice), Ellen Drew (Nina), Sonny Tufts (Vince Alexander), Percy Helton (Petey), Rhys Williams (Lt. Williams).

*The Crooked Way* is one of several film noirs made just after World War II that feature returned servicemen suffering from traumatic amnesia. The heroes of these films represent, in an exaggerated manner, the general maladjustment of the World War II veteran. However, Sergeant Eddie Rice (Silver Star) in *The Crooked Way* takes this to an extreme because his amnesia is organic rather than psychological, as in many other films. There will be no psychiatric cure for him as his memory loss stems from shrapnel deep in his brain around which scar tissue has grown. It will therefore be permanent. This situation offers Eddie the possibility of gaining a totally new identity: he has forgotten his prewar life as a criminal, and paradoxically, the battle injury allows him to be a better man than he was previously. Nonetheless he must pick up the pieces of his past experiences to assemble an identity, and some misunderstandings are inevitable. This process forces him to be passive at first, allowing experiences to come to him, such as when a police officer shows him his file, which reveals that before the war he had been suspected of murder. Like many other noir heroes, then, he is in the predicament of being an innocent man wrongly suspected of a killing. Operating with an understandable mistrust of other people, Eddie becomes a quasi-detective in search of himself. In this amnesia film, though, the hero does not really want to remember, but would rather forget much of his past life.

The film's narrative contains two early coincidences that propel its plot: the first is that two policemen who know Eddie from before the war just happen to encounter him on his initial arrival from hospital at Los Angeles's Union Station and take him in for questioning. He is quickly told by them that he is an ex-gangster and is set loose to help incriminate his old partner, Vince Alexander. The second coincidence is that on the very same day, Nina Martin (his ex-wife) by chance sees him leaving the Halls of Justice. Psychically scarred by the war, Eddie is now physically beaten by Vince's hoods for a past transgression, when he had turned state's evidence. Vince wants to pander Nina off to Eddie sexually, and she is caught up in the two men's macho rivalry. Nina, too, has scars—one physical, where Eddie had struck her back in 1943. She becomes the reason he stays in town after his beating and warning off because he reads in a newspaper that years before, she had refused to testify against him. In a sincere talk at a restaurant he tells Nina of his medical state, and she reveals that she is his wife. She calls herself the "top bait" at Vince's covert casino on Sunset Strip, where she works as a hostess encouraging "pigeons" to the betting tables. Later, she is shot, and a doctor is fetched at some risk by a newly tender Eddie. They forge a new romantic connection as she lies wounded, struck in the same shoulder where he had previously hurt her. Their new love seems free from the past and her former hatred.

*The Crooked Way*, rather unusually, has two different voice-over narrators: a neutral voice makes introductory generalized remarks about injured war veterans in the style of semidocumentary noirs, but later, this is replaced by the voice of Eddie himself, a very limited narrator, seemingly even more puzzled by the plot's mysterious events than is the audience. While the film's lethargic pace may betray its origins as a radio play, its visual style is striking, with cinematographer John Alton frequently using dramatic shadows and low angles in violent scenes combined with low lighting and high contrast. The tangled plot builds to a confrontation between Eddie and Vince. Trapped in a dragnet while attempting to clear his name, Eddie goes to a waterfront gang house after an atmospheric nighttime sequence detailing his search through the city's demimonde for Petey, a minor gang flunky. He ambushes Vince and arranges for the police to come. In the climactic fistfight, Eddie is slugged and used as a shield by Vince. After Petey distracts him and Eddie is dropped, Vince is left exposed, and the police gun him down. The film ends symmetrically as it began: in a hospital ward. This time, Eddie kisses Nina when she visits him, his new, morally sound identity expunging the old.

Brian McDonnell

**CROSSFIRE** (RKO, 1947). *Director:* Edward Dmytryk. *Producer:* Adrian Scott. *Script:* John Paxton, from the novel *The Brick Foxhole* by Richard Brooks. *Cinematography:* J. Roy Hunt. *Music:* Roy Webb. *Cast:* Robert Young (Finlay), Robert Mitchum (Keeley), Robert Ryan (Montgomery), Gloria Grahame (Ginny), Paul Kelly (the Man), Sam Levene (Joseph Samuels), Steve Brodie (Floyd), George Cooper (Mitchell).

It was very uncommon for any of those films of the late 1940s that we now call classical film noir to be considered at the time of their production A movies, or to be thought to have serious themes, or to be nominated for Oscars. *Crossfire* is very much an exception to these rules of thumb. It was adapted from a critically admired literary novel by Richard Brooks, and it is a serious examination of the theme of anti-Semitism. *Crossfire* was also nominated for five Academy Awards, including best picture, best director, and best script, although it won none. Like its contemporary drama *Gentlemen's Agreement* (also about anti-Semitism and eventually winning best picture for that year), it has ambitions to social relevance, but it presents all this in the form of a crime thriller replete with noir-style flashbacks. Dmytryk uses the same low lighting he had employed in 1944 in *Murder, My Sweet* and most memorably uses a series of shorter and shorter lenses on the face of Robert Ryan

*Crossfire* (1947). Directed by Edward Dmytryk. Shown from left: Robert Ryan (as Montgomery), Robert Mitchum (as Keeley), Robert Young (as Finlay). RKO Radio Pictures/Photofest.

as a murderer (from 50 mm down to 25 mm) to produce a compellingly distorting effect.

The story begins *in media res* with the shadowy depiction of a man's murder in a hotel room by unseen hands. The police begin their investigation after the body is found by the man's girlfriend. It emerges that the man (Samuels) has spent his last evening drinking and socializing with a group of soldiers awaiting demobilization at the end of World War II. Detective Finlay takes charge, and when he questions a soldier named Montgomery about the evening's events, Corporal Mitchell (Mitch) becomes the prime suspect for the crime. Finlay enlists the aid of Sergeant Keeley in finding Mitchell, but Keeley is keen to speak to the soldier before handing him over to the police. He sends other soldiers out to find him, which they do. Just as the police had heard one version of events given by Montgomery, Keeley hears a long description of the same evening from Mitchell as they hide out in a movie theater. Mitchell is upset and missing his absent wife and is unable to provide a clear alibi, despite having spent part of the night with a dancer named Jenny. Together, Keeley and Finlay are eventually able to characterize the murder as a hate crime and identify the killer as Montgomery, who had murdered Samuels merely because he was Jewish.

The narrative structure of *Crossfire* is typically complex in the noir manner, and this is demonstrated by the two main flashbacks. Montgomery's account is deceitful, and he presents himself to the detectives in a false and self-serving light. He describes meeting Samuels in a bar and befriending him. After they go up to Samuel's room, there is a mild dispute over drinks, and the soldiers leave. The fact that Mitchell's wallet was found in the room is seized on by Montgomery to direct suspicion at him. However, Montgomery's mentioning to Finlay that he dislikes Jews and other malingerers sticks in the mind of the detective (and the audience). Mitch's flashback by comparison is confusing but honest and presents a different point of view from Montgomery. Mitch describes getting progressively drunker through the evening. He goes to the far side of the bar from his buddies, and Samuels joins him. They talk about the war and the difficult adjustment to peace, major anxieties for Mitch. Later, in Samuel's room, he gets drunker and more confused. Ryan looks distinctly more threatening in this flashback. As Mitch leaves, he hears a quarrel. He also remembers Jenny at the dance bar. They dance together, they kiss, and she offers him a key to her apartment, telling him he can rest. Mitch goes there, but there is a strange man at the door, who tells him an odd, contradictory yarn. He calls Jenny a "tramp" and keeps changing his story. Mitch leaves. These two contradictory accounts emphasize the mood of doubt and mystery at the film's center, and this doubling is reflected in the two separate pursuits of Mitch that occur: one by the police, the other by his army buddies.

The film's theme is evident in the title: Mitch is caught in the crossfire of other people's conflicts. Like other postwar soldiers, he is maladjusted, full of self-hate. Even Keeley describes the general nervousness of people when he vividly remarks, "The snakes are loose. I get 'em myself. They're friends of mine." This postwar angst is most overtly stated when Samuels makes his famous "peanut speech" in the bar, describing how Americans are at each other's throats because they have lost the common enemy they shared in the war against Germany and Japan. Montgomery kills Samuels because he considers him a Jewish malingerer, but we find out that Samuels had actually been wounded on Okinawa. When Finlay looks for a murder motive, he asks, why would you kill someone you don't know? He theorizes about hate and prejudice being the only possible reason for the crime. To convince another soldier to help trap Montgomery, he compares anti-Semitism to prejudice against Irish Catholics in America, including his own grandfather, who was killed in a hate crime. The original novel from which the film was adapted had been about a homophobic killing, but the Production Code Office would not allow that topic on the screen in 1947.

Significantly, the film is set in Washington, D.C., the nation's capital, and the Houses of Congress are visible behind Finlay as he tells his grandfather's story. As part of the film's construction of an ideology of cooperation and commonality, Finlay persuades Keeley to work with him in solving the murder. Detective

Finlay is able to discuss the crime rationally with Keeley, proving that two heads can be better than one. While Keeley helps in the tricking of Montgomery, it is Finlay who shoots him dead when he flees. Standing over the body, he laconically instructs other cops to "clean it up."

Brian McDonnell

**CROUPIER** (Channel Four Films, 1998). *Director:* Mike Hodges. *Producers:* Jonathan Cavendish, Christine Ruppert, and James Mitchell (executive producer). *Script:* Paul Mayersberg. *Cinematography:* Michael Garfath. *Music:* Simon Fisher-Turner. *Cast:* Clive Owen (Jack Manfred), Kate Hardie (Bella), Alex Kingston (Jani de Villiers), Gina McKee (Marion), Nicholas Ball (Jack Sr.), Nick Reding (Giles Cremorne), Alexander Morton (David Reynolds), Paul Reynolds (Matt).

Mike Hodges directed the best British crime film of the early 1970s in *Get Carter* (1971) and the best British crime film of the late 1990s in *Croupier*. *Croupier* is the work of a mature filmmaker working with a limited budget to deliver a personal, multilayered film. Paul Mayersberg's script develops a world of paradoxes and metaphors based around gambling as a metaphor for life. Mayersberg's main character is the cold, detached Jack Manfred. There is, however, an inherent dichotomy within Manfred. Although he refuses to gamble, as the odds are too great, he takes great risks, risks that are rationalized through his fictional surrogate, Jake. Thus Jack the croupier, who takes perverse pleasure watching his customers lose their money, readily sleeps with Bella, a fellow croupier, and takes Jani, a South African gambler, away for the weekend, despite a prohibition from his gambling establishment that forbids croupiers from fraternizing with colleagues or customers.

The film begins with Jack, who was born in South Africa, suffering from writer's block. Although he is desperate for money, he cannot fulfill the demands of his philistine publisher, Giles Cremorne, for a soccer book with plenty of action and sex. Jack, with the assistance of his father, secures a job as a croupier, where he finds that he is fascinated (again) by the prospect of watching people lose their money. His live-in girlfriend, Marion, is less enthusiastic about the prospect of living with a croupier rather than a struggling writer. Jack, who is half in love with Marion, meets two women, Bella, a fellow croupier who also despises the punters, and Jani, a gambler who invites Jack to participate in a plan to rob the casino. Jack, rationalizing away his objections through his voice-over, agrees, leading to an unexpected, somewhat oblique ending.

*Croupier,* consistent with the world of film noir, is a deeply cynical film. Jack's publisher, Giles Cremorne, is almost a caricature of the crass publisher with little interest in quality writing, only in sales. The film's dominant motif, gambling, is a perfect expression of disaffection. Jack only succeeds through chance. Even after Marion's death and his success as an anonymous novelist, there is no sign of redemption or regeneration as Jack replaces the romantic, caring Marion with the cynical Bella. Bella is the perfect match for Jack's alienated point of view as she is a woman who spent a year as an S-M prostitute as it required no emotional or sexual interaction with her customers—a social condition that also approximates the rules of the casino for its employees. Jack's detachment and alienation from the gamblers is not moral, but sadistic—he enjoys watching people lose their money. Yet, as the narrative shows, when the price is right, he also succumbs to the temptations of illicit sex and criminal behavior.

While Hodges and Mayersberg infuse *Croupier* with a quasi-realistic atmosphere, it is a very stylized film, opening on the metal center of a spinning wheel as the carriage spins around its center, replaced by the image of Jack as the camera dollies around him in the casino. These contrasting images of stasis and movement provide an effective summary of the film's basic premise: the alienated croupier seemingly detached from the world of risk takers. As the film progresses, this duality, contrasting Jack's control with the addiction of the gamblers, is cleverly subverted by Jack's alter ego, Jake, the risk taker. Clive Owen, as Jack, is perfect as the croupier who has one good novel in him. Jack's realization of this fact begins with the pleasure he takes in his physical transformation from the bohemian would-be writer, with dyed blonde hair, to the repressed, controlled croupier with his slicked-down black hair and accompanying uniform, his impersonal evening dress.

Even the history of the distribution and exhibition of *Croupier* reinforces the film's central thesis, that life is a gamble. When the film was completed in 1998, the BBC was no longer interested in promoting the film as there had been a change in management. Paul Mayersberg complained that they did not even produce one poster for promotion as the film was destined not to have a cinema release but go straight to television. After 13 copies were sent to the American festival circuit and a subsequent theatrical release occurred, *Croupier* received glowing reviews, which led to openings in Britain, Europe, and Australia and New Zealand and a nomination for Paul Mayersberg at the 2001 Edgar Allan Poe Awards. Yet, consistent with the inherent irony of the film, because it had been shown briefly on television, *Croupier* was ruled ineligible for American awards, an unjust fate for Clive Owen, Mike Hodges, and Paul Mayersberg.

Geoff Mayer

**CRY OF THE CITY** (Twentieth Century Fox, 1948). *Director:* Robert Siodmak. *Producer:* Sol Siegel. *Script:* Richard Murphy, based on the novel *The Chair for Martin Rome* by Henry Edward Helseth. *Cinematography:* Lloyd Ahern. *Music:* Alfred Newman. *Cast:* Victor Mature (Lieutenant Candella), Richard Conte (Martin Rome), Fred Clark (Lieutenant Collins), Shelley Winters (Brenda Martingale), Betty Garde (Miss Pruett), Berry Kroeger (Niles), Tommy Cook (Tony Rome), Debra Paget (Teena Riconti), Hope Emerson (Rose Given), Walter Baldwin (Orvy), Konstantin Shayne (Dr. Veroff).

*Cry of the City* was directed by Robert Siodmak during his most creative period, a period that included key noir films such as *The Killers* (1946), *Criss Cross* (1949), and *The File on Thelma Jordan* (1950). While the basic story line of two men from the same impoverished background, New York's Little Italy, who take different paths, one a cop and the other a criminal, is familiar film material, Siodmak resolutely changes the tone of the film by refusing to sentimentalize the characters and by presenting the seemingly good character, Lieutenant Candella, as a rigid, self-righteous cop. His film differs from other films which draw on this premise, most notably the 1938 Warner Bros. film *Angels with Dirty Faces*.

Unlike the 1938 film, Siodmak virtually ignores the sociological implications and replaces it with a dark, fatalistic view of a city permeated by personal and social corruption. Siodmak's city is populated by sad, lonely, and corrupt characters totally devoid of communal spirit. The social good is replaced by personal revenge. At one point, Lieutenant Candello and his partner (Collins) wait in the early hours of the morning in an all-night diner for any news of Martin Rome, who has escaped from a prison hospital ward. Collins, who queries Candello's obsessive pursuit of Rome, notices a woman sitting in the diner by herself and asks her why she is in the diner at this hour of the morning. She is unable to give him an answer—like the other denizens of this city, it appears that she has nowhere to go and no one to go home to.

The film begins with Martin Rome recovering from severe wounds after his failed attempt to rob a store. Rome, who killed a policeman during the robbery, is questioned by Lieutenant Candello, who grew up with Rome in New York's Little Italy. Candello is also friendly with Rome's parents. Although Rome escapes, the film shows that he is trapped in the city. Whoever he meets, Rome ultimately betrays—except the masseuse Rose Given. Rome's encounter with Given reinforces Siodmak's view of the city as both sensual and highly dangerous. Given, a large woman, wants the jewels that Rome stole from a crooked lawyer, and she offers to provide relief to the stricken criminal by massaging his neck. As Rome relaxes under her skilful touch, Given's hands slowly move from his shoulders to his neck, and suddenly pleasure turns into terror as the powerful masseuse threatens to strangle him unless he provides the information she wants.

Finally, a badly wounded Candello corners Rome in a neighborhood church in Little Italy, an appropriate setting for the resolution of the conflict between a righteous cop and an unrepentant sinner. This encounter confirms Siodmak's determination not to provide a simple polarization of morality in the film between Rome, the cop killer, and Candello, the obsessive cop. Both men are seriously flawed individuals, and the film rejects the simple dichotomy between good and evil found in other variants of this story. *Cry of the City* encourages the audience to consider life as morally complex, dangerous, and lonely.

Geoff Mayer

# D

**DANCE WITH A STRANGER** (Goldcrest Films, 1985). *Director:* Mike Newell, *Producers:* Roger Randall-Cutler and Paul Cowan (associate). *Script:* Shelagh Delaney. *Cinematography:* Peter Hannan. *Music:* Richard Hartley. *Cast:* Miranda Richardson (Ruth Ellis), Rupert Everett (David Blakely), Ian Holm (Desmond Cussen), Matthew Carroll (Andy), Tom Chadborn (Anthony Findlater), Jane Bertish (Carole Findlater), Stratford Johns (Morrie Conley), Joanne Whalley (Christine), David Troughton (Cliff Davis).

After Ruth Ellis has fired six bullets into race car driver and lover David Blakely, *Dance with a Stranger* concludes with a sad, confused letter written by Ellis to David's mother trying to explain her action. In the letter Ellis blames David's friends, Anthony and Carol Findlater, for causing his death because of their class-based prejudice to Blakely's relationship with Ellis. This letter relates to one of the film's dual narrative strands—the obvious class difference between Ellis and Blakely. The other is sexual obsession, which, in the end, destroys both Ellis and Blakely. Director Mike Newell forces the audience to focus on these aspects—not only is the Ellis/Blakely relationship permeated by obsessive, irrational behavior, but the film frequently returns to the same pattern whereby Ellis and Blakely fight followed by sex followed by betrayal followed by sex followed by violence.

Although *Dance with a Stranger* is based on a true story, the film largely restricts its focus to the recurring love-hate pattern involving Ellis and Blakely. The only characters that are permitted within this pattern are Desmond Cussen, Ellis's

*Dance with a Stranger* (1985). Directed by Mike Newell. Shown: Miranda Richardson (as Ruth Ellis), Rupert Everett (as David Blakely). Samuel Goldwyn Company/Photofest.

long-suffering admirer, and Andy, her son. However, the only information we learn about Desmond and Andy is restricted to the destructive effect that Ellis and Blakely have on their lives.

Ruth Ellis, a bar manager with a shady past, divorced, and an ex-prostitute with a Marilyn Monroe hairstyle, becomes the lover of David Blakely, a spoiled, immature race car driver. Ellis murders Blakely in 1955 and becomes the last woman in England to go to the gallows. *Dance with a Stranger* does not moralize and refuses to reduce Ellis and Blakely to the melodramatic status of victims and villains. Even the immature, self-centered Blakely is allowed moments of sympathy while Ellis struggles, unsuccessfully, to establish a stable environment for Andy, who committed suicide later in life.

Ellis declares, "I've never had any kind of peace," and her inability to establish the necessary distance in her relationship with Blakely, as required by a professional workingwoman, gives the film more than a tinge of fatalism. A sense of inevitability and doom is expressed through the dark visuals, the costumes, and the settings. It is one of the finest British films of the 1980s, with its relentless focus on the destructive effects of class barriers in 1950s England, especially when combined with sexual obsession.

Geoff Mayer

**DARK CITY** (Paramount, 1950). *Director:* William Dieterle. *Producer:* Hal B. Wallis. *Script:* John Meredyth Lucas and Larry Marcus, with contributions from Leonardo Bercovici, adapted by Ketti Frings from a story by Larry Marcus. *Cinematography:* Victor Milner. *Music:* Franz Waxman. *Cast:* Charlton Heston (Danny Haley), Lizabeth Scott (Fran), Viveca Lindfors (Victoria Winant), Dean Jagger (Capt. Garvey), Don DeFore (Arthur Winant), Jack Webb (Augie), Ed Begley (Barney), Henry Morgan (Soldier), Mike Mazurki (Sidney Winant).

While its title makes it seem a quintessential noir film, *Dark City* is not quite as gloomy or pessimistic as its name suggests. In fact, the film's upbeat ending and the characterization of the story's main female figure have prompted some critics to consider it a rather marginal noir. However, these misgivings can be countered by a close consideration of the male protagonist of *Dark City*, who is very much an example of the kind of moral ambiguity that is a central concern of film noir. Danny Haley (played by Charlton Heston in his film debut) is a man of basically decent values who has crossed over to the wrong side of the law as a result of personal and historical circumstances. Finding himself compromised by his participation in criminal rackets, and shocked by the tragic consequences of his venality, he has to struggle toward some type of expiation and eventual redemption. If his final triumph seems somewhat glib, that does not negate the complex psychological tussles and vulnerabilities that precede it.

Danny is first shown as a small-time gambler and operative in an illegal betting ring in a large American city, possibly Chicago. A narrow escape from a police raid in the film's opening shows his stylishness, his presence of mind, and his flippancy. It also introduces Capt. Garvey (Dean Jagger), one of the film's several voices of moral persuasion, who tells Danny that his crimes will soon catch him. Danny visits his girlfriend, Fran (Lizabeth Scott), who is a singer in a café, and it is immediately apparent that while she loves him profoundly, he is emotionally uncommitted to her. She feels that his reluctance to be involved stems from some past hurt and encourages him to leave his criminal associates. These men, including the aging and ulcer-ridden Barney (Ed Begley) and the self-serving Augie (Jack Webb), recruit Danny into a gambling scam whereby a visiting businessman named Arthur Winant will be swindled out of $5,000 during a fixed poker game. When the man subsequently commits suicide from the shame of losing other people's money, Danny is forced to face up to the ramifications of his chosen occupation. His anxiety is amplified when the businessman's psychotic brother Sidney embarks on a program of violent revenge.

Fran feels that she has played a part in the tragedy as Winant had initially been attracted to her and was a sitting duck. She tries to convince Danny to leave the rackets, and his feelings are made more ambivalent by the number of competing voices offering possible courses of action. Barney and Augie are frustrated that they cannot clear the man's check because of police interest in his death, while an ex-boxer called Soldier (Henry Morgan) pricks Danny's conscience with talk of the inherent decency of the victim. After Barney is strangled to death by Sidney,

Danny is in real fear for his life. At this point, two key conversations allow crucial information about his back story to be revealed. During a nighttime walk along the river, Danny tells Fran about his British ex-wife who was unfaithful to him during the war. Later, in a talk with Capt. Garvey, it is revealed that Danny was an admired college-educated air force officer serving in England until he killed his wife's lover in a fight. While he was acquitted of any charges, this trauma set him in the wrong direction. The possibility of turning back from his immoral path is raised by the appearance at the police station of Winant's European-refugee widow, Victoria, who has flown in from Los Angeles.

At this stage the narrative of *Dark City* takes a curious turn. Danny and Augie fly out to Los Angeles to attempt to track down Sidney and turn the tables on him before he can attack them. Danny befriends Victoria and her young son, visiting their bright suburban home in scenes that are marked by a strong visual contrast with the shadowy city sequences earlier in the film. Through taking the boy on outings and in hearing from Victoria that the war has made everybody different, Danny comes to envisage an alternative domestic life for himself. After Augie is viciously murdered by Sidney, Danny determines to use his gambling skills to earn enough cash to help Victoria rebound from her husband's death, thus expiating his previous crime. He flies to Las Vegas to win big at craps, at the same time making himself a decoy for Sidney. Fran pursues him there and gets a job singing in the casino where Danny is working. When Sidney assaults him in his motel room, Danny is rescued by the police, who have participated in the trap. The $11,400 Danny has won is earmarked for Victoria, and in the final scene he tells Fran he is at last ready to settle down with her.

*Dark City*'s dialogue is full of moral fables. A casino manager tells of a boxing death that changed his view of life, and the police captain relates an allegory about animals in a slaughterhouse that is meant to spur Danny into taking responsibility for his actions. A scene in a planetarium, reminiscent of *Rebel Without a Cause*, highlights the insignificance of human desires in a vast universe. Such arguably nonnoir elements reinforce the way *Dark City* uses the figure of Fran. This is a thankless role for Scott whereby she repeatedly nags Danny away from crime in between singing a string of forgettable torch numbers. She exists on the fringe of the criminal world but is not evil and certainly no femme fatale. What does make the film more noir-like is the unusually nonheroic characterization of Heston as a man weighed down by moral pressures, a role so different from the standard persona he embodied later in his career. There are also the studio-bound expressionistic sets with their artificial fog and source lighting. However, there is little doubt that the film's unconvincing happy ending undercuts the noir potentiality of earlier sections of the film. Perhaps a more powerful and tough-minded conclusion would have had Danny die in his attempt to win a better life for Victoria.

Brian McDonnell

**THE DARK CORNER** (Twentieth Century Fox, 1946). *Director:* Henry Hathaway. *Producer:* Fred Kohlmar. *Script:* Jay Dratler and Bernard Schoenfeld. *Cinematography:* Joe MacDonald. *Music:* Cyril Mockridge. *Cast:* Mark Stevens (Bradford Galt), Lucille Ball (Kathleen), Clifton Webb (Hardy Cathcart), William Bendix (White Suit), Cathy Downs (Mari Cathcart), Kurt Krueger (Anthony Jardine).

Many film noir protagonists feel that the world is out to get them, or at least that some of the world's nastier inhabitants bear them malice. There are literally scores of such films that show an innocent man trapped by the vicissitudes of fate. *The Dark Corner* is one of the most famous of these films and one where the pressures on the main character are unrelenting until the very end. As Alain Silver and Elizabeth Ward phrase it in their book *Film Noir: An Encyclopedic Reference to the American Style*, this film is a "prototypical reflection of postwar malaise in film noir" (p. 82). Under the expert direction of Henry Hathaway, the audience is drawn in to the plot's morass of complex motivations and malicious conspiracies so that they come to share the near-despair of hero Bradford Galt. Galt is a tough detective caught up in a truly existential bind from which he keeps fighting to disentangle himself, aided by no one except his resourceful secretary Kathleen.

*The Dark Corner* (1946). Directed by Henry Hathaway. Shown from left: Lucille Ball (as Kathleen), Mark Stevens (as Bradford Galt). Twentieth Century Fox Film Corp./ Photofest.

Galt operates a small office in New York, and at the film's opening he is trying to rebuild his life and indulge in some mild flirtation with Kathleen, who has not long been working for him. There is a clear attraction between the two, and they banter about sex while she fends off a pass by him. But Galt is a troubled man, as his back story, described later to Kathleen in a café, indicates. Some years before, he had been incriminated in San Francisco by a blackmailer, Tony Jardine, who reacted to Galt's threat to expose his ill-gotten gains by faking a traffic accident. Jardine slugged Galt and filled him with liquor, and in the resulting car crash a man was killed. Galt served time for manslaughter. Now he finds he is being followed by a mysterious fellow in a white suit who orchestrates another attempted frame whereby Galt will be found with the dead body of Jardine (whom "White Suit" has slugged with a poker) and be wrongly convicted of his murder. Galt's supposed motive of seeking revenge over his earlier imprisonment makes him the perfect fall guy in someone else's plot to be rid of Jardine.

Galt, who has a well-practiced line in hard-boiled dialogue, beats what he thinks is a confession out of the man in the white suit, but it transpires that the man's story is yet another deceitful element in the overall conspiracy. When Galt is later chloroformed in his apartment by "White Suit" and left next to Jardine's corpse, he is saved from discovery only by the intervention of the plucky Kathleen, who cleans up the mess and gets Galt out. A kiss seals the fact that from this point on they will work as a team to expose the true villains. The people behind the plot, however, remain murky figures in the first half of *The Dark Corner*, but it eventually emerges that a wealthy art collector, Hardy Cathcart, is behind Jardine's death as that man had been having an affair with Cathcart's wife, Mari. The Cathcarts bring to the story line an upper-class milieu of art and culture that contrasts with Galt's dark world of crime and grubbiness. Their world of art galleries and glamorous parties is, of course, just as corrupt as the unlit alleys and El tracks of the gritty city where Galt normally works. By casting Clifton Webb as Cathcart, Hathaway also gains the considerable dramatic advantage of Webb's bitchily acerbic one-liners that recall his role as Waldo Lydecker in *Laura*. His voyeuristic spying on a clinch between Mari and Jardine also echoes his jealous attempts to control Laura Hunt in the earlier film.

For much of *The Dark Corner* it seems that the more Galt and Kathleen try to shed light on the enveloping frame that surrounds them, the more frustrating and intractable their predicament becomes. It is at one such moment of despair that Galt utters the classic line to Kathleen that sums up the emotions of many of the victim heroes of film noir: "I feel all dead inside. I'm backed up in a dark corner and I don't know who's hitting me." But in a proficiently constructed climax the film eventually moves into more traditional thriller territory. "White Suit" is propelled by Cathcart's cane to his death through a 31st story skyscraper window and, after a harum-scarum cab chase through downtown New York, Galt is baled up by Cathcart in the gallery vault. He appears to be about to die when Mari appears and empties her gun into her murderous husband. As she is taken into custody by a pair of cops casting sidelong sardonic glances over the modern art pieces that fill the gallery, Galt and Kathleen are able to finally relax and make verbal hints about an imminent marriage. As a team, they have wriggled out from the dark corner and given themselves the breathing space to plan a happy future.

Brian McDonnell

**DARK PASSAGE** (Warner Bros., 1947). *Director:* Delmer Daves. *Producer:* Jerry Wald. *Script:* Delmer Daves, based on the novel by David Goodis. *Cinematography:* Sid Hickox. *Music:* Franz Waxman. *Cast:* Humphrey Bogart (Vincent Parry), Lauren Bacall (Irene Jansen), Bruce Bennett (Bob), Agnes Moorhead (Madge Rapf), Tom D'Andrea (Sam), Clifton Young (Baker), Douglas Kennedy (Detective), Rory Mallinson (George Fellsinger), Houseley Stevenson (Dr. Walter Coley).

The first two films Humphrey Bogart and Lauren Bacall made together, *To Have and Have Not* (1944) and *The Big Sleep* (1946), were immensely popular as audiences welcomed their wisecracking dialogue and sensual sparring. *Dark Passage*, however, was less commercially successful. It *was* decidedly darker in tone and imbued with a strong melancholic streak. This was primarily due to its source novel by David Goodis, one of the more bizarre hard-boiled writers who worked in Hollywood in the 1940s. While the film softened the novel's presentation of

*Dark Passage* (1947). Directed by Delmer Daves. Shown from left: Lauren Bacall (as Irene Jansen), Humphrey Bogart (as Vincent Parry). Warner Bros./Photofest.

alienation and the vagaries of the criminal justice system, it retained sufficient material from the novel to make audiences uncomfortable.

The film begins with Vincent Parry escaping from prison, where he was serving a life sentence for killing his wife. Parry, who is innocent of the murder, smuggles himself out of jail in a trash can, and the film, to prevent the audience from seeing Parry's face, employs subjective narration whereby the camera presents only what Parry can see, without the conventional reverse shot showing the actor's face, for the first hour. This technique was employed for the whole film in actor/director Robert Montgomery's film adaptation of Raymond Chandler's novel *Lady in the Lake* (1947). In *Dark Passage* it appears less gimmicky as the device is motivated by the plot. Hence for the first hour the audience can only hear Humphrey Bogart's voice while the camera records what he is looking at, and so when the trash can falls off the truck transporting him out of the prison, the camera simulates the jarring motion experienced by Parry in the can. Similarly, when he moves through the undergrowth and meets Irene Jansen, everything is recorded via his point of view. Thus when Irene Jansen speaks to Parry, she talks directly into the lens of the camera.

In terms of the plot, this technique is motivated by Parry's decision to undertake plastic surgery so that he can avoid capture by the police while he searches for his wife's killer. Parry, who is dependent on Irene Jansen for much of the film, is directed by a helpful cabbie, Sam, to an unregistered doctor. This sequence, the most powerful one in the film, allows the filmmakers to explore a range of technical devices that accentuate Parry's sense of helplessness where, as a convicted killer on the run from the police, he is at the mercy of a discredited surgeon about to operate on his face in inferior facilities. This results in a surreal nightmare emanating from an aging, smoking doctor who warns Parry that he might emerge from the operation looking like a bulldog.

Parry's postoperative condition is equally tenuous. Bogart's face, seen for the first time, is covered in bandages as he walks through the San Francisco streets in the early hours of the morning while workers shout insults at his appearance. Similarly, after the bandages are removed and he leaves the security of Irene's apartment, he stops to rest in an all-night diner, only to arouse the suspicions of its only other customer, an off-duty policeman.

Parry's quest to find security, and his wife's killer, brings him into contact with a number of bizarre characters, including a petty crook who tries to blackmail him. In the novel Parry executes the crook (named Arbogast in the novel and Baker in the film) by cold-bloodedly shooting him in a field, while in the film he manages to extricate himself when the crook stumbles off a cliff and falls to his death. This change, necessitated by the Production Code Authority, had the effect of softening Parry's character.

Parry's only friend in the film, aside from Irene Jansen, is George Fellsinger, a lonely trumpeter. However, when Parry seeks his help after surgery, he discovers that Fellsinger has been murdered. To heighten Parry's despair, when he finds his friend's body lying on the floor of his apartment, director Delmer Daves and cinematographer Sid Hickox use a glass floor with Fellsinger's body on it so that they can present both Parry and Fellsinger in a single shot—this enables them to clearly to get the camera under Fellsinger, as he lies face downward, and register the dismay on Parry's face as he looks at Fellsinger's body. This results in an archetypal noir image that simultaneously links death and alienation.

*Dark Passage*, like many of Goodis's stories, is predicated on a series of coincidences and seemingly implausible events. While this does not seriously weaken the film, which is less interested in the murder plot and more concerned with establishing Parry's vulnerability, it caused concern with critics when the film was released. The climax in both the novel and the film takes place when Parry confronts Madge Rapf, a tormented former lover who killed his wife because of her jealousy. However, while a typical Hollywood crime film in the 1930s and 1940s would end with the police arresting Rapf and erasing Parry's conviction, *Dark Passage* offers no such easy solution. The demented Rapf, determined to make sure that Parry can never be acquitted, commits suicide by jumping out of her apartment window. This action must have provoked some consternation with the Production Code Authority as Parry is still legally guilty of his wife's death as well as suspected by the police for Fellsinger's death (who was actually killed by Rapf). This produces a rare 1940s film with no legal remedy as Parry is forced to leave the United States for good, and the film ends with the two lovers, Parry and Irene, together in a coastal town in Peru as the romantic tune "Too Marvelous for Words" provides an optimistic epilogue to a bleak film. The ending in the novel is much less romantic, although there is some suggestion that Irene may eventually join Parry in exile in a Peruvian coastal village.

Geoff Mayer

**DAUGHTER OF DARKNESS** (Paramount British, 1948). *Director:* Lance Comfort. *Producers:* Victor Hanbury and James A. Carter (executive). *Script:* Max Catto, based on his play *They Walk Alone*. *Cinematography:* Stanley Pavey. *Music:* Clifton Parker. *Cast:* Anne Crawford (Bess Stanforth), Maxwell Reed (Dan), Siobhan McKenna (Emmy Beaudine), George Thorpe (Mr. Tallent), Barry Morse (Robert Stanforth), Liam Redmond (Father Corcoran), Honor Blackman (Julie Tallent), David Greene (David Price), Denis Gordon (Saul Trevethick), Grant Tyler (Larry Tallent).

*Daughter of Darkness* was released in the same year, 1948, as a number of critically acclaimed British films, such as *The Winslow Boy*, *The Fallen Idol*, and *Hamlet*, and, not surprisingly, it disappeared quickly after hostile newspaper reviews. The film violated many of the canons of critical respectability prized in 1948. For a start it is thematically confronting and emotionally challenging and eschews the realist aesthetic that was celebrated at that time. It also denies the viewer the security of relating to a virtuous hero or heroine threatened with evil intent. However, with little change, it could have accommodated this need—it could have, for example, presented its theme as evil (Emmy Beaudine) permeating and violating a conventional British family (the Tallent family). To his credit, director Lance Comfort rejected this simplistic premise.

*Daughter of Darkness* dramatizes the strange story of Emmy Beaudine, a young Irish girl ejected from her village following the fears of the local women. She is sent to work on the Tallent Farm in Yorkshire. Before she leaves Ireland, however, Emmy meets a boxer, Dan, who works in a traveling carnival. Dan, excited by Emmy's presence at the ringside, batters his opponent before pursuing Emmy into the darkness, where he is seriously maimed by Emmy's nails after she rejects his sexual advances. This incident follows a recurring pattern in the film as Emmy expresses both love and hate toward her male suitors. Sexual desire repeatedly transforms into sexual violence.

Emmy, however, is not the conventional femme fatale found in many noir films. She is a victim of social repressions emanating from a patronizing class system. Unlike protagonists in films such as *Blanche Fury* (1947), she does not exploit her sexual powers in an attempt to obtain a better social position. While the Tallent farm offers Emmy an opportunity to make a new start, this is jeopardized when the local men are attracted to her. The first murder occurs when Dan's carnival sets up camp near the farm and the Tallents force a reluctant Emmy to join them at the carnival. This results in Dan's death. When a local boy also dies, Bess Stanforth, who lives on the farm with her husband, Robert, suspects Emmy after watching her playing the organ in a local church late at night. When Bess attempts to evict her from the farm, the young woman, as retribution for what she feels is victimization, seduces and kills Bess's young brother Larry. Bess retaliates by forcing Emmy onto the moors, where Dan's mongrel dog kills her.

*Daughter of Darkness* presents a society where sexual repression eventually warps women such as Emmy. To offset the repressions of the real world, she constructs an alternative world that repudiates reality. Her desire for romance and sex is perverted into overwhelming feelings of guilt and self-disgust that result in sexual violence and murder.

*Daughter of Darkness*, with a budget of £200,000 and three weeks' location shooting in Cornwall, was not a financial success and represented a setback to the career of Lance Comfort, who was relegated to low-budget films in the 1950s and 1960s. Yet the film's mixture of elements from gothic, film noir, and horror establishes it as one of the most startling British films of the 1940s. Although it was produced too late in the decade to cash in on the brief vogue for gothic melodrama in the early and mid-1940s (such as *The Man in Grey* [1943]), it is problematic that such a thematically confronting film would have attracted a large audience at any time.

Geoff Mayer

**DEAD RECKONING** (Columbia, 1947). *Director:* John Cromwell. *Producer:* Sidney Biddell. *Script:* Oliver H. P. Garrett and Steve Fisher. *Cinematography:* Leo Tover. *Music:* Marlin Skiles. *Cast:* Humphrey Bogart (Rip Murdock), Lizabeth

Scott (Coral Chandler), Wallace Ford (McGee), Morris Carnovsky (Martinelli), Charles Cane (Lt. Kincaid), Melvin Miller (Krause).

In the 1970s and 1980s feminist film theorists paid particular attention to the representation of women in film noir, often taking an equivocal stand over whether such depictions were progressive or retrogressive. On the one hand, they admired the energy and self-possession of the femmes fatales but they also felt that many noir story lines either punished these women cruelly for their independence or subjected them to harsh judgments from the male protagonists with whom they shared the screen. *Dead Reckoning* has often been cited in these discussions because of the way its script deals with the Lizabeth Scott character Coral Chandler. This may seem an overreaction to what is essentially a very male story about friendship and codes of loyalty and revenge. However, a close analysis of the film's messages shows that both aspects of the film's themes are significant.

*Dead Reckoning* opens *in media res* with Humphrey Bogart as Rip Murdock on the run in a fictional Gulf Coast city. He hides in a Catholic church, where he meets a priest dressed in the uniform of a paratrooper. Rip begins to impart his story to the priest, and a long flashback ensues, in which he confides that he himself is a returned soldier flown back stateside with a pal, Sergeant Johnny Drake, who was to receive the Medal of Honor. To Rip's surprise, Johnny is dead set against getting the medal, and he promptly disappears from the train in Philadelphia. Using a smattering of clues, Rip follows his friend's trail south and ends up in "Gulf City." A St. Louis cab company owner in peacetime, Rip now becomes a type of amateur detective as he tries to track down his friend and discover why he wanted to vanish. In local newspaper archives he discovers that Johnny was implicated some years before in the murder of a rich realtor, but almost straightaway, Rip hears of a charred body being found in a car wreck. Identifying the charred remains as Johnny, he determines to find the killers and to clear Johnny's name of the original murder so that his friend can receive his medal. One might say that the underlying theme expressed through his self-imposed task is the redemption of the reputation of the misunderstood war veteran.

In typical noir fashion, Rip soon finds himself at an upmarket nightspot called the Sanctuary Club, where Johnny used to work and where he meets Coral Chandler, widow of the murdered realtor. She is losing heavily at the gambling tables (this is later explained as a method of her paying blackmail debts). In a rather misogynistic way he is immediately distrustful of her, and his misgivings seem justified when he is given a drink he realizes has been spiked. He wakes later in his hotel room with the dead body of a barman lying on the floor. Rip is obviously being set up as a patsy, but with presence of mind he stows the body in the trunk of his car and is alone when the police arrive. The film's plot gets very complex at this point, much of the activity turning on the recovery of a letter that Johnny had written in their paratrooper unit's code (using the jump call "Geronimo") and that is in the office safe of club owner Martinelli. Rip had acquired some quite shady contacts in St. Louis, and these people put him in touch with a local safecracker who might get hold of the letter. This man, McGee, is a very good minor character played with ebullience by noir veteran Wallace Ford.

Alas for Rip, the safe is found empty, and he is soon captured by Martinelli and his sadistic goon Krause, who want the code explained to them. Rip finds that there are others who want to benefit from any discoveries he might make. As Alain Silver and Elizabeth Ward put it in their book *Film Noir: An Encyclopedic Reference to the American Style,* he is "at once the hunter and the hunted" (p. 86). By an ingenious stratagem he is able to escape them when they deliver him to a hotel, and he is happy to find the police there waiting for him. Throughout these events Rip takes Coral into his confidence, driving with her to the various locales that his investigation carries him to. It is on one of these excursions that a conversation takes place between them that is often quoted by feminist critics. He says that any woman who is involved with a man should be somehow able to change size. When the man wants her quiet and unobtrusive, she should shrink to a size tiny enough to be kept in his pocket. Only when he wants her life-size for sex should he make her swell to her full proportions. Coral seems to go along with this demeaning proposition.

The complicated plot of *Dead Reckoning* takes another twist here as the long flashback ends. Rip tells the priest that he now suspects Coral of involvement in his capture by the hoods. She later confesses to killing her husband and says that Martinelli has the gun in his possession and is blackmailing her. Using an incendiary Japanese grenade given to him by McGee, Rip confronts Martinelli and Krause at the office. A shocked Rip is informed by Martinelli that Coral is actually his wife, and when Rip tosses the grenade and Krause exits through the window, Martinelli attempts to escape. Outside, he is shot by Coral, who flees in a car with Rip. She has now turned out to be just as vicious and dissembling as all the misogynistic statements earlier had threatened her to be. When Rip says she will "fry" for her crimes, she shoots at him, and they crash. Like so many other film noirs, (such as *The File on Thelma Jordan* or *The Postman Always Rings Twice*), a fatal car crash thus resolves the moral dilemmas as if in accord with Production Code demands. *Dead Reckoning* closes with Coral dying in a hospital while Rip (his arm broken) looks on. He confirms by phone that Johnny will get his Medal of Honor posthumously. Before she dies, Coral says she wishes she could be safe in Rip's pocket. He tells her that dying is like jumping from a plane door. As he whispers "Geronimo," she succumbs, and a parachute is seen dropping through an empty sky.

Brian McDonnell

**DEAR MURDERER** (Gainsborough, 1947). *Director:* Arthur Crabtree. *Producer:* Betty E. Box. *Script:* Sidney Box and Muriel Box, based on the play by St. John Clowes. *Cinematography:* Stephen Dade. *Music:* Ben Frankel. *Cast:* Eric Portman (Lee Warren), Greta Gynt (Vivien Warren), Dennis Price (Richard Fenton),

Maxwell Reed (Jimmy Martin), Jack Warner (Inspector Pembury), Hazel Court (Avis Fenton), Andrew Crawford (Sergeant Fox), Jane Hylton (Rita).

*Dear Murderer*, based on a play by St. John Clowes, is a superior example of the British film noir cycle of the middle to late 1940s. The story involves a jealous husband, Lee Warren, his unfaithful wife, Vivien, Vivien's former lover, Richard Fenton, and her current lover, Jimmy Martin. Lee, unhinged by his wife's serial infidelity, murders Fenton and then incriminates Martin. Seemingly trapped, Vivien Warren concocts her own scheme to murder her husband, retain his money, and resume her affair with Jimmy.

Although Lee Warren's ingenious murder scheme, and the subsequent game of cat and mouse with Inspector Pembury, occupies most of the screen time, Vivien Warren dominates the film. Greta Gynt, one of the few so-called wicked women of the British cinema, has one of her best roles as a selfish, sensual woman who subjugates everything, and everyone, to her carnal and materialistic desires.

Unlike most of the femmes fatales in American film noir, Vivien wants more than material comforts—she wants sexual satisfaction, a desire not met by her husband. This is indicated by a sequence of images early in the film—stranded on business in New York, Lee phones his wife in London and seeks reassurance that she still loves him. Vivien, framed by a painting of her in the background, reassures her husband. However, as she declares her love for him, the camera pulls back to show a man's hand (belonging to Jimmy Martin) sliding into the frame to gently touch her shoulder. The narcissistic implication of her painting indicates the self-centered, pleasure-seeking basis that dominates her life.

Later, after Fenton's death and Jimmy's arrest, Lee presumes that he has the upper hand in his relationship with Vivien. While her initial reaction is to leave her husband with a note addressed "Dear Murderer," she soon returns. The fact that her power over him has not diminished is expressed in the contrasting areas of light and shadow crisscrossing Vivien's face and body as she sits in front of her triple dressing room mirror. Vivien seduces her husband into believing that she is still in love with him while plotting his death so that she may resume her sexual relationship with Jimmy Martin. As Lee dies from a fatal overdose of sleeping pills, Vivien explains to him, "You've got to die so that I may go on living as I want to." Unfortunately, Inspector Pembury traps Vivien after she leaves behind an incriminating ring.

The films of the British film noir cycle differed from the Hollywood films in terms of their overall tone. While the American films were intense and melodramatic, the British films often presented their stories of betrayal and murder in a more "civilized," less intense manner. For example, when Lee returns to London from New York to murder Richard Fenton, the two men carry on a polite discourse, despite the fact that Fenton is aware that Lee knows of his affair with Vivien. Even after Lee indicates that he is going to kill Fenton, a sense of civility remains, with Lee telling Fenton that he will let him go if he can point out flaws in his plan to murder him. After Fenton fails, Lee chides him by pointing out,

"You were a bit of a failure as a lawyer. I'm glad that my life didn't depend on your arguments."

Geoff Mayer

**DECOY** (Monogram, 1946). *Director:* Jack Bernhard. *Producers:* Jack Bernhard and Bernard Brandt. *Script:* Nedrick Young, based on an original story by Stanley Rubin. *Cinematography:* L. W. O'Connell. *Music:* Edward J. Kay. *Cast:* Jean Gillie (Margot Shelby), Edward Norris (Jim Vincent), Herbert Rudley (Dr. Lloyd Craig), Robert Armstrong (Frank Olins), Sheldon Leonard (Sergeant Joseph Portugal), Marjorie Woodworth (Nurse).

British actress Jean Gillie, who was married to the director of *Decoy* Jack Bernhard, only made one more film, *The Macomber Affair* (1947), before her death of pneumonia in 1949. Gillie's first film was *While Parents Sleep* in 1935, and for the next nine years she appeared in a number of British films, largely in ingenue and lightweight romantic roles. These films did not prepare audiences for her performance as Margot Shelby, one of the toughest femmes fatales in the 1940s, in *Decoy*. This transformation preceded a similar shift when another British actress, Peggy Cummins, was cast as the killer Annie Laurie Starr in *Gun Crazy* (1950) after years of girl-next-door roles. Just as Cummins dominates Joseph Lewis's film, Gillie holds *Decoy* together with her performance, and without her it would be just another Poverty Row film saddled with an implausible plot.

*Decoy*, which reworks aspects of the Frankenstein story, begins with a doctor, Lloyd Craig, looking at his dazed face in a cheap, dirty mirror in the washroom of a roadside gas station. He finds his way back to town and to the apartment of Margot Shelby, where a killing takes place. When Sergeant Joseph Portugal enters the room, he finds Craig dead and Shelby seriously wounded. Thereafter the bulk of the film appears as a prolonged flashback as Shelby recounts the events leading up to the shooting to Portugal, whom she calls "Jojo."

Shelby's boyfriend, Frankie Olins, who stole $400,000 in a robbery, is waiting in jail on death row for killing a policeman. Shelby, desperate to find out where Olins has hidden the money, devises a plan to steal his body after he has been executed by cyanide gas and revives him with methylene blue, a powerful antidote. However, she needs a doctor to assist her, and so she seduces Doctor Lloyd Craig, and with the assistance of mobster Jim Vincent, they bring Olins back to life after stealing his body. When Olins, brought back to life by Craig, tries to kiss Shelby, Vincent kills him, and the trio, Shelby, Craig, and Vincent, set out to find the money that is supposedly buried a couple of hundred miles away. However, greed and a desire to inflict pain motivates Shelby into murdering Vincent by running over him in her car when he stops to change a tire and then, while laughing hysterically, shooting Craig after she has recovered the box with the money inside. The flashback ends with the revelation that Olins only left one dollar in the box. Realizing that Shelby may double-cross him, he buried the money where no one would ever find it.

As she is about to die, Shelby invites Sergeant Portugal to bring his face down near her face. When Portugal agrees, expecting her to show some remorse, she humiliates him by calling him "Jojo" and laughing in his face. This is a relatively familiar motif in noir films in the 1940s, where the femme fatale, especially in low-budget films such as *Blonde Ice*, refuses to express any sense of remorse for her actions. Similarly, Margot Shelby in *Decoy* takes pleasure in ridiculing the representatives of patriarchy such as the police and the medical profession. Doctor Craig, who is shown with high ideals at the start of the film, allows sexual desire and a perverted sense of love to bring him down, even though the film provides him with a good woman, his nurse, to remind him of his duties. The focus within the film on his inner torment is commensurate with the pleasure it takes in emphasizing Shelby's destructive behavior.

Geoff Mayer

**DESPERATE** (RKO, 1947). *Director:* Anthony Mann. *Producer:* Michel Kraike. *Script:* Harry Essex. *Cinematography:* George E. Diskant. *Music:* Paul Sawtell. *Cast:* Steve Brodie (Steve Randall), Audrey Long (Anne Randall), Raymond Burr (Walt Radak), Douglas Fowley (Pete), Jason Robards (Ferrari).

Although a less unreservedly successful piece than his better-known works *Raw Deal* (1948) and *T-Men* (1948), Anthony Mann's earliest film noir *Desperate* shows some of the themes, visual style, and the exploitation of violence found in his later films. Fear, despair, suffering, an unforgiving materialistic social environment, and graphic brutality (which are all typical features of Mann's films) take center stage here. The desperation highlighted by the title increases steadily for the film's protagonist as the story advances. Steve Randall, like many other noir heroes of the late 1940s, is a returned World War II veteran scraping together a living for himself and his wife. Having learned mechanical skills in the army, he drives an ex-army truck in a one-man business operation. Unbeknownst to him, Anne is pregnant with their first child. The film's opening scenes stress their happiness despite a shortage of funds, but this early equilibrium is shattered by a phone call from an old acquaintance, Walt Radak, offering some welcome cash for a one-off nighttime job. The smooth progress of Steve's life is derailed when this job turns out to be a robbery and the unsuspecting trucker is caught up in the resulting death of a police officer, which in turn leads to his flight from imminent arrest. Just as dangerously for Steve, Walt's favored kid brother is captured by the police and faces the death penalty. Walt seeks to take out his anger on both Steve and Anne.

Steve's unselfish primary aim throughout the story is to keep his wife safe, understandable as Walt's gang has threatened her life. The biological pressure of his wife expecting a child exacerbates their perilous situation as a couple on the lam, running "like hunted animals." Indeed, the narrative of *Desperate* has lots of movement, the central characters traveling through the Midwest as far as Minnesota to hide out on a farm belonging to Anne's relatives. Walt is wounded in an ambush while trying to leave his city hideout in pursuit of the pair, his recuperation allowing narrative time to pass (and for Anne's pregnancy to develop). At the maternity hospital where his daughter is born, Steve is lectured by an insurance salesman about the risks inherent in life. In a characteristically noir move of desperation, he responds by taking out a policy that will give his family money in the event of Walt's thugs killing him. Steve is later used as bait by the police after being told he has been cleared by the district attorney of all charges, and he ends up doing the job of the police by himself shooting down the vengeful Walt.

Mann's expressionistic visual style is evident throughout in the markedly different lighting he devises for contrasting locations: the hideouts of the criminals (shadowy, high contrast, source lit) are opposed to the bright, shadow-free lighting of Anne and Steve's home. Steve is drawn out of that haven into the nighttime world of the robbery. Low-angle shots dominate Walt's standover tactics with a swinging light bulb slapping lines of shadow onto his face during his off-screen beating of Steve, and there is even a frightening subjective shot of a broken bottle threatening Steve's face. Mann defines clearly by its rural setting and brighter lighting the different world of the farm where Steve and Anne shelter. In this atmosphere of peace and nature Anne's Czech relatives plan a "wedding" ceremony for the couple. This establishment of a lighter tone and the sense of a secure haven only creates a deeper shock when Walt and his cronies eventually come to the farm, bringing the corrupt air of the city with them. They visibly violate the innocent space, a shift in tone encapsulated in Walt's action of casually helping himself to some meat. Mann often deploys a mobile camera, no more strikingly than in the film's dramatic nighttime climax with its ticking clock, its powerful suspense, and the narrative deadline created by the kid brother's imminent hanging. There is wonderful low-angled photography of a dark stairway in the final shoot-out, in which Walt dies at midnight, the exact same moment as his brother is executed.

Brian McDonnell

**DETOUR** (PRC, 1945). *Director:* Edgar G. Ulmer. *Producers:* Leon Fromkess and Martin Mooney (associate). *Script:* Martin Goldsmith, based on his novel. *Cinematography:* Benjamin H. Kline. *Music:* Erdody. *Cast:* Tom Neal (Al Roberts), Ann Savage (Vera), Claudia Drake (Sue), Edmund MacDonald (Charles Haskell), Tim Ryan (Diner Proprietor), Esther Howard (Waitress).

*Detour* is often presented as the quintessential low-budget noir film, and its reputation has grown steadily in the past four decades. This is deserved. However, its reputation as an extremely low budget film is based on false information, with many accounts inflating its achievements by claiming that the entire budget was only $30,000 with a six-day shooting schedule. In reality, the film was budgeted at $89,000, and it finally cost $117,000, which was more than four times the usual budget for a film produced by PRC, one of the poorest studios in Hollywood in the 1940s. Unfortunately, director Edgar Ulmer received very little money for his

*Detour* (1945). Directed by Edgar G. Ulmer. Shown: Tom Neal (as Al Roberts), Ann Savage (as Vera). PRC/Photofest.

film as Lew Landers, the initial director who left the project just before filming commenced, received most of the director's fee.

*Detour,* however, could have been a much different film. After author Martin Goldsmith sold the film rights to producer Leon Fromkess, John Garfield expressed interest in the film as a project that Warner Bros. could produce for him at the studio. Fromkess, however, refused Warner's offer of $25,000, and this was fortunate as no major Hollywood studio in the 1940s would have produced anything like the film that emerged from PRC. Also, Warner's would not have used Edgar Ulmer or actress Ann Savage, and a major studio would be most unlikely to have filmed Ulmer's ending.

Ulmer's most significant contribution to *Detour* was to conceive the film in terms of an internalized nightmare as experienced by the main protagonist, Al Roberts. In effect, the film takes place in Robert's head, and his narration resembles a radio drama, with many plot details explained via his voice-over. At times he even addresses the audience and tells them what they may be thinking of him, while at other moments he tries to strip away his nightmare from what normally happens in fiction—"If this were fiction," he explains, "I would fall in love with Vera, marry her, and make a respectable woman of her. Or else she'd make some supreme class-A sacrifice for me and die."

The film begins with Al Roberts sitting in a roadside diner outside Reno, wallowing in his self-pity. As the lighting on his face changes, the camera moves to an extreme close-up as Al begins his narration. He recalls a happier time in New York, where he worked as a piano player with his singer girlfriend, Sue, in a Manhattan nightclub. While Al grumbles about his lousy luck playing in a third-rate nightclub, he is moderately content until Sue rejects his offer of marriage and tells him that she is moving to Los Angeles to seek work in Hollywood. After she leaves, Al decides to hitchhike across America to join her on the West Coast. In Arizona, however, bookmaker Charles Haskell picks him up on his way to a race meeting in Los Angeles. During the journey Haskell dies of a heart attack, and Al panics when, after opening the car door, Haskell falls out and hits his head on a rock.

This is a seminal moment in the film, and Al makes his first major mistake when he assumes Haskell's identity, takes his car and money, and hides his body under a bush near the roadside. His second major mistake occurs after crossing the border into California when he picks up Vera. At a time when he should remain as anonymous as possible, this action proves to be disastrous, leading eventually to Vera's death and Al's arrest.

Vera, after a few quiet moments in the car, transforms into one of cinema's most aggressive characters as she takes control of his life—she is able to blackmail him by pointing out that she knows that Al killed Haskell as she traveled through Louisiana with him and she recognized his car. Al also recalls the deep scars on Haskell's wrist, a legacy of her response when he made sexual advances to her.

The conflict between Al and Vera intensifies during their journey to the West Coast as Vera's interest in Al shifts between tormenting him and, when aroused, expressing a predatory sexual interest. Mostly, however, her attitude is one of domination and harassment as she tells him that she knows "a wrong guy when I see one," "What'd you do, kiss [Haskell] with a wrench," "You've got all the earmarks of a cheap crook," and "Shut up! You're a cheap crook and you killed him. For two cents I'd change my mind and turn you in. I don't like you!" Her abuse is frequent and vicious. Her alternative approach, her sexual invitations to Al, gained the attention of the Production Code Authority, who forced Ulmer to rewrite some of the dialogue so as to render Vera's voracious sexual appetite, which erupts when alone with Al in a succession of cheap boarding house rooms, less obvious.

The film's sparse production values, where the trip west is presented via rear-projection scenes, seems ideal for such a tawdry couple. Ulmer's compositions, his use of shadow, fog, and street signs, combine to heighten the sense that the film is one prolonged surreal nightmare, a perception that is reinforced by the bizarre climax. Vera, drunk and bitter following Al's rejection of her offer of sex, grabs the phone and runs into the bedroom, threatening to call the police. Al, in an attempt to stop her, grabs the long phone cord, which Vera has wrapped around her neck, and accidentally strangles her. The film returns to the Nevada diner of the opening scene and concludes by providing a seeming conflict between what Al is saying and what is shown on the screen. While his narration predicts that someday, "a car will stop to pick me up. . . . Yes, fate, or some mysterious force, can put the finger on you for no good reason at all," Ulmer, to appease the Production Code Authority, shows a police car pulling alongside Roberts while he is walking along the highway as a cop takes him into custody. Hence, while the narration predicts his eventual arrest some time in the future, the film shows this happening to him after he leaves the diner.

It is not fate, or some "mysterious force," that leads to Al's downfall. He brings it on himself in the decisions he makes during his journey. However, his morbid sense of self-pity requires a scapegoat, and thus he blames his downfall on fate. This is, both thematically and aesthetically, a groundbreaking film noir.

Geoff Mayer

**DEVIL IN A BLUE DRESS** (TriStar, 1995). *Director:* Carl Franklin. *Producers:* Jesse Beaton and Gary Goetzman. *Script:* Carl Franklin, from the novel by Walter Mosley. *Cinematography:* Tak Fujimoto. *Music:* Elmer Bernstein. *Cast:* Denzel Washington (Easy Rawlins), Tom Sizemore (Dewitt Albright), Jennifer Beals (Daphne Monet), Don Cheadle (Mouse), Terry Kinney (Todd Carter), Maury Chaykin (Matthew Terell).

*Devil in a Blue Dress* marks the emergence in the neo-noir genre of stories created by black creative talents and featuring black protagonists. African American director and script writer Carl Franklin had already filmed one impressive noir story in his movie *One False Move* (1992) and, with *Devil in a Blue Dress*, he turned to the task of adapting the crime novel by Walter Mosley. Mosley had created black detective Easy Rawlins as an African American equivalent to Raymond Chandler's Philip Marlowe, setting his first crime stories back in the 1940s and filling them with the complexities, colorful language, and twists and turns of Chandler's prose. As in classical film noir, the plot of *Devil in a Blue Dress* centers on the search for a missing woman, a surface puzzle that soon reveals deeper secrets of a personal and political nature. As the earliest of a series of stories about Easy Rawlins, its subject is really the creation or formation of a detective rather than the depiction of a typical case being addressed by a seasoned investigator. The film's tone is more positive at the end than many noirs because Franklin is at pains to render favorably the postwar black community of Watts and seems nostalgic for the simpler times that prevailed before south central Los Angeles declined with the 1960s riots and the racial turmoil of 1992.

The main purpose of both novel and film is to present a dramatized image of life as it existed for American blacks in the 1940s, when society was more segregated than now. There is, throughout the film, an underlying menace that the black characters must deal with and a sense that black people must keep to their own designated areas and roles. In his voice-over narration Easy contrasts the unifying aims of World War II with the continuation of a color line in Los Angeles that cannot be crossed. The story begins with Easy being sacked from his job in an aircraft plant during the economic downturn of 1948. While drinking in a bar on Central Avenue (that lively and prosperous heart of postwar negro Los Angeles known as the "Great Black Way"), he is approached by a white man named Dewitt who is seeking help in finding Daphne Monet, the white girlfriend of a wealthy mayoral candidate called Todd Carter, and Dewitt's ostensible employer. Daphne apparently has a taste for the company of black men, and Dewitt needs a local man to unobtrusively scout for information on her. This commission leads Easy into a morass of scandal, sexual depravity, and civic chicanery that is as tangled and confusing as anything in Chandler yarns such as *The Big Sleep*. He encounters racism and thuggery from the police and from prejudiced college kids, he uncovers the pedophilia of a second mayoral candidate named Terell, and he brings to light blackmail schemes and murders arising out of hysterical concerns with miscegenation.

Easy suspects Daphne may have a black boyfriend, Frank, who is a dangerous criminal adept with a knife. Indeed, a number of people die violently in the film, often at the hands of Mouse, Easy's psychopathic friend from Louisiana played with charismatic verve by Don Cheadle. Chief among many breathless plot revelations is Daphne's confession (reminiscent of *Chinatown*) that Frank is actually not her lover but her brother. She is the daughter of a Creole, and her part-black origins are being used as a way of damaging the mayoral aspirations of Carter. This shock admission is immediately followed by Daphne's abduction by Dewitt, who is actually acting for Terell. All the villains are killed by Easy and Mouse in a climactic shoot-out in a remote cabin, after which they rescue Daphne. She is confident Carter will now take her back, but the man reluctantly breaks up with her in order to resume his political ambitions without Daphne's racially mixed status causing public disapproval. After his completed quest, Easy retreats to his pride and joy: a small bungalow in Watts from where he observes approvingly his idyllic black community.

The film makes a valiant attempt to bring most of Mosley's crowded book to the screen with the side effect that there is perhaps too much expository voice-over. Denzel Washington very ably embodies the grace, self-confidence, and tenacity that make Easy Rawlins an admirable detective figure. Like Philip Marlowe, Easy lives by a code of honor in a world full of obstacles and temptations. However, it is possibly Washington's own code that leads to a key element in the novel being absent from the film version of *Devil in a Blue Dress*: its raw eroticism. Reportedly, the actor did not want any interracial love scenes in the film, and so the sexual union between Easy and Daphne that is so vividly portrayed in the book is omitted from the movie. In fact, Daphne is not much of a character at all, more a narrative necessity than a rounded individual and definitely no femme fatale. As well, the prolific violence of Mouse, true to the novel as it may be, also frees up the character of Easy from doing much of his own dirty work. He is thus able to appear more admirable and noble, as if a Mike Hammer figure has been divided into two people instead of being a complex and morally ambivalent individual. These features slightly reduce the noir quotient of this historically important film.

Brian McDonnell

**DMYTRYK, EDWARD** (1908–1999). Although Edward Dmytryk was an important director in the formative period of film noir, his political background and subsequent involvement with the House Committee on Un-American Activities has often deflected consideration of his contribution to film noir. He was born in 1908 in Grand Forks in British Columbia to Ukrainian parents, and after his mother's death, when Dmytryk was six, he accompanied his father to San Francisco. In 1923 he got a part-time job as a messenger boy at Paramount Studios while studying mathematics and physics, and he won a scholarship to the California Institute of Technology. However, after one year, he left tertiary studies to take a full-time job in Hollywood, and between 1930 and 1939, he worked as an editor. In 1935 he directed his first film, *The Hawk*, and in 1939 he became a full-time director.

From 1939 to 1943, Dmytryk directed low-budget films at Columbia and RKO. One of these films, the propaganda exploitation film *Hitler's Children* (1943), created such an impact that Dmytryk was lifted from the ranks of B directors to A productions with respectable budgets and major stars. *Hitler's Children* had a relatively small budget of $205,000 and made $3,335,000 in its first release. Based on a book by Gregory Ziemer titled *Education for Death*, the film was supposedly a study of Nazi behavior in Germany, while in effect, it was an exploitation film that depicted the brutality inflicted on young women. In the film Bonita Granville is selected for sterilization, and she is publicly whipped by Tim Holt for defying the authorities. Both Dmytryk and screenwriter Emmet Lavary were given a $5,000 bonus because the film was so successful.

Dmytryk's adaptation of Raymond Chandler's novel *Farewell, My Lovely* is an important film with regard to the development of film noir. Made in 1944, it was renamed *Murder, My Sweet* soon after its release because audiences thought it was a musical, and not a hard-boiled detective film, due to the title and the fact that it starred ex–Warner Bros. musical star Dick Powell. Dmytryk followed with a string of commercial hits, including the John Wayne war film *Back to Bataan* (1945), a Dick Powell antifascist espionage film *Cornered* (1947), and *Till the End of Time* (1946), a sentimental story of postwar adjustment which preceded *The Best Years of Our Lives* by a few months. Dmytryk's most controversial, and possibly best, film, *Crossfire* (1947), followed. Based on Richard Brooks's novel of the killing of a homosexual, screenwriter John Paxton and Dmytryk altered the story to the brutal murder of a Jew by an anti-Semitic soldier, played by Robert Ryan. Right-wing political forces thereafter pursued Dmytryk, and he was one of the so-called Hollywood 10 brought before the House Committee on Un-American Activities. In the late 1940s he was blacklisted, and Dmytryk made three films in Britain, including the taut noir thriller *Obsession* (1949). However, it was his first British film, *So Well Remembered* (1948), scripted by John Paxton, with John Mills as a socially conscious newspaper editor who campaigns for the rights of local mill workers, that caused the most trouble. Although this earnest film was not a Communist tract but a faithful adaptation of James Hilton's novel, it attracted the attention of Hedda Hopper, the right-wing gossip columnist, and she attacked Dmytryk in print for a number of years.

Dmytryk returned to the United States in 1951 and again appeared before the House Committee on Un-American Activities to name colleagues. As a result, his blacklisting was removed, and Dmytryk was hired by Stanley Kramer's company, where he directed a number of films, including the low-budget noir film *The Sniper* (1952). Gradually, Dmytryk was offered more prestigious films, and he directed a succession of large-budget studio films in the 1950s and 1960s. Some, including the westerns *Broken Lance* (1954) and, especially, *Warlock* (1959), were very good. Others, such as *Where Love Has Gone* (1964) and *The Carpetbaggers* (1964), both based on novels by Harold Robbins, were banal films that failed to rise above their source material. When film projects dried up in the early 1970s, Dmytryk worked in universities for the rest of his life, first at the University of Texas at Austin and then at the University of Southern California.

**Selected Noir Films:** *Murder, My Sweet* (1944), *Cornered* (1945), *Crossfire* (1947), *Obsession* (1949), *The Sniper* (1952), *Warlock* (1959), *Walk on the Wild Side* (1962).

Geoff Mayer

**D.O.A.** (United Artists, 1950). *Director:* Rudolph Maté. *Producers:* Leo C. Popkin, Harry M. Popkin (executive), and Joseph H. Nadel (associate). *Script:* Russell Rouse and Clarence Greene. *Cinematography:* Ernest Lazlo. *Music:* Dimitri Tiomkin. *Cast:* Edmond O'Brien (Frank Bigelow), Pamela Britton (Paula Gibson), Luther Adler (Majak), Beverly Campbell (Miss Foster), Lynn Baggett (Mrs. Philips), William Ching (Halliday), Henry Hart (Stanley Philips), Neville Brand (Chester), Laurette Luez (Marla Rakubian), Larry Dobkin (Dr. Schaefer), Frank Jaquet (Dr. Matson), Frank Gerstle (Dr. MacDonald).

*Double Indemnity* (1944) was narrated by a dying man. *Sunset Boulevard*, which was released just after *D.O.A.* in 1950, was narrated by a dead man. *D.O.A.* went one step further—the central protagonist, Frank Bigelow, was murdered, but still alive, while he tries to find the man who killed him. He then, 48 hours after he was poisoned, dies on the floor of the homicide division of a precinct of the Los Angeles Police Department.

Loosely inspired by Robert Siodmak's 1931 German film *Der Mann, Der Seinen Mörder Sucht*, *D.O.A.* begins in a striking fashion as Frank Bigelow strides into a large building to the homicide division of the Los Angeles Police Department. Filmed with alternating point-of-view shots, Bigelow's walk, accompanied by one of Dimitri Tiomkin's most emphatic scores, is shown during the film's credit sequence. The sequence ends in a dramatic fashion, with Bigelow telling the police captain that he wants to report a murder—his own.

The film begins in Banning, a small town in California, where Bigelow, an accountant, wants to go to San Francisco for a holiday and, in effect, get away from the attentions of his personal secretary, and fiancée, Paula Gibson. In San Francisco he gets caught up with a wild bunch of promiscuous conventioneers, and while Frank is initially eager to join in their drinking and, possibly, the promise of illicit sex, he soon tires of their rowdy behavior at a hopped up waterfront nightclub called The Fisherman. When the wife of one of the conventioneers makes advances toward him, he moves down the bar and sits with a blonde. Unfortunately, he leaves his drink behind, and a mysterious man exchanges Frank's bourbon for a concoction that includes luminous toxin, a fatal poison that eventually closes down the body.

Frank wakes up the next morning feeling queasy, and after visiting a doctor, he learns that he has been fatally poisoned. Dr. Matson delivers the news: "I don't think you understand, Bigelow. You've been murdered." Frank panics and, in a visually stunning sequence, runs through the streets of San Francisco at midday as he tries to escape his fate while not knowing where he is going or what he is going to do. Finally, he stops to rest by a newsstand and, with sadness, realizes that while others are getting on with their lives, he will soon die. Thus he stands in the sun and watches a little girl playing with a ball while a young woman waves to her boyfriend.

Frank decides that in the time available to him before he dies, he will find out who poisoned him, and why. His investigation takes him to Los Angeles and brings him into contact with the gangster Majak and a convoluted plot involving the importation of the mineral iridium. However, Bigelow learns that the real reason he was poisoned was more basic. It involves a love affair between an unfaithful wife (Mrs. Philips) and one of her husband's employees (Halliday). When Bigelow notarized a bill of sale for the iridium, he, in effect, signed his death warrant as this action had the potential to expose the fact that Philips's alleged suicide was, in effect, murder committed by Halliday. Bigelow finally corners Halliday and, after Halliday fires at him, empties his gun into the killer.

D.O.A. is noteworthy not because of its complicated plot but because of the ability of the film, directed by European Rudolph Maté, who was the cinematographer on Carl Dreyer's *The Passion of Joan of Arc* (1928) and *Vampyr* (1932), to dramatize the existential premise of a man alive but dead, while others around, except his fiancée Paula Gibson, care little whether he lives or dies. Maté chooses his outdoor locations in the film very carefully to emphasize the fact that Bigelow is going to die, and he is continually overwhelmed by the settings. The film's climax, for example, is filmed in the labyrinth passageways of the atmospheric Bradbury Building in Los Angeles.

D.O.A. explores, to some degree, the familiar noir motif that shows the deadly consequences when the male libido strays from its secure environment (see, e.g., *Out of the Past* [1947], *The Big Clock* [1948], and *The File on Thelma Jordan* [1950]). However, the film is more intent on dramatizing its fatalistic basis. After recounting his tale of murder and betrayal to the police, Bigelow dies on the floor of the police station. When a policeman asks the captain what he should do, the captain, resigned to the fact that he cannot help Bigelow, tells him to stamp the file "Dead on Arrival." Bigelow's death, as the film emphasizes, was the result of an arbitrary world where simply being in the wrong place at the wrong time can lead to death. Bigelow did not deserve to die, as he points out to Paula: "All I did was notarize one little paper—one paper out of hundreds."

*D.O.A.* was remade in Australia in 1970 as *Color Me Dead* with American actors—Tom Tryon as Frank Bigelow, Carolyn Jones as Paula Gibson, and Rick Jason as the gangster Bradley Taylor (Majak in the 1950 film). It was remade again, in Hollywood, in 1988, with Dennis Quaid and Meg Ryan.

Geoff Mayer

**DOUBLE INDEMNITY** (Paramount, 1944). *Director/Producer:* Billy Wilder. *Script:* Billy Wilder and Raymond Chandler, from a novel by James M. Cain. *Cinematography:* John F. Seitz. *Music:* Miklos Rozsa. *Cast:* Fred MacMurray (Walter Neff), Barbara Stanwyck (Phyllis Dietrichson), Edward G. Robinson (Barton Keyes), Jean Heather (Lola Dietrichson), Tom Powers (Mr. Dietrichson), Byron Barr (Nino Zachette), Porter Hall (Mr. Jackson).

*Double Indemnity* (1944). Directed by Billy Wilder. Shown from left: Barbara Stanwyck (as Phyllis Dietrichson) and Fred MacMurray (as Walter Neff). Paramount Pictures/ Photofest.

*Double Indemnity* is highly impressive in its own right and stands up today as a very good film. It is one of the best films of the 1940s in any genre and represents the accomplished ensemble work of many people, especially director and co-script-writer Billy Wilder, co-scriptwriter Raymond Chandler, novelist James M. Cain, cinematographer John F. Seitz, and actors Fred MacMurray, Barbara Stanwyck, and Edward G. Robinson. In addition, it is a leading and central example of the film noir genre, being the most influential of all the early films in the classical cycle and also having a major impact on the subject matter, narration, and visual style of many of the noir films that followed its appearance in 1944. Perhaps only *Out of the Past* holds a comparable position of eminence as the quintessential film noir.

The original plot of the novel *Double Indemnity* is typical of James M. Cain's fiction. As in his other famous work *The Postman Always Rings Twice*, it is the story of a sexual triangle in which a seductive woman who is married to a dull, older man entices a younger man into both an illicit affair and a plot to kill off the husband. After the book's appearance in 1935, several film studios were interested in it, but the newly formed Breen Office banned any adaptation as being unacceptable under the Production Code. It was not until World War II had toughened American sensibilities sufficiently that Joe Breen even contemplated a film version. By that time Cain himself had left Hollywood, and producer/director Billy Wilder hired crime novelist Raymond Chandler to cowrite the script with him. Chandler (and other studio scenarists along with him) was used to writing about crime from the viewpoint of a detective or a police officer, but Cain tended to write from the point of view of the criminal perpetrators themselves. In making murderers the central characters, with all that meant about audience sympathy, *Double Indemnity* as a large-budget A feature was to prove revolutionary. The film's script writers retained much of Cain's story (while altering character names), but Chandler did introduce a flashback narration structure whereas Cain's novel had been chronological, and the novel's ending was changed to one where the murderers kill each other so that Breen's demands for justice could be met. The resulting film was to prove a sensational watershed.

Narrator Walter Neff is a smart, cocky, and overconfident insurance salesman full of repartee. As played by Fred MacMurray, who was cast against type, he conceals moral weakness under a veneer of snappy one-liners. When he meets Phyllis Dietrichson during a routine job in the Hollywood Hills, he becomes obsessed, seduced, and finally, doomed. She is (un)dressed to kill, and they banter suggestively in the style of a 1930s screwball comedy. But the film soon moves into darker territory. She wants her husband dead, preferably with a big cash payout. Walter, who has himself come to fantasize about ways of bilking his insurance company bosses, is the perfect fall guy to help implement Phyllis's scheme. They set up a way of faking the husband's death, choosing a train accident since the infrequency of such fatalities carries a multiple payout: the *double indemnity* of the title. The only apparent fly in the ointment is one of Walter's colleagues, a relentless claims investigator named Barton Keyes. The superb characterization achieved by Edward G. Robinson in this part makes Keyes much more than just a supporting role. He has a nose for fraud and is soon suspicious of the Dietrichson death. Something of a misogynist, he quickly has Phyllis in his sights but is so admiring of Walter that he never suspects his friend. The seemingly perfect crime begins to unravel when Walter learns some disturbing details about Phyllis (such as the possibility that she also murdered her husband's first wife) from her daughter-in-law Lola, with whom he has a few casual dates. Lola's regular boyfriend, Nino, is sexually involved with Phyllis, and Walter realizes he may just be one of a long line of fall guys as she moves like a black widow spider through her succession of hapless mates. At a final rendezvous in the dim interior of Phyllis's Spanish-style home, the two finally come clean about their respective motives, and Walter shoots her dead before staggering, seriously wounded, back to his office.

He is planning to leave a confession for Keyes before escaping to Mexico, and this desire to speak out produces the particular narrative structure of *Double Indemnity,* which was to prove so influential on the genre. Walter dictates his story into a recording machine, and the film actually opens with his arrival at the insurance company to carry this plan out. Once he begins his recounting of the conspiracy, there begins a series of flashbacks punctuated by brief returns to the office, where the bloodstains of his wounds steadily spread. The voice-over narration also allows Chandler to adapt and add to Cain's prose with a number of telling metaphorical phrases that, along with the sexual badinage, give a rich texture to the film's dialogue. Wilder's night-for-night shooting of the railway tracks and of the perfumed Los Angeles suburban streets works along with the expressive interior scenes to create a classic noir setting. Different audience members will be divided about which of the two protagonists they sympathize with: Walter or Phyllis? However, the nuances and complexities of scenes such as their late-night encounter in Walter's Spartan apartment will make the choice a difficult one.

Brian McDonnell

**DURYEA, DAN** (1907–1968). With his slicked-back hair, sharp features, rakish air, and wolfish grin, Duryea was one of the most distinctive figures in film noir. He seldom played an unalloyed hero, more commonly cast as the villain, or at least a fast-talking, self-serving opportunist who was out for himself. Frequently playing intense, bad-tempered characters, Duryea became known for his portrayal of cads who were not above actually striking women. Born in New York State, Dan Duryea studied at Cornell University, where he began acting in amateur theater. After leaving college, he worked in the field of advertising sales until a mild heart attack at the age of 27 encouraged his shift from that quite stressful occupation into acting. He found immediate success, and it was his role in the Lillian Hellman play *The Little Foxes* on Broadway that first brought him to Hollywood to recreate the role on film in 1941. Within four years Duryea had made three film noirs with Fritz Lang: *Ministry of Fear* (1944), *The Woman in the Window* (1944), and *Scarlet Street*

(1945). He also appeared opposite Erich von Stroheim in Anthony Mann's *The Great Flamarion* in the middle of the three Lang projects. Of particular note from these early noirs is Duryea's performance as the languorous conman Johnny, who is Joan Bennett's boyfriend in *Scarlet Street*. The oily Johnny is one of his best characterizations: he is plainly the pimp of Bennett's character Kitty, but the Production Code led to their relationship being slightly sanitized.

In 1946 *Black Angel* gave Duryea a lead role as Martin Blair, an alcoholic husband searching for his wife's killer only to eventually discover it is himself. Martin is an especially noir creation: a man suffering from amnesia who lives out a nightmare of fate and entrapment. Here Duryea is both villain and hero, an edgy mixture hinted at in the title *Black Angel*. Duryea made three film noirs in 1949: *Manhandled, Criss Cross,* and *Too Late for Tears*. In all three he plays a heavy and is frequently malicious, but he is particularly villainous as the vicious Slim Dundee in *Criss Cross*. In a paroxysm of vengeance in the climax of the film, he guns down the two leads, Yvonne de Carlo and Burt Lancaster, before being apprehended by the police. Duryea made a TV series in 1953–1954 called *China Smith,* in which he played a world-weary American detective in Singapore. In 1954 a modestly budgeted film noir called *World for Ransom* was spun off this series by Robert Aldrich, and Duryea played the lead character, a version of China Smith conveniently renamed Mike Callahan. The plot involved nuclear secrets in a way that anticipates the concerns of *Kiss Me Deadly*. Rather surprisingly, in the late noir *Storm Fear* (1956), Duryea had a complex, unusually sympathetic role as a pensive writer beset by circumstances and a criminal brother.

**Selected Noir Films:** *Ministry of Fear* (1944), *The Woman in the Window* (1944), *The Great Flamarion* (1945), *Lady on a Train* (1945), *Scarlet Street* (1945), *Black Angel* (1946), *Larceny* (1948), *Criss Cross* (1949), *Manhandled* (1949), *Too Late for Tears* (1949), *Johnny Stool Pigeon* (1949), *One Way Street* (1950), *The Underworld Story* (1950), *World for Ransom* (1954), *Storm Fear* (1956), *The Burglar* (1957).

Brian McDonnell

**FALLEN ANGEL** (Twentieth Century Fox, 1945). *Director/Producer:* Otto Preminger. *Script:* Harry Kleiner, from the novel by Marty Holland. *Cinematography:* Joseph La Shelle. *Music:* David Raksin. *Cast:* Alice Faye (June Mills), Dana Andrews (Eric Stanton), Linda Darnell (Stella), Charles Bickford (Mark Judd), Anne Revere (Clara Mills), John Carradine (Professor Madley), Percy Kilbride (Pop).

Made very early in the classical film noir cycle in 1945 and employing many of the Twentieth Century Fox team who had made *Laura* the previous year (Preminger, LaShelle, Raksin, Andrews), *Fallen Angel* is an intriguing style piece but overall not quite as satisfying as the earlier Gene Tierney classic. The story sets up a typical noir triangle consisting of Stella, a dark, sensual, seductive, independent woman; June, a blonde, domesticated, sexually inexperienced woman; and Eric, the morally ambiguous man who has relationships with both of them. Hovering around these three central figures are lesser characters, especially other men who are drawn to Stella's sexual glow and who may be responsible for her murder. While the film builds up an interesting milieu whose atmosphere is well conveyed by Preminger's direction and LaShelle's photography, the resolution of the plot is hurried, schematic, and unconvincing.

Like many another noir drifter, Eric alights by chance from a bus in a small coastal Californian town and becomes caught up in the complex dynamics of a group of townsfolk. At a diner that features as a key location throughout the film, he meets waitress Stella, her adoring boss Pop, and a brooding, phlegmatic ex-cop named Judd. Stella makes a great first entrance in the sultry form of Linda

*Fallen Angel* (1945). Directed by Otto Preminger. Shown from left: Dana Andrews (as Eric Stanton), Percy Kilbride (as Pop), and Linda Darnell (as Stella). 20th Century Fox/Photofest.

Darnell, who shows off a sexy pair of legs as she rubs a sore ankle. By chance, Eric also meets a couple of other grifters who are in town running a scam involving a fraudulent spiritualism act. By teaming up with this pair of likeable scoundrels, he comes into contact with June, a somewhat wealthy spinster who lives with a sister, also unmarried. Their substantial and decorous brightly lit home represents ideologically the polar opposite of the shadowy, raffish diner, which is redolent of obsessive desires. Eric soon wants to both satisfy his sexual needs with Stella and work on convincing June to marry him so that he can get at her substantial bank account. His scheming is put in jeopardy when the film's main object of desire, Stella, is brutally murdered, and Eric, along with other men who have romanced her, becomes a suspect. In good noir tradition he must become a quasi-detective himself to clear his name.

Eric is the "fallen angel" of the title, caught between the two women: one depicted as an angel living in the world of daylight and playing the church organ, the other as a devil, whose natural setting is night. As in 1987's *Fatal Attraction*, the plot kills off the so-called bad, independent woman (who is actually pleasant and moral in her own way) and leaves Eric with the rather boring but well-meaning June. He woos the latter by telling her she is "scared to live" and educating her in the fun of dancing, drinking, and movies. This project culminates with his cynical marriage to her. He even connives to avoid consummating the union by absenting himself from the house on their wedding night, drinking, then falling asleep. It is on the morning after that he discovers Stella is dead and that vicious cop Judd is on his tail. He and June flee to San Francisco, where Eric has a change of heart and abandons his plan to gyp June of her funds. For once, June is seen in a less salubrious setting in their tawdry hotel room, and they are even shown in bed together.

However, the film now rushes rather implausibly to its conclusion when Eric returns to the small-town diner and confronts Judd. Eric, an ex-journalist, has apparently discovered secrets about Judd's past in New York and turns the tables on his former nemesis. With police waiting outside, Judd confesses to Stella's killing, which was caused by his obsessive jealousy. There is a struggle over a gun, a cop appears, and Judd is led away to the strains of the romantic tune associated with Stella. June is waiting in the car outside, and when she asks the now redeemed Eric where he wants to go, he replies, "Home." This is the very last word of *Fallen Angel* and encapsulates the conservative ideology that finally overcomes the film's other noir aspects.

Brian McDonnell

**THE FALLEN SPARROW** (RKO, 1943). *Director:* Richard Wallace. *Producer:* Robert Fellows. *Script:* Warren Duff, based on the novel by Dorothy Hughes. *Cinematography:* Nicholas Musuraca. *Music:* Roy Webb. *Cast:* John Garfield (John "Kit" McKittrick), Maureen O'Hara (Toni Donne), Walter Slezak (Dr. Christian Skaas), Patricia Morison (Barby Taviton), Martha O'Driscoll (Whitney Parker), Bruce Edwards (Ab Parker), John Banner (Anton), John Miljan (Inspector Tobin), Hugh Beaumont (Otto Skaas).

After the United States declared war on Japan, following the December 7, 1941, attack on Pearl Harbor, there were relatively few noir films produced during 1942 and 1943. There was a sense that noir-influenced films, with their divisive attributes and inbuilt pessimistic view of the human condition, were not appropriate at a time when the nation was fighting for its survival. Unity, not disunity, was the desired state, and it was not until 1944 and 1945 that a regular production of such films commenced.

Within this context *The Fallen Sparrow* is a remarkable film as it was the first Hollywood film released during World War II to portray a psychologically scarred American who, as a result of the war (the Spanish Civil War), found it difficult to adjust to daily life and resume relationships with lovers and friends. Kit McKittrick returns to New York after suffering physical and emotional torture in a Spanish prison for the past two years. He is emotionally vulnerable, and the film constantly emphases his fragile condition. For example, as he travels by train to New York after treatment in Arizona, he takes out a newspaper and reads of the death of a close friend, Louie Lepitino. As the train passes through a tunnel, his troubled face is reflected in the train window, and his voice is heard on the sound track:

> Hide! Go on. Let's have it! Can you go through with it?
> Have you got the guts for it? Can you go through with it? Have they made you yellow?

Later, he relives the experiences of the Spanish prison when he describes the effect it had on him to Ab Parker, a friend:

> It was as if somebody stuffed you in the bottle and put the cork in. It was dark and hot [the camera slowly moves into a tight close-up of Kit's face to reveal that he is sweating]. You heard the drag of that foot, you tried to hide against the wall or crawl into a hole, only there wasn't a hole to crawl into. You try to hide in the corner and feel like a dog that's been whipped and cupped. I couldn't take it anymore.

Kit's inner turmoil continues in New York as he tries to find out what really happened to his friend Louie Lepitino while Nazis, disguised as refugees, pressure him to reveal the whereabouts of the standard of his Spanish regiment. On occasions, while alone in his apartment, he hears the dragging noise made by the man who tortured him in Spain.

After Ab Parker is murdered, Kit falls in love with Toni Donne, a woman who, she claims, is forced to work with the Nazis in New York as they have control of her three-year-old daughter back in Germany. Finally, Donne is shown to be a liar and spy after she tries to lure Kit to his death at the film's climax. However, *The Fallen Sparrow*, which is closely based on Dorothy Hughes's 1942 novel, shows Kit overcoming his torment at the end when he summons up sufficient strength to defeat the malevolent Dr. Skaas, the man who tortured him in Spain. This victory is not significant merely as another example of the hero defeating the villain but more as victory over self-doubt and internal divisions. Hence *The Fallen Sparrow*, with its the internalization of the plot and its emphasis on emotionally divided characters, a characteristic of noir films after 1945, is a noir film for most of its length. The ending, however, with its hero who sacrifices the woman he loves because she is a spy, functions as propaganda that, in 1943, was entirely appropriate.

Geoff Mayer

**FARROW, JOHN** (1904–1963). A tough, no-nonsense director, John Villiers Farrow was born in Sydney and educated in Australia and the United Kingdom before entering the Royal Naval Academy, where he earned an officer's commission. After a brief period as a first mate on various cargo ships, Farrow fought with the U.S. Marine Corps in Latin America. He arrived in Hollywood in the late

1920s, and his first screen credit was for coauthoring titles for the 1927 silent film *White Gold*. Farrow worked as a screenwriter in the 1920s and early 1930s, and he also directed two short films in 1934. In 1936 he was removed as director from his first feature film, *Tarzan Escapes*, due to censorship problems concerning the brief costume worn by the film's costar, Maureen O'Sullivan. Sullivan married Farrow in 1936, and they had seven children, including Mia Farrow.

Farrow left MGM for Warner Bros. in 1937, where he directed seven films over the next two years before moving on to RKO for a series of films including *Five Came Back* (1939), a taut melodrama written by Dalton Trumbo, Jerry Cady, and Nathanael West concerning the fate of survivors of a plane crash in a South American jungle. When the plane is reconstructed, there is space for only five passengers, and the dramatic tension emanates from the selection of those who will get a place on the plane and those left behind to die. Farrow directed a remake, *Back from Eternity*, in 1956.

Farrow served with the Royal Canadian Navy in 1940 and 1941 until he contracted a severe case of typhus. He returned to Hollywood and made *Wake Island* for Paramount, a timely propaganda film that showed the heroic, but ultimately doomed, defense of a small Pacific Island by a combination of civilians and American marines after the Japanese attack on Pearl Harbor. Farrow won the New York Film Critics Circle Award for best direction and, a first for an Australian, he received an Academy Award nomination in 1943 for best director for *Wake Island*. After *Commandos Strike at Dawn* for Columbia, a war film set in Norway, Farrow returned to Paramount for the rest of the decade, where he directed a diverse range of films. This included the popular Alan Ladd vehicles, such as *China* (1943) and *Calcutta* (1947); the propaganda film *The Hitler Gang* (1944); nautical features (*Two Years before the Mast* [1946]); aerial films, such as *Blaze of Noon* (1947); musicals (*Red Hot and Blue* [1949]); and westerns (*California* [1946], *Copper Canyon* [1950]). There was also a strong cycle of noir films, such as *The Big Clock* (1948) and *The Night Has a Thousand Eyes* (1948), which he made at Paramount before leaving the studio, after which he directed *Where Danger Lives* (1950) and *His Kind of Woman* (1951) for the Howard Hughes–controlled RKO studio and *The Unholy Wife* (1957) for Universal. *Where Danger Lives*, his most bizarre noir film, is a harrowing depiction of a young doctor, played by Robert Mitchum, who suffers headaches and intermittent paralysis due to concussion as he and femme fatale Faith Domergue try to reach the Mexican border ahead of the police.

The remainder of Farrow's output in the 1950s, with the exception of the John Wayne western *Hondo* (1953) and *A Bullet Is Waiting* (1954), is less distinguished. Farrow won an Academy Award for best screenplay for *Around the World in Eighty Days* (1956), which was cowritten with S. J. Perelman and James Poe, and he finished his career in 1962 directing episodes of the television series *Empire*. Farrow converted to Roman Catholicism and wrote a number of religious books before dying of a heart attack in Beverly Hills on January 28, 1963.

**Selected Noir Films:** *The Big Clock* (1948), *The Night Has a Thousand Eyes* (1948), *Alias Nick Beal* (1949), *Where Danger Lives* (1950), *His Kind of Woman* (1951), *The Unholy Wife* (1957).

Geoff Mayer

**FEAR IN THE NIGHT** (Paramount, 1947). *Director:* Maxwell Shane. *Producers:* William H. Pine, William C. Thomas, and L. B. Merman (associate). *Script:* Maxwell Shane, based on the William Irish (Cornell Woolrich) short story "And So to Death," which was first published in *Argosy* in 1941 and reprinted as "Nightmare" in 1943 in the Irish (Woolrich) omnibus *I Wouldn't Be in Your Shoes. Cinematography:* Jack Greenhalgh. *Music:* Rudy Schrager. *Cast:* Paul Kelly (Cliff Herlihy), DeForest Kelley (Vince Grayson), Ann Doran (Lil Herlihy), Kay Scott (Betty Winters), Charles Victor (Captain Warner), Robert Emmett Keane (Lewis Belnap), Jeff York (Deputy Torrence), John Harmon (Mr. Bilyou).

Some films use their source material merely as a pretext to move in a radically different direction. Not so *Fear in the Night*, which is dominated by Cornell Woolrich's distinctive worldview. The film is a literal rendering of Woolrich's 1941 short story "And So to Death," which was reprinted in 1943 as "Nightmare," and it encapsulates Woolrich's paranoid perspective on human existence. Just as his stories are permeated by coincidences and a constant blurring between reality and the supernatural, *Fear in the Night* jettisons the normal Hollywood emphasis on narrative coherence and plausibility.

Its basic premise, concerning a man waking up fearing that he may have killed someone during the night, was not new as Woolrich had used it in his 1940 short story "C-Jag," which was filmed by Monogram in 1947 as *Fall Guy. Fear in the Night* is a better film, and although it was produced by the notoriously parsimonious Pine-Thomas B picture unit at Paramount, this unit was still able to provide more resources than Poverty Row studios such as Monogram. *Fear in the Night* had a stronger cast, an excellent cinematographer, and a director, Maxwell Shane, who understood Woolrich's view of the world, and Shane was so taken with this story that he filmed it again as *Nightmare* in 1956.

This is an archetypal noir story dominated by a pervasive sense of paranoia and despair. Its protagonist, Vincent Grayson, suffering from a sense of entrapment and loss of personal control, remains in a semihysterical state for much of the film. At his lowest point, facing arrest for murder, he contemplates committing suicide in his barren hotel room. After considering cutting his wrist with a razor, he opens a window seven stories above the street and sits on the ledge. Just as he is about to plunge to his death, his brother-in-law, Detective Cliff Herlihy, pulls him back into the room.

Grayson's vulnerability stems from a surreal dream sequence at the beginning of the film that shows him struggling with a man in a mirrored room. As the other man gains the upper hand, a blonde woman hands Grayson a sharp instrument, and he stabs his opponent before losing consciousness. When he wakes up, he finds that his clothes have been torn, with a button missing from his jacket, cuts on his arm, thumbprints on his neck, and a strange key in his possession.

Grayson, who believes that he may have killed somebody during the night, begins to doubt his sanity. At first, nobody believes his story, but following a picnic with his sister Lil, her husband, Cliff Herlihy, and his girlfriend, Betty, incriminating evidence points to his involvement in the murder of Bob Clune, a young man who was having an affair with the wife of a wealthy businessman, Lewis Belnap. This follows a strange series of events following the abandonment of the picnic due to rain. Grayson, who has no knowledge of the area, starts giving specific directions to Herlihy as to the whereabouts of a large house. This continues when they discover that the house is empty, and Grayson immediately locates the house key beneath a flowerpot. Inside the house, he directs Herlihy to the mirrored room, and the policeman's suspicion that Grayson was involved in a crime is confirmed when a local cop, Deputy Torrence, enters the house and tells them that Bob Clune's body was discovered upstairs in the mirrored room while Belnap's wife was murdered in the driveway.

Although Herlihy fears that Grayson may be guilty of murder, he helps his brother-in-law and eventually discovers that Grayson was hypnotized by Belnap into committing the murder before running over his wife with his car. During the climax Grayson confronts Belnap in the mirrored room, where he again is hypnotized by Belnap and taken to a nearby lake. However, Herlihy rescues Grayson from drowning, and the police kill Belnap. This ending, however, is perfunctory, and the main interest in the film, and in Woolrich's story, is Grayson's inability to control the events going on around him, an unusual state for a conventional Hollywood hero but a representative condition of many noir protagonists. Woolrich's story posed a censorship problem for the filmmakers as Grayson did kill Clune while under the hypnotic control of Belnap. Hence the last scene shows him entering court with Betty, confident that he will be released.

Geoff Mayer

**THE FILE ON THELMA JORDAN** (a.k.a. *Thelma Jordan*; Paramount, 1949). *Director:* Robert Siodmak. *Producer:* Hal B. Wallis. *Script:* Ketti Frings. *Cinematography:* George Barnes. *Music:* Victor Young. *Cast:* Barbara Stanwyck (Thelma Jordan), Wendell Corey (Cleve Marshall), Paul Kelly (Miles Scott), Joan Tetzel (Pamela Marshall).

Robert Siodmak directed a succession of films, including *Phantom Lady, Cry of the City, The Dark Mirror, The Killers,* and *Criss Cross,* that are today considered noir classics. *The File on Thelma Jordan* is one of his lesser known noir titles, but it is still a very nicely nuanced example of film noir, in particular of that branch of the genre dealing with stories of professional men who are tempted by criminal women to stray from the path of righteousness. Andrew Spicer is particularly fulsome in his praise of the film in his book *Film Noir,* calling it Siodmak's "most subtle and intricate study of duality and obsession" and going on to write that Thelma is "intelligent and sophisticated, frustrated and scheming, but also capable of tenderness and love" (p. 119). Barbara Stanwyck is excellent in the title role, portraying a complex woman who has more depths and contradictions to her than many comparable movie villainesses. The plain-looking Wendell Corey also plays, with considerable skill, a complicated and believable figure in his role as the law enforcement official who compromises both his ethics and his wedding vows because of the blandishments of a femme fatale.

In the film's opening sequence, Thelma Jordan visits after hours the office of Assistant District Attorney Cleve Marshall, saying her house has been burglarized. It happens to be a night when he is complaining about his wife's family and hitting the bottle to drown his sorrows. Thelma finds him inebriated, and he begins behaving inappropriately, so she leaves. Cleve follows her and offers to fix her parking ticket (this being his first small act of corruption). He continues to act the obnoxious drunk and kisses her in her car. She responds and admits reluctantly, "Maybe I am a dame who wants to be picked up by someone on a binge." Soon they have clandestine meetings, and when the opportunity arises through Cleve's wife and children being away on vacation, begin an illicit affair. The most startling plot development occurs when Thelma's wealthy aunt is apparently killed by a burglar in her large, old house. This crime happens off-screen, with the perpetrator unseen, but when Thelma is charged with the murder after a new will is discovered, the audience begins to suspect that she has ulterior motives. An odd coincidence involving the brother of the district attorney means that Cleve officially takes the case for the state, and he deliberately prosecutes badly in court to maximize Thelma's chances of acquittal. This is a very noir situation as he is torn between different loyalties, and the film makes the most of his anguish during the long courtroom sequences. Throughout it all Thelma remains very poised, avoiding the witness stand. Hence Cleve cannot cross-examine her, and when the defense makes a strong closing, she is found not guilty.

Thus the film's central theme is the crossing of the boundary between respectability and criminality by a basically decent man and the moral paradoxes he works through as he tries to disentangle himself from the path he has taken. Cleve has been ripe for such an eventuality as he was generally unhappy in his life, a hardworking man fed up with his in-laws, chiding his blameless and pleasant wife, and drinking too much. Paul Kelly plays Miles Scott, Cleve's colleague and confidant who later begins to investigate his friend's probity. A past "husband" of Thelma's called Tony Laredo turns out to have been involved in the plot to kill the old lady for her jewels, and in climactic scenes, Cleve confronts the pair. He is called a "fall guy" by them, sapped, and they flee. Of course, the Production Code would not allow Thelma to evade punishment for her crime, and while they are speeding away, she has a crisis of conscience and pushes a cigarette lighter into Tony's face, causing a fatal crash. At the hospital she makes a dying confession to Miles

Scott but refuses to name the other man in her life. We are, however, left with the distinct impression that Miles knows exactly to whom she is referring.

As usual, Siodmak directs in a stylish manner, ably assisted by noted cinematographer George Barnes. He creates several atmospheric set pieces such as the darkened room where the aunt's body is found or the illumination by car headlights of Cleve and Thelma at one of their trysts. The film's closing ideological message is a cautionary one, but the compromised man lives to lead a better life. Unlike Walter Neff, who died along with Barbara Stanwyck's Phyllis in *Double Indemnity*, Cleve here survives as a sadder but wiser figure.

Brian McDonnell

**FORCE OF EVIL** (Roberts Productions, 1948). *Director:* Abraham Polonsky. *Producer:* Bob Roberts. *Script:* Abraham Polonsky and Ira Wolfert, from the novel *Tucker's People* by Ira Wolfert. *Cinematography:* George Barnes. *Music:* David Raskin. *Cast:* John Garfield (Joe Morse), Thomas Gomez (Leo Morse), Marie Windsor (Edna Tucker), Howland Chamberlin (Freddy Bauer), Roy Roberts (Ben Tucker), Beatrice Pearson (Doris Lowry).

*Force of Evil* has many of the ingredients of a standard film noir (the compromised hero, the criminal milieu, themes of betrayal and hypocrisy, shadowy locales), but director Abraham Polonsky overlays these elements with some of the trappings of an art film. These include a stylized poetic strain of dialogue, a lack of concern for audience expectations about action and character identification, a schematic narrative, and a rather abstracted take on social realism. All these make the film very unusual for the genre. It is thereby an attenuated emotional experience but still has strong aesthetic values. Examining the numbers racket, *Force of Evil* does not focus on the gang leaders as 1930s films might have, but instead, in true noir manner, concentrates on marginal figures such as the Morse brothers, who are involved with the gangsters and affected by them.

Protagonist Joe Morse (John Garfield) is the younger brother of Leo (Thomas Gomez) who has been like a parent to him. Joe has become a successful and rich lawyer after Leo financed his education. Leo is a minor banker in the numbers racket, which allows millions of people to enjoy small bets on lucky numbers. The film's first few scenes are heavy with expository dialogue explaining the workings of the racket. Joe is now the lawyer for syndicate boss Tucker and has become wealthy by compromising his ethics and his morals. Joe is a typical noir divided hero, enjoying, in a self-centered way, the trappings of wealth but with a core of goodness and humanity that prevails in the end. His budding relationship with his brother's young secretary, Doris, and her assertion of positive moral values are the chief spurs toward a change of lifestyle for Joe. When rival racketeers become violent, he tries to ease Leo out of the crossfire, but his attempts are futile, and Leo dies. In a restaurant scene (a forerunner of Michael Corleone's famous baptism of fire in *The Godfather*), Leo talks philosophically to a doomed companion of his failing heart: "You feel as though you're dying . . . here, and here. You're dying while you're breathing." Gunmen enter, and they take Leo outside to his fate. Sacrificing his own freedom, Joe then allows a police task force to overhear enough incriminating evidence to severely damage the racket and promises that he will even testify himself. Above and beyond this, he kills Tucker to avenge his brother.

The two Morse brothers are contrasted to underscore the themes of loyalty and betrayal, as when Joe makes a plea on behalf of Leo to allow him to be let in on a profitable fix for a particular numbers result. Leo is uninterested in personal gain from this tactic, which he views as qualitatively worse than being a banker for small-time punters. To Joe's chagrin, he even uses the analogy of Cain and Abel. Joe later meets Doris and talks of the hypocrisy he sees in Leo's attitude. He claims that Leo just wants to be forced into the new arrangement so it is not his own decision, as does Doris in her romantic association with him. Her goodness affects him, though, and later, Joe wants Leo out of the rackets altogether for his own safety. Doris tells Joe that she dislikes his world of "death" and urges him to give away his amoral life. This moral suasion, combined with Leo's murder, causes him to decide to help end the evil. The main female characters of *Force of Evil*, while less central to events than the men, are also conspicuously contrasted with each other. Doris represents a pure kind of virtue that survives despite the proximity of vice, while Tucker's wife, Edna (played with vampish verve, despite few scenes, by Marie Windsor), is beyond redemption.

*Force of Evil* has a distanced manner that elicits more a respectful appreciation from audiences rather than warm identification with its characters. However, throughout the film, John Garfield is excellent as Joe: fiery, charismatic, and fast talking. Polonsky, himself later blacklisted in the anti-Communist witch hunts, makes this rebellious figure highly attractive. He also creates a memorable visual style: the suspenseful final gunfight in Tucker's office occurs in near-total darkness, with the audience being unable to see who is shot. Poetic voice-over narration punctuates *Force of Evil*. When Joe abandons his syndicate office, he walks out to a bleak dawn vista of Wall Street, a barren streetscape devoid of people. And when he goes to search for Leo's body, discarded "like an old dirty rag," the voice-over is full of references to a journey down into a mythic underworld. Marvelous location shots beneath the George Washington Bridge add to the somber tone of the ending, but Doris's presence and the accompanying music make Joe's quest seem a liberating one.

Brian McDonnell

**FORD, GLENN** (1916–2006). Although Ford is best known for his westerns, such as *Texas* (1941), *The Desperadoes* (1943), *Jubal* (1956), *The Fastest Gun Alive* (1956), *3:10 to Yuma* (1957), *Cowboy* (1958), *The Sheepman* (1958), and *The Rounders* (1965), he also appeared in a number of key noir films. Unlike other cowboy stars, such as John Wayne and James Stewart, Ford's westerns often present him as a morally problematic and/or vulnerable character. These traits were particularly emphasized in his noir western *The Man from Colorado* (1948) as military hero Colonel Owen Devereaux, who had an uncontrollable desire to inflict pain on those around him, including his wife. Ford's performance in this film contained elements of his most famous role, the tormented, possibly bisexual nightclub manager Johnny Farrell in *Gilda* (1946).

Ford, the son of a Canadian railroad executive, was born in Quebec and moved to California with his parents when he was eight. He was active in theatrical productions in high school and worked as a theater manager when he was 18. From the mid-1930s until his first screen test in 1939 he performed on stage with a traveling theater company. Although his first film, *Heaven with a Barbed Wire Fence* (1939), in which Richard Conte also made his screen debut, was made at Twentieth Century Fox, Ford signed a contract with Columbia Studios, where he made most of his films in the 1940s and early 1950s. From the start Ford connected with audiences with his low-key, realist style of acting, and while he insisted that he never played anyone but himself on screen, his range was extensive.

Before entering the marines during World War II, where he served in France, Ford was busy at Columbia with starring roles in films such as *Texas, The Desperadoes*, and *Destroyer* (1943). However, it was *Gilda*, his second film after leaving the armed services, that made him a major star. For the rest of the 1940s he alternated between lightweight roles in romantic comedies, such as *The Mating of Millie* (1948) and *The Return of October* (1948), where Ford played Professor Bentley Bassett Jr., a psychologist treating a young woman who believes that her late uncle is reincarnated as a thoroughbred horse, and intense crime dramas such as *Framed* (1947) and *The Undercover Man* (1949).

Although he starred in a number of fine films, such as *The Big Heat* (1953) and *Human Desire* (1954), Ford's career briefly faltered in the early 1950s as some of these films were not successful at the box office. However, this changed quickly after he was cast in *Blackboard Jungle* (1955), followed by *Trial* (1955), *The Teahouse of the August Moon* (1956), *3.10 to Yuma, The Sheepman*, and *The Gazebo* (1959). In 1958 he was voted the number one male box office attraction. After the relatively disappointing box office returns for Frank Capra's *Pocketful of Miracles* (1961), which was a remake of Capra's 1993 film *Lady for a Day*, Ford's status gradually diminished in the 1960s, although he still commanded lead roles in a number of major productions, including Blake Edwards's *Experiment in Terror* (1962), *The Rounders*, and his final noir film, *The Money Trap* (1965). This film reunited him with Rita Hayworth, an actress who costarred with Ford in five films.

A series of westerns in the late 1960s, including Phil Karlson's *A Time of Killing* (1967), and a television series that lasted only one season in 1971 (*Cade's County*), followed by another series in 1975 (*The Family Holvak*), ended Ford's career as a star. Thereafter he accepted cameo roles in major films, such as *Midway*

(1976) and *Superman* (1978), where he appeared as Clark Kent's foster dad, and television movies and miniseries. Although Ford retired from acting in 1991, he made one very brief cameo appearance in the western *Tombstone* in 1993.

**Selected Noir Films:** *Gilda* (1946), *Framed* (1947), *The Man from Colorado* (1948), *The Undercover Man* (1949), *Lust for Gold* (1949), *The Big Heat* (1953), *Human Desire* (1954), *Trial* (1955), *Jubal* (1956), *Experiment in Terror* (1962), *The Money Trap* (1965), *A Time for Killing* (1967).

Geoff Mayer

**FRAMED** (Columbia, 1947). *Director:* Richard Wallace. *Producer:* Jules Schermer. *Script:* Ben Maddow, based on a story by John Patrick. *Cinematography:* Burnett Guffey. *Music:* Marlin Skiles. *Cast:* Glenn Ford (Mike Lambert), Janis Carter (Paula Craig), Barry Sullivan (Steve Price), Edgar Buchanan (Jeff Cunningham), Karen Morley (Beth Price), Jim Bannon (Jack Woodworth), Barbara Woodell (Jane Woodworth), Art Smith (Desk Clerk), Al Bridge (Judge).

*Framed* benefits from the casting of Glenn Ford as the fall guy, Mike Lambert, as Ford brings to this film the resonance of his twisted love-hate relationship with Rita Hayworth in *Gilda* (1946) the previous year. In *Framed*, Glenn Ford reprised the loser aspect of the previous role as Lambert, an unemployed mining engineer forced to take a short-term job as a truck driver. When his truck breaks down, he is rescued from a 10-day jail sentence by waitress Paula Craig, who pays his $50 fine. Craig, however, has an ulterior motive as she is planning with her lover, bank manager Steve Price, to rob his bank and substitute another body for Price when he appears to die in a car crash. They plan to transfer $250,000 to Craig's account, kill Lambert by pushing his car off a cliff, and then plant information on his body to indicate that he is Price. However, Craig falls in love with Mike, and just as she is about to murder him, she hits Price over the head and pushes his car over the cliff. As Price's car, with her ex-lover's body inside, goes over a cliff, Craig, played by Janis Carter, expresses a degree of sexual excitement in a scene reminiscent of a sequence in *Night Editor* where Carter, as Jill Merrill, suddenly goes into a sexual frenzy while watching a girl being killed.

*Framed* is a modest, competent film noir that is similar, in some ways, to James M. Cain's story *The Postman Always Rings Twice,* involving an unemployed drifter who is seduced by a glamorous woman. Similarly, the male protagonists in *Framed* and Cain's *The Postman Always Rings Twice* are basically flawed, everyday men punished by fate for being in the wrong place at the wrong time. *Framed,* on the other hand, lacks the intensity of Cain's story, and Lambert redeems himself by outwitting Paula and, unlike Cain's protagonist, hands her over to the police. In the film's final scene, a bank guard tells Lambert that he will get a reward, but to show that there is still a residue of guilt, he rejects the offer and walks away alone and still without a job.

Geoff Mayer

**FULLER, SAMUEL** (1912–1997). Fuller was a highly talented and idiosyncratic filmmaker who came rather late as a director and script writer into the classical film noir cycle. Those films of his that have noir characteristics appeared both during the 1950s and into the early 1960s. Today, even after the passage of many decades, Fuller's films still remain powerful and appear distinctly contemporary in tone and style. Born in Worcester, Massachusetts, Samuel Fuller was a precocious writing talent and became a newspaper crime reporter as a teenager. The rather lurid tabloid writing style he adopted at that time affected his later filmmaking, contributing to its oft-noted "banner headline" nature. In fact, his films, with their raw, jagged style, are widely considered to be the cinematic equivalent of tabloid journalism, and his detractors say that this can lead to thematic oversimplification. Fuller did important work as a script writer as well as being a notable director, and he was also a novelist. Both as a man and as a creative worker, he was greatly affected by his experiences as a World War II infantryman. Fuller enjoyed the greater freedom possible in working on lower-budget films rather than hugely expensive projects where studio executives were more often tempted to interfere. An unusually independent and cantankerous figure, even by Hollywood standards, he was an integrationist who showed great interest in cultures other than his own white America, such as the Asians who figure largely in films such as *House of Bamboo* and *The Crimson Kimono*. Perhaps because he had a highly individual style, Samuel Fuller became a cult figure during the 1960s, especially in France. European critics extolled his pulpy films that were always personal in some way.

In repeated public statements, he claimed that film is like a battleground, and it is not surprising that he was best known for his war films. However, he always confronted social issues head-on, no matter in which genre he was working. Indeed, in his film noirs, as in his war films, Fuller sympathized most with the ordinary foot soldiers of life, those ground-down people who have no real power. A case in point is his depiction of the trio of luckless nobodies and social peripherals in *Pickup on South Street* (1953) played by Richard Widmark, Jean Peters, and Thelma Ritter. Fuller very much liked the idea of a film centered on a pickpocket, a hooker, and a stool pigeon who would find themselves at the front line of the Cold War. In this important film he claims that there is a moral difference between everyday crooks and Communists. As well, Fuller was unafraid of moving outside his comfort zone to realize a promising story premise. For instance, he went to Japan to make the interesting color noir *House of Bamboo* (1955) with Robert Ryan as a U.S. gangster living in Tokyo and Robert Stack as an investigator. His early 1960s films *Shock Corridor* and *The Naked Kiss*, which are often included in lists of film noir titles, are very offbeat but are fascinating, bitingly satirical insights into the darker nooks and crannies of American culture. *Shock Corridor* (1963) is claustrophobic and pessimistic and challenging in its commentary on racism and sexual pathology. Fuller also relished the visual shock audiences experienced when Constance

Towers has such a savage fight near the start of *The Naked Kiss* (1964) that her wig comes off and reveals her bald head. Kelly, the prostitute she plays is shown as more moral than Grant, the supposedly upright member of the community who, in a shocking revelation for the period, turns out to be a child molester.

**Selected Noir Films:** Fuller was director and script writer for the following films: *Pickup on South Street* (1953), *House of Bamboo* (1955), *Forty Guns* (1957), *The Crimson Kimono* (1959), *Underworld U.S.A.* (1961), *Shock Corridor* (1963), *The Naked Kiss* (1964). Fuller was also script writer for *Shockproof* (1949) and *Scandal Sheet* (1952, adapted from his novel *The Dark Page*).

Brian McDonnell

# G

**GARFIELD, JOHN** (1913–1952). A compact ball of energy at just five feet seven inches, Garfield had charisma aplenty and a super-powerful acting style. He combined boyishness with an air of threat and allied both these characteristics with the independence of a loner. All of these traits made him an icon of noir. Born Jules (Julius) Garfinkel in New York, John Garfield was the son of Jewish migrants from Russia. He attended a school for problem boys, where a teacher channeled his energies into acting. At 12, Garfield suffered scarlet fever, which weakened his heart, but nevertheless he was an accomplished boxer as a schoolboy. He went from working in the politically active left-wing Group Theater in New York to taking up a contract in Hollywood with Warner Bros. (in the process changing his name) on the proviso that he could return to act on the stage once a year. In life, Garfield was a defiant loner and leftist, and his film characters often seemed to be links to the outcast American people of the Great Depression. He played in some very early proto-noirs such as *They Made Me a Criminal, Dust Be My Destiny* (both 1939), and *Out of the Fog* (1941). The first two had him playing a wrongly judged innocent, while in the last of them he was a rather sympathetic racketeer. In the early marginal noir spy story *The Fallen Sparrow* (1943), he was extremely moving as an idealistic veteran of the Spanish Civil War. However, real-life problems afflicted Garfield about this time, an example being the death of his six-year-old son, which depressed him greatly.

Later, political issues with House Committee on Un-American Activities took their toll on his career and health, in spite of his flowering career onscreen. His famous portrayal of the drifter Frank Chambers in *The Postman Always Rings Twice*

(1946) has been compared to Henry Fonda's earlier depiction of Tom Joad in *The Grapes of Wrath* (1940). Garfield became an independent contractor in 1946 after acting in the marginal noir *Humoresque* opposite Joan Crawford. His first independent production was the boxing film *Body and Soul* (1947), which reflected aspects of his own life. Here, as elsewhere, Garfield was almost the ideal noir figure. Stocky and combative, he struck out at the world with both his fists and his tongue. Despite a slight voice impediment, he could talk up a storm. Almost always an outsider and the sufferer of much hard luck, Garfield in these roles personified the loner and the rebel. Only in *Force of Evil* (1948) as seductively corrupt mob lawyer Joe Morse is he affluent and graced with power. Garfield was excellent in the underrated *The Breaking Point* (1950), which many consider the best of all cinematic adaptations of Hemingway's fiction. *He Ran All the Way* was his last film, made when he was already unhappy in his personal affairs and becoming seriously ill. Blacklisted and separated from his wife and family, Garfield died of a heart attack at the very young age of 39. A very modern figure, John Garfield was the forerunner and anticipator of Montgomery Clift, Marlon Brando and James Dean in his acting style and sexual allure.

**Selected Noir Films:** *They Made Me a Criminal* (1939), *Dust Be My Destiny* (1939), *Out of the Fog* (1941), *The Fallen Sparrow* (1943), *The Postman Always Rings Twice* (1946), *Nobody Lives Forever* (1946), *Humoresque* (1946), *Body and Soul* (1947), *Force of Evil* (1948), *We Were Strangers* (1949), *Jigsaw* (1949, uncredited), *The Breaking Point* (1950), *He Ran All the Way* (1951, and producer, uncredited).

Brian McDonnell

**GET CARTER** (MGM British, 1971). *Director:* Mike Hodges. *Producer:* Michael Klinger. *Script:* Mike Hodges, based on the novel *Jack's Return Home* by Ted Lewis. *Cinematography:* Wolfgang Suschitzky. *Music:* Roy Budd. *Cast:* Michael Caine (Jack Carter), Ian Hendry (Eric Paice), Britt Ekland (Anna Fletcher), John Osborne (Cyril Kinnear), Tony Beckley (Peter), George Sewell (Con McCarty), Geraldine Moffat (Glenda), Dorothy White (Margaret), Rosemarie Dunham (Edna), Petra Markham (Doreen), Alun Armstrong (Keith), Bryan Mosley (Cliff Brumby), Glynn Edwards (Albert Swift), Bernard Hepton (Thorpe), Terence Rigby (Gerald Fletcher).

*Get Carter* marked a return to the tough British gangster films of the late 1940s such as *They Made Me a Fugitive* (1947) and *Brighton Rock* (1947). However, although it was released with little publicity in 1971, the film has, over the past three decades, deservedly acquired a reputation as one of the finest British gangster/noir films.

Carter is working in London for Gerald Fletcher when he learns of the death of his estranged brother in Newcastle. He is warned by Fletcher not to go north and interfere with the local criminals as Fletcher has an arrangement with gangster Cyril Kinnear, who controls much of the crime in Newcastle. Carter ignores Fletcher's advice and returns home. He becomes suspicious about the circumstances concerning his brother's death in a car accident, and when he investigates, the locals turn nasty.

*Get Carter* (1971, British). Directed by Mike Hodges. Shown: Michael Caine (as Jack Carter). MGM/Photofest.

Jack is caught between the corrupt Kinnear and members of his own gang who have been sent by Fletcher to bring him back to London. However, when Fletcher learns that Carter has been sleeping with his wife, Anna, he orders Carter's death.

The turning point in the film occurs when Jack views a pornographic film showing the seduction of his brother's young daughter, Doreen. This intensifies Jack's desire to find out who killed his brother and inflict retribution on those involved in the pornographic film. There is even a vague suggestion in the film that Doreen may be Jack's daughter.

*Get Carter* transfers the setting of Ted Lewis's novel from somewhere around Doncaster, probably the steel town of Scunthorpe, to Newcastle. This proves to be an inspired choice as the city, and its pervasive atmosphere of the old mixed with the modern, is used to great effect by Hodges. For example, the setting for the final scene, by the sea at Seaham, County Durham, provides an evocative mixture of industry in conflict with nature. When Jack places Eric Paice's body in one of the coal carts heading out to sea to be dumped, he jauntily walks alongside the cart, swinging the gun that has just battered Eric to death. Carter, pleased that he has avenged his brother and the exploitation of Doreen, is then executed by an unseen hit man, and the last image shows Carter's body lying on the beach as the water washes over him. The film's violent tale of regeneration is complete.

*Get Carter,* with a reasonable budget of $750,000, was released by MGM when it was in financial trouble, and the film was virtually thrown away to the American drive-in circuit. MGM remade it as *Hit Man,* with a black American cast, the following year. The only award nomination *Get Carter* received was a 1972 BAFTA nomination for best supporting actor for Ian Hendry's performance as the chief villain Eric Paice. Mainstream critics at the time were dismayed by the film's complex plotting and Carter's lack of remorse. During the film he kills Cliff Brumby by throwing him off the roof of a car park; Albert Swift is knifed by Carter, and Eric Paice is bashed to death. Similarly, Carter shows little emotion as he watches the villains push his car, with a woman (Glenda) in the boot, off a pier into the water. Later, in an attempt to incriminate Kinnear, he injects another woman (Margaret) with drugs before drowning her in Kinnear's lagoon. While the commentators were appalled by Carter's actions, each killing is justified by the moral context established in the film. Carter is the moral agent, as Hodge signals in a scene showing him traveling to Newcastle by train and reading Raymond Chandler's *Farewell, My Lovely*—another "knight" forced to dispense his own sense of justice in a corrupt world. A third-rate Hollywood version of *Get Carter*, starring Sylvester Stallone, was released in 2000.

Geoff Mayer

**GILDA** (Columbia, 1946). *Director:* Charles Vidor. *Producer:* Virginia Van Upp. *Script:* Marion Parsonnet, adapted by Jo Eisinger from an original story by E. A. Ellington. *Cinematography:* Rudolph Maté. *Music:* Morris Stoloff. *Cast:* Rita Hayworth (Gilda), Glenn Ford (Johnny Farrell), George Macready (Ballin Mundson), Joseph Calleia ( Obregon), Steven Geray (Uncle Pio), Joe Sawyer (Casey), Gerald Mohr (Captain Delgado).

*Gilda* is a sexually provocative film—especially when you consider it was produced during a period of strict censorship under the Production Code Administration. Whereas themes involving sadomasochism underpin many noir films, they are normally kept in check, and heavily camouflaged, by familiar plot devices. In *Gilda* there are no dramatic devices to hide this aspect, and it underpins the drama. Pain and torment appear alongside suggestions of bisexuality and homosexuality, themes and actions normally summarily removed by the Production Code Administration. Yet in *Gilda* they were permitted. Why? A possible reason appears to be the film's setting, not an American city but Buenos Aires, which was perceived as a decadent location where the normal moral rules do not seem to apply. However, when the tormented couple, Gilda and Johnny Farrell, finally extricate themselves from the evil control of Ballin Mundson and prepare to leave Buenos Aires for the United States, their unhealthy obsessions and desires dissipate as they display so-called normal, sentimental behavior based on the purity of their love.

*Gilda* benefits, and extends, the challenge made to the censorship code that *Double Indemnity* achieved two years earlier in 1944. The filming of James M. Cain's story *Double Indemnity* had been opposed by Joseph Breen since its publication in 1935. Its release in 1944 represented a change as lust and adultery were seen as the motivation for why a seemingly ordinary couple murder an "innocent" man. *Double Indemnity* was followed by *The Postman Always Rings Twice* (1946) and *Forever Amber* (1947). *Gilda* continued this trend, and while this pattern was noticed by critics and others, including condemnation from the church, it was a major hit with the public and Columbia Studios. It also consolidated the career of Rita Hayworth, and she moved from film star to icon in her performance as the archetypal bad-good girl.

The film's central male protagonist, Johnny Farrell, exhibits some of the amoral qualities of Cain's drifter in *The Postman Always Rings Twice*. After winning money from gambling in a waterfront dive, he is confronted by a robber. However, he is rescued by a middle-aged man with his "little friend," a walking cane that suddenly transforms into an erect weapon with a phallic steel tip. The relationship between Mundson and Johnny, and Ballin's little friend, is presented by director Charles Vidor as perverse, with hints of a kept man (Farrell) in a relationship with an older man (Mundson). This, of course, cannot be literally presented, so Vidor combines low-level camera angles and clever editing with oblique dialogue such as the moment when Mundson compares Johnny with his phallic cane: Johnny, he explains, is "almost as sharp as my other friend, but he'll kill for me." Johnny replies, "That's what friends are for." The homosexual basis of their "friendship" was recognized at the time of the film's release, and as Glenn Ford acknowledged, the film was striving to break through some of the sexual taboos imposed by the industry and the Production Code.

The relationship between Mundson and Johnny is threatened when Ballin, away on a business trip, marries Gilda. The prospect of a woman, especially one who had an affair with him some years ago, threatens Johnny's mental equilibrium. His condition is further aggravated when Ballin orders Johnny to look after Gilda as she exploits the opportunity to punish the young man by teasing him with her supposed infidelities. His sense of frustration is evident, and after seeing her with Ballin, the basis of his reaction is evident in his voice-over: "I wanted to hit her. I wanted to go back and see them together without me watching." Mundson, on the other hand, relishes the poisonous atmosphere he has created, and as he tells Gilda, "Hate can be a very exciting emotion. Hate is the only thing that has ever warmed me."

When Mundson seemingly dies midway in the film, although an insert shows his survival, this clears the way for Gilda and Johnny to resume a normal relationship. However, Johnny's determination to hurt Gilda and make her pay for what he perceives as her sexual indiscretions only intensifies the perversity of his response to her. Determined to dedicate himself to Mundson's memory, he systematically tortures Gilda by denying her any sexual, or normal, contact with himself or others. Finally, after failing to escape Johnny's control by leaving Buenos Aires, she publicly humiliates him. At the casino controlled by Johnny, Gilda sings the torch song "Put the Blame on Mame" while seemingly stripping—in effect, she only removes her gloves, but the suggestion that she is going to strip off all her clothes combined with her body gyrations—and her invitation to two eager customers to assist her in shedding her dress—is enough to drive Johnny over the edge.

However, Mundson reappears, and it is only after he is killed that normality is restored in a happy ending that threatens the film's credibility. This ending appears contrived as Johnny, throughout the entire film, does not have a normal, or romantic, relationship with Gilda, nor she with him. Yet, at the insistence of producer Virginia Van Upp, a happy ending was imposed—possibly to gain the approval of the Production Code Administration.

Geoff Mayer

**THE GOOD DIE YOUNG** (Romulus Productions, 1954). *Director:* Lewis Gilbert. *Producer:* Jack Clayton (associate). *Script:* Lewis Gilbert and Vernon Harris, based on a novel by Richard Macaulay. *Cinematography:* Jack Asher. *Music:* Georges Auric. *Cast:* Laurence Harvey (Miles "Rave" Ravenscourt), Gloria Grahame (Denise), Richard Basehart (Joe), Joan Collins (Mary), John Ireland (Eddie), Rene Ray (Angela), Stanley Baker (Mike), Margaret Leighton (Eve Ravenscourt), Robert Morley (Sir Francis Ravenscourt), Freda Jackson (Mrs. Freeman), James Kenney (David), Susan Shaw (Doris), Lee Patterson (Tod Maslin).

*The Good Die Young* is quintessential film noir, and it benefits from an outstanding cast, including iconic Hollywood noir actors such as Gloria Grahame (*Crossfire* [1947], *In a Lonely Place* [1950], *The Big Heat* [1953]), Richard Basehart (*He Walked by Night* [1948]), and John Ireland (*Railroaded* [1947], *The Gangster* [1947], *Raw Deal* [1948]). British actors readily associated with crime films, such as Stanley Baker, Freda Jackson, James Kenney (*Cosh Boy* [1953]), and Susan Shaw (*To the Public Danger* [1948]), were also cast. The mood of the film was captured by Jack Asher's high-contrast black-and-white photography. Its use was most noticeable in Stanley Baker's death in the gutter late at night and the image of John Ireland's body lying on the railway tracks. The script by director Lewis Gilbert and Vernon Harris was based on Hollywood script writer Richard Macaulay's novel—Macaulay also scripted numerous films for Warner Bros. in the 1930s, including *Brother Rat* (1938) and *The Roaring Twenties* (1939), plus the tough RKO film noir *Born To Kill* (1947).

The film's fatalistic narrative structure focuses on the reasons why four ex-servicemen (Eddie is a deserter, while the others were discharged) decide to rob a postal van. Ex-soldier Joe returns to England from the United States to persuade his British wife Mary to return with him to America. Mary, on the other hand, is pressured by her selfish mother to stay in England. Joe, who was forced to leave his job in America, runs out of money and reluctantly participates in the robbery. Eddie deserts the American military to stay with his duplicitous actress-wife Denise when he discovers that she is having an affair with her leading man. Mike, a battered aging boxer, loses his funds for a tobacconist shop when his wife lends the money to her criminal brother. Finally, the psychotic "Rave," in need of money when his father Sir Francis Ravenscourt refuses to pay his gambling debts, convinces Joe, Eddie, and Mike to join him in the robbery of a postal van.

The robbery goes wrong, and the men are forced to hide the money in a churchyard grave. "Rave" kills Eddie and Mike before confronting Joe at the airport. Both men are killed in a shoot-out, leaving Mary alone on the airport tarmac near the plane that would have taken them back to America. The film ends with the narrator's warning that the money would not have helped the men. Nothing, he insists, would allow them to escape their fate.

Geoff Mayer

**GORING, MARIUS** (1912–1998). Marius Goring projected an urbane, educated, somewhat decadent image for much of his screen career. A typical film was his costarring role as a murderous doctor opposite Rick Jason and Lisa Gastoni in the crime melodrama *Family Doctor* (1958). This was one of five films Goring made that year, and although none of them were especially significant, he was a strong presence in each film. Although *Family Doctor* was little more than a routine murder mystery based on a series of deaths in a British village, it was typical of the type of film in which Goring labored for so many years.

Born on the Isle of Wight, Goring attended universities at Cambridge, Frankfurt, Munich, Vienna, and Paris before his first stage appearance in 1925 at Cambridge. This was followed by his London debut in 1927 and his West End debut in 1934. During the war he made many BBC service broadcasts. While he was British, he was adept at portraying foreigners such as his decadent playboy in *The Barefoot Contessa* (1954) as well as Nazi sadists in *Pastor Hall* (1940) and *I Was Monty's Double* (1958). In fact, Goring made his first major screen appearance as a German naval officer, the first of many such roles, in Michael Powell's World War I espionage thriller *The Spy in Black* (1939).

He appeared on stage in London from 1927, and it was his preferred medium. He had several Old Vic seasons in the 1930s as well as seasons at Stratford. His preferred filmmaker was Michael Powell, and his association with Powell and Emeric Pressburger proved to be rewarding for Goring as after World War II, they provided him with his most prestigious screen roles—notably as Operator 71 in the fantasy *A Matter of Life and Death* (1946) and, two years later, as the composer Julian Craster who falls in love with the tragic heroine in *The Red Shoes* (1948). Other noteworthy roles included the wealthy yachtsman who lusts after Ava Gardner in *The Barefoot Contessa* (1954), the Nazi officer who falls in love with Maria

Schell in *So Little Time* (1952), and another German in Michael Powell's war film *Ill Met by Moonlight* (1957).

By the 1950s Goring was stereotyped as the villain in most of his films—this included his evil Communist commandant Anton Razinski in Roy Ward Baker's espionage drama *Highly Dangerous* (1950), his murderous schoolmaster in Ronald Neame's film noir *Take My Life* (1947), and the relatively large number of Germans he played throughout his career. However, aside from the films for Michael Powell, there was one role that showcased Goring's abilities when the script gave him half a chance. As the tragic, vulnerable schoolmaster Vincent Perrin in Lawrence Huntington's noir film *Mr. Perrin and Mr. Traill* (1948), Goring gave a moving performance. In the film Perrin is forced to confront his own weaknesses as he reacts adversely to the arrival of David Farrar, a new teacher, and Perrin is, alternatively, vindictive, caring, jealous, and ultimately, heroic.

Goring starred in two British television series, as Sir Percy Blakeney in *The Adventures of the Scarlet Pimpernel* in the mid-1950s and in *The Expert* in the late 1960s. He died of cancer in 1998.

**Selected Noir Films:** *The Amateur Detective* (1936), *Consider Your Verdict* (1938), *The Spy in Black* (1939), *The Case of the Frightened Lady* (1940), *Take My Life* (1947), *The Red Shoes* (1948), *Mr. Perrin and Mr. Traill* (1948), *Highly Dangerous* (1950), *Circle of Danger* (1951), *Pandora and the Flying Dutchman* (1951), *Break in the Circle* (1955), *Family Doctor* (1958), *Whirlpool* (1959), *The Inspector* (1960), *The Crooked Road* (1964).

Geoff Mayer

**GRAHAME, GLORIA** (1923–1981). Appearing rather childlike in some films, and often cast as a victim, Grahame could also be sassy and sexy and hold her own in films that featured snappy dialogue and badinage. She was notable for her mousy features, her often squeaky voice, and her sensual, swollen lips that perhaps reflected the many plastic surgery procedures that reflected her insecurity about her looks. Born Gloria Hallward in Los Angeles (some sources say in 1925 rather than 1923), Gloria Grahame was first employed at MGM. But in 1947 she was loaned out by them to RKO to make the influential Edward Dmytryk film *Crossfire*. In this film she opened her noir career notably well with the small role of Ginny, the weary dance hall hostess. Grahame immediately impressed as a woman who takes a lot of punishment from men but still maintains her overall resilience. Her sexy pout that made her seem so available frequently had a propensity to break into a mischievous smile. Grahame's most nuanced and graceful role was definitely as Laurel Gray opposite Humphrey Bogart in the Hollywood noir *In a Lonely Place*, directed by her then husband Nicholas Ray. The couple were in the process of breaking up in real life, just as the main characters do in the film. This lends some poignancy to Grahame's performance as Laurel, and she is at once vulnerable and sweet in her love scenes with Bogart's violent character Dix Steele, but Laurel also has an independent mind. Incidentally, Grahame later married Ray's son Tony.

She got little value out of the controlling studio head, Howard Hughes, assigning her a small role in *Macao* but fared better in *Sudden Fear*, where she took third billing after Joan Crawford and Jack Palance. Grahame won the best supporting actress Oscar for 1952 as the unfaithful southern belle wife of Dick Powell in *The Bad and the Beautiful* (a title that features in some listings of classical noir), although her peculiar behavior after winning took some of the glow off as far as her public reception was concerned. A year later, she was highly affecting as the put-on and scarred Debby Marsh in *The Big Heat*. Disfigured by a sadistic act by Lee Marvin's character Vince Stone, she was able to get her revenge on him before he shot her. Grahame was also good in the less than perfect Fritz Lang noir *Human Desire*, again opposite Glenn Ford, the star of *The Big Heat*. She found herself back in a small part in the very late classical noir *Odds against Tomorrow* (1959), which showed her offbeat side in a nicely played scene where, with just a bra covering her upper torso, she responds sexually to Robert Ryan's description of how it felt to kill a man. By that time the Production Code allowed more openly erotic material, a concession that would have helped Grahame in some of her earlier roles.

**Selected Noir Films:** *Crossfire* (1947), *A Woman's Secret* (1949), *In a Lonely Place* (1950), *Macao* (1952), *Sudden Fear* (1952), *The Bad and the Beautiful* (1952), *The Big Heat* (1953), *The Good Die Young* (1954), *Human Desire* (1954), *Naked Alibi* (1954), *Odds against Tomorrow* (1959), *Chandler* (1971).

Brian McDonnell

**GREAT DAY** (RKO British, 1945). *Director:* Lance Comfort. *Producer:* Victor Hanbury. *Script:* John Davenport and Wolfgang Wilhelm, from Lesley Storm's play. *Cinematography:* Erwin Hiller. *Music:* William Alwyn. *Cast:* Eric Portman (Captain Ellis), Flora Robson (Mrs. Ellis), Sheila Sim (Margaret Ellis), Philip Friend (Geoffrey Winthrop), Isabel Jeans (Lady Mott), Marjorie Rhodes (Mrs. Mumford), Margaret Withers (Miss Tyndale), Walter Fitzgerald (Bob Tyndale), Maire O'Neill (Mrs. Walsh).

*Great Day* provides Eric Portman one of his first opportunities to present a male character suffering from an intense emotional crisis, a role he was to repeat with different variations throughout the 1940s. The film is also a British example of a film noir theme common to many American postwar films: the inability of the returning soldier to adjust to peacetime conditions (see, e.g., *Crossfire* [1947]).

The film, produced in the final months of World War II, begins, and ends, in a conventional manner, celebrating the strong community support for the hands-across-the-sea military alliance between Britain and the United States. The context for this expression is the proposed visit by Eleanor Roosevelt to the Women's Institute of Denley Village. The displays of patriotism and communal solidarity expressed in the film are expected of a film produced during this period. What is not expected is its emphasis on tension and division within this village community.

Within the overarching context of the Denley women preparing for the visit of the American First Lady, the film explores two narrative strands. The first, and most important, focuses on the anxieties and disintegration of Captain Ellis, a World War I veteran who, despite his superficial bluff and bravado, is alienated from his community. This is largely due to his inability to find a sufficient reason for living in a seemingly idyllic place like Denley after the glory and responsibilities he enjoyed during World War I. Ellis is particularly embittered because, as some remind him, he is nothing more than a relic of a past war. The "old days," his wife tells him, "are dead and done with," while the village barmaid complains that "he [Ellis] never lets you forget, the captain."

The second strand concerns his daughter Margaret who, despite loving a young army captain, is tempted to accept the security offered by a middle-aged farmer, Bob Tyndale. The plight of Margaret's mother, who Margaret feels is trapped by her "Dad's swaggering and drinking and clinging to the past," provides sufficient motivation for her to accept Tyndale's marriage offer and reject her young army captain. This decision is in accord with her mother's advice that "security may sound dull, but it does give you your freedom." Captain Ellis, on the other hand, warns his daughter not to get trapped, a clear reference to his own emotional predicament. The film suggests that despite the superficial attractions of the village, it provides no real outlet or satisfaction.

Ellis's self-destructive traits are activated by alcohol and a need to impress visiting American and British soldiers. However, his anger erupts when he is denied credit in the local pub and he attempts to steal a 10-shilling note from a woman's purse. After the police charge him with theft, Ellis contemplates suicide in the local river. However, unlike the ending in Lesley Storm's play, Ellis decides not to kill himself, and his daughter offers solace by telling him that "it's sometimes braver to live than to die." Margaret then decides to follow her heart and marry the young soldier rather than the middle-aged farmer. Both father and daughter, tentatively, join in the communal celebrations associated with Eleanor Roosevelt's visit at the end of the film.

*Great Day* is a complex film that exposes the plight of those, such as Ellis, who are alienated from their communities. Director Lance Comfort utilizes expressive lighting to highlight Ellis's torment, and when, for example, Ellis tries to explain his behavior to his wife prior to his attempted suicide, Eric Portman's face is partly covered in shadow while his wife is fully lit. In this scene Ellis explains, "I was never frightened during the war. But I was frightened in peace—of a wife being dependent on me." He breaks down and admits that although he was a leader of men in World War I, he has trouble with the responsibilities of a man's role in peacetime: "He's the lover, the protector, the strong man, or he wants to be. In my case, no fresh supplies came in." *Great Day* anticipated the end of the simplicities of war and the fears associated with the complexities of peace.

Geoff Mayer

**THE GREAT FLAMARION** (Republic, 1945). *Director:* Anthony Mann. *Producer:* William Wilder. *Script:* Anne Wigton, Richard Weil, and Heinz Herald, from a story by Anne Wigton based on Vicki Baum's *The Big Shot. Cinematography:* James S. Brown Jr. *Music:* Alexander Lazlo. *Cast:* Erich von Stroheim (The Great Flamarion), Mary Beth Hughes (Connie Wallace), Dan Duryea (Al Wallace), Stephen Barclay (Eddie Wheeler), Lester Allen (Tony), Joseph Granby (Detective Ramirez), Franklyn Farnum (Stage Manager).

One of the great visual stylists of the Hollywood cinema, director Anthony Mann managed to invest the most banal genre film with a strong sense of atmosphere and menace. In *The Great Flamarion* Mann invests this familiar, predictable story with a degree of perversity not always found in the Hollywood film during the 1940s. This low-budget film was produced by William Wilder, Billy Wilder's brother, for his independent company, Filmdom Productions, and distributed by Republic Pictures, a studio more commonly associated with westerns starring popular cowboy stars such as Gene Autry and Roy Rogers.

While Mann brought his customary toughness, accompanied by the familiar noir devices such as flashback narration, a tormented protagonist, and a strong

*The Great Flamarion* (1945). Directed by Anthony Mann. Shown from left: Erich von Stroheim (as The Great Flamarion), Mary Beth Hughes (as Connie Wallace). Republic Pictures Corporation/Photofest.

sexual motivation, he was assisted by an unusual group of filmmakers who provided a strong European influence on this tale of murder and betrayal. The film was co-scripted by Bavarian-born screenwriter Heinz Herald, and the lead role was played by the controversial Viennese born actor-director Erich von Stroheim. Also, the screenplay was based on Vicki Baum's 1936 short story "The Big Shot," and Baum was also born and raised in Vienna. This European influence stripped the story down to its elemental basis of three men who are seduced by a callous femme fatale, Connie Wallace. Each man is humiliated and stripped of his dignity, in a similar manner to Josef von Sternberg's breakthrough film for Marlene Dietrich, *Der blau Engel* (The Blue Angel, 1930), which follows the moral descent of a schoolteacher due to his obsession for a nightclub singer.

This film's emphasis on masochism and humiliation is also accompanied by a strong sense of fatalism as the fate of the central protagonist in *The Great Flamarion* is known from near the start of the film as it is told in a prolonged flashback by Flamarion as he is dying after Connie has shot him. The film also has, for a Hollywood film produced during the strict censorship regime of the Production Code Administration, an outrageous sexual metaphor: as Connie tries to convince the aging vaudevillian sharpshooter to kill her husband, she strokes the barrel of his pistol.

The story concerns a rigid, sexually repressed vaudeville artist, a sharpshooter, who falls under the spell of a scheming woman wishing to kill her husband. Her plan is based on the nature of their vaudeville act, where the sharpshooter, Flamarion, shoots various objects around the bodies of the husband and wife dancing team, Connie and Al Wallace. The film's predictable narrative trajectory traces his fall from grace when he eventually falls in love with Connie. Wallace, who seduces Flamarion into killing her husband during their act, abandons the lovesick artist after he commits the murder. She humiliates him by promising to meet him in a Chicago hotel when, in reality, she runs away to South America with another vaudeville artist, trick cyclist Eddie Wheeler. The film's final section traces Flamarion's degradation and ruin as he loses his career and his money searching for Connie. Finally, after more than a year, he locates her in Mexico. When she ridicules him by telling him that she could never love him as he is old and ugly, he attacks her. Connie retaliates by shooting him, and mortally wounded, Flamarion kills Connie by strangling her. The film ends with the Flamarion's death while recounting his story to Tony, a vaudeville artist.

The casting of von Stroheim gives *The Great Flamarion* a theatrical edge, although his performance is low key compared with other roles during this period. Von Stroheim, who was unable to obtain a job with the major studios following his dismissal from the Gloria Swanson film *Queen Kelly* in 1929, was reduced to working as an actor in low-budget films in Hollywood in the 1940s, with an occasional supporting role in large-budget studio films such as *Five Graves to Cairo* (1943). Nevertheless, *The Great Flamarion* was an ideal part for von Stroheim as it exploited his public reputation as an autocratic performer that makes his fall from grace more profound. This aspect, his degradation, is detailed in the film that shows his humiliation and torment while waiting in vain for Connie in Chicago. His decline is foreshadowed by Connie's treatment of Al, her husband. Like Flamarion, he also loves Connie and is prepared to suffer at her hands. When she fails to return his affectation, he turns to the bottle. This pattern is repeated at the end of the film, and when Flamarion tracks her down to Mexico, she has already cuckolded Wheeler by chasing after another vaudeville performer. By the end of the film, all the main characters are dead.

Geoff Mayer

**GREER, JANE** (1924–2001). Despite her small number of film roles, Greer's compelling characterization of Kathie Moffett in Jacques Tourneur's *Out of the Past* (1947) has become one of the classic femme fatale figures. This role alone has made her an important noir actress. She was born Bettejane Greer into a prosperous family living in Washington, D.C. During her childhood, Greer suffered from Bell's palsy, which paralyzed the left side of her face, but through her adolescence, she overcame this setback. The palsy did have the ongoing effect of leaving her with a slightly crooked smile, but that merely added to her beguiling charms. When Greer moved to Hollywood, she (like dozens of other young female hopefuls) became a "protégé" of the womanizing Howard Hughes when he was an independent producer. Her alleged refusal to join his stable of mistresses led him to drop her. Greer then married crooner Rudy Vallee, who had pursued her since she was 17. It was Vallee who helped her get an acting contract with RKO, ironically later to be taken over by Howard Hughes. After a minor role in the obscure 1945 amnesia-themed noir *Two O'Clock Courage*, Greer played a more substantial part as a good girl rather than a vamp in the suspenseful *They Won't Believe Me*. Greer was only 22 when she played her most famous role in *Out of the Past*. At that time Hollywood friends were still describing her as a mixture of a girl and a woman, but the femme fatale part of Kathie Moffett showed her to be capable of all the necessary womanly wiles. Kathie is spoken of early in the film but is not seen until the story is well advanced. She makes a wonderful entrance into a bar in Acapulco: Greer's beauty combined with Nicholas Musuraca's lighting and Robert Mitchum's wistfully romantic voice-over create her as an immediate icon of noir. For the rest of the film, Kathie becomes steadily more deadly, killing off Steve Brodie, Kirk Douglas, and Mitchum before expiring herself in a fusillade of bullets in a police ambush. Sadly, Hughes, when he took over the RKO studio, later stifled the development of Greer's career. With several less memorable roles under her belt, she retired early after marrying a wealthy businessman. The year 1984 saw her briefly brought out of retirement to appear in an ill-advised remake of *Out of the Past*: the terminally clunky *Against All Odds*. This time, Greer played the mother of British actress Rachel Ward, who played the Kathie Moffett role.

**Selected Noir Films:** *Two O'Clock Courage* (1945), *They Won't Believe Me* (1947), *Out of the Past* (1947), *The Big Steal* (1949), *The Company She Keeps* (1950), *The Outfit* (1973), *Against All Odds* (1984).

Brian McDonnell

**GUN CRAZY** (United Artists, 1950). *Director:* Joseph H. Lewis. *Producers:* Frank and Maurice King. *Script:* MacKinlay Kantor and Milliard Kaufman, based on the *Saturday Evening Post* story "Gun Crazy" by MacKinlay Kantor. (Much of the script was written by Dalton Trumbo, who remained uncredited because of the Hollywood blacklist. Kaufman fronted for Trumbo, a reasonably common practice during the years of the blacklist.) *Cinematography:* Russel Harlan. *Music:* Victor Young. *Cast:* Peggy Cummins (Annie Laurie Starr), John Dall (Bart Tare), Berry Kroeger (Packett), Ned Young (Dave Allister), Harry Lewis (Clyde Boston), Morris Carnovsky (Judge Willoughby), Rusty Tamblyn (Bart Tare, aged 14), Annabel Shaw (Ruby Tare).

Gun Crazy is generally acknowledged to be one of the finest, if not the finest, B film produced in Hollywood. This, however, is a retrospective judgment, and at the time of its release in 1949—and its rerelease in 1950 (the film was produced under the title *Deadly Is the Female,* and it was released in July 1949 before United Artists rereleased the film in August 1950 as *Gun Crazy*)—it received little attention from the critics. This was primarily due to the fact that it was an independent production released by United Artists and not a major studio film. There was also the fact that the film was produced by the King brothers, who did not have a good reputation in Hollywood—primarily because of their dubious background in borderline criminal activities associated with the installation of slot machines. This fact discouraged major stars from appearing in the film, and the producers could only secure a British actress, Peggy Cummins, who had failed to make her mark on Hollywood in the middle and late 1940s, and a minor male star, John Dall. After World War II, Peggy Cummins was brought to Hollywood by Twentieth Century Fox to star in its controversial production of *Forever Amber* (1947), but when studio head Darryl F. Zanuck viewed the rushes, he replaced her with Linda Darnell. Cummins stayed in Hollywood at Fox for a few years, but when they did not renew her contract in 1949, she decided to return to London. However, before leaving, the King brothers offered her the part of Annie Laurie Starr in *Gun Crazy.* Her performance was so good in *Gun Crazy* that it should have reignited her Hollywood career, but after completing the film, she returned to London and spent the next decade, with a few exceptions, such as *Hell Drivers* in 1957, in thankless romantic comedy roles. In *Gun Crazy,* on the other hand, Cummins gives the performance of a lifetime as the psychotic carnival sharpshooter-turned-robber who cannot control her fetish for guns and an uncontrollable desire to kill.

John Dall, who had costarred as a gay thrill killer in Alfred Hitchcock's *Rope* in 1948, plays Bart Tare, an ex-veteran who complements Annie Starr with his

*Gun Crazy* (1950, also called *Deadly is the Female*). Directed by Joseph H. Lewis. Shown: John Dall (as Bart Tare), Peggy Cummins (as Annie Laurie Starr). United Artists/Photofest.

own lifelong fascination with guns. However, unlike Starr, he cannot kill. This emanates from an incident when as a young boy, he killed a baby chick with his BB gun. After a period in reform school and the army, Bart returns to his hometown and visits a traveling circus, where he accepts a challenge from sharpshooter Annie Laurie Starr to compete on stage in a shooting contest. This sequence, replete with Lewis's customary skill involving dramatic compositions and expert editing, is a textbook example of how skilled filmmakers could bypass censorship prohibitions imposed by the Production Code Authority. Instead of a literal depiction of lust, Lewis exploits the obvious phallic sensuality of the gun and, via a series of clever inserts and low-level compositions, immediately establishes the sexual attraction between this sharp, knowing woman and passive, alienated male, who are bonded together through their fascination with the power and danger of the handgun.

Tare and Starr leave the circus and marry. However, when their money runs out, Starr makes it quite clear that if he wants her to remain, he will have to join in her criminal activities. Despite Bart's superiority with the "gun," it is Annie who is dominant in the relationship ("I want action," she tells Bart), and the sequences where she puts her demands to Bart again demonstrate how Lewis could bypass the Production Code through the staging of Cummins on her bed and the reaction of Tare to the implications of her demand for money. Bart, however, is a tormented figure. He is disgusted by her behavior during a major robbery, which results in the killing of two innocent people: "Two people dead! Just so we can live without working. Why? Why do you have to murder people? Why can't you let them live?" However, he remains loyal to her, even after Annie, unapologetic about her sadistic tendencies, tells him, "I told you I was no good, and I didn't kid you." Only guns and the power of life and death can make her feel that she is alive.

There is one sequence in *Gun Crazy* that challenged the formal basis of the classical Hollywood film. When they rob a small-town bank, Lewis decided to abandon the script and not film the sequence in a studio interior and, instead, filmed the entire sequence in one four-minute take, without any cuts, on the street in Montrose, California. He prepared the action by staging it, initially, with two extras, and filmed it with his own 16-mm camera. He then shot the footage as the actors ad-libbed the dialogue. When it came to the actual film, he repeated this approach, with Dall and Cummins in a renovated stretch limousine. He had everything behind the front seats of the car removed to make room for the crew. Cinematographer Russell Harlan sat on a jockey's saddle as the crew struggled to allow Harlan to complete a dolly shot by pushing the cinematographer and his camera along a plank inside the car. The dialogue, which was improvised by Dall and Cummins to fit the circumstances, was recorded on tiny microphones under the sunshades, while two technicians strapped to the roof of the car captured sounds outside the vehicle. In three hours, Lewis shot what had been scheduled for four days in the studio.

Starr and Tare finally run out of luck after they rob the payroll at the Armour meatpacking plant. Again, Annie cannot control her bloodlust and shoots the office manager when she triggers an alarm. Bart and Annie flee from the police and return to his small town in California. However, after seeking refuge with his family, Annie destroys the possibility of hiding from the police by threatening Bart's sister Ruby and her small child. They are chased into the mountains, and in a scene reminiscent of the climax in *High Sierra* (1941), the police corner Bart and Annie. Hiding out in a foggy marshland, Annie panics when Bart's childhood friends, Sheriff Clyde Boston and journalist Dave Allister, approach them. She loses control and tells them, "Come any closer and I'll kill you! I'll kill you all!" To stop Annie killing Boston and Allister, Bart shoots Annie. The final irony in the film is that the only person Bart kills is the person he loves most—Annie. Bart is then shot by the police.

Two decades later, with a much larger budget, *Bonnie and Clyde* (1967) captured some of the subversive excitement of *Gun Crazy*. Yet Joseph Lewis, with a budget of $450,000 and a 30-day filming schedule, easily surpasses Arthur Penn's film. While Penn resorts to a spectacular, bloody finale, where the lovers are repeatedly shot by the police, Lewis utilizes cheap studio interiors to recreate a foggy marshland, to generate considerable more empathy for his doomed couple. *Gun Crazy* has been copied many times but never surpassed.

Geoff Mayer

**GYNT, GRETA** (1916–2000). Greta Gynt was the closest the British film industry had in the late 1930s and 1940s to the so-called bad girl, or sensually promiscuous girl, that was reasonably common in Hollywood at that time (e.g., Ann Savage, Jane Greer, Audrey Totter, Marie Windsor, and Gloria Grahame, to name just a few). Yet there were not many opportunities for Gynt to display her talent in this regard, and her popularity was restricted to a brief period in the 1940s. However, for a few short years, especially in the immediate postwar period, Gynt, with her long blonde hair and assertive, sensual demeanor, gave British audiences an alternative to the respectable, sexually repressed women, such as Celia Johnson, that dominated British cinema in the 1930s and early 1940s. Gynt was born Margrethe Woxholt in Oslo in 1916. She began dancing and acting in Norway, and encouraged by her mother, she came to England when she was only 19. Gynt, who selected her name because of the *Peer Gynt Suite* by Edvard Grieg, was naturally dark haired but changed her hair color to blonde after arriving in the United Kingdom. This was done at the suggestion of her agent, Christopher Mann, whom she married. Mann also had success with Madeleine Carroll's career when she changed her dark hair to blonde.

Gynt's major break, after a couple of years of low-budget thrillers (such as *Sexton Blake and the Hooded Terror* [1938]) and comedies (*Boys Will Be Girls* [1937]), was in the Thorold Dickinson murder mystery *The Arsenal Stadium Mystery* (1939) as the sexually permissive Gwen Lee, a persona that characterized her subsequent film roles. In the middle and late 1940s this persona matured in films such as *Take My Life* (1947) and *Dear Murderer* (1947). In *Take My Life,* a superb film noir, Gynt has the best role of her career as Philippa Shelley, an opera singer forced to investigate the circumstances leading to the death of her husband's (Hugh Williams) former girlfriend. When her husband is convicted of the murder, Shelley's enquiries lead to a remote public school in Scotland and Marius Goring, the murderous headmaster. Gynt's next film was also a fine film noir. As Vivien Warren, an adulterous woman who betrays her husband (Eric Portman) in *Dear Murderer,* Gynt convincingly plays a promiscuous woman who does not hesitate to commit murder, if necessary to achieve her goals. Her next noir film, *Mr. Perrin and Mr. Traill* (1948), provided Gynt with yet another variation of this persona as the vivacious school nurse Isobel Lester who attracts the attention of both Marius Goring and David Farrar. This proves fatal to Goring. She was also a nightclub singer in *Easy Money* (1948).

Gynt, who would have been more comfortable in Hollywood films, finally got her chance when MGM invited her to appear in *Soldiers Three* (1951), but this film, which was relatively late in Gynt's career, offered little, and she soon returned to Britain and a succession of mediocre, low-budget crime films in the 1950s. She did, however, outshine the imported Hollywood star Arlene Dahl in the noir film *Fortune Is a Woman* (1957). Greta Gynt died in London on April 2, 2000.

**Selected Noir Films:** *The Last Curtain* (1937), *Sexton Blake and the Hooded Terror* (1938), *Too Dangerous to Live* (1939), *Dark Eyes of London* (1939), *The Arsenal Stadium Murder Mystery* (1939), *Two for Danger* (1940), *Bulldog Sees It Through* (1940), *Take My Life* (1947), *Dear Murderer* (1947), *Easy Money* (1947), *Mr. Perrin and Mr. Traill* (1948), *I'll Get You for This* (1951), *Whispering Smith Hits London* (1952), *The Ringer* (1952), *Three Steps in the Dark* (1953), *Forbidden Cargo* (1954), *Devil's Point* (1954), *See How They Run* (1955), *Dead on Time* (1955), *Fortune Is a Woman* (1957), *Morning Call* (1958), *The Witness* (1959), *Bluebeard's Ten Honeymoons* (1960).

Geoff Mayer

# H

**HATTER'S CASTLE** (Paramount British, 1941). *Director:* Lance Comfort. *Producer:* Isadore Goldsmith. *Script:* Paul Merzbach and Rudolph Bernaur, with scenario and dialogue by Rodney Ackland, from the novel by A. J. Cronin. *Cinematography:* Max Greene. *Music:* Horace Shepherd. *Cast:* Robert Newton (James Brodie), Deborah Kerr (Mary Brodie), James Mason (Dr. Renwick), Beatrice Varley (Mrs. Brodie), Emlyn Williams (Dennis), Enid Stamp-Taylor (Nancy), Henry Oscar (Grierson), Anthony Bateman (Angus Brodie), Stuart Lindsell (Lord Winton).

After his debut feature film, the dull *Penn of Pennsylvania* (1941), Lance Comfort established his credentials with this version of A. J. Cronin's popular novel, which was first published in 1931. Comfort heightens the melodramatic potential of the novel and provides a filmic adaptation, as opposed to a literal translation, of Cronin's story of a patriarchal bully whose overwhelming desire to perpetuate, and elevate, his name through his "castle." Ultimately, his actions result in pain and death to his family.

In 1879, in the Scottish town of Levensford, James Brodie bullies his family, his employees, and the local townspeople, carrying on a brazen affair with the local barmaid Nancy while preventing Mary, his daughter, from engaging with the outside world, particularly young Doctor Renwick. Brodie also prevents Renwick from treating his wife, and his dictatorial behavior prevents Mary from attending the county ball. Nancy's lover, Dennis, sneaks away from the festivities and seduces Mary, who falls pregnant. After learning of Mary's condition, Dennis rejects her, and her father forces her to leave his house.

A rival hat shop exposes Brodie's vulnerable financial situation and, combined with a reluctance to adjust his extravagant lifestyle, this results in economic ruin. At the same time he exerts pressure on his son to win a scholarship and be the best student at school. The boy responds by breaking into the headmaster's office so that he can read the exam questions. Brodie's reaction to his son's disgrace causes Angus to commit suicide and, with his wife and son dead, his wealth gone, and Mary believed dead, Brodie attacks the symbol of his ambitions—his castle. He dies in the ensuing blaze while Mary, who lost Dennis's child, is reunited with Renwick at her father's funeral.

*Hatter's Castle* was a perfect vehicle for Robert Newton's florid acting style, and he excels in this biting study of ambition and patriarchal tyranny. Comfort emphasizes the melodramatic basis of Cronin's story—even including a snowstorm as Brodie heartlessly ejects his pregnant daughter from the family castle. *Hatter's Castle* is a strong, unflinching example of British melodrama with a bleak, noir outlook.

Geoff Mayer

**HAYDEN, STERLING** (1916–1986). A stalwart of low-budget crime melodramas and westerns in the 1950s, Hayden's tall, lumpy body and lived-in face gave the audience a sense that the hardened characters he played were based on real-life experiences. He was, in the 1950s at least, the antithesis of the glamorous Hollywood movie star. Born in New Jersey, his father died when he was nine, and Hayden left school when he was 16 to work as a seaman on schooners. His love of the sea never waned, and acting was merely a quick way of generating sufficient money to satisfy this need. He sailed around the world a number of times as a teenager and was a ship's captain before he was 20. In search of quick money to purchase his own vessel, he began modeling, and after meeting director Edward H. Griffith, he signed a contract with Paramount.

Hayden's first two films for Paramount were directed by Griffith. In the first, *Virginia* (1941), a romantic melodrama, he had a supporting role to Fred MacMurray and Madeleine Carroll and, at this stage of his career, was an imposing figure—six feet fives inches tall, with blonde hair. These attributes encouraged the studio to elevate this 25-year-old into a starring role in his second film, opposite Madeleine Carroll, *Bahamas Passage* (1941). The film was financially successful, and Paramount, who billed him as "the most beautiful man in the movies," thought that they had a major star on their hands. However, Hayden, in the first in a series of disastrous career decisions, left Hollywood to become a commando. After marrying Carroll, he enlisted under the name of John Hamilton and eventually operated a fishing boat off Yugoslavia, where he was ordered to pick up allied pilots and supply Tito's Communist partisans who were fighting the Germans. He affection for the partisans and friendship with Communists in the Hollywood community, including Karen Morley and Abraham Polonsky, motivated him to join the Communist

Party when he returned from overseas. This action had a profound effect on his career in the early 1950s. Although Hayden was too much of a maverick to function as a committed Communist, he was forced to cooperate and name names when called before the House Committee on Un-American Activities, an action he deeply regretted the rest of his life.

When he returned to acting in 1945, he found that public interest in him had waned, and after a supporting role in John Farrow's romantic melodrama *Blaze of Noon* (1947), starring William Holden, Hayden was content to collect his Paramount salary of $70,000 a year without making any film appearances. Hayden had little respect for acting as a career and despised the way in which actors were accorded a privileged status merely because they photographed well and could deliver dialogue. However, he needed the money, and in 1949 he began a decade-long process of alternating between crime melodramas and westerns.

*Manhandled* (1949), a pedestrian noir film costarring Dorothy Lamour, and a John Payne western, *El Paso* (1949), both produced by the William Pine–William Thomas B unit, were his final films at Paramount. While the next phase of Hayden's career began with his best and most prestigious role as Dix Handley, a criminal out for just one more robbery in John Huston's masterly caper film *The Asphalt Jungle* (1950), he failed to build on the film's success and worked (mostly) in B films for the rest of the decade. His films included a number of noir films. In *Crime Wave* (1954) he is surly Detective Sergeant Sims, who believes that ex-convict Gene Nelson is implicated in a holdup. In *Naked Alibi* (1954) he is the obsessive chief Joe Conroy, who believes that Gene Barry has killed three detectives. While Hayden is wrong in *Crime Wave*, he is correct in *The Naked Alibi*, although he has to leave the police force and pursue Barry and Gloria Grahame to Mexico to prove that he is right.

*The Killing* (1956), Stanley Kubrick's brilliant reworking of the caper film, offered Hayden another chance at the big time as ex-convict Johnny Clay, a small-time criminal who devises an ingenious plan to rob a racetrack. However, he immediately returned to B films. In *The Come-On* (1956) Hayden is cast as a seafaring wanderer, his real-life preoccupation, who falls in love with a con artist, played by Anne Baxter. Baxter convinces Hayden to kill her partner, John Hoyt, in this low-budget variation on *Double Indemnity*. Hayden's last film noir in the 1950s, *Crime of Passion* (1957), was also one of his best. He is Detective Bill Doyle, a solid cop who marries ambitious reporter Kathy Ferguson (Barbara Stanwyck). Dissatisfied with her role as a domestic housewife, Ferguson seduces Doyle's boss, Inspector Tony Pope (Raymond Burr), so as to advance her husband's career. However, when Pope appoints another cop ahead of her husband, Ferguson kills Pope, and Doyle is forced to arrest his wife.

Hayden's dislike of Hollywood intensified, and he defied a court order so that he could sail to Tahiti with his children following a bitter divorce—he had four children with Betty Ann de Noon, and the couple married and divorced three times. Hayden did not act for six years and only returned to filming in London when he was offered his most bizarre role as the psychotic brigadier general Jack D. Ripper in Stanley Kubrick's brilliant satire on global politics, *Dr. Strangelove or: How I Learned to Stop Worrying and Love the Bomb* (1964). He left the film industry again, only returning to Hollywood in 1969 for a spate of films including a supporting role in *Loving* (1970), Irving Kershner's insightful film on how corporate pressures can derail a marriage. He followed this with one of his best roles as the corrupt Irish police captain Mark McCluskey in Francis Ford Coppola's masterpiece *The Godfather* (1972). The following year, Robert Altman cast him as the alcoholic Roger Wade in his revisionist version of Raymond Chandler's *The Long Goodbye* (1973).

Hayden continued acting sporadically until 1983, although, like most of his career, there were missed opportunities. He was, for example, cast as the villainous Quint in Steven Spielberg's blockbuster hit *Jaws* (1975), but tax problems prevented him from entering the United States. None of this affected Hayden—to him, filmmaking was inconsequential compared to life on the sea, and he brought to his noir films a sense of weariness, distrust, and a positive revulsion of sentimentality and artifice—the perfect attributes of a noir actor.

**Selected Noir Films:** *Manhandled* (1949), *The Asphalt Jungle* (1950), *Crime Wave* (1954), *Naked Alibi* (1954), *Suddenly* (1954), *The Killing* (1956), *The Come-On* (1956), *Crime of Passion* (1957), *Valerie* (1957), *The Godfather* (1972), *The Long Goodbye* (1973), *Winter Kills* (1979).

Geoff Mayer

**HEFLIN, VAN** (1910–1971). Not conventionally good looking but with an energetic charm, Van Heflin was essentially a character actor who, even in his leading roles, came to personify the average American. Heflin's highly expressive face and his ability to suggest moral ambivalence made him particularly suited to film noir roles. He was born Emmett Evan Heflin Jr. in Oklahoma, but in his early teens his parents separated, and he moved with his mother from Oklahoma to Los Angeles. Heflin had what he later described as a disastrous acting debut, which led to him spending three years working around the world as a merchant seaman. When he returned to the United States and to acting, he appeared first on stage, then got a contract in Hollywood with RKO, before moving to MGM. In these early years, Heflin made a solid reputation as a ruggedly handsome supporting actor while gaining a few lead roles in lower-budget films. It was at this point in his career that the newly emerging classical film noir became an important factor. Heflin won the 1942 best supporting actor Oscar for his performance as the sidekick in his first film noir *Johnny Eager*, with Robert Taylor in the leading role as a gangster masquerading as a taxi driver. Heflin played his alcoholic friend who is nevertheless the conscience of his racketeering pal. The outbreak of World War II interrupted his film career, and Heflin served as a combat photographer throughout the hostilities. After the war was over, he made *The Strange Love of Martha Ivers*

(1946) with Barbara Stanwyck and Kirk Douglas, where he persuasively depicted a man's moral ambiguity and temptation but also the capacity to overcome them. In *Possessed* (1947), opposite Joan Crawford, Heflin was effective and subtle as an exploitative, self-serving man whose complacency is fatally challenged when he is shot at the end by a woman who is obsessed with him. Fred Zinnemann's atmospheric film noir *Act of Violence* (1949) provided Heflin with an edgy role he once more impressively well, that of a socially prominent man whose past secrets undercut his surface respectability. Frank Enley is a construction executive pursued by an embittered fellow ex-serviceman, and Frank's haunted flight through the dark underbelly of inner Los Angeles is one of the most vivid evocations of paranoia in all the noir genre. During the early 1950s, many film noirs had as their protagonists corrupt policemen, in contrast to the damaged war veterans of the 1940s such as Frank Enley. In *The Prowler* (1951), made for United Artists, Heflin plays such a bad cop role, but one that was quite daring for its time with its open dramatization of a sexual affair and a subsequent unplanned pregnancy. Through that decade, Heflin also appeared in a number of westerns, most famously in *Shane* (1953).

**Selected Noir Films:** *Johnny Eager* (1942), *Kid Glove Killer* (1942), *The Strange Love of Martha Ivers* (1946), *Possessed* (1947), *Act of Violence* (1949), *The Prowler* (1951), *Black Widow* (1954).

Brian McDonnell

**HELL DRIVERS** (Rank-Aqua, 1957). *Director:* C. Raker ("Cy") Endfield. *Producer:* Benjamin Fisz. *Script:* C. Raker Endfield and John Kruse, based on a story by John Kruse. *Cinematography:* Geoffrey Unsworth. *Music:* Hubert Clifford. *Cast:* Stanley Baker (Tom Yately), Herbert Lom (Gino), Peggy Cummins (Lucy), Patrick McGoohan (Red), William Hartnell (Cartley), Wilfred Lawson (Ed), Sid James (Dusty), Jill Ireland (Jill), Alfie Bass (Tinker), Gordon Jackson (Scottie), David McCallum (Jimmy), Sean Connery (Tom), George Murcell (Tub), Wensley Pithey (Pop), Marjorie Rhodes (Ma West), Beatrice Varley (Mrs. Yately), Robin Bailey (Assistant Manager), John Horseley (Doctor).

*Hell Drivers,* a tough action melodrama, consolidated Stanley Baker's status within the British film industry and provided Sean Connery with a strong supporting role as a reckless lorry driver before his major film break as James Bond in *Dr. No* (1962). Tom Yately, who has just been released from prison, gains a job as a lorry driver with a shady company that only hires men prepared to break the speed limit while delivering gravel. To meet the company-imposed deadline, they are forced to drive dangerously on narrow rural roads. Yately takes up residence with the other drivers at the local boarding house, run by Ma West, but when a fight breaks out at the village dance, he refuses to join in, fearing that he will jeopardize himself due to his prison record. The rest of the men, lead by Red, try to drive Yately out of the company, and when Gino supports Yately, he is killed by Red. Yately then exposes the corrupt collusion between Red and the company manager, Cartley.

The appeal of the film resides in Baker's performance and Endfield's robust direction. Endfield makes sure that the film moves at a breakneck pace, not only on the roads with some superb action scenes, but also in the boarding house and café scenes, which crackle with a sense of violence and sharp dialogue. The only time sentimentality threatens to stall the film occurs when Yately visits his crippled brother Jimmy in London. However, the arrival of Beatrice Varley, as Tom's mother, who vents her bitterness toward her ex-convict son, dissipates any chance that the film will become sentimental. Similarly, the lorry drivers, who are presented as a group of social misfits working only for their bonus money, are shown to be, with the exception of Gino, a vicious pack driven only by self-interest. *Hell Drivers* is a tough, uncompromising film that emphasizes the corruption, not the sense of community, of the drivers.

Geoff Mayer

**HIGH SIERRA** (Warner Bros., 1941). *Director:* Raoul Walsh. *Producers:* Mark Hellinger (associate) and Hal B. Wallis (executive). *Script:* John Huston and W. R. Burnett, based on Burnett's novel. *Cinematography:* Tony Gaudio. *Music:* Adolph Deutsch. *Cast:* Ida Lupino (Marie Garson), Humphrey Bogart (Roy "Mad Dog" Earle), Alan Curtis (Babe Kozak), Arthur Kennedy (Red Hattery), Joan Leslie (Velma), Henry Hull ("Doc" Banton), Henry Travers (Pa Goodhue), Cornel Wilde (Louis Mendoza), Willie Best (Algernon).

*High Sierra* is both an important film noir and one of the earliest Hollywood examples as well as a landmark film in the history of the gangster genre. While the gangsters in key films of the early 1930s, such as *Little Caesar* (1930), *The Public Enemy* (1931), and *Scarface* (1932), were characterized by their strength, aggression, self-confidence, and ability to overcome all obstacles blocking their way to the top, *High Sierra* represents a virtual inversion of these traits. The early gangsters had to die—the censorship regime demanded it. Yet their fall was brief and lacked impact as the films celebrated their rise, not their deaths. Such characters displayed strength, ambition, and aggression, qualities associated with the actors, such as James Cagney and Edward G. Robinson, who played them.

*High Sierra* marks a profound change in the genre. Its protagonist, Roy Earle, is an aging gangster who is not only well past his prime, but living in the past. After eight years in prison, Earle is paroled following the intervention of Big Mac on the condition that Earle will take charge of a robbery planned by Big Mac. Earle is sent to a Californian resort, Tropico Springs, to survey the place where it will take place, and during his trip west he encounters a rural family, the Goodhues. Roy takes a liking to their young daughter Velma, who needs an operation on her clubfoot. Arriving at the resort, he is dismayed when he discovers that his two young associates, Red and Babe, have taken in a dance hall girl, Marie. Roy, however, comes to trust Marie, and she falls in love with him—a feeling that is not, initially, reciprocated as Roy loves Velma.

*High Sierra* (1941). Directed by Raoul Walsh. Shown: Humphrey Bogart (as Roy Earle), Ida Lupino (as Marie Garson). Warner Bros./Photofest.

Velma, after allowing Roy to pay for her operation, rejects him as being too old for her. Roy's pain is compounded by the fact that the robbery goes wrong and Red and Babe are killed while Roy and Marie flee, trying to elude the police. Trapped in the Sierra Mountains, Roy dies when a sniper shoots him. The film concludes with Marie's realization that death is the best result for Roy as he is finally released from a society that offers him nothing but pain and disillusionment.

While a sense of fatalism is intrinsic to the gangster film—in the sense that it is virtually mandatory that he dies at the end—at least in Hollywood films produced before the 1970s, the fatalism that pervades *High Sierra* is both stronger and evident right from the start. The film shows only Earle's downward trajectory and not, as in the earlier films, his rise to the top. In this film, aggression is replaced by pain, humiliation, and confusion. Roy is shown to be a man who has trouble comprehending the world after eight years in prison. As he tells Big Mac soon after his release, "You know, Mac, sometimes I feel that I don't know what it's all about anymore."

This theme, which dominates the film, is visually encapsulated by the first shot of Earle as he leaves Mossmoor Prison at the start of the film. The camera tilts up Earle's back as he slowly turns to reveal a pale, graying, aged gangster, a perception reinforced by the reaction of gangster Jake Kranmer, who asks Earle at their first meeting, "Aren't losing your touch, are you?" Later, Kranmer comments, "You can have your Roy Earle. He don't look much to me. He's getting gray. He may be a powerhouse to some, but he looks like a blown-out fuse to me." This is reinforced when Earle makes a visit to Tropico Springs as he looks out of place, despite his attempt to blend in by carrying a tennis racquet and taking off his black suit jacket.

Roy's response to a changed world is to try to recreate the rural innocence of his youth. This, the film repeatedly shows, is futile. When Roy visits a park as soon as he is released from prison, to "make sure that the grass is green and the trees are growing," his initial sense of contentment in watching the children play ball is soon jarred by workmen collecting rubbish. As the camera moves in on a newspaper headline, "Citizens Protests Ignored" as "Roy Earle Famous Indiana Bank Robber Wins Pardon," Roy is forced to move on. Similarly, driving across country to Tropico Springs, Roy decides to pay a nostalgic visit to the old Earle farm in Indiana. Again, his tranquility is shattered when the present owner recognizes Roy, forcing the gangster to leave.

Roy's relationship with the impoverished rural family the Goodhues, especially their daughter Velma, also ends in humiliation and pain. Roy, oblivious to Velma's selfishness, is embarrassed when she rejects his offer of marriage—after allowing him to pay for the operation on her leg. Only Marie, who, like Roy, has suffered rejection and humiliation, understands his torment, which erupts during a nightmare while he is sleeping:

> No, no, I say. Can't hold me. Take the gates away, I'm crashing out. Yeah, sure, sure, I'll go back to the sweet Indiana farm. But you're holding me back. I'll crash out. I tell you, I'll crash out . . .

This nightmare prefigures Roy's death in the rural setting of the Sierra Mountains as Roy "crashes out" in a lonely death on a barren mountain peak.

As the strength of the gangster diminishes in *High Sierra,* and in subsequent gangster films in the 1940s, the collective power of society correspondingly increases. However, society's increased power is not always shown to be a positive quality. Trapped on Mt. Whitney, a radio reporter describes Roy's plight to his audience, who waits for the kill:

> Whenever the flares are lit the faces of the crowd gathered here look like white masks of snow. They look dead, all but their eyes. . . . Any minute now it looks curtains for Roy Earle. This seems to be the coldest place in the world tonight, cold and unreal. One is awestricken with the gruesomeness of this rendezvous with death. The morbidly curious onlookers standing by as if they watched a game, the tall pine trees clustered around like a silent jury. The stern-faced officers of the law waiting for the

kill. And up above a defiant gangster from a simple farm on the flats of Indiana about to be killed on the highest peak in the United States.

Roy is shot in the back as he attempts to crash out of a hostile, uncaring society. While death in the early gangster films is shown to be necessary in that it punishes the aggressive behavior of the gangster, death for Roy Earle in *High Sierra* and other gangster films of the 1940s, such as *The Killers* (1946), *The Gangster* (1947), and *Raw Deal* (1948), is almost welcomed as it represents a release from their anxieties. It is presented not necessarily as a social good, in removing a threat to society, but in an existential manner as an end to personal pain and torment. It is society, not the individual, that is shown to be greedy, cynical, and threatening.

Geoff Mayer

**A HISTORY OF VIOLENCE** (New Line Productions, 2005). *Director:* David Cronenberg. *Producers:* Chris Bender, David Cronenberg, J. C. Spink, Kent Alterman (executive), Cale Boyter (executive), Josh Braun (executive), Toby Emmerich (executive), Justis Greene (executive), Roger Kass (executive), and Jake Weiner (coproducer). *Script:* Josh Olson, based on a graphic novel by John Wagner and Vince Locke. *Cinematography:* Peter Suschitzky. *Music:* Howard Shore. *Cast:* Viggo Mortensen (Tom Stall), Maria Bello (Edie Stall), Ed Harris (Carl Fogarty), William Hurt (Richie Cusack), Ashton Holmes (Jack Stall), Peter MacNeill (Sheriff Sam Carney), Stephen Hattie (Leland Jones), Greg Bryk (William Orser), Heidi Hayes (Sarah Stall).

At first glance, this screen version of John Wagner's graphic novel would seem to be an unlikely project for Canadian director David Cronenberg as it has a much stronger generic basis than his previous films. Working with a much larger budget than usual (US$32 million), and using actors such as Viggo Mortensen, William Hurt, and Maria Bello, *A History of Violence* is a complex discourse on the simultaneous appeal and repulsion expressed toward the use of violence. To achieve this, Cronenberg has utilized the most simplistic story line, the contemporary revenge film, and employed many of the archetypal characters associated with both American mythology and the Hollywood crime film.

Essentially, Cronenberg questions the simultaneous, somewhat contradictory response involved in the pleasure, the attraction, and the repulsion expressed toward violence. To explore this issue, he sets up a series of contrived scenarios that lead to a violent response. He shoots these scenes in real time with no slow motion and no jump cuts, never forgetting to show the brutal aftermath. He also refuses to provide easy answers or simple solutions by refusing to present the violence as cathartic or redemptive. Yet the film can be enjoyed on a number of different levels—as a conventional crime film involving character regeneration and personal revenge as well as a treatise on a complex moral issue. The film as Cronenberg

A *History of Violence* (2005). Directed by David Cronenberg. Shown from left: Heidi Hayes (as Sarah Stall), Maria Bello (as Edie Stall), Viggo Mortensen (as Tom Stall), Ashton Holmes (as Jack Stall). New Line Cinema/Photofest.

acknowledges, also, has an oblique political context concerning the issue of the television coverage of violence in Iraq and elsewhere and the way it exploits the spectacular imagery while censoring the aftermath—the bodies left behind.

The film's opening scene shows two men leaving a small-town motel. One man, Leland Jones, enters the main office of the motel, while the younger man, Greg Bryk, waits outside in their car. When Jones returns, he tells Bryk that he had "a little trouble with the maid." Returning to the motel office to get more water, Bryk discovers two bodies and a terrified little girl, who approaches him for protection. However, as he coaxes the child to come forward, he slowly raises his gun and points it at her. The film then cuts to the scream of another frightened child, the daughter of Tom Stall, who reassures her that "there is no such thing as monsters."

This masterly opening shows the deceptive appearance of evil and the fact that, in the most banal settings, violence resides just beneath the surface of everyday life. This dual reality involving violence and normality permeates every scene. When Jones and Bryk violate a waitress in Tom Stall's diner, he mercilessly executes both men, an act praised by the media and the local community. However, when Stall's son Jack is victimized at school, his physical response, which is the same as his father's, is criticized at school and at home. When Tom tells Jack that "in this family we do not solve problems by hitting people," Jack replies, "No, in this family we shoot them." Tom then hits his son across the face.

The setting for *A History of Violence* is Millbrook, Indiana (although much of the film was shot in the Canadian town of Millbrook, Ontario). This is mythic Americana, the seemingly serene countryside and the overly friendly small town. Here lives the perfect family man, Tom Stall, with his perfect family—wife Edie, teenage son Tom, and young daughter Sarah. Tom owns the local diner, and Edie is the local lawyer. However, when news of Tom's actions in the diner reach Philadelphia, his dark past begins to show, and mobster Carl Fogarty arrives in Millbrook with two men. Fogarty accuses Tom of being Joey Cusack, a former hit man who escaped the mob after mutilating Fogarty by tearing an eye out of its socket with barbed wire. After Jack is kidnapped, Stall responds by killing Fogarty and his men, an action witnessed by Edie, who begins to doubt Tom's denial that he is Cusack.

Stall's emotional façade begins to disintegrate, and Cronenberg shifts the focus of the film away from the external threat to the Stall family to its internal tensions. In the film's most disturbing scene Edie Stall comes to realize that she is both stimulated and frightened by her husband's violence. When he struggles with her on the stairs within their home, she responds sexually, followed by a strong display of self-disgust. This scene provides a dark rejoinder to an earlier one where, before the arrival of Fogarty, she seduced her husband dressed as a cheerleader. Now that Stall's secret life has been exposed, fantasy is replaced by a dark reality.

Fearing another attack on his family, Tom travels to Philadelphia to make peace with his estranged older brother Richie, a middle-level mobster. However, when Richie tells Tom that only his death will rectify the problem he caused years ago with his mutilation of Fogarty's face, Tom kills his brother and his associates. He then travels back to Millbrook and the film's ambiguous ending. Desperate for redemption, Stall throws his gun away and slowly enters a lake, hoping to wash away his sins. His return to his family is equally problematic—his young daughter Sarah welcomes him back, while Jack and Edie watch him cautiously across the family dinner table. Jack eventually responds to his father, although Edie maintains her distance as the film ends.

Cronenberg refuses to provide a simple ending. Violence, the film suggests, provides pleasure and, in certain situations, is sought after. Similarly, its origin is also a matter of conjecture—is it inherited through specific families, or is it a normal part of the human condition? When is it justified, and why do we seek it? There is, however, one aspect that the film shows—it should never be perceived as merely pleasurable, nor should it provide the basis of popular entertainment without exploring its ugly consequences.

Geoff Mayer

**HITCHCOCK, ALFRED** (1899–1980). Without doubt the most celebrated film director of the twentieth century, Hitchcock was renowned as a creator of cinematic suspense who exerted an almost Pavlovian control over the emotions and reactions of his audiences. He worked with great success for half a century in a wide range of genres, from spy films to gothic romances to glossy adventure films, but among his best films are several that lie clearly within the parameters of film noir. This entry will concentrate on his work on these titles rather than on his overall movie career. Born in London, England, at the end of the Victorian age, Alfred Hitchcock grew up in a lower-middle-class Catholic family and attended a Jesuit school, where he famously learned the temporal and religious consequences of both sin and crime. His movie career started in silent film in the 1920s, and his very first job involved the designing of title cards. In subsequent years he learned the skills of script writing, art direction, editing, and directing. Hitchcock worked in England until 1939, and then at the outbreak of World War II he moved to the United States and settled in Los Angeles. Even during the 1930s, he had been interested in the theme of the so-called wrong man, that is, the plight of a man wrongly accused of a crime he did not commit. In such films as *The 39 Steps* (1935) he explored these issues, concentrating on the predicaments of ordinary people wrenched out of their routine lives. Disliking clichéd visual motifs, Hitchcock often chose unlikely settings for the commission of the dark deeds usually associated with crime films. Interested also in the potential violence within people and the turmoil of inner conflicts characteristic of film noir, he sometimes embodied these features in contradictory figures such as Norman Bates in *Psycho* (1960) or Uncle Charlie in *Shadow of a Doubt* (1943).

Hitchcock made many popular entertainments but also hankered after the kind of serious critical respect for his art that came only belatedly and from people outside American mainstream culture. This ambition for serious recognition may have helped fuel his desire to anchor even his entertainments with a more sober underlying commentary on the darker side of human nature. For example, in the manner of gothic romance, he built up the suspense inherent in a wife's doubts about her husband's character, both in *Rebecca* (1940) and in the aptly named *Suspicion* (1941). He also depicted a niece suspicious of her adored uncle, who may be a serial killer, in *Shadow of a Doubt*. Hitchcock may have made most of his films outside of the noir tradition, but he was always fascinated by crime, by guilt, and by the temptation to transgress society's mores felt by basically moral people. Often, if an individual stands between a Hitchcock character and that person's desires, the obstacle is soon eliminated. In *Strangers on a Train* (1951) this is clearly the case with Bruno, who is keen to be rid of an inconvenient parent and seeks to enlist Guy in a murder exchange. Hitchcock's Catholic upbringing, sense of sin, and interest in the secrets of the confessional helped make *I Confess* (1953) a dark and intriguing glimpse into the conflicting loyalties of a professional, in this case a priest who maintains his vow of silence even when he himself is tried for the murder confessed to him by the man he protects. Hitchcock's later film *The Wrong Man* (1956) in its very name points to a theme at the heart of film noir as well as to one central to his own works: an innocent man who is hounded by a malign fate. The resulting mental collapse of the man's wife (played by Hitchcock favorite Vera Miles) is a particularly bleak feature of this film's narrative. These two films were nowhere near as popular with the public as other Hitchcock entertainments, but they are truly noir. While some critics regard it as a marginal noir only, the themes of death, betrayal, conspiracy, and obsession in the haunted film *Vertigo* (1958) place it firmly within the ambit of film noir. Some historians feel that with *Psycho* Hitchcock brought to an end the kind of subtle and ambiguous filmmaking that characterized classical noir and led Hollywood more in the direction of the type of sheer spectacle that the 1960s and 1970s would offer as standard fare. It is certainly true that he always wanted to operate beyond the limits of subject matter and treatment imposed by the Production Code, and so when Hitchcock made *Frenzy* in 1972, he was able to depict the depraved killings of the serial murderer known as the Necktie Killer in a much more explicit manner than in *The Lodger* (1926) or even in *Psycho*.

**Selected Noir Films:** *Rebecca* (1940), *Suspicion* (1941), *Shadow of a Doubt* (1943), *Spellbound* (1945), *Notorious* (1946), *The Paradine Case* (1947), *Rope* (1950), *Strangers on a Train* (1951), *I Confess* (1953), *The Wrong Man* (1956), *Vertigo* (1958), *Psycho* (1960), *Marnie* (1964), *Frenzy* (1972).

Brian McDonnell

**HOLLOW TRIUMPH** (a.k.a. *The Scar*, Eagle-Lion, 1948). *Director:* Steve Sekely. *Producer:* Paul Henreid. *Script:* Daniel Fuchs, from the novel by Murray Forbes. *Cinematography:* John Alton. *Music:* Sol Kaplan. *Cast:* Paul Henreid (John Muller/Dr. Bartok), Joan Bennett (Evelyn Hahn), Eduard Franz (Frederick Muller), John Qualen (Swangron), Leslie Brooks (Virginia Taylor), Mabel Paige (Charwoman).

*Hollow Triumph* is an underrated and understudied example of the film noir genre. It is a film that deploys, in an entertaining and suspenseful way, important noir themes such as identity, the doppelganger, and the actions of fate, exploring existential doubt about identity and positing the notion that in the final analysis people are unable to escape their doom. Paul Henreid plays the double role of John Muller, a psychopathic career criminal, and also of Dr. Bartok, a well-established psychiatrist who is physically Muller's double. On the run from avenging criminals, Muller usurps the identity of the doctor to find sanctuary from danger, but he then finds that he is pursued even in his new identity. A typical noir hero on the run, ironically, he cannot escape his fate, even when he has successfully hoodwinked people about who he is. In fact, it is the high quality of his deception that traps him at the end.

The first 15 minutes of *Hollow Triumph* could make viewers believe they are watching a straightforward caper film as Muller's gang attacks a casino and earns the implacable vengeance of its gangster owner. From that point on, though, the narrative is full of twists, turns, and surprises that help turn the movie into something more thought provoking. The first twist occurs when Muller discovers his resemblance to Dr. Bartok and determines to usurp that man's life. Since Bartok has a noticeable scar on his cheek, this requires Muller (who has had medical training), in a particularly harrowing sequence, to cut an identical mark into his own face. A second twist occurs when he finds that he has cut the scar into the wrong cheek because a guiding photo he has taken of Bartok has been inadvertently flipped during processing. Strangely enough, after Muller murders Bartok and takes over his practice, no one seems to notice this discrepancy, underscoring how unobservant and preoccupied most people can be. Nonetheless Muller remains anxious for his own security, particularly as he has begun an affair with the doctor's receptionist, Evelyn. Later, there is a third twist when Muller's brother tells him he is no longer being chased by the gangsters and that all his extraordinary efforts have now proved unnecessary. The narrative's last devastating twist occurs when he is mistaken for Bartok by thugs and realizes that Bartok (a reckless gambler who has run up huge debts) is also a wanted man. Muller, in this instance absolutely innocent, must face the wrath of another casino owner.

The plot of *Hollow Triumph* is at pains to present Muller as a very clever, accomplished, but amoral figure. He is a mentally nimble risk taker, showing great presence of mind when imitating Bartok. Furthermore, the sequence where he treats Bartok's psychiatric patients offers wider insights into the neuroses of the general society. Despite his intelligence, his hubris and his contempt for people eventually contribute to his downfall, and fate trips him up. In the film's downbeat ending, when he is shot dead while trying to escape by ship, Muller has finally outsmarted himself. The character of Evelyn presents something of a moral balance to his sociopathic character. She is no innocent dupe but a self-possessed, mature woman, hardened by experience and proud of her cynicism. She correctly diagnoses Muller's rampant egotism but still loves him. Evelyn has a tough exterior when they first meet but is given a soft heart in later scenes. Joan Bennett carries off skillfully this shift of character despite its seeming like a requirement of Production Code approval. The film also has an impressive roll call of quirky minor characters, such as an inquisitive dentist, a garage attendant who wants to be a dancer, and a humane charwoman who is the only person to notice that Muller's scar has miraculously changed cheeks. John Alton's deep focus photography and use of source lighting, seen to best effect in the scenes involving the gang, give *Hollow Triumph* a highly stylish look. A plethora of mirror shots also contributes to the sense of introspection and the questioning of identity.

Brian McDonnell

**THE HOUSE ACROSS THE LAKE** (Hammer, 1954). *Director:* Ken Hughes. *Producer:* Anthony Hinds. *Script:* Ken Hughes, based on his novel *High Wray*. *Cinematography:* Walter Harvey. *Music:* Ivor Slaney. *Cast:* Alex Nicol (Mark Kendrick), Hilary Brooke (Carol Forest), Paul Carpenter (Vincent Gordon), Hugh

Dempster (Frank), Peter Illing (Harry Stevens), Sid James (Beverly Forest), Alan Wheatley (Inspector MacLennan), Susan Stephen (Andrea Forest).

*The House Across the Lake*, based on the novel *High Wray* by the film's director, Ken Hughes, is an archetypal example of the low-budget British hybrid film noir. Hughes incorporates many archetypal elements found in seminal noir films such as *Double Indemnity* (1944)—most notably the sexual entrapment of the male character by a femme fatale desirous of killing her husband for material reasons. In *The House Across the Lake*, duplicitous Carol Forest schemes to kill her wealthy husband after she learns that he is dying and plans to cut off his financial support after his death. Consequently, Carol exploits the sexual hunger of jaded, failed novelist Mark Kendrick, who lives across the lake from the Forest mansion. Kendrick, for his part, struggles with his conscience as he forms a friendship with Carol's husband, Beverly, and his daughter.

The film's short running time necessitates that little time is wasted on subplots, and the film strips the thematic and narrative basis of noir back to its iconic essence. Consequently, the viewer is readily aware that Kendrick's attempts to break away from Carol are futile and that, eventually, he will participate in Beverly's death. Also, a rudimentary familiarity with film noir means that once the murder is executed, the affair between Carol and Kendrick will sour, resulting in his confession. This is an assured film providing minor Hollywood actor Alex Nicol with a rare opportunity to star in a nonwestern role.

Geoff Mayer

**HUSTON, JOHN** (1906–1987). Important as both a director and a script writer, Huston confounded auteurists by having no consistent thematic preoccupations. After immediate acclaim as a young director, he experienced some mid-career wobbles but came impressively back into form in his later years. Born in Missouri, John Huston was the son of famous actor Walter Huston and, in turn, the father of actress Anjelica Huston. They are, in fact, the first three-generational family to all win Academy Awards. John Huston led a very eventful life, albeit with some self-mythology built up around its details. In his youth he was a boxer and apparently served for a time in the Mexican cavalry. He joined the film industry when he became a script writer at Warner Bros. Huston made an immediate splash and launched his reputation with his directing debut *The Maltese Falcon* (1941). In that seminal film, he was able to maintain the core strengths of the Dashiell Hammett story and also to elicit fine performances from his ensemble cast, including Humphrey Bogart, Mary Astor, Sydney Greenstreet, Peter Lorre, Ward Bond, and Elisha Cook Jr. A distinguished wartime documentarian with films such as *The Battle of San Pietro* (1944), Huston also made one documentary about the rehabilitation of psychologically damaged soldiers that is mandatory viewing for anyone interested in the end-of-war malaise that helped create the classical film noir cycle. *Let There Be Light* (1946), about the psychiatric treatment of veteran soldiers suffering war neuroses, was suppressed by the Defense Department for more than 30 years but emerges today as a haunting factual counterpart to the amnesia noirs such as *Somewhere in the Night* (1946), *High Wall* (1947), *The Crooked Way* (1949), and *The Clay Pigeon* (1949).

Huston had written the script for the Universal film noir *The Killers* (1946) without credit as he was working at Warner Bros. at the time, but his first post-war directing success was when he made *The Treasure of the Sierra Madre* in 1948. In this film, which some have characterized as film noir, Huston portrayed the dynamics of a group working together on a quest, which became a pattern in his films, a recurrent Huston preoccupation being the behavior of ordinary men under tough and extreme circumstances. Some critics thought that the generally admired *Key Largo*, which he made that same year, betrayed its stage origins and was less cinematic than *Sierra Madre*. Huston made the most of his chance to helm a caper film with *The Asphalt Jungle* in 1950, a film that had an inspirational effect on many later heist movies. In a radical move he made the criminals themselves the centre of audience attention and sympathy, not the authority figures, and the resulting film was marvelously atmospheric. The curious and self-indulgent semiparody *Beat the Devil* (1953), made with Humphrey Bogart, was an attempt to revive the spirit of *The Maltese Falcon* and featured Robert Morley in a Sydney Greenstreet role. After this, Huston's career was turbulent, and the quality of his films was mixed, but his later adventure story, the Rudyard Kipling adaptation *The Man Who Would Be King* (1975), was considered a classic piece, as was his 1979 film version of Flannery O'Connor's *Wise Blood*. John Huston's greatest contribution to neo-noir, however, was as an actor. His compelling performance as the thoroughly corrupt Noah Cross in *Chinatown* (1974) established a solid link between his place in old noir and in neo-noir.

**Selected Noir Films:** Huston was director for the following films: *The Maltese Falcon* (1941, and script writer), *The Treasure of the Sierra Madre* (1948), *Key Largo* (1948, and script writer), *The Asphalt Jungle* (1950, and script writer), *Beat the Devil* (1953, and script writer). Huston was also a script writer for *High Sierra* (1941), *Dark Waters* (1944, uncredited), *Three Strangers* (1946), *The Stranger* (1946, uncredited), and *The Killers* (1946, uncredited). Huston also acted in *Chinatown* (1974).

Brian McDonnell

**I**

**I WAKE UP SCREAMING** (Twentieth Century Fox, 1941). *Director:* H. Bruce Humberstone. *Producer:* Milton Sperling. *Script:* Dwight Taylor, from the novel by Steve Fuller. *Cinematography:* Edward Cronjager. *Music:* Cyril J. Mockridge. *Cast:* Betty Grable (Jill Lynn), Victor Mature (Frankie Christopher), Carole Landis (Vicky Lynn), Laird Cregar (Ed Cornell), William Gregan (McDonald), Elisha Cook Jr. (Harry).

This movie is a significant but undervalued example of the classical film noir cycle coming extremely early (1941) and forging a link between the screwball comedies of the late 1930s, the Thin Man series of light-hearted mystery movies, and film noir proper. Given limited screenings in 1941 under the title *Hot Spot*, it received its main release under the present title in 1942. With its morally ambivalent authority figures, its obsessive tone, and moments of dark perversity, *I Wake Up Screaming* deserves to be counted as one of the more important forerunners to the wave of noir movies to follow in 1944, including *Laura, Murder My Sweet*, and *Double Indemnity*.

Opening on a sensational newspaper story about a "beautiful model" being murdered, *I Wake Up Screaming* quickly introduces man-about-town Frankie Christopher, who had sponsored the dead woman, Vickie Lynn, in a *Pygmalion*-like scheme to have her accepted into high society despite her modest origins. As both Frankie and Vickie's sister Jill are interrogated by police, the early part of the film incorporates a series of flashbacks depicting the last months of Vickie's life. A number of murder suspects are proffered, including Frankie and his chums,

*I Wake Up Screaming* (1941). Directed by H. Bruce Humberstone. Shown in foreground: Laird Cregar (as Ed Cornell), Betty Grable (as Jill Lynn). Fox/Photofest.

who are all attracted to Vickie (and who all feel used by the ambitious young model), and Harry, the surly switchboard boy at her apartment building. Jill also says she had noticed someone suspicious stalking Vickie at the restaurant where she worked, ogling her like the "wolf at the three little pigs." It transpires that this obsessed figure is police detective Cornell, who is himself now investigating Vickie's death.

After some initial animosity, Frankie and Jill gradually become romantically involved. She seems to him to be different from Vicky, and he eventually shows Jill a new, nicer side of himself by being kind to people. Seemingly omnipresent, the sinister and looming Cornell watches their socializing. In these central sequences, which involve swimming excursions, slapstick scenes in bedrooms, and the couple hiding out in an adult movie theater, the otherwise dark tone of the film lightens to resemble a screwball comedy such as the contemporaneous Preston Sturges film *Sullivan's Travels*. Jill and Frankie become quasi-detectives as they attempt to learn the truth about the killing. They soon implicate the switchboard boy, Harry, and trap him into confessing to the crime. He reveals that Cornell had known of his guilt all along but had hidden his knowledge to wreak revenge on Frankie for appearing to steal away Vickie's affections away from him. The film reaches its climax when Frankie visits Cornell's apartment and discovers that it is a shrine to Vickie, with lots of flowers and photos and posters of her. The desperate detective then poisons himself. Jill arrives as Cornell slumps dead.

The themes of *I Wake Up Screaming* are those staples of the noir genre: obsessive love and the predicament of a man wrongly accused of a crime. Even the film's name has the nightmarish ring of a Cornell Woolrich title. At one point, Cornell says to Frankie, "You're like a rat in a box with no holes," indicating that he is trapped existentially, with little prospect of escape. The characters, too, are stock noir figures: Frankie the cocky figure who learns humility, Vickie the siren who draws men to her blatant sexuality, Jill (played by glamorous star Betty Grable) the somewhat stuffy voice of reason and caution, Cornell the respectable professional with a dark secret. As played by Laird Cregar, Cornell is emphatically a heavy and one of the film's most memorable figures. The visual style of *I Wake Up Screaming* is often striking right from the credits, which are made up of neon lights seen against the nighttime skyline of Manhattan. Source lighting features in the shadowy fight in an interrogation room that resembles the similar location in *Murder, My Sweet*. Noir lighting dominates whenever Cornell is on the prowl, and Frankie is effectively shown hiding in the chiaroscuro shadows of an elevator framework while pressuring Harry into a confession. The very quick entry into and exit out of many early flashbacks (some so quick it is almost like inter-cutting) is a major feature of the narrative, and it is notable that we never see the murder of Vicky, even in a flashback.

With its strong performances, busy plotlines, and overall style, it is a pity the film falls a little flat at the end with a conventional happy romantic conclusion. In its closing, as at other points, the film seems unsure of exactly what genre it wishes to belong to. A deleted scene at the department store where Jill works (and included in a new DVD version of the film) would have taken *I Wake Up Screaming* even more in a lighter (and less noirish) direction. This scene, which depicts Jill's overly amorous boss and shows an old lady who wants to buy song lyrics to stimulate her husband's waning ardor, seems mainly designed to allow Grable to sing a song. Despite these features, the film has a strong noir basis and contains instances of unusual pithiness such as its use of the expression "just because he didn't give you a tumble" during the police questioning of Jill. This was a very frank term for Hollywood in 1941. The film's story was used again later in the classical film noir cycle when *I Wake Up Screaming* was remade as *Vicki* (1953).

Brian McDonnell

**I WOULDN'T BE IN YOUR SHOES** (Monogram, 1948). *Director:* William Nigh. *Producer:* Walter Mirisch. *Script:* Steve Fisher, based on a short story by Cornell Woolrich. *Cinematography:* Mack Stengler. *Music:* Edward J. Kay. *Cast:* Don Castle (Tom), Elyse Knox (Ann), Regis Toomey (Judd), Charles D. Brown (Inspector Stevens), Rory Mallinson (Detective).

The dominant influence in *I Wouldn't Be in Your Shoes* is Cornell Woolrich. His short story was first published in *Detective Fiction Weekly* in 1938 and republished in

1943. For more than a decade Woolrich reworked variations of the story of a man imprisoned for a murder he did not commit, thereby forcing his wife, or girlfriend in some stories, to exchange her mainstream world for the underworld. During the investigation the woman has to assume some of the traits of the femme fatale as she ruthlessly uses any man who gets in her way. Popular Woolrich novels, such as *Phantom Lady* and *The Black Angel,* as well as short stories, such as *Murder in Wax, Face Work,* and *Those Who Kill,* utilize this premise.

Tom and Ann, husband and wife dance team, are between jobs when they find a parcel of money. The money is traced to a murdered recluse, and Tom, through discarded dancing shoes, is arrested and convicted. Only Ann, who works in a dance hall teaching lonely men to "dance," believes in his innocence, and she persuades an admirer, policeman Judd, to assist her in her search for the real killer. Judd, who is in love with Ann, offers to help her after she offers to cement their relationship, and marry him, if he will help her.

In a typical Woolrich plot contrivance, which is implausible in terms of the overall story, Judd is revealed to be the murderer, and he is shot by a colleague when he resists arrest. This low-budget Monogram film suffers from poor production values that constrain the actors and limit the action by the small number of sets and scenes, which lack the requisite sense of atmosphere. However, the film does have one startling moment, typical of Woolrich's fiction, when Ann offers herself to Judd if he will help her find the real killer. This reaction of the seemingly virtuous woman to offer her body in exchange for assistance is, in the context of the censorship imposed by the Production Code Administration in the 1940s, a striking sequence. Also, Judd, the sad, obsessive policeman who assists in his own demise, is a true noir protagonist who incriminates himself on behalf of a woman who has no real interest in him.

Geoff Mayer

**IMPULSE** (Tempean Films, 1954). *Director:* Cy Endfield (Charles de Lautour). *Producers:* Robert S. Baker and Monty Berman. *Script:* Cy Endfield (Jonathan Roach) and Laurence Huntington, based on a story by Robert S. Baker and Carl Nystrom. *Cinematography:* Jonah Jones. *Music:* Stanley Black. *Cast:* Arthur Kennedy (Alan Curtis), Constance Smith (Lila), Joy Shelton (Elizabeth Curtis), Jack Allen (Freddie), James Carney (Jack Forrester), Cyril Chamberlain (Gray), Cameron Hall (Joe).

*Impulse* was directed and written by American Cy Endfield, who, as he was forced to do throughout the period from 1952 to 1955, used a series of different names, such as Hugh Raker and C. Raker, so that he could continue to work in Britain. *Impulse,* for example, was supposedly directed by Charles de Lautour, but in practice, Endfield directed the film. Similarly, Endfield, as Jonathan Roach, cowrote the screenplay with Lawrence Huntington. This situation was forced on Endfield following his flight from the United States in the early 1950s after he was named as a Communist in the hearings conducted by the House Committee on Un-American Activities. This was Britain's gain and America's loss as Endfield brought enormous energy and talent to the sometimes staid British film industry during this period as he labored on cheap coproduction films produced by Robert Baker and Monty Berman for their company, Tempean Films.

*Impulse* also benefited from the presence of American actor Arthur Kennedy, who, although not a major Hollywood star, was one of the more talented American imports brought out to Britain in the 1950s so that their films would have some chance of a release in the United States. Kennedy stars in *Impulse* as real estate agent Alan Curtis, who operates a small agency with his partner Freddie in the quiet Sussex village of Ashmore. Curtis lives a modest middle-class life with his wife, Elizabeth, and a weekly bridge game with Freddie appears to be their only outlet. While Curtis clearly loves his wife, he is bored with this situation and longs for excitement away from Ashmore.

When Elizabeth decides to spend the weekend with her mother in London, after rejecting Alan's plea to fly to Paris with him, he goes to the local hotel for a drink, where he spots an attractive brunette, Lila. Driving home in the rain, he notices that her car has broken down, so he offers to take her back to his house. While making arrangements for the local garage to repair her car, Lila decides to take a bath, and she flirts openly with Curtis—even though she knows he is married. When two men, posing as policemen, stalk Lila, Alan takes her to London, where he becomes embroiled in a jewel robbery and with a shady nightclub owner, Jack Forester, who is interested in the stolen jewelry.

*Impulse* is a modest film that reveals some of the essential differences between British and American noir films in the late 1940s and 1950s. The film's central theme, based around a bored, discontented married man seeking adventure and excitement, is a familiar one in the 1940s as it is found in Hollywood noir films such as *The Woman in the Window* (1945), *Pitfall* (1948), and *The File on Thelma Jordan* (1949). *Impulse*, however, while conforming to this basic pattern involving a femme fatale (Lila) and a bored husband, is less melodramatic. The femme fatale genuinely cares for the husband and, finally, sacrifices her chance to escape by returning to the police and telling them that he is innocent.

The film's determination to avoid the excesses of the American cinema extends to its leisurely pacing as Endfield spends considerable time detailing the bland lifestyle of middle-class England. Hence Alan Curtis's decision to spend the night with Lila and subsequently run away with her comes as a shock, and although the audience is aware that his interest in her is primarily sexual, as she offers the excitement missing in his life, the film is also careful to show that he has a loving relationship with his wife, Elizabeth. On this level, *Impulse* reiterates a familiar noir theme showing how the daily routine of everyday life can disturb a normal, loving relationship and that, if the circumstances are right, a partner's affections can be easily deflected. While sharing little of the stylish visual appeal of its Hollywood counterpart, *Impulse* has a quiet, low-key charm representative of the best British films of this period.

Geoff Mayer

**IN A LONELY PLACE** (Santana/Columbia, 1950). *Director:* Nicholas Ray. *Producer:* Robert Lord. *Script:* Andrew Solt, adapted by Edward H. North from the novel by Dorothy B. Hughes. *Cinematography:* Burnett Guffey. *Music:* George Antheil. *Cast:* Humphrey Bogart (Dixon Steele), Gloria Grahame (Laurel Gray), Frank Lovejoy (Brub Nicolai), Carl Benton Reid (Capt. Lochner), Art Smith (Mel Lippman), Jeff Donnell (Sylvia Nicolai), Martha Stewart (Mildred Atkinson), Robert Warwick (Charlie Waterman), Jack Reynolds (Henry Kesler).

"I was born when she kissed me; I died when she left me; I lived a few short weeks while she loved me." These are the most famous and poignant lines from *In a Lonely Place*, an intriguing noir collaboration between director Nicholas Ray and star Humphrey Bogart. Made by Bogart's independent company, Santana Pictures, and set in the world of Hollywood filmmaking, it is a somber, broodingly romantic,

*In a Lonely Place* (1950). Directed by Nicholas Ray. Shown from left: Frank Lovejoy (as Det. Sgt. Brub Nicolai), Carl Benton Reid (as Capt. Lochner), Gloria Grahame (as Laurel Gray), Humphrey Bogart (as Dixon Steele). Columbia Pictures/Photofest.

existential tale of two people trying to make a relationship work against the odds. Some might view the comparatively small part that crime plays in the film as a sign that it is only marginally a film noir and that its lasting value really lies in its nature as an adult love story constructed with intelligence. However, its themes of distrust, suspicion, betrayal, loss, alienation, and paranoia are all ones crucial to a noir sensibility.

Laurel Gray (Gloria Grahame), a would-be starlet, provides an alibi for her neighbor, the conflicted screenwriter Dix Steele (Bogart), who is suspected of the murder of a young woman named Mildred. This accidental link leads on to a romantic relationship, during which Laurel becomes the muse who helps him work. Their love, though, is plagued by the deleterious effects of Dix's inner demons and by his violent jealousy. His sense of alienation pulls him away from those closest to him, as is hinted at by the title's multiple meanings, reflecting both the isolation of the hero and his predicament being caught between the past and the future. Indeed, as the title comes onto the screen in the credit sequence, Dix's volatility is already apparent in a verbal joust he has with a stranger in the street. By the time he and Laurel part for good at the conclusion, he is clearly right back in that same lonely place. *In a Lonely Place* is a very loose adaptation of its source book. In the original novel, written by Dorothy B. Hughes, Dix is guilty of Mildred's murder, while the film reveals her boyfriend, Kessler, as the culprit. Dana Polan, in his British Film Institute monograph on the film, points out that in Andrew Solt's final written script version, Dix kills Laurel (although he is innocent of Mildred's death), and he writes the last line of his own screenplay just before his arrest—Polan believes this ending was perhaps shot. In Ray's screen version Laurel does not die, but Dix is seen to be capable of murder, and his violence and complexity certainly kill off the possibility of happiness for the couple.

*In a Lonely Place* was perhaps Nicholas Ray's most personal film, and James Naremore, in his book *More Than Night: Film Noir in Its Contexts*, refers to its "densely self-referential or autobiographical quality" (p. 128). Ray was married to Grahame, but they had separated by the time production began (she later married his son by a previous marriage). Ray put a lot of himself into the character of Dix, especially the mixture of charm, cold-bloodedness, and rebelliousness. The film's main constructed set was a replica of Ray's first apartment in Los Angeles, and he even slept there during filming. At the time, Ray described himself as the man who took the gun out of Bogart's hand, putting him in a film that was character driven rather than action driven. Bogart here plays a much more complex figure than in *Casablanca* or *The Big Sleep*. Dix is a borderline psychotic screenwriter slumming in the Hollywood scene, a self-destructive, volatile alcoholic with a bad, almost hair-trigger temper, a vulnerable aesthete who feels he is surrounded by phonies and bullies. Dix has a retinue of faithful friends, especially an old ham actor and his agent Mel. Detective Brub Nicolai, who investigates Mildred's death and who, along with his wife, Sylvia, befriends Laurel, is a former wartime buddy of Dix's.

Dix's potential for murder is dramatized in his smug reaction to the death of Mildred and by the morbidly obsessive reenactment of the killing that he performs for Brub and Sylvia. Dix may well be paternally protective of his agent and the broken-down actor, but he attacks a college kid, taking out on that innocent bystander his aggression toward Laurel. She devotes herself to him but frets about his violence, wanting to back out of the marriage he proposes but too scared to tell him. Laurel is provided with her own bizarre supporter as well: a lesbian masseuse who calls Laurel "Angel." A nightmare she has about her suspicions of Dix is given a strongly subjective treatment, and the identification of the audience definitely shifts from Dix to Laurel before the end. The film's narrative operates through a sophisticated double plot interweaving the murder investigation and the love affair. It cleverly keeps up audience intrigue about Dix's true nature, emphasizing both his viciousness and his tenderness in key major sequences. Along with the murder reenactment and the postpicnic attack on the college boy, these include the famous breakfast love scene between Laurel and Dix in her kitchen one morning and Dix's unprovoked eruption at a restaurant when Mel gets slapped. The film's sad conclusion ironically comes after two pieces of good news: Dix's new script is praised and offers the prospect of a much needed lift to his career, and Kessler confesses to murdering Mildred.

Some have asked the question, Is *In a Lonely Place* really a film noir? Certainly it is a bleak portrayal of life and of repressed violence. However, the murder mystery is not central, and the narrative does not care too much about its solution. Certainly it is concerned with whether Dix is guilty or innocent, but this is as much because of its possible effect on his relationship with Laurel as for any sense of justice being done to a criminal. Although he is found to be innocent of Mildred's death, Dix is nevertheless capable of killing, and that proves to be the main thing in the end. Instead, *In a Lonely Place* is about a romance that was very adult for its time. As in much noir, there is no traditional Hollywood happy ending. In fact, the film questions the romanticism of Hollywood, even indicting it. Dana Polan, in his monograph *In a Lonely Place*, says that generically, the film lies somewhere between film noir, screwball comedy, and gothic romance (pp. 18, 21). This view should not be surprising to students of Ray's films as the director mixed genres throughout his career. The role of Dix was arguably the closest Bogart ever came to portraying himself. It was certainly his last great performance (exempting the self-parody of *The African Queen* and *The Caine Mutiny*) and may have been his best.

Brian McDonnell

**INTERRUPTED JOURNEY** (Valiant, 1949). *Director:* Daniel Birt. *Producer:* Anthony Havelock-Allen. *Script:* Michael Pertwee. Cinematography: Erwin Hillier. *Music:* Stanley Allach. *Cast:* Valerie Hobson (Carol North), Richard Todd (John North), Christine Norden (Susan Wilding), Tom Walls (Mr. Clayton), Ralph Truman (Inspector Waterson), Vida Hope (Miss Marchment), Alexander Gauge (Jerves Wilding), Dora Bryan (Waitress), Vincent Ball (Workman).

Richard Todd, who burst into prominence with his second film, *The Hasty Heart* (1949), changed direction with his third film, *Interrupted Journey*. Todd, as John North, plays a weak, unfaithful husband caught up in a desperate situation triggered by his sexual desire for another woman. The moral context for the film is established early when North, a relatively unsuccessful writer, decides to leave his wife, Carol, and run away with Susan Wilding, the wife of his publisher. North panics when he sees Susan's husband on the same train that is taking them to an illicit hotel. He pulls the emergency cord and then runs across a field to his wife, who lives close by. Just as North returns home, however, he hears the train crash, and many of the passengers, including Susan Wilding, are killed. Although he denies being on the train, a railway officer (Mr. Clayton) suspects that North pulled the emergency cord.

Gradually, North's nightmare intensifies as evidence is produced that he was on the train with Susan Wilding. Eventually, he breaks down and confesses to Carol and Clayton. When new evidence is discovered that the accident was not caused by North's actions, he is reassured. However, more evidence reveals that Susan was not killed in the train accident but died from a bullet lodged in her back. North now becomes the prime suspect. With Carol's support he evades the police and confronts the real killer, Susan's husband (Jerves) in a hotel room. However, just as Jerves fires his gun into North, he wakes up from his nightmare and tells Susan that he is not going away with her. He then returns to his wife.

Although the dream ending appears contrived, the film carefully simulates the qualities of a nightmare through the unmotivated use of coincidence in the story line. These plot twists, accentuated by the sparse production values and Erwin Hillier's low-key lighting, result in a superior film noir, with Richard Todd and Valerie Hobson expressing the requisite degree of angst as the troubled husband and wife. The ending is similar to, but not as morally complex as, Fritz Lang's *The Woman in the Window* (1944).

Geoff Mayer

**IT ALWAYS RAINS ON SUNDAY** (Ealing, 1947). *Director:* Robert Hamer. *Producers:* Michael Balcon and Henry Cornelius (associate). *Script:* Henry Cornelius, Robert Hamer, and Angus MacPhail, based on the novel by Arthur La Bern. *Cinematography:* Douglas Slocombe. *Music:* Georges Auric. *Cast:* Googie Withers (Rose Sandigate), Jack Warner (Detective-Sergeant Fothergill), Edward Chapman (George Sandigate), Susan Shaw (Vi Sandigate), Patricia Plunkett (Doris Sandigate), John McCallum (Tommy Swann), Sidney Taffler (Morry Hyams), John Slater (Lou Hyams), Jimmy Hanley (Whitey), Alfie Bass (Dicey), John Carol (Freddie), David Lines (Alfie Sandigate), Michael Howard (Slopey Collins), Nigel Stock (Ted Edwards), John Salew (Caleb Neesley), Frederick Piper (Detective-Sergeant Leech), Jane Hylton (Bessie Hyams).

From 1945 to 1949 Robert Hamer directed four of the best noir, or ironic, melodramas produced by the British film industry—*Pink Sting and Sealing Wax* (1945),

*It Always Rains on Sunday, Kind Hearts and Coronets* (1949), and *The Spider and the Fly* (1949). However, when *It Always Rains on Sunday* was released in the United States, Joseph Breen and the Production Code Administration objected to the casual manner in which Rose Sandigate invites her former lover, the escaped convict Tommy Swann, to strip off his prison clothes in front of her as it clearly suggests a sexual relationship between them before he went to jail. The local censorship board in Massachusetts demanded the deletion of this scene.

Set in London's East End, *It Always Rains on Sunday* focuses on the activities of the Sandigate family and members of the local community from dawn to midnight on a rainy Sunday. Rose Sandigate is married to George, a dull man, 15 years her senior, whom she does not love. She takes her frustrations out on his daughters, particularly the sexually active Vi, who is having an affair with a married man (Morry Hyams). The other daughter, the dutiful Doris, is embroiled in a minor row with her boyfriend, Ted, over an offer from Lou Hyams to work in one of his establishments. Doris eventually declines his offer.

When Tommy Swann enters her life, Rose sees a chance for sexual fulfillment and romance. Frustrated by her family responsibilities, Rose tears the dress off Vi, leaving her exposed in her underwear. Vi is presented in the film as a younger mirror image of Rose—only Vi now has the freedom that Rose covets. A flashback shows Rose with Tommy, and he is arrested as they attempt to leave Bethnal Green. Now, at least in Rose's imagination, Tommy represents a chance to escape. After finding him hiding in the Anderson shelter in the backyard, she moves him into the house and, when George goes out for his weekly darts match at the pub, allows him into their bedroom and, more suggestively, their bed. In this manner Hamer bypassed the stringent censorship restrictions while making quite explicit the carnal attraction between Rose and the gangster Swann.

Finally, Slopey Collins, a local newspaperman, suspects that Rose may be hiding Swann. When he enters the Sandigate house, Swann erupts and attacks both the newspaperman and Rose. After an exciting, noirish chase through the dark streets of London, culminating in a railroad marshalling yard, Swann is captured by Detective Sergeant Fothergill (Jack Warner). The film ends with George forgiving Rose, thereby condemning her to a life that will never again experience passion in the East End, a place she has been trying to escape since puberty.

Geoff Mayer

# J

JOHNNY O'CLOCK (Columbia, 1947). *Director:* Robert Rossen. *Producers:* Edward G. Nealis and Milton Holmes (associate). *Script:* Robert Rossen, from an unpublished story by Milton Holmes. *Cinematography:* Burnett Guffey. *Music:* George Duning. *Cast:* Dick Powell (Johnny O'Clock), Evelyn Keyes (Nancy Hobbs), Lee J. Cobb (Inspector Koch), Ellen Drew (Nelle Marchettis), Nina Foch (Harriet Hobbs), Thomas Gomez (Pete Marchettis), John Kellogg (Charlie), Jim Bannon (Chuck Blayden), Jeff Chandler (Turk).

This was the first film directed by Robert Rossen, who had been a prolific, and successful, screenwriter of crime and gangster films (including *Marked Woman* [1937], *Racket Busters* [1938], and *The Roaring Twenties* [1939]) in the late 1930s and early 1940s. Rossen, who was blacklisted in the late 1940s, focused on the dark side of American capitalism by exposing aspects of its hypocritical social values and corrupt institutions—especially the police.

*Johnny O'Clock* was primarily a star vehicle for Dick Powell, who was enjoying resurgence in the mid-1940s after his success as Philip Marlowe in *Murder, My Sweet* (1944). After his initial career as a lightweight leading man and singer at Warner Bros. in the 1930s, *Murder, My Sweet* represented a complete change in his screen persona as he emerged as a tough, cynical protagonist. *Johnny O'Clock* continued this pattern with Powell as the vaguely crooked junior partner of Pete Marchettis, who owns a casino in New York. When a cop associated with both Marchettis and O'Clock is murdered, along with his ex-girlfriend, Inspector Koch applies pressure to both Marchettis and O'Clock by exploiting Marchettis's suspicions that his wife, Nelle, is still in love with O'Clock and is having an affair with him. Nelle, the film's femme fatale, encourages her husband's paranoia by giving both men identical watches as presents. When Koch informs Marchettis of this action, he orders O'Clock's death. O'Clock is forced to kill Marchettis, and when he refuses Nelle's advances, she lies to the police, saying that O'Clock killed her husband in cold blood. The film ends with O'Clock's regeneration, which is largely due to Nancy Hobbs, his new lover.

Although the film's sentimental conclusion is disappointing and dissipates the sense of perversity that permeates much of the film, especially the scenes involving Nelle, her husband, and Johnny, Rossen is more interested in this curious arrangement than the routine plot involving the murder of a corrupt cop and his ex-girlfriend. Thomas Gomez, as Pete Marchettis, reinforces the film's subtle exploration of racial prejudice within the limitations of the crime thriller as Gomez is able to imbue his otherwise conventional gangster role with a layer of pathos mixed in with his murderous traits. When Marchettis explains to Nelle that she considers him inferior to Johnny because of his Mexican heritage, Rossen's script heads off in a political direction that, in the next few years, would lead to Rossen's blacklisting within the film industry following the anti-Communist crusade conducted by the House Committee on Un-American Activities.

Geoff Mayer

**K**

KANSAS CITY CONFIDENTIAL (United Artists, 1952). *Director:* Phil Karlson. *Producer:* Edward Small. *Script:* George Bruce and Harry Essex, based on an unpublished story by Harold R. Greene and Rowland Brown. *Cinematography:* George E. Diskant. *Music:* Paul Sawtell. *Cast:* John Payne (Joe Rolfe), Coleen Gray (Helen Foster), Preston Foster (Tim Foster), Neville Brand (Boyd Kane), Lee Van Cleef (Tony Romano), Jack Elam (Pete Harris), Dona Drake (Teresa), Howard Negley (Scott Andrews), Carleton Young (Assistant District Attorney Martin), Charles Cane (Detective Mullins).

*Kansas City Confidential* is a stylish noir film, typical of director Phil Karlson's tight, emphatic style of direction, and he regularly transformed formulaic scripts into some of the finest noir films of the 1950s. In *Kansas City Confidential* Karlson is assisted by cinematographer George Diskant's low-key lighting and one of the best casts for this type of film, especially Neville Brand, Jack Elam, and Lee Van Cleef as a trio of murderous hoods forced to participate in an armored car robbery. Assisted by the film's stylized hard-boiled dialogue, *Kansas City Confidential* is a key noir; as a low budget film, it forced the filmmakers to be inventive in suggesting the Kansas City and Mexican settings while never leaving a Hollywood soundstage, enhances the film's pervasive sense of desperation and entrapment.

Tim Foster, an embittered former Kansas City police captain who was forced to retire, devises a clever plan to rob an armored car. He blackmails three gangsters, Boyd Kane, Tony Romano, and Pete Harris, into executing a meticulous plan whereby each gangster is forced to wear a mask at all times so that they cannot identify their partners if they are captured by the police—only Foster knows

*Kansas City Confidential* (1952). Directed by Phil Karlson. Shown: John Payne (as Joe Rolfe). United Artists/Photofest.

the identity of the men. The plan also depends on exact timing as the armored car arrives at an inner city bank at the same time each morning as a nearby florist van. The robbers utilize a similar van so as to divert police attention onto the innocent florist driver. The robbery is successful, and the police detain Joe Rolfe, the driver of the florist van, for questioning. Karlson exploits this setup fully as he shows in detail the arbitrary, brutal methods employed by the police to extract a confession from Rolfe, an ex-convict. However, when the getaway van is found, Assistant District Attorney Martin reluctantly releases Rolfe. Rolfe, angered by his treatment by the police and the criminals, goes after them. Following a tip from an underworld figure, he finds Harris in Tijuana, and he employs the same brutal methods used by the police to force a confession from Harris. When Harris is killed by the local police, Rolfe assumes his identity and travels to a small Mexican resort where the other participants are waiting. A cat-and-mouse situation follows as the criminals try to get their share of the robbery, and only the intervention of Foster's daughter Helen, a law student who is vacationing with her father, saves Rolfe's life when his true identity is revealed. The film climaxes on a boat anchored in the bay, and following a shoot-out, Kane, Romano, and Foster die. Rolfe, to protect Helen, decides not to expose Foster's involvement in the crime.

*Kansas City Confidential* is one of the best noir films of the 1950s with its tough, uncompromising view of life. It reworks some of the familiar noir themes of the postwar period, most notably the problems facing the veteran's assimilation back into society. This film, however, extends this motif by showing that a man's war record is less important than his prison sentence. During Rolfe's brutal interrogation by the police, his war record, which includes a Bronze Star and a Purple Heart, is read out. Realizing that this is not going to help him, he bitterly tells the cops, "Try and buy a cup of coffee with them." The police, interested only in a conviction, are not impressed with his military achievements, and the subsequent action confirms the film's point of view that there is little difference between law officers and criminals.

Geoff Mayer

**KARLSON, PHIL** (1908–1985). Phil Karlson is the most important noir director in the 1950s. His unrelenting depictions of the vulnerability of the individual when confronted by large institutions, government, and criminals shifted the focus of film noir. His films reworked many of the themes and conventions of 1940s noir cinema into a distinctive series of high-quality films. This disappeared in the 1960s when, due to the changes within the Hollywood cinema, he was forced to accept superficial projects such as *Kid Galahad* (1962), starring Elvis Presley, and the last entry into the Matt Helm series, *The Wrecking Crew* (1968), starring Dean Martin as the extraordinary secret agent. These empty, facile films are a far cry from the personal melodramas that Karlson directed in the previous decade, with extraordinary films such as *Scandal Sheet* (1952), *Kansas City Confidential* (1952), *99 River Street* (1953), *The Phenix City Story* (1955), and *The Brothers Rico* (1957).

Karlson was born and raised in Chicago and studied at the Art Institute before undertaking a law degree at Loyola University in Los Angeles. While studying law, Karlson accepted a part-time job at Universal, where he worked in various menial jobs. Gradually, he was offered more responsible positions, such as assistant director on a number of Abbott and Costello films, and during this period he also worked as an editor on films directed by William Wyler and John Ford. Karlson offered gags to Lou Costello, and the star repaid him by bankrolling Karlson's first film as director, *A Wave, A Wac, and a Marine* (1944), a low-budget comedy at the Poverty Row studio Monogram. However, his second film at Monogram, *G.I. Honeymoon* (1945), was successful, and his career as a film director was under way; for the next two years he churned out more than a dozen low-budget films for Monogram, including the socially conscious melodrama *Black Gold* (1947), starring Anthony Quinn as an Indian who discovers oil on his land and trains an orphan to be a jockey for his thoroughbred horse.

Throughout the 1940s and early 1950s Karlson was working at the lowest level of the Hollywood system, at studios such as Monogram and Eagle-Lion, and even when he had a film at a major studio, such as Columbia, including Marilyn Monroe's first film *Ladies of the Chorus* (1949), he remained in their B units. Nevertheless, although some of his films cost as little as $250,000, they were invariably interesting, with sudden bursts of physical or emotional violence and, within the budgetary limitations, a sense of energy and vitality. His opportunities increased in the early 1950s with crime films that presented the world as an intrinsically dangerous place as institutional corruption was pervasive.

In his first major noir film, *Scandal Sheet*, which was based on Samuel Fuller's novel *The Dark Page*, the institutional corruption is evident in the newspaper business, where a ruthless editor, Mark Chapman, and an ambitious reporter, Steve McCleary, seek to boost circulation by exploiting the material dreams of newlyweds by offering them the chance to win a bed with a built-in television. However, their scheme exposes Chapman's dark past, and it leads to betrayal, guilt, and murder. Karlson followed this with two noir films starring John Payne, an actor who revitalized his career in the 1950s when he transformed his screen persona with a succession of tough roles. In *Kansas City Confidential* and *99 River Street* Payne plays characters that are nearly broken by the system. In *Kansas City Confidential* he is an ex-convict harassed by the police after he is wrongfully suspected of participating in an armed robbery. Fittingly, the man who planned the robbery is a bitter ex-detective. In *99 River Street* Payne is again wrongfully suspected of killing his wife, and he is hunted throughout the film.

In *The Brothers Rico* Karlson reiterates his view that society has become totally dehumanized by placing an ex-mobster-turned-businessman, Eddie Rico, in the terrifying situation whereby he unwittingly leads gangsters to his younger brother Johnny. Eddie is forced to passively wait in a hotel room while they kill his brother. This follows the murder of his other brother, Gino, by the same criminal syndicate controlled by a family friend. Based on the novel *Les Frères Rico* by Georges Simenon, Karlson and screenwriters Lewis Meltzer and Ben Perry transform this French novel into a film that epitomizes the flat, realist style of American film noir in the middle to late 1950s.

Karlson remained prolific throughout the 1960s, although he never surpassed his 1950s cycle of noir films. A taut crime melodrama, *Key Witness* (1960), was followed by an unusual war film, *Hell to Eternity* (1960), a true story of an American soldier, Guy Gabaldon, raised by Japanese foster parent who fought the Japanese in the Pacific during World War II. A violent western, *A Time for Killing* (1967), starring Glenn Ford, preceded Karlson's biggest commercial hit, *Walking Tall* (1973), a simplistic revenge story involving a southern sheriff, Buford Passer, and the corruption in his town. This film spawned a television movie in 1978 and a television series as well as a puerile remake in 2004 starring the Rock. Karlson's last film, *Framed* (1975), was also a violent revenge story. Both films shifted the emphasis from the vulnerability of his protagonists in his 1950s films to the self-righteousness of their 1970s counterparts.

**Selected Noir Films:** *The Missing Lady* (1946), *Scandal Sheet* (1952), *Kansas City Confidential* (1952), *99 River Street* (1953), *Tight Spot* (1955), *Hell's Island* (1955), *5 Against the House* (1955), *The Phenix Story* (1955), *The Brothers Rico* (1957), *Key Witness* (1960), *Walking Tall* (1973), *Framed* (1975).

Geoff Mayer

**THE KILLERS** (Universal International, 1946). *Director:* Robert Siodmak. *Producer:* Mark Hellinger. *Script:* Anthony Veiller, from the short story by Ernest Hemingway. *Cinematography:* Woody Bredell. *Music:* Miklos Rozsa. *Cast:* Burt Lancaster (Swede), Ava Gardner (Kitty Collins), Edmond O'Brien (Riordan), Albert Dekker (Colfax), Sam Levene (Lubinsky), Jack Lambert (Dum Dum), John Miljan (Jake), Charles McGraw (Al), William Conrad (Max).

Despite its rather unusual narrative structure and its lack of a strong link between its main continuing character and its chain of story events, *The Killers* is still considered to be one of the more stylish and accomplished noir films of the mid-1940s. It is essentially an expansion of the famous Ernest Hemingway story of the same name into a long investigation that is assembled using a narrative structure based on the model of *Citizen Kane*. The content of Hemingway's story acts like a prologue to *The Killers*'s central events, but his hard-boiled dialogue and laconic style

*The Killers* (1946). Directed by Robert Siodmak. Shown from left: Ava Gardner (as Kitty Collins), Burt Lancaster (as "the Swede"). Universal Pictures/Photofest.

pervade much of the extra original material appended to his own creation. A great deal of the dash and polish of the film is due to the storytelling and visual skill of director Robert Siodmak, and a large contribution is also made by Edmond O'Brien, who brings his usual energy, verve, and self-belief to the largely functional role of investigator Riordan.

Hemingway's story sketched in a cryptic account of the death in a small town of an ex-boxer Olly Anderson, better known as the Swede (played by Burt Lancaster in his film debut), at the hands of a couple of ruthless hit men. Script writer Anthony Veiller (assisted greatly, it is said, by an uncredited John Huston) and Siodmak use this material to create a suspenseful and atmospheric opening to their film. In expressionistically lit scenes in a cheap hotel and a diner that looks like an Edward Hopper painting, psychopathic killers Charles McGraw and William Conrad coldly stalk and then blast into oblivion the Swede, who seems completely fatalistic about his impending doom. Burt Lancaster became famous for his later acrobatic, swashbuckling parts, but here, in his first starring role, he shows another side: passive, still, and unresisting. He makes a laconic remark about having done one bad thing in the past, then awaits his fate stoically. Whereas Hemingway left it at that, the film version introduces a new character, insurance investigator Riordan, who attempts to piece together the back story of Olly Anderson by interviewing many of those who had known him.

In this function Riordan resembles the reporter in *Citizen Kane* trying to solve the mystery of Charles Foster Kane. There is even an equivalent of the earlier film's iconic child's sled Rosebud in the form of an Irish-themed handkerchief that the Swede has kept. The chief contrast in *The Killers*, though, is that Riordan is a much more visible person and an important agent of the plot, and there are a crowded 11 separate flashbacks here rather than the 5 in *Kane*. Highly fortuitous occurrences help him gain vital information to make progress just when he needs it most, and he succeeds in constructing a coherent (if complex) story. It turns out that Anderson was a broken-down boxer who fell into crime and became involved in a major robbery. The caper's kingpin, Colfax, was the boyfriend of Anderson's ex and, along with her, plotted an elaborate double-cross concerning the crime's proceeds. It was Colfax who had sent the hit men to eradicate the Swede after a chance encounter between them threatened his own exposure, but Colfax gets his comeuppance when he and another gang member gun each other down in the film's climax.

As Riordan (yet another film noir quasi-detective) goes about his quest to reconstruct the Swede's life, the film's story line is able to include many exciting set pieces, which are all handled skillfully by Siodmak. These include a bravura three-minute crane shot that depicts a payroll robbery without any editing (a forerunner of the more celebrated extended crane shot in Orson Welles's *Touch of Evil*). However, the piecemeal nature of the plot as Riordan assembles his jigsaw of clues from the testimony of a large number of witnesses tends to create a kind of vacuum at the centre of the film. The Swede remains an elusive figure, hard to pin down or understand, almost two-dimensional. In particular, his relationship with femme fatale Kitty Collins seems to occur between the flashbacks rather than being dramatized within them. This is not a criticism: the tangential narrative of the romance and subsequent betrayal is actually arresting in its originality and poignant in its understatement. Furthermore, its effectiveness is greatly assisted by the vividness of Ava Gardner's portrayal of Kitty. She is photographed erotically throughout, and her sexual allure is extraordinarily powerful in every scene where she appears. Her first appearance at a glamorous party 40 minutes into the film is a key scene. Here the Swede first becomes infatuated with her and is fatefully smitten from that point on.

The film's theme is basically the question Riordan sets himself: why does Olly Anderson not care that he is about to die? What in his life has made him so accepting of the idea of a violent end? The film seeks to answer these questions. The Swede's fate is a product of mishap (a broken hand) and misplaced trust (believing Kitty's promises of lasting love). He should have listened to his philosophizing cell mate, who had ruminated on the tiny scale of human existence when compared to the scope of the solar system and the stars. After all the killings and the deceptions and the tangled motives and dreams, even after much of the robbery money is recovered, Riordan's boss at the insurance company blithely tells him that his good work will result in their next year's premiums varying by just half a cent. In their book *Film Noir: An Encyclopedic Reference to the American Style*, Alain Silver and Elizabeth Ward sum up well these contradictions of *The Killers*: "an undercurrent of violence exists throughout the film and there is also an existential anger present that serves to create a chaotic environment, dark motives, and hopeless situations" (p. 154).

Brian McDonnell

**THE KILLING** (United Artists, 1956). *Director:* Stanley Kubrick. *Producers:* Stanley Kubrick and Morris Bousel. *Script:* Stanley Kubrick, with dialogue by Jim Thompson, from the novel *The Clean Break* by Lionel White. *Cinematography:* Lucien Ballard. *Music:* Gerald Fried. *Cast:* Sterling Hayden (Johnny Clay), Coleen Gray (Fay), Vince Edwards (Val Cannon), Jay C. Flippen (Marvin Unger), Marie Windsor (Sherry Peatty), Ted deCorsia (Randy Kennan), Elisha Cook, Jr. (George Peatty).

Early in his career, and long before gaining fame with landmark movies such as *Dr. Strangelove* (1963), *2001: A Space Odyssey* (1968), and *A Clockwork Orange* (1971), Stanley Kubrick made two films that belong to the classical noir cycle: *Killer's Kiss* (1955) and *The Killing*. A claim could even be made that he returned to the noir world for his last film, *Eyes Wide Shut* (1999), as well. Kubrick's experience as a photographer for *Look* magazine helped his black-and-white compositions when he moved into filmmaking. As with many of his movies, there is something of a coolly distant and academically detached tone to *The Killing*, as if he were more interested in trying out the heist subgenre as an experiment in narrative and photographic techniques (such as source lighting), rather than being fully involved in the fates of his characters. Nevertheless, this film, which ostensibly concerns a robbery at a horse racetrack, remains a taut, well-acted, and stylish example of the cycle and is impressively succinct.

The narrative structure of *The Killing* is particularly interesting. A voice-over narration by a documentary-type voice (an uncredited Art Gilmore) helps link the separate story strands as the early expository scenes are built up. A series of suspenseful vignettes introduces the main players, while the voice-over refers to their being "pieces of a jigsaw." First, Marvin (Jay C. Flippen) is shown behaving rather cryptically. Second, we see a cop, played by Ted deCorsia, who is described as owing large sums of money. Third, Sterling Hayden, who is the heist mastermind Johnny, appears with his wife, Faye. He has been in jail for the past five years. Fourth, a racetrack bartender is glimpsed with his sick wife. Fifth, track cashier George (Elisha Cook, Jr.) is shown arguing with his unsatisfied wife, Sherry (Marie Windsor). He is a little man who is clearly sexually impotent. Sixth, Windsor goes to see her more virile boyfriend, Val (Vince Edwards), whom she is desperate to keep. She foolishly tells Val about the upcoming robbery. Thus she betrays George doubly by her sexual infidelity and by enabling Val to plan a hijacking of his own. Johnny recruits two specialist workers for the caper: a Russian wrestler to distract the attention of security officers and Nicky, a sniper who will create a diversion by gunning down the favorite during the running of a feature race.

The film's narrative progresses conventionally after these vignettes until the day of the race itself, when Kubrick creates a special time scheme. In that section of the narrative we see the day's events broken up and repeated from different characters' points of view. Some of these overlap to show the same occurrences from the perspective of different characters. This involves a little repetition, but the voice-over allows the audience to keep a handle on the exact times things happen. As in most heist films, even the most clinical of plans tend to go wrong because of human frailty. An instance of this is that Nicky the sniper calls a parking lot attendant at the track a "nigger" to get rid of him. The man summons the police and, just after Nicky brings down the leading horse, a cop kills him in a shoot-out. Even more devastating is the scene where most of the gang gather after the successful robbery to await Johnny's divvying up of the spoils. Marvin (who reveals a touch of homoeroticism as well as paternal solicitude in his fawning attention to Johnny) fusses about his absence. Val bursts in on them armed with a shotgun. But the cuckolded George kills him in a sudden burst of incredibly violent mayhem that prefigures 1994's *Pulp Fiction*. Abruptly, all gang members present are dead, except George, and he will soon die after dispatching the faithless Sherry. Johnny misses the carnage as he is running 15 minutes late: this unpunctuality saves his life.

The themes of *The Killing* are thus similar to many noir films: little stories of little people who are leading lives of desperation. Right from the start, there is a sense of the continual accretion of unhappiness. Venality combines with betrayal, futility allies itself with fatalism. This air of existential gloom is assisted by the pithiness of Jim Thompson's dialogue, which is as terse and understated as is Kubrick's overall direction. The whole film has a hard-boiled style with no unnecessary padding. This can be discerned most clearly in the way it concludes. Johnny is faced with the attractive prospect of having all the cash to himself, but he has to transport it out of town. He buys a big suitcase, despite its faulty lock, and meets Faye at a small civic airport. We then see an old lady fussing with her poodle. An argument ensues with check-in staff over whether such a big case can go on the plane as hand baggage and Johnny is forced to check it through. In a succinct and suspenseful series of camera shots, all now goes horribly wrong. The dog runs from its mistress, the baggage cart swerves to miss the animal, Johnny's case falls off, the lock fails, and the robbery money flies like confetti in a plane's propeller wash. When Faye asks Johnny if he will run or give himself up as two armed cops come through the terminal's glass doors to approach him, his laconic reply is, "What's the difference?"

Brian McDonnell

**KISS ME DEADLY** (United Artists, 1955). *Director/Producer:* Robert Aldrich. *Script:* A. I. Bezzerides, from the novel by Mickey Spillane. *Cinematography:* Ernest Laszlo. *Music:* Frank DeVol. *Cast:* Ralph Meeker (Mike Hammer), Albert Dekker (Dr. Soberin), Paul Stewart (Carl Evello), Maxine Cooper (Velda), Gaby Rogers (Gabrielle/Lily Carver), Wesley Addy (Pat), Nick Dennis (Nick), Cloris Leachman (Christina).

One of the more significant and interesting examples of film noir, 1955's *Kiss Me Deadly* is definitely a salient example from the last years of the classical cycle. In some ways it represents the culmination of the private-eye subgenre within noir, while in others its depiction of Mickey Spillane's Mike Hammer marks a radical subversion and undercutting of the tradition of such private detectives as Sam Spade and Philip Marlowe. *Kiss Me Deadly* looks both back to the postwar period of tangled mysteries with murkily motivated crimes and looks forward to the glamorous consumerist world of the 1960s. Private eye Hammer flaunts his souped-up cars, wears narrow-lapelled suits with narrow ties, and resides like a *Playboy* magazine reader (or a forerunner of James Bond) in a modern apartment with a television and an answering machine. Yet he prowls the darkly lit Victorian buildings of the old Los Angeles seeking out marginal and displaced souls. Ralph Meeker absolutely inhabits the role of Hammer in a memorable manner.

The film's narrative follows a standard formula for much of its length. Hammer by chance meets a vulnerable young woman named Christina on the coast highway and, after her death, becomes entangled in a tortuous investigation into why she was killed and by whom. He becomes involved with a parade of dangerous and duplicitous men and women who put in peril both the detective and his associates such as assistant Velda and mechanic Nick. Like his forebears Spade and Marlowe, he deals out some rough justice and suffers the odd beating and drugging himself. He encounters femmes fatales such as Lily/Gabrielle, who mix sex

*Kiss Me Deadly* (1955). Directed by Robert Aldrich. Shown from left: Gaby Rodgers (as Gabrielle/Lily Carver), Ralph Meeker (as Mike Hammer). United Artists/ Photofest.

and violence when they direct both kisses and gunfire in Mike's direction. But in the culmination of the story, the plot moves beyond the usual types of crime into a modern nightmare world of atomic energy and an illegal trade in nuclear fuel. The ominous names "Manhattan Project, Los Alamos, Trinity" presage the almost apocalyptic climax to Hammer's search for the truth.

This new political edge to the film's noir ingredients is supplemented by an equally dramatic shift in the story's treatment of Hammer as a heroic detective figure. As Andrew Spicer puts it in his book *Film Noir*, "*Kiss Me Deadly* continues a left-liberal critique of capitalism by turning the self-righteousness and brutal pragmatism of Hammer's world inside out" (p. 73). Essentially, the film subverts and deconstructs the masculinist ethos of traditional private eye films and Spillane's own novels, where the protagonist's violence and ruthless egotism are valorized. In their dialogue the film's characters instead frequently attack Hammer (e.g., Christina undercuts his male vanities, the Crime Commission mocks his work practices, Velda ironically refers to his quest for "the great whatsit," and Gabrielle questions his emotional honesty). After his friend Nick is crushed under a car by the villains, Hammer seeks vengeance by either killing or causing to die those responsible. But the film portrays this appetite for revenge as reprehensible in its brutality. Even the cops, with whom he has the expected strained relationship of the noir private eye, criticize his narrow and selfish range of vision. As Alain Silver and Elizabeth Ward claim in their book *Film Noir: An Encyclopedic Reference to the American Style,* the film's "central character is less heroic than he is ego-centric, callous and brutal" (p. 157).

Mike Hammer as director Aldrich and screenwriter Bezzerides depict him does have his good points: he is, for example, quite liberal in his attitude to blacks. He is friendly with several negro characters and seems at home in black bars and nightspots. He is protective of a promiscuous young woman whom he advises to say no and of young boxers ripe for exploitation by their self-interested managers. But he can also be malicious, mean-spirited, and avaricious in his hunger for the money he feels must attach to the big secret he is pursuing. His faithful researcher Velda, whom he could not operate without and who loves him, is nonetheless virtually pandered by him to a succession of victimized men in divorce cases. Hammer knows the popular culture of the city well, and *Kiss Me Deadly* presents an impressive portrait of 1950s Los Angeles in its many examples of location shooting. But Mike has no time for the finer things in life, and the film emphasizes his lack of sympathy with poetry, classical music, modern art, ballet, and opera. He is contrasted with admirable and not-so-admirable people who love these things; whose apartments are full of books, paintings, and records; and whose speech is peppered with allusions to the Medusa, Lot's wife, Lazarus, Pandora, and Cerberus.

From the startlingly upside-down credits onward, *Kiss Me Deadly* is highly stylish. Major action set pieces are photographed in a bravura manner, and the inventive night-for-night shooting is augmented by high-contrast lighting. This is especially apparent in the scenes that foreground the antiquely gothic nature of the Bunker Hill tenements. Cinematographer Ernest Laszlo achieves almost abstract diagonal shots in their stairways or around the Angel's Flight inclined rail line. Recently, Robert Aldrich's approved ending has been restored to DVD and other copies of *Kiss Me Deadly,* and this affects in an important way the received wisdom about the film's ultimate message. The studio's former ending had Mike and Velda apparently killed in an explosion of fissionable material in a Malibu beach house. The restored ending, which matches Aldrich's original intentions, shows them escaping to the nearby sea and sheltering from the fireball in the Pacific breakers. Thus the film ends not, as many earlier commentators had claimed, with nuclear holocaust and the end of the world, but by a narrow escape and a blasting and impactful lesson in priorities for the bloodied but wiser noir detective figure.

Brian McDonnell

**KISS OF DEATH** (Twentieth Century Fox, 1947). *Director:* Henry Hathaway. *Producer:* Fred Kolmar. *Script:* Ben Hecht and Charles Lederer, based on a story by Eleazar Lipsky. *Cinematography:* Norbert Brodine. *Music:* David Buttolph. *Cast:* Victor Mature (Nick Bianco), Brian Donlevy (Louis DeAngelo), Coleen Gray (Nettie), Richard Widmark (Tommy Udo), Karl Malden (Sergeant William Cullen), Mildred Dunnock (Rizzo's mother).

The publicity and prologue to the film stressed that *Kiss of Death* was entirely filmed on location in New York. Hence appropriate scenes were filmed in the Chrysler Building, Tombs Prison, Criminal Courts Building, Marguery Hotel, Sing Sing Penitentiary, and an orphanage in New Jersey. In most of these scenes, cinematographer Norbert Brodine presents a realistic veneer, with flat photography and natural compositions. This is particularly evident when ex-convict Nick Bianco bids farewell to his family at a suburban railway station prior to his final confrontation with gangster Tommy Udo. However, *Kiss of Death* is a melodramatic film with a conventional Hollywood story line, and Brodine's photography also utilizes expressive, low-key lighting and dramatic close-ups to generate tension when required. For example, when Nick waits in his darkened house for an anticipated onslaught from Udo, the film employs the same stylized use of sound and imagery found in many studio-bound noir films of the 1940s.

*Kiss of Death* is a noir film with a soft centre. While it begins with a degree of social criticism, it soon reverts to a melodramatic confrontation between good, Nick Bianco, and evil, Tommy Udo, and the social elements disappear. However, the film opens on a promising note with Nettie, Nick's second wife, narrating the reasons why ex-convict Nick Bianco is forced to participate in a jewelry robbery just days before Christmas. Nick is shown to be a caring family man who, because employers refuse to hire an ex-convict, cannot buy Christmas presents for his daughters, so he takes part in an armed robbery in the Chrysler Building. However, when a shop assistant trips an alarm, Nick is cornered and shot by a policeman as he leaves the building. This mixture of pathos and tension characterizes the entire film.

Nick is sentenced to a long prison term after he refuses to cooperate with the police. However, after a period in prison, he becomes alarmed when his letters to his wife are returned unopened. He soon learns that she put her head in a gas oven and committed suicide due to a lack of money as Nick's associates failed to look after his family. Nick decides to cooperate with Assistant District Attorney Louis DeAngelo, and as part of the terms of his offer of a pardon, they require that Nick insinuate himself into the confidence of gangster Tommy Udo, a giggling, sadistic psychopath. Nick provides information leading to Udo's arrest, and he has to testify against Udo in court. In return, Nick is allowed to marry Nettie, his former babysitter, and reestablish himself away from New York. However, Udo is found not guilty, and Nick sends his family away and offers himself up as a sacrifice so that the police can arrest Udo. Udo fires a number of bullets into Nick's body, but Nettie's voice-over indicates that Nick will survive as he is carried away by an ambulance.

Unlike similar film noirs, such as Robert Siodmak's *Cry of the City* (1949), *Kiss of Death* is a sentimental tale with little tension between Nick, the convict, and DeAngelo, the assistant district attorney. Instead of the protagonist being presented as alienated from society, a characteristic of the tough noir films, Nick, after the opening scenes, becomes an agent working on behalf of society to eradicate aberrant elements such as Tommy Udo. Thus evil in *Kiss of Death* can be marginalized to one character, Udo, and the film does not present evil and corruption as permeating every level of society, as in similar films such as *Cry of the City* and *Raw Deal* (1948).

The film is best remembered for Richard Widmark's debut as Tommy Udo, a criminal psychopath with an ambivalent sexual orientation and a love of inflicting pain. Widmark's most notable scene takes place when he gleefully pushes an elderly woman in a wheelchair to her death down a flight of stairs. His giggling, excessive performance resulted in his only Academy Award nomination. *Kiss of Death* was remade in 1958 as a western, *The Fiend Who Walked the West*, starring future Paramount Studio mogul Robert Evans in the Richard Widmark role. A more literal remake, titled *Kiss of Death*, was released in 1995. Directed by Barbet Schroeder, the film starred David Caruso as the ex-con trying to go straight and Nicolas Cage as the crazed gangster.

Geoff Mayer

**KISS THE BLOOD OFF MY HANDS** (Universal International, 1948). *Director:* Norman Foster. *Producer:* Richard Vernon. *Script:* Leonardo Bercovici, from the novel by Gerald Butler. *Cinematography:* Russell Metty. *Music:* Miklos Rozsa. *Cast:* Joan Fontaine (Jane Wharton), Burt Lancaster (Bill Saunders), Robert Newton (Harry Carter), Lewis L. Russell (Tom Widgery).

This minor but interesting noir is set, like *Night and the City* (1950), in postwar London. In *Kiss the Blood Off My Hands*, that bombed-out city becomes an appropriate metaphor for the situation of the main character, a burned-out case damaged by his war experiences. Bill (Burt Lancaster) is a man on the run (often through bombed and ruined locales), under multiple pressures, resentful of everyone, and inarticulate about his feelings. Bill is nervous and jumpy, identifying himself verbally during a trip to the zoo with caged animals such as stressed-out monkeys and chimps and later visually compared to a goldfish flopping helplessly on the floor. Audience curiosity is aroused about what has made him such an emotionally bruised figure. The origin of his anxiety turns out to be his two years spent in a Nazi prison camp, and his resulting volatile temper is such that he cannot stay out of trouble. Indeed, in the film's very first scene, Bill, while drinking in a pub, accidentally kills a man in a knee-jerk reaction. Lancaster's acrobatic athleticism is exploited in such action scenes, as is his propensity to seem vulnerable to pain, even to appear masochistic. However, he does gain one ally, a sympathetic nurse named Jane, in his quest to put his life back together.

Bill is very much a typical noir protagonist in that he is caught between good and bad influences: Jane offering a push toward the good and a shady underworld figure called Harry Carter a spur toward the bad. The developing relationship between Bill and Jane is a constant thread throughout the film's plot. His first meeting with the girl has a threatening tone as he climbs through her bedroom window to escape his pursuers. He gradually becomes obsessed by her, while Jane's witnessing of his violent temper leads her to think of him as a "vicious bully." Bill's jailing and sentence of corporal punishment for hitting a policeman lead to a disturbingly masochistic scene of his beating (18 strokes of the cat-o'-nine-tails), during which he is stripped to the waist, and there is an almost fetishistic concentration on his bondage. The brutality of this event is lessened only a little by the camera's indirect presentation of the effects of the whipping. After his release, Jane gets him a job as a driver at the clinic where she works. This appears to offer him a new start, but his nemesis, Harry, who had observed the original pub killing, tempts him to hijack a shipment of clinic drugs. Bill wants money from what he terms a one-off crime, then hopes to leave, keeping his relapse into criminality hidden from Jane. But on the stormy night of the crucial penicillin delivery, she decides to accompany him in the truck. Bill has a change of heart when he encounters a sick child, doing something kind both for her sake and Jane's. Joan Fontaine, who mostly plays the saintly Jane very much in the style of woman as helpmeet, has her one big moment of self-assertion when Harry attacks her sexually and she stabs him in self-defense.

The darker aspects of the film's primary setting in inner London are stressed, and the city emerges as a clear symbol for entrapment. This is first seen in the film's shadowy opening scenes, where Bill flees from the fateful pub fight and the cobbled streets are photographed from odd angles. There are subjective close-ups of Jane's face during the attempted rape by Harry and accompanying tilted, distorted mirror shots in which her obvious anguish is intensified by her echoing, disembodied voice-over. There is obvious symbolism in the repeated shots of a ruined bombed building next to Jane's flat (it becomes an analogue of the damaged hero). This recurring image reflects the tenor of the film's opening words written on the screen, which ruminate about the wounds of war, about there being visible in the postwar world both the rubble of cities and the rubble of men. This constrictive milieu is contrasted with the happier tone of the location shooting of scenes at a racetrack, at the zoo, and along the skylines of summer fields, where Bill and Jane enjoy a brief respite from their pressured lives. One message of *Kiss the Blood Off My Hands* may be that a committed love might be the only hope for the redemption of damaged souls. The film's memorable title, which, like those of *Kiss of Death*, *Kiss Me Deadly*, and *Murder My Sweet*, provocatively blends sex and violence, certainly suggests that love can redeem someone. In the concluding moments Bill and Jane, both now with blood on their hands, decide not to run away but to face the authorities together.

Brian McDonnell

**KLUTE** (Warner Bros., 1971). *Director/Producer:* Alan J. Pakula. *Script:* Andy and Dave Lewis. *Cinematography:* Gordon Willis. *Music:* Michael Small. *Cast:* Jane Fonda (Bree Daniel), Donald Sutherland (John Klute), Charles Cioffi (Peter

Cable), Roy Scheider (Frank Ligourin), Dorothy Tristan (Arlyn Page), Vivian Nathan (Psychiatrist).

In the early 1970s, when English-language film critics, historians, and other academics first began to write about the phenomenon of film noir and to identify contemporary films as marking the beginnings of a neo-noir genre, *Klute* was one of the first films discussed as a prime example of the latter development. This was most clearly marked by the prominence given the film by Christine Gledhill and E. Ann Kaplan in *Women in Film Noir* (1978), a pioneering piece of feminist film criticism. Much attention was paid to the ideological messages of the film, and contrasts were drawn between the unswerving independence of many of the femmes fatales of classical noir and the seeming shift from independence to dependence of the female protagonist of *Klute*. In the decades since then, the film has enjoyed less attention, but it remains one of the more important and interesting 1970s examples of the genre. It has also become clearer that the strength of Jane Fonda's central performance tends to counteract the more conservative ideology of the plot. Furthermore, if placed alongside other later films directed by Alan J. Pakula, such as *The Parallax View* (1974), *All the President's Men* (1976), and *Presumed Innocent* (1990), *Klute* can be seen as illustrating his views of urban paranoia and the breakdown in American family and community values.

*Klute* begins in a small town where a respected businessman, Tom Gruneman, is missing, believed dead, but the action soon shifts to New York, where he has disappeared and where the search for him is centered. Although the film is named after the detective who works on the central investigation (John Klute), it could just as easily be called "Bree" after the prostitute Bree Daniel, whose experiences lie at the core of the film and who is actually a much more nuanced and interesting character than the eponymous Klute. Early scenes show her life as a high-class call girl and her attempts to break into more legitimate careers such as modeling or stage acting. Indeed, a modeling casting call makes it clear that the women are treated more or less as "meat," in a comparable manner to prostitutes. Bree is seen in her spooky and lonely studio apartment, where the ringing of her phone late at night shows how vulnerable she is to the crazier denizens of the city. She regularly meets with a therapist to whom she confesses the attractiveness of maintaining sexual and emotional "control" when she is with her tricks, as opposed to the raw exposure of feelings required by conventional relationships. When John Klute comes calling on her as a key contact and possible witness, Bree tells him she had once been cruelly beaten by a businessman who may have been Gruneman. After she discovers Klute has been tapping her phone, she offers him sex in exchange for the tapes. The pair are interrupted by an intruder on the roof, and Klute searches for the man he believes to be his friend Tom. This man, whose actions show that he must be the killer, is soon revealed (just one-third of the way through the story) as Tom's boss Peter Cable, and thus any last-minute plot revelations assigning guilt are deliberately done away with.

The film's narrative develops in two ways from this point. First, more details of Bree's life are shown: there is more of the therapist, there is an old man she talks with erotically, there is her pimp Frank, and there are more auditions for acting parts. Second, she helps Klute in his search by helping him find a junkie hooker named Arlyn Page who may have more information. In the meantime, she has sex with Klute, but this action may be as much a ploy as a sign of growing affection. In tracing Arlyn's decline into full-on drug addiction, Bree and Klute take the audience on a journey into increasingly down-market areas of city vice and crime. Bree is spooked by Arlyn's condition (the addict is eventually fished dead out of the harbor) and veers uncertainly between reliance on Klute and on her pimp Frank. She confides to her therapist that she is actually enjoying sex with Klute and sometimes pines for the "numbness" of her former profession. When Cable violates her room, she runs away while Klute sets a trap for the man. A botched communication leads Bree herself into the trap, and the scary climactic scene has her threatened by Cable, who confesses to killing Gruneman to conceal his shame over a vicious beating of a prostitute his employee had witnessed. When Klute belatedly arrives, Cable falls backward to his death through a window. The epilogue shows Bree leaving the city with Klute for a new start, despite her voice-over claiming she cannot remain involved with him.

This ending has caused concern for some critics who see it as the logical culmination of the film's conservative values. They see it as supporting the "redemption" of an independent, if transgressive, woman by a man who offers her a traditional life as a wife. They link it to an earlier scene where a statement by Arlyn may indicate that prostitutes are implicated in any violence meted out to them. Certainly one of the questions the film raises is, What risks may ensue if your occupation (e.g., Bree's job as a call girl) is to ask people to shed all their inhibitions? Prostitution is definitely shown as dangerous, but it is depicted as just one part of the general atmosphere of peril that pervades the city. Pakula constantly underlines this with images of funeral homes, skid row dives, and shots of Cable alienated from his surroundings by barriers of glass. The film was the most clear-headed and insightful dramatization of a prostitute's lot that Hollywood had ever attempted up to its release (even the topic itself was out of bounds in the 1940s and 1950s), and since Fonda's performance is so vividly memorable compared to Sutherland's bland impassivity, Bree's humanity is able to balance the film's more reactionary messages.

Brian McDonnell

# L

**L.A. CONFIDENTIAL** (Warner Bros./Regency Enterprises, 1997). *Director:* Curtis Hanson. *Producers:* Arnon Milchan, Curtis Hanson, and Michael Nathanson. *Script:* Brian Helgeland and Curtis Hanson, from the novel by James Ellroy. *Cinematography:* Dante Spinotti. *Music:* Jerry Goldsmith. *Cast:* Kevin Spacey (Jack Vincennes), Russell Crowe (Bud White), Guy Pearce (Ed Exley), Kim Basinger (Lynn Bracken), James Cromwell (Dudley Smith), David Strathairn (Pierce Patchett), Danny DeVito (Sid Hudgens), Ron Rifkin (D. A. Ellis Loew).

The most significant figure in the literary revival of noir subject matter during the late 1980s and early 1990s was California crime novelist James Ellroy (1948–), especially in his four novels that are now collectively known as the *L.A. Quartet* (*The Black Dahlia, The Big Nowhere, L.A. Confidential,* and *White Jazz*). Ellroy set this loosely connected group of novels in the Los Angeles of the 1940s and 1950s and concentrates his attention on obsessive police officers, corrupt civic officials, ambitious boosters and developers, and a gruesome band of psychopathic killers and drug-fuelled sadists. His writing style is exciting, vivid, and overwrought, and the writer presents himself as almost as obsessive as his driven protagonists, particularly by highlighting in interviews the unsolved murder of his own mother when he was 10 years old. Furthermore, Ellroy has often mentioned the formative effect classical film noir had on his imagination during his childhood, and so it is not surprising that filmmakers have been drawn to the plots of his period crime novels. A movie version of *The Black Dahlia* was released to mixed reviews in 2006 under the direction of Brian De Palma, but by far the best-known neo-noir film adapted from Ellroy's fiction is 1997's *L.A. Confidential.*

254

Script writers Brian Helgeland and Curtis Hanson (Hanson also directed) took on the daunting task of boiling down the extremely complex plot lines and crowded cast of heroes and villains in Ellroy's novel to produce a coherent feature film version. They had to shed many of his characters and eliminate entire plot strands in order to reduce their script to a manageable length. The resulting film still has a complicated narrative and can still be a little confusing on first viewing. However, it remains one of the most thought-provoking, profound, and moving of all neo-noir films, and Hanson also succeeded in making it stylish and beautiful, both to look at and to listen to. The core story involves three detectives, working in the Los Angeles Police Department under the command of Captain Dudley Smith, whose characters are quite dissimilar. Bud White is a burly, quick-tempered hard case whose childhood memories of his mother's death at the hands of his father still affect his explosive responses to both men and women. Ed Exley is a buttoned-down, intelligent, and highly ambitious officer who, despite being somewhat disparaged by his more macho colleagues, generally goes by the book, but he is also open to finding a shortcut if it will help achieve his own aims. Jack Vincennes is a media-savvy show pony who advises on a TV police drama akin to the real-life *Dragnet* and who sets up self-serving arrests in concert with Sid Hudgens, the editor of a scurrilous scandal rag called *Hush-Hush*. The plot gives all three men the chance to transcend their initial limitations and to grow morally. For Bud this lies in his personal crusade to prove himself as a capable investigator, particularly as a way of impressing his new love: high-class call girl Lynn Bracken. For Ed it comes with his realization that he has to free himself from the Faustian temptations and blandishments of corrupt and murderous Captain Dudley Smith. And for Jack it is an epiphany in which he sees for the first time the shallowness of his "gone Hollywood" life and the tragic consequences of his conniving with the unscrupulous bottom-feeders of Los Angeles. The three police officers come together during the investigation of two violent crimes: the Nite Owl Diner massacre and the kidnapping and gang rape of a Latina girl. Ed and Bud emerge more or less unscathed from their life-changing experiences; Jack, though, dies shockingly at the hands of Dudley Smith.

The overall plot outline of *L.A. Confidential* illustrates clearly an important noir theme, namely the danger inherent in crossing moral borderlines, especially for those entrusted with upholding society's standards. Dudley Smith has gone completely over the line, not just committing murder, but ruthlessly establishing a drug ring that seeks to dominate the entire city's supply and distribution. By contrast, the misdemeanors of Ed, Jack, and Bud are less serious, and their characters are redeemable. Beyond these individual figures, though, the city itself becomes a functioning character in the film, a felicitous outcome since Ellroy has claimed that the subject of his original novel was the "secret history" of Los Angeles largely unseen due to its veneer of glamour. Hanson foregrounds this aspect by having Sid Hudgens narrate parts of the story in a muckraking *Hush-Hush* tone that sounds like a Californian Walter Winchell. This is especially apparent in the film's opening, where a collage of newsreel and documentary images of L.A. in the 1950s brilliantly establishes the period feel of *L.A. Confidential* to introduce this theme of image versus reality. It is further developed by the painstaking choice of urban locations that have remained unchanged since the mid-twentieth century. A contributing factor to this successful evocation of the 1950s is Hanson's decision to shoot the period film as if it were a contemporary story: the old houses and cars are not italicized with special compositions and lighting, just treated as incidental items, albeit ones scrupulously researched for authenticity.

Two sequences near the end of *L.A. Confidential* sum up its considerable achievements and its minor shortcomings. The climactic shoot-out in a derelict motel where Bud and Ed battle with Dudley and his minions is a complete addition by the script writers: no such scene occurs in Ellroy's novel. Hanson directs this set piece brilliantly, tying together several plot and character developments into a tour de force (and truly noir) action sequence that is played out virtually free of dialogue. It is, however, followed by a lengthy and overly wordy epilogue, in which Ed Exley has to spell out in grinding detail a mass of expository information for his police bosses and, by implication, for puzzled audience members. This turgid sequence is at odds with the snappy pace of much of the rest of the film but cannot diminish its overall effect of period style and noir atmosphere.

Brian McDonnell

**LADD, ALAN** (1913–1964). A highly enigmatic actor, Ladd impressed audiences and critics more through his stillness, handsomeness, and presence than through his range of theatrical tricks or his refined technique. Despite his small stature (he stood just five feet five inches), he was able to convey toughness through his impassivity, self-possession, and his surprisingly deeply timbered voice. Born in Hot Springs, Arkansas, Alan Ladd endured quite an underprivileged childhood. As a young boy, he moved from Arkansas firstly to Oklahoma and then to California. He became a very good athlete and swimmer, despite his lack of height. Ladd's first gained experience in the film industry when he worked as a grip at Warner Bros., but around this time, he was hit hard emotionally by his mother's suicide in 1937. At the beginning of the 1940s, he moved slowly into movie acting, having a tiny, almost invisible part in *Citizen Kane* (1941). Ladd was not at all well known when the release of *This Gun for Hire* in 1942 made him an instant star: his inscrutable presence as the cold killer in *This Gun for Hire* (Ladd was cast in the role purely through his looks, as demonstrated in publicity photos), and his pairing with the equally glamorous Veronica Lake, helped make the noir story a hit. Critics called him the "baby-faced killer," but playing a psychopath in his first starring role did Ladd no harm at all. He and Lake rapidly made the follow-up film noir *The Glass Key* (1942), where he played a slightly more conventionally heroic character. Soon after this, Ladd married his agent, Sue Carol, who was 10 years his senior. Despite mixing his acting with wartime entertainment service in the military, by the mid-1940s he had become a big Paramount star. His third pairing with Veronica Lake in *The Blue Dahlia* (scripted by Raymond Chandler) revealed his best performance so far. Ladd's character in this film, Johnny Morrison, is a truly noir figure: a returned serviceman who first discovers that his wife has been unfaithful and then that she has been murdered. Although he made a number of minor and undistinguished film noirs subsequent to *The Blue Dahlia*, Ladd was best known in the 1950s as the titular figure in the classic western film *Shane*. After that appearance, he found little success as his career stuttered along. Ladd was considered by many observers to be a bland, inexpressive actor who failed to develop in his middle years and, like Lake, too, was thought to be more mannequin-like than skilled. Others though looked more favorably on his acting as being minimalist and praised his stoical work in *Shane*. Ladd became an alcoholic in his later years, and heavy drinking hurt his career prospects as his looks faded.

**Selected Noir Films:** *This Gun for Hire* (1942), *The Glass Key* (1942), *The Blue Dahlia* (1946), *Calcutta* (1947), *Chicago Deadline* (1949), *Appointment with Danger* (1951), *A Cry in the Night* (1956, voice-over narrator), *The Man in the Net* (1959).

Brian McDonnell

**LAKE, VERONICA** (1919–1973). As one of the most sweetly beautiful actresses of her time and sporting a hairstyle that became her trademark, Lake was briefly a popular star, but her career waned as quickly as it had burgeoned. She was the partner of Alan Ladd in three accomplished film noirs and made a few quite effective comedies, but she later disappeared from prominence, ending her life in virtual obscurity. Born Constance Ockleman in Brooklyn, New York, Veronica Lake was discovered by Paramount and had her name changed by the studio to reflect what was thought to be her cool, unflappable style, literally as calm as a lake. They also gave her a characteristic hairdo, with her long locks shading one eye, and she was promoted as the girl with the "peek-a-boo bang." The tiny Lake was often cast in roles where she was a helper of the leading man, but she complemented this task with her unforced sexiness, aplomb, and poise. She was perhaps better suited to comedy than to film noir (as shown by her excellent work in 1941's *Sullivan's Travels*); indeed, that Preston Sturges comedy opposite Joel McCrea helped propel her to stardom. Paramount then cast her opposite the equally diminutive Alan Ladd in 1942 in both *This Gun for Hire* and *The Glass Key*. For some critics of these films it was more her presence and sexiness than her acting talent that shone through, although she showed a real propensity for snappy dialogue, and she could be subtly appealing in such scenes as the magic act she performed in *This Gun for Hire*. Furthermore, Lake gave an excellent performance in the wartime melodrama *So Proudly We Hail* (1943) as a heartbroken nurse who sacrifices her own life for her friends and colleagues by becoming a suicide bomber. On a less positive note, Lake gained a reputation around the studios as something of a troublemaker. Among many relationships in the 1940s, she married noir director André De Toth. Lake's last true high point in film acting was making *The Blue Dahlia* in 1946, once more with Ladd. In this film, she plays the estranged wife of the man with whom Ladd's wife has had an affair, and the violent deaths of both their spouses allow Lake and Ladd to end up romantically paired. Her career, alas, did not last, and she suffered a sudden decline into comparative poverty. Like many another actors out of work (including Alan Ladd), Lake became an alcoholic who eventually died destitute of hepatitis. Her characteristic image was evoked again in the neo-noir film *L.A. Confidential* (1997) by Kim Basinger's character Lynn Bracken, who is employed in a high-class prostitution ring where the women trade on their resemblance to Hollywood stars.

**Selected Noir Films:** *This Gun for Hire* (1942), *The Glass Key* (1942), *The Blue Dahlia* (1946), *Ramrod* (1947).

Brian McDonnell

**LANCASTER, BURT** (1913–1994). With his handsome features, agreeably wide and toothy grin, powerful physique, and regal air, Burt Lancaster became a major Hollywood star in the middle decades of the twentieth century. Although he had a long and distinguished career in a wide variety of genres, from swashbuckling roles to such serious artistic projects as Luchino Visconti's *The Leopard* (1963), Lancaster got his start in film acting in several classical film noirs, and he remains an iconic figure from that cycle of films. His audience appeal in noir was often a product of his combination of physical strength and the propensity to be easily hurt, of a robust body joined with a damaged soul. Lancaster could be at times aggressive and violent and at others strangely passive. He was able to show the vulnerability of a classic antihero as he was knocked about by both uncaring women and brutal authority figures. Born Burton Stephen Lancaster in New York, he was an acrobat and a gymnast as a young man but was forced to retire from professional acrobatics when an injured hand became badly infected. Lancaster's career in film noir began with his debut in 1946 in *The Killers* and was quickly followed by leading roles in *Brute Force* and *Desert Fury*. His introduction as the Swede in the opening sequence of *The Killers* is quintessential noir: lying supine on a bed as hired assassins arrive to dispatch him, he accepts his death stoically as just punishment for a vague past wrongdoing. In *Brute Force* he is effective as the natural leader of disaffected convicts rioting in protest against sadistic treatment. In the curiosity *Desert Fury* Lancaster is one of a group of sexually ambivalent characters caught up in melodramatic circumstances in a desert community. He worked opposite Kirk Douglas in the gangster noir *I Walk Alone* in 1948, one of many fruitful film collaborations between the two friends, and the same year, he made *Sorry, Wrong Number*, where he appeared in a number of flashbacks explaining the present situation of protagonist Barbara Stanwyck. After forming his own production company with agent Harold Hecht, Lancaster made *Kiss the Blood Off My Hands*, a little-known film noir set in England and costarring Joan Fontaine. This film contains perhaps the clearest depiction of the masochism that was a feature of many of Lancaster's roles: at one point, he is literally whipped in a strangely fetishized scene. One of his best roles was as Steve Thompson in Robert Siodmak's *Criss Cross* (1949), where once again he conveyed a vulnerable side at odds with his powerful physical presence. Yvonne de Carlo plays the woman who manipulates him as she seduces him into a risky double-crossing of her criminal boyfriend. Much later, in the 1950s, he played a very different kind of role in a marginally noir film called *Sweet Smell of Success*. Cruel power plays and a pathological desire for control give Lancaster a sinister strength in the role of the egomaniac columnist J. J. Hunsecker in this film (a characterization based on Walter Winchell) with disturbing hints of an incestuous desire within Hunsecker for his youthful sister. The role was one of the few outright villains he played. After his time in film noir, Lancaster matured into a thoughtful actor in high-budget dramas. He won the best actor Oscar for the title role in *Elmer Gantry* in 1960 and made a number of serious films in association with leading directors for another 25 years, both in the United States and in Europe.

**Selected Noir Films:** *The Killers* (1946), *Brute Force* (1947), *Desert Fury* (1947), *I Walk Alone* (1948), *Sorry, Wrong Number* (1948), *Kiss the Blood Off My Hands* (1948), *Criss Cross* (1949), *Sweet Smell of Success* (1957, and executive producer).

Brian McDonnell

**LANG, FRITZ** (1890–1976). Émigré directors from Germany and Austria played a large part in establishing the style, tone, and preoccupations of classical film noir. Among them, Fritz Lang was a central figure, contributing in a substantial way to the cycle and directing a dozen films that are emphatically noir. Lang was born in Vienna, Austria, and as a teenager, he studied architecture and painting at his parents' request. His privileged upbringing also allowed him to travel the world as a young man. Lang though did have to face the grimmer aspects of life, serving in World War I in the Austrian army. At the war's end he joined the Decia studio in Berlin as an editor and soon progressed to directing. He is best remembered from that period as the director of the science fiction allegory *Metropolis* in 1927, but he also made the proto-noir *Mabuse* films over a number of years. Like many another filmmaker, Lang ran into trouble with the Nazis after Hitler's accession to power, and he fled to France in 1933 (making just one film there), then with the onset of war in 1939, he went on to America, where he worked until 1956. Lang certainly had a temperament suited to involvement in the emerging cycle of film noir, and it is a tribute to his skills that almost all his American films still have a distinctly modern feel. With the possible exception of Robert Siodmak, he could be said to have made more substantial and important film noirs than any other single director. While many associate him, because of *Metropolis*, with German expressionism, Lang's visual style became more pared down in his American films, but he remained a strong believer in the power of visual material (especially mise-en-scène). Among his recurrent themes were notions of people being entrapped and of the unforeseen consequences of chance encounters. These can be detected in such films as *The Woman in the Window* (1944), *Scarlet Street* (1945), and *Beyond a Reasonable Doubt* (1956). He also explored the subtleties and ramifications of revenge in his fine police thriller *The Big Heat* (1953), among other movies.

Lang's noir remakes (*Scarlet Street* [1945] and *Human Desire*[1954]) were colder in tone than the French originals (*La Chienne* [1931] and *La Bête Humaine* [1938]), and he was more disciplined in his treatment, as detached as Hitchcock might have been in using such material. Despite depicting a range of psychopathic characters well and sympathetically, Lang denied that he was a pessimistic filmmaker, claiming he had evolved from being a fatalist. In recent years, some critics and historians have called his noirs, especially *The Woman in the Window* and *Scarlet Street*, male melodramas, but his last two film noirs, *While the City Sleeps* and *Beyond a Reasonable Doubt* (both 1956) reflected his interest in social problem films with their partly documentary method and intention. They clearly show the ambiguities of moral justice, Lang stating that this emphasis revealed his essentially Catholic viewpoint that man makes his own destiny. He definitely identified with the average man in most of his best noir stories. In *The Big Heat,* for instance, corruption, violence, and greed seem to pervade society, and ordinary-Joe protagonist Dave Bannion must struggle against these malign forces as best he can. Lang's final film of the classical noir period, *Beyond a Reasonable Doubt,* was a film noir disguised as a social problem film on the topic of capital punishment, and its place in the cycle is achieved partly through its clever employment of suppressed narrative information. As in many Lang films, its existential hero finds poetic justice. In the late 1950s, failing eyesight sadly truncated his career.

**Selected Noir Films:** *Dr. Mabuse: Der Spieler* (1922, and script), *M.* (1931, and script), *You Only Live Once* (1937), *Hangmen Also Die* (1943, and script), *The Ministry of Fear* (1944), *The Woman in the Window* (1944), *Scarlet Street* (1945), *Secret Beyond the Door* (1948), *House by the River* (1949), *Rancho Notorious* (1952), *Clash by Night* (1952), *The Blue Gardenia* (1953), *The Big Heat* (1953), *Human Desire* (1954), *While the City Sleeps* (1956), *Beyond a Reasonable Doubt* (1956).

Brian McDonnell

**THE LATE EDWINA BLACK** (Romulus, 1951). *Director:* Maurice Elvey. *Producer:* Ernest Gartside. *Script:* Charles Frank and David Evans, based on the play by William Dinner and William Moray. *Cinematographer:* Stephen Dade. *Music:* Allan Gray. *Cast:* David Farrar (Gregory Black), Geraldine Fitzgerald (Elizabeth Grahame), Roland Culver (Inspector Martin), Jean Cadell (Ellen), Mary Merrall (Lady Southdale), Harcourt Williams (Dr. Septimus Prendergast).

When Edwina Black dies, suspicion is immediately cast on her husband, Gregory, and Edwina's maid Elizabeth Grahame as they had been carrying on an affair for some time. Ellen, the elderly housekeeper, loved Edwina and disapproved of Gregory's relationship with Elizabeth. Enter Inspector Martin from Scotland

Yard, who demonstrates that Edwina was murdered by arsenic poisoning. After Martin leaves, the love between Gregory and Elizabeth turns sour as each suspects the other of the murder. Eventually, Martin rounds the suspects up in the kitchen and recreates the crime before exposing Ellen as the murderer. Knowing that she was about to die, Edwina convinced Ellen to administer poison to her so that Gregory would be blamed for her death—thereby destroying the love affair between Gregory and Elizabeth. Gregory and Elizabeth reconcile at the end, determined that Edwina's malice will not prevent their marriage and subsequent honeymoon in Venice.

*The Late Edwina Black* draws on a sturdy mixture of conventions from the classical detective genre, film noir, and gothic fiction. The legacy of the dead wife haunts the illicit lovers throughout the film, perpetuating guilt, dread, and death. Her memory permeates the house, particularly the wind chimes that ring out at key moments to remind the lovers of the dead wife's presence. Similarly, Edwina's housekeeper Ellen remains obsessively faithful to the memory of her dead mistress (as in the archetypal gothic film *Rebecca* [1940]).

The film is basically restricted to four characters, although Mary Merrall has one effective scene as Lady Southdale. After Edwina's funeral, she reminds Elizabeth that the world is a cruel place for penniless young women and old women, as the events in the film readily demonstrate.

Geoff Mayer

**LAURA** (Twentieth Century Fox, 1944). *Director/Producer:* Otto Preminger. *Script:* Jay Dratler, Samuel Hoffenstein, and Betty Reinhardt, from the novel by Vera Caspary. *Cinematography:* Joseph La Shelle. *Music:* David Raksin. *Cast:* Gene Tierney (Laura Hunt), Dana Andrews (Mark McPherson), Clifton Webb (Waldo Lydecker), Vincent Price (Shelby Carpenter), Judith Anderson (Ann Treadwell).

In significant ways, *Laura* is a far from typical film noir since it has no femme fatale and, unusually, its story is set in an upper-class world of privilege rather than in the criminal demimonde. Although made during World War II, director Otto Preminger scrupulously avoids the topic of the war in his pursuit of a tone of escapist glamour. As Andrew Spicer puts it in his book *Film Noir*, "*Laura* does not move out into New York's 'mean streets,' but instead remains in the rarified world of expensive restaurants, luxurious apartments, modern offices and art galleries" (p. 52). Despite this surface gloss, the 1944 film played a vital role in the beginnings of the classical noir genre, establishing not just the popularity of mystery stories, but also some of the basic themes and preoccupations of the cycle.

The plot follows the investigation of a violent death, but one that occurs not in the criminal world, but in a world of affluence, style, and high fashion. *Laura* opens with the voice-over of effete social gadfly Waldo Lydecker remembering how he heard of Laura's death and introducing the character of Mark McPherson, the detective investigating her apparent murder by shotgun blast. Fifteen minutes into

*Laura* (1944). Directed by Otto Preminger. Shown: Dana Andrews (as Mark McPherson), Gene Tierney (as Laura Hunt). 20th Century Fox/Photofest.

the film, there occurs a flashback of much the same length, in which Waldo tells Mark of his first inauspicious meeting with Laura and then of helping Laura's career and coming to admire her. As McFarlane tries to interview other acquaintances of Laura, all the main suspects tail along with him as he does his rounds. The most dramatic, startling, and famous aspect of the film's narrative, though, is the shock plot twist halfway through, when Laura turns up alive and an utterly astounded Mark has to identify the real victim. Laura and Mark become romantically entangled. Waldo is eventually revealed as the killer, trying to eliminate Laura because he did not want to lose her in marriage to the charming wastrel Shelby Carpenter. A model called Diane Redfern is killed in Laura's apartment doorway when Waldo mistakes her for Laura because she has a similar build and is wearing Laura's negligee. He fires both barrels of buckshot into her face.

The film is full of wonderful characterizations. Waldo is a shrewd judge of character, witty and trenchant, but also waspish, vindictive and egotistical, possessive, jealous, and controlling. He is like Shakespeare's Iago in the way he manipulates people, weaving webs of suspicion. He snobbishly puts down McFarlane's character, telling Laura that the detective refers to women as "dames" and that he offers only an "earthy relationship." McFarlane, of course, changes halfway through from grim investigator to smitten romantic. Laura herself is the chief object of desire but becomes more independent and stronger on her return from the dead. She is able to front up to Waldo at last. One of the most moving sequences in *Laura* is when the lovelorn Mark returns to her apartment late one rainy night. Still believing her to be dead, he stares at her portrait as music plays. We learn from Waldo (whose arrival interrupts this reverie) that Mark has tried to buy the painting, and indeed, it plays an almost fetishistic role in the film's dramatization of obsession. Waldo says that Mark will end up in a psychiatric ward, where he will be the "first patient who fell in love with a corpse." After Waldo leaves, Mark drinks and falls asleep (one might ask whether the rest of the film is his dream). As he sleeps, the camera dollies in and out, and then Laura Hunt, oblivious to all the tragedy and fuss, walks through the door. A triangular composition shows her, the portrait, and Mark. Dana Andrews is able to subtly imply the joy going through McPherson's mind when he discovers she is alive.

This happiness is, however, tempered by his knowledge that a murder is still unsolved. He determines to use Laura's reappearance to shock some unguarded reactions from his suspects. The next morning, Waldo faints when he sees her, later blaming this on epilepsy. A celebration party is held (never mind poor Diane) during which Mark, using theatrics, tells a telephone caller that he has found the killer, then arrests Laura at the party and takes her to the station. He interrogates Laura, questioning her personally as well as professionally, and satisfies himself that she is innocent of Diane's death. Later, he goes to Waldo's apartment and is searching for the shotgun when a decorative pedestal clock chimes. He examines it, then smashes it with his foot. Waldo meanwhile has gone to Laura's place. When Mark arrives there, Waldo turns spiteful and appears to leave, but instead hides. Mark finds the gun in the clock base and describes to Laura how Waldo committed the murder. Mark and Laura kiss good-bye. Once the living room is empty, the hidden Waldo emerges and takes the gun. Laura tunes into his radio program (aptly, it is on the topic of love, and his voice appears by electrical transcription). He loads the gun and fires at Laura, but she deflects the shot. The cops gun him down as he fires toward them, destroying the face of his own clock.

The film is highly stylish, with evocative music. It foregrounds glamour in clothes and fancy apartments. As Andrew Spicer writes, "*Laura* is a Hitchcockian romance-thriller which exploits sexuality in a complex and quite daring way through the suggestiveness of décor" (p. 52). There is one example of high-contrast lighting at the police station as Laura moves into McFarlane's world for once. Most of the camera work is deliberately objective, avoiding close-ups, but an exception is the subjective method used in the dreamlike sequence where McFarlane prowls around her apartment drinking until he slumps asleep beneath her portrait. This film, like Hitchcock's *Vertigo*, is about obsession: Waldo's with Laura and Mark's with the same woman. Mark is a deeply noirish figure who cannot separate the personal from the professional, for example, taking Laura to the police station because he does not trust himself to be with her elsewhere.

Brian McDonnell

**LEAVE HER TO HEAVEN** (Twentieth Century Fox, 1945). *Director:* John M. Stahl. *Producer:* William A. Bacher. *Script:* Jo Swerling, from the novel by Ben

Ames Williams. *Cinematography:* Leon Shamroy. *Music:* Alfred Newman. *Cast:* Gene Tierney (Ellen Berent), Cornel Wilde (Richard Harland), Jeanne Crain (Ruth Berent), Vincent Price (Russell Quinton), Darryl Hickman (Danny Harland), Ray Collins (Glen Robie), Chill Wills (Thorne).

A rare example of a Technicolor film that in thematic terms definitely belongs within the classical film noir cycle, *Leave Her to Heaven* has engendered questions about how its being in color affects its generic status. For much of its length, events take place in bright sunlight in both the western and eastern locations, while at other times the lighting is of the more familiar low-key variety noir often prefers. The film's themes and characterizations, though, place it firmly within the noir genre. *Leave Her to Heaven* is, like a number of other classical noirs, strongly related to the tradition of women's melodrama, and it is female protagonist Ellen Berent who is the most arresting and unforgettable of the film's elements. Ellen, who is one of the most fascinating and monstrous characters in classical Hollywood history, combines in her person elements of domesticity with the attributes of a femme fatale. The film is unusual in privileging the female gaze, something that is apparent even from its opening scenes.

A book cover forms the film's title in the credits, alluding both to the fact that it is an adaptation of a popular novel and to the fact that its chief male character, Richard Harland, is himself a novelist. Sections of the story are given chapter titles, also like a book. The plot opens in the present, with Richard returning from jail to his lakeside house, and then, when his watching lawyer talks of jealousy having caused his incarceration, we go into an extended flashback that is completed only near the end of the film. The lawyer feels he is the only one privileged with enough knowledge to tell the story, although he retards disclosure of some of this information until the end. He relates the story of Richard meeting Ellen by chance on a holiday in New Mexico and of her claiming a striking resemblance between him and her beloved deceased father. A whirlwind romance ensues, and they marry after she jilts her current fiancé. Her love for Richard becomes increasingly possessive and pathological after she discovers his continuing support and hospitality to his kid brother Danny, who has polio. Ellen later arranges for Danny to drown in a cold lake called Back of the Moon and then forces the miscarriage of her unborn child when she believes it may become a rival for Richard's attention. This crazed behavior culminates in her suicide by poisoning, the circumstances of which she engineers to look like murder to stop Richard leaving her for her demure cousin Rose. The film's melodramatic plot ends with the reunion of Rose and Richard after his release from prison.

As this summary indicates, *Leave Her to Heaven* is essentially a character study of an obsessive, even insane individual. Ellen is the main subject for scrutiny, but the film holds up both her and Rose as contrasting examples of femininity. At one point, her nice-girl cousin compares Ellen to a Salem witch, and the film certainly highlights her seductiveness. This emphasis on her sexuality is remarkable for a 1940s film, and Gene Tierney seldom retreats from the challenge of conveying this physicality in arresting ways. Ellen's lone ride with her father's ashes is photographed to highlight her breasts. She complains that the bedroom walls at Back of the Moon are too thin for privacy during their honeymoon, and in one scene, where she kneels to beg for Richard's attention, her pose clearly suggests oral sex. Ellen seems a creature of the water, propelling herself powerfully underwater and winning a swimming race against children in a way that reveals her determination. Ruth, by contrast, is of the earth, always pruning or planting. Ellen wants Dick all to herself, telling him, "I'll never let you go—ever, ever, ever!"

This possessiveness creates a fatal sense of rivalry with Danny, who even interrupts their incipient lovemaking at Back of the Moon. Ellen calls Danny a "cripple" in an unguarded moment, just as she later refers to her unborn child as a "little beast." Her hatred for Danny culminates in the most chilling scene in *Leave Her to Heaven* when, from her vantage point in a rowboat, she watches him drown in the lake. Ellen puts her sunglasses on to shut off any human sympathy and coldly witnesses his death, calmly talking to him as he flounders around and then sinks. The tone is highly sinister, despite the beautiful scenery and setting, reinforcing the idea of the evil that lies within Ellen, despite her outer beauty. The film goes so far as to hint at incest when her mother says Ellen loved her father too much. She takes up with Dick as a replacement for him the very day she symbolically cast her father's ashes to the winds in New Mexico. Ultimately, though, her possessiveness drives Dick into the arms of Ruth. When the story moves out of flashback at the end, the observing lawyer remarks that this was the only time Ellen ever lost. When Dick paddles across the lake, we see Ruth waiting. He kisses her, and sweetness finally prevails over monstrous jealousy.

Brian McDonnell

**LEWIS, JOSEPH H.** (1907–2000). When Joe Lewis was shooting westerns starring Bob Baker, Charles Starrett, Bill Elliott, and Johnny Mack Brown at Universal and Columbia studios in the late 1930s and early 1940s, he was confronted by small budgets, poor production values, and impossibly short shooting schedules—often only 12 days. Yet Lewis was determined to make these films visually dramatic, and he gained a reputation for constantly placing objects between the camera and the action so as to break up the so-called dead space and enliven the scene. However, this was not always appreciated by penny-pinching studio executives, who merely wanted the films brought in on time and within the budget. Hence when producer Oliver Drake wanted to hire Lewis in 1942 for a series of westerns starring Johnny Mack Brown, studio executives warned Drake that they did not want "Wagon Wheel Lewis" because he was always filming through a wagon wheel—Lewis even took a box filled with wagon wheels with different spokes into each production. Universal relented, and while the feisty Lewis did not use a wagon wheel on *The Silver Bullet* (1942), he did film one scene through a wheel of fortune, which simulated the same effect. Consequently, Universal let his contract lapse, and Lewis was forced further down the Hollywood system; his next film was made for the Poverty Row studio PRC, where he directed *Secrets of a Co-Ed* (1943).

Lewis, the son of Russian Jewish immigrants, was born in New York in 1907. He came to Los Angeles in 1925, and his first job was as a gofer in the editorial department at MGM. When he left in 1934, he talked his way into Mascot Pictures when the head of the studio, Nat Levine, confused Joe Lewis with his brother Benny, an editor at MGM, and offered him the job as supervising editor. When Mascot merged with a number of other small studios to form Republic Pictures in 1935, Lewis continued as an editor until the middle of 1936, when he walked out of the studio when Levine reneged on a promise to let Lewis direct. Lewis joined another Poverty Row studio, Grand National, and was offered a film, *Navy Spy* (1937), as codirector when the studio became disenchanted with the scenes directed by the veteran Crane Wilbur. Later that year, producer Trem Carr at Universal, who owed Lewis a favor, hired him to direct a series of westerns starring Bob Baker. Each film had a shooting schedule of only six days. Lewis left when Universal wanted to loan him out to other studios while only paying him $100 a week in between films. Lewis could not find steady work until 1939, when Columbia hired him for a series of westerns starring Charles Starrett. A year later, after fighting with studio executives, Lewis walked out and was forced into assignments at Monogram, another low-budget studio, before rejoining Universal just prior to the Japanese attack on Pearl Harbor on December 7, 1941.

In 1943 Lewis was drafted into the army, and he spent the next two years making army training films in New York. After directing *The Falcon in San Francisco* in 1945, he finally received his big break when Columbia offered him the low-budget gothic-noir film *My Name Is Julia Ross* (1945), a suspense story about a young woman who is tricked by a man and his mother into living with them in a remote part of the Cornwall coast, where they plan to murder her as part of their scheme to cover up the killing of the man's wife. The studio, however, only gave Lewis a 10-day shooting schedule, and when the production fell behind, Lewis was threatened with dismissal. This time he was saved by the head of the studio, Harry Cohn, who had been viewing the rushes and was impressed by his direction. Cohn extended the filming schedule to 18 days, and the film was a great success.

Lewis's next film was another low-budget noir, *So Dark the Night* (1946), one of the strangest studio films produced in Hollywood in the 1940s. Lewis converted part of the Columbia back lot into a French village, and with the assistance of mirrors and other devices, he was able to suggest a much larger budget than was offered to him. The film also had no stars and a bizarre plot with a downbeat ending that surprised audiences.

Lewis worked as a contract director at Columbia between 1945 and 1949, including on the excellent noir film *The Undercover Man* (1949), starring Glenn Ford as a federal agent trying to bring down Al Capone (Capone's name is never mentioned in the film, and he is only referred to as the Big Fellow). He followed this with his masterpiece *Gun Crazy* (1950), a low-budget film he made for independent producers: the King brothers, Frank and Maurice. However, the film was poorly distributed by United Artists, and it did not receive any sustained critical attention for many years after its release.

Lewis spent the early part of the 1950s as a contract director at MGM before directing his last great noir film, *The Big Combo* (1955), for Allied Artists, which was formerly Monogram Films. This story of an obsessive cop, played by Cornel Wilde, pursuing sadistic mobster Richard Conte was characterized by its elegant style, and here the director was assisted by talented cameraman John Alton. He followed this with a number of excellent westerns, such as *A Lawless Street* (1955), starring Randolph Scott, and *The Halliday Brand* (1957), starring Joseph Cotten. Fittingly, Lewis's last film was a 10-day western, *Terror in a Texas Town* (1958), which he directed as a favor to his old friend Ned Young, who could not find work in the 1950s because he was blacklisted. The climax of the film is a bizarre confrontation between a gunman, Johnny Crale (Ned Young), and the hero, George Hansen (Sterling Hayden), in the dusty western street. Instead of a gun, however, Hansen is armed only with a harpoon, with which he impales Crale. For the next 10 years Lewis directed numerous television series, including *The Rifleman, Bonanza, Daniel Boone, Gunsmoke,* and *The Big Valley*.

**Selected Noir Films:** *My Name Is Julia Ross* (1945), *So Dark the Night* (1946), *The Undercover Man* (1949), *Gun Crazy* (1950), *A Lady without Passport* (1950), *The Big Combo* (1955).

Geoff Mayer

**THE LONG MEMORY** (Rank, 1952). *Director:* Robert Hamer. *Producer:* Hugh Stewart. *Script:* Frank Harvey, based on the novel by Howard Clewes. *Cinematography:* Harry Waxman. *Music:* William Alwyn. *Cast:* John Mills (Phillip Davidson), John McCallum (Superintendent Bob Lowther), Elizabeth Sellars (Fay Lowther), Eva Bergh (Ilse), Geoffrey Keen (Craig), John Chandos (Boyd), John Slater (Pewsey), Thora Hird (Mrs. Pewsey), Vida Hope (Alice Gedge), John Horseley (Bletchley), Laurence Naismith (Hasbury), Michael Martin Harvey (Jackson), Mary Mackenzie (Gladys), Harold Lang (Boyd's Chauffeur).

Phillip Davidson leaves prison after serving 12 years for a murder he did not commit. He was convicted primarily because of the testimony of brain-damaged boxer Pewsey and Fay, Davidson's ex-girlfriend. Fay lied to protect her father at the trial. Davidson, bent on revenge, moves into a cabin on an abandoned barge on the coast of Kent. Director Robert Hamer uses this bleak setting to establish a close association between the bleak imagery of this desolate area, with its sparse, windblown vegetation, poverty-ridden shacks, and abandoned boats, and Davidson's sense of alienation. "Home" has never been depicted in such a stark manner.

Davidson's desire for revenge takes him to London, where Fay now lives with her husband, Superintendent Bob Lowther. Phillip learns that the man he supposedly killed, Boyd, is alive and prosperous, operating his black market activities on the Thames. Davidson's only ally in this story of redemption and regeneration is a displaced woman, Ilse, who comes to live with him after he rescues her from a rape attack. Although Davidson initially wants nothing to do with Ilse, her belief in his innate goodness and her devotion to him gradually temper his obsession for revenge.

Finally, he decides that it "is not worth it." Although there is a perfunctory climax, with Boyd attempting to kill Davidson, the focus of *The Long Memory* remains with Davidson's (and Ilse's) sense of alienation and estrangement. The film also shows the breakdown of traditional/populist values and presents a pessimistic view of the role of basic social institutions such as the media and the justice system. For example, Superintendent Lowther, appointed to uphold the law, lives with Fay, a woman that he knows is guilty of perjury.

As a way of showing that people rendered marginalized in the community, such as Davidson and Ilse, can have a stronger relationship than seemingly respectable members of society, Hamer crosscuts from a bedroom conversation between Lowther and Fay, shown isolated in their single beds, to an angled shot of Davidson and Ilse, with their heads nearly touching, in their cabin. While Lowther and his wife, Fay, are presented as repressed and anxious, Ilse and Davidson, perceived as society's outcasts, are shown to be intimate and open.

Ilse and Phillip Davidson function as parallel characters within the film—both have been unjustly treated. Ilse, a victim of war ("Our village was burned. What happened to my father and mother I never knew? Since then, I've never had a place to be where I was happy"), shows Phillip how to recover ("Bad things have happened to me, but I'm not bad"). After Boyd's death and Lowther's apology to Davidson, Ilse tells the policeman that Davidson "does not need anything that you can do. He just needs to be alone" as the two wounded lovers retreat back to their isolated cabin on the coast. Although *The Long Memory* is a story of regeneration, it is not a story of assimilation, as the two lovers remain estranged from society.

Geoff Mayer

**LUPINO, IDA** (1918–1995). Ida Lupino was in the unique position of both acting in a large number of classical film noirs and directing several of them. She is the only woman credited with being a director of classical American film noir and one of a small number of women who were able to helm commercially successful feature films during the classical Hollywood period. As an actress, Lupino was one of the most important figures in the classical noir cycle. Not a conventional beauty, she showed intelligence in her acting roles as well as strength, loyalty, and independence. Born in London, England, Lupino came from an English acting dynasty. Her classical training in Britain contributed to her wide range of technical skills, including a well-modulated voice and expressive face. After some initial struggles settling into the Hollywood studio system, her considerable natural abilities began to draw her favorable attention. Lupino's efforts in the early Warner Bros. noir *They Drive by Night* (1940) gained her the main female role in that studio's *High Sierra* (1941). In that influential film she is radiant and very convincing as the tough dance hall girl who forms a passionate love for Humphrey Bogart's humane but doomed criminal Roy Earle. Another successful film noir was *Road House* (1948), where she is caught up in the rivalry between male leads Richard Widmark and Cornell Wilde, her character, Lily, ending up shooting Widmark dead. Lupino was also able to show off her sultry singing style in this role. She was compelling and affecting as Mary, the blind girl who is able to humanize the Robert Ryan character in *On Dangerous Ground* (1952), and she also appeared that same year opposite him as a vulnerable woman trapped in her own home in *Beware My Lovely*. Both these films are well thought of today, but they were relatively unpopular with audiences of the time.

Lupino was also a script writer and songwriter as well as a director. The significance of her work as a director was really brought to wide attention by feminist historians in the 1970s and 1980s. Lupino formed a production company with her husband, Collier Young, a Columbia executive, and directed their first film, *Not Wanted* (1949), when the original director assigned to the project became ill. Her impressive directing talents were immediately obvious, as was her skill in presenting material of interest to both male and female moviegoers. *The Hitch-hiker* (1953) maintained tension as the two travelers (Frank Lovejoy and Edmond O'Brien) are terrorized by the crazed killer to whom they offer a ride. *The Bigamist* (1953) was an unusually ambiguous film for its time. The topic of bigamy was controversial on its own, but the film is remarkably even-handed in its judgment of the principals, showing a degree of compassion and tolerance not often associated with America in the 1950s. In *The Bigamist* Lupino became the first woman to both act in and direct a Hollywood film. Her general qualities as a director might be summed up as being very good at conveying tone subtly, being open to offbeat subjects, and being sensitive to the stories of people living on the edge, alienated individuals who are suffering stress.

**Selected Noir Films:** Lupino was an actress in the following films: *They Drive by Night* (1940), *High Sierra* (1941), *Out of the Fog* (1941), *The Man I Love* (1947), *Deep Valley* (1947), *Road House* (1948), *On Dangerous Ground* (1952), *Beware My Lovely* (1952), *The Bigamist* (1953), *Private Hell 36* (1954), *The Big Knife* (1955), *While the City Sleeps* (1956). Lupino directed the noir films *Outrage* (1950, and script writer), *On Dangerous Ground* (1952, uncredited assistance to Nicholas Ray), *The Hitch-hiker* (1953, and script writer), and *The Bigamist* (1953). Lupino was also a script writer on *Private Hell 36* (1954, directed by Don Siegel).

Brian McDonnell

# M

**MACMURRAY, FRED** (1908–1991). Born in Illinois in 1908, Fred MacMurray was a multitalented performer who began as a musician and finished his career as a Disney Studios stalwart and popular television actor. His contribution to film noir, like Billy Wilder, was relatively short but extremely important. His Everyman protagonist in *Double Indemnity* gave Hollywood an alternative villain, a character that blurred the rigid distinction between good and bad. As Walter Neff, he was likeable, ambitious, and fallible. He was also capable of murder and adultery.

MacMurray was the son of a concert violinist, and he was educated at a military academy before studying in Chicago. However, it was music, not education, that appealed to him, and he worked as a professional saxophonist in a number of bands in Chicago. In the late 1920s he traveled with a band to Hollywood and began moonlighting as an extra before moving on to Broadway for the 1930 revue *Three's a Crowd*. After the show closed, he returned to vaudeville and nightclubs.

MacMurray came back to Hollywood and was placed under contract by Paramount in 1934. In 1935 he made an impact in the romantic comedy *The Gilded Lily*, costarring Claudette Colbert. His career received a boost when Katherine Hepburn requested MacMurray as her costar in *Alice Adams* (1935), and he followed this with *Hands Across the Table* (1935). He worked in a number of different genres, including the outdoor melodrama *The Trail of the Lonesome Pine* (1936), which was the first outdoor film in full Technicolor, and the historical melodrama *Maid of Salem* (1937) with Claudette Colbert, which involved witch burning in seventeenth-century Massachusetts and was a rare commercial failure for MacMurray at the time. However, the public and the studio wanted to see MacMurray in comedies and musicals, and he met this need from 1936 to 1944. A typical 1930s film for MacMurray was *The Princess Comes Across* (1936), a clever blending of elements from romantic comedy with murder mystery. This film teamed MacMurray with Carole Lombard, one of his regular costars during this period. MacMurray played a musician with Lombard as a Brooklyn showgirl, and while traveling to the United States from Europe by ship, they solve a murder.

*Swing High, Swing Low* was a popular 1937 romantic melodrama with MacMurray as a professional trumpeter who marries Carole Lombard. The marriage fails when he is tempted to stray with Dorothy Lamour, although the film presents a happy ending with his reconciliation with Lombard. MacMurray followed this with four films with Madeleine Carroll, and in 1940 he costarred with Barbara Stanwyck in the romance *Remember the Night*.

There was nothing in MacMurray's career prior to 1944 to prepare audiences for his performance as Walter Neff in *Double Indemnity*. MacMurray initially resisted the role as he was worried about the effect it would have on his screen persona—Neff was motivated to murder because of lust, greed, and ambition. However, even though this film was an outstanding success, he immediately returned to comedy and romance in films such as *Practically Yours* (1944), with Claudette Colbert, and *Murder, He Says* (1945), with MacMurray as an insurance salesman who visits a family of homicidal hillbillies. Jean Heather, who played Lola in *Double Indemnity*, had a supporting role in this film.

After leaving Paramount, MacMurray joined Twentieth Century Fox and, later in the decade, Universal, where he starred in the 1947 comedy *The Egg and I*, a film so popular that Universal produced a series of Ma and Pa Kettle films, without MacMurray.

After rejecting the lead role in Billy Wilder's *Sunset Boulevard* (1950), there are few highlights in MacMurray's subsequent film career, except his performance as a duplicitous naval officer in *The Caine Mutiny* (1954) and in *Pushover* (1954), where he reprised the type of character he played in *Double Indemnity*. In this film he is a cop who falls from grace when he meets Kim Novak. Aside from a couple of interesting westerns, such as *At Gunpoint* (1955) and *Good Day for a Hanging* (1958), MacMurray had one more great performance as the adulterer in Billy Wilder's *The Apartment* (1960) before spending the rest of his career with Disney and the 1960s television program *My Three Sons*.

**Selected Noir Films:** *Double Indemnity* (1944), *Pushover* (1954).

Geoff Mayer

**THE MACOMBER AFFAIR** (United Artists, 1947). *Director:* Zoltan Korda. *Producers:* Benedict Bogeaus, Casey Robinson, and Arthur M. Landau (associate). *Script:* Casey Robinson and Seymour Bennett, based on Seymour Bennett's and Frank Arnold's adaptation of Ernest Hemingway's *The Short Happy Life of Francis Macomber*. *Cinematography:* Karl Struss. *Music:* Miklós Rózsa. *Cast:* Gregory Peck

(Robert Wilson), Joan Bennett (Margaret Macomber), Robert Preston (Francis Macomber), Reginald Denny (Police Commissioner), Jean Gillie (Aimee).

Most of *The Macomber Affair* takes place on the plains of Kenya, or the Hollywood back lot that matches the African footage, and this film, more than any other 1940s film, shows that film noir was not dependent on, or confined to, the dark, urban landscapes generally associated with this kind of film. More important than the physical setting are the humans that inhabit these films, with their twisted emotional desires—and *The Macomber Affair* is predicated on a classic noir situation involving lust, domination, and humiliation.

Although the film uses extensive location footage shot by Osmond Borradaile in Africa, Karl Struss's black-and-white cinematography and Zoltan Korda's compositions eradicate the exhilarating sense of freedom and space generally associated with big-game hunting in Africa. This is replaced by a claustrophobic environment showing the three main characters trapped within a warped situation. Professional hunter Robert Wilson becomes embroiled in the intense battle between a married couple, Francis and Margaret Macomber, for control within the marriage. As the theme of domination and submission could not be explicitly presented, the film is partially reliant on Miklós Rózsa's evocative score to suggest those aspects of human desire that the Production Code Authority would not allow in terms of the dialogue and action.

Francis and Margaret Macomber, in a belated attempt to save their ailing marriage, hire hunter Robert Wilson to take them deep into Kenya so that, on one level, Francis can kill a dangerous animal and prove to his wife that he is not a coward, and, on another level, their sadomasochistic relationship can continue without the daily distractions of urban living. Wilson, a professional hunter, is caught between this disturbed couple, and he makes the mistake of falling in love with the wife after, the film implies, consummating a sexual relationship while her husband is sleeping.

The relationship between these three people deteriorates when Francis wounds a lion that subsequently escapes into a bushy area. However, when Francis insists on accompanying Robert into the bushes to put the lion out of his misery, he panics when the lion charges. Wilson is forced to complete the kill, and Francis's cowardice provides further ammunition for Margaret to taunt her husband. Now she openly flirts with Wilson, and Francis compounds his humiliation by attacking two helpless guides assisting Wilson on the safari.

This proves to be a turning point. The next day, Francis redeems himself during a buffalo shoot, and his newfound confidence upsets his wife more than his cowardice as she realizes that he will regain control of their marriage. When, in a similar incident, a wounded buffalo seeks shelter in the bushes, Francis again insists on accompanying Wilson into the area. However, when the buffalo charges the men, Francis does not run this time. Margaret then shoots her husband in the head, and though Wilson testifies that it was an accident, the film ends with Margaret about to defend her actions at an inquest into her husband's death.

*The Macomber Affair* rarely appears on lists of noir films, yet the plot is pure film noir. While the film has to be indirect in its suggestion of a sexual relationship between Robert and Margaret—with Francis waking up to find that his wife is not in her bed—this provides the only explanation for the scenes in Nairobi that begin and end the film. Both clearly have formed a relationship that is never specified during their time on the plains. The casting of Joan Bennett is important in this respect as Bennett appeared as the dangerous femme fatale in two popular noir films—*The Woman in the Window* (1944) and *Scarlet Street* (1945)—prior to *The Macomber Affair*. Similarly, the possibility that Francis was accidentally killed does not make much sense as she shoots him while standing by their vehicle with Francis in front of her. His death provides the logical outcome of the struggle for ascendancy within their troubled marriage.

*The Macomber Affair* is a significant film noir and, along with more well-known films such as *The Maltese Falcon* (1941) and *Out of the Past* (1947), documents the battle for control between the sexes that occupied many 1940s films. Francis is no threat to Margaret for much of the film. Only when he regains his confidence does she kill him.

Aside from the husband and wife, *The Macomber Affair* was a strange role for Gregory Peck as Robert Wilson, who breaches his ethical code, and loses his license, by succumbing to the temptation of Margaret Macomber. Aside from borderline noir films such as *The Paradine Case* (1948) and *Cape Fear* (1961), Gregory Peck did not appear in a similar role for the rest of his career. Yet his screen persona, which was based on honor, strength, and virtue, adds to the moral ambivalence expressed in this film. Wilson's fall from grace, which is confirmed when he confesses to Francis that he loves Margaret , and repeated in Nairobi, paradoxically shows that as Francis Macomber was regenerated by his experience on the plains, Robert Wilson, the sturdy, heroic big-game hunter, suffers a moral decline. When Margaret leaves him to face the inquest at the end of the film, Wilson is left in the darkness to confront an even more difficult problem—himself.

Geoff Mayer

**MACREADY, GEORGE** (1899–1973). One of the screen's best villains, Macready's most important contribution to film noir was as Ballin Mundson, the bisexual German sadist in *Gilda* who, as he admits to Gilda, only feels alive when he can experience hate. Macready was born in Providence, Rhode Island. After graduating from Brown University, he worked as a reporter in New York before making his Broadway debut in 1926. While Macready was able to play a variety of characters on stage, his screen persona was strictly that of a villain, due mainly to his rasping voice and his angular facial features, which included a scar on his cheek.

Macready first appeared in films in 1943, and typical of his early work was his role as Harry Wharton in *The Missing Juror* (1944), directed by Oscar (Budd) Boetticher for Columbia Studios. Macready plays an innocent man convicted and sentenced to death for a murder he did not commit. However, even though he is pardoned, the torment proves too much, and after he is sent to a psychiatric institution, members of the jury begin to die. Similarly, his role of Ralph Hughes, the mother-dominated killer in Joseph Lewis's gothic noir *My Name Is Julia Ross* (1945), crystallized Macready's screen image as the cultured sadist, forever tormenting poor Nina Foch on a lonely estate in Cornwall. *Gilda* gave him a chance to refine these traits even further. In the film he dominates Glenn Ford to the extent that Ford spends the entire second half of the film punishing Rita Hayworth for her supposed infidelities while married to Mundson.

In *The Big Clock* (1948), Macready is Steve Hagen, Charles Laughton's loyal assistant, who devises the scheme to implicate an innocent man for the murder of Laughton's mistress, Pauline Delos. Stanley Kubrick's great antiwar film *Paths of Glory* (1957) gave Macready his last great role as Paul Mireau, a French general who orders his men to undertake a suicidal mission during World War I. Enraged when the mission fails, Mireau selects three men to be tried for cowardice. Throughout the 1950s and 1960s he also appeared in many television series. Off-screen, he was an art connoisseur and operated an art gallery with his friend Vincent Price. In 1970 he played U.S. Secretary of State Cordell Hull in *Tora! Tora! Tora!*, the large-budget film detailing the events leading up to the Japanese attack on Pearl Harbor. Macready's final film was the low-budget horror film *The Return of Count Yorga* (1971). He died two years later.

**Selected Noir Films:** *The Missing Juror* (1944), *I Love a Mystery* (1945), *My Name Is Julia Ross* (1945), *Gilda* (1946), *The Walls Come Tumbling Down* (1946), *The Man Who Dared* (1946), *The Big Clock* (1948), *Knock on Any Door* (1949), *Alias Nick Beal* (1949), *Johnny Allegro* (1949), *A Lady without Passport* (1950), *Detective Story* (1951), *A Kiss Before Dying* (1956), *Dead Ringer* (1964).

Geoff Mayer

**MADELEINE** (Cineguild, 1950). *Director:* David Lean. *Producer:* Stanley Haynes. *Script:* Stanley Haynes and Nicholas Phipps. *Cinematography:* Guy Green. *Music:* William Alwyn. *Cast:* Ann Todd (Madeleine Smith), Norman Wooland (William Minnoch), Ivan Desny (Emile L'Anglier), Leslie Banks (James Smith), Barbara Everest (Mrs. Smith), Elizabeth Sellars (Christina), Patricia Raine (Bessie Smith), Eugene Deckers (Thuau), Andre Morell (Defending Counsel), Barry Jones (Prosecuting Counsel), Ivor Barnard (Mr. Murdoch), Jean Cadell (Mrs. Jenkins).

*Madeleine* is one of David Lean's finest films. His precise, almost clinical visual style is ideally suited to the film's emotionally complex subject matter, and the director cleverly exploits the recessive screen persona of Ann Todd as the enigmatic Madeleine Smith. Cinematographer Guy Green, at the request of Lean, transformed Green's normal desire to achieve a realistic look into an expressionistic lighting style emphasizing Todd's cheek bones via an overhead lighting pattern, similar to the style devised by Josef von Sternberg for Marlene Dietrich in her Paramount films in the early 1930s (see, particularly, *The Devil Is a Woman* [1935]).

Todd, who began in the British cinema in 1932, enjoyed great success as the masochistic, emotionally fragile pianist Francesca in *The Seventh Veil* (1945), and her performance as Madeleine Smith exploits, and subverts, the submissive basis of her earlier films. Early scenes in the film seemingly emphasize this trait, as she appears vulnerable before the two males in her life—her lover, Emile L'Anglier, and her father, James Smith. However, Madeleine Smith is not a submissive Scottish lady torn between the forbidden pleasures offered by Emile and the social demands of Victorian society. Madeleine subtly resists the pressure from her father to marry the wealthy, but dull, William Minnoch and tries to seemingly live within the constrictions imposed by Victorian society while indulging her sexual desire for Emile. After Emile rejects Madeleine's offer to run away and get married, she realizes that her French lover is more interested in her family's social position and wealth than in marriage to her.

Emile's rejection follows the sexual consummation of their relationship, and Lean leaves little doubt as to their sexual behavior through his judicious insertion of a passionate dance sequence at a highland festival as Madeleine and Emile engage in foreplay. When Madeleine falls over in a dark forest and looks up with anticipation at Emile towering over her, Lean cuts to the frenzy of the dancers performing in the village below. Following the purchase of arsenic by Madeleine from a local chemist, Emile suffers two bouts of poisoning, with the last one being fatal. Madeleine is tried for murder, and the jury finds the charge "not proven." The film concludes with a voice-over pointing out that she is deemed neither innocent nor guilty, but Lean's final close-up of Madeleine's sly smile as she leaves the court leaves little doubt as to her guilt.

Lean, together with script writers Stanley Haynes and Nicholas Phipps, transformed a real court case that took place in Glasgow in 1857 into a study of the destructive power of Victorian patriarchy. The film makes it quite clear that the real motivation for Madeleine's actions emanate from James Smith's authoritarian control over his family, in particular, the (lack of) rights accorded to women. The repression of female desire leads to betrayal and murder. The scenes between Todd and Banks are both revealing and powerful as the patriarch tries to impose his will on Madeleine. She, in turn, subverts his authority.

Geoff Mayer

**THE MAN FROM COLORADO** (Columbia, 1948). *Director:* Henry Levin. *Producer:* Jules Schermer. *Script:* Robert Hardy Andrews and Ben Maddow, based on an original story by Borden Chase. *Cinematography:* William Snyder. *Music:* George Duning. *Cast:* Glenn Ford (Owen Devereaux), William Holden (Del Stewart), Ellen Drew (Caroline Emmett), Ray Collins (Big Ed Carter), Jerome Courtland (Johnny Howard), James Millican (Jericho Howard), William "Bill"

Phillips (York), Denver Pyle (Easy Jarrett), James Bush (Dickson), Ian MacDonald (Jack Rawson), Myron Healey (Powers).

In the late 1940s a cycle of westerns presented a radically different view of the West by shifting from its traditionally optimistic view of human behavior to a more problematic presentation of psychologically disturbed characters fighting their inner demons. This cycle of westerns combined elements of the traditional western with an emphasis on entrapment that was more generally associated with urban noir crime films. A key film in this cycle was the 1947 Warner Bros. production *Pursued*, starring Robert Mitchum as a young man haunted by a childhood trauma. This somber film, influenced by Hollywood's fascination with psychoanalysis, transformed the familiar western setting of Monument Valley in Utah, the location for many of John Ford's westerns, into a nightmarish landscape by cinematographer James Wong Howe. *Pursued* was accompanied in 1947 with another noir western, *Ramrod*, directed by Andre De Toth and starring Joel McCrea as the cowboy caught up in the destructive behavior of an obsessed female landowner, played by Veronica Lake.

*Blood on the Moon*, also starring Robert Mitchum, was released the following year by RKO, and director Robert Wise, assisted by cinematographer Nicholas Musuraca (who photographed many of RKO's noir films, including *Out of the Past* [1947]), presented a claustrophobic environment that reinforced the sense of personal entrapment. Columbia's contribution to this cycle in 1948 was *The Man from Colorado*, starring two popular contract players at the studio, Glenn Ford and William Holden. In 1941, at the start of their careers, both men had costarred in *Texas*, an upbeat western that presented Ford and Holden as two cowboys who end up on different sides of the law. Seven years later, *The Man from Colorado* presented a more troubling view of human behavior, and although it does not have the superior direction of and expressive cinematography of *Pursued* or *Blood on the Moon*, thematically, it is the most extreme noir western of the late 1940s.

If *The Man from Colorado* did not have a western setting and mid-nineteenth-century background, it would have been a typical film noir in the late 1940s as it dramatizes the fears and anxieties, especially involving a strong sense of disillusionment and dislocation, found in many urban noir films released between 1946 and 1949 (including *The Blue Dahlia* [1946], *Crossfire* [1947], *Ride the Pink Horse* [1947], *Dead Reckoning* [1947], and *Act of Violence* [1949]). *The Man from Colorado* adapts, and transforms, these aspects from 1945 to 1865 and the post–Civil War period, and the film suggests that whatever the war, its destructive effects are the same as some men never recover from its aberrant condition, where killing is presented as morally and socially acceptable.

The film begins on the final day of the Civil War as a strong force of Union soldiers, led by Colonel Owen Devereaux, corner a small band of Confederate soldiers. When the Confederates try to surrender by flying a white flag, Devereaux pretends that he does not see their surrender and opens fire with his artillery. A close-up of Devereaux, with Glenn Ford uncharacteristically presented with curly hair and a grim visage, shows his evident pleasure in the suffering inflicted by his artillery on the helpless soldiers.

After the war, Devereaux, accompanied by his close friend Captain Del Stewart, returns to his hometown in Colorado, where he is welcomed as a war hero. Devereaux accepts an appointment as a federal judge, while Stewart becomes the town marshal. As a federal judge, Devereaux is able to operate without scrutiny whereby he can inflict pain without the fear of prosecution or legal retribution. However, his biased support for the major capitalist in the region, Big Ed Carter, who is exploiting and persecuting the local miners who have lost their rights while fighting in the Civil War, forces Del Stewart to abandon the law and wage guerrilla warfare against Carter and Devereaux.

The conventional western plot, which sides with the miners against the corporate greed of Carter, is pushed into the background as the film focuses on Devereaux's fragile mental condition. Devereaux, unlike most other western characters, is a divided figure, fighting his inner turmoil, which surfaces in a need to inflict pain. This link between psychosis and war makes *The Man from Colorado* a topical film in 1948, when many ex-army personnel were required to adjust to peacetime following an extended experience with the abnormal and atrocities of war.

The film, however, extends this link by also including a thinly veiled attack on large-scale capitalism. Hence the insane federal judge (Devereaux) uses his position to support the unscrupulous entrepreneur (Big Ed Carter). This link is strengthened by the nominal hero's (Stewart) vigilante in rejecting the law as impotent in protecting the helpless miners from Devereaux and Carter.

In some ways Glen Ford's behavior in *The Man from Colorado* represented a continuation of the unstable character he portrayed in *Gilda* (1946). His psychotic judge in this western contained many of the qualities of the neurotic, tormented lover he played in *Gilda*. Both men are unable to find comfort and solace with their lovers—in *The Man from Colorado* Devereaux's willful actions destroy his marriage. Whether this illness is a direct result of the war or whether the war merely provides the opportunity for such tendencies to erupt is not clear in either *Gilda* or *The Man from Colorado*. However, while audiences in the 1940s were prepared to enjoy such qualities in a contemporary melodrama such as *Gilda*, which was Columbia's most commercially successful film in 1946, they were more hesitant to see them displayed in a western such as *The Man from Colorado*.

Geoff Mayer

**MANN, ANTHONY** (1906–1967). Mann was one of the best and most significant Hollywood directors of the middle decades of the twentieth century. A superb storyteller and a fine stylist, he made compelling films in several genres. Perhaps best remembered today for the dark westerns he made with James Stewart in the 1950s, Mann began his directing career with a number of memorable contributions to the classical film noir cycle. Sometime shocking in their bursts of brutality, these films were always well paced and replete with striking visuals, thought-provoking subject matter, and strong acting performances. Mann was born Emil Bundmann (some sources say Bundsmann) in San Diego, California. From his late teens he worked on the theater stage in New York and became a successful Broadway director. Mann went to Hollywood in 1940 and was soon directing low-budget films for Republic and RKO. At this time Mann worked as an assistant director on Preston Sturges's classic, self-reflexive comedy of Hollywood life *Sullivan's Travels* (1941). He began his own directing career with films that have since been defined as noirs, then moved on to make a number of westerns, which also had a noticeably dark tone to them. Mann, early on, exhibited a very expressive visual style. His films featured lots of tracking shots as early as *Dr. Broadway* (1942) and *The Great Flamarion* (1945). Already, too, he was showing a thematic preoccupation with characters who were trapped in a bleak and hostile world and who could find no escape other than death or madness. What some now consider as being his first full-fledged film noir was *Desperate* (1947). This small-budget feature displayed Mann's excellent use of light, which was to reach its culmination in *T-Men* (1947) and *Raw Deal* (1948), where he worked with John Alton, perhaps the greatest of the many superb cinematographers who worked in noir. *Desperate* had a memorable suspenseful set piece as a group waits in a darkened building for the midnight execution of a young thug. *T-Men* combined a semidocumentary story structure with bold chiaroscuro lighting and chillingly subjective depictions of despair and impotence in the face of violence. *Raw Deal* included a rare female voice-over in a tale that featured outbreaks of sadistic viciousness. These are among the finest of all classical noirs: their dark world of pessimism (even of nihilism) is crammed with danger, tension, violence, and drama. With *Border Incident* (1949), Mann continued his skilful exploitation of the potential of noir story lines in unusual settings through his location shooting on the U.S.–Mexican frontier. A continuing and sustained theme of revenge can be found in his work, beginning with *Raw Deal* and going through to the dark James Stewart westerns such as *The Naked Spur* (1953) and *The Man from Laramie* (1955). The bridging films between his noir period and the thematically similar westerns were *Border Incident* (1949) and *The Devil's Doorway* (1950). The former showed the western landscape in a dark way (including a hideous encounter with quicksand), and the latter's somber story of an American Indian's tragic fate has undeniably noirish elements. Mann died comparatively young while filming the drama *A Dandy in Aspic* in 1967.

**Selected Noir Films:** *Dr. Broadway* (1942), *The Great Flamarion* (1945), *Two O'Clock Courage* (1945), *Strange Impersonation* (1946), *Desperate* (1947, and story), *Railroaded!* (1947), *T-Men* (1947), *Raw Deal* (1948), *He Walked by Night* (1948, uncredited), *Follow Me Quietly* (1949, uncredited and story), *Reign of Terror* (a.k.a. *The Black Book*, 1949), *Border Incident* (1949), *Side Street* (1950), *The Furies* (1950), *Devil's Doorway* (1950), *The Tall Target* (1951).

Brian McDonnell

**THE MARK OF CAIN** (Two Cities/Rank, 1947). *Director:* Brian Desmond Hurst. *Producer:* W. P. Lipscomb. *Script:* W. P. Lipscomb (adaptation), Francis Crowdy, and Christianna Brand, based on the novel *Airing in a Closed Carriage* by Joseph Shearing. *Cinematography:* Erwin Hillier. *Music:* Bernard Stevens. *Cast:* Eric Portman (Richard Howard), Sally Gray (Sarah Bonheur), Patrick Holt (John Howard), Dermot Walsh (Jerome Thorn), Denis O'Dea (Sir William Godfrey), Edward Lexy (Lord Rochford), Therese Giehse (Sister Seraphine), Maureen Delaney (Daisy Cobb), Helen Cherry (Mary), Vida Hope (Jennie), James Hayter (Dr. White).

Four novels written by Joseph Shearing, a pseudonym for Gabrielle Margaret Vere Long, were produced as films in 1947 and 1948. Whilst *Moss Rose* was produced in Hollywood, *Blanche Fury* (1948), *So Evil My love* (1948), and *The Mark of Cain* were all produced in England. All four films involve female protagonists in situations involving betrayal, murder, and unhappy relationships. *The Mark of Cain* is consistent with this pattern, although its female protagonist is not as complex, assertive, or interesting as her counterparts in *So Evil My Love* and *Blanche Fury*. Instead, the virtues of *The Mark of Cain* reside more in Alex Vetchinsky's striking Victorian sets and Erwin Hillier's low-key photography.

Two brothers, Richard and John Howard from the north of England, fall in love with French-raised, British-born Sarah Bonheur when they visit France to purchase cotton for their mill. Sarah is initially attracted to Richard's high-culture leanings, although she ultimately favors the masculine prowess of John. Although the marriage produces a child, Sarah is unhappy with John's dictatorial, boorish behavior and, encouraged by Richard, investigates the possibilities of a divorce. When Sarah learns that Victorian law favors the husband and that she will have to leave her daughter with John if she abandons the marriage, she decides to stay. Ironically, as John's health and overt masculine power deteriorate, Sarah is increasingly attracted to her husband. Richard, thwarted by Sarah's reconciliation with John, poisons his brother and frames Sarah for the crime, planning to save her at the trial. Richard's bizarre performance in the courtroom fails to save Sarah, and she is found guilty. Only the intervention of Jerome Thorn, who is attracted to Sarah, saves her from the gallows when he plays on Richard's mental disintegration.

*The Mark of Cain* is less interesting than either *Blanche Fury* or *So Evil My Love* due to the fact that Sally Gray's Sarah Bonheur is little more than a victim, or pawn, of the sibling rivalry involving Richard and John. Nevertheless, director Brian Desmond Hurst, supported by Erwin Hillier's superb cinematography, provides a strong dramatic visual basis for this elemental melodrama and its biblical subtext. Primarily, it is a story of virtue (Bonheur) struggling to survive, and overcome, the demands of the Howard family in particular, and the iniquities of Victorian patriarchy in general.

Geoff Mayer

MASON, JAMES (1909–1984). James Mason's film career was built on the enthusiastic reaction, mainly from women, to his sadistic treatment of a number of young women in a series of films in the early and mid-1940s. His "dangerous" persona at that time was a revelation to British audiences more accustomed to the cultured, sexually restrained style of theatrically trained actors such as Laurence Olivier, Ralph Richardson, and John Gielgud. Mason, on the other hand, was tall, dark, and brooding, and he became, for a period, every woman's favorite brute, which made him a huge box office draw.

After studying architecture at Cambridge, Mason made his professional stage debut with a repertory company in Croydon. In the 1930s, after stage work with the Old Vic and Dublin's Gate Company, Mason appeared in low-budget "quota quickies," such as *Late Extra* (1935), with supporting roles in better films such as *Fire over England* (1936) and *The Return of the Scarlet Pimpernel* (1937). In 1941 he had a key role as the sensitive hero in Lance Comfort's gothic noir film *Hatter's Castle* (1941). More important to the development of his "dangerous" persona was his starring role as the brooding war-affected composer in *The Night Has Eyes* (1942) who arouses strong passions in the vulnerable, repressed heroine (Joyce Howard). The film's pervasive sense of danger was reinforced by the fact that the characters were trapped in an isolated mansion on the Yorkshire moors.

Mason's ability to convincingly project a feeling of repressed violence and sexual sadism, coupled with suggestions of emotional disturbance, was further developed in his breakthrough role as the sadistic Lord Rohan in *The Man in Grey* (1943). While Rohan was an unmitigated villain, Mason's character as Nicholas, Ann Todd's perverse mentor in *The Seventh Veil* (1946), was also disturbing, especially in his overt hostility to women, as he explains to Todd in their first encounter. However, Todd, like Howard in *The Night Has Eyes*, welcomes Nicholas's firm control, and the immense popularity of this film reinforced the desire of producers to continue casting Mason in similar roles. In both *The Seventh Veil* and *The Man in Grey* Mason inflicts physical damage on his women—beating Margaret Lockwood to death in *The Man in Grey* and thrashing the delicate fingers of pianist Todd in *The Seventh Veil*. Mason's highwayman, Captain Jackson, opposite Lockwood in *The Wicked Lady* (1945), was more of the same for Mason; the only difference is that this time, Lockwood kills him. There was also his persecution of Phyllis Calvert in *Fanny by Gaslight* (1944).

A welcome change for Mason was his performance as the vulnerable Northern Irish gunman Johnny McQueen in Carol Reed's *Odd Man Out* (1947). This critically celebrated film depicts the last hours in McQueen's life after he has been fatally wounded in a raid on a linen mill to obtain money for the IRA. Before he left for Hollywood, following the success of *Odd Man Out*, Mason gave a less showy performance as a doctor avenging the death of his lover in Lawrence Huntington's film noir *The Upturned Glass* (1947), where Mason costarred with his wife, Pamela Kellino, whom he murders in the film.

Mason was voted number one male star in Britain in the mid-1940s. It took time to establish himself in Hollywood—an early film role was as a sympathetic doctor with a working-class clientele in Max Ophuls's noir film *Caught* (1949), with Mason, now the hero, opposite the archetypal screen villain Robert Ryan. A more significant noir performance by Mason was in his next film for Ophuls, *The Reckless Moment* (1949), as Martin Donnelly, a small-time criminal who tries to blackmail Joan Bennett but gradually falls in love with her. His regeneration is complete when he protects Bennett from his boss and dies taking the blame for an earlier murder he did not commit to prevent Bennett and her daughter from facing an investigation from the police. This was Mason's most important role in a film noir produced in Hollywood.

After essaying the famed German General Rommel in two films for Twentieth Century Fox, *The Desert Fox* (1951) and *The Desert Rats* (1953), and the notorious espionage agent Ulysses Diello ("Cicero") in *Five Fingers* (1952), Mason played Norman Maine, the fallen movie star, in the Technicolor remake of *A Star Is Born* (1954). This role earned him his first Academy Award nomination. As Mason gradually moved into character parts in Hollywood in the 1950s, he produced a number of his films, including Nicholas Ray's bold melodrama *Bigger Than Life* (1956), a story of a teacher who terrorizes all around him after becoming affected by prescription drugs. Later, Mason was cast as Professor Humbert, who becomes infatuated with underage Sue Lyon, in Stanley Kubrick's *Lolita* (1962). In 1969 Mason traveled to Australia to portray a painter, loosely based on the activities of artist Norman Lindsay, who gains inspiration from young Helen Mirren in *Age of Consent* (Mason also produced this film, directed by Michael Powell).

The 1970s and early 1980s were less rewarding as he walked through numerous European coproductions, although he gave a mannered performance as the cruel plantation owner in *Mandingo* (1975), and he was a fine Dr. Watson in *Murder by Decree* (1979). The standout performance by Mason in his final decade was as the amoral lawyer Edward Concannon in Sidney Lumet's courtroom drama *The Verdict* (1982), demonstrating again that when the script and direction were right, James Mason was a fine actor. He died in Switzerland in 1984. Aside from his nomination for *A Star Is Born*, Mason also received Oscar nominations for *Georgy Girl* (1966) and *The Verdict* (1982). Mason was nominated for best British actor at the 1963 BAFTA Film Awards for *Lolita* (1962) and at the 1968 Awards for *The Deadly Affair* (1967).

**Selected Noir Films:** *Late Extra* (1935), *Troubled Waters* (1936), *Twice Branded* (1936), *Prison Breaker* (1936), *Catch As Catch Can* (1937), *I Met a Murderer* (1939), *Hatter's Castle* (1941), *The Night Has Eyes* (1942), *Alibi* (1942), *The Man in Grey* (1943), *They Met in the Dark* (1943), *Fanny by Gaslight* (1944), *A Place of One's Own* (1945), *The Seventh Veil* (1945), *Odd Man Out* (1947), *The Upturned Glass* (1947), *Caught* (1949), *The Reckless Moment* (1949), *One Way Street* (1950), *Lady Possessed* (1952), *The Man Between* (1953), *Bigger Than Life* (1956), *Cry Terror!* (1956), *The Deadly Affair* (1966),

*11 Harrowhouse* (1974), *The Marseille Contract* (1974), *Murder by Decree* (1978), *A Dangerous Summer* (1982), *The Verdict* (1982).

Geoff Mayer

**MEMENTO** (Newmarket/Summit Entertainment, 2000). *Director:* Christopher Nolan. *Producers:* Suzanne Todd and Jennifer Todd. *Script:* Christopher Nolan, from a short story by Jonathon Nolan. *Cinematography:* Wally Pfister. *Music:* David Julyan. *Cast:* Guy Pearce (Leonard), Carrie-Anne Moss (Natalie), Joe Pantoliano (Teddy), Mark Boone Junior (Burt), Jorja Fox (Leonard's Wife), Stephen Tobolowsky (Sammy), Harriet Sansom Harris (Mrs. Jankis).

Insurance investigator Leonard Shelby, protagonist of Christopher Nolan's *Memento*, suffers from a special type of short-term amnesia that prevents him creating any new memories. This disability struck him at the time of the rape and murder of his wife. Despite the obstacles his amnesia creates, he tries to solve the mystery of her death by tattooing his torso with important instructional statements and by recording precautionary instructions and details using annotated Polaroid photographs. As if to mimic his situation, the film's plot unfolds in reverse chronology. Early in the film, but late in Leonard's story, Leonard shoots dead a man named Teddy. He had been guided to Teddy by a mysterious woman named Natalie, whose motives in doing so are highly suspect. The core of the film involves Leonard's bewildering interactions with Teddy, Natalie, and a drug-dealing associate named Dodds, all this mixed up with another narrative line depicting the plight of a second short-term amnesia victim, Sammy Jankis, whose situation is analogous to Leonard's. It is possible that Leonard is being set up as a convenient fall guy/assassin by Teddy, who exploits his condition to persuade him to kill off Teddy's rivals and then to promptly forget what he has done. Can Leonard possibly extricate himself from this entrapped existence?

*Memento* has been widely praised for its ingenuity, originality, and complexity and its innovative, experimental story structure. As a murder mystery whose narrative has been dismembered and reassembled so that its plot is presented in reverse chronological order, *Memento* recalls the time-reversal devices of Harold Pinter's *Betrayal* (1983) and the fractured storytelling of John Boorman's 1967 classic revenge movie *Point Blank*. In making amnesia its central subject matter, *Memento* also looks back to the classical film noir tradition of stories about amnesiac World War II veterans and about men and women accused of crimes they had possibly committed prior to temporary memory loss. The ambitions of *Memento*, however, go far beyond those earlier films. In this film the narrative building blocks are laid out in reverse order, and such a reverse assembly requires the viewer to deal with what is, in effect, the opposite of the usual cause-and-effect narrative logic. In order to make sense of this back-to-front storytelling, the viewer has to take each successive scene and mentally place it before the preceding scene. *Memento* has a very complex story line that is further complicated by its unique narrative structure. It is a film that in its overall story content conforms to the thriller tradition, but it is a thriller that is not about what happens *next,* but about what happened *before,* and why what we see happening now has come about. Director Nolan says it is about the "existential conditions of identity," and its amnesiac hero, Leonard, has a virtually unmatched opportunity to freely choose his own destiny, if only he can escape other people's traps.

In thematic terms, the film is thus clearly an example of the neo-noir genre. The plot of *Memento,* like those of many film noirs both old and new, has the framework of a (distorted) detective story. A man is trying to track down the killer of his wife to exact revenge. In experiencing the film, we in the audience are forced into the same position as Leonard as protagonist, a process helped by Guy Pearce's compelling performance in the leading role. Seen generically in this way, the film fits well the noir pattern of extreme subjectivity. Typically enough, *Memento* starts with the killing of Teddy, and by the end we know how that death has come about and why. Seen from this viewpoint, the plot is a process of the accumulation of evidence until we have sufficient knowledge to explain the enigmas of the story. In setting, too, we get an appropriate (even classical) film noir landscape: the unspecific, unmemorable, interchangeable, and architecturally anonymous world of Los Angeles motels and shopping strip streets in the northern suburbs of the San Fernando Valley. Los Angeles has always been the *locus classicus* of urban film noir, exemplified either by its rain-slicked nighttime streets or its burned-out, semiurban no-man's-land.

*Memento* is also very similar thematically to a cycle of wartime and (more commonly) postwar film noirs on the subject of amnesia such as *Street of Chance* (1942), *Spellbound* (1945), *Black Angel* (1946), *Crack-Up* (1946), *Somewhere in the Night* (1946), *Fear in the Night* (1947), *High Wall* (1947), *The Clay Pigeon* (1949), *The Crooked Way* (1949), and *The Blue Gardenia* (1953). Several of these films concern returning World War II veterans rendered amnesiac by wartime traumas. In those examples of the sub-genre where women are the central characters, the memory loss may be short-term through blacking out due to alcohol or being drugged. Men in some such films are likewise framed with drugs by unscrupulous villains or have committed crimes while drunk, only to forget them after blacking out. Their lead characters frequently have to become quasi-detectives in order to discover the truth about how they had actually come to be in the pickles in which they currently find themselves. Leonard's story in *Memento* takes this a step further because his amnesia is of a different order. So, too, is his predicament, which could be framed as a question: how do you manage to pursue a quest when you keep forgetting "what" and "why"? Leonard's life has come to resemble a nightmare where he cannot progress. Many detectives in such classical and neo-noir films are seeker-heroes who have quests, mysteries to solve. Leonard, as the main character of *Memento,* is one such, but he is also a noir-style fall guy, the unwitting tool of both Natalie's and Teddy's duplicity. His peculiar situation therefore makes him as much a victim-hero as a seeker-hero. But in this instance the tables can be turned, on Teddy at least: Leonard gets revenge on him for his exploitative deceit. In effect, Teddy has, by setting Leonard up as a hunter of criminals, created a Frankenstein monster who then kills him.

Brian McDonnell

**MILDRED PIERCE** (Warner Bros., 1945). *Director:* Michael Curtiz. *Producer:* Jerry Wald. *Script:* Ranald MacDougall, based on the novel by James M. Cain. *Cinematography:* Ernest Haller. *Music:* Max Steiner. *Cast:* Joan Crawford (Mildred Pierce), Jack Carson (Wally Fay), Zachary Scott (Monte Beragon), Eve Arden (Ida Corwin), Ann Blyth (Veda Piece), Bruce Bennett (Bert Pierce), Lee Patrick (Maggie Biederhof), Moroni Olsen (Inspector Peterson), Veda Ann Borg (Miriam Ellis), Butterfly McQueen (Lottie), John Compton (Ted Forrester).

In the middle and late 1940s, there was a cycle of noir films that focused on middle-class dissatisfaction with the so-called American dream. In films such as *The Woman in the Window* (1945), *Nora Prentiss* (1947), and, especially, *Pitfall* (1948), normal, reliable men were presented as dissatisfied with their steady jobs, loving partners, and traditional families. These protagonists were male, and their problem was usually instigated by an infatuation with *la belle dame sans merci*, the "fatal woman." However, on a deeper level, these films represented a change in the balance of power between men and women. As the men became less heroic and more vulnerable, the women were seen as more independent and assertive. *Mildred Pierce* represented an assimilation of this trend with the twist that the protagonist was a woman, and the basis of the film represented a critique of the very basis of society, the normal love of a parent for a child.

This theme is established in the film's opening narration as Mildred expresses her dissatisfaction with the monotony and routine of domesticity:

> We lived on Corvallis Street, where all the houses looked alike. I was always in the kitchen. I felt as though I had been born in a kitchen and lived there all my life, except for the few hours it took to get married.
> I married Bert when I was 17. I never knew any other kind of life. Just cooking, ironing, and washing.

When Bert loses his job as a real estate broker, and Mildred suspects he is having an affair with a wealthy woman, she forces him out of the house. Mildred, determined that her daughters will avoid the domestic drudgery that dominates her life, works hard baking pies to raise money for music and ballet lessons for her children Veda and Kay. Mildred takes a job as a waitress, and after learning the restaurant business, she joins with Bert's former real estate partner Wally Fay to open her own restaurant. This is achieved when playboy Monte Beragon provides the land.

The restaurant is successful, but the price that Mildred has to pay for deviating from social norms is high. While Mildred is making love to Monte Beragon in his beach house, her youngest daughter, Kay, dies of pneumonia. Although both events are geographically separate, the editing establishes a thematic link suggesting that maternal neglect was motivated by illicit sex as Mildred and Bert are still married. Although Mildred works long hours, and eventually establishes a chain of restaurants, she cannot acquire what she wants most—Veda's love and respect. Instead, her daughter openly despises her mother and her work ethic, preferring the company of dilettante Monte Beragon, Mildred's erstwhile lover. When Veda seduces a wealthy young man, Ted Forrester, into marriage and then forces his family into a financial settlement after a false claim of pregnancy, Mildred confronts her daughter in the film's most powerful scene. Here Veda's thinly veiled contempt for Mildred explodes in her display of overt hatred. Mildred tells Veda to leave and pays off Beragon, who has been romancing both women.

Mildred's obsession with Veda, however, is so warped that she humiliates herself by marrying Beragon in an attempt to attract Veda back into her home. The price of the marriage, a third share in Mildred's restaurant chain, eventually leads to her financial ruin when Beragon sells his share and Mildred goes into debt providing for her daughter's materialistic needs. Mildred's final humiliation occurs when she discovers Veda and Beragon making love in the same beach house where she had sexual intercourse on the night that Kay died. When Beragon refuses to marry Veda, she shoots him, and although Mildred attempts to take the blame, the police arrest Veda as she attempts to flee the country.

By the close of the film Mildred has lost her once-thriving business and her family has been destroyed—Veda has been arrested for murder, and Kay is dead. Her only alternative is to return to Bert, the ineffectual husband she left at the beginning of the film. As they leave the police station, director Michael Curtiz provides one of Hollywood's most devastating gender images, showing two women on their knees scrubbing the floor in the right-hand corner of the frame. This sad, prophetic symbol of Mildred's futile attempt to break away from her domestic prison suggests not only her fate, but also points to the power of patriarchal norms, which can turn the normal love for a child into an unhealthy obsession.

Joan Crawford deservedly won an Academy Award for her performance as Mildred Pierce, and the role was the high point of a long career. Born into poverty as Lucille Fay LeSueur in San Antonio, Texas, she was recreated by MGM in the 1920s as Joan Crawford. However, in 1943, it appeared that her days of a star were over when, approaching 40 years of age, MGM did not renew her contract. Crawford signed with Warner Bros., and after a two-year wait for a suitable role, *Mildred Pierce* represented one of the best comebacks in the history of Hollywood. It extended her acting career until 1970 and the low-budget British horror film *Trog*.

Geoff Mayer

**MINE OWN EXECUTIONER** (London Film Productions, 1947). *Director:* Anthony Kimmins. *Producers:* Anthony Kimmins and Jack Kitchin. *Script:* Nigel Balchin, based on his novel. *Cinematography:* Wilkie Cooper. *Music:* Benjamin

Frankel. *Cast:* Burgess Meredith (Felix Milne), Dulcie Gray (Patricia Milne), Kieron Moore (Adam Lucian), Christine Norden (Barbara Edge), Barbara White (Molly Lucian), John Laurie (Dr. James Garsten), Michael Shepley (Peter Edge), Walter Fitzgerald (Dr. Norris Pile), Edgar Norfolk (Sir George Freethorne).

Following the end of World War II, a cycle of films was produced in Hollywood and London that examined the psychological and physical effects of the war on the combatants. *Mine Own Executioner*, produced by Alexander Korda's London Films, was a strong example of this cycle, and despite overt signs of studio (and possibly censorship interference) affecting the character motivation and narrative coherence, the film retained its bitter, downbeat climax. After Adam Lucian tries to murder his wife, Molly, she approaches London psychoanalyst Felix Milne to treat her husband. Milne reluctantly accepts the case and quickly realizes that Adam Lucian is schizophrenic as a result of the torture and mental anguish inflicted on him by the Japanese during the war. While Milne seemingly makes rapid progress with Lucia, the psychoanalyst realizes that his early success with his patient is misleading as Lucian's problems are deep seated and will not respond easily to treatment.

There are a number of fascinating, if underdeveloped, subplots in *Mine Own Executioner.* These include the personal and professional tensions emanating from that fact that Milne is not a qualified doctor and only practices due to the support of eminent Harley Street specialist Dr. James Garsten. Milne's lack of qualifications in turn threatens the funding of his institute. Milne also suffers from his own form of schizophrenic behavior with regard to his marriage. While he loves his long-suffering wife, Patricia, under pressure, he is drawn to the sensual charms and forbidden excitement offered by a family friend, Barbara Edge. Patricia Milne is aware of this relationship and, in an unlikely plot device, accepts Felix's relationship with Barbara Edge, despite her anguish and misgivings.

These narrative strands come together when Milne, feeling poorly because of the flu, fails to follow his intuition when he allows Lucian to postpone treatment until the next day. Milne, realizing that Lucian's mental condition represents an immediate threat to his wife, Molly, is distracted because of his own problems, including the news that the institute will be denied funding because of his lack of formal qualifications. As the pressure on the psychoanalyst intensifies, Milne resumes his affair with Barbara Edge, and just as they are about to have sex, he receives news (from his wife, Patricia, who knows that he is spending the night with Edge) that Lucian has fired four bullets into Molly. Milne tries to redeem himself by climbing a long fire ladder to speak to Lucian, who is poised on the roof of a building. However, this fails, and Lucian shoots himself in the head. Only the support of Dr. Garsten at the subsequent inquest saves Milne's position at the institute.

After the death of Lucian and Milne's humiliation at the inquest, the ending of the film is less than satisfactory. Although Milne has failed to heal Lucian, which resolves the main narrative thread, other issues, notably the funding of the institute and, more important, Milne's relationship with wife, Patricia, and mistress, Barbara, are basically ignored. This, however, did not weaken support for the film, which was both a critical and commercial success.

Geoff Mayer

**MITCHUM, ROBERT** (1917–1997). The night after Robert Mitchum died on July 1, 1997, James Stewart died, and Stewart's death overshadowed the media coverage of Mitchum's death. And Robert Mitchum would not have had it any other way. He, unlike Stewart or Wayne, was perceived as unpredictable, edgy, even dangerous, qualities that made him such a fine noir actor. While his range was extensive, from the passive schoolteacher in David Lean's *Ryan's Daughter* (1970) to the psychotic religious fanatic in Charles Laughton's *The Night of the Hunter* (1955), from the Irish-Australian itinerant worker in Fred Zinnemann's *The Sundowners* (1960) to Raymond Chandler's detective Philip Marlowe in *Farewell, My Lovely* (1975) and *The Big Sleep* (1978), he was most known in the 1940s and early 1950s as the preeminent film noir actor with morally problematic characters.

Throughout his career Mitchum expressed contempt for Hollywood and found little pleasure in acting. Yet he was the consummate professional actor—well prepared and reliable—and he made acting deceptively easy. These qualities, however, resulted in critics underestimating his performances. He was born Robert Charles Durman Mitchum in Bridgeport, Connecticut, and his father was one-quarter Scottish, one-quarter Irish, and half Blackfoot Indian, while his mother was a Norwegian immigrant. His father, a railroad worker, died in an accident at work in 1917. Aged 11, Mitchum ran away from home but was soon caught. In 1928 he was expelled from Felton High School for fouling a girl's shower cap, and although he was eventually reinstated, on the eve of his graduation, after being named Felton High's valedictorian, he left for good after failing to collect his diploma. In the next few years he worked as a deckhand; rode the boxcars; was arrested for vagrancy in Savannah, where he escaped the chain gang; and worked as a dishwasher, truck driver, forest laborer, coal miner, bouncer, and part-time prize fighter while drifting throughout the United States.

In 1937, following pressure from his sister, he joined the Long Beach Player's Guild and began appearing on stage—including the role of gangster Duke Mantee in *The Petrified Forest*—and in 1939 he wrote and directed two children's plays. In 1940 he married Dorothy Spence and took a job at the Lockheed aircraft factory in Burbank while continuing to appear on stage. In 1942, while working as a shoe salesman, he debuted on the screen as a model in the short film *The Magic of Make-Up*. The same year, the producer of the Hopalong Cassidy series, Harry Sherman, hired Mitchum for supporting roles—mainly villains. He also appeared in a number of nonwesterns, such as *Cry Havoc* and *Gung-Ho*, both released in 1943. In 1944 RKO selected Mitchum to replace Tim Holt, who was in the military, to star in their western series based on novels by Zane Grey. Mitchum appeared in two of these films, *Nevada* (1944) and *West of the Pecos* (1945). He also starred in two low-budget films for Monogram, the film noir *When Strangers Marry* (1944), as the murderer, and the topical comedy *Johnny Doesn't Live Here Anymore* (1944).

Mitchum's big break came in 1945 when he was cast as Lieutenant Walker in William Wellman's *The Story of GI Joe*. This prestigious film was based on war correspondent Ernie Pyle's factual account of his experiences with Company C of the 18th U.S. Infantry during their North African campaign. In Italy, Walker is promoted to captain and dies when the unit attacks a mountaintop monastery—a battle that was also featured in John Huston's documentary *Battle of San Pietro* (1944). In the film Mitchum gives a moving performance as a leader who has seen too many of his men die. He was rewarded by an Oscar nomination for best supporting actor, although, characteristically, he did not attend the ceremony. This was his only nomination in a long career. Before the film was released, Mitchum was drafted into the military and served for eight months.

With the release of *The Story of GI Joe*, Mitchum's status in Hollywood was strong, and he was offered major roles in big-budget films, such as *Undercurrent* (1946), as well as lead roles in medium-budget films at RKO such as *Out of the Past* (1947) and *Blood on the Moon* (1948). It was during this period that he developed a screen image of a problematic figure who was physically strong but emotionally and morally vulnerable. In *The Locket* (1947) he commits suicide when he is tormented by a psychotic woman; in *Out of the Past* he jeopardizes his vocation and life when he falls under Jane Greer's spell; in *Pursued* (1947) he is tormented by a childhood trauma that emanates from the repressed memory of his father's adulterous affair with Judith Anderson; in *Where Danger Lives* (1950) he suffers from concussion and the manipulative behavior of Faith Domergue; and in *Angel Face* (1952) he cannot disentangle himself from the psychotic behavior of a young woman determined to kill her stepmother.

This list does not include noir-inflected westerns, such as *Blood on the Moon* and *Track of the Cat* (1954), as well as Nicholas Ray's elegiac rodeo film *The Lusty Men* (1952), where Mitchum plays the veteran rider whose death causes an arrogant man, played by Arthur Kennedy, to reassess his life on the rodeo circuit. When this cycle ended in 1954, Mitchum began appearing in more straightforward action-romantic films in less neurotic roles such as the *River of No Return* (1954) with Marilyn Monroe and *Heaven Knows, Mr. Allison* (1957) with Deborah Kerr.

While Mitchum continued acting until his death in 1997, with a number of roles in television films and miniseries in the 1980s, his career as a film star lasted only until the late 1970s. During the 1960s and 1970s he returned to film noir, beginning with his sadistic Max Cady in *Cape Fear* (1962), the middle-aged small-time criminal in *The Friends of Eddie Coyle* (1973), and the retired private eye in Sidney Pollack's underrated film *The Yakuza* (1975), which is set in Japan and parallels *Chinatown* (1974) in that its detective (Mitchum) inadvertently causes pain to the innocent. Mitchum also gave a world-weary interpretation of Raymond Chandler's detective Philip Marlowe in *Farewell, My Lovely* (1975) and *The Big Sleep* (1978).

**Selected Noir Films:** *When Strangers Marry* (1944), *Undercurrent* (1946), *The Locket* (1946), *Pursued* (1947), *Crossfire* (1947), *Out of the Past* (1947), *Blood on the Moon* (1948), *The Big Steal* (1949), *Where Danger Lives* (1950), *His Kind of Woman* (1951), *The Racket* (1951), *Macao* (1952), *The Lusty Men* (1952), *Angel Face* (1952), *Second Chance* (1953), *Track of the Cat* (1954), *The Night of the Hunter* (1955), *Cape Fear* (1962), *The Friends of Eddie Coyle* (1973), *The Yakuza* (1975), *Farewell, My Lovely* (1975), *The Big Sleep* (1978), *Cape Fear* (1991).

Geoff Mayer

**THE MONEY TRAP** (MGM, 1965). *Director:* Burt Kennedy. *Producers:* Max E. Youngstein and David Karr. *Script:* Walter Bernstein, based on a novel by Lionel White. *Cinematography:* Paul C. Vogel. *Music:* Hal Schaefer. *Cast:* Glenn Ford (Detective Joe Baron), Elke Sommer (Lisa Baron), Rita Hayworth (Rosalie Kelly), Joseph Cotten (Horace van Tilden), Ricardo Montalban (Detective Pete Delanos), James Mitchum (Detective Wolski), Ted de Corsia (Police Captain), Eugene Iglesias (Father), Teri Lynn Sandoval (Daughter), Than Wyenn (Phil Kenny).

Released at a time (1965) when there were very few noir films, *The Money Trap* has been ignored by most studies of film noir. Aside from the fact that its plot was a relatively common one in the late 1940s and 1950s, the film was also notable for being one of the last studio films shot in both CinemaScope and black and white. *The Money Trap*, based on a novel by Lionel White, who also wrote the source novel for Stanley Kubrick's *The Killing* (1956), was directed by Burt Kennedy, a writer more famous for his scripts for Budd Boetticher, who directed Randolph Scott in a series of westerns such as *Seven Men from Now* (1956) and *The Tall T* (1957). Kennedy also directed a number of successful comedy westerns such as *The Rounders* (1964) and *Support Your Local Sheriff* (1968).

*The Money Trap* was a rare excursion for Kennedy into film noir, and the film reworks the familiar noir plot of an essentially good man (Joe Baron) lured into crime by his need to satisfy the materialistic needs of an attractive young woman, in this case, his wife, Lisa. The film's moral basis, which emphasizes the folly of obsessing about material possessions, is conveyed in the final moment, which ends in Joe's opulent house, complete with a spectacular swimming pool, large garden, and spacious interior, which is extravagant for a man whose annual income of $9,200 barely supports the servants. Initially, Joe is financially dependent on his wife's inheritance, and when her dividends fail, he is faced with the prospect of returning to his working-class neighborhood and, possibly, losing his young wife. Instead, he decides to rob the safe of a crooked doctor, Horace van Tilden, who has been trafficking in heroin. However, when his partner in the police force, Pete Delanos, discovers the plan, he insists on joining in.

The film begins with the failed attempt of a drug addict, Phil Kenny, to rob van Tilden. The investigation takes Joe back to his working-class neighborhood and the wife of the dead man, Rosalie Kenny, Joe's childhood sweetheart, who now works in a bar and takes home men to supplement her meager income. Actress

Rita Hayworth, in one of her final roles as Rosalie, is reunited with Glenn Ford, her costar in the memorable 1946 film noir *Gilda*. Twenty years later, both actors are allowed one night of tired passion as a sad reminder of the sparkling energy, and torment, they inflicted on each other in *Gilda*. In *The Money Trap*, they are disillusioned and doomed.

Van Tilden kills Rosalie and traps Joe and Pete when they rob his safe. Pete, obsessed by the prospect of money after years of hard work and little personal or material reward, dies from a gunshot wound, and Joe, also wounded, kills van Tilden before limping home to his wife. While awaiting death, or imprisonment, he tells Lisa that it is "never the money" that corrupts, "it's people and the things they want."

*The Money Trap* is one of the final noir films in a cycle that began in the 1940s to trace the corruption of a basically good man who, through sexual desire, greed, or even boredom, falls from grace. Other films in the cycle include *Night Editor* (1946), *Pitfall* (1948), and *The File on Thelma Jordan* (1949). There is a subplot within *The Money Trap* that reinforces this theme and shows a loving husband who murders his wife when she tries to supplement their income by working as a prostitute. Joe traps the man at an amusement park when he takes his young daughter on a trip for her birthday. Happiness, in this filmic universe, is never lasting.

Geoff Mayer

## MR. PERRIN AND MR. TRAILL (Two Cities, 1948).

*Director:* Lawrence Huntington. *Producer:* Alexander Galperson. *Script:* T. J. Morrison and L.A.G. Strong, based on the novel by Hugh Walpole. *Cinematography:* Erwin Hillier. *Music:* Allan Gray. *Cast:* David Farrar (David Traill), Marius Goring (Vincent Perrin), Greta Gynt (Isobel Lester), Raymond Huntley (Moy-Thompson), Mary Jerrold (Mrs. Perrin), Edward Chapman (Birkland), Finlay Currie (Sir Joshua Varley), Ralph Truman (Comber), Viola Lyel (Mrs. Comber), Don Barclay (Rogers).

Although *Mr. Perrin and Mr. Traill* is largely forgotten today, it exemplifies many of the virtues of the British film industry in the 1940s and early 1950s. The story concerns a new teacher, David Traill, fresh from the army and successes on the rugby field, who fails to pay appropriate respect to the obsessive rituals of Vincent Perrin, a master in an elite private boarding school. The conflict between the two teachers escalates from small issues, such as Perrin's perceived right to the first reading of the daily newspaper and the sole occupancy of the communal bathroom, to larger issues, such as romancing local nurse Isobel Lester. The news of Traill and Lester's engagement results in the total breakdown of Perrin's fragile grasp on reality.

The film refuses to replicate the sentimental stereotypes in films such as *Goodbye, Mr. Chips* (1939), and it also does not present the conflict between Perrin and Traill as one of virtue versus evil. In fact, Traill, the film's so-called normal character, gains most of his sympathy from the craven behavior of the other masters who, faced with a tyrannical headmaster, lack his spirit. On the other hand,

Perrin's virtues, such as his dedication to the students and their education, are overwhelmed by his obsession with the trivialities of daily life—until the climax of the film, when circumstances transform him into a hero who saves Traill's life after he falls down the side of a cliff. After Perrin loses his life while rescuing his nemesis, Traill exposes the real villain, the despotic headmaster Moy-Thompson, by accusing him of systematically breaking the spirit of Perrin and the other masters.

Geoff Mayer

**MURDER, MY SWEET** (RKO, 1944). *Director:* Edward Dmytryk. *Producer:* Adrian Scott. *Script:* John Paxton, from the novel *Farewell, My Lovely* by Raymond Chandler. *Cinematography:* Harry J. Wild. *Music:* Roy Webb. *Cast:* Dick Powell (Philip Marlowe), Claire Trevor (Velma/Mrs. Grayle), Anne Shirley (Ann), Otto Kruger (Amthor), Mike Mazurki (Moose Molloy), Miles Mandor (Mr. Grayle), Don Douglas (Lieutenant Randall), Ralf Harolde (Dr. Sonderborg).

Along with *Double Indemnity, Laura, The Woman in the Window*, and *Phantom Lady, Murder, My Sweet* marks the release, in 1944, of the first substantial group of Hollywood films that helped establish what we now call the classical noir cycle. It was the first film adaptation of one of Raymond Chandler's Philip Marlowe novels, and it built on the start made with *The Maltese Falcon* in setting up the tradition of noir private eye stories. In addition, through Paxton's script and Dmytryk's directorial style, it went far beyond the 1941 film in developing the narrative form, the lighting policy, and the general look that has since come to be associated with film noir. In regard to the contrast between these trailblazing films, in his book *Film Noir*, Andrew Spicer writes that the team of producer Adrian Scott, script writer John Paxton, and director Edward Dmytryk was "determined to make its mark through a radically different approach that would approximate much more closely to the novel's cynical, dispassionate take on American society" (p. 54). *Murder, My Sweet* also successfully transformed crooner Dick Powell into a convincing tough guy who could walk the mean streets of the dark city along with the best of them.

In plot the film employs the standard private eye formula whereby the detective is approached by a bizarre client, is given the quest of finding a missing person, and then becomes personally involved in all the adventures and risks such a task can entail. The giant figure of Moose Molloy appears in Marlowe's Los Angeles office wanting to find long-lost love Velma. But the path of the subsequent investigation is far from straight. Marlowe finds himself with multiple clients, each seeking contradictory outcomes and all prepared to lie to him to further their own ends. In the course of his investigation he is often in personal jeopardy and is beaten, drugged, slugged, and kissed by a variety of devious men and women. Frequently he must use his wits, his smart talk, and his presence of mind to keep ahead of both the bad guys and the abrasively unsupportive police. There are shocks, twists, and turns, seemingly unconnected cases finally blend, and Marlowe's realization that he has been used comes only just in time to allow him to put all the tangled

*Murder My Sweet* (1944). Directed by Edward Dmytryk. Shown from left: Dick Powell (blindfolded as Philip Marlowe), Don Douglas (far right as Lieutenant Randall). RKO/ Photofest.

pieces together and emerge relatively unscathed. From time to time he is forced to reexamine his own code of conduct by which he tries to function, despite the mix of danger and temptation he confronts. The chronological unfolding of the quest is contained (in flashback form) within a frame where a blindfolded Marlowe is being interrogated by police detectives, and thus the audience is kept intrigued by never knowing more than the hero at any stage.

Apart from Marlowe, the film has a rich complement of well-drawn supporting characters, from Moose himself; through the super-rich Mr. Grayle, who is a far-from-virile old man with a sexually voracious and desirable younger wife, the "paltry foppish," sexually ambiguous Marriott; the spunky daughter Ann; the urbane and ruthless blackmailer Anthor; and, naturally, one of the finest of noir's femmes fatales, Velma herself (or Helen, as she calls herself for much of the film), who is first seen with much of her legs dangling bare for Marlowe's delectation. Expressionistic lighting is used right from the credits, and subjective camera work is foregrounded in the scenes where Marlowe receives blows to the head or is pumped full of drugs at a sinister private clinic. Nightmare sequences feature visual and aural distortions, and throughout, Marlowe's voice-over narration consciously conveys the hard-boiled tone of Chandler's original prose style. In the film's climactic scene at an expensive beach house, all the plot complexities are explained in a rush of bewildering dialogue, but of much more impact are the strong visuals as gunfire flashes in the darkened room, temporarily blinding Marlowe. In a gush of violent death, all at once, Moose, Grayle, and Velma are dead. The cynical Marlowe is collaterally maimed, and the one pure soul, Ann, is left to inherit the family fortune and to bestow a final, tender kiss on knight errant Marlowe.

Brian McDonnell

**MY BROTHER'S KEEPER** (Gainsborough, 1948). *Director:* Alfred Roome. *Producers:* Anthony Darnborough and Sidney Box (executive). *Script:* Frank Harvey, based on the story by Maurice Wiltshire. *Cinematography:* Gordon Lang. *Music:* Clifton Parker. *Cast:* Jack Warner (George Martin), Jane Hylton (Nora Lawrence), George Cole (Willie Stannard), David Tomlinson (Ronnie Waring), Yvonne Owen (Meg Waring), Raymond Lovell (Wainwright), Bill Owen (Syd Evans), Beatrice Varley (Mrs. Martin), Garry Marsh (Brewster), Wilfrid Hyde-White (Harding), Brenda Bruce (Winnie Forman), Susan Shaw (Beryl).

Alfred Roome, one of Britain's top editors for more than 40 years, directed only two films: *My Brother's Keeper* and *It's Not Cricket* (1948). Roome, uncomfortable directing actors, was assisted by Roy Rich on both films. Although *My Brother's Keeper* is marred by a distracting subplot concerning a young journalist (Ronnie Waring) on his honeymoon, the film is tough and unsentimental. *My Brother's Keeper* also provided Jack Warner with his most complex and, arguably, best screen performance as the hardened criminal George Martin.

*My Brother's Keeper* is, despite the light-hearted scenes showing the marital and vocational problems of Ronnie Waring, a bleak film. It presents a postwar society devoid of compassion and lacking the communal spirit of the war years. The film is sometimes associated with the racial drama *The Defiant Ones* (1958) because both films share the basic premise of two contrasting convicts handcuffed together on the run. However, *My Brother's Keeper* has little in common with Stanley Kramer's 1958 Hollywood production, and it is a much tougher film, marked by an absence of sentimentality. Only with the offer of Martin's mistress, Nora Lawrence, to testify to the police on behalf of the hapless Willie Stannard, and thereby incriminate herself, does the film display any hint of human generosity. In all other respects the basic institutions of society, including the media and the police, lack compassion, as does George Martin.

The dramatic focus in *My Brother's Keeper* is the complex character of George Martin, a man who can use his literary knowledge and street cunning to charm people, including Willie Stannard, who idolizes Martin; his mistress, Nora Lawrence, who assists the convict; and Martin's wife (Beatrice Varley), who tells Nora at the end of the film that in her 22-year marriage to Martin, she never really knew her husband as he spent 14 years in jail, 5 years in the army, and only 3 years with her (during which time she, presumably, shared Martin with Nora Lawrence). Both Stannard and Lawrence eventually realize that Martin cares for no one except himself. As Martin tells Stannard, "There's no such things as friends. People are either useful or useless. You're useless!"

Most of the film is concerned with Martin's and Stannard's attempts to elude capture. After Martin is able to free himself from Stannard, who is presented as basically an innocent young man, the film focuses on Martin's flight from the police. In this situation, audience sympathy normally gravitates toward the hunted, but director Alfred Roome steadfastly refuses to present Martin as a victim—the closest we come to understanding his lack of compassion for other people comes from his wife's suggestion that the army, and his years in jail, played a part in molding his character. Essentially, the film is content to reinforce her conclusion that "there's something in his mind that's not quite right. He's just a misfit."

Geoff Mayer

**MY NAME IS JULIA ROSS** (Columbia, 1945). *Director:* Joseph H. Lewis. *Producer:* Wallace MacDonald. *Screenplay:* Muriel Roy Bolton, based on the novel *The Woman in Red* by Anthony Gilbert, the pseudonym of Lucy Beatrice Malleson. *Cinematography:* Burnett Guffey. *Music:* Mischa Bakaleinikoff. *Cast:* Nina Foch (Julia Ross), Dame May Whitty (Mrs. Hughes), George Macready (Ralph Hughes), Roland Varno (Dennis Bruce), Anita Bolster (Sparkes), Doris Lloyd (Mrs. Mackie), Leonard Mudie (Peters).

Director Joseph H. Lewis made more than 20 films prior to *My Name Is Julia Ross*. Most critical studies of Lewis, however, begin with this noir/gothic hybrid. The gothic influence on film noir is evident in the 1940s, particularly in the early years of the decade with films such as *Among the Living* (1941), *Experiment Perilous* (1944), and *Gaslight* (both the 1940 British version directed by Thorold Dickinson and the more well-known but inferior MGM version directed by George Cukor, and released in 1944 starring Ingrid Berman and Charles Boyer). *My Name Is Julia Ross*, with only a fraction of the budget lavished on the MGM film, is superior and confirmed the ability of Lewis to inject vitality and a visual sophistication into films that, in the hands of a lesser director, would be utterly conventional and banal.

With a small budget, less than $150,000, and a short shooting schedule of 10 days, this 64-minute film was intended as merely another disposable B film from Columbia Studios. Lewis, however, had other ideas and was able marginally to extend the shooting period and increase the budget after Harry Cohn, the head of production at Columbia, was impressed by footage from the first day of shooting. Also, Lewis insisted that the film receive a preview, which was rare for a B film

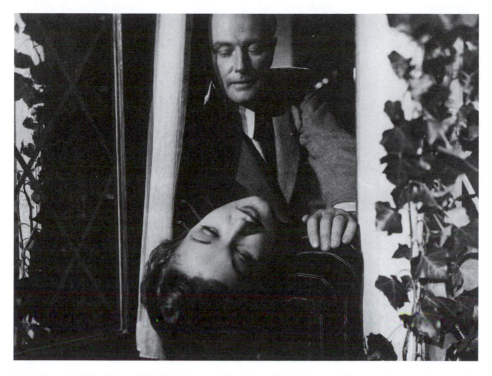

*My Name Is Julia Ross* (1945). Directed by Joseph H. Lewis. Shown: George Macready (as Ralph Hughes), Nina Foch (as Julia Ross). Columbia Pictures/Photofest.

from Columbia. The result was that *My Name Is Julia Ross* was a financial and critical success and gave Lewis the career breakthrough he had been seeking after more than a decade working on low-budget films.

Julia Ross is unemployed in England when she receives an offer to act as secretary to Mrs. Hughes and her son Ralph. Julia is in a vulnerable state due to the fact that the man she loves, Dennis Bruce, has rejected her so that he can marry another woman. After Mrs. Hughes administers a drug, Julia wakes up in bed in a large house situated on a lonely stretch of the Cornwall coast. Being a young woman alone and threatened by sinister forces in a large, isolated house is conventional material to those familiar with gothic stories. When Hughes and Ralph attempt to eliminate Julia's identity by calling her "Marian," the name of Ralph's dead wife, the film's gothic basis is reinforced.

Julia learns that Mrs. Hughes and Ralph plan to kill her as part of the cover-up for Ralph's murder of his wife, and the body of the film is concerned with Julia's attempts to escape the Hughes household. Her inability to convince the locals that she is not Ralph's dead wife generates a powerful sense of frustration in the viewer, leading to an equally powerful sense of catharsis when her attempt to contact Dennis in London succeeds and he arrives just as the psychotic Ralph is about to smash in Julia's head with a rock.

This is almost the perfect low-budget film. Taut, suspenseful, with strong performances from Nina Foch as the resolute heroine; George Macready, who, by 1945, had perfected the mannerisms of the gleefully sadistic, psychologically unstable villain, traits that he fully displayed the following year in *Gilda* (1946); and Dame May Whitty, cast against type as the ruthless mother determined to protect her insane son from a murder charge.

Geoff Mayer

**THE NAKED CITY** (Universal International, 1948). *Director:* Jules Dassin. *Producer:* Mark Hellinger. *Script:* Albert Maltz and Marvin Wald, based on a story by Marvin Wald. *Cinematography:* William Daniels. *Music:* Miklos Rozsa and Frank Skinner. *Cast:* Barry Fitzgerald (Lt. Dan Muldoon), Howard Duff (Frank Niles), Dorothy Hart (Ruth Morrison), Don Taylor (Jimmy Halloran), Ted de Corsia (Garzah), House Jameson (Dr. Stoneman), Anne Sargent (Mrs. Halloran), Mark Hellinger (Narrator).

*The Naked City* is perhaps the best known of a group of films made in the immediate postwar period that are commonly referred to as semidocumentary film noirs or as semidocumentary crime films. Some historians exclude them from the canon of classical film noir for ideological reasons, claiming that their political values are conservative rather than radical, while others are more inclusive and consider them an important subgroup within the overall genre. It is widely accepted that during World War II, there was a softening of the control that the Production Code Administration exerted over the content of Hollywood films, especially of violence. As part of the war effort, newsreel footage of battles, along with somber documentaries showing such enemy atrocities as concentration camps, included images of brutality that would not previously have been allowed on American screens. These nonfiction films, with their authoritative (even strident) voice-over narrations, helped foster a desire in the public for a greater realism in fictional movies. The classical film noir cycle helped satisfy that appetite.

Louis De Rochemont had been a producer on the weekly newsreel series *The March of Time*. At the end of the war he moved to the Twentieth Century Fox

*The Naked City* (1948). Directed by Jules Dassin. Shown: Ted de Corsia (as Garzah). Universal Pictures/Photofest.

studio, and with the encouragement of production head Darryl F. Zanuck, he began to make fictional films that employed techniques taken from documentaries and newsreels. The first of these was a spy film titled *The House on 92nd Street* (1945), directed by Henry Hathaway. This film combined actual FBI surveillance footage with dramatized scenes involving actors shot on actual locations and narrated by the stentorian voice of a newsreel announcer. Later examples, which were also influenced by such Italian neo-realist films as *Rome: Open City* (1945), included *Boomerang!* (1947) and *The Street with No Name* (1948). The popularity and success of these rather cheap films spurred other studios to follow suit. Theatrical journalist and film producer Mark Hellinger, who had worked as a war correspondent, produced *The Naked City* at Universal and also narrated it (he died of a heart attack before its general release). Its visual style was influenced by realist photographer Weegee (Arthur Fellig), who had published *Naked City,* a book of photographs of crime scenes and other stark urban images, in 1945, although his contribution to the film is not credited.

Essentially a police procedural, *The Naked City* traces the investigation into the murder of a young woman in New York, leading up to the identification and pursuit of her killer. Many of the scenes are filmed in the standard dramatic style of

Hollywood filmmaking, but the story is framed by documentary-style shots of the city that place the woman's individual fate in the context of the organic life of the whole metropolis. The narration generalizes about work and crime and psychology, personalizes the city itself as an emotional entity, and even verges on self-congratulation in its description of the way in which the production has used the actual city locations of the story's events. The opening aerial shots of Manhattan give way to a montage of vignettes of ordinary New Yorkers going about their lives. This begins in the predawn hours of a hot summer's night, and among its shots of night workers and revelers, it shows the murder of a young clothing model by two men. Later, one of the men ruthlessly kills his accomplice, who has shown weakness and remorse. A veteran police lieutenant Dan Muldoon (played with an air of wisdom and world weariness by Barry Fitzgerald) leads the investigation. The film emphasizes the unglamorous routines of Muldoon and his team, their doggedness and the way in which progress is made by legwork and thoroughness rather than through spectacular insightfulness or violent action. His associates are mostly young family men, and the film conveys a sense of America reconstituting itself as the baby boom generation settles energetically into postwar domesticity.

The first suspect grilled about the killing is an interesting character and represents at least one way in which *The Naked City* could be said to be authentically a film noir. Frank Niles (Howard Duff) is a close friend of the dead woman and appears at first to be an all-American nice guy from a respectable family and with a sound war record. It soon emerges, though, that he is actually a pathological liar, a con man, an unfaithful Lothario engaged to another woman, and at least indirectly connected with the murder. Always ready with a new story or a plausible excuse, he has a superficial charm and, as Duff plays him, is a complex mixture of strength and weakness. In a film with many stark contrasts between good and bad, he has the morally ambivalent nature of many characters in film noir. It turns out that Niles (in league with the dead woman) had been running an operation involving high-society jewel thefts. As a source of intelligence on desirable gem collections, he had used a socially prominent doctor who unwittingly provided helpful information on the dead woman, who was his mistress. Two thugs in Niles's gang had committed the murder for money, and *The Naked City* culminates in a fairly conventional chase sequence where the surviving killer (Garzah, a harmonica-playing wrestler) is pursued up into the superstructure of the Williamsburg Bridge until he plummets to his death.

These climactic scenes make excellent use of the real bridge and its environs, and their verisimilitude must have been a novelty on the movie's release in 1948. The milling multiethnic crowds filmed in the teeming streets of the Lower East Side have the feel of an Italian neo-realist film by Roberto Rossellini or Vittorio De Sica. The whole enterprise is also greatly aided by the underplaying and whimsicality of Fitzgerald in the main role. Certainly, like other semidocumentaries, *The Naked City* is plainly on the side of authority and shows scant sympathy for the predicaments of its lawbreakers, but it does have a place within a broad definition of film noir. Over the closing credits, Hellinger's narration famously states that "there are eight million stories in the naked city—this has been one of them." The popularity of the film and of this catchphrase led to the production of a long-running (1958–1963) and high-quality television crime-drama series of the same name.

Brian McDonnell

**NEAL, TOM** (1914–1972). Tom Neal is not much more than a bizarre footnote to the history of film noir, although his real life parallels aspects of his most famous film, *Detour* (1945). Neal was born into a middle-class family; his father was a banker in Evanston, Illinois. While the family favored a career in the legal profession for Tom, he, a keen boxer, preferred acting and entered summer stock at West Falmouth.

Neal made his Broadway debut in 1935, and he soon left Broadway for Hollywood, where he was offered a contract by MGM, who saw him as another Gable due to his athletic build and rugged good looks. MGM started Neal in small parts in series films, such as *Out West with the Hardys* (1938) and *Another Thin Man* (1939), as well as in more significant roles in B films such as Jacques Tourneur's *They All Come Out* (1939). However, by 1941, Neal had left MGM and was freelancing. His first lead role was opposite Frances Gifford in *Jungle Girl* (1941), Republic's exciting 15-episode serial directed by William Witney and John English. He also had a prominent role as Dave Williams in *The Courageous Dr. Christian* (1940), the second in RKO's series of six Dr. Christian films starring Jean Hersholt.

Neal alternated between small roles in big-budget studio films, such as Warner Bros.'s war film *Air Force* (1943), and lead roles in low-budget films such as *Two Man Submarine* (1944), where he costarred with Ann Savage, his nemesis in *Detour*. Neal's career received a (brief) boost after starring in RKO's low-budget exploitation film *First Yank into Tokyo* (1945), where he played Major Steve Ross, whose face is transformed by plastic surgery so that he can move freely in Japan during World War II. However, after principal photography was finished, the studio shot extra material so as to change the reason for Ross's motivation to enter Japan. In the original screenplay he seeks an American scientist who has invented a new gun. This was changed to the A-bomb, making *First Yank into Tokyo* the first Hollywood feature film to use the atomic bomb as part of its plot. The film was a financial success as it was released one month after atom bombs were dropped on Hiroshima and Nagasaki.

Neal's first starring role in a film noir was as crime reporter Jim Riley in *Crime, Inc.* (1945), who befriends a crime boss fighting the growing power of a crime syndicate composed of businessmen and criminals. When he refuses to reveal his sources, Riley is arrested and threatened with jail by the leader of the syndicate, who poses as a respectable businessman and controls the jury investigating Riley. *Crime, Inc.* enjoyed a larger budget than most films produced at PRC, and Neal followed it with *Detour*, another film produced at PRC on a miniscule budget. Nevertheless, it gave Neal his most famous role as the hapless Al Roberts who, through a combination of personal weakness and fate, falls under the control of Ann Savage in *Detour*. This ends in her death and his arrest. Unfortunately, the film's virtues were not recognized at the time, and Neal did not progress beyond low-budget films for the next few years. He followed *Detour* with *Blonde Alibi* (1946), another low-budget noir in which he played Rick Lavery, a pilot accused of murdering his ex-girlfriend's rich lover. By 1949 he was no further advanced than he was in 1941 as his most significant role that year was the lead in Columbia's 15-episode serial *Bruce Gentry—Daredevil of the Skies*.

The following year, he was reduced to an appearance in a low-budget Lash La Rue western, *King of the Bullwhip* (1950). However, worse was to come, and his off-screen behavior effectively ended his career. In 1951, Neal, who had a reputation for brawling, was involved in a scandal when his girlfriend, actress Barbara Payton, decided to leave him and marry Franchot Tone. Neal reacted violently and smashed Tone's cheekbone, broke his nose, and inflicted concussion. Fifty-three days after the marriage, Payton decided to return to Neal. She started divorce proceedings against Tone, and Neal was in the headlines again as he was named in the suit. Except for a few appearances in television series, such as the *Adventures of Wild Bill Hickok*, he was finished in the entertainment industry, and Neal left Hollywood and moved to Palm Springs, where he married Patricia Fenton and started a landscaping business. Neal tried a comeback in the late 1950s but was unable to find work, except appearances in the television series *Tales of Wells Fargo* and *Mike Hammer*. Fenton died of cancer a year after giving birth to their son in 1958, and in 1960, Neal married Gale Kloke. However, in 1965, Neal killed her by putting a .45-caliber bullet through the back of her head, and while the prosecution sought the death penalty, the jury returned a verdict of involuntary manslaughter. Neal was sentenced to 10 years in jail, and on December 7, 1971, he was released on parole after serving six years. Tom Neal, aged 58 years of age, died less than nine months later after suffering heart failure.

**Selected Noir Films:** *Sky Murder* (1940), *Under Age* (1941), *The Racket Man* (1944), *Crime, Inc.* (1945), *Detour* (1945), *Blonde Alibi* (1945), *The Hat Box Mystery* (1947), *The Case of the Baby Sitter* (1947), *Fingerprints Don't Lie* (1951), *Danger Zone* (1951).

Geoff Mayer

**NIGHT AND THE CITY** (Twentieth Century Fox, 1950). *Director:* Jules Dassin. *Producer:* Samuel G. Engel. *Script:* Jo Eisinger, based on the novel by Gerald Kersh. *Cinematography:* Max Greene. *Music:* Franz Waxman. *Cast:* Richard Widmark (Harry Fabian), Gene Tierney (Mary Bristol), Googie Withers (Helen Nosseross), Hugh Marlowe (Adam Dunne), Francis L. Sullivan (Phillip Nosseross), Herbert Lom (Kristo), Stanislaus Zbyszko (Gregorious), Mike Mazurki (the Strangler), Edward Chapman (Hoskins), Maureen Delaney (Anna O'Leary), James Hayter (Figler).

*Night and the City* (1950). Directed by Jules Dassin. Shown: Richard Widmark (as Harry Fabian). Twentieth Century Fox Film Corporation/Photofest.

This key noir film was filmed in London in 1949. Darryl F. Zanuck, the head of production at Twentieth Century Fox, sent director Jules Dassin to Britain as he was about to be expelled from the studio following orders from New York because of his left-wing political sympathies. Zanuck told Dassin to start filming Jo Eisinger's script for *Night and the City* as soon as he could, and he also told Dassin to film the most expensive scenes first so that it would be costly for the studio to remove him from the film. Zanuck also asked Dassin if he could develop a role for one of the studio's most important female stars, Gene Tierney, as he wanted to get her away from Hollywood following a failed romance.

Dassin did not have time to read Gerald Kersh's book, published in 1938, and his interest in the project was both formal and ideological. He wanted to present London as an urban nightmare with night-for-night shooting at a time when it was still difficult to generate sufficient light for extended night scenes, especially those filmed in long shot. Dassin, however, received the cooperation of many London businesses, who agreed to leave their lights on at night so as to assist the filming. As a result, *Night and the City* is one of the strongest examples of film noir expressionism, and it presents London as an urban hell—a world of dark shadows, desperate individuals, and derelict buildings. Tourist landmarks such as Trafalgar Square and Piccadilly Circus, along with other parts of the city, were transformed into a consistent vision of urban hell, a perfect encapsulation of a dark, threatening world permeated by betrayal, fall guys, and moral corruption.

Dassin was also attracted to the film's overarching theme based on the destructive effect of money and ambition, and *Night and the City* is one of the toughest, bleakest films ever produced by a major Hollywood studio. The film's opening sequence was developed by Zanuck, who jettisoned the more conventional, and softer, opening scenes in Eisinger's script. Zanuck wanted to emphasize Fabian's vulnerability from the start. The film begins with Harry Fabian, a cheap American-born scam artist, running through the desolate streets of London, and the film ends in the same way, with Fabian running for his life through the same wasteland until he is executed by his nemesis, the Strangler, with his body dumped into the Thames at Hammersmith. In between these events, the film traces the downward spiral of Fabian as he tries to live down failed investments and "be somebody." In the past Fabian's activities have caused suffering to his girlfriend, Mary Bristol. Now he is doomed. He overreaches himself when he tries to compete with men such as Kristo when, striving to lift himself out of the world of small-time crime, he manipulates himself into the position of wrestling promoter when Kristo's father, Gregorius, and his wrestling protégé Nikolas become disenchanted by Kristo's demeaning exploitation of the wrestling business. Fabian exploits this rift by promising Gregorius that he will promote classical Greco-Roman wrestling, but short of funds, Fabian gets caught between Helen Nosseross's desire to leave her husband and start up her own nightclub and Phil's jealousy and sexual frustration. Fabian accepts money from both parties, and this eventually leads to his downfall when, in financial desperation, he tries to provoke Gregorius into fighting the Strangler. Fabian loses control of the situation, and when Gregorius dies after subduing the Strangler, Kristo sets the London underworld onto Fabian with the promise of a bounty for his head.

This sets up the film's magnificent final act as Harry seeks refuge among the denizens of London's underworld only to discover that, except for his surrogate mother, Anna, and Mary, nobody will help him. His unsentimental death lacks any sense of glamour. Fabian, as Dassin constantly reminds us with his mise-en-scène, is doomed from the start. He is a tragic figure who, as one character tells him, is "an artist without art," who overreaches himself. Fabian's grasp of an unstable world is shown to be untenable right from the start, and at the film's conclusion he runs through the nightmarish streets lamenting that he "was so close to being on top." The film concludes with his death as his body is dumped into the Thames.

At times, the doomed protagonists of film noir assume some of the dramatic characteristics of tragedy, particularly when they overstretch themselves. Richard Widmark's Harry Fabian at times assumes this tragic persona. At other times he approximates his giggling psychopath persona from his trademark performance as Tommy Uddo in his debut film *Kiss of Death* (1947). Overall, he is a slacker, a con man sent out to The American Bar to persuade gullible American tourists to follow him back to Nosseross's Silver Fox club, where "hostesses," trained and drilled by Helen Nosseross, can fleece their victims. He dies when he tries to move out of this limited sphere. In his attempt to "be somebody" and raise money to promote a legitimate wrestling match, Fabian takes the audience on a tour of London's underbelly as he visits, first, the Fiddler, who runs a scam involving beggars with fake disabilities (the Fiddler, who eventually betrays Harry near the end of the film, offers to set Harry up with his own operation involving "a few good beggars"), then Googin, who forges birth certificates, passports, and medical licenses, and finally, Anna O'Leary, who deals in stolen nylons and cigarettes. This is a world devoid of so-called normal people.

*Night and the City* was a startling production from a major Hollywood studio due largely to its almost total lack of sentimentality. American director Jules Dassin and actors Richard Widmark, Gene Tierney, and Hugh Malowe joined talented British actors such as Francis L. Sullivan as the love-stricken Phillip Nosseross and Googie Withers as his venal wife, Helen, and German cinematographer Max Greene, who gave Dassin the depth of field and unusual compositions he wanted. Greene and Dassin filmed many scenes just prior to sunrise so as to accentuate the film's sense of fatalism.

When Dassin returned to the United States for postproduction work on *Night and the City*, he was, due to the fact that his left-wing past had become public, prevented from entering the studio and had to convey his ideas with regard to the film's postproduction to editors Nick De Maggio and Sidney Stone and composer Franz Waxman by phone as they were too frightened to meet him in person due to the possibility that any direct association with Dassin might have damaged their careers. The film received mostly negative reviews in the United States and Britain, possibly affected by the political climate, and performed poorly at the box office. Dassin did not direct another film, until the wonderful *Rififi*, for five years. *Night and the City* was remade in 1992 with Robert DeNiro as the doomed protagonist, but the change of setting to New York, and a more sentimental perspective, weakened the film, and it is an inferior version.

Geoff Mayer

**THE NIGHT HAS EYES** (Associated British Picture Corporation, 1942). *Director:* Leslie Arliss. *Producer:* John Argyle. *Script:* Leslie Arliss, based on the novel by Alan Kennington. *Cinematography:* Gunther Krampf. *Music:* Charles Williams. *Cast:* James Mason (Stephen Deremid), Wilfred Lawson (Jim Sturrock), Mary Clare (Mrs. Ranger), Joyce Howard (Marian Ives), Tucker McGuire (Doris), John Fernald (Barry Randall).

The damaging social and or psychological effects of war were utilized as a plot element in a number of films such as *Mine Own Executioner* (1947) and *They Made Me a Fugitive* (1947). *The Night Has Eyes*, in this respect, is a rarity as the film was produced at a time (1942) when most British and American films were focused not on the destructive physical and emotional effects of war, but on the need for communal solidarity to defeat the Axis powers. James Mason's Stephen Deremid in *The Night Has Eyes* is a tormented, broken man following his return from fighting for the Republican side in the Spanish Civil War. With his career as a composer and pianist in tatters, Deremid is bitter and estranged from normal society. He is nursed back to health by his housekeeper, Mrs. Ranger, although he still fears that he has not conquered his murderous impulses.

He lives an isolated existence on the Yorkshire moors, and he is not happy when two schoolteachers on holiday, Marian Ives and her American friend Doris, seek the safety of his house during a storm. Marian, however, has her own emotional problems due to the loss of a close female friend who disappeared in the area 12 months earlier. Marian, sexually repressed and introverted, is immediately attracted to Deremid, especially after he explains to her what a "queer fascination cruelty has." He begins dressing her in his grandmother's clothes, physically carrying her around, and, on occasion, humiliating her with vicious taunts: "What've you got? No beauty. No brains. Just a lot of half-digested ideas about life picked up in a teachers' common room." This does not, however, deter Marian.

This bizarre premise is let down by the film's perfunctory climax. Deremid's aberrant mental condition, aggravated by the regular appearance of dead animals, is shown to be caused by the actions of his greedy housekeeper, Mrs. Ranger, and the handyman, Jim Sturrock, who are determined to keep Deremid dependent on them. They killed Marian's friend when she threatened to upset their scheme by bringing in a medical specialist. Deremid, after saving Marian from Ranger and Sturrock, drives the crooked pair to their deaths on the moors.

*The Night Has Eyes* was released twice in the United States under two different titles. In 1943 PRC released the film as *Terror House.* In 1949, after James Mason had left England and was working successfully in Hollywood, Cosmopolitan Pictures released the film as *Moonlight Madness*.

Geoff Mayer

**NIGHT MOVES** (Warner Bros., 1975). *Director:* Arthur Penn. *Producer:* Robert M. Sherman. *Script:* Alan Sharp. *Cinematography:* Bruce Surtees. *Music:* Michael Small. *Cast:* Gene Hackman (Harry Moseby), Jennifer Warren (Paula), Edward Binns (Joey Ziegler), James Woods (Quentin), Melanie Griffith (Delly Grastner), Susan Clark (Ellen), Janet Ward (Arlene Iverson).

Much has been made of the fact that the neo-noir genre emerged in American film in the early 1970s when a public mood of pessimism was being identified by many social commentators. Much of this mood was ascribed to a kind of psychological hangover from the heady excesses of the 1960s, to ambivalence about the U.S. military failure in Vietnam, and to a feeling of political disenchantment associated with the damaged Nixon presidency after the Watergate scandal. Comparisons have been made to the disillusionment that accompanied the end of World War II and that saw the establishment of the classical film noir cycle. Characteristic neo-noir movies released in the early 1970s, full of references to paranoia and futility, included *The Parallax View* (1974), *Chinatown* (1974), *Three Days of the Condor* (1975), and Arthur Penn's private eye drama *Night Moves*. Penn had tapped into the violent American zeitgeist with *Bonnie and Clyde* in 1967, and he has spoken about the way the tone of *Night Moves* reflected a national malaise. He told *Sight and Sound*'s Tag Gallagher in 1975, when asked about the film's pessimism, "I feel that way about the country . . . I really think we're bankrupt, and that the Watergate experience was just the coup de grâce." At that time the ideological content of many Hollywood genres was also undergoing reexamination, prompted partly by changes in the film industry itself. It is not surprising then, given such social and industrial ferment, that in 1975 Penn should produce a private eye film noir that is as morally murky as *Night Moves*.

Harry Moseby (intelligently played by Gene Hackman with antiheroic traits similar to those he employed in 1974's *The Conversation*), is a Los Angeles private detective feeling alienated from his regular case load and dealing with the shock of his wife, Ellen's, infidelity. In the film's opening sequence he is given the standard sort of commission that noir private eyes have been offered ever since Sam Spade and Philip Marlowe: to find a missing teenage daughter. An aging minor actress named Arlene says that her 16-year-old daughter Delly has run away, and Harry quickly discovers from Delly's friend Quentin that she had been involved in an affair with a movie stuntman on location in New Mexico. Thus the plot of *Night Moves* touches on the edges of Hollywood itself. It appears that Delly may be attempting to punish her mother by having sex with Arlene's ex-lovers, including Delly's own stepfather, Tom Iverson. As Tom lives in the Florida Keys, Harry heads off there, and much of the film's action takes place in and around those subtropical isles. Delly is indeed living there, and the task of restoring her to her mother seems straightforward, but the plot thickens when Harry becomes entangled with Tom's girlfriend Paula and when a body is spotted in a sunken light aircraft during a nighttime boating excursion.

Soon after Delly returns to L.A., and after he has attempted a reconciliation with his wife, Harry is shocked to learn that Delly has been killed in a car crash resulting from a movie set stunt gone wrong. He suspects her mother may be involved since Delly was due to inherit a large sum of money from her dead father when she turned 18. Further information from Quentin that the body in the sunken aircraft was Delly's stuntman lover leads Harry to fly to Florida once again to unravel the mystery of her death. The final quarter of *Night Moves* is crowded with confusion, twists and turns, and abrupt revelations about hidden motivations. It transpires that the stuntmen, in association with Tom, have been smuggling Indo-American artifacts out of the Yucatan into Florida and that Delly has been killed to prevent her exposing the illegal trafficking. Harry fights with Tom and travels out with Paula to the area of the sea where the smuggled objects are hidden. While Paula dives down to the site of the concealed statuary, Harry is attacked in the boat by a seaplane. In a rapid, culminating series of violent acts, Harry is wounded in the thigh by submachine gun fire, Paula is killed by the pontoon of the plane as it touches down on the water, and the aircraft itself crashes and sinks after colliding with a large statue. Harry sees that it is piloted by the stuntman involved in Delly's car crash. The film's final shot shows the boat alone on the empty ocean, circling in a compelling symbol of futility as Harry struggles to reach its controls.

Harry Moseby thus becomes another of those frustrated detectives found in many of the films of the early modernist phase of neo-noir. He is particularly comparable to Jake Gittes in *Chinatown* (1974) in his inability to intervene successfully in the complex events and schemes in which he finds himself embroiled. Harry complains bitterly to Paula near the end that he has actually solved nothing. As well, he had talked earlier in the film of his fondness for chess and used an anecdote about a famous chess maneuver to raise the topic of lost opportunities. His abortive attempts to save Delly, or to catch her killers, seem analogous to those of a stymied chess player. The film's title *Night Moves*, with its pun on the chess piece the knight, hints at this notion of noble intentions going awry and also plays on the metaphor of the detective an knight errant found as far back as the novels of Raymond Chandler. By the mid-1970s, the film seems to claim, such questing figures can only be depicted with irony, and the lasting impression of the investigator in *Night Moves* remains that encapsulated by the image of a tiny craft circling in existential futility.

Brian McDonnell

**NIGHTMARE ALLEY** (Twentieth Century Fox, 1947). *Director:* Edmund Goulding. *Producer:* George Jessel. *Script:* Jules Furthman, from the novel by William Lindsay Gresham. *Cinematography:* Lee Garmes. *Music:* Cyril Mockridge. *Cast:* Tyrone Power (Stanton "Stan" Carlisle), Joan Blondell (Zeena Krumbein), Colleen Gray (Molly), Helen Walker (Dr. Lilith Ritter), Taylor Holmes (Ezra Grindle), Mike Mazurki (Bruno), Ian Keith (Pete Krumbein), Julia Dean (Addie Peabody), James Flavin (Hoatley), Roy Roberts (McGraw), James Burke (Town Marshall).

Tyrone Power was Twentieth Century Fox's main matinee idol in the late 1930s and early 1940s. He was Jesse James in *Jesse James* (1939) and Zorro in *The Mark of Zorro* (1940) as well as the star of *Blood and Sand* (1941), Fox's remake of the Valentino silent film. Prior to leaving Hollywood for military service, he was a swashbuckler in *The Black Swan* (1942), and he returned briefly from active duty for the submarine melodrama *Crash Dive* (1943). After the war, Power wanted a change from adventure films, and in 1946 he starred in Fox's adaptation of Somerset Maugham's *The Razor's Edge*. He also persuaded the studio to purchase the rights to *Nightmare Alley,* William Lindsay Gresham's powerful exposé of carnival life. However, the head of production at the studio, Darryl Zanuck, was reluctant to risk Power in this role of an amoral con man who seduces two women and tries

*Nightmare Alley* (1947). Directed by Edmund Goulding. Shown: Joan Blondell (as Zeena Krumbein), Tyrone Power (as Stanton "Stan" Carlisle). 20th Century Fox/ Photofest.

to fleece a wealthy businessman when he forms an alliance with a ruthless psychiatrist, Dr. Lilith Ritter.

The film begins with Stan working in a mind-reading act in a second-rate carnival. Away from the stage, he amuses himself with an affair with Zeena, a middle-aged married woman and star of the act. When Stan learns that Zeena and her alcoholic husband Pete were once headliners in major nightclubs with a mind-reading act, he initiates a scheme to acquire the code from Zeena. When Pete dies after drinking wood alcohol given to him by Stan, Zeena teaches him the code. However, when Stan seduces another carnival woman, Molly, her partner forces him to marry the young woman.

Stan, now Stanton, takes his act to Chicago and, with the assistance of Molly, is a great success in a major nightclub. During one of his performances he meets Dr. Ritter, an unscrupulous psychiatrist, and they devise a plan to swindle a wealthy businessman, Ezra Grindle, by using information given to Ritter in her professional relationship with Grindle. However, their plan disintegrates when Molly, dressed as Grindle's long-lost lover, fails to complete her part of the scam. Stan is forced to flee from the police and sends Molly back to the carnival. Hiding out, and in disgrace, he begins drinking heavily. Finally, in need of alcohol and desperate for money, he accepts a position only available in small, disreputable carnivals—the geek who, in exchange for a bottle of bourbon, bites off the heads of live chickens.

This morality tale is Power's best role. His striking features and easy charm seduces both Zeena into giving him the code and also Molly into running away with him. For most of the film he is the homme fatal, the duplicitous and destructive counterpart of noir's femme fatale. In the latter part of the film, however, he occupies the more traditional role of the noir protagonist who falls victim to his overwhelming ambition.

The film is faithful, except for the last scene between Stan and Molly, to the tone of Gresham's novel. Gresham was fascinated by the dark underbelly of the entertainment industry in general, and carnival life in particular, and he uses his story to question the basis of religious faith and the gullibility of its adherents. Nevertheless, the film places Gresham's story within a moral context, and Stan's scam collapses when Molly, the only virtuous character, realizes that there is a difference between the entertainment of low-level carnival tricks and the fraud that Stan and Ritter try to perpetuate on Grindle.

Two of the film's recurring motifs—alcohol and the geek—open and close the film and, in the process, document Stan's fall from grace. At the beginning he watches the geek run wildly in a drunken frenzy and wonders how a man can be reduced to such a pathetic state. By the end of the film he is the geek, running in a crazed fashion from carnival workers who are trying to calm him down. The geek, the film's metaphor for human weakness, is universal, and when Stan's ambition exceeds accepted moral codes, his "inner geek" appears.

*Nightmare Alley* emerged from filmmakers not generally associated with film noir. Director Edmund Goulding was responsible for a series of literate, so-called quality films such as *Grand Hotel* (1932), *Dark Victory* (1939), and *The Razor's Edge* (1946). Much of the film's credit can be attributed to cinematographer Lee Garmes's imagery—most notably when Stan confronts Ritter in her office just before they form a partnership to deceive Grindle. Garmes's lighting fractures the frame, creating a distorted world, which is reinforced by Ritter's masculine attire, consisting of a black business suit. Although Stan believes he is in control of the situation, the lighting and costume indicate otherwise. Finally, screenwriter Jules Furthman wrote many of Josef von Sternberg's 1930s films starring Marlene Dietrich such as *Morocco* (1930) and *Shanghai Express* (1932).

Geoff Mayer

**99 RIVER STREET** (United Artists, 1953). *Director:* Phil Karlson. *Producer:* Edward Small. *Script:* Robert Smith, based on a story by George Zuckerman. *Cinematography:* Franz Planer. *Music:* Emil Newman and Arthur Lange. *Cast:* John Payne (Ernie Driscoll), Evelyn Keyes (Linda James), Brad Dexter (Victor Rawlins), Frank Faylen (Stan Hogan), Peggie Castle (Pauline Driscoll), Jay Adler (Christopher), Jack Lambert (Mickey), Eddy Waller (Pop Dudkee), Glen Langan (Lloyd Morgan),

John Day (Bud), Ian Wolfe (Walde Daggett), Peter Leeds (Nat Finley), William Tannen (Director), Gene Reynolds (Chuck).

Director Phil Karlson was one of the best, if not *the* best, director of low- to medium-budget black-and-white film noirs in the early 1950s. He could take what would be conventional stories in the hands of a less talented director and imbue his films with a pervasive sense that the world was an endlessly violent, arbitrary place, and 99 *River Street* is a strong example of his style and worldview. He even presents a story within a story when actress Linda James convinces taxi driver Ernie Driscoll that she has killed a man who tried to molest her. This melodrama within a melodrama not only does not jeopardize the film's main story line, but also serves to complement the film's main premise, which involves murder and betrayal.

A similar deception occurs at the start of the film. It begins with a boxing match between the champ and Ernie Driscoll. Driscoll, who comes within one second of winning the title, eventually loses the fight when a punch opens up his eye. However, after he is defeated, the camera pulls back to reveal Driscoll watching this match on a television set—the fight was three years ago, and now Driscoll is a taxi driver in an unhappy marriage to his wife, Pauline. This deception, however, performs a number of functions in the film: it conveys Pauline's disappointment that Ernie, as a taxi driver and no longer a prizefighter, cannot meet her material aspirations. Second, Driscoll's disappointment at losing the fight functions to spur him on during the film's climax when all appears lost—when Pauline's lover, gangster Victor Rawlins, shoots Driscoll, he draws on the fight to summon sufficient strength to eventually overpower Rawlins.

Near the start of the film, Ernie, in an attempt to rekindle his relationship with Pauline, arrives at her workplace with a box of candy. However, he sees his wife kissing a man (Victor Rawlins) and, in a scene handled effectively by Karlson, arrives with a satisfied smile on his face, and as he moves out of his cab into a close-up, he records Driscoll's reaction to his wife's betrayal. Angry, he allows actress Linda James to take him back to the theater, where she claims that she has killed a casting director. This also proves to be a lie designed to show off James's acting skill for the director of a new play. Doubly humiliated, Driscoll storms off after starting a fight.

Rawlins kills Pauline and frames Driscoll for the murder, and the second half of the film sees Driscoll on the run trying to clear himself. This is pure melodrama with pulp dialogue, pulp characters, and a noir sensibility. Driscoll has only one choice—to fight for his survival—and he has two allies: Linda James, who is remorseful after her attempt to exploit his kindness, and the dispatcher at Driscoll's taxi company, Stan Hogan, who diverts the police away from Driscoll. Driscoll, with their assistance, exposes Rawlins as the killer and finds love with a good woman, Linda James.

When 99 *River Street* was released in 1953, it provoked discussion because of its realistic violence. Aside from the boxing match that opens the film, there are two prolonged fight scenes—between Driscoll and a killer, Mickey, in a small apartment, and the climactic fight between Driscoll and Rawlins. Both are, for the early 1950s, savage. Karlson even wanted to film these sequences in slow motion to maximize the violent effect—similar to the way that, 16 years later, Sam Peckinpah used this device to capture the bloodletting in *The Wild Bunch* (1969). However, producer Edward Small would not allow Karlson to use slow motion and told the director that it was only suitable for comedy shorts, not a feature-length drama. Nevertheless, Karlson, with enthusiastic support of lead actor John Payne and veteran cinematographer Franz Planer, transformed Robert Smith's familiar story into a powerful film noir that bypassed the conventional basis of the story line to emphasize the pain of marginalized people such as Ernie Driscoll and Linda James—people who aspire to reach the top but, through circumstances beyond their control, realize that they will never make it and that they have to adjust to this realization.

Geoff Mayer

**NO ORCHIDS FOR MISS BLANDISH** (Renown Pictures, 1948). *Director:* St. John Leigh Clowes. *Producers:* Oswald Mitchell and A. R. Shipman. *Script:* St. John Leigh Clowes. *Cinematography:* Gerald Gibbs. *Music:* George Melachrino. *Cast:* Jack La Rue (Slim Grisson), Linden Travers (Miss Blandish), Hugh Mc-Dermott (Fenner), Walter Crisham (Eddie), Danny Green (Flyn), Lila Molnar (Ma Grisson), Richard Nelson (Riley), Frances Marsden (Anna Borg), Percy Marmont (Mr. Blandish), Leslie Bradley (Bailey), Zoe Gail (Margo), Charles Goldner (Louis).

The hostile critical reception that *No Orchids for Miss Blandish* received in 1948 was only surpassed by the hysterical critical reaction to Michael Powell's *Peeping Tom* 12 years later. The film was little more than a low-budget gangster film that tried to replicate many of the conventions of its Hollywood counterparts. The weaknesses of the film are obvious—the phony American dialogue and accents; the small budget that renders much of the film static by limiting the number of interior sets; the mediocre night club acts and variability of the performances, as some British actors, such as the South African-born Sid James, struggle to duplicate the speech patterns of Hollywood gangsters. Perennial American B actor Jack La Rue, as the love-smitten gangster Slim Grisson, having spent the bulk of his career in such films, flourishes in the role, as does Linden Travers, who reprises her 1942 stage role as the wealthy Miss Blandish, who prefers the masculine pleasures of gangster Slim Grisson to the dull respectability and sexless existence of the Blandish family.

The casual way the film utilizes violence, especially early in the film, when Richard Nelson's "Riley" tries to maim most members of the cast, caused problems for the film. However, it is a gangster film, and most of the violence is contained within its generic context. It is mainly implicit and conveyed by the reaction of the other actors. What may have really upset the British critics was the film's attempts to replicate what was perceived as a lowbrow strand of American popular culture: the hard-boiled novel, which author James Hadley Chase tried to emulate.

Chase—in actuality, Rene Raymond, a librarian and wholesale bookseller—wrote a more lurid story than the film, focusing on the sexual harassment of a heiress who is kidnapped and repeatedly raped by gang members. Eventually, she falls prey to the attentions of Slim Grisson, a sexually disturbed member of the Grisson gang, which is headed by his mother, Ma Grisson. The novel concludes with Blandish's death. She kills herself because she feels degraded by the experience. The 1948 film changes the motivation for Blandish's suicide, a factor that may have inflamed the critics of the film even more. She chooses death in the film because she is separated from her lover. She would rather die than return to her family. Significantly, Miss Blandish, after the initial violation of other gang members, is shown enjoying and soliciting Slim Grisson's attentions, even after he offers her the opportunity to escape.

Geoff Mayer

# O

**O'BRIEN, EDMOND** (1915–1985). O'Brien was a rather ordinary-looking character actor who had a surprising number of leading roles through both the 1940s and 1950s. He was energetic and credible in a wide variety of roles and used his strong, expressive voice well. O'Brien played the lead in a number of the most interesting and significant films of the classical noir cycle. Solidly built, he was not handsome, with his heavy facial features lending themselves to scowling rather than a winning smile. Hence O'Brien had few romantic roles, but specialized in playing intelligent versions of men who show moral ambiguity. Born in New York, he briefly attended Fordham University, then went on to study acting in New York and played a number of roles on Broadway. O'Brien was a member of Orson Welles's Mercury Theater group on radio and stage, then moved out to Hollywood after gaining a contract at RKO. *The Killers*, directed by Robert Siodmak, was his first noir in 1946. In this film O'Brien played the crucial linking narrative role of the insurance investigator who tries to piece together the reasons for the death of the Swede (Burt Lancaster), a man gunned down by hired assassins. O'Brien had a major role in the James Cagney classic *White Heat* (1949) for Warner Bros., where he played an undercover man infiltrating Cagney's gang. From that point on O'Brien freelanced at a number of different studios. He was eminently employable because his screen persona was that of a likeable, Everyman figure. This is clearly evident in the very important noir *D.O.A.* (1950), a film whose relentless narrative momentum he effectively drives by himself. O'Brien plays Frank Bigelow, a man poisoned with a drug that will inevitably kill him but who fights to solve his own murder, despite the pressures of a literal deadline. He was also highly effective as the morally equivocal protagonist of the undervalued film noir *711 Ocean Drive* (1950), in which he evinces a complex set of values interacting with financial and sexual temptations. One of his most intriguing projects was in *The Bigamist* (1953), a marginal noir directed by Ida Lupino, who also directed O'Brien in *The Hitch-Hiker* the same year. *The Bigamist* is a very unusual and interesting film for its time. As its title indicates, it concerns a man (O'Brien) who is bound up in the continuing crime of bigamy, but the film treats his situation with sympathy and a subtle approach seemingly at odds with the Production Code. Around this time, O'Brien played a number of tough-cop roles, as in *Shield for Murder* (1954), where he is an example of the corrupt policeman figure often seen in the 1950s (e.g., *Rogue Cop, Pushover,* and *Private Hell 36,* all from 1954). The minor film noirs *Man in the Dark* and *The 3rd Voice* also show him at his best. O'Brien won the best supporting actor Oscar for *The Barefoot Contessa* in 1954, and despite never becoming a first-rank star, he made memorable character acting appearances through the 1960s in films such as *The Wild Bunch* (1969).

**Selected Noir Films:** *The Killers* (1946), *The Web* (1947), *Brute Force* (1947, uncredited), *A Double Life* (1947), *An Act of Murder* (1948), *White Heat* (1949), *Backfire* (1950), *D.O.A.* (1950), *711 Ocean Drive* (1950), *Between Midnight and Dawn* (1950), *Two of a Kind* (1951), *The Turning Point* (1952), *Man in the Dark* (1953), *The Hitch-Hiker* (1953), *The Bigamist* (1953), *Shield for Murder* (1954, and codirector), *A Cry in the Night* (1956), *The 3rd Voice* (1960).

Brian McDonnell

**OBSESSION** (An Independent Sovereign Film, 1949). *Director:* Edward Dmytryk. *Producer:* N. A. Bronsten. *Script:* Alec Coppel, based on his novel *A Man About a Dog. Cinematography:* C. M. Pennington-Richards. *Music:* Nino Rota. *Cast:* Robert Newton (Dr. Clive Riordan), Sally Gray (Storm Riordan), Phil Brown (Bill Kronin), Naunton Wayne (Superintendent Finsbury), James Harcourt (Aitken), Ronald Adam (Clubman), Michael Balfour (American Sailor).

In the late 1940s Edward Dmytryk left Hollywood for London due to pressure from anti-Communist forces within the United States. He was a director familiar with the conventions of film noir, although the term had not yet been used in Hollywood. *Obsession* offered Dmytryk an opportunity to rework this type of film in Britain. The outcome is a fascinating mixture of styles and narrative modes as American film noir mutates into a different mode due to a different cultural context. Yet, despite the film's civilized tone, which emphasizes the superficial display of civility and manners between the three central characters (and a characteristically perceptive, if eccentric, English police detective), *Obsession* preserves one of the most common themes within film noir: the destructive power of sexual repression. Similarly, the characters belong to the hard-boiled world of film noir—the bitter husband (Riordan) who wants to preserve his marriage by killing his latest rival (Kronin), despite the fact that his adulterous wife (Storm) despises him.

The basic dramatic situation in *Obsession* is a familiar one—Harley Street specialist Dr. Clive Riordan resents the succession of lovers attracted to his wife, Storm. Thus Riordan kidnaps Storm's latest lover, American Bill Kronin, and chains him to the wall in a bombed-out, abandoned building. Riordan's plan is to keep Kronin alive so that if things go wrong, he can produce him to the police. In the meantime, Riordan brings Kronin food, drinks (martinis), and the newspaper as he prepares to kill the American in an acid bath—in a characteristic English touch, each time Riordan visits Kronin with supplies, he also carries acid in a hot water bottle.

It is worth noting that the nationality of Storm's lover (American) is not an accident as early scenes involving Riordan at his private club show the elderly men discussing world politics, where they bitterly resent the decline of the British empire and the dependency of Britain on American aid. This aspect is not fully developed as audience sympathy, almost by default, drifts toward the hapless American chained to the wall (symbolic revenge on the part of the British?) as Riordan's superior, calculating manner destroys any semblance of audience support for his marital situation. Similarly, Storm is depicted as shallow and totally self-absorbed. At the end of the film, when Storm visits Kronin in a hospital, she tells him that she plans to recover from her ordeal with a South American holiday. Kronin, who is fortuitously saved by the actions of the Riordan family dog and an alert policeman, indicates to Storm that he prefers the family dog to her company—a satisfying end to a superior film noir.

Geoff Mayer

**THE OCTOBER MAN** (Two Cities, 1947). *Director:* Roy Baker. *Producer:* Eric Ambler. *Script:* Eric Ambler. *Cinematography:* Erwin Hillier. *Music:* William Alwyn. *Cast:* John Mills (Jim Ackland), Joan Greenwood (Jenny Carden), Edward Chapman (Peachey), Kay Walsh (Molly Newman), Joyce Carey (Mrs. Vinton), Catherine Lacey (Miss Selby), Patrick Holt (Harry Carden), Jack Melford (Wilcox), Felix Aylmer (Dr. Martin), Frederick Piper (Detective Inspector Godby), James Hayter (Garage Man), Juliet Mills (Child).

Jim Ackland, an industrial chemist, suffers both physically and mentally following a bus crash that kills a young child in his care. After a year in the hospital, Ackland leaves his home in Sheffield for a new start in London. He moves into a second-rate establishment, the Brockhurst Common Hotel, on the edge of Clapham Common. Although Ackland still suffers from periodic bouts of depression and thoughts of suicide, his life gradually turns around, particularly after falling in love with Joan, the sister of a fellow worker (Harry Carden). However, when a resident of his boarding house, Molly Newman, is strangled on the common, the police, and a vindictive boarder (Mrs. Vinton), quickly assume that Ackland killed Newman.

The identity of the killer is unclear until late in the film, when another boarder, Peachey, reveals that he killed Newman after she rejected him. Prior to this confession, Ackland suffers regular bouts of self-doubt as no one, except Joan Carden, will believe he did not murder the woman. However, *The October Man* is more than just a crime thriller. It is a story of psychological trauma and regeneration as Ackland fights to control his impulse to commit suicide by jumping from a railway bridge as a train passes below. He visits the bridge three times in the film, and each time, he is tempted to jump. Director Roy Baker utilizes the motif of Ackland's habit of twisting his handkerchief into the symbol of a rabbit as an indication of his torment, and it is used to signify his victory over this impulse in his final visit to the bridge.

*The October Man* was Baker's first film as director. It was a somewhat troubled project, and producer/writer Ambler lost faith in Baker due to the slow pace of production (the film was scheduled for 12 weeks and took 17). Nevertheless, it is a remarkably assured debut film. Baker uses composition, lighting, and sound to advance the story, and he generates a degree of romantic warmth through editing and composition to show the immediate attraction between Ackland and Joan Carden at a dinner dance. While Joan Carden, the only person who supports Jim throughout the film, is a relatively conventional character, Joan Greenwood imbues the role with her customary sensuality and screen presence.

*The October Man* represented a significant shift in the British crime film/melodrama as noir attributes found their way into the genre. For example, a plaque on the wall in Ackland's barren room reads "From ghoulies, ghosties and short-legged beasts that go bump in the night, Good Lord deliver us." Unfortunately, *The October Man,* like other postwar British films, reveals a universe where such hopes for personal security are shown to be simplistic and obsolete.

Geoff Mayer

**ODDS AGAINST TOMORROW** (United Artists, 1959). *Director/Producer:* Robert Wise. *Script:* Abraham Polonsky (as John O. Killens) and Nelson Giddin, from the novel by William P. McGivern. *Cinematography:* Joseph Brun. *Music:* John Lewis. *Cast:* Harry Belafonte (Johnny Ingram), Robert Ryan (Earl Slater), Shelley Winters (Lorry), Ed Begley (Burke), Gloria Grahame (Helen), Will Kuluva (Bacco).

Released in 1959, *Odds Against Tomorrow* is a very late and very accomplished example of the noir genre. Indeed, it is often thought of as the last film of the classical cycle, supplanting in the view of many historians Orson Welles's 1958 *Touch of Evil* in that role. Looking back from the perspective of the early twenty-first century, *Odds Against Tomorrow* is clearly marked by precise historical placing in the transition from the 1950s to the 1960s. The presence of old hands Robert Ryan, Shelley Winters, Gloria Grahame, and Ed Begley links it to earlier films. However, characters also talk of Cape Canaveral and Sputnik. The credit sequence is abstract and, like much of the film, is accompanied by a very 1960s jazz score featuring a vibraphone. There is also considerable evidence of the impact of the Production

Code having weakened from earlier years. Bullets, for instance, are seen to actually hit people and leave bloody wounds. Sex is treated more openly than in previous noirs and is even linked to violence, as in Helen's erotic interest in Earl's killing. Gloria Grahame's torso is seen clad only in a bra, and a minor hood named Coco is flamboyantly homosexual. The film's interest in racial questions too looks forward to the flowering of the civil rights movement in the 1960s. Unsurprisingly, since it was made by HarBel (Harry Belafonte's own independent production company), there is a sense of a complex negro culture rather than just the inclusion of the odd black maid or Pullman attendant. James Naramore, in his book *More Than Night: Film Noir in Its Contexts* (p. 241), claims that script writer Killens was black, but recent evidence indicates that this name was a pseudonym for the blacklisted Abraham Polonsky.

*Odds Against Tomorrow* is an unsentimental and fatalistic example of the heist (or caper) subgenre of film noir, and this makes it similar to famous earlier versions of that type such as *The Asphalt Jungle* and *The Killing*. All three main characters have a beef against the system. Their lives have varying degrees of isolation: the most extreme is Burke, who lives alone with his dog in a room full of photos from the irretrievable past. He is old, corrupt, and embittered. Each man has goals; they are looking for just "one roll of the dice." Ryan plays Earl, an aging man (Ryan was 50 when the film was made) pressured by time passing him by: "They're not gonna junk me like an old car." He is an Okie (similar to Ryan's early noir character in *Crossfire*), an example of damaged masculinity, as seen in an incident where he strikes a young soldier in a bar or in his picking up of dry-cleaning or his babysitting. Earl's wife earns more than him. He has a criminal record of manslaughter and is a racist: "You didn't tell me the third man was gonna be a nigger." Earl is correct to have misgivings about how he will go with the "colored boy." Johnny is an affluent stylish negro with a sports car and snappy clothes. Johnny is a gambler with debts as well as alimony payments. A musician, he views himself as a "bone player in a four-man cemetery." His wife mixes with whites, whom he calls "ofey." Burke likes Johnny and kills himself at the end to try to save him. The film is virtually allegorical in its thematic intentions, with its three main characters being representative of both clear social placement and common noir situations. The irrelevance of ethnicity is highlighted when at the film's end the burned bodies of Earl and Johnny (incinerated in an explosion of huge gas tanks) are indistinguishable, with an ambulance officer unsure which is which. The social compact of World War II is plainly now over, despite references to it and to wartime commonality across the race divide. The film's view of criminal morality is summed up by the gangster Bacco: "I'm a little bit on the inside, a little bit on the outside" of the law.

The film has a typical heist film narrative structure, being a film of two halves: 60 minutes of the story is set in New York, where the raid is planned, 30 minutes on the robbery itself in the upstate town of Melton. As the team is assembled, their initial reluctance is overcome by the various pressures on their lives. Things go wrong (of course) during the heist, chiefly through the thieves falling out with each other, as has happened in almost every crime story since Chaucer's "The Pardoner's Tale". Director Robert Wise creates a consistent and intriguingly developed visual style through his coldly alienating urban and rural landscapes. There is a motif of murky water featuring images of ominous flotsam and jetsam such as broken dolls, and even Central Park looks inhospitable. The sound track adds to the perilous atmosphere with a shock balloon burst in a phone booth or raucous zoo noises. The location shooting includes some very early use of a zoom lens and of an infrared filter to emphasize the wintry sky. On an overnight reconnoiter of the bank, a hotel window view is used for quick exposition, as in Kurosawa's *Yojimbo*. Symbolism dominates the allegorical epilogue filmed in a wasteland of gas tanks reminiscent of *Touch of Evil*. A post closely resembles a cross, and the words *dead end* on a road sign are portentous. There is almost a pre-echo of James Baldwin's 1963 book *The Fire Next Time* in the cataclysm at the end. Thus, while *Odds Against Tomorrow* neatly closes off the classical noir cycle, it helps usher in the mood of the 1960s both in terms of Hollywood and of American culture in general.

Brian McDonnell

**ON DANGEROUS GROUND** (RKO, 1952). *Director:* Nicholas Ray. *Producer:* John Houseman. *Script:* A. I. Bezzerides, adapted by A. I. Bezzerides and Nicholas Ray from the novel *Mad with Much Heart* by Gerald Butler. *Cinematography:* George E. Diskant. *Music:* Bernard Herrmann. *Cast:* Ida Lupino (Mary Walden), Robert Ryan (Jim Wilson), Ward Bond (Walter Brent), Charles Kemper (Bill Daly), Anthony Ross (Pete Santos), Ed Begley (Captain Brawley), Ian Wolfe (Sheriff Carrey), Summer Williams (Danny Malden), Gus Schilling (Lucky), Frank Ferguson (Willows), Cleo Moore (Myrna Bowers), Olive Carey (Mrs. Brent).

*On Dangerous Ground* is a film of two halves, although both are thematically related. The first section of the film focuses on an urban feel and the way it affects one man, New York policeman Jim Wilson. The second half shows Wilson's regeneration when he leaves New York for a case in a rural area upstate. The transformation from the grimy, hothouse streets and apartments to the snow-covered landscape mirrors Wilson's change, and this provides the setting for his redemption. Director Nicholas Ray uses the landscape as not only a physical but also an emotional setting to show how the healing power of nature overcomes the psychic pain that the large city invokes in Wilson's tormented cop.

Although Ray was unhappy with the film, it represents one of his best. The film's first image, a close-up of a black gun on the white linen of a bed, is an effective visual motif that dominates the film and reveals the transformation in the character whereby the purity of the snow eventually subjugates the arbitrary violence of the gun. Three policemen, Jim Wilson, Pete Santos, and "Pop" Day, investigating the killing of a cop, receive information from a prostitute, Myrna Bowers, regarding the whereabouts of her former boyfriend, Bernie Tucker. Tucker, the police

*On Dangerous Ground* (1952). Directed by Nicholas Ray. Shown from left: Robert Ryan (as Jim Wilson), Cleo Moore (as Myrna Bowers), Anthony Ross (as Pete Santos). RKO Radio Pictures/Photofest.

believe, will be able to help them solve the murder. Wilson sends Santos away and "interrogates" Myrna alone, and the film's depiction of sadomasochism is startling for a studio film in the early 1950s. Wilson's eagerness to exploit Myrna's masochistic tendencies with his own sadism and anger, which, the film suggests, emanate from his disgust with the promiscuous behavior of young women, is very raw.

Earlier, when a girl flirts with him in a bar, he has her removed, and when the topics of marriage or family are raised by his colleagues, he ignores or rejects their comments. So when Myrna reveals that she likes it rough, Wilson accommodates her on the pretext that he is gathering vital information. After showing him the bruises on her arm inflicted by Bernie Tucker, Myrna tells Wilson that "he [Tucker] was real cute" and that Wilson "is cute, too." She then invites more of the same by telling him, "You'll make me talk, you'll squeeze it out of me with those big strong arms . . . won't you?" Wilson, who is standing next to Myrna, replies in a soft voice, "That's right, sister." Wilson the policeman is, at this point in the film, no different from Tucker the hoodlum—both enjoy inflicting pain on Myrna.

As a result of information supplied by Myrna, Wilson corners Bernie in a dingy apartment. With the policeman towering over the gangster, who is lying on a bed, Wilson attacks, after which the hood taunts him with "go on, hit me, hit me." As

Wilson smashes into Tucker's body, the cop cries out, "Why do you make me do it? You know you're gonna talk. I'm gonna make you talk. I always make you talk. Why do you do it? Why? Why?"

Wilson lives alone in a sparsely decorated apartment, and after 11 years in the force, his existence is defined by his obsession to apprehend, and hurt, the criminals. After chasing the "garbage" down an alley and responding with characteristic violence, Pop Daly tells Wilson that he should know "the kind of job it is" and come to terms with it. Wilson, however, asks Daly how he manages to divorce himself from this life when he goes home ("How do you live with yourself?"). Daly tells Wilson that, unlike him, he "lives with other people" and that when he goes home, he does not take "this stuff" with him.

The urban landscape, composed of expressionist lighting, rapid editing, and a prowling camera captures Wilson's torment, and only when he reluctantly goes upstate does he achieve some kind of equilibrium in his life. While the rural destination, Westham, shelters its own perverse killer, Wilson, when he confronts the killer, a young boy, is able to show compassion. This occurs due to his regeneration through a relationship with a blind woman, Mary Walden.

During the last section of the film, the noir elements recede in favor of classical melodrama, as purity and virtue (mainly through the effect Mary has on Wilson) combine to regenerate the tormented cop so that, by the end of the film, he is rational and humane. The price for Mary, however, is the death of Danny, her shy, retarded brother who has killed a young girl. When the boy invites Wilson to hit him, the policeman responds by offering to protect him from the father of the dead girl, Walter Brent. However, after the boy falls to his death, Mary asks Wilson to return to the city. During the trip back Wilson recalls Mary's warning about loneliness as well as Pop Daly's advice about the violence within him. Wilson turns the car around and goes back to Mary. This was not the ending Ray favored. He wanted Wilson to return to the streets of New York, with the suggestion that he may even return to his old ways. This would have been a true noir ending. However, the studio and the two stars favored a more optimistic ending showing Wilson's redemption through his love for Mary.

While this decision ruptures the noir basis of the film, it is a logical ending as it completes Wilson's spiritual regeneration. The film is especially noteworthy for Robert Ryan's performance as the tormented policeman. Following powerful performances in *Crossfire* (1947) and *The Set-Up* (1949), *On Dangerous Ground* confirmed Ryan as one of Hollywood's best, and most underrated, actors, especially in his ability to convey a sense of inner torment and repressed violence. This quality is also reinforced by Bernard Herrmann's superb score, which captures the seething violence of the urban sequences, the pulsating excitement of the chase across the snow, and the lyrical, tender moments between the blind woman and the big-city policeman.

Geoff Mayer

**OUT OF THE PAST** (RKO, 1947). *Director:* Jacques Tourneur. *Producer:* Warren Duff. *Script:* Geoffrey Homes, from his novel *Build My Gallows High*. *Cinematography:* Nicholas Musuraca. *Music:* Roy Webb. *Cast:* Robert Mitchum (Jeff Bailey/Jeff Markham), Jane Greer (Kathie Moffett), Kirk Douglas (Whit Sterling), Rhonda Fleming (Meta Carson), Richard Webb (Jim), Steve Brodie (Fisher), Virginia Huston (Ann), Paul Valentine (Joe), Dickie Moore (The Kid), Ken Niles (Eels).

Often described as the quintessential film noir, Jacques Tourneur's 1947 classic *Out of the Past* is certainly one of the finest, most accomplished, and most moving films in the genre, representing the combined talents of many individuals working at their peak with the support and encouragement of the RKO production team system. Tourneur was a master of atmosphere and tone, Nicholas Musuraca created a luminous black-and-white aesthetic both in his location and studio-bound cinematography, and the three leads (Robert Mitchum, Jane Greer, and Kirk Douglas) forge characterizations that have become the standard for particular genre types: the fated man, the duplicitous femme fatale, and the rich and ruthless criminal boss. In addition, *Out of the Past* examines what Alain Silver and Elizabeth Ward call, in their book *Film Noir: An Encyclopedic Reference to the American*

*Out of the Past* (1947). Directed by Jacques Tourneur. Shown: Robert Mitchum (as Jeff Bailey), Jane Greer (as Kathie Moffett). RKO/Photofest.

*Style*, a subject central to the noir genre: the "destruction of a basically good man by a corrupt woman he loves" (p. 218).

Mitchum plays this "basically good man" as someone seeking a moral life but unable to escape his fate. As Jeff Bailey, garage owner, he dwells in the present in a small Californian mountain town, living quietly and wooing a wholesome local lass named Ann. But, as the title warns us, into this apparent idyll comes a figure from his past to upset the equilibrium. Joe Stephanos is a messenger from a wealthy gambler, Whit Sterling, who wants Jeff to do one more job for him. Jeff explains the background to this surprise development to Ann as they drive to Whit's compound on Lake Tahoe. Jeff's story, narrated as a 30-minute flashback, tells how he had once been a detective in New York and had been hired by Whit to find errant girlfriend Kathie Moffett, who had shot Whit and decamped with $40,000. Jeff tracks her down in Acapulco and, perhaps predictably, falls in love with her. They evade Whit and return from Mexico to the United States, where they hide out in San Francisco. All is well until Jeff's business partner Fisher finds them and is shot dead by Kathie, who then drives off and out of Jeff's life.

In the story's present day, Ann leaves Jeff at Tahoe, where he finds that Kathie has reunited with Whit and that Whit wants him to retrieve some incriminating tax documents from his accountant Eels in San Francisco. Jeff's suspicions that he is being framed are confirmed when the accountant turns up dead, and Jeff is determined not to become a fall guy. Events become very complicated as double-crossings multiply and several characters are killed. Jeff has to juggle his genuine love for Ann with his increasing mistrust of Kathie's motives. Back in the mountains, he pretends to want to escape justice with Kathie, who has murdered Whit, but both figures perish in a police roadblock arranged by a pessimistic, even fatalistic, Jeff. Ann is left free to go on with her life in the belief that Jeff was planning to abandon her for Kathie.

The chief theme that emerges from this convoluted story line is a mainstay of film noir: the presence of a fate that you cannot escape, a fate embodied by a figure from your past. Jeff Markham is such a fated figure but one marked by a streak of passivity. At one stage he responds to a question of Kathie's with the remark, "Baby, I just don't care." A sense of how chance plays a part in his destiny can be seen in the fact that he finds the Acapulco telegraph office closed when he goes to wire Whit that he has found Kathie. In effect, he shrugs his shoulders, and his life changes course. It would, though, be an oversimplification to consider him merely passive. At times he can take charge in an assertive way, as when he breaks free of the frame Whit and others attempt to bind him in over the murder of Eels. In this case he effortlessly turns the tables on the double-crossers. He is also able to manipulate Kathie at the end so that she is trapped by the authorities. But he more or less accepts that in doing this, he will lose his own life and his chance of happiness with Ann. His philosophy could be summed up in his rueful claim that "if I have to [die], I'm going to die last."

Ann is set up as a direct contrast to Kathie, being the trusting, faithful, domestic woman who is essentially good. This tends to make her less interesting to the audience, and she plays a far smaller role than Kathie. The latter is one of noir's greatest spider women. As played by Jane Greer, she is at once seductive and deadly. Her early appearances in the film are given every rhetorical device to maximize her attractiveness. Jeff's voice-over describes her as repeatedly materializing into his view either out of the bright Mexican sunlight or the tropical moonlight. Andrew Spicer, in his book *Film Noir*, says this of her appearances: "Kathie thus emerges as if out of a dream and her delicate ethereality makes her seem both innocent and overwhelmingly desirable" (p. 55).

Later, of course, Jeff sees the other side to her: her unwavering will and determination to achieve her own selfish ends. Her betrayals and amorality cause him to say that she resembles a "leaf that blows from one gutter to another." She personally kills his partner, Fisher, then Whit (after having wounded him years before), and she colludes in the killing of Eels and arranges Joe's abortive attempt to kill Jeff. But there is also a feeling that this is what many women in her situation might be forced to do by circumstance. And there is no denying her overarching sexiness, as in the erotic scene in an Acapulco rainstorm where lovemaking is suggested strongly for a 1947 film. The Production Code, however, forced some compromises in the directness with which such sexual activity could be suggested, just as it played a role in the obligatory resolution by car crash that brings the deaths of the two main characters.

The heavy hand of censorship cannot, though, obscure the many pleasures of *Out of the Past*: the snappy dialogue, full of banter and badinage, the shadowy lighting of the fistfight between Markham and Fisher, the refreshingly nontoken representation of black characters at the Harlem nightclub. Such a black milieu was highly unusual in classical noir. In fact, the range of different locations, each with their different lighting patterns, is a major feature of the film. There are the clear skies of Bridgeport, with its small-town gossip and mountain streams; bustling New York; the exoticism of Acapulco; the nighttime murk and intrigue of San Francisco; and the sinister stillness of Lake Tahoe. Despite his careening around all these disparate places, Jeff Markham actually meets his end at Kathie's side right in the same kind of woodland where we first met him, fishing and dreaming of marriage to Ann.

Brian McDonnell

# P

**PARIS BY NIGHT** (Film Four/Cineplex Odeon, 1988). *Director:* David Hare. *Producers:* Edward Pressman and Patrick Cassavetti. *Script:* David Hare. *Cinematography:* Roger Pratt. *Music:* Georges Delerue. *Cast:* Charlotte Rampling (Clara Paige), Michael Gambon (Gerald Paige), Iain Glen (Wallace Sharp), Robert Hardy (Adam Gillvray), Jane Asher (Pauline), Andrew Ray (Michael Swanson), Niamh Cusack (Jenny Swanton), Linda Bassett (Janet Swanton), Robert Flemying (Jack Sidmouth).

Celebrated British playwright David Hare wrote and directed this subversive political thriller, which works on many levels—as a straight thriller concerned with Clara Paige's attempts to evade detection after killing a former business associate in Paris and also as a metaphor for the changing social, economic, and political climate in Britain in the late 1980s. Clara Paige is invested with sufficient recognizable traits, notably her emphasis on self-discipline and accountability, to provide a link to the uncompromising characteristics celebrated in the early Thatcher years. Yet the film is much more than a reductionist, crude metaphor and takes the viewer on an emotional ride, beginning with a problematic presentation of Clara Paige who, at times, is invested with a degree of sympathy and audience empathy as she confronts a potential blackmailer. This perception only makes the final section of the film even more effective as Clara metaphorically removes her mask to reveal a self-interested, pragmatic, and hypocritical woman who publicly supports traditional values while repudiating them through her actions.

Clara Paige is a politically successful Conservative member of the European Parliament, with a less successful marriage to aging British politician Gerald Paige.

The failure of the marriage does not unduly concern Clara, whose political star is on the rise. The only clouds on her horizon are the repeated calls from a former business associate, Michael Swanson, and fearing blackmail, she has him removed from a political meeting. While in Paris, however, she sees him again, and when she confronts him, he falls to his death. Clara panics and runs away, leaving her handbag at the scene of the crime. After failing to retrieve it, she seeks sexual solace in the arms of young Wallace Sharp. When Wallace learns of Clara's actions, he is persuaded not to go to the police after she offers to divorce her husband and marry him. But Gerald Page, finally realizing the extent of his wife's deceit, has other ideas, and he kills her when she returns home.

The political ramifications of this film go beyond its literal subject matter and extend to the allegorical level of a strong female politician at a time when Margaret Thatcher was in power. Importantly, the film systematically undermines the operation of traditional conservative values, based on the family and the need for self-discipline and moral behavior.

Charlotte Rampling, as usual, is effective as Clara Paige. The film exploits her cool beauty to gradually peel away the layers to reveal the monster lurking beneath this attractive facade. Her apparent vulnerability is interspersed with moments of ruthlessness early in the film such as the brutal dressing down of her distressed husband. These early scenes foreshadow the revelation of her true character in the last part of the film, when expediency and self-preservation overwhelm integrity. Hare's script skillfully probes Clara's character, placing her in a series of morally problematic situations that reverse earlier expectations. For example, the film reveals that Michael Swanson, the potential blackmailer, was harmless and merely wanted financial assistance from his former business associates (Clare and Gerald Paige) as they had duped him in a financial transaction. After his murder, the murderer (Clare) is forced to comfort Swanson's wife and daughter. Full of subtle ironies and dramatic twists, *Paris by Night* is one of the best noir films produced in Britain in the 1980s.

Geoff Mayer

**PAYNE, JOHN** (1912–1989). John Payne's screen career in some ways followed the same path as Dick Powell's, although Payne was never as popular as Powell. Payne began his entertainment career as a singer, moved into summer stock, and began his film career as the male lead in musicals at Twentieth Century Fox. Later, when he had lost his boyish looks, Payne, in the 1950s, switched to action and crime films. John Payne came from a musical family. He was the son of an opera singer and studied voice at Julliard. Although he made his film debut in the domestic melodrama *Dodsworth* (1936), where he was billed as John Howard Payne, he was soon cast in musicals: in his second film, *Hats Off* (1936), he was a press agent romancing Mae Clark; in *Garden of the Moon* he replaced Dick Powell as a band leader and sang frequently throughout the film; in Twentieth Century Fox's *Tin*

*Pan Alley* (1940), the studio's follow-up to *Alexander's Ragtime Band* (1938), Payne replaced Tyrone Power and costarred opposite Alice Faye and Betty Grable; in *Sun Valley Serenade* (1941) he starred opposite skating star Sonja Henie; in *Weekend in Havana* (1941), a large-budget Technicolor musical, he starred opposite Alice Faye and Carmen Miranda; in *Springtime in the Rockies* (1942), an even more lavish Technicolor musical extravaganza, Payne costarred opposite Betty Grable; in *Footlight Serenade* (1942) he costarred with Betty Grable; in *Iceland* (1942) he was again opposite Sonja Henie; in *Hello Frisco, Hello* (1943), another lavish period musical, he appeared with Alice Faye; and in his final musical at Fox, *The Dolly Sister* (1945), another period film, Payne appeared once again with Betty Grable. Although he was the star, Payne appeared only briefly in *Wake Up and Dream* (1946) at the beginning and end of the film as a soldier believed lost in battle. While Payne starred in nonmusicals at Fox, such as the patriotic melodrama *To the Shores of Tripoli* (1942), he was more closely associated with its lavish musicals. His final film at the studio was the sentimental Christmas film *Miracle on 34th Street* (1947).

Payne's first film away from Fox was the crime melodrama *Larceny* (1948) for Universal Studio, with Payne starring as a con man in league with Dan Duryea, Richard Rober, and Dan O'Herlihy, who try to swindle a war widow. This film represented a significant departure for Payne in shedding his lightweight romantic persona for a more mature, tough screen image. He followed *Larceny* with another crime film, *The Crooked Way* (1949), an independent film released through United Artists, with Payne emerging from the army with a piece of shrapnel in his head and a doctor telling him that he is suffering from "organic amnesia." Payne discovers, during the course of the film, that he was a racketeer before embarking on military service and that he turned state's evidence against his former partner. Also, he is not welcome in Los Angeles as his ex-wife and former criminal associates want him dead.

In the next 10 years Payne alternated between action films, including many westerns, and noir films. The highlight during this period was his series of tough crime films with director Phil Karlson, who claimed that Payne collaborated in developing the script for their first film, *Kansas City Confidential* (1952). Karlson and Payne followed with *99 River Street* (1953) and *Hell's Island* (1955), all violent, bleak films devoid of sentimentality.

Payne's final two noir films in the 1950s were also excellent. The first, *Slightly Scarlet* (1956), was based on James M. Cain's novel *Love's Lovely Counterfeit*, and the film benefited greatly from John Alton's sumptuous Technicolor photography. Payne plays a shady political operator for the syndicate who inveigles himself into control of the organization until his former boss returns and empties his gun into Payne's body. This was followed by a similar film, *The Boss* (1956), with Payne as a ruthless politician who extends his corrupt political influence so that it extends across an entire Midwestern state. While the film's credits claim that the film was scripted by Ben L. Perry, he was only the front for Dalton Trumbo, who was blacklisted at the time.

Payne starred in a western television series in 1958 and 1959, *The Restless Gun*, even writing some episodes. After more television work in the early 1960s, he was involved in a automobile accident in 1962, which resulted in considerable injuries and facial scarring, and he did not work again until *They Ran for Their Lives* in 1968, a film that he also directed. Payne retired in 1975 after sporadic television appearances in the early 1970s.

**Selected Noir Films:** *Larceny* (1948), *The Crooked Way* (1949), *Kansas City Confidential* (1952), *99 River Street* (1953), *Hell's Island* (1955), *Slightly Scarlet* (1956), *The Boss* (1956).

Geoff Mayer

**PHANTOM LADY** (Universal, 1944). *Director:* Robert Siodmak. *Producer:* Milton Feld. *Script:* Bernard C. Schoenfeld, from the novel by William Irish. *Cinematography:* Woody Bredell. *Music:* Hans J. Salter. *Cast:* Franchot Tone (Jack Marlow), Ella Raines (Carol "Kansas" Richman), Alan Curtis (Scott Henderson), Aurora (Estela Monteiro), Thomas Gomez (Inspector Burgess), Fay Helm (Ann Terry), Elisha Cook Jr. (Cliff), Andrew Tombes (Bartender), Regis Toomey (Detective).

One of the seminal early films in the classical noir cycle, 1944's *Phantom Lady* was the first reasonably large budget film adaptation of a novel by Cornell Woolrich (writing here under the pseudonym William Irish), and it brought to a wider audience his nightmarish world of entrapment, victimhood, and wrongful imprisonment. It was also the first American film noir directed by Robert Siodmak, one of the genre's leading figures. In this film he helps bring into being the visual style of noir, especially the studio-bound variety prevalent in the mid 1940s. In their book *Film Noir: An Encyclopedic Reference to the American Style*, Alain Silver and Elizabeth Ward accurately describe Siodmak's contribution to the look of the genre: "the whole noir world is developed here almost entirely through mise-en-scène" (p. 226). Like *Laura*, released in the same year, *Phantom Lady* is set in a wealthier, more glamorous ambience than is the usual noir story.

The film's narrative setup is typical of Woolrich's fiction and representative of that subgroup of noir that depicts the plight of male victims, men who are essentially passive, trapped individuals almost powerless to resist their fate. New York architect Scott Henderson is such a figure. Out on the town one night drinking away his marriage blues, he encounters a woman in a bar. The paths of two unhappy people thus cross in a fateful way. This stranger spends the evening with him but, for her own reasons, wants no names exchanged. The only memorable thing about her is the extravagant hat she wears. When Scott, later that night, finds his estranged wife, Marcella, murdered and the police at her apartment, he becomes caught up in a Kafkaesque series of events that lead to his conviction, incarceration, and sentence of death. The hat woman, who could provide an alibi, is not to be found and becomes the "phantom lady" of the title.

*Phantom Lady* (1944). Directed by Robert Siodmak. Shown in silhouette in background: Ella Raines (as Carol "Kansas" Richman), Alan Curtis (as Scott Henderson). Universal Pictures/Photofest.

As Andrew Spicer points out in his book *Film Noir*, the film's nominal hero, Scott, is actually "weak, passive and lachrymose, assaulted by doubts" (p. 113). Indeed, the truly dynamic figure in *Phantom Lady* is his secretary, Carol (dubbed throughout the film because of her origins in Wichita as "Kansas"). Played with great verve by Ella Raines, she is secretly in love with her boss and is made of stern stuff. She determinedly sets out to prove his innocence, which basically entails finding the phantom woman with the hat. This quest is initiated after she visits Scott in prison in a strikingly expressionistic scene reminiscent of the library sequence in *Citizen Kane*. Through the middle section of the story the audience follow Kansas's search for the witness. She thus becomes a kind of temporary detective, a plot development common in the genre. Like an avenging Fury, she doggedly pursues a bartender (an odd instance of an innocent party following a guilty one) until he dies in a bizarre traffic accident.

Most memorably, she sets out to entrap Cliff, a drummer from the musical show Scott had attended with the phantom lady. Kansas believes rightly that he may have been bribed not to give evidence about seeing the woman with Scott. The craven Cliff (played with effective creepiness by ubiquitous noir actor Elisha Cook, Jr.) takes her to a late-night jam session, and in the film's most notorious scene, he drums furiously, reaching a sexually charged percussive crescendo, while Kansas, tarted up for the occasion, encourages his overwrought pounding of the drum. Declaring herself a "hep kitten," she is quite prepared to use her sexuality to gain information and transforms herself with tight clothing, net stockings, garish makeup, and chewing gum. It is in this part of the film that Siodmak employs tilted angles and high-contrast lighting as Kansas prowls the nighttime streets and El stations of the noir city.

Despite Franchot Tone's top billing, his character, Jack Marlow, does not enter the story until 50 minutes into the film. He is a friend and colleague of Scott's who has been away on a trip to Brazil at the time of the killing. Jack is, however, a sinister and disturbed person, and the audience soon suspects him of involvement in the wife's murder. He is provoked, by comparison with Dr. Crippen, by a particularly helpful policeman, Inspector Burgess, who calls him a "paranoiac." Siodmak places great emphasis on Jack's powerful and restless hands, and the impression is given that he harbors violent, murderous impulses that cannot be repressed. Jack appears to be willing to help Kansas, but when her resourceful sleuthing actually uncovers the phantom lady (who turns out to be another psychologically fragile soul), he realizes he must kill Kansas as well. In the film's climactic scene he attempts to strangle her in his sinister, modernist apartment. Suspense is created after she finds incriminating evidence in a drawer and Jack confesses to having killed Marcella in order to stop her laughing at him. He had then flown to Havana to create an alibi for himself. The police burst in just in time, and Jack leaps to his death out the window.

After the film's male hero has thus been saved by the female lead, a neat little epilogue in Scott's office allows a romance to begin between him and Kansas. He leaves a dinner invitation on the office Dictaphone, which promptly jams, so that the phrase indicating he wants to be with her "every night, every night" keeps repeating. A similar device of a conveniently inoperative recording machine was used at the end of the film version of Graham Greene's *Brighton Rock* three years later.

Brian McDonnell

**PICKUP ON SOUTH STREET** (Twentieth Century Fox, 1953). *Director:* Samuel Fuller. *Producer:* Jules Schermer. *Script:* Samuel Fuller, from a story by Dwight Taylor. *Cinematography:* Joe McDonald. *Music:* Leigh Harline. *Cast:* Richard Widmark (Skip McCoy), Jean Peters (Candy), Thelma Ritter (Moe), Murvyn Vye (Captain Don Tiger), Richard Kiley (Joey), Willis B. Bouchey (Zara), Milburn Stone (Winoki).

Created by the talented but idiosyncratic Sam Fuller, *Pickup on South Street* is a difficult film to categorize. Essentially a character piece, it curiously shies away from action while relishing its long, carefully choreographed scenes and its vivid, colloquial dialogue. It freely uses the Cold War terminology of the McCarthy era (e.g., *Commies*), but in its celebration of eccentricity and marginality it cannot

*Pickup On South Street* (1953). Directed and written by Samuel Fuller. Shown from left: Richard Widmark (as Skip McCoy), Jean Peters (as Candy). Twentieth Century Fox Film Corp./Photofest.

be characterized as having a conservative or reactionary ideology. Most striking of all perhaps is the film's Dickensian panorama of people and places (despite all the supposed New York street scenes being shot in Los Angeles). Its three central characters are a cocksure pickpocket named Skip (Richard Widmark), a beaten-down but feisty police informer named Mo (Thelma Ritter), and a none-too-bright whore with a heart of gold called Candy (Jean Peters). They live in a low-rent riverside district of Manhattan in cramped tenements, cold-water apartments, or shacks that stand on poles above the waves of the Hudson. It is a vividly evoked milieu that could practically have sprung from the pages of Dickens's *Our Mutual Friend*.

In the film's opening sequence Skip rifles through Candy's handbag inside a crowded subway car. He is unaware that she is also being targeted by some FBI officers who know she is carrying a microfilm destined for Communist agents. Candy realizes her loss and calls her agitated contact. After Skip's escape from the pursuing officers, they seek the assistance of local New York police. Mo is called in as an informer who knows the city's pickpockets (or "cannons") well, and she obliges by identifying Skip. This sets up a generally straightforward narrative involving a triple pursuit of Skip by the police, by Candy, and by the Communists, who all desire the microfilm. It transpires that Candy is an unknowing dupe of a Communist operator Joey (Richard Kiley), who had once been her lover. Despite the fulminations of the FBI and the police, the microfilm never gains much more status in the story than one of Hitchcock's McGuffins. Certainly Skip will have no truck with pompous talk of the possible effect on national security of its loss: "Are you waving the flag at *me?*" he asks cockily.

Of more importance to Fuller than the spy plot are the interactions between his colorful central characters. Candy quickly falls for Skip and follows him doggedly, even though he inadvertently slugs her when he discovers her searching through his shack in the dark. When Mo is first brought in to the station to help find Skip, she is shown (especially through Ritter's excellent portrayal) as a semicomic character. She is saving up to pay for a burial plot and bargains entertainingly with the detectives for her modest reward money. Later, when the ruthless Joey calls at her apartment with evil intent, Mo is seen in a far more poignant and tragic light. Making a vivid speech about the pains of aging, she compares herself to an "old clock winding down." When he threatens to kill her if she does not give up the location of Skip, she declines, saying, "I'm so tired, you'd be doing me a big favor if you blew my head off." An off-screen shot is heard as the needle of her record player slides from music to a harsh scratching.

*Pickup on South Street* features several excellent set pieces that reveal Fuller's talent for managing scenes that involve complex camera work. The opening scene on the subway train is one such. Filmed on a specially constructed studio set at Fox, it is both realistic and stylized. Fuller concentrates on the faces of the bored passengers and conveys all his information without dialogue. Something similar happens with the climactic fight between Skip and Joey after the microfilm has been exchanged in a public toilet. Again, the action happens in the subway. However, after Joey escapes and Skip pursues him onto the tracks, there is an abrupt, anticlimactic end to their fight, and a jarringly cute epilogue occurs in which Candy and Skip form a romantic bond in a hospital ward. This seems lightweight, but there is a serious thematic point made in the closing sequences. Skip learns the meaning of decency and commitment, mainly from Mo's example in sacrificing her life for him. His change of heart is shown when Mo is bound for Potter's Field on a boat full of coffins. Skip, looking more sober and serious than at any other time, redeems her body for the kind of burial she always hankered after.

Brian McDonnell

**PINK STRING AND SEALING WAX** (Ealing, 1945). *Director:* Robert Hamer. *Producer:* Michael Balcon and S. C. Balcon (associate). *Script:* Diana Morgan and Robert Hamer, based on the play by Roland Pertwee. *Cinematography:* Richard Pavey. *Music:* Norman Demuth. *Cast:* Mervyn Johns (Edward Sutton), Googie Withers (Pearl Bond), Gordon Jackson (David Sutton), Jean Ireland (Victoria

Sutton), Sally Ann Howes (Peggy Sutton), Mary Merrall (Ellen Sutton), John Carol (Dan Powell), Catherine Lacey (Miss Porter), Garry Marsh (Joe Bond), Pauline Letts (Louise), Maudie Edwards (Mrs. Webster).

This film is concerned with betrayal and domestic unhappiness, a theme that director Robert Hamer also explored in a contemporary setting in *It Always Rains on Sunday* (1947). *Pink String and Sealing Wax*, set in 1890s Brighton, begins with members of the Sutton family anxiously waiting the arrival of Edward Sutton, the stern head of the family. Sutton returns home for his evening meal after testifying, in his capacity of consulting pharmacist, at the trial of a woman arrested for poisoning her husband. When Peggy Sutton notices her father's jaunty approach to the house, she realizes that the woman on trial has been condemned to death.

Patriarchal punishment of the fallen woman is a central motif in the film. Sutton's stern discipline of his family prohibits son David's courtship of a young woman and daughter Victoria's desire to train as an opera singer. Both desires, Edward Sutton tells his children, are immoral. He explains to his long-suffering wife, Ellen, his philosophical rationale for controlling the family in such a manner: "Love and

*Pink String and Sealing Wax* (1946, British). Directed by Robert Hamer. Shown from left: Googie Withers (as Pearl Bond), Garry Marsh (as Joe Bond). Eagle-Lion/Photofest.

fear are inseparable. God is love but we are taught to fear him." The film subjects this philosophy to a rigorous examination. Both David and Victoria disobey their father. David's rebellion, however, leads him to the marital problems of Pearl Bond. Her situation, in some way, parallels David's sense of entrapment within the Sutton family. Pearl suffers in a loveless marriage to a drunken, abusive publican, Joe Bond.

Pearl seeks solace with local womanizer Dan Powell. When David Sutton enters her world, she sees a means of escape from her intolerable situation. David takes Pearl back to the pharmacy to bandage her hand after her husband accidentally strikes her, and Pearl steals poison to kill her husband. This action eventually implicates David after suspicions are raised about Joe Bond's death. The situation becomes more complicated when Edward Sutton is commissioned to carry out the examination on the dead man. Sutton resists Pearl's attempt to blackmail him into falsifying his report by threatening to implicate David. When this fails, and Dan Powell abandons her, Pearl commits suicide.

Hamer is less concerned with the melodramatic details of the plot than in the dark ambience emanating from the repressive social context. Hence the film concentrates on the ramifications of Sutton's unyielding control of his family. The film consists of a series of failed love affairs extending from David's disastrous infatuation with Pearl, to Pearl's betrayal by Dan, and minor figures, such as Louise's doomed love of Dan. Only a brief photograph at the end of the film, showing David's marriage to his first love, provides any semblance of a successful romance and a brief glimpse of so-called normality.

Hamer presents the restoration of normality in a cursory fashion, preferring to emphasize the cost of its restoration—the suicide of Pearl Bond. This is presented as the visual set piece of the film with a long track following Pearl before she plunges to her death. The suicide of this strong, sensual woman, the film suggests, is a necessary precondition for the restoration of patriarchal rule. Googie Withers is outstanding as the sensual, complex Pearl Bond, and she is matched by Catherine Lacey as the cynical prostitute Miss Porter. The overt references to Porter's profession, together with Pearl's suicide and the detailed poisoning of her husband, denied *Pink String and Sealing Wax* a Production Code certificate of approval. The release of the film in the United States was delayed until 1950, when it was shown in New York without a certificate.

Geoff Mayer

**PITFALL** (Regal Films/United Artists, 1948). *Director:* André de Toth. *Producer:* Samuel Bischoff. *Script:* Karl Kamb, from the novel *The Pitfall* by Jay Dratler). *Cinematography:* Harry Wild. *Music:* Louis Forbes. *Cast:* Dick Powell (John Forbes), Lizabeth Scott (Mona Stevens), Jane Wyatt (Sue Forbes), Raymond Burr (MacDonald), John Litel (District Attorney), Byron Barr (Bill Smiley), Jimmy Hunt (Tommy Forbes), Ann Doran (Maggie).

A somber and fascinating film noir, *Pitfall* dramatizes the consequences on an average middle-class American male (John Forbes) of a single indiscretion. It was called by Alain Silver and Elizabeth Ward, in their book *Film Noir: An Encyclopedic Reference to the American Style*, "the key noir detailing the fall of the errant husband from the grace of bourgeois respectability" (p. 228). John's fall is brought about largely by boredom, his frustration with conformity, and his sense that his daily routine has become a rut. He remarks in the opening scene that he feels he is a "wheel within a wheel within a wheel." A rare example in the genre of a film centered on family and suburbia, *Pitfall* is quite moralistic in theme, hammering home the burdensome fallout of a brief extramarital liaison. James Naramore, in his book *More Than Night: Film Noir in Its Contexts,* has compared it to 1987's *Fatal Attraction,* saying that both films show suburban America as an "iron cage" for both husband and wife (p. 264). The film's polysemic title (a typical feature of noir) encapsulates this view through its literal meaning of an animal trap, while at the same time being a metaphorical reference to the snares and temptations that can ambush us in life.

Unsurprisingly, the equilibrium of John's life is broken early in the film's narrative. After an opening scene full of snappy dialogue and drolleries set in the Forbes's spanking-new kitchen, John encounters a young woman named Mona who makes a huge change in his life. He is an insurance man (rather like Walter Neff in *Double Indemnity*) sent to reclaim gifts made to Mona by her imprisoned boyfriend, Smiley. John is tempted to conceal a small boat she treasures, in effect to steal from his employer. He also begins a brief romance with the girl, but Mona is no femme fatale: as soon as she knows he is married, she stops the affair. On visiting his home, discovering the true situation and attempting to explain her presence there, she says meaningfully to his wife, "I think I'm on the wrong street." John's wife, Sue, is a poised figure, down to earth and loyal but not blindly supportive of her errant husband. In fact, *Pitfall,* unusually for film noir, is full of funny and accurate insights into family life. The true villain of the piece is insurance investigator MacDonald, played impressively by Raymond Burr and accurately described by Mona as "gruesome." A creepy mischief maker, he uses his friendship with his former police colleagues to abet his mistreatment of both her and Forbes (of whose intimacy with Mona he is envious). Mac is, in effect, the id equivalent to John, manifesting the latter's darker impulses and showing him the danger of untrammeled desire in the outer world, away from the restraints of family. A central scene depicting Mac's malevolent treatment of Mona is when Mac ogles Mona at the department store where she is a clothes model. Under the pretext of being a customer, he leers at her while she parades a series of frocks and orders her around in a strikingly unpleasant manner.

A broader social commentary about transgression can be seen in the visits made to the incarcerated Smiley with prison bars prominent. This seedy jail setting and Mac's office resemble more traditional noir milieu, and both Mac and Smiley bring their taint to the Forbes's suburban house with them. For most of its length, *Pitfall* is brightly lit and has little of the conventional high-contrast look of film noir. However, when the Forbes home is invaded, it becomes visibly more sinister. The house is threatened with violence, and while John waits there fearfully at night, it turns into a noir setting: dark and shadowy. Even Sue's face is in darkness when he tells her the bitter truth about his affair. It is in this murky setting that John shoots and kills Smiley, who, egged on by Mac, has come to murder him. This symbolic use of setting is continued at the end, when Mona is seen in an elevator descending to a lower level of the Halls of Justice. The turning of suburban dream into nightmare is also suggested by a nightmare suffered by John and Sue's son, his bad dream an indicator of the more general malaise of middle-class life. A perplexed John tells the boy that "the mind is like a camera" recording our days and that its accumulated pictures make up our dreams at night. He advises him to take nice pictures.

*Pitfall* thus occupies a central place in the genre through its potent depiction of transgression, of an ordinary man caught up in extraordinary events. However, what is probably more apparent today than on the film's release in 1948 is the poignancy of the fate of Mona after she shoots the relentless Mac. John Forbes escapes relatively unscathed from his experiences, wiser certainly, but punished far less than the unfortunate Mona, who is a thoroughly innocent and decent person. John is let off what is viewed by the authorities as the justifiable killing of a prowler, merely being admonished by a detective in a Production Code–style ideological homily that he should have contacted the police instead of taking the law into his own hands. The overarching sadness of Mona's situation is that she has been trapped between three men: John, Mac, and Smiley. Real questions at the end about what will happen to her as well as to Johnny contribute to the somber ending. The epilogue, too, suggests a subdued future for the Forbes when the wife promises only to "try" to keep the marriage going. As in many 1940s films, fear of scandal is much stronger than it would be today, and Sue tells John to continue lying about what has occurred for the family's sake. She does not want them dragged through the dirt.

Brian McDonnell

**POINT BLANK** (MGM, 1967). *Director:* John Boorman. *Producers:* Judd Bernard and Robert Chartoff. *Script:* Alexander Jacobs, David Newhouse, and Rafe Newhouse, from the novel *The Hunter* by Richard Stark. *Cinematography:* Philip H. Lathrop. *Music:* Johnny Mandel. *Cast:* Lee Marvin (Walker), Angie Dickinson (Chris), Keenan Wynn (Yost), Carroll O'Connor (Brewster), Lloyd Bochner (Frederick Carter), Michael Strong (Stegman), John Vernon (Mal Reese), Sharon Acker (Lynne).

Coming as it did in 1967 halfway between the end of the classical noir cycle and the beginning of the main revival of noir subject matter in the early 1970s, *Point Blank* was a historically crucial bridging film. It was directed by Englishman

John Boorman, who was to stay on in Hollywood after this film to make other meditations on violence such as *Deliverance* (1972). In many ways a continuation of both film noir and the gangster genre, *Point Blank* shows clearly the influence of the French new wave and art cinema movements on its formal properties, especially its narrative flourishes. As the famous *TIME Magazine* cover article on *Bonnie and Clyde* in December 1967 concluded, "*Point Blank* . . . is in its plot an old-fashioned shoot-'em-down but in its technique a catalogue of the latest razzle-dazzle cinematography." Its vulpine protagonist, Walker, has a pronounced lack of affect comparable to the single-minded heroes of the French noir films of Jean-Pierre Melville such as *Le Samouraï* (1967). While Walker may progress through the shiny modern landscape of 1960s Los Angeles, he also shares many of the existential quandaries of his generic forebears in the classical film noir cycle.

Walker is gunned down in the opening seconds of the film during a robbery of syndicate funds in the derelict Alcatraz Prison in San Francisco and has his $93,000 share of the mob's loot purloined by his erstwhile partner, Mel Rhys. The remainder of the film follows Walker's dogged pursuit of those responsible for his loss and his attempts to retrieve his money, no matter how high up the hierarchy of the criminal organization he has to reach. He is encouraged in this revenge by a mysterious man who seems to be a policeman. Walker's wife, Lynne, has decamped to Los Angeles with Rhys, but abandoned by her fickle lover, she commits suicide soon after Walker tracks her down. He intercepts her next allowance from Rhys and follows the money trail via a lecherous car dealer named Big Jim Stegman to Rhys himself. Stegman also alerts Walker to the fact that Rhys is currently pursuing Lynne's sister Chris. A set piece triple-cross ensues in which Rhys and his boss, Carter, set a trap for Walker at Rhys's penthouse suite while Walker himself plans to use Chris as bait in an attempt to breach the gang's defenses. While Chris is in bed with Rhys, Walker sneaks in, and during a struggle between the men, Rhys falls to his death off the balcony.

Carter is unnerved by this mishap and pretends that he will pay off Walker while secretly arranging for a sniper to kill him when he collects the money at a rendezvous in the storm drains of the Los Angles River. Again, Walker trumps the double-cross by sending Carter out into view for the cash, and the mob man is shot dead by his own assassin. Along with Chris, Walker then camps out in the Hollywood Hills mansion of Carter's boss, Brewster. After an evening of conflict in which she repeatedly slaps him, slugs him with a pool cue, and even produces an assaultive wave of noise from the house's appliances to prompt an emotional response from him, they make love. Walker confronts Brewster when he arrives in the morning, and the syndicate boss promises him his $93,000 after making arrangements on the phone with mob accountant Fairfax. They then return to San Francisco for the pickup in an empty warehouse. While Walker hides and watches, Brewster is gunned down by a sniper. The cop from the beginning of the film emerges from the shadows and is revealed as Fairfax: he has cynically used Walker to help him eliminate all his syndicate rivals. In a closing example of symmetry the camera tilts up and zooms through the darkness toward Alcatraz Island. It is left unclear whether Walker will get his money back or not. There is even a suggestion that most of the film may actually have been the dying reverie of Walker when he was shot in the opening scene.

In generic terms, the freshest aspect of *Point Blank*, then, is the way in which its elliptical narrative breaks away from the classical, coherent storytelling style of most Hollywood B thrillers. It has the same obsession with vengeance and the same ironies surrounding the notion of the hero as dupe that were found in classical noir, but these themes are combined with a depiction of an alienated society that links it with such 1960s nonnoir classics as *The Graduate* (1967) and *Petulia* (1968). Abrupt flashbacks, the juggling of time, and fragmentation also help give *Point Blank* the feel of a 1960s art film. Its very clean-cut criminals with educated accents underline the fact that old-style gangsters have been replaced by corporate types wearing snappy suits. They make Walker seem even more old-fashioned in his dogmatic demands for satisfaction. The film's use of the Los Angeles landscape, especially the river bed and the concrete drains, echoes old classical film noirs such as *Roadblock* (1951) while also looking forward to the vision of another British expatriate director in Christopher Nolan's *Memento* (2000). Perhaps the most lasting impression from *Point Blank* is that established by Lee Marvin as Walker, who maintains a resolutely stoic determination throughout, punctuated by abrupt explosions of violence such as his emptying of his pistol into the mattress of Lynne's adulterous bed in a volley of shots that resembles a sexual ejaculation.

Brian McDonnell

**PORTMAN, ERIC** (1903–1969). Eric Portman was an unusual British film star in the 1940s and a character actor in the 1950s and 1960s. He was an unlikely star due to the fact that his characters were often tormented or disturbed by personal flaws or suffered from unrequited love. His characters were remote, obsessed, and repressed with suggestions of perversity or psychological disturbance. Portman made his stage debut in 1924 and his film debut in 1933. A succession of minor film roles in the 1930s, including a brief, unsuccessful stint in Hollywood with a small role in *The Prince and the Pauper* (1937), followed. However, as the ruthless, pragmatic Nazi U-boat commander Hirth forced to travel across Canada in Michael Powell's *49th Parallel* (1941), Portman made a strong impression with audiences. Roles as a member of the British bomber crew in *One of Our Aircraft Is Missing* (1942) and a factory foreman in *Millions Like Us* (1943) restored Portman to more positive characterizations. However, his next role gave an indication to the perverse, troubled characters he would play in the next few years. As the tragic Captain John Ellis in Lance Comfort's noir film *Great Day* (1945), Portman gives his finest screen performance in this underrated film. Ellis, a figure who lives only in the past glories of his military achievements in World War I, finds it almost impossible to adapt to the demands of World War II. He resists any attempt to subjugate his achievements in the past, and he shows little interest in communal village life. Finally, his reckless actions culminate in thoughts of suicide. Portman's Ellis, with his unrelenting focus on the past, is similar to his Thomas Colpeper in Michael Powell's *A Canterbury Tale* (1944), a justice of the peace who diverts soldiers away from the local women, and toward his lectures on his native Kent, by placing glue on the hair of the women.

Portman portrayed a succession of vulnerable characters in noir films between 1946 and 1949. One of the best was his performance in Lawrence Huntington's underrated noir film *Wanted for Murder* (1946), which was loosely based on the real-life case of Neville Smith. His introspective, psychologically damaged serial killer is motivated to kill by the legacy of his grandfather, a Victorian public hangman. In his next film, *Daybreak* (1947), Portman is the troubled hangman involved in a doomed love affair with Ann Todd. Next, he was Paul Mangin, an artist living in the past and obsessed with the image of Edana Romney, in Terence Young's visually splendid film noir *Corridor of Mirrors* (1948). This was followed by his effete Richard Howard in *The Mark of Cain* (1948), Brian Desmond Hurst's melodrama of desire and sibling rivalry. A more straight noir film was Arthur Crabtree's *Dear Murderer* (1947), with Portman as the husband driven to murder by his unfaithful wife (Greta Gynt). Finally, in Robert Hamer's *The Spider and the Fly* (1949), Portman, as policeman Fernand Maubert involved in a game of cat and mouse with safecracker Guy Rolfe, demonstrated more than a hint of sexual ambiguity in his "strange friendship" with the thief.

The 1950s and 1960s were less rewarding as Portman had less opportunity to essay his morally problematic characters. His major roles included the stolid Colonel Richmond in the popular prisoner of war film *The Colditz Story* (1954); the trade union leader turned governor in *His Excellency* (1952); Commodore Wolfgang Schrepke in the revisionist Cold War melodrama *The Bedford Incident* (1965), starring Richard Widmark and Sidney Poitier; a supporting role in John Huston's *Freud* (1962); and, before his death in 1969, two films directed by Bryan Forbes: *The Whisperers* (1966), opposite Edith Evans, and *Deadfall* (1967), with Portman as an aging, homosexual safecracker who is the tormented father of the film's heroine.

**Selected Noir Films:** *Maria Marten* (1935), *The Crimes of Stephen Hawke* (1936), *The Great Day* (1945), *Wanted for Murder* (1946), *Dear Murderer* (1947), *The Mark of Cain* (1947), *Corridor of Mirrors* (1948), *Daybreak* (1947), *The Spider and the Fly* (1949), *Cairo Road* (1950), *The Naked Edge* (1961), *The Man Who Finally Died* (1962), *West 11* (1963), *Deadfall* (1967), *Assignment to Kill* (1968).

Geoff Mayer

**POSSESSED** (Warner Bros., 1947). *Director:* Curtis Bernhardt. *Producer:* Jerry Wald. *Script:* Silvia Richards and Ranald MacDougall, from the story by Rita Weiman. *Cinematography:* Joseph Valentine. *Music:* Franz Waxman. *Cast:* Joan

Crawford (Louise Howell), Van Heflin (David Sutton), Raymond Massey (Dean Graham), Geraldine Brooks (Carol Graham), Stanley Ridges (Dr. Harvey Willard), John Ridgely (Harker), Moroni Olsen (Dr. Ames), Gerald Perreau (Wynn Graham).

*Possessed* remains one of the central film noirs of the late 1940s, combining as it does important aspects of the genre at that time: a female-centered story focusing on a woman's psychological vulnerability, postwar alienation, and a foregrounding of Freudian analysis. In this troubling vision of a society where civilization itself is largely to blame for people's ills, America is seen more as a nation of nightmares than of dreams. Curtis Bernhardt's direction pursues these themes with a particularly strong visual style. Joan Crawford, playing one of her most complex characterizations, conveys effectively the roller-coaster ride of Louise Howell's emotions.

The film has a famous and notable opening in which an isolated, somnambulistic, and almost catatonic Louise wanders at dawn through the empty streets of downtown Los Angeles. This sequence introduces the film's themes of powerlessness, alienation, and unrequited, obsessive love. When Louise is subsequently hospitalized in a "psychopathic ward," the doctors there claim they encounter 20 such cases a day of people who have disengaged from an inhospitable world. While she lies in bed as rigid as the robot from *Metropolis*, they discuss her in the Freudian terms that were much bandied about in the culture of the time. In fact, *Possessed* is one of the most emphatic elaborations of Freudian analysis in the noir canon.

The film's narrative is constructed out of the drug-assisted interrogations the chief psychiatrist conducts on Louise, leading into a very long, interrupted flashback concerning her fraught relationships with two men: David Sutton and Dean Graham. She had worked as a nurse tending Graham's ailing wife, Pauline (who, in her own madness, is a character analogue for Louise), at the couple's lakeside home. While there, Louise falls profoundly in love with neighboring engineer Sutton, an independent man more concerned with mathematical posers than with committed relationships. On the other hand, Louise feels things deeply, despite being considered rather detached as a nurse, and this makes her a very vulnerable woman. She becomes unhealthily obsessed with David, so possessive that she claims a "monopoly" on him, leading him to say he feels "smothered." To escape her demanding attentions, he takes up a job offer from Graham to work in a distant Canadian oil field.

This coincides with the death by suicide of Pauline (a scene gruesome by 1940s Hollywood standards shows her drowned body being pulled from the lake), which initiates a worsening of Louise's condition. Her mental state deteriorates, and the filmmakers trace her decline in a manner that anticipates Roman Polanski's *Repulsion* (1965). As the film's title suggests, she is like someone possessed by a demon, but in this instance it is the demon of a mind-destroying compulsive infatuation. Louise comes to experience aural hallucinations in which she hears Pauline's false accusations that she was having an affair with Dean. Later, his daughter Carol echoes these claims, and Louise consults a doctor about her fears for her own sanity. When he speaks of her symptoms, her medical knowledge allows her to recognize incipient schizophrenia, and this prospect terrifies her. Things become acute when David (something of an *homme fatal*) returns to town and, despite a 15-year age gap, begins an intense relationship with Carol, who long before had had a girlish crush on him. Louise, by now in a passionless marriage to Dean, becomes jealous. After a brief respite from her mania after Dean helps her "exorcise" the maddening memories of Pauline's death, she finally topples over the edge into psychosis when David tells her that he and Carol are to marry. To prevent this ultimate loss, she shoots him dead, an event that triggers the catatonia seen in the film's opening minutes. Nevertheless, the present-day doctors hold out hope for a recovery after their therapy, and Dean swears he will stand by her.

Much of the camera work of *Possessed* is subjective, leading the viewer to share in Louise's mental disintegration. Apart from early scenes where we share her view from a hospital gurney as she is examined in her traumatized state, there is one frightening later sequence in which she prowls the rooms of a Gothic mansion lit in high contrast that shows, through its visual distortions, her unbalanced mind. She appears to catch Carol kissing David, then confronts the girl and throws her down a staircase. This violent episode is immediately revealed as one imagined by the frantic Louise. The extreme visuals here are matched by the powerful Franz Waxman piano-dominated score, whose classical motifs are justified by David's earlier delight in playing the works of Robert Schumann. All this adds to the hypnotic atmosphere of the film. As Alain Silver and Elizabeth Ward remark in their book *Film Noir: An Encyclopedic Reference to the American Style*, *Possessed* is "a prime example of oneirism, the dreamlike tone that is a seminal characteristic of film noir" (p. 231).

Brian McDonnell

**THE POSTMAN ALWAYS RINGS TWICE** (MGM, 1946). *Director:* Tay Garnett. *Producer:* Carey Wilson. *Script:* Harry Ruskin and Niven Busch, from the novel by James M. Cain). *Cinematography:* Sidney Wagner. *Music:* George Bassman. *Cast:* Lana Turner (Cora Smith), John Garfield (Frank Chambers), Cecil Kellaway (Nick Smith), Hume Cronyn (Arthur Keats), Leon Ames (Kyle Sackett), Audrey Totter (Madge Gorland), Alan Reed (Ezra Liam Kennedy).

*The Postman Always Rings Twice* contains one of the most quintessential noir situations, collections of characters, and plot structures, centering as it does on a sexual triangle in which a young man has an affair with the youthful wife of an older husband and then plots with her to murder the cuckold. Yet in its visual style it seldom uses the conventions associated with film noir. Made by a studio (MGM) more often linked to glamorous subject matter, it is nevertheless an important example of the classical cycle in its formative years in the mid-1940s. The film seems today overstuffed with plot as if the adaptors included too much material

*The Postman Always Rings Twice* (1946). Directed by Tay Garnett. Shown from left: Cecil Kellaway (as Nick Smith), John Garfield (as Frank Chambers), Lana Turner (as Cora Smith). MGM/Photofest.

from the original novel for any single feature film to bear. Some scenes therefore feel sketchy, but overall, it remains a powerful melodramatic work, and John Garfield and Lana Turner make a charismatic team as the two lead characters.

*The Postman Always Rings Twice*, James M. Cain's first novel, was optioned in 1935, but the studios only felt it could be made after 1944 saw the acceptance by the Production Code Administration of Cain's other novel, *Double Indemnity*. The success of the Billy Wilder film helped *Postman* get under way, and the book was still sensational enough for the producers to use its dust jacket as the basis of the film's main titles. It was unusual for MGM to make such a crime movie: they were better known for musicals, prestige dramas, and Technicolor epics. As if to emphasize their unfamiliarity with this territory, they borrowed Garfield from Warner Bros. to play the role of drifter Frank Chambers. He narrates almost the entire story in a flashback that is only broken at the end, where Frank is seen in a death cell confessing his tale to a priest. Because the audience is unaware of his eventual fate, the film is less fatalistic in tone than such examples of flashback as *Mildred Pierce* or *Double Indemnity*.

Frank's partner in crime, Cora Smith, is much less nasty than Cain's femme fatale Phyllis Dietrichson was in *Double Indemnity*. Cora is seen as much more a figure of desperation and inner goodness than Phyllis, who is murderous from beginning to end. Frank first meets her when he arrives by chance at the roadside diner/garage she runs with her elderly husband, Nick. The sign outside reading MAN WANTED is the first visual item in the film and carries a sexual double meaning that introduces the atmosphere of passion and erotic tension that features in the first half of *Postman*. Their meeting is an example of the noir theme of fate, and the bond of desire between the two is clearly established when a lipstick tube rolling across the floor draws Frank's attention to Cora's arresting figure as she stands posing in a white bare-midriff outfit with short shorts and a tight turban. He literally burns his hamburger meat as he stares at her. Nick soon hires Frank, who impresses with his entrepreneurial flair for marketing. He toils in the gas station by day and pursues Cora by night, accompanying her on moonlight swims. Their forays into the sea continue throughout the film, and the dark ocean waters come to symbolize the world of danger that surrounds their passion. They attempt to run away together, and Cora even sullies with dirt and oil her immaculate white skirt and shoes as they hitchhike. They return, however, because Cora cannot face a penniless future with the feckless Frank.

The only real option for them is to kill Nick, and they have one abortive attempt at this before they eventually succeed. On the first occasion, their plan to fake an accident by striking him over the head while he is in the bath goes awry when a motorcycle cop notices a ladder placed to aid escape and when a cat blows the fuses by electrocuting itself on the roof. This blackly humorous sequence leads to hospitalization for Nick and is quickly followed by his decision to sell the business and take Cora with him to Canada. She cannot contemplate a life nursing his paralyzed sister, and so she and Frank conspire to fake a car accident. Nick often drives drunk, so they feel it will be believed. When Frank is also inadvertently injured in the crash, this detail seems to make it all even more credible. However, a suspicious district attorney charges Cora with murder, and the film's narrative accelerates through a bewildering trial full of lawyer manipulation and double dealing. The two conspirators fall out through infidelity and mutual mistrust; only Cora's pregnancy and their fight against a common foe (a blackmailer) draw them back together. They have one last moonlight swim, during which Cora tests Frank's confidence in her love by offering to drown if he cannot trust her. All seems settled and a happy future beckons, but the Production Code Administration could not allow the audience to receive such an unconventional ideological message. As in many classical noirs, a car crash on their way home resolves the moral dilemma: Cora is killed, and Frank is convicted of her murder.

The film has a much brighter and glossier look than most examples of film noir. The MGM house style is evident in the lighting, which has much more fill and far fewer shadows than is characteristic of noir. Turner is always glamorously lit, and there are no sequences that use distortion to suggest nightmare or a subjective viewpoint. Despite the high production values and presentation, though, *The Postman Always Rings Twice* is thematically as noirish as it is possible to be. The main compromise that distinguishes it from many grittier examples of the same period is the rather awkward ending of the story. When the flashback that takes up nearly all the film's running time finally ends, Frank is shown in jail talking to a Catholic priest. As if especially designed to appease Production Code Administration head (and prominent Catholic layman) Joe Breen, the closing scene brings in compensating moral values and underlines the fact that both killers are punished for their crimes. The film's complicated title metaphor is explained in some mumbo-jumbo dialogue from Frank concerning messages from God, and he closes with a plea that the priest pray for him and Cora to be together through eternity. It is arguable whether this brief sugary closing can outweigh the darker passions on display earlier in the story.

A remake of *The Postman Always Rings Twice* directed by Bob Rafelson was released in 1981, with Jack Nicholson and Jessica Lange in the main roles. Unsurprisingly, this version was able to adhere much more closely to Cain's original novel.

Brian McDonnell

**POWELL, DICK** (1904–1963). Powell was a multitalented individual who was able to achieve highly in a number of entertainment fields. He began his working life as a musician and singer who later turned to hard-boiled dramatic roles in one of the most successful career shifts in Hollywood history. He was even a notable director and producer in both cinema and television. Dick Powell was born in Arkansas and toured the South and other regions as a singer before hitting Hollywood and trying his luck at the big studios. He became a prominent song-and-dance man, known best as a crooner in musicals such as *42nd Street* (1933) and the Gold Diggers series (1933-1937). His persona was that of a likeable and affable, handsome young man who was a witty and charming romancer of the ladies. However, Powell was able to make a complete and successful change of image midcareer, moving from Paramount to RKO to get the different sorts of roles that he hankered after and which his home studio would not offer him. At RKO he was given the lead as detective Philip Marlowe in the 1944 adaptation of Raymond Chandler's novel *Farewell, My Lovely*. Thus he became the first actor to play Marlowe and was widely admired for his performance, overcoming the reservations of many people who thought he could not pull it off. Even Chandler thought him closer to his own view of the character than Bogart was later in *The Big Sleep*. Powell eclipsed his old image as a sweet singer to become a totally convincing tough guy who evinced endurance and resilience, although RKO helped dampen audience expectations associated with his old persona by retitling the film *Murder, My Sweet*. He was especially skilled in the delivery of the film's voice-over narration, a key component in evoking the spirit of Chandler's prose. In 1945 he made the noir story *Cornered*, in which he played a pilot handy with his fists, demonstrating that *Murder, My Sweet* was certainly not a one-off. His depiction of the suave gambler in *Johnny O'Clock* added urbanity to Powell's tough image, and he was able to combine a streak of ruthlessness with a hint of chivalry in a similar way to Bogart. Powell was also very capable and effective in the complex leading role of John Forbes in *Pitfall* (1948), one of the central masculine roles in classical film noir. In this film he plays a husband caught in a brief adulterous affair who has to extricate himself from association with murder, manslaughter, and jealousy to rebuild his marriage. His leading role as Rocky in the underrated film *Cry Danger* (1951) shows him up well in a story that vividly illustrates conditions for everyday people in postwar Los Angeles. Powell later directed the little-known film noir *Split Second*, a tightly suspenseful, claustrophobic film depicting a group of people trapped near an atomic test site. When he moved into the production and direction of television drama, Powell had even greater popular success, particularly with the highly regarded *Dick Powell Show*.

**Selected Noir Films:** *Murder, My Sweet* (U.K. title *Farewell, My Lovely*, 1944), *Cornered* (1945), *Johnny O'Clock* (1947), *Pitfall* (1948), *Cry Danger* (1951), *The Tall Target* (1951), *The Bad and the Beautiful* (1952). Powell also directed *Split Second* (1953).

Brian McDonnell

**PREMINGER, OTTO** (1906–1986). Known for his long takes, mobile camera, attacks on conservative censorship practices, and romantic themes, Preminger was one of the more distinctive directors of the mid-twentieth century and one of a group of émigré filmmakers from central Europe who played a very substantial role in the shaping of classical film noir. Preminger was born in Vienna, Austria, into a wealthy family and studied to be a lawyer like his prominent father, who was the attorney general of the Austrian Empire. However, he abandoned his legal ambitions to be a stage actor and a director in Viennese theater. Preminger made just one film in German and then traveled to the United States in 1935 at the invitation of the Twentieth Century Fox studio. He saw this as a way of escaping Nazism. Throughout his time at Fox Preminger was a contrary character to deal with, his volatile temperament causing conflict with authority figures such as production chief Darryl Zanuck, and only the success of *Laura* in 1944 established his career there. A film with a distinctly dark tone and cool elegance, *Laura* was his only great noir work. It is set, not on the rough-and-tumble streets of the American city, but in a high-class swanky world of glamour, privilege, and fashion. Through Gene Tierney's playing, the title character, Laura Hunt, becomes one of the signal objects of desire in the noir cycle. Clifton Webb's Waldo Lydecker and other secondary characters have an underlying sexual ambivalence about them. Preminger masterfully balances this effete milieu with the down to earth doggedness of Dana Andrews's sometimes dreamy policeman Mark McPherson.

Preminger did not make a large number of film noirs, although those he made were almost all stylish thrillers. *Fallen Angel* (1945) is involving for most of its length and is atmospheric in its settings but opts for a dull and conventional narrative resolution at the end. In this film, one intriguing twist is that a morally ambivalent man comes to fall in love with the woman he meant to exploit. Some of Preminger's films have a recurring theme of obsession and misunderstanding. This is well delineated in both *Laura* and in his final film noir, *Angel Face* (1952). The protagonist of the latter film, Diane Tremayne, played in mesmerizing fashion by Jean Simmons, is insanely nasty, unlike Laura Hunt, but she remains fascinating and alluring. Diane hardly understands what makes her behave the way she does, an incomprehension that lasts until she dies at her own hand along with her lover. Sometimes criticized for his objective style, with its prolonged takes and paucity of cuts, Preminger was the opposite of someone like Nicholas Ray, who identified himself deeply with his films' romantic characters. Despite this, Preminger was able to elicit affecting acting performances such as those of Gene Tierney in *Whirlpool* (1949) and Dana Andrews in *Where the Sidewalk Ends* (1950). At a more contextual level Otto Preminger was part of the erosion of the power of the Hollywood Production Code in some challenging films he made in the 1950s and 1960s, such as *The Moon Is Blue* (1953), *The Man with the Golden Arm* (1955), and *Anatomy of a Murder* (1959), proving to be a tireless fighter against censorship.

**Selected Noir Films:** *Laura* (1944), *Fallen Angel* (1945), *Whirlpool* (1949), *Where the Sidewalk Ends* (1950), *The 13th Letter* (1951), *Angel Face* (1952).

Brian McDonnell

**THE PROWLER** (Horizon Pictures/United Artists, 1951). *Director:* Joseph Losey. *Producer:* S. P. Eagle (Sam Spiegel). *Script:* Hugo Butler. *Cinematography:* Arthur Miller. *Music:* Lyn Murray. *Cast:* Van Heflin (Webb Garwood), Evelyn Keyes (Susan Gilvray), John Maxwell (Bud Crocker), Katherine Warren (Grace Crocker), Emerson Tracy (William Gilvray), Madge Blake (Martha Gilvray), Wheaton Chambers (Doctor James).

One of the most relentlessly tough and uncompromising of all classical film noirs, Joseph Losey's *The Prowler* creates in its protagonist Webb Garwood, an impressive portrait of an *homme fatale*. James Naremore, in his book *More Than Night: Film Noir in Its Contexts* (p.125), has attributed some of its "despairing tone" to the uncredited influence of blacklisted writer Dalton Trumbo. One of a large group of film noirs about bad cops, including *Where the Sidewalk Ends* (1950), *Rogue Cop* (1954), *Shield for Murder* (1954), and *Pushover* (1954), —even the neo-noir *Unlawful Entry* in 1992—*The Prowler* explores the theme of a man crossing the line from law enforcer to law breaker. While this theme is common in noir, *The Prowler* is less typical than many others because the impression is given that Webb has always had a weak character and has always been tempted to take the easy way. He is therefore a little different from the more honest souls who go astray in other films. When he and his partner attend a nighttime call-out concerning a Peeping Tom at the affluent home of Susan Gilvray, his weak hold on moral probity proves no match for his immediate attraction to her and his desire for a shortcut to an easy life. There is also an undercurrent of voyeurism signaled by the film's opening shot: a man looking at a naked woman through a bathroom window, an image echoed when we see Webb's face in the same window as he investigates the original prowler.

Webb is an all-American guy: well-spoken, handsome, and good at sports, but he has a big chip on his shoulder, having expected to achieve social mobility through his athletic prowess. From the beginning of the film he has an unappealing swagger and smugness to him. He is cocky and full of fresh talk with Susan. Like many sociopaths, Webb is generally resentful of other people and their supposed advantages over him: he talks of people who "had it in" for him, or some setback as being "another one of my lousy breaks." He is a schemer full of blandishments who plays Susan along in a passive-aggressive way, manipulating her love. When Susan's husband is an obstacle, he has no qualms about murdering him and tricking Susan into believing the death was accidental. There are clear class differences between the two lovers dating back to their shared youth in Indiana. But Susan finds Webb far more exciting than her radio announcer husband. They marry after the fuss of the husband's shooting has died down, but the happy start to their married life in his dream motel in Las Vegas is shattered in a plot twist whereby Susan announces that she has been pregnant for several months. Since the husband had been sterile, the publicity of the birth threatens to reveal their affair. This development is discussed in a fairly candid way for Hollywood of the period. Webb's tactic is to secrete Susan away in a desert ghost town until the birth and pretend the baby arrives later than it actually does. The sense of a biological trap is deepened by the geographical dead end of the desert hideout, and the tragic plot plays itself out against sere images of futility, with Webb meeting his fate on the steep slopes of a Sisyphean waste heap.

Alain Silver and Elizabeth Ward say in their book *Film Noir: An Encyclopedic Reference to the American Style* that *The Prowler* is typical of director Joseph Losey's examination of social issues and "reveals the dark underside of the US dream of status and success" (p. 234). Losey's visual style in *The Prowler* has some highly expressive touches, including the mise-en-scène depicting Webb's bachelor room. A very high angle shot of him lying in bed using a light fitting as a basketball hoop emphasizes his pathological lack of emotion when Susan makes distraught phone calls to him during an early break in their relationship. One wall of his room has a police target dominating it, indicating his marksmanship and foreshadowing his shooting of Susan's husband. The sound track, too, is used to intensify the impact of certain scenes. A prophetic emergency vehicle siren is heard as they argue on their wedding night, and monotonous traffic noise outside their motel suite represents the pressure they are already under. Later, at their desert hideout, a recording of the dead husband's voice is accidentally played, an unwelcome reminder of the regrettable events that have brought the couple there. The interlude in the desert prior to the birth is cleverly foreshadowed in early dialogue about ghost towns between Webb and his rock hound police partner, Bud.

Production Code Administration correspondence (written by Joe Breen himself while *The Prowler* was in preproduction) described the moral tone of the script as low, ordered that their attraction should be portrayed as love rather than lust, and insisted that the filmmakers take out a reference to the husband's impotence and remove the discussion about a possible abortion. Characteristically, Breen wanted Susan to be a convincing "voice for morality."

Brian McDonnell

**PUSHOVER** (Columbia, 1954). *Director:* Richard Quine. *Producer:* Jules Schermer. *Script:* Roy Huggins, from stories by Thomas Walsh and William S. Ballinger. *Cinematography:* Lester H. White. *Music:* Arthur Morton. *Cast:* Fred MacMurray (Paul Sheridan), Kim Novak (Lona McLane), Phil Carey (Rick McAllister), Dorothy Malone (Ann), E. G. Marshall (Lt. Carl Eckstrom), Allen Nourse (Paddy Dolan).

At most a minor film noir, 1954's *Pushover* is most notable as an intriguing variation of the prevalent noir topic of a man, in this instance a police detective, breaking the normal constraints of the law and his professional duty for a woman and for money. The fact that the detective is played by Fred MacMurray creates inevitable comparisons with his role as Walter Neff in *Double Indemnity* 10 years earlier. As well as these thematic and character features, the film definitely has a noirish look throughout, set mainly at night in interior spaces such as shadowy rooms and stairways or outside on dimly lit streets. *Pushover* also marked the debut of Kim Novak, who gives early glimpses of the brooding air of mystery and sensuality which were to be exploited more fully by Alfred Hitchcock when she appeared opposite James Stewart in *Vertigo* four years later.

The film's story line features extreme narrative compression, with events concentrated over a few, very action packed nights. After a brief opening scene showing a bank robbery in which a twitchy guard is shot dead, the plot quickly moves to an encounter between Paul Sheriden (MacMurray) and Lona McLane (Novak) outside a movie house. Their apparent chance meeting, which is prompted by her car not starting, leads to a night of sex between the two. We soon learn that Paul is a police detective who has set things up to win the trust of Lona, who is the girlfriend of Harry, the chief bank robber. Paul and his partner, Rick McAllister, are put (along with the alcoholic cop Paddy Dolan) on a stakeout to see if the robber will show up at her apartment. While watching Lona, Rick notices her next-door neighbor Ann (a nurse played by Dorothy Malone) and becomes attracted to her. When Lona discovers the truth about Paul's job, she at first chides him, but then suggests they should kill Harry and take the robbery proceeds ($200,000) for themselves. After some initial misgivings, Paul accedes to her suggestion.

Like Walter Neff in *Double Indemnity*, Paul believes he has every angle covered, but the plan soon unravels. He needs to catch Harry alone, but because the lookout, Paddy, strays into a local bar, Paul is unable to accost Harry unaccompanied.

He has to extemporize and shoots the robber, claiming to Paddy that Harry was about to jump him. Paddy is naturally suspicious, but Paul still thinks smugly that he can get away with everything through his own cunning. Unfortunately for him, things get worse as Ann spots him in Lona's apartment when she calls asking for ice. Desperate to untangle himself, Paul argues with Paddy, who accuses him of exactly the crime he has embarked on, and in a struggle over a pistol, Paddy is killed. From this point on, the trap tightens around Paul, and he is trapped within the investigation (both pursued and pursuer), rather like Ray Milland's character in *The Big Clock*. Rick's suspicions have been raised by Ann's description of the man she saw, and the chief investigator calls in more support to help search for the suspect. Paul makes a wild dash for freedom but is shot down by Rick. He dies with a remorseful Lona attempting to comfort him. In the closing scene, Rick and Ann walk away as a prospective couple.

The main theme of *Pushover* is indicated by the double meaning of the title. The term *pushover* refers both to the notion of a line of behavior being transgressed and to Paul's weak character. He is a pushover for Lona's scheme because of his own cupidity. In an early stakeout scene, Paul and Rick talk about the importance of money. Paul says his parents always fought about it, their quarrelling upsetting him, so that he now wants plenty of it. When he is shot, Lona says belatedly, "We didn't really need that money, did we?" There is also a distinct subtext of voyeurism present in the film, dramatized by the nature of the stakeout. As in *Rear Window* (also 1954), much is made of men looking surreptitiously at women across a courtyard. The police resemble filmgoers as they watch the brightly lit rectangles of the windows of Ann's and Lona's rooms. Furthermore, the film's story clearly sets up parallels and contrasts between the two detectives and between the two women they are interested in. Lona is a femme fatale somewhat softened by Novak's genuine tenderness and fragile demeanor, while Ann is a wholesome, domesticated, nurturing nurse figure given some sex appeal by Malone.

Lona is no Phyllis Dietrichson to Paul's Walter Neff, not only because she is far less vicious than the spider woman of *Double Indemnity*, but because she is so much younger (Novak, at 21, was 25 years McMurray's junior). There is, however, no denying Lona's sexual allure right from her first appearance outside the movie theater. The excitement evident in her husky, sexy voice combines with the forwardness embodied in her frank question: "Want to take me home?" Back at Paul's apartment, they quickly kiss, and Lona is shown to be scantily clad: braless in a dress that is split down the back. When a two-hour delay occurs with her car repairs, she settles down for what is plainly a night of lovemaking, and both Lona and Paul are seen equally to be pushovers.

Brian McDonnell

**RAW DEAL** (Eagle-Lion, 1948). *Director:* Anthony Mann. *Producer:* Edward Small. *Script:* Leopold Atlas and John C. Higgins. *Cinematography:* John Alton. *Music:* Paul Sawtell. *Cast:* Dennis O'Keefe (Joe Sullivan), Claire Trevor (Pat Regan), Marsha Hunt (Ann Martin), John Ireland (Fantail), Raymond Burr (Rick Coyle), Curt Conway (Spider), Chili Williams (Marcy).

*Raw Deal* is a remarkable example of the creative tensions that can energize classical film noir. It combines the toughness of the male criminal world, including some of the most brutal violence of that period in Hollywood, with the foregrounding of a woman's point of view by including a rare example of a female voice-over narration. Made at the short-lived British/U.S. production house Eagle-Lion, *Raw Deal* is hugely advantaged by the fact that director Anthony Mann and cinematographer John Alton were working together at the peak of their stylistic powers. Its existential main character is drawn through an insurmountable series of events to his doom so that he very much comes to embody the raw deal of the title.

The film opens with an eerie and somewhat stilted sequence at the state prison. The voice of narrator Pat is heard on the sound track backed by ethereal theremin music. She is at the jail to arrange the escape of her lover Joe but is disconcerted to find that he has another female visitor. This is Ann, a paralegal who has formed an interest in his case—and an attraction to him. After the escape, certain setbacks force Joe and Pat to take Ann with them. Joe is trying to reach San Francisco, where his criminal boss, Rick, operates a casino on Corkscrew Alley. Scenes in the casino reveal that Rick has actually facilitated the initial breakout in the hopes that Joe will be killed. His sadistic nature is also highlighted by his casual brutality toward a girlfriend. The film's central sequences are thus intercut between the threesome on the run and events in San Francisco, where Rick tries to have Joe intercepted by his henchmen. One of these goons, Fantail, has a vicious fight with Joe and is shot by Ann, whose attachment to Joe has been building during their flight from the authorities. She is later abducted by the wounded Fantail and taken to Rick's place. Pat hears of this and faces the dilemma of whether or not to tell Joe. Eventually, she does so, even though Ann is her rival for his love. Joe heads off to Corkscrew Alley to rescue Ann, but after managing to kill Rick, he himself dies.

*Raw Deal* reiterates the noir catch cry that there is no escape from your fate. It is full of images of entrapment such as roadblocks and brief sieges. It has an emphasis on pursuit and is permeated by a sense of the pursuers closing in. The central relationships feature subtle shifts in their dynamics. Ann is morally compromised when she shoots Fantail, but overall, she stands for decency. She has a definite code of behavior, which she tries to have Joe adopt. Ann admires his childhood heroism when he saved some other kids from a fire. Telling him that her upbringing was as tough as his, she helps ensure that the film's theme of determinism is not too overt. However, Joe remains steadfast in wanting to get revenge on Rick, for whom he had taken the original fall that brought him to prison. Like other noir heroes before him, Joe decides Ann is too good for him and that staying with him will only ruin her prospects. Although he does not love Pat, he suggests a life together for them, even talking of a marriage at sea. His remark to her that he wants to do "the whole thing right" pricks Pat's conscience, and she tells him of Ann's predicament. In spite of his ingenious sneak entry into the casino, Rick treacherously shoots him, and they fight at the center of a searing fire. Amid the flames, Rick topples to his death through a window, and Joe hears a hammering noise, which leads him to Ann. He rescues Ann from the fire in a scene that anticipates the ending of *Kiss Me Deadly*. He is badly wounded and dies in Ann's arms, while Pat watches, realizing he is happy at last. Joe's final words are "I got my breath of fresh air."

Joe is played with appropriate gruffness by Dennis O'Keefe, who was like a poor man's Dana Andrews in several low-budget noirs. The two women are contrasted, and both Claire Trevor and Marsha Hunt are effective in showing the way they chafe each other. In a similar manner to many of his other film noir appearances, Raymond Burr as Rick makes a very impressive heavy. Often seen in a dressing gown, he seems effete, but this surface impression masks his violent nature. He is sadistically cruel to his girlfriend when, in annoyance at a trifle, he tosses a burning dessert over her. Rick also threatens to torture Ann with a cigarette lighter, making him one of the nastiest villains in the classical noir canon. In fact, *Raw Deal* is one of the most violent films of its time, with the fight between Fantail and Joe containing an attack with a broken bottle and a man being pushed onto the antlers of a stuffed animal head. The shock effect of these moments is to no small degree made even more emphatic by the stark black-and-white images created by ace cinematographer John Alton.

Brian McDonnell

**RAY, NICHOLAS** (1911–1979). Viewed by his admirers as an engaged and committed director of young passion, Nicholas Ray came to be identified with the misfits and vagrants, the romantic couples, who people his films. While many in the public would link his name primarily to James Dean and *Rebel Without a Cause* (1955), Ray actually made a surprisingly large number of films that have come to be included in the canon of classical film noir. Born Raymond Nicholas Kienzle in Wisconsin, his precocious skills as a writer gave him a scholarship to the University of Chicago. There he studied architecture with Frank Lloyd Wright (his architectural training was later said to have helped his widescreen CinemaScope compositions), then moved on to political theater and radio in New York working with Elia Kazan and John Houseman. Ray went out to Hollywood in 1945 as assistant director to Elia Kazan on *A Tree Grows in Brooklyn*. He served an apprenticeship at RKO, and his first film as a full director was *They Live by Night* (produced in 1947 but released in 1948). Adapted from the 1937 Edward Anderson novel *Thieves Like Us*, it was the poignant tale of a young criminal, Bowie, on the run along with his naïve girlfriend, Keetchie. Owing to Ray's manifold talents, it became one of the great directorial debuts of all time. The original novel had been a radical critique of America in which Keetchie and the baby died, along with Bowie, at the end. Marxist critics disliked the lack of social analysis and determinism in Ray's version, but film noir is actually more about entrapment, victimization, and an inability to escape the past than it is about confidence in the perfectibility of human beings. Ray showed a passionate identification with his characters, in contrast to Fritz Lang's distancing techniques in telling a similar story in *You Only Live Once* (1937). *They Live by Night* emphasized how Ray's romanticism could work against noir's pervasive bleakness and it established his continuing interest in lonely young innocents, anxious outsiders, and solitary misfits.

His 1949 film *Knock on Any Door*, which, on release, was viewed as a sizzling exposé, today seems to be preachy and stagy, as is evidenced in the very long address to the jury by attorney Humphrey Bogart, which leads to several extended flashbacks. On the other hand, Ray's brilliant *On Dangerous Ground* (1952) stands up extremely well. It is very much a film of two unlike halves. The first is a noirish portrayal of a bustling city where a brutal cop (Jim, played by Robert Ryan) chases baddies along darkened streets. The second is a fable of a man's redemption through the ministry of a blind woman (Ida Lupino) set in a snowy mountainous region virtually devoid of people. While resisting the temptation to depict a facile change in Jim, Ray had a happy ending pressed on him by the studio and the film's stars, both of whom were operating at the peak of their powers.

However, Ray's most personal film in the noir style (and perhaps his greatest achievement in the genre) was *In a Lonely Place* (1950), which starred his wife, Gloria Grahame, from whom he was at the time in the process of separating. Made for Humphrey Bogart's Santana Productions, it showed a different side of the star in the central role of script writer Dix Steele, a violent, contradictory figure who owed a lot to Ray's own personality. Ray said subsequently, "I was the man who took the gun out of Bogart's hand." *In a Lonely Place* is unparalleled in film noir for its poignancy and its complex and convincing dramatization of love between a man and a woman.

**Selected Noir Films:** *They Live by Night* (1948, and adaptation), *Knock on Any Door* (1949), *In a Lonely Place* (1950), *The Racket* (1951, uncredited), *On Dangerous Ground* (1952, and adaptation), *Macao* (1952, uncredited), *Bigger Than Life* (1956), *Party Girl* (1958).

Brian McDonnell

**THE RECKLESS MOMENT** (Columbia, 1949). *Director:* Max Ophuls. *Producer:* Walter Wanger. *Script:* Henry Garson and Robert W. Soderberg, from the short story "The Blank Wall" by Elisabeth Sanxay Holding. *Cinematography:* Burnett Guffey. *Music:* Hans Salter. *Cast:* James Mason (Martin Donnelly), Joan Bennett (Lucia Harper), Geraldine Brooks (Bee Harper), Henry O'Neil (Mr. Harper), Shepperd Strudwick (Ted Darby), David Bair (David Harper), Roy Roberts (Nagle), Frances Williams (Sybil).

Long undervalued in many surveys of the classical noir cycle because of its surface resemblance to a woman's melodrama, *The Reckless Moment* is now gaining wide appreciation as one of the most significant and accomplished examples of noir themes and preoccupations being played out in a film narrative. In its dramatization of the plight of protagonist Lucia Harper, it provides one of the deepest and most subtle portrayals of a woman caught between respectability and crime to be found in any film noir of the classical period. In achieving this, it is a good example of the subgenre of the woman-centered noir story similar to *Mildred Pierce* or *The Blue Gardenia*. Max Ophuls (credited here as Max Opuls) combines the sustained atmosphere of melodramatic domestic anguish that he had perfected in films such as *Letter from an Unknown Woman* (1948) with a sordid urban milieu of felonious intent, violence, and immoral behavior.

A brief anonymous voice-over opens the film, setting the scene as the fictional suburban boating community of Balboa Island on the southern edge of Los Angeles and introducing Lucia as a mother going into the city to extricate her teenage daughter from an unsuitable relationship. Lucia warns off the middle-aged Ted Darby, and he responds by attempting to be paid for his trouble. He visits the 17-year-old daughter Beatrice (Bee), argues with her in the family's boathouse, then falls through a rotten balustrade unseen by Bee, who retreats into the house. Early the following morning, Lucia finds Ted's dead body on the sand: he has impaled himself on an anchor. Fearing that Bee had pushed him, Lucia dumps the body across the lagoon. She has to act alone as her engineer husband is absent overseas. Lucia's situation becomes more complicated when a man called Donnelly arrives from the city and demands $5,000 for Bee's love letters to Darby. Without her husband's authorizing signature, she is unable to raise the cash. There is a plot twist when Donnelly tells her that it does not matter about the money as another criminal has been arrested for the murder. Donnelly, who has become attracted to Lucia, claims that he wants to abandon his ideas of extortion but says that his unscrupulous partner, Nagle, still wants the money. When Nagle comes to the boathouse to pressure Lucia, he and Donnelly fight. Nagle dies in the struggle, and despite Lucia's plans to belatedly contact the police, a bleeding Donnelly drives off with Nagle's corpse. He is mortally injured in a car crash and makes a false dying confession that he had also killed Darby. Lucia's plight is ended, but she has been deeply affected by all that has happened.

The main theme of *The Reckless Moment* concerns the multiple pressures on a mother and how she copes, especially with an absent husband. Lucia has to negotiate with crooks while she wrangles the boisterous members of her family. The fact that Christmas is approaching only adds to the pressures on her. A second theme is that indicated by the film's title: a good person can transgress the law through a momentary lapse of judgment or through a hasty decision. The figure of Donnelly conveys yet another message: that any human being, no matter how compromised by a life of crime, can have a change of heart. Donnelly's softening toward Lucia may seem unlikely, but it is made much more credible by the thoughtful performance of James Mason in the role. Lucia herself is a very interesting character, pragmatic and resourceful, as when she discovers Darby's body and has the presence of mind to swiftly hide it in a suspenseful and wordless Hichcockian sequence. She is unable even to cable her husband for advice and support because of the public nature of such communication. The difficulties for a woman of accessing money at that time are stressed by showing Lucia's descent through several social layers as she seeks a loan. Lucia goes first to her bank, then to an unhelpful loan company, and finally to a pawn shop, where she is appraised of the harsh facts of life affecting those whose need for cash is desperate.

Ordinary American families do not feature greatly in film noir, where many of the characters lead solitary and isolated lives. *The Reckless Moment* is a striking exception, with Lucia having to be the main support for her children and having to keep her household running as well as dealing with the unwelcome incursion of crime into her life. Donnelly calls Lucia a "prisoner," adding that "family can surround you." She demurs by claiming that "everyone has a mother like me." Interestingly, Donnelly becomes a truly noir figure of moral ambivalence through his contact with Lucia, caught between her goodness and the evil of Nagle. He sides with Lucia's virtue when he kills Nagle, and this allegiance is stressed by the intimacy of their pose as she kneels over him trying to help at the scene of the car crash. His last words to her are "have courage."

Max Ophuls creates a visual language that greatly aides the impact of his messages in the film. He sets up a sharp visual contrast between the clean open spaces of Balboa Island and the much less respectable interiors of the city scenes. When Lucia goes to visit Darby or when Donnelly seeks out Nagle, these visits occur in seedy bars full of gamblers, brassy blondes, and drunks. The boathouse is dark and sinister, and in the nighttime fight between Nagle and Donnelly, the shadows of windblown trees shiver on the walls. At a strictly domestic level Ophuls makes of Lucia's house a complex warren full of obstacles and winding staircases. Lucia is frequently photographed through the barrier of banisters, no more emphatically than in the film's final scene, where she talks to her absent husband in Berlin. She suppresses the urge to unburden herself of all that has happened and merely wishes him a merry Christmas.

The basic storyline of *The Reckless Moment* was used again in the 2001 neonoir film *The Deep End,* in which Tilda Swinton plays the Joan Bennett role, Goran Visnjic the James Mason role, and the teenage child (now a boy) has a homosexual affair rather than a heterosexual one.

Brian McDonnell

**RIDE THE PINK HORSE** (Universal International, 1947). *Director:* Robert Montgomery. *Producer:* Joan Harrison. *Script:* Ben Hecht and Charles Lederer, from the novel by Dorothy Hughes. *Cinematography:* Russell Metty. *Music:* Frank Skinner. *Cast:* Robert Montgomery (Lucky Gagin), Wanda Hendrix (Pila), Thomas Gomez (Pancho), Andrea King (Marjorie), Art Smith (Bill Retz), Fred Clark (Frank Hugo), Richard Gaines (Jonathan).

A pervasive sense of alienation from mainstream society is a recurring motif in film noir in the 1940s. It also dominates Dorothy Hughes's 1946 novel *Ride the Pink Horse* as well as the 1947 film adaptation. Gagin, an ex-GI, believes that he "fought a war for three years and got nothing out of it but a dangle of ribbons." He arrives in a small New Mexico town during the annual fiesta to blackmail a mobster, Fred Hugo, into giving him $30,000. In exchange, Gagin offers Hugo possession of a check that implicates the mobster in a criminal conspiracy involving a corrupt politician. During the protracted negotiations Gagin is followed around the town by Bill Retz, an FBI agent.

When he is unable to secure a hotel booking, Gagin is forced to seek shelter and assistance among the disenfranchised members of the town, such as the young Indian girl Pila, who attaches herself to the ex-GI, and Pancho, who operates an amusement ride, the Tio Vivo Carousel, for young children. This carousel provides the film's dominant metaphor involving the irrationality of the universe and Gagin's inability to discern his place in it. Just like the carousel, Gagin goes around and around seeking, but unable to achieve, his objective. When Pila asks him which horse she should ride in the carousel he tells her to take the pink one—it does not matter to him which direction you select as you always seem to end up in the same place. Pila, on the other hand, recognizes the significance of the pink horse as she knows that all actions have significance, and because of this belief, she is able to protect Gagin and restore his belief in a moral universe and an ordered society. This represents a significant change in the film compared with the novel as Hughes's story ends with Gagin running wildly away from the town in complete disarray, while the film traces Gagin's regeneration as he hands over the evidence to Retz.

*Ride the Pink Horse* is a strange film. With Robert Montgomery as director and star, the claustrophobic, studio-bound setting captures Gagin's sense of entrapment in the novel—forever repeating his journey in a futile attempt to establish meaning in his life. Unable to find lodging in the local hotel, Gagin goes to a Mexican bar, the patrons of which initially express only hostility to the American. However, away from the corrupt, dissolute lifestyle of the luxurious hotel, his redemption begins when he befriends the impoverished Pancho and the virginal Pila. Gradually, his bitterness and mercenary ambitions recede, and when Hugo repudiates these values, Gagin joins forces with the police, foregoing the $30,000 that prompted his journey in the first place.

Geoff Mayer

**ROADBLOCK** (RKO, 1951). *Director:* Harold Daniels. *Producer:* Lewis J. Rachmil. *Script:* Steve Fisher and George Bricker. *Cinematography:* Nicholas Musuraca. *Music:* Paul Sawtell. *Cast:* Charles McGraw (Joe Peters), Joan Dixon (Diane Marley), Lowell Gilmore (Kendall Webb), Louis Jean Heydt (Harry Miller), Milburn Stone (Egan), Joseph Crehan (Thompson).

Designed, like many other low-budget dramas of the 1940s and 1950s, to fill the bottom half of a double bill, this film is an above-average example of an RKO B crime melodrama. Its visual style is enhanced (particularly in the action sequences) by the participation of cinematographer Nicholas Musuraca, a master of film noir lighting (see *Out of the Past* [1947]). *Roadblock* is also a rare example of tough character actor Charles McGraw appearing in a leading role. McGraw plays Joe Peters, an honest insurance investigator who turns bad, a variation on the common noir theme of police officers corrupted by sex and money. Joan Dixon plays Diane, the beautiful and sexy woman who tempts him to betray his loyalty to the firm employing him. When the two first become involved, a theme of avarice quickly emerges, with her telling Joe that she likes to "travel first class" and that in her material ambitions she is "aiming for the World Series." Envious of her conspicuously affluent and smoothly spoken racketeer boyfriend, Kendall Webb, Joe feels that he, too, must become rich to win Diane's love. He decides to steal a fortune in currency insured by his own company by supplying inside information to Webb on its shipment by train.

McGraw is thus morally weaker here than in his usual noir roles and becomes a typical trapped noir protagonist (as in the double meaning of the film's title),

*Roadblock* (1951). Directed by Harold Daniels. Shown: Charles McGraw (as Joe Peters), Joan Dixon (as Diane Marley). RKO Radio Pictures/Photofest.

tempted by an alluring combination of sex and riches. The story's chief irony is that Diane could have been gained by Joe without any need for criminality. While early dialogue describes her as a "chiseller," and while even Joe distrusts her sincerity, she later finds a conscience and changes from her mercenary ways. After making repeated claims that he is too underpaid to afford someone like her, Diane visits Joe's flat and says that money does not matter; but it is too late for her honesty to have a good effect as he is already inextricably involved in planning the hijacking. He cannot pull out, even though she declares herself to be crazy about him. In contrast to her character shift toward morality (perhaps a result of Production Code Administration influences on the script), he changes the other way, from "Honest Joe" to someone who betrays his employer and eventually even commits murder.

Instead of containing the sort of surprise ending common in the noir genre, *Roadblock* includes an opening twist in which the audience believes that McGraw is a killer until he reveals himself to be an insurance investigator. The film begins with a nighttime shooting in which Joe guns down a man in front of a startled bystander. He then threatens the witness, who pleads for his life by telling Joe about a nearby stash of cash. When this is produced, the apparently dead man turns up alive, and he and Joe arrest the "witness" for insurance fraud. In actual fact, two scams occur at the start of the film: as well as Joe's playacting to locate the missing money, Diane, at her first appearance, plays a duplicitous trick on Joe at the Cincinnati airport. Despite being a total stranger, she pretends to an airline agent (in a clever product placement for RKO boss Howard Hughes's airline TWA) that she is Joe's wife to gain a cut-price ticket to Los Angeles. The couple are thrown closer together by fate when a storm forces their plane to land in Missouri. As an apparently married couple, they are roomed together in a hotel (a rather risqué topic for a 1950s film), where they get to know each other better, and Joe is set on his course of transgression. When he next encounters Diane, she is dressed symbolically in a sumptuous fur coat supplied by her criminal boyfriend, but the film emphasizes the emptiness of her life as a rich man's mistress by showing her alone at Christmas beside a forlorn Christmas tree while Webb is away with his family.

Joe's wrongdoing escalates after the train robbery when he murders Webb, rendering the protagonist's actions beyond the pale even for his friend and partner Harry Miller. Joe the investigator now comes under the insurance company's scrutiny himself, and his own team's efficiency gets him in the end. The film culminates in a police chase filmed in exciting semidocumentary style, and in the film's downbeat ending, the roadblocks of the title eventually entrap Joe in the maze of the concrete-bound course of the Los Angeles River. The high and steep sides of the riverbed symbolize the blockage of his desire for escape, and while attempting to scale them, he is gunned down in front of a distraught Diane.

Brian McDonnell

**ROBINSON, EDWARD G.** (1893–1973). Edward G. Robinson was the third film star to benefit from the success of *Double Indemnity* in 1944. This film regenerated Robinson's film career, and he remained a prominent actor for the next 30 years. Robinson was born Emmanuel Goldenberg in 1893 in Romania, and he accompanied his parents to the United States when he was 10 years old. Robinson chose an acting career, rejecting his initial ambition to be a rabbi or lawyer after studying at City College in New York. He received his initial training in summer stock companies before making his Broadway debut in 1915, where he remained for the next 15 years.

Goldenberg changed his name to Robinson at the beginning of his acting career, and while he appeared in a couple of silent films, he did not express any interest in Hollywood until after the advent of sound. Following his performance as Rico, the gangster boss in Warner Bros.'s 1931 film *Little Caesar*, Robinson became a major star, and his performance provided the prototype for the screen gangster for many years. However, he was not confined to gangster roles, and throughout the 1930s he demonstrated his versatility in films such as *Five Star Final* (1931), *Tiger Shark* (1932), *Confessions of a Nazi Spy* (1939), and *Dr. Ehrlich's Magic Bullet* (1940), where Robinson starred as a nineteenth-century German scientist who develops a cure for venereal disease, and as the sadistic, intellectual sea captain Wolf Larsen in Warner's 1941 version of Jack London's *The Sea Wolf*.

In the early 1940s Robinson's film career began to wane, and initially, he rejected the role of Barton Keyes in *Double Indemnity* because he was the third listed actor after Barbara Stanwyck and Fred MacMurray. However, as he was now more than 50 years of age, he reconsidered his decision and reasoned that if he was going to transform his career from film star to character actor, he would not find a better role. His success in *Double Indemnity* restored his status in Hollywood, and he soon starred in noir films such as *The Woman in the Window* (1944) and *Scarlet Street* (1945).

In the 1950s his career suffered as a result of the anti-Communist witch hunt, and he was forced to appear before the House Committee on Un-American Activities. Also, his personal life was affected by his divorce in 1956 when he was forced to sell his large art collection as part of the settlement. In 1956 he costarred in *Nightmare* as the tough policeman who solves the murder involving his brother-in-law in Maxwell Shane's remake of his 1947 film *Fear in the Night*. Robinson's last film was the 1973 science fiction thriller *Soylent Green*, and he died two weeks after completing his scenes.

**Selected Noir Films:** *The Sea Wolf* (1941), *Manpower* (1941), *Double Indemnity* (1944), *The Woman in the Window* (1944), *Scarlet Street* (1945), *The Stranger* (1946), *The Red House* (1947), *Key Largo* (1948), *Night Has a Thousand Eyes* (1948), *House of Strangers* (1949), *Vice Squad* (1953), *Hell on Frisco Bay* (1955), *The Violent Men* (1955), *Tight Spot* (1955), *A Bullet for Joey* (1955), *Illegal* (1955), *Nightmare* (1956).

Geoff Mayer

**THE ROCKING HORSE WINNER** (Two Cities/Rank, 1949). *Director:* Anthony Pelissier. *Producer:* John Mills. *Script:* Anthony Pelissier, based on the story by D. H. Lawrence. *Cinematography:* Desmond Dickinson. *Music:* William Alwyn. *Cast:* Valerie Hobson (Hester Grahame), John Howard Davies (Paul Grahame), Ronald Squire (Oscar Cresswell), John Mills (Bassett), Hugh Sinclair (Richard Grahame), Charles Goldner (Mr. Tsaldouris), Susan Richards (Nannie), Cyril Smith (Bailiff).

In 1949 John Mills produced and acted in two films for Rank. The second, *The Rocking Horse Winner*, is a bizarre film. Based on a story by D. H. Lawrence, this cautionary fable warns of the dangers of greed and the disastrous effects it has on a family. Hester Grahame's greedy, materialistic desires not only emasculate her husband (Richard), but also kill her son Paul. As her demands intensify, Paul begins hearing voices within the house, and the only way he can silence them is to ride his rocking horse in a frenzied manner, whipping his horse as he throws himself about in the saddle. This behavior not only silences the voices (temporarily), but also enables Paul to pick the winner of forthcoming horse races. Eventually, his riding kills him.

*The Rocking Horse Winner* functions as a morality play, warning of the dangers of material excess by showing how maternal greed and family disharmony cause the death of an innocent young boy. At this level, the meaning of the film is clear. Hester, whose affection for Paul and her other children is subsumed by her desire for wealth, learns that her greed directly killed her son—hence she refuses to touch Paul's winnings (£80,000), and director Anthony Pelissier closes the film in a redemptive manner by showing the distressed Hester, dressed in black with her hair pulled tightly to her head, watching Paul's rocking horse burn. However, there is a symbolic dimension to the film concerned with the financially and sexually impotent father, the frustrated mother—it is Hester's distorted voice within the house that disturbs Paul—and Paul's masturbatory riding of his rocking horse. It is only Paul's ability to produce wealth from his racing predictions, resulting from his frenzied riding, that can satisfy Hester—all the other men in her life are symbolically impotent, due to financial weakness (her husband), age and kinship (her brother Oscar), or class differences (Bassett, the family handyman). In a period of strict censorship, *The Rocking Horse Winner* is a fascinating film that weaves its disturbing ramifications within a symbolic form not common in the British cinema in the late 1940s.

Geoff Mayer

**RYAN, ROBERT** (1909–1973). Ryan's angular, sharp facial features, his ability to convincingly suggest violence and a seething hatred, meant that he, after an initial phase, was more often cast as a villain or, at least, a morally problematic protagonist. Yet the same man who could brilliantly portray an anti-Semite bigot in *Crossfire* (1947) was a resolute liberal throughout his entire life, a man who did not waver in his social and political convictions, even at the height of the anti-Communist hysteria in the late 1940s and 1950s, and even when costarring with Hollywood's most trenchant political conservative, John Wayne, in Nicholas Ray's wartime aerial melodrama *Flying Leathernecks* (1951).

Robert Ryan was born in Chicago and educated at Dartmouth College, where he was its heavyweight boxing champion for four years—which gave him credibility for his favorite role as the over-the-hill boxer "Stoker" Thompson in *The Set-Up* (1949). Ryan graduated in 1932, intending to establish himself as a playwright. However, finding work as a playwright during the Depression years was difficult, and to support himself, he worked at a number of different jobs, including stoking coal on a ship traveling to Africa and herding horses in Montana. He joined a theater group in Chicago and began acting, making his professional stage debut in 1940. He also made his screen debut at Paramount in 1940 in *Queen of the Mob*, followed by small roles in *The Ghost Breakers* (1940), *Golden Gloves* (1940), *Texas Rangers Ride Again* (1940), and *Northwest Mounted Police* (1940).

Paramount did not show any interest in Ryan, and he returned to the stage. While appearing in *A Kiss for Cinderella* with Luise Rainer, her husband, Clifford

Odets, offered Ryan the part of Joe Boyle in his Broadway production of *Clash by Night*, starring legendary actress Tallulah Bankhead. Ryan also appeared in Fritz Lang's film version 11 years later, although he was now too old to play Boyle and instead costarred as Earl Pfeiffer opposite Barbara Stanwyck. After receiving good reviews for the Broadway production, RKO signed Ryan to a contract and placed him in the aerial film *Bombardier* (1943), followed by a series of supporting roles in war-related films. In 1944 Ryan joined the U.S. Marines, and he did not return to RKO until 1947, when he was cast in Jean Renoir's final American film, *The Woman on the Beach* (1947), a poetic, albeit incoherent, domestic melodrama. However, Ryan's powerful performance as the rabid anti-Semitic soldier in *Crossfire* changed his career, and only rarely would Ryan play a straightforward character in subsequent years.

The late 1940s was a rich period for Ryan. He followed *Crossfire* with two films for RKO: Jacques Tourneur's espionage drama *Berlin Express* (1948) and *The Boy with the Green Hair* (1948), Joseph Losey's cinematic plea for tolerance. Two of MGM's best noir films of the 1940s followed: in Fred Zinnemann's *Act of Violence* (1949), Ryan is a bitter ex-army veteran determined to punish the man, Van Heflin, who betrayed his colleagues in a German prisoner of war camp; in *Caught* (1949) Ryan is compelling in Max Ophuls's visually splendid film noir dealing with spousal abuse. As the psychologically disturbed Smith Olrig, Ryan is at his neurotic best tormenting Barbara Bel Geddes. *The Set-Up* ended a rich period for Ryan.

Although Ryan worked steadily throughout the 1950s, most of his roles were simplistic variations of the characters he played after World War II. One exception was Roy Ward Baker's *Inferno* (1953), which was filmed in Apple Valley on the edge of the Mojave Desert in 3-D. This story of regeneration starred Ryan as Donald Carson, a wealthy, selfish man left to die in the desert with a broken leg by his wife (Rhonda Fleming) and her lover (William Lundigan). As most of the film focused on Carson alone in the desert, the actor and director had to convey the story through Ryan's physical actions and reactions as well as through his voice-over. The fact that the film is so successful is a tribute to Ryan's skill as an actor as well as to the visual capabilities of Baker, ably assisted by one of Hollywood's finest cameramen, Lucien Ballard.

Other highlights in the 1950s included *Bad Day at Black Rock* (1955) and Sam Fuller's crime film set in Japan, *House of Bamboo* (1955), although both films only offer Ryan an opportunity to reprise the psychotic villain he had perfected in earlier films. An exception was *On Dangerous Ground* (1952), Nicholas Ray's story of redemption, with Ryan as the troubled cop dispatched to the country where he eventually finds peace and salvation. However, Ryan was becoming disillusioned with most of the roles offered to him. To find diversity, he had to return to the stage, which he did frequently throughout the 1950s and 1960s.

Ryan remained one of America's most respected actors. In 1971 he starred on stage as James Tyrone in a revival of *Long Day's Journey into Night*, and he followed this in 1973 in the cinema with the role of Larry Slade in John Frankenheimer's film adaptation of *The Iceman Cometh*, even though he knew, while filming, that he was dying of lung cancer. His role as the terminally ill political activist was an appropriate end for a man who had championed progressive causes throughout his life yet was mostly cast in roles that represented the antithesis of the values he believed in.

**Selected Noir Films:** *The Woman on the Beach* (1947), *Crossfire* (1947), *Berlin Express* (1948), *Act of Violence* (1949), *Caught* (1949), *The Set-Up* (1949), *The Woman on Pier 13* (1949), *Born to Be Bad* (1950), *The Secret Fury* (1950), *The Racket* (1951), *On Dangerous Ground* (1952), *Clash by Night* (1952), *Beware, My Lovely* (1952), *The Naked Spur* (1953), *Inferno* (1953), *Bad Day for Black Rock* (1955), *House of Bamboo* (1955), *Odds against Tomorrow* (1959), *The Outfit* (1973).

Geoff Mayer

**SAVAGE, ANN** (1921–). More vicious than Barbara Stanwyck in *Double Indemnity* (1944), more sensual than Jane Greer in *Out of the Past* (1947), Ann Savage's performance in *Detour* (1945) as the harridan who makes Tom Neal's life a misery should have catapulted Savage into A list films—instead, it marked the high point of a decade-long career.

Ann Savage was born Bernice Maxine Lyon in South Carolina, although her father, a jeweler, kept the family moving. Finally, after they had settled in Dallas, Texas, he ran off with another woman. After a teenage marriage with a Norwegian hot rod fanatic, and a quickie divorce, Bernice took a job at Max Reinhardt's acting school in Los Angeles under an arrangement with the school's manager, Bert D'Armand, that her wage would pay the tuition for her acting lessons.

Talent scouts from Columbia Studios and Twentieth Century Fox chased Bernice for her signature, and following D'Armand's advice, she signed with Columbia. D'Armand also suggested that Bernice change her name to Ann Savage. After modeling for the requisite studio "cheesecake" photos, Columbia put Savage to work in low-budget series films, including *One Dangerous Night* (1943), which was part of their Lone Wolf series starring Warren William, and *After Midnight with Boston Blackie* (1943), starring Chester Morris as the former jewel thief and con artist turned detective. Savage also costarred in two low-budget westerns with Russell Hayden, and when she began dating the actor, who was in the midst of divorce proceedings, studio executives told Savage to stay away from him. Savage, however, ignored the studio.

Columbia continued to build Savage's career with lead roles in low-budget films such as *Klondike Kate* (1943), the first of four films Savage would star in opposite Tom Neal. *Klondike Kate* was a dramatization of the life of Kate Rockwell Matson, a real-life larger than life character involved in the 1890s Alaskan gold rush, and Columbia's decision to cast Savage in this role indicated that at this stage, the studio was serious about building her career. They also hired glamour photographer George Hurrell to shoot Savage in a series of pin-ups, and one of the photos appeared in the March 1944 issue of *Esquire* magazine. However, after suffering pneumonia during the filming of the war film *Two Man Submarine* (1943), opposite Tom Neal, Savage verbally abused the first assistant director because he insisted that she jump into a cold studio tank when she had a heavy cold. The intensity of her abuse damaged her standing at the studio. Her reputation was damaged even further in 1944 and 1945 following adverse publicity after her two-month (unconsummated) marriage to a gay film editor was terminated.

When Columbia decided not to renew her contract, Savage accepted a two-picture deal with PRC after Tom Neal, who was working at PRC, recommended her to Leon Fromkess, the head of production at the studio. Edgar Ulmer, the talented director who was churning out low-budget films at the studio, immediately cast her as Vera in *Detour*. Even though Vera only appears in the second half of the film, Savage realized that this was a major chance and threw herself into the role. With stringy hair, a result of the judicious application of cold cream to her luxuriant mane, a constantly strident voice, and a less than glamorous wardrobe, Savage was immortalized as one of the screen's most vicious femmes fatales. Ulmer encouraged this change and insisted that she deliver her dialogue at a rapid, breathless pace. Savage was so successful in her transformation that when her husband, Bert D'Armand, tried to promote Savage's career with screenings of *Detour,* producers and filmmakers were shocked at her appearance.

Savage followed *Detour* with another strong performance as Toni Kirkland in *Apology for Murder* (1945), PRC's noir film that copied *Double Indemnity* so closely that Paramount insisted that the film be removed from circulation soon after its release. Hence Savage's two best roles, for different reasons, failed to ignite her career. If these films had been produced and distributed by a major studio, even Columbia, Savage's career may have extended beyond the early 1950s. However, PRC was at the bottom of the Hollywood barrel, its films were rarely reviewed, and they received only limited distribution in third-rate theaters.

Savage's career went nowhere after *Apology for Murder.* A starring role in a noir film at Republic, *The Last Crooked Mile* (1946), costarring cowboy star Don "Red" Barry, followed by a programmer at Universal, *The Dark Horse* (1946), and a starring role in another noir film at PRC, *Lady Chaser* (1946). Savage's best role during this period was a characteristically forceful character, Jean Shelby, in the western *Renegade Girl* (1946). However, by 1949, Savage was relegated to roles in low-budget series films such as the Cisco Kid series, where she costarred in *Satan's Cradle* (1949), and worse was to come the next year with her role in *Jungle Jim in Pygmy Island* (1950) as Captain Ann Kinglsey, a Women's Auxiliary Corps captain lost in the jungle and dependent on Jungle Jim and a tribe of white pygmies to rescue her.

With her film career finished, Savage appeared in a few television plays and series before giving up completely in 1953 and leaving Hollywood with her husband, D'Armand. An appearance in an episode of *The Ford Television Theatre* in 1955 and a supporting role as Sister Harriet in the low-budget romantic film *Fire with Fire*, starring Craig Sheffer and Virginia Madsen, in 1986 completed Savage's acting career. The three days she spent shooting *Detour* in June 1945 were the pinnacle of her career.

**Selected Noir Films:** *One Dangerous Night* (1943), *After Midnight with Boston Blackie* (1943), *Murder in Times Square* (1943), *Passport to Suez* (1943), *Dangerous Blondes* (1943), *Scared Stiff* (1945), *Midnight Manhunt* (1945), *Detour* (1945), *Apology for Murder* (1945), *The Spider* (1945), *The Dark Horse* (1946), *The Last Crooked Mile* (1946), *Lady Chaser* (1946), *Pier 23* (1951).

Geoff Mayer

**SCANDAL SHEET** (Columbia, 1952). *Director:* Phil Karlson. *Producer:* Edward Small. *Script:* Eugene Ling, James Poe, and Ted Sherdeman, based on the novel *The Dark Page* by Samuel Fuller. *Cinematography:* Burnett Guffey. *Music:* George Duning. *Cast:* Broderick Crawford (Mark Chapman), Donna Reed (Julie Allison), John Derek (Steve McCleary), Rosemary DeCamp (Charlotte Grant), Henry O'Neill (Charlie Barnes), Harry Morgan (Biddle), James Millican (Lieutenant Davis), Griff Barnett (Judge Hacker).

Prior to the United States entering World War II, Sam Fuller began writing the source novel for *Scandal Sheet*, *The Dark Page*, based on his experiences as a journalist on Park Row in the late 1920s and early 1930s,. After its publication in 1944, Howard Hawks bought the rights and tried to interest Warner Bros. in a film version starring Edward G. Robinson as the editor of a New York tabloid newspaper who, after murdering his wife, is exposed as a the killer by his favorite reporter, played by Humphrey Bogart. When Hawks was unable to get a green light from the studio, he sold the film rights to Columbia for six times the amount he paid Fuller.

Although Fuller was unhappy with the resultant film, as he often was with anything he did not write or direct himself, *Scandal Sheet* retains his fascination with the power and exploitative tactics used by tabloid newspapers to boost circulation. The film begins with a young reporter, Steve McCleary, deceiving a witness to a brutal murder by encouraging her to believe that he is a police detective. McCleary's tactics are endorsed by Mark Chapman, the domineering editor of *The New York Express*. Chapman, who is in line for a substantial bonus for increasing the paper's circulation, is a kind of mentor for McCleary. This motif of an older man's professional affection for a young colleague is relatively common in noir films—most notably *Double Indemnity* (1944), *Apology for Murder* (1945), and *The File on Thelma Jordan* (1950). The difference in *Scandal Sheet* is that this time, it is the older man who transgresses, and the younger man who finally brings him down.

Mark Chapman, as a circulation gimmick, organizes a Lonely Hearts Ball, where people are encouraged to get married with the promise of a grand prize, a bed with a built-in television set. However, Charlotte Grant, the wife Chapman abandoned many years before, sees her husband at the ball, and when she threatens to expose him, he pushes her over, accidentally killing her when her head hits a protruding pole. Chapman tries to cover up his crime, but McCreary, in search of another story to exploit, decides to investigate the murder.

The central drama in *Scandal Sheet* is similar to *The Night Editor* (1946), *The Big Clock* (1948), its 1987 remake *No Way Out*, and *The Man Who Cheated Himself* (1950) as well as *Fear in the Night* (1947) and its 1956 remake, *Nightmare*. The plot focuses on a protagonist who, having murdered, or is likely to be accused of murder, is forced to investigate the crime knowing that eventually, the trail will lead back to him. This dynamic is a key element as it shifts the focus to the protagonist's anxiety and torment as he tries desperately to extricate himself. *In Scandal Sheet*, this leads to an additional murder when Chapman is forced to kill a former colleague, Charlie Barnes, because he has acquired evidence that implicates Chapman. He traps Barnes, an aging alcoholic, in an alley, and in a scene found in other films directed by Karlson, the anticipation of violence is palpable as Chapman prepares to murder Barnes. Filming with low-key lighting, Karlson cuts between close-ups of the editor and his desperate quarry, who knows that he is about to be killed. Lastly, a medium shot shows Chapman killing the helpless Barnes.

Finally, after McCreary traps Chapman in his office late at night, the editor chooses suicide at the hands of the police, rather than killing his protégé. Surrounded by the police, Chapman tells McCreary that "we're just too close, kid" and that he (McCreary) now has the scoop of his career. Chapman then deliberately fires his gun into the floor, causing the police to shoot him. The film concludes on an ironic note by showing the newspaper's circulation reaching 750,000, which would, if he was still alive, have increased his bonus. Instead, he lies dead on the floor of his office.

Geoff Mayer

**SCARLET STREET** (Universal, 1945). *Director/Producer:* Fritz Lang. *Script:* Dudley Nichols, from the novel and play *La Chienne* by Georges de la Fouchardiere. *Cinematography:* Milton Krasner. *Music:* H. J. Salter. *Cast:* Edward G. Robinson (Christopher Cross), Joan Bennett (Kitty Marsh), Dan Duryea (Johnny Prince), Margaret Lindsay (Millie Ray), Rosalind Ivan (Adele Cross), Jess Barker (Janeway).

Based on the prewar French film *La Chienne* (1931), Fritz Lang's *Scarlet Street* is (along with the roughly contemporary *The Woman in the Window*, also starring Joan Bennett and Edward G. Robinson) one of the most significant and influential examples of film noir from the mid-1940s. In Kitty Marsh it has a memorable femme fatale, in Christopher Cross it has a classic fallen hero, and in Johnny Prince (Dan Duryea) it has a notably charming but egocentric rogue. It helps that all these figures are superbly portrayed by the respective cast members. In addition, *Scarlet Street* was quite daring for the time in its challenges to Production Code conventions, especially in its refusal to parcel out neatly moralized destinies for its chief characters. Lang brings a mordant European sensibility to what is a quintessentially American story of a middle-aged man seeking an exciting new life that will improve on the old.

The initial respectability of that middle-aged man, Chris Cross, is stressed in the opening scene where his 25 years of loyal service as cashier to a large New York company are rewarded at a celebratory dinner with a gold watch. Immediately after this, however, the course of his life will change. On his way home he sees a man striking a woman in the street and intervenes. He misinterprets what he has seen. It is actually just part of the rambunctious relationship between Kitty and Johnny, but Chris believes that he has saved her from a mugger. Kitty also misinterprets what Chris tells her and forms the impression that he is a wealthy man. When he writes to her, she and Johnny plan to bilk him of his money. Chris is an amateur painter, and Kitty suggests that he avoids the objections of his shrewish wife, Adele, by painting at a studio apartment that Kitty will also occupy. The trickery escalates when Johnny passes off Chris's paintings as being done by Kitty and the works start to attract buyers and the esteem of art critics. Two twists bring the plot to its climax: Adele's supposedly dead husband turns up, thus offering Chris the freedom to marry Kitty if he wishes, and Chris catches her canoodling with Johnny when he arrives to tell her the good news. In a fit of passion at her mockery of his love for her, he stabs Kitty to death with an ice pick. Unexpectedly, he escapes undetected, and Johnny is convicted and executed for the murder. In the following years, a haggard and babbling Chris is seen guiltily wandering the streets, haunted by the consequences of his actions.

Chris is a rather pathetic figure, a true noir victim of fate. Unhappy in his personal life, he ponders what it would be like to be loved by a young woman. He dreams of being an artist and confides to Kitty his feelings as he paints. The emptiness of his marriage is revealed when he admits he has never seen a nude woman. Kitty, too, has dreams (of being an actress), but unlike Chris, she is a selfish manipulator. A practiced liar, she claims that Johnny is the boyfriend of her friend Millie. The sexual bond between her and Johnny is plain, and it enables Johnny to use her the way she uses Chris. Johnny longs to go to Hollywood and is interested only in moneymaking. He is repeatedly physically violent to Kitty and even panders her to the art critic Janeway. These ironies are supplemented by the disdain in which Adele holds Chris, always comparing him unfavorably with her first husband. When that man turns out to be a corrupt ex-detective who has faked his death to escape both her and the authorities for a new life in Honduras, her bogus values are exposed.

Thus one strong theme that Lang postulates is the universality of greed, deceit, and egocentric behavior. Women are dissembling creatures: born liars and actresses. Chris himself exemplifies the notion of obsessive love leading to the downfall of an individual. He not only comes to kill Kitty out of a jealous rage, he also has earlier robbed his company of the money to support her (and Johnny's) extravagances. His boss declines to have him charged, sympathizing with Chris's apparent motive ("It's a woman, isn't it?"). Chris looks very guilty, but in actuality his boss is no better than him. We have in a prior scene seen that man with a young mistress.

What makes *Scarlet Street* most remarkable, though, for a 1940s film is not this list of moral transgressions, but the fact that it disobeys one of the Production Code's chief rules: that no serious crime should ever go unpunished. There is no getting around the fact that Johnny dies for the murder Chris has committed. The film dodges some of the ramifications of its radical narrative conclusion by having a newspaperman remark to Chris that a person's conscience can punish him far more strictly than any judge. He may not be penalized conventionally with an arrest and jail time, but he is nonetheless doomed to be remorseful. The film's last view of him is shuffling through Christmas shoppers with the voices of Kitty and Johnny echoing in his head.

Brian McDonnell

**SCOTT, LIZABETH** (1922–). With her distinctive, low, husky voice and her rather unconventionally angular looks, Lizabeth Scott was often compared to Lauren Bacall, and she definitely became one of the most iconic bad girls of film noir. Her time at the top was brief, but it contained a number of memorable noir roles. Born Emma Matzo in Scranton, Pennsylvania, Scott later renamed herself after Mary Queen of Scots. She came comparatively late to film after being a stand-in on the theatrical stage for Tallulah Bankhead and eventually received her Hollywood call-up because of a modeling spread in the magazine *Harper's Bazaar*. After a debut in *You Came Along* (1945) that was given lukewarm reviews, Scott gained positive reaction the next year for her work in *The Strange Love of Martha Ivers* (her first role in a noir film) in the august company of Barbara Stanwyck, Van Heflin, and Kirk Douglas in his film debut. Her next noir role was opposite Humphrey Bogart in *Dead Reckoning* in 1947, where she was more than adequate in something of a thankless role, but some reviewers compared her unfavorably with Lauren Bacall as a foil for Bogart. His notorious speech in that film about women being most suited to a role as the toys of men is directed at her. That same year, she also appeared in the bizarre Technicolor noir *Desert Fury*, a heady melodrama involving the contorted relationships between John Hodiak, Burt Lancaster, Wendell Corey, Mary Astor, and herself. An accomplished torch singer, Scott sang sultry numbers in several films (e.g., *Dead Reckoning* [1947], *I Walk Alone* [1948], *Dark City* [1950]). She was very sympathetic in a rare nice-girl role as Mona Stevens, the model used by men in *Pitfall* (1948), her fate at the end being contrasted with that of Dick Powell as her lover John Forbes, who dodges a bullet. The most definitively nasty femme fatale Scott played was in *Too Late for Tears* (1949) as the avaricious Jane Palmer, a role that allowed her to overcome the tepid reviews of her work in *I Walk Alone* the year before. When $60,000 of ill-gotten gains literally falls in her lap, Jane conspires to kill her squeamish husband (Arthur Kennedy), and then murders her criminal accomplice (Dan Duryea) when he proves surplus to requirements before herself dying in a fall. Scott plays Jane as a woman completely lacking in any conscience or remorse. She was rather more clingy and pliant in *Dark City* (1950) opposite Charlton Heston in his screen debut, a role that prefigured the lower-profile parts she had in a number of minor film noirs in the next few years. In 1954 *Confidential* magazine made scandalous allusions to her sexual orientation, and Scott retired, entirely of her own volition, comparatively early. One later curiosity related to the noir tradition was her appearance in the British film *Pulp* made in the early 1970s, a story about a writer of pulp fiction also featuring Mickey Rooney, Michael Caine, and Lionel Stander.

**Selected Noir Films:** *The Strange Love of Martha Ivers* (1946), *Dead Reckoning* (1947), *Desert Fury* (1947), *I Walk Alone* (1948), *Pitfall* (1948), *Too Late for Tears* (1949), *Paid in Full* (1950), *Dark City* (1950), *The Company She Keeps* (1951), *Two of a Kind* (1951), *The Racket* (1951), *Stolen Face* (1952), *Pulp* (1972).

Brian McDonnell

**SE7EN** (New Line Cinema, 1995). *Director:* David Fincher. *Producers:* Arnold Kopelson and Phyllis Carlyle. *Script:* Andrew Kevin Walker. *Cinematography:* Darius Khondji. *Music:* Howard Shore. *Cast:* Brad Pitt (Detective Wills), Morgan Freeman (Detective Somerset), Gwyneth Paltrow (Tracy), Kevin Spacey (John Doe), Richard Roundtree (Talboy), R. Lee Ermey (Police Captain).

David Fincher's bleak and harrowing film *Se7en* made a big impact in the middle of the 1990s with its grotesque, even revolting, crime scenes, its infernal urban milieu of rainy sordid streets and decaying neighborhoods, its darkly shadowed cinematography, its sparing use of traditional action scenes, its Manichean view of the world, and above all, its devastating ending. Harking back to the "city as purgatory" imagery of Martin Scorsese's *Taxi Driver*, *Se7en* was an even harsher morality tale than the 1976 classic. Using as its unifying motif the seven deadly sins of early Christian teaching, the film's script imagines a crazily rational criminal known simply as John Doe who attempts to teach a decadent society moral lessons by committing seven murders in a single week, each crime exemplifying one of the cardinal sins of pride, avarice/greed, lust, envy, wrath, gluttony, and sloth. Against the scheming of this misanthropic, murderous zealot is ranged a disparate pair of detectives, Somerset and Mills, one old, one young, one black, one white, one a meditative philosopher, the other a hothead. As they struggle to keep pace with the rising body count of John Doe's accelerating homicides and to unravel the cryptic clues with which he tantalizes them, they and the audience have their

*Se7en* (1995). Directed by David Fincher. Shown: Brad Pitt (as Detective David Mills), Morgan Freeman (as Detective Lt. William Somerset). New Line Cinema/ Photofest.

noses rubbed in the odorous residue of human vice. Paradoxically, the very stylishness of the film's grubby content made it highly influential so that *Se7en* had a considerable influence on the spate of television police forensic programs that were developed in the following decade (e.g., the *CSI* franchise, *Special Victims Unit*, *Bones*, and even the family drama *Six Feet Under*).

The film's opening scenes establish the characters of the two detectives, who have been newly put together as investigative partners. Somerset is near retirement, a fastidious and solitary man who deliberates methodically over his work, is highly cultured, and is well read. Mills, on the other hand, is young, brash, short-tempered, devotedly married, emotionally volatile, and temperamentally inclined to try shortcuts. Unsurprisingly their relationship is scratchy, even though they are equally determined to catch the killer. The first victim they encounter is grossly obese (gluttony) and discovered dead at his dining table along with written messages apparently deliberately left by the killer. One of these is from Milton's *Paradise Lost*, which sends booklover Somerset off to the library to research the topic of sin in classical and Renaissance texts. He uses actual books rather than computers, and this methodology is in line with the other old-fashioned objects associated with him: manual typewriters, vinyl records, the hat he wears while working. Mills's only way of coping with his partner's book learning is to buy sets of Cliff's study notes on all the literary classics that Somerset sends him. While the bodies of such victims as a high-profile lawyer (greed) and a semimummified serial rapist (sloth) accumulate, Mills's wife, Tracy, begins to befriend Somerset. She invites him to a dinner in their unappealing apartment, which is regularly shaken by the vibrations of subway trains. Tracy stresses to Somerset that she is unhappy and scared of the city, especially now that she is pregnant. The two officers almost catch the elusive John Doe when Somerset tracks his address down by pulling a list of his library borrowings off an illicit FBI database. After two women are killed, one genitally mutilated by a bayonet-style dildo and the other having the skin of her face removed (lust and pride), John Doe abruptly surrenders. He offers to take Somerset and Mills to the desert where the final two of the seven victims are buried, but his offer turns out to be another appallingly manipulative trick. Horrifically, it is revealed that he has beheaded Tracy, supposedly because he feels jealous of Mills's relationship with her (envy) with the added intention of provoking Mills to kill him (wrath). Thus he hopes to complete his theatrically atrocious publicizing of all seven sins. In the film's final sequence Mills does angrily shoot him dead, despite Somerset's frantic attempts to prevent Doe's perverse scheme reaching fruition.

As this summary indicates, the film's overall tone is almost despairing. The anonymous city of *Se7en* becomes an allegorical character in itself: it seems perpetually caught up in a stultifying miasma of acid rain and rotten garbage. From the marvelous credit typography to the décor of the interior murder scenes, Fincher's experiments with special resilvered film stock contribute to the film's highly expressive shadows, dark blacks, muted settings, and pervasive air of pessimism. Even the unprecedented sunshine that bathes the climactic scenes in the desert somehow manages only to emphasize the stark horror of Tracy's tragic death. *Se7en* sets up a dystopian vision of a society so mired in self-interest that a twisted individual such as Doe might come to believe that even the carnage of successive murders may be a legitimate form of protest. John Doe is, in some ways, like a biblical prophet in the form of a serial killer (or a 1990s version of *Taxi Driver*'s Travis Bickle trying to clean out society's scum), but Somerset's sanity and erudition are the true antidotes to this madness: culture becomes a means of salvation. In the last lines of *Se7en* Somerset quotes Ernest Hemingway's line that "the world's a fine place and worth fighting for." Somerset's rueful amendment to this sentiment is "I agree with the second part."

Brian McDonnell

**THE SET-UP** (RKO, 1949). *Director:* Robert Wise. *Producer:* Richard Goldstone. *Script:* Art Cohn, based on a poem by Joseph Moncure March. *Cinematography:* Milton Krasner. *Music:* Constantin Bakaleinikoff. *Cast:* Robert Ryan (Bill "Stoker" Thompson), Audrey Totter (Julie), George Tobias (Tiny), Alan Baxter (Little Boy), Wallace Ford (Gus), Percy Helton (Red), Hal Fieberling (Tiger), Darryl Hickman (Shanley), James Edwards (Luther Hawkins).

Robert Ryan, a key noir actor in the 1940s and 1950s, was able to express inner torment and submerged violence—aspects missing in most of the major male stars of the 1930s, such as James Cagney and Clark Gable, where violence and torment were conveyed externally and expressively. In *The Set-Up* Ryan expertly utilizes this aspect of his persona as an aging boxer, Stoker Thompson, wanting to have one last success. Although Thompson is well past his prime, he brings a sense of dignity to an activity, as depicted in the film, riddled with corruption and deceit, a world where working-class men and women, and petty criminals, alleviate the boredom of their meaningless lives by waiting for somebody, such as Stoker, to receive a thrashing in the boxing ring.

The film is told in real time in that the 72 minutes of its running time represent 72 minutes in the life of Stoker Thompson. Not only does the film record Stoker's triumph, and his pain, but it also presents a desperate world of the Paradise City Athletic Club. This is a world of gangsters, cocky young boxers, and aging fodder such as Stoker who, at 35 years of age, is considered too old to win a title, and so he is relegated to the last fight on the card, a match that follows the main event. After leaving his wife Julie in a shabby room at the Hotel Cozy, Stoker wanders down to the Paradise Athletic Club, hoping that Julie will follow him and watch the bout. However, she is sick of seeing him battered in each fight and wants him to retire from the ring ("Don't you see, Bill, you'll always be one punch away").

Stoker no longer has any currency in the boxing world, except as a punching bag for younger, ambitious fighters and his crooked manager, Tiny, who expects Stoker to lose and accepts money for Stoker to take a dive in his bout with Tiger, an up-and-coming fighter who is being groomed by the gangster Little Boy. Tiny is so sure that Stoker will lose that he does not even tell his fighter that he has accepted the money.

The first section of the film captures the ugly milieu of this world better than any other Hollywood boxing film prior to Martin Scorsese's *Raging Bull* (1980). The pain, the futility, and the violence is shown by director Robert Wise in Stoker's dingy hotel room, the gaudy streets, the dressing room, the boxing ring, and, above all else, the crowd's reactions to the violence, who share one thing in common—a desire to escape, if only for a brief time, their everyday world. At one point the film shifts from the boxing to show Julie pensively walking through the streets around the Athletic Club as he wonders whether she will attend Stoker's fight. Here the gaudy neon signs, which advertise enterprises such as the Dreamland Chop Suey Restaurant, offer the same empty promise that awaits the fighters in the boxing ring.

The second half of the film shows Stoker's fight in graphic detail, and Robert Ryan, who was a boxer for a period, brings a sense of realism to these scenes. Stoker believes he can beat the young fighter Tiger, and when he starts to get on top, Tiny is forced to tell him that he has taken money off a gangster for Stoker to take a dive. Stoker, however, refuses to go along with the deal and eventually knocks Tiger out. The price of retaining his dignity is high—the gangster's men crush Stoker's hands in a violent sequence set in a dark alley. The film ends with Julie comforting the battered boxer and offering him hope—because he will never be able to fight again, the film offers some hope of finally escaping from this sordid existence.

Geoff Mayer

***711 OCEAN DRIVE*** (Columbia, 1950). *Director:* Joseph M. Newman. *Producer:* Frank N. Seltzer. *Script:* Richard English and Francis Swann. *Cinematography:* Franz F. Planer. *Music:* Sol Kaplan. *Cast:* Edmond O'Brien (Mal Granger), Joanne Dru (Gail Mason), Otto Kruger (Carl Stephans), Donald Porter (Larry Mason), Sammy White (Chippie Evans), Dorothy Patrick (Trudy Maxwell), Barry Kelly (Vince Walters), Howard St. John (Lt. Pete Wright), Robert Osterloh (Gizzi).

Hollywood's gangster films of the 1930s were in some ways precursors of classical film noir, but whereas many of those earlier films tracked the rise to power of criminal overlords almost as if lauding their capitalistic enterprise, similar noir narratives tend to depict basically decent individuals who are tempted into organized crime because of their inherent weaknesses and internal contradictions. *711 Ocean Drive*, with its swaggering central turn by a charismatic Edmond O'Brien, is one of the most assured of these gangster noirs, and it moves more away from the margins of the genre and closer to its heart than most of them. With its voice-over commentary by an establishment figure (a police officer) being indicative of its links to the semidocumentary subgenre and its flashback structure adding a sense of fatalism, *711 Ocean Drive* is a cautionary tale about greed and an obsession with success. The film explores themes of avarice, gambling, opportunism, and technology being corrupted. It clearly identifies a national crime syndicate centered in Cleveland (this illegal organization representing the corrupt side of capitalistic endeavor), and a rather self-congratulatory written note in the opening credits mentions threats by organized crime to stop the film's release and to carry out reprisals on the filmmakers.

The film's protagonist, Mal Granger, is shown from the start to be both a bold risk taker and a man seriously short of money. He begins poor but rises rapidly through the horse gambling rackets by using his electronic know-how after accepting an almost Mephistophelean temptation by a gangster to join the organization. Mal is very cocky and turns his skills into money, rapidly becoming upwardly mobile. He gets more assertive with his success, for example, extorting a bigger share from his boss by making the new communication system crash. Mal's relationships with women are also fairly cynical, at least until he meets Gail (Joanne Dru), and he smugly flaunts the trappings of his new wealth, including the Malibu address of the title. His climactic scam can thus be seen as an instance of Faustian overreaching. Gail comes from a higher social class ("the country club set") but is slumming in her loveless marriage to Larry, a mid-level gang functionary. Chippie (Sammy White), Mal's assistant and confidant, remains the typical Hollywood loyal and devoted sidekick throughout, while Mal's earlier girlfriend, Trudy, exhibits compensating moral values and finally leaves the rackets for an honest life.

With its double-dealing and its brutal violence, the film is rather like *The Godfather* or a Martin Scorsese gangster film. A clear instance of this is the assassination by hit man Gizzi of Larry as he sits by his pool, a vengeance shooting prompted by Larry's beating up of Gail because of her affair with Mal. Another key scene occurs on Malibu Pier, where Mal himself kills someone (Gizzi) for the first time. He tries to manufacture an alibi that he was actually in Palm Springs by setting up a bogus long-distance phone connection with Gail on a relay amplifier he has developed, thus using his technical knowledge to evade suspicion. Ironically, the police also use technology to catch him out by recording the conversation and noting the sound of a Santa Monica streetcar in the background. These crime activities are mostly portrayed in standard Hollywood style. However, while *711 Ocean Drive* does not have the pervasive expressionistic lighting of some film noirs, much of its nefarious activity does occur in darkly lit rooms, and the racetrack racket is literally seen as a shadowy business.

*711 Ocean Drive* climaxes in a complex sequence involving a futile attempt by Mal to bilk the syndicate of millions of dollars through an elaborate "past-the-post" scam. Predictably, it goes wrong, and although Mal flees from Las Vegas toward the Arizona state line, like many a noir hero, he finds himself trapped. The towering iconic concrete structure of Boulder Dam becomes an appropriate Hitchcock-like setting for Mal's final pursuit, entrapment, and death. The electricity the dam produces is, of course, what powers his particular racket. The impressively edited chase through the labyrinthine passages of the dam resembles the famous sewer sequence of the previous year's *The Third Man*. Like Harry Lime in the earlier film, Mal is cornered and then shot down in a hail of bullets in front of Gail. This exciting story, which frequently valorizes Mal's glamorous ruthlessness, is framed at the end by a montage of shots of ordinary bettors, such as college students, accompanied by a moralizing voice-over narration telling audiences that when they make even a seemingly harmless two-dollar illegal bet, it is about "as innocent as germs in an epidemic."

Brian McDonnell

**THE SEVENTH VEIL** (Ortus Films, 1945). *Director:* Compton Bennett. *Producer:* Sydney Box. *Script:* Muriel Box and Sydney Box. *Cinematography:* Reginald Wyer. *Music:* Benjamin Frankel. *Cast:* James Mason (Nicholas), Ann Todd (Francesca Cunningham), Herbert Lom (Dr. Larsen), Hugh McDermott (Peter Gay), Albert Lieven (Maxwell Leyden), Yvonne Owen (Susan Brook).

*The Seventh Veil* was not only the most successful British film commercially of the mid-1940s it is also one of the strangest. Perhaps its emphasis on the recuperative powers of psychology and the fact of the film's overall plot, the musical career and psychological "cure" of young, fragile pianist Francesca Cunningham, camouflaged the film's more disturbing elements. The film begins with a failed suicide attempt by Francesca, who then relates her story, in flashback, to Dr. Larsen. After the death of her parents, Francesca, a shy schoolgirl, is sent to Nicholas, a relative. Nicholas, who suffered when his mother abandoned him in favor of a lover, shows little affection to Francesca and appears to have little interest in women in general (his home only has male servants). This, plus the film's emphasis on his crippled state and his dependency on a cane, symbolizes a flaw in his masculinity. His lack of interest in a normal sexual relationship is reiterated when Nicholas points out to Francesca that in devoting himself to her career, he expects nothing in return.

Nicholas guides and shapes Francesca's career as a classical pianist while systematically removing her lovers along the way. Francesca's desire to marry musician Peter Gay is destroyed when Nicholas takes her to the continent for seven years. Later, artist Maxwell Leyden's interest in Francesca provokes Nicholas's vicious attack on her hands with his cane while she is playing the piano. At the end of the film, a "cured" Francesca has the choice of three suitors—Peter Gay, Maxwell Leyden, and Nicholas. She chooses Nicholas, the man who has ruled her with strong discipline and the only one of the three men she has not slept with. Nicholas, unlike Gay and Leyden, has displayed little or no affection toward her—a truly perverse choice considering that the film provides little evidence of any substantial change in their relationship of guardian and ward. The film implies that Francesca is clearly comfortable occupying a submissive position and accepts, even welcomes, the repression of her sexual/romantic inclinations.

Francesca is one of the more overt masochistic heroines in the cinema, and the film dramatizes numerous situations where she is powerless under the control of a dominant figure—beginning with her assertive girlfriend at school, who leads Francesca into trouble and a caning from the headmistress. This causes Francesca to miss an opportunity for a musical scholarship. Subsequent (male) authority figures include conductors, lovers, doctors, and, of course, Nicholas. All exert control over Francesca. This quality is accentuated by her narration, which approximates the submissive tones associated with the fragile heroines of gothic fiction. At one point in the film, as Nicholas strikes Francesca across the face, director Compton Bennett presents this action via a subjective close-up, presumably to intensify this display of female submissiveness and male sadism. This may have reinforced James Mason's popularity in Britain in the mid-1940s following his brutal treatment of Margaret Lockwood in *The Man in Grey* (1943).

Geoff Mayer

**THE SEVENTH VICTIM** (RKO, 1943). *Director:* Mark Robson. *Producer:* Val Lewton. *Script:* DeWitt Bodeen, based on a story by Charles O'Neal. *Cinematography:* Nicholas Musuraca. *Music:* Roy Webb. *Cast:* Kim Hunter (Mary Gibson), Tom Conway (Dr. Louis Judd), Jean Brooks (Jacqueline Gibson), Isabel Jewell (Frances

Fallon), Evelyn Brent (Natalie Cortez), Hugh Beaumont (Gregory Ward), Erford Gage (Jason Hoag), Elizabeth Russell (Mimi), Ben Bard (Mr. Brun).

Visual and thematic conventions from the 1930s Hollywood horror genre, which owed much to German expressionism in the 1920s, were assimilated into a number of 1940s noir films—most notably in the early 1940s in a cycle of superb horror and supernatural thrillers produced by Val Lewton at RKO. Lewton, who was born in Russia, worked as a script consultant with David O. Selznik in the 1930s before moving over to RKO, where he was provided with his own unit to produce a series of low-budget horror films. Aside from the imposition of pulp titles such as *Cat People* (1942), *I Walked with a Zombie* (1943), and *The Leopard Man* (1943), Lewton was allowed considerable freedom by the studio as the films did not cost very much and the financial risk was minimal. As a consequence, the 11 films produced by Lewton represented a high point in the Hollywood cinema and, despite their low budgets, outclassed most of the A films produced by the major studios.

*The Seventh Victim* was one of Lewton's best films, and it has not, until recently, received its due recognition by critics and scholars. While it was not as visually accomplished as Lewton's first two films, *Cat People* and *I Walked with a Zombie*,

*The Seventh Victim* (1943). Directed by Mark Robson. Shown: Jean Brooks (as Jacqueline Gibson), and Feodor Chaliapin Jr. (as Leo). RKO Radio Pictures/Photofest.

which were both directed by Jacques Tourneur, thematically, *The Seventh Victim* is one of most pessimistic and fatalistic films ever produced—not just in Hollywood, but anywhere. It makes almost no concession for the conventional Hollywood demand for a happy or sentimental ending as the film does not deviate from its desire to dramatize the quotation from John Donne's "Holy Sonnet" that opens the film:

> I run to Death and Death meets me as fast,
> and all my Pleasures are like Yesterday.

Each character in the film is doomed to despair or death. Its central protagonist, Mary Gibson, a young girl who leaves Highcliff Academy to come to New York to search for her sister, is warned at the start of the film not to return to school and take up a teaching position—even if she fails to locate her sister. Even school, the film suggests, does not offer security, as a young female assistant warns her:

> Mary, don't come back, no matter if you never find your sister. No matter what happens to you, don't come back.

This woman explains to Mary that once she was in the same position as Mary and about to leave the school. Instead, she made the mistake of coming back.

In New York Mary appears lost, and during her search, she visits a number of places, which only intensifies her fears that something awful has happened to her sister Jacqueline. For example, at a missing person's bureau, the camera tracks down a long row of people searching for lost loved ones. Similarly, when she goes to the dark offices of the cosmetic company where Jacqueline works, a pathetic little private eye is murdered while Mary waits in the darkness. Later that night, on the subway, Mary is threatened by two men carrying the body of the detective. Even when taking a shower, Mary, in a vulnerable state, is confronted by a sinister woman, Mrs. Redi, in a scene which, to some extent, foreshadows the shower sequence in Alfred Hitchcock's *Psycho* (1960). Finally, her sister Jacqueline is systematically tormented by the Palladists, a group of middle-class devil worshippers wishing to kill her.

Mary's journey through New York also brings her into contact with characters who are spiritually lost in a cruel, joyless urban world—such as Jason Hoag, the failed poet who attempts to help Mary after falling in love with her. When his love is not reciprocated, he tells her,

> I am alive yet every hope I had is dead.
> Death can be good. Death can be happy.

There is also the psychoanalyst Dr. Judd, who protects Jacqueline from the Palladists but lacks the confidence to treat patients anymore. Finally, Gregory Ward,

Jacqueline's husband, still cares for his wife while she appears to no longer feel anything for him. Ward accepts this situation and the fact that Jacqueline prefers to live in a rented room, which is empty, except for a chair and a rope noose hanging from the ceiling.

Although *The Seventh Victim* contains a characteristic Lewton suspense sequence made up of expressive lighting, with deep shadows broken up with bright lighting, clever editing, and menacing sounds as Jacqueline tries to escape a killer in the dark street of New York, this is primarily a film that documents morbid despair on many levels. At the end, while Gregory and Mary discuss the futility of their love for each other as Gregory is still married to Jacqueline, Jacqueline prepares to commit suicide in her near-empty room. Just before she enters the room where she will hang herself, she meets another lost character, her neighbor from next door, Mimi, who is dying from consumption:

| | |
|---|---|
| Jacqueline: | Who are you? |
| Mimi: | I'm Mimi, I'm dying. |
| Jacqueline: | No! |
| Mimi: | I've been quiet, ever so quiet. I hardly move, yet it [death] keeps coming all the time, closer and closer. I rest and I rest and yet I am dying. |
| Jacqueline: | And you don't want to die. I've always wanted to die. Always. |
| Mimi: | I'm afraid. I'm afraid of being afraid, of waiting. |
| Jacqueline: | Why wait? |
| Mimi: | I'm not going to wait. I'm going out, laugh, dance, do all the things I used to do. |
| Jacqueline: | And then? |
| Mimi: | I don't know. |
| Jacqueline: | You will die! |

After two short sequences—one with Mary telling Gregory that although she loves him, she will have to leave New York, and the other whereby Judd and Hoag confront the Palladists—this bleak film concludes in the hallway outside Jacqueline's room. Mimi, dressed up for a final night on the town, emerges from her room, and as she walks past Jacqueline's room, we hear a chair topple over—Jacqueline has finally achieved the death she always wanted. As Mimi continues walking down the corridor, Jacqueline's voice-over repeats the quotation from Donne that opened the film ("I run to Death and Death meets me as fast, / and all my Pleasures are like Yesterday").

Geoff Mayer

**SHALLOW GRAVE** (Channel Four Films/The Glasgow Film Fund, 1994). *Director:* Danny Boyle. *Producers:* Andrew Macdonald and Allan Scott (executive). *Script:* John Hodge. *Cinematography:* Brian Tufano. *Music:* Simon Boswell. *Cast:* Kerry Fox (Juliet Miller), Christopher Eccleston (David Stephens), Ewan

McGregor (Alex Law), Ken Stott (Detective Inspector McCall), Keith Allen (Hugo), Colin McCredie (Cameron), John Hodge (Detective Constable Mitchell).

*Shallow Grave* was Britain's most commercially successful film of 1995 and provided screenwriter John Hodge, director Danny Boyle, and producer Andrew Macdonald with the opportunity to make the even more commercially successful, and confronting, *Trainspotting* (1996) two years later. *Shallow Grave*, a surprising hit, was cleverly promoted, and it tapped into a niche market of savvy filmgoers and young viewers. It also provided an effective launching pad for the career of Ewan McGregor. Overall, *Shallow Grave* received a positive critical reaction, especially in Britain, although some critics, notably in the United States, objected to the film's "mean-spirited" quality, its unrelenting cynicism and lack of sentiment. These qualities are particularly evident in the ending, which adopts a similar tone (irony) to the closing moments in *The Treasure of the Sierra Madre* (1948).

*Shallow Grave* was celebrated by British critics for its effective use of local (Edinburgh and Glasgow) settings. It was presented as a successor to the dark strain of British comedy that seeped through the conventional surface of the British cinema in the late 1940s and 1950s in films such as Ealing's *Kind Hearts and Coronets* (1949) and *The Ladykillers* (1955). Yet the story line and characterizations of this film, unlike the Ealing films, are more universal and could be found in any city,

*Shallow Grave* (1994). Directed by Danny Boyle. Shown: Kerry Fox (as Juliet Miller), Ewan McGregor (as Alex Law), Christopher Eccleston (as David Stephens). Gramercy Pictures/Photofest.

as David points out at the start of the film. This extends to the film's simple theme concerning the association between personal corruption and money, a theme found in many films.

*Shallow Grave* is impatient to show evidence of its mean-spirited tone right from the start as accountant David, doctor Juliet, and journalist Alex humiliate a succession of applicants who subject themselves to ridicule in an effort to rent an empty room in their apartment. Juliet, who refuses to take phone calls from a former boyfriend (Brian) because he displays "certain personal weaknesses," is impressed by the worldly Hugo. Hugo tells Juliet that he is writing a novel about a priest who dies. However, it is Hugo who dies the next day with a large amount of money in a suitcase beside his body. Although Alex, Juliet, and David agonize over whether to take the money to the police or keep it, there is little doubt what their decision will be. When David pulls the short straw, he is forced to mutilate Hugo's body so that it will not be recognized when discovered. This decision takes the occupants on a dark journey leading to death and betrayal as the initial skirmishes for power within the group blossom into full-blown paranoia.

Although John Hodge, Andrew Macdonald, and Danny Boyle keep pushing the darker elements of the story, they provide just enough character detail to make Alex, David, and Juliet interesting. Thus Juliet, the doctor, smokes while David, the only member of the group to display remorse, cuts through tissue and bone in an effort to destroy Hugo's identity. Ironically, Alex, the journalist, receives the best break of his short career when he is assigned to investigate the discovery of three bodies in the countryside. These are the bodies they have tried to conceal. David, on the other hand, following the mutilation of Hugo, becomes mentally unhinged and moves into the small space between the ceiling and roof of their flat. This action proves useful when two criminals burst into the apartment and terrorize Juliet and Alex. When they enter David's domain, between the roof and ceiling, they die.

Juliet, the most calculating member of the group, fulfils the function of the femme fatale as she moves between David and Alex late in the film. However, Hodge and Boyle provide an early indication of her true nature when, during a charity function, Alex trips while dancing with Juliet. At this point, Boyle, with a low-angle shot from Alex's point of view, emphasizes Juliet's power when she places her foot on Alex's chest as he licks it before she dances away. Later, Juliet betrays both men by purchasing a one-way plane ticket to South America, and she reveals the extent of her corruption, and ruthlessness, when she takes the shoe off her foot and bangs at a knife impaled in Alex's shoulder in a scene reminiscent of the earlier episode on the dance floor. A final, and obvious, twist denies her the money she covets so badly, and David's voice-over concludes the film, in a kind of homage to *Sunset Boulevard* (1950), as he laments the failure of their friendship, despite the fact that he is now dead, courtesy of a knife through his neck from Juliet.

*Shallow Grave* walks a fine line between cynicism and calculation, combining Grand Guignol moments, film noir sensibilities, and Boyle's showy visual style matched by a dramatic use of color and music. The discovery of Hugo's body draped over a red satin bed cover is accompanied by Nina Simone's "My Baby Just Cares for Me" on the sound track. *Shallow Grave* won the Alexander Korda Award for best British film at the 1995 BAFTA Film Awards, and director Danny Boyle won the Best Newcomer Award from the 1996 London Film Critics Circle.

Geoff Mayer

**SIN CITY** (Dimension Films/Troublemaker Studios/Miramax, 2005). *Directors:* Frank Miller and Robert Rodriguez. *Special Guest Director:* Quentin Tarantino. *Producer:* Elizabeth Avellán. Based on the Sin City graphic novels by Frank Miller. *Cinematography:* Robert Rodriguez. *Music:* Robert Rodriguez, John Debney, and Graeme Revell. *Cast:* Bruce Willis (John Hartigan), Mickey Rourke (Marv), Clive Owen (Dwight), Jessica Alba (Nancy Callahan), Jaime King (Goldie/Wendy), Rosario Dawson (Gail), Benicio Del Toro (Jackie Boy), Elijah Wood (Kevin), Nick Stahl (Roark Jr./Yellow Bastard), Brittany Murphy (Shellie), Devoni Aoki (Miho), Powers Boothe (Senator Roark), Rutger Hauer (Cardinal Roark), Carla Gugino (Lucille), Josh Hartnett (The Man), Alexis Bledel (Becky).

By the time *Sin City* (adapted from the graphic novels of Frank Miller) was released in 2005, there was such familiarity in American culture with the notion of *film noir* that discussion of the new film frequently used the term as a point of reference, even in newspaper and television reviews and in descriptions by members of the public. What most people meant by the word *noir* in connection with *Sin City* was the high-contrast black-and-white look of its comic book urban landscapes and the hard-boiled brutality of both its voice-over narration and violent action. In short, the film was viewed as having a style that paid tribute to the noir tradition rather than as being an expression of noir's thematic preoccupations. Such stylistic homage is not uncommon in movies of the early twenty-first century, and a comparable instance is Steven Soderbergh's black-and-white period film *The Good German* (2006), where a use of vintage lenses, high-contrast color film stock with the color pulled out, and stock footage of Berlin that had been shot immediately after World War II by Billy Wilder and William Wyler helps produce a classical noir look. However, while *The Good German* has a serious message to convey through the fate of its morally compromised hero, *Sin City* seems more an exercise in impressively high-impact style than a statement about substantial ideas.

Robert Rodriguez, who had multiple creative roles in the film's production, designed a circular narrative structure, assembling a complicated mass of material from three different Miller Sin City novels or "yarns" (*That Yellow Bastard, The Hard Goodbye, The Big Fat Kill*) and one short story ("The Customer Is Always Right"). Rodriguez shuffled the chronology in a manner reminiscent of Quentin Tarantino's 1994 film *Pulp Fiction*. In fact, Tarantino guest-directed one scene in the film involving a talking corpse. *Sin City*'s three main plot threads begin after a prefatory precredit sequence on a balcony above Basin City where a man shoots a woman dead after seeming to be seducing her. In the first plotline, middle-aged police officer John Hartigan rescues 11-year-old Nancy Callahan from the pedophile Roark Jr., whom he shoots in the groin before being himself shot by his corrupt partner. The second plotline has the extremely tough Marv wake up next to a woman's corpse after she has made love to him, despite his ugliness. He swears revenge, and like Lee Marvin in *Point Blank,* he works his way up the criminal food chain to find Goldie's killer. Marv learns that the murderer is a cannibal called Kevin who is able to move about in a silent and deadly manner. In sadistic revenge he gets Kevin's pet wolf to eat his flesh, then beheads him. Marv also kills the cardinal, who has shared human flesh with the cannibal, and then is himself executed in the electric chair.

In the third plot, fugitive Dwight wants to kill a bully named Jackie Boy who is violent toward Dwight's waitress girlfriend, Shellie. Dwight pursues Jackie into the Old Town area of Basin City, a district ruled over by hookers under the leadership of Gail and martial-arts exponent Miho, who dispatch Jackie with a samurai sword. Dwight tries to bury Jackie's body in the local tar pits, but Irish mercenaries ambush him. The hookers, likened by Dwight to Valkyries, help him kill all the Irishmen and other assorted gang members. The narrative of *Sin City* then returns to the first plot strand after eight years have elapsed. Hartigan, who has been wrongly imprisoned for raping Nancy, is released and reunited with Nancy, who is now 19, an exotic dancer, and in love with him. He wants to save her from the violent retribution of the emasculated Roark Jr. and his vile family. Unwittingly, he leads the young Roark (now disfigured and a bright yellow color after undergoing procedures to restore his manhood) to Nancy. Hartigan and Nancy hide out together, and she wants sex, but the 60-year-old Hartigan declines. In a suspenseful series of fast-moving scenes, he is trussed up by Roark before escaping, then rescues Nancy, rips off young Roark's reconstructed genitals, and punches him to death. To protect Nancy from further Roark family vengeance, Hartigan kills himself. A brief epilogue turns back to the figure of the prologue's assassin, who now has a new target.

*Sin City* is clearly not a realist story, preferring the stark and simplistic oppositions of comic books or martial arts films to the moral subtleties usually associated with film noir. There is a disturbing amount of extremely brutal violence meted out through the film, including decapitation, dismemberment, and emasculation. The film's theme, shared by its three main story lines, is of existential heroes with preternatural powers who absorb terrible punishment to save sexy but angelic women from evil villains. This moral polarization is not really reflective of the ambivalence of noir, but *Sin City* does have a consistent visual sense of entrapment. The film uses original story panels from Frank Miller's graphic novels, and Rodriguez views it as more of a "translation" than an adaptation. The film's characters were shot on high-definition video in front of green screens so that computer-generated backgrounds could be added in instead of building traditional studio sets, and this method results in a strikingly brilliant visual tone. The stark black and white of

*Sin City* is sometimes augmented by splashes of bright color, such as a red evening gown in the opening scene or the sickly yellow skin of pedophile Roark Jr.

Interestingly, Frank Miller's own visual style in his graphic novels (especially their depiction of city life) itself owed a debt to classical film noir. When he first conceived the original Sin City series, Miller was a fan of both film noir and the hard-boiled detective novels of Raymond Chandler and Mickey Spillane. He was also influenced by comic book artist Will Eisner, who, between 1940 and 1952, drew a series called *The Spirit* which was published in Sunday newspapers. The hero was a noir detective called Denny Colt whose visage (often masked) was based on actor Dennis O'Keefe. These comics, which became legendary for their expressionistic visuals, sexy women, and existentialist themes, were analogous to the contemporaneous films of classical noir. However, just as the violence and nudity of the film *Sin City* would never have been allowed by the Production Code Administration in Old Hollywood, so, too, would the similar features in Miller's modern novels have been censored by the Comics Code Authority back in the 1950s. A sequel to *Sin City* (one of a number planned by Rodriguez) was in preproduction early in 2007.

Brian McDonnell

**SIODMAK, ROBERT** (1900–1973). In terms of the creation of a distinctive visual style in the early years of the classical film noir cycle, Robert Siodmak is without equal as a director. The catalogue of his films in the late 1940s includes many of the most impressive and influential noirs produced at that time. Born in Memphis, Tennessee, while his German parents were in the United States on a business trip, Siodmak grew up in Leipzig and Dresden. He trained as an actor and flirted with the idea of joining his father's banking business, but not for long. He collaborated with Edgar Ulmer, Fred Zinnemann, and others on directing *Menschen am Sonntag* (*People on Sunday*, 1929) and worked at UFA in Berlin. The influence of expressionism is clearly evident in his early German films. However, along with many other Jewish artists, Siodmak fled Nazi persecution to settle in Paris in 1934. Reichminister Goebbels had labeled him as a subversive because of one of his films which was dubbed: "a corrupter of the German family." He stayed in France until the German invasion in 1940 making sexually charged melodramas. Before the Nazis arrived in Paris, Siodmak fled once more to Hollywood, and after making B films at various studios, in 1943 he began work at Universal. He quickly came to be acknowledged as a master of the deployment of lighting and other atmospheric effects in psychological thrillers. *Phantom Lady* (1944) showed the way he could brilliantly combine expressionistic elements into the mode of Hollywood realism to evoke a morbid atmosphere that was haunting and gloomy. *Phantom Lady* also introduced into the nascent noir cycle the motif of a weak man matched by a potent woman (not long before the more widely influential *Double Indemnity* did something similar). These figures were to be present in many of Siodmak's subsequent noirs. The film has a tour-de-force visual style, as in the notorious scene where Elisha Cook Jr. orgiastically smashes his drums virtually to smithereens inspired by the arousing presence of amateur detective Ella Raines.

*The Killers* (1946) was a virtual masterpiece for Siodmak, adding a deft handling of a multiple flashback narrative structure to his usual visual panache. There are Gothic influences in many of Siodmak's films that particularly show up female terror, a good example being *The Spiral Staircase* (1946) with its psychological mise-en-scène. The characteristically divided personalities of the obsessive protagonists in his stories literally became divided into two separate people with the good and evil twins played by Olivia de Havilland in *The Dark Mirror* (1946). While he was instrumental in making popular the studio-bound style associated with the budget controls of the war years, Siodmak later effectively used location shooting in *Cry of the City* (1948) and *Criss Cross* (1949). These two films display a mastery of style just as complete as had been evident in earlier works such as *Phantom Lady*. At the end of his Hollywood career Robert Siodmak returned to Germany in 1951 without too much recognition for his achievements. However, he is today universally recognized as one of film noir's most significant artists.

**Selected Noir Films:** *Phantom Lady* (1944), *Christmas Holiday* (1944), *The Suspect* (1944), *The Strange Case of Uncle Harry* (1945), *The Spiral Staircase* (1946), *The Killers* (1946), *The Dark Mirror* (1946), *Cry of the City* (1948), *Criss Cross* (1949), *The File on Thelma Jordan* (1950). Siodmak also coauthored the original story "The Pentacle" on which was based the film noir *Conflict* (filmed before *Phantom Lady* but not released until 1945).

Brian McDonnell

**SLIGHTLY SCARLET** (RKO, 1956). *Director:* Allan Dwan. *Producer:* Benedict Bogeaus. *Script:* Robert Blees, based on the novel *Love's Lovely Counterfeit* by James M. Cain. *Cinematography:* John Alton. *Music:* Louis Forbes. *Cast:* John Payne (Ben Grace), Rhonda Fleming (June Lyons), Arlene Dahl (Dorothy Lyons), Kent Taylor (Frank Jansen), Ted de Corsia (Solly Caspar), Frank Gerstle (Dave Dietz), Lance Fuller (Gauss), Buddy Baer (Lenhardt), Roy Gordon (Norman B. Marlowe), Ellen Corby (Martha), Myron Healey (Wilson).

*Slightly Scarlet* is a gangster film that challenged the restrictions of the Production Code Authority by absorbing elements of the adult melodrama, such as *The Magnificent Obsession* (1954), *All That Heaven Allows* (1956), and *Written on the Wind* (1957), within the narrative conventions of the 1950s crime film. This hybrid quality, with its emphasis on sex, is superbly conveyed by John Alton's lurid cinematography, which renders *Slightly Scarlet* one of the most striking color noir films. Alton's use of color in *Slightly Scarlet* performs the same effect as Leon Shamroy's cinematography in *Leave Her to Heaven* in 1945: rendering the film less realistic so as to direct the audience's attention towards sexual and psychological aspects that were normally prohibited by censorship restrictions.

In *Slightly Scarlet* this is especially evident in the characterization of Dorothy Lyons, who is determined to enjoy the pleasure of transgression, whatever the cost. When mobster Sol Caspar prepares to shoot June Lyons, her sister Dorothy is shown behind Caspar urging him on while in the heightened state of perverse sexual excitement. Years later, director Allan Dwan complained that restrictions imposed by the Production Code limited his ability to fully capture the extent of Dorothy's perversity, but Alton and Dwan, assisted by Arlene Dahl's performance, expertly conveyed this aspect through a combination of color, costume, and body language.

The film's opening credits, with Alton's lurid color, signal that *Slightly Scarlet* is a different crime film. June greets Dorothy outside the local penitentiary following Dorothy's imprisonment for stealing—she suffers from kleptomania as well as nymphomania. In the background Ben Grace, the ideas man for Solly Caspar, photographs the reunion as part of an attempt to gather information to discredit reform mayoral candidate Frank Jansen (Dorothy is Jansen's personal assistant). However, the plan falters when Grace falls in love with Dorothy, and he devises an alternative strategy that involves betraying Caspar, forcing the gangster to leave town and thereby allowing Grace to take over the mob. Grace, to assist his romance with Dorothy, allows the reformist Jansen to win the mayoral election.

There are two interrelated plot strands in *Slightly Scarlet*. The crime element follows Grace's control of Caspar's mob. This is the familiar plotline, while a second strand is the strange love-hate relationship between Dorothy and June, and this aspect is more controversial as it details June's erratic behavior—which includes lusting after her sister's boyfriend (Grace) and shoplifting, which the film links with her nymphomania. Ultimately, June's sexual and criminal predilections provoke the events that lead to Grace's downfall. During the film's bizarre climax, following Caspar's attempt to regain control of the mob, Grace offers his body up to Caspar's bullets in an attempt to save June and ensure Caspar's capture by the police.

*Slightly Scarlet* is based on James M. Cain's novel *Love's Lovely Counterfeit*, and the film, despite Dwan's complaint that the Production Code restricted him too much, captures Cain's interest in the association between aberrant sexual desire and criminal activity. Dorothy's masochism in protecting a sister who despises her is matched by June's nymphomania and Grace's regeneration in inviting Caspar to shoot him. These aspects, combined with the hard-boiled dialogue, the casting of redheads Rhonda Fleming and Arlene Dahl, and John Alton's use of garish colors, such as orange and green, make *Slightly Scarlet* one of the more bizarre noir films produced in Hollywood while the Production Code was still in operation.

Geoff Mayer

**SO DARK THE NIGHT** (Columbia, 1946). *Director:* Joseph H. Lewis. *Producer:* Ted Richmond. *Script:* Martin Berkeley and Dwight V. Babcock, from an unpublished story by Aubrey Wisberg. *Cinematography:* Burnett Guffey. *Music:* Hugo Friedhofer. *Cast:* Steven Geray (Henri Cassin), Micheline Cheirel (Nanette

Michaud), Eugene Borden (Pierre Michaud), Ann Codee (Mama Michaud), Egon Brecher (Dr. Boncourt), Helen Freeman (Widow Bridelle), Paul Marion (Leon Archard), Gregory Gay (Commissioner Grande).

Director Joseph Lewis followed *My Name Is Julia Ross* with *So Dark the Night*, another low-budget film for Columbia. Set in the French village of St. Margot, the studio gave Lewis a short shooting schedule (12 days, which Lewis extended to 18), no sets, virtually no money to construct a French village, and no stars. Harry Cohn, head of production at Columbia, also demanded that Lewis abandon the film so that he could assist director Alfred E. Greene on a more prestigious Columbia film, *The Jolson Story* (1946). Lewis rejected Cohn's request to leave *So Dark the Night*, although he filmed the musical sequences for *The Jolson Story* after completing the former film.

Lewis was an ingenious director and disguised the fact that Columbia refused to build a French village for the film by dressing up a standing set on the Columbia back lot that depicted a bombed-out wartime village. With the assistance of a bull-dozer, Lewis cut out a rough road in the studio paddock and hid the bomb-damaged

*So Dark the Night* (1946). Directed by Joseph H. Lewis. Shown: Micheline Cheirel (Nanette Michaud), Steven Geray (as Henri Cassin). Columbia Pictures/Photofest.

buildings with a few walls and thatched roofs. Then, through the judicious selection of camera angles and other tricks, such as the use of black velvet and mirrors to create the effect that there were a number of buildings in the village—when, in effect, there were none—Lewis was able to generate the illusion that the actors were moving around a French village.

The film's sense of authenticity was assisted by the casting of character actors who were virtually unknown to the American public at that time. For example, Czechoslovakian actor Steven Geray, as the film's main protagonist, Paris detective Henri Cassin, had no major roles in Hollywood prior to this film. Lewis was so successful that he convinced some American critics that *So Dark the Night* was a French production.

Even with a short running time of 71 minutes, *So Dark the Night* is a significant film noir in the way it dramatizes mental illness, specifically amnesia, as a pretext for murder, and many films soon followed this example—including *Fear in the Night* (1947) and its remake *Nightmare* (1956), *The Guilty* (1947), *A Double Life* (1948), and, more recently, *Angel Heart* (1987), *Memento* (2001), and *The Machinist* (2004).

The protagonist in *So Dark the Night,* Henri Cassin, is conservative, disciplined, and intelligent. He is the top detective at the Paris Súreté, and overworked, he takes his first vacation for more than a decade and leaves Paris for the small village of St. Margot. He immediately attracts the interest of the villagers, especially Mama Michaud, who sees in the unmarried Cassin an opportunity to break the engagement between her daughter Nanette and a local farmer, Leon Archard. She encourages Nanette to seduce Cassin so that he will marry her and take her to Paris. Although Nanette thinks Cassin is too old, she is intrigued with this idea, and when Leon leaves the village for a few days, she encourages the detective's interest in her. Cassin falls for Nanette and proposes marriage. However, on the night of their wedding ceremony, Leon appears and tells Cassin that he wants Nanette back. Upset, Nanette follows Leon from the reception. Cassin, humiliated and frustrated, is devastated when, a few days later, Nanette is found dead in the river and, a few hours later, Leon's body is discovered at his farm.

Cassin vows to find the killer who has strangled both Nanette and Archard. However, his investigations are not successful, even after he receives a note stating that more people will die. When the body of Mama Michaud is discovered, Cassin returns to Paris to consult with Commissioner Grande, who suggests that an artist draw the killer based on the known clues. When the artist jokingly tells Cassin that the drawing looks like him, he realizes that the reason he has been unable to find the murderer is because it is him. A doctor tells the commissioner that Cassin is suffering from schizophrenia, and Cassin is shot by Grande when he attempts to murder Nanette's father.

This is a startling film with the shock discovery that Cassin is the murderer. Lewis, even within the small budget and short shooting schedule, consistently devises ways to reinforce Cassin's plight, and many scenes are filmed with depth staging through obstacles such as windows so as to visually reinforce the film's dominant motif involving Cassin's split personality. This is most evident in the final scene: as Cassin lies fatally wounded on the floor of the village inn he peers through the window, which shows an image of him when he first appeared in the village as a man seemingly without a worry in the world. This tranquil image is then replaced by his present predicament as a disgraced serial killer. Cassin smashes the window in a vain attempt to destroy this image, and his final comment acknowledges his illness—"Henri Cassin is no more. I have caught him and killed him."

Geoff Mayer

**SO EVIL MY LOVE** (Paramount British, 1948). *Director:* Lewis Allan. *Producer:* Hal Wallis. *Script:* Ronald Miller and Leonard Spigelgass, based on the novel by Joseph Shearing. *Photography:* Max Greene. *Music:* William Alwyn (additional music by Victor Young). *Cast:* Ray Milland (Mark Bellis), Ann Todd (Olivia Harwood), Geraldine Fitzgerald (Susan Courtney), Leo G. Carroll (Jarvis), Raymond Huntley (Henry Courtney), Raymond Lovell (Edgar Bellamy), Marita Hunt (Mrs. Courtney), Moira Lister (Kitty Feathers), Roderick Lovell (Sir John Curle), Muriel Aked (Miss Shoebridge), Finlay Currie (Dr. Krylie).

*So Evil My Love* is a superior film noir and one of the finest films produced by any Hollywood studio in Britain in the 1940s. The Hollywood contingent comprised Ray Milland, who was born in Wales in 1905, and director Lewis Allan, who was born in Shopshire in Britain in 1905. Both men, however, achieved fame due to the films they made in Hollywood in the 1930s and 1940s. *So Evil My Love* was produced by veteran Hollywood producer Hal Wallis for Paramount British, and it was filmed at the British D&P Studios. The focus of the film is Olivia Harwood, expertly played by Ann Todd. While the other characters (skillfully) fulfill their conventional roles, the film concentrates on Harwood's transformation from a missionary's widow to the sensual, conniving mistress of a thief and murderer. This transformation is neither linear nor simplistic as her moral code clashes with her carnal desires throughout the film. A notable example of this occurs near the end of the film, when, distressed at the prospect that her friend Susan will hang (because of Olivia's actions), she is able to relieve the sense of guilt by replacing it with lustful thought at the prospect of a reunion with Mark Bellis.

On a boat returning to England from Jamaica, Harwood reluctantly nurses typhoid victim Mark Bellis back to health. Bellis, hiding from the police, takes a room in Olivia's house and gradually exploits the widow's desire for a satisfying sexual relationship. He also convinces her that she has not fulfilled her ambitions in life (OLIVIA: "My life was to be rich and full and complete"). When a former school friend, Susan Courtney, makes contact with Olivia, Bellis encourages her to insinuate herself into Susan's household and exploit Courtney's growing dependency on her. Susan is even more vulnerable because she is married to the tyrannical, impotent Henry Courtney, a wealthy barrister.

In a perverse way Olivia enjoys her power over Susan ("poor Susan, so pampered, such a fool"), and when she believes that she also has control over Henry due to incriminating letters in her possession, Olivia Harwood's transformation, and corruption, is complete. She tells Mark Bellis, after demanding $5,000 from Henry Courtney,

> Olivia: I had the whip hand and he knew it. I was utterly in command.
> Mark:   You enjoyed yourself.
> Olivia: Yes, the power of it. It was a wonderful sensation. I've never had it before. I was quite calm, my heart wasn't pounding and my mouth wasn't dry. I was utterly in possession.
> Mark:   I am beginning to know you Olivia.
> Olivia: I am beginning to know myself.

When the blackmail scheme fails, and Henry has a heart attack, Olivia manipulates Susan so that she inadvertently kills her husband with poison. Olivia, however, discovers that Mark has another mistress, and despite his pledge that he loves her, Harwood stabs him and gives herself up to the police.

*So Evil My Love* was one of four films in the 1940s based on the novels of Joseph Shearing. Shearing was the pseudonym for Gabrielle Margaret Vere Long, and the title of her novel *For Her to See* was changed for the cinema to *So Evil My Love*.

Geoff Mayer

**SOMEWHERE IN THE NIGHT** (Twentieth Century Fox, 1946). *Director:* Joseph L. Mankiewicz. *Producer:* Anderson Lawler. *Script:* Howard Dinsdale and Joseph L. Mankiewicz, from the story "The Lonely Journey" by Marvin Borowsky, adapted by Lee Strasberg. *Cinematography:* Norbert Brodine. *Music:* David Buttolph. *Cast:* John Hodiak (George Taylor), Nancy Guild (Christy Smith), Lloyd Nolan (Lt. Donald Kendall), Richard Conte (Mel Phillips), Josephine Hutchinson (Elizabeth Conroy), Fritz Kortner (Anzelmo), Margo Woode (Phyllis).

*Somewhere in the Night* was described by Alain Silver and Elizabeth Ward, in their book *Film Noir: An Encyclopedic Reference to the American Style*, as the "quintessential noir whose protagonist is an amnesiac veteran" (p. 262). A group of such films with themes of amnesia and a search for identity were released between 1946 and 1949 and had plots that essentially were more extreme versions of the general idea of the need for readjustment to postwar U.S. life by all ex-servicemen. In this film the individual soldier is ex-marine George Taylor, who engages in a search for his own identity (it being, of course, a typical noir task to search for one's self). And in terms of having any sense of who he is, Taylor begins with a pretty clean slate. Not only is he amnesiac, but plastic surgery has altered his facial features enough for him to be unrecognizable by any former acquaintances. His "face was pushed around at Okinawa" and "the docs patched [him] up." Indeed, he is given the name George Taylor by doctors from a clothing tag. The film's narrative

*Somewhere in the Night* (1946). Directed by Joseph L. Mankiewicz. Shown: John Hodiak (as George W. Taylor). 20th Century-Fox/Photofest.

involves his search for hard evidence, actively seeking to solve the mystery of who he could be. Intrigue (which is inherent in amnesia stories) prevails: for much of the film, we and he do not know what is going on. He has, in effect, to become a detective and, appropriately, it turns out that he was once a private eye.

*Somewhere in the Night* opens in a military hospital to close-ups of the hero's bandage-swathed face. A feature of this opening is its prolonged subjective camera work, with the main character's point of view made more emphatic by his voice-over heard on the sound track as he lies silent (at that point, his jaw is wired up). Taylor determines to work step by step until his past can be recreated. His starting point is a letter from a Larry Cravat conveniently containing $5,000. He soon meets a gang who have their own reasons to seek revenge. The rather obscure driving force for these criminals' actions is $2 million worth of precious Nazi war booty, which apparently went missing along with Cravat after a violent struggle on a dock. Not knowing why anyone might wish him harm, Taylor becomes paranoid, and he pours his heart out to a nightclub singer named Christy. Christy thinks she is tough and hardened by life experience: "I'm the girl with the cauliflower heart." Apart from this main romantic pairing, there are a large number of well-crafted minor characters. Harry Morgan plays a sinister guy at a bathhouse similar to his dangerous flunky in *The Big Clock*. There is a sexy floozy named Phyllis who is married to a rough San Pedro hoodlum. Mid-level hood Anselmo wheezes melodramatically and pontificates like a cross between Peter Lorre and Sydney Greenstreet. Most important is Mel Philips (Richard Conte), who is poised and self-confident but who turns out to be duplicitous and murderous. Lloyd Nolan is police lieutenant Kendall.

The film does not overlook the fact that there were many physically and mentally wounded ex-soldiers in the United States of the immediate postwar years, and *Somewhere in the Night,* like many other noirs of the period, acknowledges that. Taylor is just one of many damaged men in his Honolulu hospital ward. Early scenes also dramatize the huge scale of the process of the demobilization of troops. This film has a longer running time than most film noirs (108 minutes) and has narrative space for a very wide catalogue of sinister and mysterious Los Angeles settings, including a Turkish bathhouse, a nightclub, a restaurant in Chinatown, houses in San Pedro, the Terminal dock, the slums of Bunker Hill, the Lambeth sanatorium, and a seaman's mission. There is a narrative twist when Anselmo says that Taylor may be the third man from the killing on the dock and another when George discovers that he actually is Larry Cravat. Anselmo, in a torture scene where he interrogates Taylor, talks of the room's lighting (in this case, underlighting) being highly suitable for a "mood of mystery and intrigue." This is somewhat self-reflexive for a 1940s Hollywood film and illustrates the way *Somewhere in the Night* plays with the conventions of the emerging noir cycle at the same time that it is establishing a new variant of the generic story line.

Brian McDonnell

**SORRY, WRONG NUMBER** (Paramount, 1948). *Director:* Anatole Litvak. *Producers:* Hal B. Wallis and Anatole Litvak. *Script:* Lucille Fletcher, based on her radio play. *Cinematography:* Sol Polito. *Music:* Franz Waxman. *Cast:* Barbara Stanwyck (Leona Stevenson), Burt Lancaster (Henry Stevenson), Ann Richards (Sally Hunt Lord), Wendell Corey (Dr. Alexander), Harold Vermilyea (Waldo Evans), Lief Erickson (Fred Lord), Ed Begley (James Cotterell), William Conrad (Morano).

On first inspection, *Sorry, Wrong Number* may appear to be merely a film with an intriguing narrative gimmick: the central character is virtually confined to her bed, and all the plot events must therefore be based on this extremely constrained setting. But the film actually transcends this novelty limitation by spinning a suspenseful story out of its radio play origin using the formidable powers of Barbara Stanwyck in the central role of Leona Stevenson. Leona is a house-bound neurotic wife whose chronic anxiety is amplified by receiving incoming phone calls that are sinister and threatening. *Sorry, Wrong Number* thus illustrates the prominent noir theme of a woman in domestic jeopardy who, from her virtually helpless situation, tries to investigate a possible threat issuing from her own husband. This is a prevalent plot device in that subgroup of classical film noir that shares common ground with the genre of gothic romance. The filmmakers develop Leona's phone conversations so that they expand visually into flashbacks which thereby dramatize what might otherwise be discerned only aurally as voices by the audience. Thus, although Stanwyck must carry much of the film through her strong performance, she is aided by a vivid succession of scenes located outside Leona's room which add a sense of mobility and dynamism that her invalid status cannot provide.

The story of *Sorry, Wrong Number* begins with the following words on the screen, which set up the film's theme and dominant motif: "In the tangled networks of a great city, the telephone is the unseen link between a million lives." Leona, who lies in bed with cigarettes, radio, and medicine all to hand, overhears on crossed telephone lines what sounds like a murder plot. As she attempts to interest the police in her discovery, she also seeks to track down her absent husband, Harry. The couple are staying in borrowed accommodations in New York, where Harry works for her tycoon father, James Cotterell. Leona is able to contact Sally, an ex-girlfriend of Harry's (and college classmate of Leona's), who is now married to an FBI agent. Their dialogue conveys several important facts to the audience: that Leona had stolen Harry away from Sally; that Leona has long suffered from a psychosomatic illness which leads her to be self-absorbed, possessive, and hysterical; and that Harry is now in trouble with the federal authorities. Sally has learned this by acting as an amateur detective: following her husband to Staten Island, where the FBI has staked out a house in which Harry and his accomplices are conducting industrial espionage with organized crime figures and foreign agents.

This news makes the bed-bound Leona even more frantic and agitated, and her appearance becomes steadily more disheveled. She intensifies her phone calls searching for Harry and contacts her doctor, whose explanatory responses trigger several more complex flashbacks. These explain more about Leona's neurotic heart condition and about Harry's frustration at her bossiness, which leads him to seek greater independence from her and her bullying father. It is implied that the father may be the source of Leona's neuroses through his tyrannical attitude to all those around him. Harry's dalliance with criminals eventually creates a financial crisis for him when the chief gangster, Morano, demands the repayment of $200,000 in missing funds. The possibility emerges that the solution to Harry's plight may be to collect on Leona's life insurance by arranging for her to be murdered (the very plot she overheard in the opening sequence).

In the climactic scenes of the film a terrified Leona hears an intruder, and the audience sees a shadowy figure prowling through the house. When she finally manages to contact Harry, she avows her love for him, promises him any money he may need to get out of trouble, and he then begs her to flee the house before it is too late. This change of heart by Harry underscores the ambivalent status of his character. The film seems unable to decide whether he is a sympathetic figure or not, just as Leona herself can sometimes appear likeable and at others almost despicable. However, escape for her proves impossible; the murderous conspiracy is now unstoppable. The shadowy figure of the hired killer enters her room and, when

Harry desperately rings back, a gloved hand lifts the receiver, and a sinister voice says, "Sorry, wrong number."

Brian McDonnell

**THE SPIDER AND THE FLY** (Mayflower/Setton-Baring/Rank, 1948). *Director:* Robert Hamer. *Producer:* Aubrey Baring. *Script:* Robert Westerby. *Cinematography:* Geoffrey Unsworth. *Music:* Georges Auric. *Cast:* Eric Portman (Ferdinand Maubert), Guy Rolfe (Philippe de Ledocq), Nadia Gray (Madelaine Saincaize), George Cole (Marc), Edward Chapman (Minister for War), Maurice Denham (Colonel de la Roche), John Carol (Jean Louis/Alfred Louis).

Robert Hamer left Ealing Studios soon after the completion of *Kind Hearts and Coronets* and made *The Spider and the Fly* for an independent company. Both films were criticized, unfairly, as cold and remote. The basis for this reaction came from their less than optimistic presentation of human nature and morally problematic characters. Intelligence, not the law, becomes the prime determinant of human worth in *The Spider and the Fly*, which focuses on the powerful bond between three

*The Spider and the Fly* (1949, British). Directed by Robert Hamer. Shown from left: Guy Rolfe (as Philippe de Ledocq), Eric Portman (Ferdinand Maubert). Eagle-Lion/ Photofest.

characters—Inspector Ferdinand Maubert, the criminal Philippe de Ledocq, and the woman they both desire, Madelaine Saincaize. While Maubert's aim initially is to capture Ledocq, Ledocq's aim is to commit robberies. Both men wish to be friends as neither receives adequate stimulation or satisfaction from their incompetent colleagues. Madelaine is in love with Ledocq, but she is courted by Maubert. Because of circumstances beyond her control, she cannot form a lasting relationship with either man.

The film begins in France in 1913 as Ledocq uses Madelaine to commit a robbery. When it is completed, he rejects her offer to continue the relationship. Maubert, in turn, utilizes Madelaine to capture Ledocq. Faced with the choice between both men, she chooses the criminal by providing a false alibi for him. However, Maubert also rejects her. Madelaine, never the less, is a survivor, and although both men come to love her, circumstances, such as Maubert's arrest of Ledocq, keep them all apart. However, in 1916, Maubert, now working for the military, needs Ledocq's criminal skills to break into the German legation in Bern to steal a list of enemy agents in France. After Ledocq acquires the list of names, they discover that Madelaine, to survive during the war years, has been working as a German agent. Consequently, Madelaine is arrested in front of both men. Ledocq joins the French army, and the film concludes as Maubert stands at the station to bid farewell to his friend and adversary. Ledocq is sent to the front and his probable death.

When Maubert tells an incompetent military officer who objects to Ledocq working on behalf of the French government that it is "better [to use] a knave than a fool," he articulates the film's main theme. *The Spider and the Fly* refuses to endorse conventional moral values or conventional presentations of sexual desire and attraction. The three central characters are presented as intelligent, flawed, and attracted to each other, although circumstances conspire to keep them apart. The ending, with Madelaine's arrest, comes as a shock as it is likely that both Madelaine and Ledocq will die.

Geoff Mayer

**STANWYCK, BARBARA** (1907–1990). Barbara Stanwyck was the consummate film actor, and although she was not confined to noir films, she popularized the prototype of the dangerous woman who kills to get her way. Born Ruby Stevens in Brooklyn in 1907, Stanwyck's early life was tough. Her mother died when she was four, and she spent time in orphanages as well as periods with her showgirl sister. Stanwyck danced in speakeasies before employment as a Ziegfeld chorus girl at the age of 15. In 1926 she made her Broadway debut in *The Noose*, although it was her next production, *Burlesque*, that established her acting career.

In 1928 Stanwyck traveled to Hollywood with her husband, comedian Frank Fay, and her first screen success was in the Frank Capra melodrama *Ladies of Leisure* (1930). For much of the early 1930s she was shared by two studios, Columbia and Warner Bros., and in films such as *Illicit* (1931), *Night Nurse* (1931), *Forbidden*

(1932), *Ladies They Talk About* (1933) and, especially, *Baby Face* (1934), Stanwyck epitomized a tough, no-nonsense woman determined to get ahead in the world—whatever the cost. In 1937 she received the first of her four Academy Award nominations as the working-class mother who sacrifices her own happiness so that her daughter can marry into a wealthy, respectable family in *Stella Dallas*.

Stanwyck's career went from strength to strength in the late 1930s and early 1940s in a succession of popular films, including Preston Sturges's *The Lady Eve* (1941), Howard Hawk's *Ball of Fire* (1941), and Frank Capra's *Meet John Doe* (1941). In 1944 she was listed as the highest paid woman in America with an annual income estimated to be $400,000. Stanwyck, like Fred MacMurray, initially resisted Billy Wilder's invitation to appear in *Double Indemnity*, and only when Wilder challenged her as an actress did she agree. This film consolidated her persona as a tough, dangerous woman, and while she appeared in a variety of roles after 1944, she was the first choice of film producers wanting an assertive, sensual woman not afraid to break the law. These traits can be found in her noir films produced between 1946, *The Strange Love of Martha Ivers*, and 1957, *Crime of Passion*.

**Selected Noir Films:** *Baby Face* (1934), *Double Indemnity* (1944), *The Strange Love of Martha Ivers* (1946), *Sorry, Wrong Number* (1948), *The File on Thelma Jordan* (1950), *No Man of Her Own* (1950), *The Furies* (1950), *Blowing Wild* (1953), *Witness to Murder* (1954), *The Violent Men* (1955), *Forty Guns* (1957), *Crime of Passion* (1957).

Geoff Mayer

**STRANGER ON THE THIRD FLOOR** (RKO, 1940). *Director:* Boris Ingster. *Producer:* Lee Marcus. *Script:* Frank Partos. *Cinematography:* Nicholas Musuraca. *Music:* Roy Webb. *Cast:* Peter Lorre (Stranger), John McGuire (Michael Ward), Margaret Tallichet (Jane), Charles Waldron (District Attorney), Elisha Cook Jr. (Joe Briggs), Charles Halton (Albert Meng), Cliff Clark (Martin), Oscar O'Shea (Judge), Ethel Griffies (Mrs. Kane), Alec Craig (Defense Attorney).

*Stranger on the Third Floor* is often cited as the first film noir. While this is debatable as there are a number of 1930s films that could claim this title, such as Paramount's 1935 version of Dashiell Hammett's *The Glass Key*, it could be argued that *Stranger on the Third Floor* is the most fully developed film noir prior to the surge in noir films after 1944. The film contains many of the visual and thematic motifs that were associated with film noir long after its release. In 1940, however, it was perceived as a psychological horror film. Today, the film's reliance on the tilted camera, chiaroscuro lighting, and expressionistic sets, especially in the film's dream sequence, as well as the three flashbacks and distinctive use of first-person narration to convey the protagonist's vulnerability elevates *Stranger on the Third Floor* to a paramount position in the history of film noir.

The story is, today, familiar from many noir films—a protagonist accused and sentenced for a crime that he did not commit but secretly desired would happen.

*Stranger on the Third Floor* (1940). Directed by Boris Ingster. Shown: Charles Waldron (as the District Attorney). RKO Radio Pictures/Photofest.

The film begins with the murder trial of young taxi driver Joe Briggs, accused of slashing the throat of Nick, the owner of a neighborhood diner. The prosecution's star witness is reporter Michael Ward, who saw Briggs with Nick just prior to his death. Although Ward did not see Briggs kill Nick, his testimony convicts the young taxi driver. However, Jane, Ward's fiancée, is not convinced that Briggs committed the murder and becomes very upset when the jury delivers their verdict. Michael, on the other hand, is convinced that the taxi driver is guilty, and he eagerly anticipates a bonus from his newspaper for an exclusive story following his involvement in the trial. This bonus will enable him to leave his shabby boarding house and marry Jane.

When Michael returns to his boarding house after the trial, he cannot hear his nemesis, Meng, snoring in the next apartment. Suddenly, Ward speculates what might have happened to Meng, and his voice-over expresses his sense of fear and excitement as the film deploys the first flashback depicting a confrontation between Michael and Meng. This provides the motivation for Ward's arrest—in the same way that Briggs was convicted by circumstantial evidence—when Meng is found with his throat cut, just like Nick.

*Stranger on the Third Floor*, released in September 1940, differs from most 1930s crime films because of its emphasis on Ward's sense of guilt. While there is a plotline involving the capture of the psychotic killer (Peter Lorre) responsible for the murders, the film is more interested in the fallibility of the police and the judiciary—and the vulnerability of the ordinary person within this system.

Ward is also presented as a flawed protagonist who shares some of Meng's traits—both men are sexually frustrated. Meng, because of his age and appearance, can only leer at young women, while Ward, because of his financial situation, is forced to live in a boarding house where sexual repression is evident, and his romance with Jane is consigned to movie theaters and cold nights in the park. On the one occasion when he is able to persuade Jane to come back to his room and change out of her wet stockings, any chance of sex is destroyed when Meng brings Mrs. Kane, the landlady, into the room. Frustrated, Ward threatens to kill Meng.

Michael's nightmare just prior to his arrest for Meng's murder is the film's set piece and one of the highlights of film noir. This dream sequence captures the affinity, however illusive, between Hollywood film noir and 1920s German expressionism. The film's director, Boris Ingster, worked at the German studio UFA in the early part of his career, and it is likely that he drew on this experience in presenting the surreal aspects of Ward's nightmare. In this sequence Michael is tried for Meng's murder in a huge, distorted court and jail cell. His trial repeats, and magnifies, the injustice suffered by Briggs, showing a judge and a jury member unable to concentrate on the trial and a media desperate for a conviction. Huge diagonal shadows are thrown across the set, which is extended out of perspective by an abstract design reminiscent of many German films in the 1920s, including *The Cabinet of Dr. Caligari* (1919). At one point the judge transforms into a composite image showing the scales of justice in one hand and a scythe in the other. Ward's nightmare ends with his conviction as the jury tells him that he is pronounced guilty.

*Stranger on the Third Floor* jettisons the melodramatic suspense of the crime thriller to emphasize a world predicated on guilt and paranoia. Ward's nightmare is the reality of the film, and after his arrest, he is saved from execution only by the efforts of his girlfriend, Jane, who exposes the real killer, played by Peter Lorre. This last section of the film anticipates the subsequent film noir cycle of avenging women forced to leave their secure worlds and enter the dark side of society to save their male partners in films such as *Phantom Lady* (1944), *Black Angel* (1946), and *I Wouldn't Be in Your Shoes* (1948) as well as in the British film noir *Take My Life* (1947).

Geoff Mayer

**STREET OF CHANCE** (Paramount, 1942). *Director:* Jack Hively. *Producer:* Burt Kelly. *Screenplay:* Garrett Fort, based on the novel *The Black Curtain* by Cornell Woolrich. *Cinematography:* Theodor Sparkuhl. *Music:* David Buttolph.

*Cast:* Burgess Meredith (Frank Thompson), Claire Trevor (Ruth Dillon), Louise Platt (Virginia Thompson), Sheldon Leonard (Joe Marucci), Frieda Inescort (Alma Diedrich), Jerome Cowan (Bill Diedrich), Adeline de Walt Reynolds (Grandma Diedrich).

In 1938 Columbia Studios released *Convicted,* starring Rita Hayworth and Charles Quigley and based on Cornell Woolrich's short story "Face Work," which was published in the pulp magazine *Black Mask* in October 1937. Although this was the first screen adaptation of Woolrich's pulp/suspense stories, it was not the first adaptation of his fiction as his prepulp novels *Children of the Ritz* and *Manhattan Love Song* were filmed in 1929 and 1932, respectively. Thus, while it is debatable whether *Street of Chance,* based on his 1941 novel *The Black Curtain,* was the first noir adaptation of his work, it is the first significant noir adaptation of a Woolrich story.

Both the novel and the film establish what would become in the next few years key noir motifs involving a heightened sense of paranoia and vulnerability. Both the novel and the film begin in Tilley Street, where Frank Thompson in the film, Frank Townsend in the novel, survives a near-death experience after loose materials from a building site fall on him as he is walking down the street. After recovering consciousness, Thompson goes home to find that his wife no longer lives there—in fact, she has moved out more than a year ago. Thompson tracks her down and realizes that he has been suffering from amnesia. When he returns to his former job as an accountant, Thompson notices a sinister man constantly observing him, and when he begins following him home, Thompson begins to feel anxious and threatened.

This feeling is reinforced when his house is raided late at night and, surviving the raid, Thompson relocates his wife and returns to Tilley Street, his street of chance. Eventually, a woman, Ruth Dillon, recognizes Thompson as Dan Nearing, a man wanted for the murder of Harry Diedrich. Thompson/Nearing also learns that the man searching for him is Detective Joe Marucci. Mindful of the need to avoid Marucci, Thompson persuades Ruth to take him back to the scene of the crime at the Diedrich estate where, after establishing a form of communication with an elderly mute invalid, Grandma Diedrich, Thompson learns that Ruth, who works on the estate, killed Harry Diedrich. Marucci shoots Ruth, and her deathbed confession clears Thompson of the murder.

While the film offers a different ending than Woolrich's novel, both involve a problematic moral situation with regard to Frank and Ruth. Ruth loves Frank, and he lived with her, as Dan Nearing, while suffering amnesia. Clearly, in both the film and the novel, they had an intimate relationship as she was not aware that he was married—nor was he at the time. Her dedication to him is strong, and Claire Trevor gives a typically moving performance that establishes Ruth as a victim, not as a femme fatale. Although she is exposed as the killer, her decision to protect him leads to her downfall. Her situation in the novel is even worse when she is shown not to be the killer but is murdered while assisting Frank.

Amnesia in film noir provides the pretext for dramatizing the male protagonist's loss of control and his vulnerability in a difficult environment, and it was used a number of times in the immediate postwar period as aftermath to the terrors of war (see, e.g., *Somewhere in the Night* [1946] and *High Wall* [1947]). *Street of Chance*, however, is more effective as it presents the state, in the form of the police, as the sinister force for the first half of the film. While it does not have the star power or the budget of later films from MGM, where the sinister force is confined to an aberrant criminal element, *Street of Chance* creates a hostile world that is shown to be more universal and pervasive.

Geoff Mayer

**SUNSET BOULEVARD** (Paramount, 1950). *Director:* Billy Wilder. *Producer:* Charles Brackett. *Script:* Charles Brackett, Billy Wilder, and D. M. Marshman Jr. *Cinematography:* John F. Seitz. *Music:* Franz Waxman. *Cast:* William Holden (Joe Gillis), Gloria Swanson (Norma Desmond), Erich von Stroheim (Max von Mayerling), Nancy Olsen (Betty Schaefer), Fred Clark (Sheldrake), Lloyd Gough (Morino), Jack Webb (Artie Green). *As themselves:* Cecil B. DeMille, Hedda Hopper, Buster Keaton, Anna Q. Nilsson, H. B. Warner, Ray Evans, Jay Livingston.

Some attempts to define the subject matter of film noir have claimed that almost all noir scenarios contain a crime. Technically, Billy Wilder's 1950 masterpiece *Sunset Boulevard* fits this prescription because it certainly begins with a man's body being recovered by the police from a swimming pool where rats once scurried, and it ends with the public surrender to law officers of that man's killer. However, most of the film in between these moments has little to do with the literal breaking of statute law, but instead has everything to do with relentlessly and insightfully depicting a shadowy world of self-serving, self-deceit, and exploitation which both embodies the thematic preoccupations of film noir and excoriates the very Hollywood system that produced the classical cycle. Like the equally accomplished but more romantic film *In a Lonely Place, Sunset Boulevard* is a rare noir in which the characters actually work in the film industry. In the process it offers in its own surface beauty and its visual brilliance one of the finest examples of the studio system at work.

Joe Gillis is a hack script writer down on his luck who, to escape some repo men, turns his car into the driveway of a moldering old mansion on the eponymous Sunset Boulevard. There he encounters the bizarre figure of Norma Desmond, an aging silent screen star whose career has long since collapsed and who lives an eccentric, reclusive life that Gillis compares with Dickens's Miss Havisham. Norma is served by faithful servant Max von Mayerling (played wonderfully by real-life silent director Erich von Stroheim), who feeds her fantasies of enduring popularity while tending her fragile, suicide-prone personality. He also turns out to be the ex-director who had discovered Norma and who was her first husband. Joe is mistaken on his arrival for a pet undertaker and is temporarily assigned to the burial of her dead chimpanzee. The impecunious Joe settles in to life at the mansion, at first to work on doctoring a script (*Salome*) that Norma is touting as a vehicle for her screen comeback, but he later graduates to the role of insincere lover. Despite fits of self-loathing, he perseveres in what he views as a sick lifestyle because of the material benefits and perquisites. Andrew Spicer says in his book *Film Noir* that Joe "plumbs the depths of abjection in becoming the grinning gigolo for the increasingly possessive and unstable silent film star Norma Desmond" (p. 85). Joe is the real noir figure of the film, not Norma, who is merely delusional. He is caught in a noirish moral bind between a call to genuine love with a young aspiring writer named Betty on one hand, and his exploitative, parasitic existence providing sexual favors to Norma on the other.

Around the three denizens of the decaying house, Wilder assembles a breathtaking cast of subordinate characters with casting that strengthens the cynical subtext of the film. There are Norma's bridge-playing friends from the silent era, known to Joe as the "waxworks" and played by real-life silent film figures Buster Keaton, Anna Q. Nilsson, and H. B. Warner. Cecil B. de Mille (who cast Warner as Christ in his 1927 version of *King of Kings*) and Hedda Hopper play themselves, and the Paramount studio even "plays" itself in this Paramount production. In dramatizing the plight of an old star attempting to resurrect her career, Wilder pulls out of obscurity an actual silent screen star in Gloria Swanson and, incidentally, draws a fine performance from her. He and the other script writers have inordinate fun mocking the carnivorous world of studio wheeler-dealers, while channeling through Joe Gillis many of their own sardonic observations on the life of Hollywood scribes. Since Joe narrates the film, they can put into his mouth many funny and mordant summations of such views, for example, his description of the best script he ever wrote: "It was a beautiful script about Okies in the Dust Bowl. When it reached the screen, it took place on a torpedo boat." Representative of Wilder's daring in *Sunset Boulevard* is the fact that Joe is the man seen floating dead in the swimming pool in the opening sequence, thus providing the film with a narrator who is already dead. The original script even suggested that Joe's corpse would sit up on its mortuary slab and (in the tone of the recent television series *Six Feet Under*) narrate the film as if speaking to his fellow cadavers.

Joe's original submission to Norma's wish that he become her lover is prompted by pity after she despondently cuts her wrists from unrequited love. But he determines to abandon her when she discovers his liaisons with Betty and then poisons his character to the younger woman. Joe makes the decision that he will free Betty of any bond to him (allowing her to marry her dull but worthy fiancé) by pretending he will stay with Norma. When he then packs to leave the mansion, Norma shoots him, and he topples into the pool. The trauma of the shooting pushes Norma over the edge into mental collapse, and when reporters and newsreel cameras arrive at the house, she imagines that they are there as part of her new film project *Salome*. In one of the most devastating closures to any film, noir or otherwise, the brokenhearted Max indulges her fantasy and directs the cameras as if it were all real. As Norma Desmond/Gloria Swanson sways toward her "close-up," the *Sunset Boulevard* camera becomes the *Salome* camera, and Joe's disembodied voice-over reflects that life has "taken pity" on her and that her "dream has enfolded her." It is an acutely affecting encapsulation both of the fragility of the noir world and of the mysterious power of Hollywood film.

Brian McDonnell

# T

**TAKE MY LIFE** (Cineguild, 1947). *Director:* Ronald Neame. *Producer:* Anthony Havelock-Allan. *Script:* Winston Graham, Margaret Kennedy, and Valerie Taylor. *Cinematography:* Guy Green. *Music:* William Alwyn. *Cast:* Hugh Williams (Nicholas Talbot), Greta Gynt (Phillipa Shelley), Marius Goring (Sidney Fleming), Francis L. Sullivan (Prosecuting Counsel), Henry Edwards (Inspector Archer), Rosalie Crutchley (Elizabeth Rusman), Leo Bieber (Parone), Marjorie Mars (Mrs. Newcombe), David Walbridge (Leslie Newcombe), Maurice Denham (Defending Counsel), Ronald Adam (Detective Sergeant Hawkins).

Within little more than 12 months, Marius Goring starred in three very different films. In *Red Shoes* (1948) he played the young composer in love with the tragic heroine, followed by the middle-aged schoolmaster who makes life difficult for David Farrar in *Mr. Perrin and Mr. Traill* (1948). Goring, however, preceded these roles with a very different schoolmaster (Sidney Fleming) in *Take My Life*, who murders his wife (Elizabeth Rusman) when she threatens to divorce him on the grounds of cruelty, thereby threatening his reputation and career as the headmaster of an elite private boys' school in Scotland.

Nicholas Talbot is charged with murdering Elizabeth Rusman. This is based on the circumstantial evidence that he was in the vicinity of the murder and that he had a relationship with her some years earlier (and, coincidentally, his forehead is injured following an argument with his wife). Talbot's wife, Phillipa, is forced to investigate and seek evidence that will establish her husband's innocence. Phillipa's search initially proves fruitless, until she discovers a piece of music that leads her to Fleming's school in Scotland. Here a tense cat-and-mouse sequence follows, culminating in the deserted school as Fleming and Phillipa confront each other. The tension is carefully orchestrated during these scenes, especially when Phillipa plays the incriminating tune on the school's organ while Fleming moves closer and closer to her exposed back.

Although the basic narrative structure of the film is, by its very nature, based on coincidence and contrivances, it marks a smooth, skilful directorial debut for cinematographer Ronald Neame. The film also gave Greta Gynt, as the wife whose investigations finally establish her husband's innocence, one of her best dramatic roles. It is worth comparing *Take My Life* with the American film noir *Phantom Lady* (1944) as both films share similar plots—a woman trying to establish the innocence of her lover who is in jail. While Ella Raines in *Phantom Lady* is forced to inhabit a succession of dives that reek of desperation and sexuality, Phillipa in *Take My Life* moves through a different world of class, propriety, and repression. Thus, while both films share a similar premise, both also reflect crucial differences between each country.

Geoff Mayer

**TAXI DRIVER** (Columbia, 1976). *Director:* Martin Scorsese. *Producer:* Michael Phillips and Julia Phillips. *Script:* Paul Schrader. *Cinematography:* Michael Chapman. *Music:* Bernard Herrmann. *Cast:* Robert De Niro (Travis Bickle), Jodie Foster (Iris), Albert Brooks (Tom), Harvey Keitel (Sport), Leonard Harris (Senator Charles Palantine), Peter Boyle (Wizard), Cybill Shepherd (Betsy).

The film *Taxi Driver* was very controversial on its release in 1976 because of its extreme violence, but it was also immediately praised for the panache of Martin Scorsese's direction and the power of Robert De Niro's performance in the central role of Travis Bickle. Its notoriety was reignited, though, five years later when real-life events became caught up with details of the film's fictional story. John Hinkley Jr., who attempted to assassinate President Ronald Reagan in 1981, stated publicly that his motivation was because of his obsession with actress Jodie Foster and the character of the child prostitute Iris that she played in the film. In *Taxi Driver* Travis Bickle stalks a presidential candidate and later conducts a violent rescue of Iris from her pimp. Hinkley saw the film an alleged 15 times and grew to identify with Bickle. The attendant publicity caused by the assassination attempt lent support to conservative calls for greater control and censorship of films but also distracted attention from the messages of the film itself, which were quite moralistic. Essentially, the film is a character study of alienation and psychosis, and its depiction of what occurs when a disaffected working-class white male goes off the rails constitutes a salutary warning to society.

Ex-marine Travis Bickle applies for a job as a New York cab driver and agrees to work the unpopular night shift. As the weeks and months pass by, he records in a diary his impressions of his job and of the city he moves through. These thoughts are conveyed to the viewer through his voice-over narration, which tracks his deteriorating mental condition as he becomes more angered by what he sees as the moral degeneration of the city's people, whom he describes as "scum." In his misanthropic outlook he resembles the character John Doe in 1995's neo-noir film *Se7en*. He pops pills to keep him alert and frequents porn theaters in his time off. The campaign headquarters of presidential hopeful Senator Palantine happens to be near Travis's workplace, and there he becomes drawn to a beautiful, preppy worker named Betsy. She has little interest in him beyond mild curiosity but agrees to one date. This proves disastrous when Travis takes her to a soft-porn film and she angrily leaves. He becomes obsessively involved with her boss, Palantine, and conceives a crazy plan to assassinate the senator. He buys an arsenal of pistols, and in front of his mirror, he practices accosting people. His mental decline is tracked in his narration (describing himself as a "man who would not take it anymore"), and when he witnesses a convenience store robbery, he shoots the perpetrator dead.

After Betsy refuses to speak with him anymore, Travis transfers his obsession to a 12-year-old hooker (Iris) whom he has seen around the streets. He arranges with her pimp, Sport, to have an assignation, during which he declines sex but offers to free her of her pernicious lifestyle. Iris seems bemused by his plans but does not actively discourage him. Travis shaves his head into a Mohawk style and attempts to kill Palantine at a rally, but his risible threat is swiftly thwarted by the Secret Service, and he flees. At night, he goes to collect Iris from her pimp's place, and this action launches the infamously violent climax of the film. In the ensuing shoot-out he kills not only Sport, but two other gangsters and is himself wounded in the neck. Iris screams at the bloodbath surrounding her, and the police arrive to find the deracinated Travis miming with a pointed finger the act of blowing out his own brains. Perversely, this carnage renders him a local hero, with headlines announcing "TAXI DRIVER BATTLES GANGSTERS." It is revealed that Iris has been returned to her parents in Pittsburgh. Even Betsy is impressed when she later travels in his cab.

This summary of events does not do justice to the potency of the film, which arises not just from the work of De Niro, Scorsese, and the excellent Foster, but also from the strongly admonitory script written by Paul Schrader, himself an expert in film noir. Schrader has said that the taxicab itself is a metaphor for loneliness and isolation and that he wanted the city to be seen as a region of hell. Scorsese (who had once trained for the Catholic priesthood) also mentioned the term *purgatory* in this connection. *Taxi Driver*, as a character portrait of the urban, white, working-class male in the years following the Vietnam War, has much to say about alienation. Travis resents almost everyone he meets: the rich and powerful, blacks of any social status, those he feels are corrupting the young. The viewer is meant to see that his violence grows out of his inarticulate rage, but the voice-over narration is that of an articulate man (e.g., he uses the term *venal*). The cinema literacy of Schrader and Scorsese is highlighted by the way in which Travis's rescue of Iris resembles Ethan Edward's rescue of Debbie in *The Searchers* or the echoes of the ending of *The Wild Bunch* in the climactic gun battle. The subjective slow-motion photography in neon hues of the cab's progress through the steamy nighttime streets has a noir quality. Scenes such as the shoot-out look like a horror film: Scorsese has described the film's visual style as "New York gothic." Cinematographer Michael Chapman said that censorship worries with the Ratings Board led them to desaturate the color of the climactic bloody scene to get an R certificate. The oneiric tone of *Taxi Driver* is further augmented by the moody saxophone score written by Hitchcock favorite Bernard Herrmann, who died days after completing it.

Brian McDonnell

**THEY MADE ME A FUGITIVE** (Alliance/Warner Bros., 1947). *Director:* Alberto Cavalcanti. *Producer:* Nat Bronsten. *Script:* Noel Langley, based on the novel *A Convict Has Escaped* by Jackson Budd. *Cinematography:* Otto Heller. *Music:* Marius-Francois Gaillard. *Cast:* Sally Gray (Sally), Trevor Howard (Clem Morgan), Griffith Jones (Narcy), Rene Ray (Cora), Mary Merrall (Aggie), Charles Farrell (Curley), Michael Brennan (Jim), Jack McNaughton (Soapy), Cyril Smith (Bert), Eve Ashley (Ellen), Vida Hope (Mrs. Fenshaw), Maurice Denham (Mr. Fenshaw), Ballard Berkeley (Inspector Rockcliffe), Peter Bull (Fidgety Phil), Sebastian Cabot (Tiny), Ida Patlanski (Soho Girl).

About one-third of the way through *They Made Me a Fugitive*, Clem Morgan, a recently demobbed RAF pilot, escapes from jail and heads toward London in search of the criminal (Narcy—short for Narcissus) who framed him for the murder of a policeman and stole his girlfriend, Ellen. After receiving a load of buckshot in his back, fired by an irate farmer, Morgan stumbles into the rural household of Mr. and Mrs. Fenshaw. Although Mrs. Fenshaw recognizes Morgan as the escaped convict, she offers him food, clothing, and a bathroom to shave and wash in exchange for a small favor. Morgan readily agrees, and after cleaning himself up and eating Fenshaw's food, he learns the nature of the favor. Mrs. Fenshaw wants Morgan to kill her husband. After Morgan refuses to cooperate and leaves her house, Mrs. Fenshaw picks up the gun she offered to Morgan (with Morgan's fingerprints on the barrel of the weapon) and fires six bullets into Mr. Fenshaw as he wanders down the stairs in search of a drink.

This incident encapsulates the film's abrasive tone, which is tinged with a lingering sense of melancholy. Mrs. Fenshaw, who appears only briefly in the film, wants her husband dead—other than the fact that he is drunk, the film is not interested in establishing a motivation for her action. Similarly, Morgan's refusal to participate, which is the appropriate moral decision under the circumstances, only causes him further trouble as Mrs. Fenshaw blames the killing on the escaped convict. The media readily accept her story. This is the arbitrary world of film noir, where detailed motivation for perverse desires, such as killing one's spouse, is not necessary. In such as world, it comes as no surprise when Morgan is jailed for 15 years for a crime he did not commit.

Morgan is essentially a moral man who has trouble making the adjustment to civilian life after the excitement of World War II. He is happy to participate in black-market criminal behavior as long as it is restricted to items such as nylons, cigarettes, and bacon, but he draws the line at drugs ("sherbet"). Unfortunately, he discovers that he cannot be so selective. The film also highlights the problems of postwar adjustment for men such as Morgan. The special needs of a wartime situation that sanctions killings (Morgan kills a German after escaping from a prison camp) make it difficult for men like Morgan to adjust to peacetime conditions, a point made by Morgan when he explains that he "gave up [killing] when it went out of season."

Similarly, Narcy is established as a new kind of criminal who is identified by his sadism and perversities, qualities that emerged toward the end of World War II. Sally describes Narcy as "not even a respectable crook, just cheap, rotten after-the-war trash." Narcy, unlike earlier criminals, does not just hunger for wealth and power but wallows in the misery of others, particularly Morgan and the two women (Sally and Cora) he brutalizes in the film.

There are many fine moments in *They Made Me a Fugitive*, including the final shoot-out in the Valhalla funeral parlor where Morgan, assisted by Sally, defeats Narcy's gang, forcing its leader onto the roof, where he falls to his death. However, the film maintains its bleak mood to the very end and resists a conventional, sentimental resolution. As Morgan and Sally plead with the dying Narcy to confess that he set Morgan up for the killing of the policeman, Narcy, true to form, dies cursing Morgan and Sally. The film ends with Morgan facing the resumption of his long prison sentence for a crime he did not commit (there is a small degree of hope as Inspector Rockcliffe tells Morgan that if new evidence comes to light, he will reopen the case). The final image shows Sally alone on the dark, wet streets, watching the police car drive away. This is an appropriate ending to a strange love story where the most affectionate, and erotic, moment takes place when Sally removes the inflamed pellets from Morgan's back—a superbly realized sequence as director Alberto Cavalcanti skillfully cuts from close-ups registering Sally's horror to the stoic reaction of Morgan as he is forced, finally, to trust someone other than himself.

Geoff Mayer

**THEY WON'T BELIEVE ME** (RKO, 1947). *Director:* Irving Pichel. *Producers:* Joan Harrison and Jack J. Gross (executive). *Script:* Jonathan Latimer, based on a story by Gordon McDonell. *Cinematography:* Harry J. Wild. *Music:* Roy Webb. *Cast:* Robert Young (Larry Ballentine), Susan Hayward (Verna Carlson), Jane Greer (Janice Bell), Rita Johnson (Greta Ballentine), Tom Powers (Trenton), George Tyne (Lieutenant Carr), Don Beddoe (Thomason), Frank Ferguson (Cahill), Harry Harvey (Judge Fletcher), Milton Parsons (Court Clerk).

*They Won't Believe Me* ends on a close-up of the clerk of court announcing that Larry Ballentine, who is accused of murdering his wife, Greta, is judged not guilty.

*They Won't Believe Me* (1947). Directed by Irving Pichel. Shown: Susan Hayward (as Verna Carlson), Robert Young (as Larry Ballentine). RKO Radio Pictures/ Photofest.

However, just before the verdict is read out to the court, Ballentine is shot dead while trying to climb out of the courtroom window in a failed suicide attempt. This ironic twist reiterates one of noir's enduring themes concerning moral guilt, which almost always overrides any criminal transgression.

*They Won't Believe Me* benefits from the casting of MGM stalwart Robert Young. Young, the normally likeable leading man at MGM, is cast against type as the weak-willed, selfish Larry Ballentine who somehow manages to attract three beautiful women to fall in love with him. Young's pleasant, if passive, screen persona creates a similar effect to the casting of a similar studio actor associated with lightweight roles, Fred MacMurray, in Billy Wilder's *Double Indemnity* four years earlier. Both men generate a similar kind of moral ambivalence in the audience—they want to like them, but both are seriously flawed. Their superficial charm provides a veneer that covers their faults. They are not, however, traditional screen villains but everyday males who transgress by lusting after women who cause their downfall.

The three women in *They Won't Believe Me* represent three noir archetypes ranging from the controlling wife to the sexually promiscuous seductress. While the film begins with Larry Ballentine in court charged with his wife's murder, much of the story is concerned with Larry's relationship with each woman and is told in a flashback as Larry explains the events leading up to his wife's death. This opens with Ballentine spending his Saturday afternoons with Janice Bell, played by Jane Greer just prior to her seminal performance as Kathie Moffat in *Out of the Past* (1947). Bell, after spending the past 11 Saturdays with Ballentine in New York, gives him an ultimatum—leave his wife and travel with her to Montreal, or she will never see him again. Ballentine agrees. However, when he goes home to pack, Greta buys his affections by purchasing a limited partnership in a prestigious Beverly Hills stock brokerage firm. Consequently, Ballentine abandons Bell and travels to Los Angeles with Greta.

After a short period, Larry becomes bored with the day-to-day responsibilities of the brokerage firm and the patronizing attitude of its major partner (Trenton), and he begins an affair with the mercenary Verna Carlson, a secretary in the firm. Verna's blatant offer of sex for money is indicative of the liberalization of sexual matters in the period after World War II. While Verna eventually falls in love with Ballentine, her initial interest is purely financial, and her bargaining weapon is clearly sex. Again, Greta secures her husband with a financial inducement—providing he will leave Los Angeles and live with her on a secluded ranch. Ballentine agrees.

Greta is the third woman in Ballentine's life. She is prepared to suffer the humiliation of his affairs, and despite buying his affection, she is the most sympathetic character in the film. Finally, after realizing that he will never change, she commits suicide, and this action leads to her husband's death.

Fate, a major factor in many key noir films, plays a crucial role and conspires to bring Ballentine down. When Verna and Ballentine appear to redeem themselves by rejecting an opportunity to embezzle funds from Greta as they head toward Reno so that Larry can divorce his wife, Verna is killed in a car accident. At the same time that Verna dies, Greta commits suicide on the family ranch miles away. However, before Ballentine learns of his wife's death, he encourages the authorities to believe that it was Greta, not Verna, who died in the car accident. Later, when Greta's body is discovered, Larry is charged with her murder.

Although Ballentine is not guilty of any serious criminal charge, not having murdered Greta or Vera, he dies because he transgresses society's moral strictures. His passive, indecisive behavior is matched by his loose moral code, and he lacks focus and ambition. He is similar to the characters in another 1947 film: *Crossfire*. Both films present, in different ways, the sense of dislocation that was evident in the immediate postwar years. Although this emphasis on listless males would soon dissipate, both films document a unique historical period where the national energy and focus needed to defeat the Axis was no longer needed, resulting in a loss of unity as the nation, and the Hollywood film industry, began to fragment during the divisive Cold War period of the late 1940s and 1950s.

Geoff Mayer

**THE THIRD MAN** (London Films, 1949). *Director:* Carol Reed. *Producers:* Carol Reed, David O. Selznick, and Alexander Korda. *Script:* Graham Greene. *Cinematography:* Robert Krasker. *Music:* Anton Karas. *Cast:* Joseph Cotten (Holly Martins), Alida Valli (Anna Schmidt), Orson Welles (Harry Lime), Trevor Howard (Major Calloway), Bernard Lee (Sergeant Paine), Wilfred Hyde-White (Crabbin), Ernst Deutsch ("Baron" Kurtz), Siegfried Breuer (Popescu), Geoffrey Keen (British Policeman).

Graham Greene never intended *The Third Man* to be a serious film, yet it remains one of the great films. There are numerous highlights, including the memorable first shot of Orson Welles, as Harry Lime, exposed in a doorway by an overhead light, together with the famous climax in the sewers beneath Vienna. But the film is also notable in its clever reworking of familiar narrative conventions to form a coherent, fatalistic mosaic that captures the despair, pain, and corruption of

*The Third Man* (1949). Directed by: Carol Reed. Shown at left: Alida Valli (as Anna Schmidt). Center background: Joseph Cotten (as Holly Martins). Selznick Releasing Organization/Photofest.

postwar Europe. The genesis for the film came from Graham Greene's experiences in Vienna in the winter of 1948, when he was told of the enormous system of sewers beneath the city that breached the tightly sequestered national zones because the Russians refused to lock the thinly disguised advertisement kiosks that covered the various entrances.

American pulp author Holly Martins arrives in Vienna at the invitation of Harry Lime only to find that his friend has been killed in an automobile accident. Once Martins discovers discrepancies in the eyewitness accounts, he behaves in a similar manner to the simple-minded heroes of his western novels in their search for the so-called truth. Martins blunders toward the revelation that Lime is not dead and that, even more shockingly, his friend is living off the proceeds of his penicillin racket in the Russian sector—at the expense of children and adults deformed by his criminally adulterated medicine. Martins gradually realizes that the moral complexities of postwar Vienna cannot be equated to the simplicities of his pulp stories, and he agrees to participate in Sergeant Calloway's plan to lure Lime from the Russian zone, after which they trap and kill him in the sewers under Vienna.

The two American characters in the story occupy different positions in the film's moral spectrum—Lime's callous black-market racketeer and Holly Martins's naïve "hero" (Anna, in disgust at Martins's betrayal of Lime, tells him that Holly is such a "silly name"). The characterization of Martins as gullible and out of his depth also provides an indication of Graham Green's low opinion of postwar America and its tendency to reduce complex world problems to simplistic platitudes. Major Calloway provides a more realistic view of the world that includes making deals with the Russians. He, unlike Anna or Holly, is aware of the ramifications of Lime's callous disregard for humanity.

The other major figure in the film, and perhaps the most enigmatic character of all, is Anna Schmidt. The film does not romanticize her but emphasizes her loyalty to Lime, whatever the cost. When she discovers the horrific nature of Lime's crimes, she cannot reject her former lover and align herself with Holly. Nor can she forgive Holly—even though she initially agrees to participate in Calloway's plan so that she will not be transported back to the Russian section. Anna not only rejects Holly in the film's famous last scene, where she walks past the American, but also refuses to avail herself of the protection of the British authorities as this protection has caused Lime's death. Instead, she faces the prospect of deportation and possibly death.

Robert Krasker won the 1950 Academy Award for best black-and-white cinematography, Carol Reed was nominated as best director, and Oswald Hafenrichter was nominated for best film editing. The film also won best British film at the 1950 BAFTA Awards, and Carol Reed won the Grand Prize of the Festival at the 1949 Cannes Film Festival. The memorable zither score of Anton Karas, who Carol Reed noticed playing in a Vienna club, was a sensation at the time of the film's release (the theme from the film was a major hit in the early 1950s) and added another original touch to a film that benefited from the collaboration of many artists—including Orson Welles's contribution of his own dialogue during the Ferris wheel scene when he tries to rationalize Lime's callous behavior:

> In Italy for 30 years under the Borgias they had warfare, terror, murder, and bloodshed, but they produced Michelangelo, Leonardo da Vinci, and the Renaissance. In Switzerland they had brotherly love. They had 500 years of democracy and peace, and what did they produce? The cuckoo clock!

Yet it was director Carol Reed who opposed Selznick's attempt to shoot the film in the studio, and he also opposed the casting of Noel Coward as Harry Lime in line with Selznick's plan for a more upbeat, conventional story. Above all else, it was Reed who insisted on the despairing tone of the film's last scene, the long-held shot showing Anna's lengthy walk past Holly in the avenue near the cemetery as the remaining leaves fall from the almost barren trees.

Geoff Mayer

**THIS GUN FOR HIRE** (Paramount, 1942). *Director:* Frank Tuttle. *Producer:* Richard M. Blumenthal. *Script:* Albert Maltz and W. R. Burnett, from the novel *A Gun for Sale* by Graham Greene. *Cinematography:* John F. Seitz. *Music:* David Buttolph. *Cast:* Veronica Lake (Ellen Graham), Robert Preston (Michael Crane), Alan Ladd (Phillip Raven), Laird Cregar (Williard Gates), Tully Marshall (Alvin Brewster), Marc Lawrence (Tommy), Victor Kilian (Brewster's Secretary), Frank Ferguson (Albert Baker).

Diminutive, baby-faced Alan Ladd had appeared in small roles in minor Hollywood films for nearly a decade before his breakthrough performance as the hired killer Phillip Raven in *This Gun for Hire*, and for the most past, he captured the nihilistic basis of Graham Greene's protagonist in his 1936 novel titled *A Gun for Sale*. Raven's vocation is quickly established at the start of the film when he kills Albert Baker and his secretary. The film, similar to *Among the Living* (1941), even provides a psychological explanation for his antisocial behavior—his violation by his aunt when he was child, after his parents died, provoked his amoral view of human life—which begins with her death. Unable to relate to people, his kindness is reserved for cats.

Williard Gates, an effeminate employee of wealthy industrialist Alvin Brewster, who is selling his chemical formulas to the Japanese, pays Raven for Baker's murder. However, Gates deceives Raven with marked money as he hopes that the police will kill the young gunman. At the same time, nightclub singer Ellen Graham is recruited by the federal authorities to infiltrate Gates's club as they believe that he may be a fifth columnist selling secrets to a foreign power. These plot strands come together on a train from San Francisco to Los Angeles when Raven sits next to Graham. However, Raven takes her as a hostage when her boyfriend, policeman Michael Crane, searches the train during his investigation of Baker's murder.

*This Gun for Hire* (1942). Directed by Frank Tuttle. Shown: Alan Ladd (as Phillip Raven). Paramount Pictures/Photofest.

Raven's revenge against Gates and Graham's desire to expose Gates as a spy come together in the film's final act when Raven sacrifices his life for Graham by exposing Gates as a spy. The final moments weaken the film's noir attributes as it becomes an overt propaganda vehicle designed to warn Americans about the actions of fifth columnists undermining the war effort. Just as Warner Bros. exploited Humphrey Bogart's gangster image in the similarly themed film *All through the Night* (1942), Paramount reworked Graham Greene's novel to show that even amoral killers, such as Phillip Raven, would sacrifice themselves if they could help save their country from foreign elements.

While there are a number of visually striking scenes in the film, including a chase through a freight yard culminating in Raven's successful attempt to elude the police by jumping from a railway bridge to a moving train, the film's contribution to film noir occurs mostly in the early scenes, such as the murder of Baker and a woman, which concludes with a striking close-up of Alan Ladd's sensual reaction to Baker's death. This scene is later paralleled by his failed attempt to murder Ellen Graham in a deserted warehouse. However, as the film shifts to propaganda, the amoral killer is gradually sentimentalized into the service of his country.

Geoff Mayer

**TIERNEY, GENE** (1920–1991). Best remembered for her haunting beauty (she was one of the most glamorous and sexy of all noir actresses) and for her tragic personal life, Tierney will always be associated with the classic title role in Otto Preminger's *Laura* (1944). Born in Brooklyn, New York, into an affluent family, she attended a Swiss finishing school. Tierney then worked as a model, and after some stage work in New York, she went to Hollywood, where she was briefly contracted to Columbia. A return to New York and positive publicity about her stage acting renewed the calls from the studios. She won a contract at Twentieth Century Fox and married Paramount dress designer Oleg Cassini. She split with her father over questions involving money and his treatment of her mother. Tierney's first film noir role was in *The Shanghai Gesture* in 1941, where she played Poppy, a socialite who falls into a decadent lifestyle at a Chinese gambling house. Poppy dies at the end at the hands of the woman Gin Sling, who runs the place and who turns out to be her mother. Tierney herself had a very tragic life especially with her ill daughter, Daria. Tierney had contracted German measles early in her pregnancy, being exposed to the infection while volunteering at the Hollywood Canteen. Later, the badly retarded child was a constant source of anxiety for her.

Tierney was forever to become associated with the dreamlike Laura Hunt in the Otto Preminger–directed film of the same name. With her beautiful, often sultry face, used positively in *Laura,* where she is the object of desire for a number of men, Tierney is, however, actually more nuanced and complex in her role as a possessive bitch in *Leave Her to Heaven* (1945). In that film, her lovely features are merely a mask over her innately obsessive, psychopathic nature as she impassively watches her husband's crippled young brother drown and later deliberately procures a miscarriage for the unborn child she considers a rival. For her work in this role of murderously possessive love, she was nominated for the Academy Award for best actress. Tierney had a brief romance with rising politician Jack Kennedy while she was shooting the gothic noir *Dragonwyck* (1946). In a reversal of *Leave Her to Heaven,* she played a kleptomaniac woman who was the victim of a male plot in *Whirlpool* opposite Richard Conte. Tierney had a secondary part in the excellent London-set noir *Night and the City* (1950), in which she was visibly less glamorous than in her earlier roles. She also appeared that same year opposite her *Laura* costar Dana Andrews in the underrated film noir *Where the Sidewalk Ends,* directed once again by Otto Preminger. Andrews plays a brutal cop who kills Tierney's estranged husband. She falls for him and stands by him at the end when he admits to his crimes. This role as a vulnerable woman is one of her most human, and Tierney combines a more earthy realism with her usual eroticism. In her later life Gene Tierney suffered extensive periods of depression and was hospitalized on a number of occasions.

**Selected Noir Films:** *The Shanghai Gesture* (1941), *Laura* (1944), *Leave Her to Heaven* (1945), *Dragonwyck* (1946), *Whirlpool* (1949), *Night and the City* (1950), *Where the Sidewalk Ends* (1950), *Black Widow* (1954).

Brian McDonnell

**TIGHTROPE** (Warner Bros./Malpaso, 1984). *Director:* Richard Tuggle. *Producers:* Clint Eastwood and Fritz Manes. *Script:* Richard Tuggle. *Cinematography:* Bruce Surtees. *Music:* Lennie Niehaus. *Cast:* Clint Eastwood (Wes Block), Genevieve Bujold (Beryl Tribodeaux), Dan Hedaya (Detective Molinari), Alison Eastwood (Amanda Block), Jennifer Beck (Penny Block), Marco St. John (Leander Rolfe).

In some ways, Clint Eastwood's 1984 film *Tightrope* is an unremarkable thriller and an unexceptional example of neo-noir. It is notable, though, for its exploration of themes and character features that were important in the classical noir cycle, elements that are revisited here in a story line that reflects both the influence of second-wave feminism and the relaxation of Hollywood censorship rules since the mid-twentieth century. *Tightrope* revives the old noir fascination with police officers who are possibly corrupt and with the close similarities between the inner demons faced by both the perpetrators of crime and those investigating them. It also delves uninhibitedly into the sordid world of prostitution in a way that would have been impossible for films of the 1940s and 1950s to contemplate, let alone attempt. This alone makes it an intriguing text to compare with those earlier films. Furthermore, Eastwood himself plays the central role of detective Wes Block, and he makes Wes a much more complex and equivocal law enforcement figure than he had done with the definitive Eastwood role of the early 1970s: "Dirty" Harry Callaghan.

Wes is a solo father looking after his two daughters while he works as a homicide detective in New Orleans. The city is being racked by a series of violently sexualized murders of prostitutes and other women, who are being killed around the red light precincts of the French Quarter. Whenever Wes attends the crime scene of one of these killings, the body is inevitably nude, and there is evidence of rape or other sexual violation. These deaths bring Wes face-to-face with unsavory misogynistic rage, and he is forced to address some of his own attitudes toward women, especially toward his estranged wife. While he is essentially a good man (and a loving father), his own predilection for sex workers and his haunting of bars, brothels, and sex clubs lead him to believe that there are uncomfortable similarities between himself and the killer he is chasing. Wes definitely has baser urges that he must overcome to distinguish himself from those whose aberrations take a more felonious turn.

This is a situation characteristic of a number of noir heroes over the years, but here it is taken to a greater degree of explicitness. It is also a mark of social changes in the 1980s that the film's main female character, Beryl Tribodeaux, is a prominent feminist figure in New Orleans who works at a rape center, where she runs self-defense classes for women, and who challenges Wes to work harder to protect the city's vulnerable female population. His growing relationship with Beryl (in which she encourages him to be more open emotionally) prompts him to reconsider some of his views about the benefits of candor in regard to his feelings and the necessity for close, caring sexual relationships. This aspect of the story foregrounding the plight of modern women is bolstered by a number of scenes showing Wes with his daughters, particularly the older one, Amanda (played by Eastwood's own daughter), in which he is shown to be empathetic and considerate. The progressive tone of such sequences is undercut a little, though, by the mildly exploitative nature of the camera work in some of the sex crime scenes and by a corny and very 1980s quasi-erotic encounter between Beryl and Wes as they work out on gymnasium equipment.

The quieter sequences contrast in tone with the many action scenes, chases, and murders, which verge on the repellent in their exposure of human cruelty, malice, and weakness. Kinky sex and sadomasochistic practices are detailed as Wes trawls the sleazier environs of the city's vice districts. Halfway through *Tightrope*, a police profiler mentions to Wes that everybody walks a tightrope in life between maintaining control of bad desires or acting out vicious impulses. This notion, embodied in the film's title, draws attention to the disturbing ties that unite the killer with Wes, sometimes even tempting the audience to believe that they might be one and the same person. At one point Wes uses handcuffs for sex and even awakes sweating from a nightmare in which he himself was a masked man strangling Beryl. However, *Tightrope* is a more conventional thriller than these details might suggest, and it is soon made clear that the real culprit is an ex-cop named Leander Rolfe, whom Wes had once arrested for the rape of two teenagers and who had been thrown off the force and imprisoned in Angola for 11 years. Rolfe eventually turns his fury directly on Wes by murdering a young hooker Wes had had sex with, then by attacking his home and menacing his girls, and ultimately, by attempting to throttle Beryl.

She fights back, but it is Wes's timely arrival that causes the man to flee. *Tightrope*'s climactic nighttime pursuit through a wasteland of railway sidings and freight cars is both exciting and an appropriate culmination to the film's examination of questions of identity, doubling, and the assigning of sexual guilt. When Leander and Wes are finally face-to-face, there are physical similarities between the men that make it seem that Wes is looking into a mirror, one that shows his darker shadow side. Their fight on the railway tracks is close and intimate. Leander attempts to strangle Wes, and when the wheel of a passing train shockingly severs the attacker's arm, Wes is left holding the amputated limb in his own hand as the dead man's grip is still around his throat. This macabre image suggests that in a way, Wes has been fighting some part of himself from which he must wrench free to become a better man. His status as just such an emotionally liberated person is clinched in the final moments, when, at last, he is able to resist flinching when Beryl touches his face.

Brian McDonnell


**T-MEN** (Eagle-Lion, 1948). *Director:* Anthony Mann. *Producer:* Aubrey Schenck. *Script:* John C. Higgins, story by Virginia Kellogg. *Cinematography:* John Alton. *Music:* Paul Sawtell. *Cast:* Dennis O'Keefe (Dennis O'Brien/Vannie Harrigan), Alfred Ryder (Tony Genaro/Tony Galvani), Mary Meade (Evangeline), Wallace Ford (The Schemer), June Lockhart (Mary Genaro), Charles McGraw (Moxie), Anton Kosta (Carlo Vantucci), John Wengraf ("Shiv" Triano), William Malten (Paul Miller), Reed Hadley (Narrator), Elmer Lincoln Irey (Himself).

*T-Men* is one of a group of postwar semidocumentary crime films (such as 1948's *The Naked City* and *Call Northside 777*) that some film historians consider marginal to true film noir. The glamorization of law enforcement officers in these films, their conservative politics and clear moral contrasts between good and bad, seem to set them apart from noir's usual concern with life's victims and with moral ambivalence. It is true that *T-Men* shares some of the establishment values of the semidocumentary subgenre, but both its contradictory dramatization of the murky behavioral codes of undercover officers and its darkly expressionistic visual style (courtesy of director Anthony Mann and cinematographer John Alton) allow it a genuine place within any comprehensive definition of classical film noir. The short-lived Eagle-Lion organization (formed from a combination of Poverty Row studio PRC and the British company Rank), which produced *T-Men*, also made such film noirs as *Hollow Triumph* and *Raw Deal* (both 1948). The new Eagle-Lion combine attempted to upgrade the traditional Hollywood B picture, and this project helped give a higher than usual budget to Mann.

*T-Men* opens with a prologue typical of semidocumentary noir. A real-life U.S. Treasury official Elmer Lincoln Irey (who had been involved in the investigation of both the Al Capone tax evasion case and the baby Lindburgh kidnapping, and who died within months of *T-Men*'s release) introduces the Treasury Department and its six branches: the Coast Guard, the Secret Service (protecting the president and stopping currency counterfeiting), and its units combating income tax evasion, smuggling, narcotics, and bootlegging. Irey says that *T-Men* will dramatize a composite counterfeiting investigation called the Shanghai paper case. The film then immediately cuts visually away from Washington officialdom to depict a darkly noirish, Alton-photographed world of crime with the cold-blooded nighttime killing of an informer in Santa Monica. The craggy face of gang assassin Moxie emerges like a snake from the blackness of a shadow to gun down the man, whose death frustrates the plans of the Treasury Department to uncover a counterfeiting ring. They decide to have two of their men go in undercover but, because the Los Angeles gang is very clever, they intend to approach the ring obliquely by having the agents first infiltrate an associated gang (the Ventucci mob of bootleggers) in Detroit. Two suitable men (O'Brien and Genaro) who can pass convincingly as gangsters are selected, the latter able to speak Italian and recently married. The two men carry out painstaking library research to prepare their cover, and posing as wanted men, they get jobs in Ventucci's liquor racket. They start out putting stolen government stamps on his bootleg bottles, these false stamps coming from the counterfeiters in Los Angeles. Fortunately, *T-Men's* narration provides the audience with a continuing guide to this complex plotline.

To speed the overall investigation, O'Brien goes to Los Angeles to locate a contact man known as the Schemer. He knows the man uses both Chinese therapeutic products and steam baths, and with the assistance of these clues, O'Brien successfully tracks him down. From Union Station he goes to steam baths in Los Angeles's Chinatown, where he identifies Schemer by a scar. O'Brien then engineers a meeting by passing counterfeit money at a crap game. Schemer notes the illegal currency and is impressed by the quality of the printing, but not by the paper. O'Brien suggests a deal where they combine his hand-engraved printing plates with the ring's high-quality Chinese-sourced paper, hoping to use Schemer to gain access to people higher up in the gang. He is taken to meet a boss figure called Shiv in a plush Beverly Hills house, but the gang soon suspects both him and Genaro of possibly being government agents. The film ramps up the potential danger of the men's situation when Genaro is brought out to the West Coast from Detroit to produce the plates. At the Farmers Market, by a wild chance, Genaro bumps into his wife and has to desperately cover up their relationship when her friend identifies him in front of Schemer. At this point, the whole undercover project seems doomed, with Schemer being brutally eliminated by Moxie in a steam bath (Alton's shooting of this scene is an expressionistic highlight) and then Genaro being shot dead in front of O'Brien, who cannot intervene for fear of exposing himself. Genaro had found a diary of Schemer's that contained information that could help break the case, and he sacrifices himself to pass on the clue to O'Brien. It is in these scenes showing the deception, ethical dilemmas, and moral impotence inherent in undercover work that *T-Men* most displays its noir character.

As the film hastens to its climax, Mann intensifies the suspense in several scenes as the audience speculates first if O'Brien can retrieve the plate while being observed by a couple of thugs, then wonders what will happen if an expert examination of the plate will expose his true identity. This tension culminates in a brilliant action sequence aboard a ship as the gang fight it out with the authorities while O'Brien gets the opportunity to kill Moxie despite himself being wounded. A brief epilogue includes a *Look* magazine layout showing the gang's big boss being apprehended, O'Brien recuperating in hospital, and Genaro's widow remembering her husband's valor. The style of *T-Men*, with its mix of a semidocumentary script and a noir mise-en-scène created by Mann and Alton, has been described as "hybrid and elastic" by Andrew Spicer in his book *Film Noir* (p. 58). In a way, the film is a celebration of the Treasury Department and does include some documentary coverage, but the central sequences of the drama are definitely immersed in a noir milieu, and the two agents fit disturbingly well into the criminal world. The critical and commercial success of *T-Men* did have one immediate good effect for its makers: soon after its release, both John Alton and Anthony Mann were given contracts at MGM.

Brian McDonnell

**TODD, ANN** (1909–1993). Compton Bennett's *The Seventh Veil* (1946), in which Ann Todd played Francesca Cunningham, the masochistic, tormented pianist, was not only Todd's breakthrough film to stardom, but was one of the most perverse love stories in the history of the British cinema. Cunningham, trained and molded (and disciplined) by her woman-hating uncle (James Mason) into a world-renowned pianist, has a variety of lovers to choose from but, ultimately, returns to the cruel, controlling arms of her uncle. Todd reprised this role in a stage version with Leo Genn, but it failed to capture the powerful screen chemistry between Todd and Mason that elevated *The Seventh Veil* to be the most popular British film in 1946–1947. The relative failure of the play compared with the film may also have had something to do with Todd's ease in front of the camera and her ability to suggest emotional turmoil within layers of repressions beneath her seemingly fragile beauty, a quality that was exploited over the next four years as Todd enjoyed her greatest film roles.

Ann Todd was trained at Central School to be a drama teacher, although she soon turned to acting, especially film acting. Following the success of *The Seventh Veil*, Todd essayed a series of emotionally and morally divided women who were unable to maintain so-called normal relationships with lovers or husbands. This series begins with Compton Bennett's bleak film noir *Daybreak* (1947), in which Todd plays the vulnerable wife of Eric Portman who, through circumstances and personal weakness, falls for the superficial sexual attentions of Maxwell Reed. This leads to suicide and murder. Todd followed this with one of the best films produced in England during the 1940s, a Paramount British film noir, *So Evil My Love* (1948), with Todd as Olivia Harwood, the sexually repressed widow of a missionary who is seduced by Ray Milland into blackmailing a vulnerable friend (Geraldine Fitzgerald). This results in humiliation, murder, and a bleak ending as Harwood tries to recover lost dignity by killing Milland and surrendering herself to the police.

In another American film shot in London, Alfred Hitchcock's *The Paradine Case* (1948), Todd is betrayed by her lawyer husband, Gregory Peck, who becomes infatuated with murderess Valli. This position is reversed in David Lean's domestic melodrama *The Passionate Friends* (1949), with Todd, as Mary Justin, trapped in a compassionate, but sexless, marriage to Claude Rains. After betraying her husband with lover Trevor Howard, Justin's equilibrium is disturbed years later when he reappears in her life, forcing her to contemplate suicide before an emotional reconciliation with Rains.

Ann Todd worked with film director–husband David Lean in three films. *The Passionate Friends*, the first, was followed by *Madeleine* (1950), a cold film that detailed the events leading up to a (possible) murder. In this film Lean exploited Todd's characteristic projection of vulnerability with less appealing character traits involving deception and betrayal. However, the film's refusal to clarify her exact moral and criminal status jeopardized its chance of attracting a large audience. At the end of the film, the jury at her trial for poisoning her lover delivers an inconclusive verdict of not proven. A third film with Lean, *The Sound Barrier* (1952), gave Todd little to do as it concentrates more on the men and their airplanes. Todd ended her eight-year marriage to Lean in 1957.

*The Green Scarf* (1954), a courtroom thriller set in Paris involving a blind man (Kieron More) accused of murder, directed by George More O'Ferrall, marked the end of Todd's career as a major star, and only Joseph Losey's *Time without Pity* (1957) and Seth Holt's convoluted psychological thriller *Taste of Fear* (1960), written by Jimmy Sangster, were of interest in the final phase of her film acting career as she moved into character roles. *The Son of Captain Blood* (1962), a Spanish/Italian/American coproduction shot in Spain, saw Todd playing Sean Flynn's (son of Errol Flynn) mother. This lackluster pirate story presented Sean Flynn as following in his father's footsteps. After stage work in the 1950s with the Old Vic, Todd returned to film in the 1960s, this time as the writer, producer, and director of travel documentaries. Ann Todd's autobiography, *The Eighth Veil*, was published in 1980.

**Selected Noir Films:** *The Return of Bulldog Drummond* (1934), *The Squeaker* (1937), *The Seventh Veil* (1945), *Daybreak* (1947), *So Evil My Love* (1948), *The Paradine Case* (1948), *The Passionate Friends* (1949), *Madeleine* (1950), *The Green Scarf* (1954), *Time without Pity* (1956), *90 Degrees in the Shade* (1965), *The McGuffin* (1985).

Geoff Mayer

**TOTTER, AUDREY** (1918–). In 1946, producer Mark Hellinger was at Universal Studios in preproduction for his adaptation of Ernest Hemingway's short story "The Killers." He selected Audrey Totter for the role of Kitty, the sultry femme fatale who brings down the hapless Burt Lancaster. Totter, however, was also offered the female lead in Robert Montgomery's "daring" adaptation of the Raymond Chandler novel *Lady in the Lake*. The film was considered daring because Montgomery planned to subvert the classical Hollywood system by shooting virtually all of the film with a subjective camera, whereby the actors delivered their dialogue directly into the lens, because the camera represented Chandler's detective, Philip Marlowe. Robert Montgomery, as Marlowe, would only be seen when the camera picked up reflected images such as a mirror. While filming for *The Killers* took place between June 28 and August 28, 1946, the schedule for *Lady in the Lake* was moved forward to begin on July 5, 1946. Hence Audrey Totter had to choose which role to accept. She selected Adrienne Fromsett in *Lady in the Lake*, and the role of

Kitty went to newcomer Ava Gardner. While *The Killers* went on to be a critical and commercial success, *Lady in the Lake* proved to be a disaster—both financially and critically—and Robert Montgomery left the studio after 17 years. While Ava Gardner became a major star, Audrey Totter, despite a series of strong roles in the late 1940s, saw her film career dissipate in the early 1950s.

Totter was born into a middle-class household in Joliet, Illinois, in 1918. Her father had served in the Austrian army, her mother was Swedish, and she learned the virtues of discipline and self-restraint from an early age. Totter began working in radio soap operas in Chicago when she was a teenager and made her stage debut in a touring production of *My Sister Eileen*. This production took her to New York. After more radio work, MGM offered her a contract, starting at $300 a week, and cast her in *Main Street after Dark* (1945), a low-budget crime film starring Edward Arnold. Totter also provided Phyllis Thaxter's "demonic" voice in *Bewitched* (1945) Arch Oboler's bizarre story of a woman suffering multiple personality disorder. She also made an impact as Madge Gorland, the temptress who lures John Garfield away from Lana Turner, for a brief period, in *The Postman Always Rings Twice* (1946). In this film Totter was required to darken her blonde hair to distinguish her from Lana Turner.

Totter's next appearance in a film noir was in *The Unsuspected* (1947), Michael Curtiz's independent production filmed at Warner Bros. Totter played the sensual, slightly kinky niece of Claude Rains. However, it was Totter's next film noir, *High Wall* (1947), that provided her best role to date as a psychiatrist determined to help ex–army pilot Robert Taylor, who suffers from amnesia, find his wife's killer. However, MGM was never entirely comfortable with film noir in the 1940s as its head of studio, Louis B. Mayer, disliked them, and Totter never received the buildup accorded actresses, such as Greer Garson, who worked in other genres.

Her last major role at MGM was one of the studio's best noir films, *Tension* (1950), starring Totter as Claire Quimby, the coldhearted wife of Richard Basehart. This taut noir was directed by John Berry, who, soon after the film was completed, was forced to flee the United States for Paris after Edward Dmytryk's testimony at the House Committee on Un-American Activities exposed Berry as the director who made the documentary supporting the Hollywood 10.

After her moving performance as Robert Ryan's wife in *The Set-Up*, where she was loaned out to RKO, and the femme fatale in *Tension*, no significant roles were offered to Totter. However, her contract with MGM prevented her from accepting the role of Montgomery Clift's pregnant girlfriend in George Steven's acclaimed film *A Place in the Sun* (1951). The role went to Shelley Winters, and her career soared after she received an Academy Award nomination. Totter left MGM and worked as a freelance actor.

*Under the Gun* (1951), a powerful noir film made at Universal, should have attracted attention, but her career was slipping at this stage. While she continued to costar in genre films until the mid-1950s, she decided to downgrade her acting ambitions after marrying doctor Leo Fred in 1953. Totter worked in television throughout the 1960s and 1970s, including a four-year stint as Nurse Wilcox in

*Medical Center* between 1972 and 1976. She finally retired after a guest role on *Murder, She Wrote* in 1987.

**Selected Noir Films:** *Main Street after Dark* (1945), *Dangerous Partners* (1945), *Bewitched* (1945, voice), *The Postman Always Rings Twice* (1946), *Lady in the Lake* (1947), *The Unsuspected* (1947), *The High Wall* (1947), *Alias Nick Beal* (1949), *The Set-Up* (1949), *Tension* (1950), *Under the Gun* (1951), *FBI Girl* (1951), *The Sellout* (1952), *Man in the Dark* (1953), *Women's Prison* (1955), *A Bullet for Joey* (1955).

Geoff Mayer

**TOUCH OF EVIL** (Universal International, 1958). *Director:* Orson Welles. *Producer:* Albert Zugsmith. *Script:* Orson Welles, from the novel *Badge of Evil* by Whit Masterson. *Cinematography:* Russell Metty. *Music:* Henry Mancini. *Cast:* Charlton Heston (Ramon "Mike" Vargas), Janet Leigh (Susan Vargas), Orson Welles (Hank Quinlan), Joseph Calleia (Pete Menzies), Akim Tamiroff (Uncle Joe Grandi), Marlene Dietrich (Tanya), Mercedes McCambridge (Hoodlum), Zsa Zsa Gabor (Owner of Nightclub), Ray Collins (Adair), Dennis Weaver (Motel Manager).

*Touch of Evil* (1958). Directed by Orson Welles. Shown from left: Orson Welles (as Police Captain Hank Quinlan), Janet Leigh (as Susan "Susie" Vargas), Akim Tamiroff (as "Uncle" Joe Grandi). Universal Pictures/Photofest.

The major burst of production of those films which are considered part of the classical film noir cycle occurred at the end of the 1940s and in the early 1950s, and there are usually only a handful of titles included after 1955. *Touch of Evil* is probably the best known of these, and several historians claim it as the very last film of the cycle. Although this has been disputed, with 1959's *Odds Against Tomorrow* given that place by many writers today, *Touch of Evil* certainly lays claim to being the final great flourish of expressionistic style within the classical noir era. Its use of a rock 'n' roll soundtrack and the presence of late 1950s cars mark it out as both visually and aurally distinct from the noir films of the 1940s, but Orson Welles (the film's director, script writer, and star) still employs the same odd angles and chiaroscuro lighting that distinguished many of the noir movies of that earlier period, along with their disconnected and subjective narrative structure. He even smuggles several major stars into his narrative by way of striking cameo roles.

Some critics have found his camera style unusual, even deliberately incoherent and confusing, noting, for instance, the absence of master shots. Andrew Spicer, in his book *Film Noir*, calls this visual strategy "baroque expressionism" (p. 63) and links it with Welles's characteristic overlapping dialogue, which is prominent in the film. Also of vital importance to the look of *Touch of Evil* is its geographical setting: the colonnades, canals, and strip clubs of a fictitious Tijuana-style frontier settlement often filmed night-for-night in the then seedy backwaters of the Los Angeles suburb of Venice. The film's famous opening sequence sets up the atmosphere of a corrupt border town as well as conveying important expository information. The much-admired four-minute crane shot that culminates in a car exploding is not only a "look at me!" device by Welles, it also provides a sense of how fluid things are in this marginal world, in what Spicer (p. 61) says is a "liminal space between Mexico and the United States."

The film's thriller plot makes no great claim for lasting significance, but what passes for its main theme is delivered by the way the story's different crimes become interlinked. These two criminal activities are the opening car bombing, with its attendant murder, and the Grandi drugs case, which has dragged on for months. The two crimes are paralleled by the interlinked nature of the town's sections (American and Mexican) and by the two contrasting law enforcement officials involved: the upright Mexican Mike Vargas and the crooked American Hank Quinlan. Vargas is stolid, pompous, physically tough, and self-righteous and is played almost woodenly by Charlton Heston with a moustache and a fake tan. Vargas, who is bringing the Grandi drug empire to book, claims defensively to his American wife Susie that "all border towns bring out the worst in a country." And to Quinlan, whom he accuses of planting evidence, he remarks that "a policeman's job is only easy in a police state." Hank Quinlan (portrayed by Welles himself, without any Hollywood vanity, as obese and slobbish) works by instinct and intuition, which serves him well. Whereas Hank tries to frame the guilty, Vargas is more a man for principle, with close connections to the Mexican government, the United Nations, and so on. When the car bomb kills a prominent businessman, Hank chases the dynamite used and pounces on a possible personal motive that implicates a young Mexican man, Sanchez, who is living with the rich man's daughter. Quinlan railroads him with planted evidence, but at the film's end his hunch about the young man's guilt proves correct.

One of the local Grandis (Uncle Joe) wants to warn Vargas off the drugs prosecution by threatening his wife. Susie is thus used as a pawn in the conflict, becoming isolated from her husband at the Mirador Motel outside town. Because Susie is played by Janet Leigh (as well as for other reasons), the motel seems a precursor of the Bates Motel in *Psycho*. Just as in Hichcock's film two years later, there is much emphasis throughout *Touch of Evil* on Leigh's breasts. A sense of threat from the Grandis pervades her time at the motel, where she is tormented by youths in hot rods, including a sinister butch lesbian. Sleep deprivation helps break her spirit, and she is forced to take drugs. There are even vague hints that she has been raped as one punk instructs the others to "hold her legs." Welles crosscuts frequently between events at the motel and what Susie's husband is doing in town. By entrapping Susie, Grandi forms an alliance with Quinlan against Vargas to discredit him as a drug addict, which will, of course, affect his credibility in the narcotics case. Quinlan, who wants Vargas out of his hair but does not want any deaths, falls off the wagon after 12 years not drinking. Later, in a hotel room where Susie lies drugged, Quinlan overcomes his compunction, and in a scene memorably employing a hand-held camera, he pursues and kills Grandi, hoping to frame Susie for his death.

Also linking the two main characters is Quinlan's very loyal friend and fellow detective Pete Menzies. He sticks by his belief in Hank's honesty despite evidence to the contrary, but he changes his mind when he hears of similar cases from Vargas, then sees Susie so damaged by his friend's actions. Menzies finds Hank's cane in the hotel room by Grandi's body and then combines with Vargas in the film's climax to gain an incriminating admission from Hank. In this nighttime sequence among the oil pumps, a rambling conversation between a drunk Hank and Menzies is listened in on by Vargas, who tapes them. Welles uses a complex sound track of echoes and distorted sound to augment his usual expressive camera angles. Hank cottons on to what is happening with the electronic eavesdropping and shoots Menzies, then washes his hands in slime. He threatens to shoot Vargas, but Menzies shoots Hank before dying and the obese, corrupt policeman sinks like a dinosaur into the oily water. In a rush of late exposition, we hear of Sanchez confessing to the car bombing, and Susie appears, suddenly recovered from her drug experience to embrace Vargas, whose virtue has overcome the viciousness of Quinlan and Uncle Joe Grandi.

Brian McDonnell

**TOURNEUR, JACQUES** (1904–1977). While Jacques Tourneur was an excellent director in his own right, working across the spectrum of Hollywood genres in the 1940s and 1950s, in terms of the development of film noir, his name is often linked with the producer of his first three films at RKO, Val Lewton. Both men played an important part in developing the morbid sensibility that came to characterize many noir films, a sensibility that was largely foreign to the Hollywood cinema prior to the Tourneur/Lewton films of the early 1940s. Both men were born overseas and both men remained mavericks, or outsiders, within the mainstream Hollywood system—rarely did Tourneur have access to substantial budgets, and Lewton never did.

The son of legendary silent film director Maurice Tourneur, Jacques was born in Paris and came to the United States with his father in 1914; after an initial education in New York, he joined his father in California in 1918, where he attended Hollywood High School. At school he befriended Joel McCrea, who made three westerns with Tourneur in the 1950s: *Stars in My Crown* (1950), *Stranger on Horseback* (1955), and *Wichita* (1955).

It was at high school where Tourneur decided to follow his father into the film industry. After completing high school, he worked as a script clerk on a number of his father's films, and he remained in Hollywood when his father returned to Europe. He supported himself with small acting parts and other odd jobs in Hollywood. However, as his acting failed to excite the studios, in 1928 Jacques rejoined his father in Berlin, where he was directing *Das Schiff der verlorenen Menschen*. From 1930 to 1934 Jacques worked as assistant director and editor on a number of his father's films before graduating to the director's chair in 1931, and he made four films in Paris before returning to MGM in Hollywood in 1934.

Jacques Tourneur remained at MGM from 1934 to 1939 as a second-unit director on feature films and as a director on short subjects, such as *Romance of Radium* (1937), which was nominated for an Academy Award. When the head of the studio, Louis B. Mayer, expressed his satisfaction with one of Tourneur's *Crime Doesn't Pay* shorts, the studio decided to upgrade it to feature length, and it became his first Hollywood feature film, *They All Come Out* (1939). After two more feature films at MGM, *Nick Carter, Master Detective* (1939) *and Phantom Raiders* (1940), both starring Walter Pidgeon as Nick Carter, and a low-budget quickie at Republic, *Doctors Don't Tell* (1941), Tourneur was invited to join producer Val Lewton, who was forming a small production unit at RKO to make horror films. Because the budgets were small, the Lewton unit enjoyed considerable freedom from studio interference, and Tourneur was assigned to the direction of its first three films: *Cat People* (1942), *I Walked with a Zombie* (1943), and *The Leopard Man* (1943). The only real interference from the studio came from the head of production, Charles Koerner, who gave the title of each film to Lewton before production.

These three films, designed by the studio to satisfy the demand for exploitation films by shift workers during the early years of World War II, are among the finest films produced in Hollywood. The relationship between the Russian-born Lewton and the visually literate French director was immediately strong, and they formed the ideal creative partnership. They decided to jettison the popular Universal approach to horror, based on iconic monsters such as Dracula and Frankenstein, and develop their supernatural thrillers around everyday people living their lives in familiar urban settings. These films, however, presented a delicate balance between the rational basis of ordinary life and the terrors presented by the supernatural. This proved to be a fertile basis for exploring contemporary anxieties.

Lewton and Tourneur were assisted on the first film, *Cat People*, by cinematographer Nicholas Musuraca, who heightened the sinister atmosphere of the film with dramatic, low-key photographic effects. This form of expressive lighting became widely associated with film noir in the middle and late 1940s, and Lewton and Tourneur consistently utilized this style at least four years before it became the norm. Tourneur, owing to the unexpected financial success of *Cat People*, was promoted out of Lewton's B unit by RKO. Although he was subsequently offered films with larger budgets, he expressed regret that was no longer able to work with Lewton.

Tourneur went on to work on a number of key noir films—especially *Out of the Past* (1947), which is now regarded as the archetypal Hollywood film noir. In this film Tourneur was assisted by cinematographer Musuraca and, together with Daniel Mainwaring and Frank Fenton's script, combined a sense of personal entrapment with a mood of melancholy and loss. Earlier, in 1944, he directed *Experiment Perilous*, which was part of a cycle of gothic melodramas. In 1951 he went to England for *Circle of Danger* (1951), starring Ray Milland as man who returns to Britain to find out who killed his brother.

Tourneur's most significant noir film in the 1950s was *Nightfall* (1957), based on a novel by David Goodis and starring Aldo Ray as a man trapped between killers who believe that he has a satchel full of money in his possession and the police, who claim he killed his partner. The film is similar to *Out of the Past* in the way in which it utilizes flashbacks and thematic parallels between the city and the country. However, *Nightfall* does not match the perfection of *Out of the Past*, and its upbeat ending fails to capture the sense of loss that pervades *Out of the Past*.

Tourneur's previous film, *Great Day in the Morning* (1956), is a strange western which Tourneur imbues with a sense of fatalism and irony, characteristics not readily associated with this genre. However, with the decline in the medium-budget genre films in the late 1950s and early 1960s, Tourneur's film career came to a premature end, and his final films were low-budget exploitation productions: *La Battaglia di Maratona* (1959), an MGM "sword and sandal" coproduction starring Steve Reeves and filmed in Italy and Yugoslavia; *The Comedy of Terrors* (1963), a horror spoof for American-International Pictures starring Vincent Price, Peter Lorre, Basil Rathbone, and Boris Karloff; and *War-Gods of the Deep* (1965), also for American International, filmed in England and starring Hollywood actors Vincent Price and Tab Hunter.

**Selected Noir Films:** *Cat People* (1942), *I Walked with a Zombie* (1943), *The Leopard Man* (1943), *Experiment Perilous* (1944), *Out of the Past* (1947), *Circle of Danger* (1951), *Great Day in the Morning* (1956), *Nightfall* (1957), *The Fearmakers* (1958).

Geoff Mayer

**TREVOR, CLAIRE** (1910–2000). A very talented actress, Trevor was an iconic figure in noir, usually playing a kindhearted woman of questionable morals who loves the hero, even if she may prove unsuitable as a permanent match for him. Claire Trevor was the actress perhaps best known for such floozy roles as well as for being a more heartless femme fatale. Born Claire Wemlinger in New York, she attended the University of Michigan and the American Academy of Dramatic Arts, then went on to Broadway, where her good reviews gained her an invitation to work in Hollywood. Through the mid-1930s she played mostly in westerns and melodramas, earning the sobriquet "Queen of the Bs," but in the A feature *Dead End* (1937) she was nominated for an Academy Award as best supporting actress. Trevor was first noticed by many people as the saloon girl/whore-with-a-heart-of-gold Dallas in John Ford's *Stagecoach* in 1939. As this role showed, she could be a rather hard, vamp figure, later even a gangster's moll. Trevor plays a cruel and vicious killer in *Street of Chance* (1942), an early film noir about amnesia. In *Murder My Sweet* (1944) her character Velma shows signs of her tarty origins as the moll of Moose Molloy despite her move upmarket as Mrs. Grayle. Trevor described this kind of woman by saying that "during the War, it was the girls in the bars and that risqué stuff, the kind of girls that soldiers met everywhere, that you saw in pictures . . . seeing the little girl at home sitting under the apple tree with blonde curls would not be strong enough." Trevor, however, played a virtuous woman in *Crack-Up* (1946), a noir set in the New York art world where she is the girlfriend of hero Pat O'Brien. In *Born to Kill* (1947) she is back in normal mode as a morally decadent woman caught up in a passionate relationship with a thug (Lawrence Tierney), a woman who is willing to overlook his killings because he excites her so much. Trevor is much more sympathetic in *Raw Deal* (1948), where, in a move unusual in classical noir, she is given the voice-over narration. She once again plays a woman in love with a man on the wrong side of the law who fears losing him to a more prim and proper rival. Trevor is excellent throughout *Raw Deal* but reaches her best in the climax, where (ironically) her conscience forces her to rescue her rival from death at the hands of a sadistic gangster. She won the 1948 best supporting actress Oscar for playing the alcoholic moll of Johnny Rocco (Edward G. Robinson) in *Key Largo*.

**Selected Noir Films:** *Crossroads* (1942), *Street of Chance* (1942), *Murder, My Sweet* (1944), *Johnny Angel* (1945), *Crack-Up* (1946), *Born to Kill* (1947), *Raw Deal* (1948), *The Velvet Touch* (1948), *Key Largo* (1948), *Borderline* (1950), *Hoodlum Empire* (1952).

Brian McDonnell

**TRUE CONFESSIONS** (United Artists, 1981). *Director:* Ulu Grosbard. *Producers:* Irwin Winkler and Robert Chartoff. *Script:* John Gregory Dunne and Joan Didion, from the novel by John Gregory Dunne. *Cinematography:* Owen Roizman. *Music:* Georges Delerue. *Cast:* Robert De Niro (Des Spellacy), Robert Duvall

*True Confessions* (1981). Directed by Ulu Grosbard. Shown from left: Robert Duvall (as Tom Spellacy), Robert De Niro (as Des Spellacy). United Artists/Photofest.

(Tom Spellacy), Charles Durning (Jack Amsterdam), Ed Flanders (Dan Campion), Burgess Meredith (Seamus Fargo), Cyril Cusack (Cardinal Danaher), Kenneth McMillan (Frank Crotty), Rose Gregorio (Brenda Samuels).

On its initial release, *True Confessions* received little attention and few favorable reviews, with most criticism centering on its slow pace and the lackluster direction by Ulu Grosbard. A quarter of a century on, however, it commands respect as one of the most thoughtful, ruminative, and serious films of the neo-noir genre. Essentially a character study of two brothers who reveal themselves to be at once similar and different, it relies on the central performances of Robert De Niro and Robert Duvall, both of whom inhabit their roles and lend strength to this moody and introspective example of retro noir. Adapted by John Gregory Dunne (with the help of his wife, Joan Didion) from his own novel, *True Confessions* examines civic, ecclesiastical, and personal corruption at several social levels in postwar Los Angeles in a manner reminiscent of the concerns of *Chinatown* seven years before. Through the working environments of its two leading characters, *True Confessions* is able to highlight contrasts between a veneer of respectability and the reality of sleaze hidden below the good-mannered surface.

Des and Tom Spellacy are a Catholic priest and a city cop, respectively, and the plot unites their professional lives by parallels and coincidences that are mostly quite convincing. Des is an ambitious and skilled administrator in the Archdiocese of Los Angeles, favored for his business acumen by the Cardinal, who is grooming him for elevation to the rank of bishop. Despite frugality in his personal life, Des enjoys the privileges and prestige of his position with a warmly indulgent round of society weddings and public social functions. Tom, on the other hand, is a struggling detective, a former bagman for vice lords who now has to deal with the dirtiest and most disreputable levels of crime in the city. While Des celebrates a lavish nuptial mass for the daughter of prominent Catholic contractor and builder of parochial schools Jack Amsterdam, Tom is covering up the discovery at a down-market brothel of the body of a local priest who had died while breaking his vow of celibacy. Although Des is grateful for Tom's discretion in this instance, the two brothers are unable to resolve as easily their moral dilemma when Jack Amsterdam becomes associated with the gruesome murder of Lois, a young singer whose dismembered corpse (along with other details of the crime) strongly evokes the real-life Black Dahlia case of 1947. Des comes to realize, partly through the curmudgeonly example of an old-style priest called Seamus, that his advancement through the church's hierarchy may be achievable only at the cost of his integrity and his duty of pastoral care. Despite the police department treating it as a "no overtime" case, Tom is determined to find the killer of the young singer (dubbed the "Virgin Whore" by crime reporters in search of lurid headlines) precisely because she was an unvalued pawn of the rich and powerful.

Most of the narrative of *True Confessions* is in the form of a long flashback springing from a framing sequence set in 1963 in a remote desert church, where, 15 years after the main events, Tom is visiting the dying Des, now a humble pastor to a poor and largely Hispanic parish. This framing device adds to the noir determinism of the story since the audience is aware from the beginning of Des's fall from favor. The sere desert landscape aptly evokes the pared-down essence of a vocation to the priesthood. The murder investigation that dominates the centre of the film becomes somewhat incidental to its meditative examination of social injustice and morality, the comparison of those two very Irish American professions, priest and policeman, allowing the guilty underside of humanity to be exposed. The "confessions" of the film's title refer not only to sins that might be aired in a Catholic confessional, but also to the scandalous misdemeanors that police officers uncover in their everyday investigations. Both Des and Tom encounter hypocrisy, exploitation, and corruption at all levels. While both in effect work as bagmen for their superiors, they both get a chance to regain their virtue: in fact, Des claims that Tom's forcing him into exposing Jack Amsterdam as morally corrupt has been his "salvation." This redemption comes, however, at the price of a penitential exile in the desert, emphasizing (as does the sadistic death of Lois in the tatty location of a sordid porn film set that obliterates her naïve dreams of Hollywood fame and fortune) the film's theme of the vanity of human wishes.

In style, *True Confessions* is very atmospheric, conjuring up a persuasive period milieu through judicious use of both real locations and rear-projected reconstructions. Telling juxtapositions, such as the sumptuous Catholic Layman of the Year dinner thrown for Jack being placed next to Tom's poignant farewell to Lois's parents as they ship her coffin back to the Midwest, help underscore thematic points. The plot gives short shrift to certain minor characters, such as the ailing mother of the Spellacy brothers and a careworn brothel proprietor named Brenda, whose abrupt suicide is dramatically underexplained. The film also lacks a powerful narrative resolution to its main investigatory plot strand, and Des's ousting from his church position provides a rather weak climax to the story. These shortcomings, though, cannot detract from the film's overall thought-provoking contribution to the subgenre of retro noir or obscure its accomplishment in raising deep questions about class conflicts in American society and about the rise and fall of successful men.

Brian McDonnell

# U

ULMER, EDGAR G. (1904–1972). A rather enigmatic figure whose biography contains some mysterious elements, Ulmer is said, along with others, to have been the "King of the Bs" in Hollywood because so many of his films were made for between $20,000 and $40,000. He claimed to have been born in Vienna, Austria, but actually, his birthplace was in Czechoslovakia. This is an example of the way Ulmer often romanticized his past. He did, though, study architecture in Vienna and worked as a set designer there. He was an assistant to F. W. Murnau (maker of *Nosferatu* [1922] and *The Last Laugh* [1924]), whose trademark was his use of tracking shots, the development of which Ulmer claimed to have influenced. He also worked with Robert Siodmak, Billy Wilder, and Fred Zinnemann on *Menchen am Sonntag* (*People on Sunday*, 1929). Ulmer traveled backward and forward between the United States and Germany throughout the 1920s, but in 1930 he moved to America permanently. There he made more than 100 obscure movies from 1933 onward. A few of his films from this period have attained classic status. For example, horror film *The Black Cat*, made on minimal resources and alluded to admiringly in Vincente Minnelli's *The Bad and the Beautiful* (1952), became a classic for Universal in 1934. Ulmer's career was said to be adversely affected around this time by his romancing and later marrying Shirley Alexander, who was already married to a nephew of Carl Laemmle (who ran Universal Studios). Ulmer and his wife moved to New York to produce ethnic pictures, sometimes making films in Yiddish or Ukrainian that at times anticipated the look and style of Italian neo-realism. In 1941 Ulmer returned to Hollywood, but his grand ambitions were unrealized, and he ended up working at PRC, with the lowest in status of the Poverty Row studios.

He later justified this career move by saying that he did not want "to be ground up in the Hollywood hash machine." Ulmer's 1944 film *Bluebeard* (starring John Carradine) had noir elements in its story of a murderous painter. His most famous film noir, *Detour* (1945), was one of a series made for PRC on a miniscule budget. It is uncertain whether these films took 6 days to shoot or 14 days. They never had real stars, but Ulmer used his abundant camera style and ingenuity to overcome the cheapness of the films. *Detour* stands out not only for these skills, but for the acidic performance he elicited from Ann Savage as the femme fatale and for the overall tone of existential doom that pervades the narrative. Ulmer also gained a fine acting performance from torpedo guidance engineer Hedy Lamarr in *The Strange Woman* (1946), an interesting period noir. This film had a larger budget than Ulmer was accustomed to receiving, as did *Ruthless* in 1948, a story of a man's rise to prominence that is reminiscent of *Citizen Kane* (1941) in its narrative structure. After making the science fiction film *The Man from Planet X* (1951), Ulmer's career faded out in a succession of European B films. His last film was *The Cavern* in 1964. Ulmer had failing health through these years and suffered a number of strokes before his death in 1972.

**Selected Noir Films:** *Bluebeard* (1944), *Strange Illusion* (1945), *Detour* (1945), *The Strange Woman* (1946, and script writer), *Ruthless* (1948), *Murder Is My Beat* (1955).

Brian McDonnell

**UNDER THE GUN** (Universal, 1951). *Director:* Ted Tetzlaff. *Producer:* Ralph Dietrich. *Script:* George Zuckerman, based on a story by Daniel B. Ullman. *Cinematography:* Henry Freulich. *Music:* Joseph Gershenson. *Cast:* Richard Conte (Bert Galvin), Audrey Totter (Ruth Williams), Sam Jaffe (Samuel Gower), John McIntire (Sheriff Bill Langley), Phillip Pine (Gandy), Gregg Martell (Henchman), Shepperd Strudwick (Milo Bragg), Royal Dano (Sam Nugent).

This little-known film noir, scripted by George Zuckerman, is based on a story by Dan Ullman, who wrote many series westerns in the early 1950s. However, instead of the usual good/bad characterizations of his westerns, the script for *Under the Gun* is a fascinating mixture of moral ambiguities within a conventional crime story. The film begins in Florida, where gangster Bert Galvin, accompanied by his two henchmen, romances nightclub singer Ruth Williams. Williams reluctantly agrees to accompany Galvin back to New York after he promises to promote her career. On the way, he stops off and kills an informer, and following Williams's testimony, Galvin is sentenced to a 20-year imprisonment on a state prison farm.

Frustrated by prison life, Galvin devises a plan to gain his freedom when he learns of an idiosyncratic regulation that any prison trusty who shoots a prisoner trying to escape is entitled to an early release. After goading a prisoner into an escape attempt, whereupon he is shot by a prison trusty (Sam Nugent), Galvin replaces Nugent as the trusty with the gun. The body of the film is concerned with Galvin's persuasion of long-serving prisoner Samuel Gower into an escape attempt. Galvin offers to pay money to Gower's wife if Gower will make a run for it. If Gower is killed by Galvin, Galvin will be entitled to an early release.

This strong dramatic premise is bolstered by Richard Conte's performance as the cold-blooded gangster. While the film begins in a conventional manner, with Galvin killing an informer, it systematically develops its psychological basis as Galvin plots Gower's demise. Only the mandatory action sequence at the film's conclusion, involving a chase through the swamps as Sheriff Langley pursues Galvin, who has kidnapped Williams, weakens an otherwise strong film.

Geoff Mayer

**THE UNDERCOVER MAN** (Columbia, 1949). *Director:* Joseph H. Lewis. *Producer:* Robert Rossen. *Script:* Sydney Boehm. *Cinematography:* Burnett Guffey. *Music:* George Duning. *Cast:* Glenn Ford (Frank Warren), Nina Foch (Judith Warren), James Whitmore (George Pappas), Barry Kelley (Edward J. O'Rourke), David Wolfe (Stanley Weinberg), Frank Tweddell (Inspector Herzog), John F. Hamilton (Sergeant Shannon), Sydney Gordon (Leo Penn), Rosa Rocco (Joan Lazer), Salvatore Rocco (Anthony Caruso).

*The Undercover Man*, Joseph Lewis's final noir film for Columbia, is not as interesting as his low-budget films for the studio in the mid-1940s—*My Name Is Julia Ross* (1945) and *So Dark Is the Night* (1946)—even though it had a more a generous shooting schedule, a longer running time, a substantial budget with a popular leading man, Glenn Ford, and a cast of strong supporting actors, including Nina Foch. Also, Lewis's customary visual flamboyance seemed constrained by the film's dramatic context, the procedural thriller, and the film's quasi-realist subject involving the investigation by treasury agents Frank Warren, George Pappas, and Stanley Weinberg into the illegal activities of the "Big Fellow," Al Capone, although he is never directly named in the film.

Producer Robert Rossen and Sydney Boehm's routine script is only occasionally enlivened by Lewis's expressionist style, involving depth staging, low-angled compositions, and chiaroscuro lighting, as the film's pseudo-documentary approach clearly inhabits his direction. However, this is another example of a familiar theme found in Rossen's scripts involving the sacrifice of the individual for the greater good. Agent Frank Warren is forced to leave his wife, Judith, for extended periods while he painstakingly builds a case against the Big Fellow. Their separation provides one of the film's best sequences when, after months apart, Frank visits Judith's rural hideout and tries to convey to her the emotional anguish he experiences when they are forced to live apart. However, after the murder of two informants, the suicide of a policeman, and a long sequence involving a young girl who explains the moral necessity of pursuing evil wherever it exists, Warren pushes aside his reservations and fights against organized corruption. His decision is vindicated when the Big Fellow is sentenced to 20 years for tax evasion.

Geoff Mayer

**VICTIM** (Rank, 1961). *Director:* Basil Dearden. *Producer:* Michael Relph. *Script:* Janet Green and John McCormick. *Cinematography:* Otto Heller. *Music:* Philip Green. *Cast:* Dirk Bogarde (Melville Farr), Sylvia Syms (Laura Farr), Dennis Price (Calloway), Anthony Nicholls (Lord Fullbrook), Peter Copley (Paul Mandrake), Norman Bird (Harold Doe), Peter McEnery (Jack Barrett), Donald Churchill (Eddy Stone), Derren Nesbit (Sandy Youth), John Barrie (Detective Inspector Harris), John Cairney (Bridie), Alan MacNaughtan (Scott Hankin), Nigel Stock (Phip), Noel Howlett (Patterson).

When Detective Inspector Harris tells embattled lawyer Melville Farr that the British law that criminalizes male homosexuality is the "blackmailer's charter," he is spelling out the central theme in *Victim*. The film is, paradoxically, both courageous and flawed: brave in openly dramatizing the intolerable situation faced by homosexual men in Britain at that time through their vulnerability to blackmail, and flawed by depicting the central character, Melvin Farr, as a married gay man and as a *nonpracticing* homosexual. Thus the film compromises, or weakens, the injustice it seeks to expose by making Farr perform the function of the "hero," investigating the death of a young man, Jack Barrett, who was infatuated with him. While Barrett, and all the other homosexuals shown in the film, remain at the level of the victim, Farr, through his ability to deny his sexual impulses, is elevated to a different (higher?) status. In a crucial scene late in the film Farr admits to his wife that although he desired Barrett, he did not act on it. Farr's denial of his sexual desires also makes possible a reconciliation between

*Victim* (1961). Directed by Basil Dearden. Shown from left: Sylvia Syms (as Laura Farr), Dirk Bogarde (as Melville Farr). Home Vision Entertainment/Photofest.

Laura and Farr—if he had sex with Barrett, this would not have been available as a viable ending.

Farr's heroic status is enhanced by his decision to destroy his legal career by testifying against the vicious blackmail ring, conducted by the psychotic Sandy Youth and Miss Benham (who is described in the film as "half avenging angel and half Peeping Tom"). Indeed, the film's depiction of Youth and Benham as demented grotesques serves to foreground its social message and reflects the intentions of script writer Janet Green to assimilate a social message into the conventions of the crime film, a tactic endorsed by director Basil Dearden and producer Michael Relph, who had examined racial issues in much the same manner in *Sapphire* (1959).

Dirk Bogarde was not the first actor offered the lead role in *Victim*, and his decision to accept the role marks a seminal point in his career. In *Victim* his character, for the first time on the British screen, confesses that he desires another man. This admission occurs late in the film in a scene especially written by Bogarde, and this, in itself, makes *Victim* a significant film. As a result of the film's sympathetic depiction of homosexual desires, *Victim* was denied a certificate by the Production

Code Administration in the United States, although *Oscar Wilde* was granted one in the same year. The sympathy the film evinced for Bogarde's Melville Farr was a factor in *Victim* not gaining a certificate.

While most critics have acknowledged the courage of *Victim* in its depiction of the male characters, the repressive characterization of Laura has been treated less charitably as some suggest that the film blames exploitation of homosexuals on the two women in the film—the blackmailing hysterical spinster Benham and the repressed wife Laura, who, it has been suggested, sadistically pursues and interrogates her husband until he admits his "deviance." Yet, as actress Sylvia Syms points out, "In those days women of a certain class were very innocent. The wife's knowledge of sex would be very limited; she may have had her suspicions but I think that it was perfectly possible for her to love Dirk's character and have a reasonably happy marriage." In fact, the relationship between Farr and Laura is one of the more complex aspects of the film, with director Basil Dearden emphasizing that their home is weakened by its lack of children, compensated for by her work with handicapped children. Yet, as Farr admits in the final scene, he needs her, and she replies that *need* is a "bigger word than *love*." This suggests that she will return to him. While for some, this is a compromised ending, *Victim* paved the way for valid alternative representations of sexual desire that, prior to 1961, were subject only to ridicule.

Geoff Mayer

# W

**WHERE DANGER LIVES** (RKO, 1950). *Director:* John Farrow. *Producers:* Irving Cummings Jr. and Irwin Allen (associate). *Script:* Charles Bennett. *Cinematography:* Nicholas Musuraca. *Music:* Roy Webb. *Cast:* Robert Mitchum (Jeff Cameron), Faith Domergue (Margo Lannington), Claude Rains (Frederick Lannington), Maureen O'Sullivan (Julie), Charles Kemper (Police Chief), Ralph Dumke (Klauber), Billy House (Mr. Bogardus), Harry Shannon (Dr. Maynard), Philip van Zandt (Milo DeLong), Jack Kelly (Dr. Mullenbach).

This relatively unknown film noir deserves greater recognition. While it is not in the same class as *Out of the Past* (1947), it shares many of the same qualities. This includes the important casting of Robert Mitchum as the film's central male protagonist, Dr. Jeff Cameron, as he is allowed to extend, and intensify, the passive, masochistic traits that he exhibited in the 1947 film. In each film Mitchum's character delegates, for slightly different reasons, control to a beautiful, scheming, murderous female who readily exploits his feelings for her. Three years after *Where Danger Lives*, in one of his last films for RKO, Mitchum completed this cycle with a similar performance in *Angel Face*.

*Where Danger Lives* was one of a small cycle of noir films directed by Australian-born director John Farrow in the period from 1948 to 1951. In the 1940s Farrow was a contract director at Paramount, where he directed *The Big Clock* (1948) and *The Night Has a Thousand Eyes* (1948), which was based on Cornell Woolrich's 1945 novel (written under one of his pseudonym's, George Hopley). In 1950 he switched to RKO, and while he directed a variety of genres in the early 1950s, he followed *Where Danger Lives* with another noir film starring Robert Mitchum, *His Kind of Woman*, which was released in 1951.

Amnesia, fate, even kindness (see, e.g., *The Chase* [1946]) provided the pretext for noir films to dramatize the inability of the male protagonist to control the world around him—whether it is amnesia in films such as *Street of Chance* (1942), *Deadline at Dawn* (1945), *Somewhere in the Night* (1946), *High Wall* (1947), and *The Clay Pigeon* (1949), or the drug-induced confusion of *Crack-Up* (1946), or hypnosis in *Fear in the Night* (1947) and its 1956 remake, *Nightmare*, the effect is the same. The male character suffers confusion and, for much of the film, loses the ability to control, and sometimes understand, his world. In some of these films it provides a camouflage for depicting the repressed masochistic desires of the protagonist. In this situation the amnesia or hypnosis operates as a dramatic contrivance to make sure that the psychological and/or sexual implications are not directly rendered as they may prove too confronting for mainstream audiences seeking "entertainment." *Where Danger Lives* goes very close to exposing this practice as the male protagonist exerts very little influence on the world around him as he cedes control to the female. In this film, however, prolonged concussion, which renders him helpless and confused for much of the film, operates as the motivation for his passivity.

Jeff Cameron, a young doctor, is called out to the wealthy Lannington house to treat a young woman, Margo, who has attempted suicide. Although Cameron has a steady girlfriend, Julie, he is immediately attracted to Margo's vulnerability and sensuality. Margo initiates an affair with Cameron and complains that her "father," Frederick, brutally mistreats her. When Cameron confronts Frederick, he discovers that he is not Margo's father but her wealthy husband. Frederick and Cameron fight, and after Frederick hits the young doctor on the head, he blacks out, only to wake up suffering from concussion. Margo tells him they must flee as he has killed Frederick during their fight.

The main body of the film shows Cameron racked by violent headaches as, under the direction of Margo, they try to evade the police by driving from northern California to the Mexican border. Margo exerts control with a combination of sexual promise and mental and physical violence. Finally, in a seedy border town, he realizes the extent of Margo's psychosis, as she is suffering constant delusions associated with acute schizophrenia. He also learns that she killed Frederick while he was unconscious. Exposed, Margo tries to kill Jeff by smothering him with a pillow. She then tries to cross the border into Mexico, and when he follows, she wounds him before the police shoot her.

While Cameron's masochism is evident throughout the film, it intensifies in the final act in a seedy border hotel room as Jeff threatens to lose consciousness altogether. As his strength diminishes, Margo's physical and emotional power over him intensifies, and the stylized lighting from veteran RKO cinematographer Nicholas Musuraca, who also shot *Out of the Past*, captures the bizarre sexual and psychological implications of this scenario. Cameron, wracked by pain, crawls around the hotel room, while Margo, impatient with his helplessness, paces and taunts Cameron with the revelation that she killed Frederick. Cameron, the hapless doctor, finally realizes the extent of her deranged mental condition. Only a tepid attempt at a happy ending, with Cameron reunited with his long-suffering girlfriend (Julie), weakens *Where Danger Lives*, which is one of Hollywood's most extreme representations of the damaged male threatened by a psychotic woman.

Geoff Mayer

**WHERE THE SIDEWALK ENDS** (Twentieth Century Fox, 1950). *Director/Producer:* Otto Preminger. *Script:* Ben Hecht, from the novel *Night Cry* by William L. Stuart. *Cinematography:* Joseph LaShelle. *Music:* Cyril Mockridge. *Cast:* Dana Andrews (Mark Dixon), Gene Tierney (Morgan Taylor), Gary Merrill (Scalise), Bert Freed (Klein), Tom Tully (Jiggs Taylor), Karl Malden (Lieutenant Thomas), Ruth Donnelly (Martha), Craig Stevens (Ken Paine).

Several historians of film noir have claimed that the all-too-common hero of the postwar movies, the maladjusted veteran, was gradually replaced in the films of the early 1950s by an equally marginal figure: the rogue cop. Thus one type of morally ambiguous protagonist was replaced by another who was perhaps more suitable to the times. Andrew Spicer, in his book *Film Noir*, claims that some of these men "became violently unstable through their contact with criminals" (p. 87). One such character is Mark Dixon, the violent New York police detective at the centre of Otto Preminger's *Where the Sidewalk Ends*. As played by Dana Andrews looking much more dissipated than he had in Preminger's *Laura* or *Fallen Angel*, Dixon's anger and temper seem natural outcomes of a society that is itself violent. Alain Silver and Elizabeth Ward, in their book *Film Noir: An Encyclopedic Reference to the American Style*, sum him up as a "hero of questionable virtue and limited potency trying to react to a society of confused moral values" (p. 310). He cannot help getting into trouble with his superiors, but he also tries the patience of his friends. It is only his innate decency that gives him any chance of overcoming the obstacles of background and conditioning so that he may prevail at film's end.

At the outset of the story, Dixon is demoted by new precinct lieutenant Andrews for his insubordination and liking for dealing out rough justice to crooks. Like the Robert Ryan character in Nicholas Ray's *On Dangerous Ground*, Dixon seems to be a loose cannon. This impression is quickly confirmed when he investigates a gambling session run by a gangster called Scalise, where a man is stabbed and a pretty young model, Morgan Taylor (played by Andrews's romantic partner from *Laura*, Gene Tierney), is struck in the face. Dixon braces the culprit and accidentally kills him. He hides the body in a closet, but his troubles are far from over. It transpires that the dead man was a war hero with a metal plate in his head. He had fallen on hard times, and his battle injuries had contributed to his surprise death. In many another film noir, such a man could himself easily become the protagonist. It also turns out that Morgan's own father had threatened the men who hit her, and this innocent old man becomes a prime suspect. The lonely Dixon is caught in a dilemma as he becomes increasingly attracted to Morgan but is unable to supply a confession that would clear her father. Cinematographer Joseph LaShelle makes the most of Tierney's beauty as the good woman who may redeem Mark, and one close-up shot of her sleeping is startlingly erotic.

An almost masochistic Dixon fronts up to Scalise at a massage parlor, but he is badly beaten by Scalise's goons. He then shows up at Morgan's room like a beaten dog, seeking her tenderness. He may ask her, "Why did I come here?" but the audience can see exactly why. He explains his own back story about his criminal father, a thief who was shot trying to escape. Mark Dixon is attempting to be different, to prove as a lie the old saying "blood will out." In an elaborate scheme he keeps to himself, Mark decides that death is the only way out of his dilemma, and he sets out to trap Scalise for his own murder. In a climactic sequence very nicely rendered by Preminger, Mark, at great personal risk, confronts Scalise in an East River parking garage. When the gangster tries to escape, Mark captures him by halting the vehicle elevator. He preserves his own life, and when lauded by Lieutenant Thomas, he insists that his confession for the accidental death is opened and read. He faces up to the consequences, but the film ends without the audience being sure just what fate awaits him. The one certainty, though, in this open ending is that Morgan will stand by him.

*Where the Sidewalk Ends* is set in a gritty, naturalistic milieu far removed from the glamour of *Laura*. It is particularly good in showing the down-and-dirty precinct procedures, the car patrols, the floating crap games, the sympathetic café owners, and the shabby rooms that make up the cops' daily routine. Despite this, the presence of the ethereally beautiful Tierney provides the promise of a different level of life. The film is also peopled with a number of cleverly written minor characters, such as Dixon's partner and his wife, who begrudgingly gives up some jewelry as pawn items to pay for a lawyer for Mark. Throughout, LaShelle conveys well the atmosphere of the nighttime city, and the film is full of judicious small details, such as the credits, which are presented as chalk writing on a concrete sidewalk, or the bandage on Mark's jaw, which becomes a visual symbol of the inner damage the man carries. All in all, it is an effective portrait of a flawed individual who finds the strength to defy his destiny, to climb out of the gutter and get back onto the safety of the pavement.

Brian McDonnell

**WIDMARK, RICHARD** (1914–). Surviving well into the early twenty-first century as the grand old man of film noir, Richard Widmark established himself (often in villainous or morally dubious roles) as an iconic figure of the genre. With his wolfish face and maniacal grin, he was a memorable presence from his very first appearance in *Kiss of Death*. Born in Minnesota, Widmark taught speech and drama at the Illinois college he had himself attended as a student. He then became a professional actor and worked in radio and on Broadway before his 1947 debut in *Kiss of Death* caused a sensation. In a secondary but unforgettable role, he played the psychopathic killer Tommy Udo, who memorably pushes a wheelchair-bound old lady down a set of stairs to her death. Udo was the nemesis of stolid hero Nick Bianco (Victor Mature), and with his fair hair, highly strung personality, wildly hysterical eye movements, and sadism, Widmark was a sharp contrast to the swarthy Mature. The following year, *Road House* saw him play a rival of Cornell Wilde for the love of Ida Lupino as the three actors played out a claustrophobic drama set in a rural diner. The film that provided Widmark with his finest noir role, Jules Dassin's *Night and the City* (1950), shows him as a Graham Greene–style pursued man. Harry Fabian is a man on the run from the film's opening sequence through to its tragic climax. In Widmark's playing, Fabian is a manic (bipolar) figure, a con man who lives on his wits and has tremendous pent-up energy. Widmark made a rare appearance as a law-abiding man when he played Clint Reed, a navy doctor fighting an outbreak of bubonic plague in New Orleans in *Panic in the Streets* (1950). Sam Fuller's *Pickup on South Street* shows him more characteristically as a mixture of admirable and venal traits: pickpocket Skip McCoy is casually violent, even toward women, but abides by a code of his own. His loyalty to murdered snitch "Mo" Williams (Thelma Ritter) is admirable. In the late 1960s Widmark returned to the noir world in Don Siegel's tough cop film *Madigan*, where he plays a hardened veteran cop. *Madigan* marked, along with John Boorman's *Point Blank* (1967), a bridge between classical film noir and the modernist neo-noir films of the 1970s. It was, however, shot using real New York locations, whereas films such as *Pickup on South Street* had used Los Angeles soundstages and second-unit work to replicate the streets of New York. Along with Jane Greer, he was asked in 1984, as a kind of in-joke, to participate in the neo-noir film *Against All Odds*, an ill-judged remake of *Out of the Past*.

**Selected Noir Films:** *Kiss of Death* (1947), *The Street with No Name* (1948), *Road House* (1948), *Night and the City* (1950), *Panic in the Streets* (1950), *No Way Out* (1950), *Don't Bother to Knock* (1952), *Pickup on South Street* (1953), *The Trap* (1959), *Madigan* (1968), *Against All Odds* (1984).

Brian McDonnell

**WILDE, CORNELL** (1915–1989). Mostly a minimalist and undemonstrative actor, Cornell Wilde developed into a performer who could convey subtle and complex emotions. He sometimes played the blander of two male protagonists who reacted temperately to more flamboyant figures such as Richard Widmark, Richard Conte, or Gene Tierney, but in a number of films he embodied tellingly the moral ambiguity endemic in the noir world. Born Cornelius Louis Wilde in New York, he spent part of his childhood in Hungary, from where his father had migrated. Wilde's European sojourn led him to be multilingual as well as cementing his general sophistication. Academically very able, he had ambitions to be a doctor before turning to acting. Wilde was selected for the 1936 U.S. Olympic fencing team that was headed for Berlin but turned down the opportunity to pursue his acting. In due course, this talent as a fencer won him the role of Tybalt in Lawrence Olivier's 1940 Broadway production of *Romeo and Juliet*. Wilde then had a minor role in *High Sierra* (1941) as a gang henchman that attracted attention and gave him the chance to work with Humphrey Bogart. He garnered what was to be his best-known role of the 1940s when he played the less histrionic role of the put-on husband in *Leave Her to Heaven*, while Gene Tierney was able to command most audience attention. The film's opening shows Wilde as a mature writer who reminds Tierney of her own beloved and deceased father. From that point on he has to endure her pathological and possessive jealousy. In 1945 he also starred as composer Frederic Chopin in *A Song to Remember*. Wilde was in *Road House* with Richard Widmark and Ida Lupino, and typically, he was the quiet, more sober man competing with Widmark for Lupino's love. He had a more interesting role in *Shockproof* (1949), where he played a parole officer who falls in love with one of his charges and is tempted away from his professional ethics. In this he is a morally compromised figure in the tradition of the protagonists of such films as *Double Indemnity* (1944), *Pitfall* (1948), and *The Prowler* (1951). In *The Big Combo* (1955) Wilde played a similar role as Lieutenant Leonard Diamond, an obsessive cop attracted to a woman who has become sexually implicated with a gangster. Furthermore, Diamond dallies with a prostitute, who eases his frustrations. Wilde's *Big Combo* costar Jean Wallace was also his wife. His last classical noir was the impressively capable chamber drama *Storm Fear* (1955), which saw him direct as well as star as a criminal who threatens the foster family of his young son. Later, in the 1960s, Cornell Wilde became even more noted and praised for his directing of nonnoir films such as *The Naked Prey* (1966) and *Beach Red* (1967).

**Selected Noir Films:** *High Sierra* (1941), *Leave Her to Heaven* (1945), *Road House* (1948), *Shockproof* (1949), *The Big Combo* (1955), *Storm Fear* (1955, and director/producer).

Brian McDonnell

**WILDER, BILLY** (1906–2002). Although Billy Wilder's contribution to film noir was small in terms of the number of films he worked on, it was immense in terms of the influence *Double Indemnity* had on film noir. The premise of the film, based on betrayal, lust, and murder, was not new, but the tone of the film and the fact that it did not have a moral voice in the guise of one of the two main characters was considered, at the time, radical for a large-budget Hollywood film. There was also the film's endorsement by the critics and the industry with Academy Award nominations. This had the effect of legitimizing this type of story, and it was now respectable for the major studios to produce similar films. Prior to 1944, the type of film we now consider film noir was largely the province of independent filmmakers, the small studios, or relegated to the B units of the major studios.

Born Samuel Wilder in 1906 in Austria-Hungary, he was called "Billy" by his mother, who was fascinated by American culture. After studying law, he worked as a journalist in Vienna before moving to Berlin in 1927. He supplemented his income as a journalist in Berlin by teaching women to dance the Charleston, and in 1929, he was also working as a screenwriter. However, when Hitler consolidated his power, Wilder, a Jew, left Germany in 1933 for France, where he codirected his first film, *Mauvaise Graine*, an experience he disliked.

Wilder, after some difficulty with immigration officials, maneuvered himself across the Mexican border into the United States, where he shared an apartment in Hollywood with fellow émigré Peter Lorre. Wilder's first Hollywood project was the Jerome Kern/Oscar Hammerstein musical *Music in the Air*. Although his English was poor, Wilder was offered a contract with Paramount in 1936, where he developed a writing partnership with Charles Brackett. During this period Wilder also immersed himself in mainstream American culture, where he developed a lifelong interest in sports, particularly horse racing.

He formed a writing partnership with the patrician Charles Brackett, who had little in common with Wilder. While this was a volatile setup, they cowrote a succession of successful films, including *Midnight* (1939), *Ninotchka* (1939), and *Ball of Fire* (1941). However, the feisty Wilder was unhappy with the way directors, especially Mitchell Leisen, altered his scripts, and he decided to become a writer-director. This decision was not supported by everybody at Paramount, and some executives wanted him to fail. While Wilder's first two Hollywood films as a director were commercially successful, they did not have the impact he sought. The first was the subversive romantic comedy *The Major and the Minor* (1942), with Ginger Rogers disguising herself as a 12-year-old so that she can purchase a half-price train ticket before becoming involved with Ray Milland's military academy. This was followed by the espionage propaganda film *Five Graves to Cairo* (1943). Both films were cowritten with Brackett.

Charles Brackett, however, refused to work with Wilder on his next project, a film version of James M. Cain's novella *Double Indemnity*. Brackett considered Cain's story sordid and immoral, the very qualities that attracted Wilder to the adaptation. He was looking for a film that would shake Hollywood, and while he wanted to adapt Cain's 1934 controversial novel *The Postman Always Rings Twice*, MGM owned the rights to that book, and following the success of *Double Indemnity*, they finally put the film into production in October 1945.

It is not entirely clear how Wilder discovered Cain's story. *Double Indemnity* was first serialized in *Liberty* magazine in 1935–1936. It is most likely that Paramount producer Joseph Sistrom gave the story to Wilder, who requested Cain to work on the script with him. Cain, however, was under contract with Twentieth Century Fox, so Sistrom suggested Raymond Chandler. Wilder and Chandler detested each other, but their collaboration produced a superb script, superior to Cain's story, as the writer later acknowledged. It was nominated for a 1944 Academy Award and gave Wilder's career the impetus he sought. He followed it with *The Lost Weekend* (1945), which detailed the plight of an alcoholic played by Ray Milland. This film won Oscars for best picture, best director, best actor, and best screenplay (Wilder cowrote the film with Brackett).

In their last screenplay together, Wilder and Bracket wrote, and Wilder directed, *Sunset Boulevard* (1950), and the 1950s proved a rich period for Wilder with films such as *The Big Carnival* (1951), *Stalag 17* (1953), *The Seven Year Itch* (1955), and his homage to his mentor Ernst Lubitsch, *Love in the Afternoon* (1957). Wilder cowrote this romantic comedy with I.A.L. Diamond, who collaborated with him for the next two decades. Wilder began the 1960s with one of his best films, *The Apartment* (1960), and while he continued to direct and write until his retirement in 1981, the post-1960s were, comparatively, a letdown.

**Selected Noir Films:** *Double Indemnity* (1944), *The Lost Weekend* (1945), *Sunset Boulevard* (1950), *The Big Carnival* (*Ace in the Hole*, 1951).

Geoff Mayer

**WINDSOR, MARIE** (1922–2000). Marie Windsor's two best roles were both in noir films: Richard Fleischer's *The Narrow Margin* (1952) and Stanley Kubrick's *The Killing* (1956). Both, however, were produced by studios that, at the time, were in trouble, and neither film received the promotion or distribution it deserved. *The Narrow Margin* was produced at RKO when the studio was owned, and controlled, by Howard Hughes, and his eccentric behavior affected many films that year—1952 was, financially, the worst year experienced in the studio's history. *The Killing*, on the other hand, was affected by studio executives at United Artists who disliked the film and virtually threw it away by releasing it on the bottom half of a double bill beneath a Robert Mitchum western. This virtually destroyed any chance that the film, and Marie Windsor, would receive adequate recognition from either the critics or the industry.

Marie Windsor was born Emily Marie Bertelsen in Marysvale, a small town in Utah that once had been a thriving gold mining community. After winning local beauty contests and schooling at Brigham Young University, where she majored in art and drama, Windsor left for Hollywood, where she expected to be placed under contract. However, after training at Marie Ouspenskaya's drama school, Paramount rejected her, and Windsor was forced into bit roles in low-budget films such as *Call Out the Marines* (1942). Her one moment of fame at this stage was giving Leo Gorcey, one of the Dead End Kids in *Smart Alecks* (1942), his first screen kiss.

With her film career languishing, Windsor left Hollywood for New York to work on radio and revues. Her work as a vamp in one of Jackie Gleason's revues attracted the attention of an MGM executive, who organized a screen test, and MGM promoted her as the "New Joan Crawford." Although she was cast in a number of large-budget films, Windsor was given only small roles, and her contract was not renewed in 1948. Her savior was screenwriter Abraham Polonsky, who was adapting Ira Wolfert's novel *Tucker's People* for the small, independent Enterprise

Studio. When fellow liberal John Garfield agreed to play the central role of the brash gambling syndicate lawyer Joe Morse, Polonsky got the go-ahead for *Force of Evil* (1948). Marie Windsor was cast as Edna Tucker, the tough wife of the head of the syndicate. Although she only appears in two scenes, she makes a strong impact, especially when she tries to seduce Morse. Although this socially conscious crime film was released by MGM, it fared poorly at the box office. Its dense, metaphorical structure and poetic dialogue did not appeal to audiences. Politically it was also running against the tide in its association between Wall Street and criminal activities.

A number of low-budget genre films followed, including another potential star-making role in the western *Hellfire* (1949). However, *Hellfire* was a Bill Elliott western (who was previously billed "Wild" Bill Elliott) produced by Republic Studios, which was not a combination likely to attract the attention of the critics or executives at the major studios. Similarly, she appeared in a Preston Sturges comedy, *The Beautiful Blonde from Bashful Bend* (1949), but this film was late in his career and a far cry from his comedic gems of the early 1940s.

Windsor's best performance was in *The Narrow Margin* as Mrs. Neil, a racketeer's widow who is accompanied on a crowded train by two detectives, Brown and Forbes, to provide evidence against a crime syndicate. When Forbes is killed, Brown expresses his resentment that the life of his colleague was worth more than the woman he is protecting. However, when she is murdered, and Brown learns that she was actually a policewoman posing as the widow so as to deflect attention away from the real woman, he feels remorse for the way he treated her.

Windsor was again typecast, in Edward Dmytryk's *The Sniper* (1952), as the blowsy entertainer who arouses the psychotic passion of Eddie Miller, a young man whose twisted sexual desires erupt into a killing spree directed at women through the telescopic sights of his rifle. Windsor is Miller's first victim in the film. By this stage she was resigned to her stereotype as the femme fatale or fallen women. Stanley Kubrick, however, gave new life to this stereotype. Earlier, in 1953, Windsor appeared in the crime melodrama *City That Never Sleeps*. In this film Windsor appears as Lydia Biddle, a woman conducting an affair with a gangster, Hayes Stewart, behind her husband's back. When the husband confronts the lover, Stewart kills him and runs away with Lydia. In *The Killing* Windsor is Sherry Peatty, married to George Peatty (Elisha Cook Jr.). Sherry is cheating on her husband by having an affair with small-time crook Val Cannon (Vince Edwards). She ruins the carefully planned heist by telling her boyfriend. This time, however, the cuckolded husband kills her. The difference between these two films resides in the quality of the writing by Kubrick and hard-boiled novelist Jim Thompson and the direction.

*The Killing* failed to generate interest in Windsor from the major studios, even after *Look* magazine selected her performance for their Best Supporting Actress Award for 1956. In desperation, Windsor took out a full-page advertisement in *Variety* commending her own performance, but the Academy Award nomination never eventuated. She continued to work in crime films and westerns, and many television series, throughout the 1950s, 1960s, and 1970s, only slowing down in the 1980s. Her last role was in 1991, in the series *Murder, She Wrote*, when Windsor was 69 years of age.

**Selected Noir Films:** *Eyes in the Night* (1942), *Song of the Thin Man* (1947), *Force of Evil* (1948), *The Narrow Margin* (1952), *The Sniper* (1952), *City That Never Sleeps* (1953), *No Man's Woman* (1955), *The Killing* (1956), *The Unholy Wife* (1957), *The Girl in Black Stockings* (1957).

Geoff Mayer

**THE WINGS OF THE DOVE** (Miramax/Renaissance Dove, 1997). *Director:* Iain Softley. *Producers:* Stephen Evans and David Parfitt. *Script:* Hossein Amini, based on the novel by Henry James. *Cinematography:* Eduardo Serro. *Music:* Edward Shearmur. *Cast:* Helena Bonham Carter (Kate Croy), Linus Roache (Merton Densher), Alison Elliott (Milly Theale), Elizabeth McGovern (Susan), Michael Gambon (Mr. Croy), Alex Jennings (Lord Mark), Charlotte Rampling (Aunt Maud).

Arguably the best British film of the 1990s, *The Wings of the Dove* is that rare adaptation that captures the essence of its source while establishing its own status as a great film. In early-twentieth-century London, Kate Croy lives with her wealthy Aunt Maud but loves (relatively) poor radical journalist Merton Densher. Maude, however, opposes this union and promotes Lord Mark as a more suitable partner for Kate. Kate, who is forced to meet Densher secretly, is dependent on Maud for the financial support of her drug-addicted father. Thus, while Kate wants financial security, she also wishes to retain Densher as her lover. To this end, Kate develops a diabolical plan to replace the patronage of Aunt Maud with the financial support of a wealthy American visitor, Milly Theale ("the world's richest orphan").

At the dinner party that reunites Kate with Merton she also meets Milly and her companion, Susan. They meet again in a London bookshop, where Kate boldly leads Milly to the pornographic section at the rear of the shop and picks up one of the books, opening it to the sexual image of two women sharing one man, a revealing image that foreshadows events in Venice when Densher joins Kate and Milly. When Lord Mark tells Kate that Milly is dying, she devises her plan with Densher as the (romantic) bait.

In Venice Kate brings Merton and Milly together, first in a gondola ride at night, and then on the night of carnival. In between these two events, Kate outlines aspects of her plan to Merton, after telling him that Milly is dying. When Merton asks if that is why Kate wanted him to come to Venice, Kate replies, "For her . . . and for us." However, the seeds of Kate's downfall also begin that night as she watches Milly and Merton dance together, followed by a kiss from the American. Confusion begins to erode her confidence as she fears that Merton may actually fall in love with the beautiful American. To reassure herself, Kate takes Merton into the darkness and encourages a sexual response from him. However, when Kate stops short of sexual intercourse, Merton blackmails her into sexually consummating their relationship as his price for participating in her scheme.

This troubling scene allows the audience an insight into another, less complimentary aspect of Merton. Similarly, Kate's doubts concerning Milly and Merton mark the start of her transformation from melodramatic villain to tragic heroine. Eventually, Kate's fear that she will lose Merton overcomes her desire for financial security, and this fear destroys not only her scheme, but also her relationship with Merton. In the film's final scene she finds that even after Milly's death, she cannot accept Merton unless he is able to convince her that he is not in love with Milly's memory. Merton is unable to answer this request from Kate. Kate leaves Merton, and he returns to Venice to assuage his guilt.

The three principals are totally convincing, with Helena Bonham Carter a standout as the complex Kate Croy. Bonham Carter was nominated for the 1997 best actress Academy Award.

Geoff Mayer

**WINSTONE, RAY** (1957–). Ray Winstone is the most formidable actor currently working in the British cinema. Although underused, he holds his own with an imposing array of American actors, including Jack Nicholson, in Martin Scorsese's violent gangster film *The Departed* (2006). Earlier, Gary Oldman (*Nil by Mouth* [1997]) and Tim Roth (*The War Zone* [1999]) both cast Winstone in the lead roles in their debut films. As the brutal, wife-bashing, foul-mouthed Ray in *Nil by Mouth* and the psychologically disturbed father who regularly commits incest with his daughter in *The War Zone*, Winstone's performances added depth to vile characters who could have so easily been stereotyped as purely evil. In *The War Zone*, for example, Winstone, as a serial sexual offender, avoids any hint of melodramatic traits that would signal his behavior as aberrant. Instead, much of the film's power emanates from his ability to convincingly present himself as a normal, caring parent. This, in turn, creates a disturbing moral dimension within the overall film.

Thick-set and physically imposing, it is no surprise that Winstone's background included a long stint as an amateur boxer, beginning when he was 12 and winning medals, trophies, and English representation in the sport. He also admired James Cagney. Both actors often portrayed a streetwise, aggressive image, and both projected a sense of danger and confrontation, even in their tender scenes. Winstone studied acting as a teenager, before expulsion, at the Corona School. This did little for his employment prospects, and he had decided to forgo acting when director Alan Clarke cast him in the lead role in *Scum*, a television film focusing on violence within a reform school. When the BBC shelved *Scum*, Winstone worked in a range of low-paying jobs, such as selling fruit, before the decision to convert *Scum* into a feature film revived his acting ambitions. He followed it with other dramas involving teenage violence, such as *Quadrophenia* (1979) and

*That Summer* (1979). This film consolidated his career with a BAFTA nomination for the most promising newcomer to a leading film role.

Winstone was prolific in television throughout the 1980s and early 1990s and in films from the mid-1990s, with a lead role in Ken Loach's *Ladybird, Ladybird* (1994); in the tough crime/revenge drama *Face* (1997) as Dave the robber, who betrays fellow criminal Robert Carlyle; and in *Nil by Mouth*, winning international recognition for Winstone and a BAFTA best actor nomination. Winstone also costarred with Ben Kingsley in *Sexy Beast* (2000), and although Kingsley had the more extroverted role as the psychotic hit man, it was Winstone's film as the ex-criminal retiring to Spain while trying to extricate himself from his criminal associates in Britain. *Sexy Beast* also established him as a leading man, albeit a dangerous one with a criminal past.

In 2000 he costarred with Jude Law and Jonny Lee Miller in the gangster film *Love, Honour and Obey*, followed by a more successful film, Fred Schepisi's bittersweet *Last Orders* (2001), which details the journey of four men who decide to scatter the ashes of an old friend, Michael Caine, in the sea. *Ripley's Game* (2002), Liliana Cavani's failed attempt to bring duplicate the success of *The Talented Mr. Ripley* (1999), was next. Winstone also worked regularly in television with his own crime series *(Vincent)*, as well as visiting the United States to act in films such as *Cold Mountain* (2004). He even spent time in Australia as Captain Stanley, opposite Guy Pearce and Danny Huston, in *The Proposition* (2005), John Hillcoat's bleak, violent revenge tale set in the Australian outback in the nineteenth century.

**Selected Noir Films:** *Scum* (1979), *Ladybird, Ladybird* (1994), *Nil by Mouth* (1997), *Face* (1997), *Final Cut* (1998), *The War Zone* (1999), *Agnes Browne* (1999), *Love, Honour and Obey* (2000), *Sexy Beast* (2000), *Ripley's Game* (2002), *Everything* (2004), *The Proposition* (2005), *The Departed* (2006).

Geoff Mayer

**THE WOMAN IN THE WINDOW** (RKO, 1944). *Director:* Fritz Lang. *Producer:* Nunnally Johnson. *Script:* Nunnally Johnson, based on the novel *Once Off Guard* by J. H. Wallis. *Cinematography:* Milton Krasner. *Music:* Arthur Lange. *Cast:* Edward G. Robinson (Richard Wanley), Joan Bennett (Alice Reed), Raymond Massey (Frank Lalor), Dan Duryea (Heidt), Edmond Breon (Dr. Barkstane), Thomas E. Jackson (Inspector Jackson), Arthur Loft (Claude Mazard).

In 1944 and 1945, director Fritz Lang made two noir films in Hollywood that reflected his background in the Weimar cinema in Germany in the 1920s. Both films, *The Woman in the Window* at RKO in 1944 and *Scarlet Street* at Universal in 1945, starred Edward G. Robinson, Joan Bennett, and Dan Duryea, and each is a key film in the development of film noir in Hollywood in the 1940s as both films confronted the normal Hollywood tendency to polarize characters as being either good or evil. In these films, however, he portrays an unassuming, middle-aged,

*The Woman in the Window* (1944). Directed by Fritz Lang. Shown from left: Joan Bennett (as Alice Reed), Edward G. Robinson (as Richard Wanley). RKO Radio Pictures Inc./Photofest.

normal man who, through different circumstances, is forced to kill. Also, each film refused to abide by the classical Hollywood convention that normally requires films to resolve their plots with a clear-cut and logical ending.

*The Woman in the Window* begins with the central protagonist, Professor Wanley, delivering a lecture to his students that explores situations in which a person may commit murder. His lecture foreshadows the film's plot, which provides an opportunity for a conservative, middle-class male, Wanley, to act out his repressed desires, desires that involve the possibility of illicit sex and, as a consequence, lead to death and, seemingly, suicide. After bidding farewell to his wife and young children at a train station in New York as they leave town for a vacation, Wanley goes to his all-male club for a drink with friends, district attorney Frank Lalor and surgeon Dr. Barkstane. Lalor and Barkstane jokingly tease Wanley with the possibilities offered by his so-called freedom and the fact that for the next few days he can live a bachelor's life. After they leave, he goes into the club library and falls asleep reading a sensual text. He then stops in front of an art gallery window to admire a portrait of a beautiful woman, an action that he has told his friends earlier in the evening he has done before. On this occasion, however, a woman, Alice Reed, who posed for the painting, appears next to him on the street. Her startling costume of dark feathers and a black dress with a matching hat indicates that she may be a high-class call girl, a notion that is reinforced by her invitation to Wanley to join her for a drink. Wanley accepts her offer, and they go back to her apartment so that she can show him other sketches by the same artist.

Their intimacy is suddenly violated by a jealous lover who enters Reed's apartment and attacks Wanley. To protect himself, he accepts the scissors handed to him by Alice, and he stabs and kills the intruder, who is revealed to be Reed's benefactor, wealthy businessman Claude Mazard. Thereafter Wanley's life becomes a nightmare. Fearing a scandal, he drives in the early hours of the morning along the Henry Hudson Parkway with Mazard's body in his car trunk. The road is deserted, except for a lone motorcycle cop waiting to book unsuspecting motorists at a traffic light. Wanley then dumps the body in parkland at one of the exits just outside of Manhattan.

The investigation into the killing involves his friend district attorney Frank Lalor, and Lalor insists that Wanley accompany him during the investigation, including a visit to the parkland, where Wanley nearly takes Lalor directly to the body. This scene is indicative of the investigation where, the film suggests, Wanley harbors a repressed desire to be caught and punished as he makes a number of "Freudian" slips to Lalor. However, his friend is oblivious to these mistakes as Wanley is too respectable to be a murderer. His situation deteriorates when a blackmailer, Heidt, learns that Wanley and Reed killed Mazard. Finally, after failing to poison Heidt, Wanley realizes that the situation is hopeless, and he commits suicide by taking a fatal overdose of tablets prescribed to him by his friend Dr. Barkstane. Director Fritz Lang shows Wanley's "death" via a slow track-in and a slow track-out to reveal that everything in the body of the film, after Wanley had fallen asleep at his club, was a dream.

While this deception may have been motivated, in part, by a need to accommodate the demands of the Production Code Authority, it serves a clever ideological purpose since it allows *The Woman in the Window* to function as a conservative morality play while simultaneously indulging the audience in the vicarious pleasure of watching a middle-aged man being punished for acting on his repressed desires while mitigating his punishment with a happy ending. After waking up, Wanley leaves the club and passes by the gallery window, with its painting of the beautiful woman he desires. Another young woman in a provocative costume approaches him for a match for her cigarette. Wanley's reaction is to run away from the woman and from his repressed desire for the forbidden pleasure she offers.

On this level *The Woman in the Window* functions as a conservative parable that warns of the dangers in following one's desires and straying too far from home and family. Yet it is also a fascinating exploration of the thin line between immorality and respectability and how easy it is for the normal person to be caught up in death and deceit. When Lang continued this theme in his next film, *Scarlet Street,* the middle-class protagonist, played by Edward G. Robinson, does not survive through the convenient device offered by dream in *The Woman in the Window;* this time, insanity results from acting on his repressed desires.

Geoff Mayer

# Selected Bibliography

Altman, Rick. *Film/Genre*. London: British Film Institute, 1999.

Andrew, Geoff. *The Films of Nicholas Ray*. London: British Film Institute, 2004.

Bassett, Mark T., ed. 1991. *Blues of a Lifetime: The Autobiography of Cornell Woolrich*. Bowling Green, OH: Bowling Green State University Popular Press.

Biesen, Sheri C. *Blackout: World War II and the Origins of Film Noir*. Baltimore: John Hopkins University Press, 2005.

Borde, Raymond, and Etienne Chaumeton. *Panorama du film noir Américain (1941–1953)*. Paris: Éditions de Minuit, 1955. Translated by Paul Hammond as *A Panorama of American Film Noir, 1941–1953* (San Francisco: City Lights Books, 2002).

Bould, Mark. *Film Noir: From Berlin to Sin City*. London: Wallflower Press, 2005.

Buss, Robin. *French Film Noir*. London: Marion Boyars, 2001.

Cameron, Ian, ed. *The Movie Book of Film Noir*. London: Studio Vista, 1992.

Chibnall, Steve, and Robert Murphy, eds. *British Crime Cinema*. London: Routledge, 1999.

Christopher, Nicholas. *Somewhere in the Night: Film Noir and the American City*. New York: Free Press, 1997.

Clark, Al. *Raymond Chandler in Hollywood*. Los Angeles: Silman-James Press, 1996.

Cochran, David. *America Noir: Underground Writers and Filmmakers of the Postwar Era*. Washington, DC: Smithsonian Institution Press, 2000.

Copjec, Joan, ed. *Shades of Noir: A Reader*. London: Verso, 1993.

Crowther, Bruce. *Film Noir: Reflections in a Dark Mirror*. London: Columbus, 1988.

Dargis, Manohla. *L.A. Confidential*. London: British Film Institute, 2003.

Dickos, Andrew. *Street with No Name: A History of the Classic American Film Noir*. Lexington: University Press of Kentucky, 2002.

Dimenberg, Edward. 2004. *Film Noir and the Spaces of Modernity*. Cambridge, Massachusetts and London, England: Harvard University Press.

Dixon, Wheeler Wilson, ed. *American Cinema of the 1940s: Themes and Variations*. Oxford, UK: Berg Publishing, 2006.

Dyer, Richard. *Se7en*. London: British Film Institute, 1999.

Eaton, Michael. *Chinatown*. London: British Film Institute, 1997.

Friedrich, Otto. *City of Nets: A Portrait of Hollywood in the 1940s*. Berkeley and Los Angeles: University of California Press, 1986.

Fujiwara, Chris. *The Cinema of Nightfall: Jacques Tourneur*. Baltimore: John Hopkins University Press, 1998.

Gates, Philippa. *Detecting Men: Masculinity and the Hollywood Detective Film*. Albany: State University of New York Press, 2006.

Gifford, Barry. *Out of the Past: Adventures in Film Noir*. Jackson: University Press of Mississippi, 2001.

Hare, William. *Early Film Noir: Greed, Lust, and Murder Hollywood Style*. Jefferson, NC: McFarland, 2003.

Heimann, Jim. *Sins of the City: The Real Los Angeles Noir*. San Francisco: Chronicle Books, 1999.

Higham, Charles, and Joel Greenberg. *Hollywood in the Forties*. New York: A. Zwemmer and A. 8S. Barnes, 1968.

Hirsch, Foster. *The Dark Side of the Screen: Film Noir*. New York: Da Capo Press, 1983.

———. *Detours and Lost Highways: A Map of Neo-Noir*. New York: Limelight Editions, 1999.

Kaplan, Elizabeth Ann. *Women in Film Noir*. London: British Film Institute, 1998.

Kitses, Jim. *Gun Crazy*. London: British Film Institute, 1996.

Krutnik, Frank. *In a Lonely Street: Film Noir, Genre, Masculinity*. London: Routledge, 1991.

Leitch, Thomas. *Crime Films*. Cambridge: Cambridge University Press, 2002.

Love, Damien. *Robert Mitchum: Solid, Dad, Crazy*. London: B. T. Batsford, 2002.

Luhr, William. *Raymond Chandler and Film*. Tallahassee: Florida State University Press, 1991.

Lyons, Arthur. *Death on the Cheap: The Lost Movies of Film Noir*. New York: Da Capo Press, 2000.

Maxfield, James F. *The Fatal Woman: Sources of Male Anxiety in American Film Noir, 1941–1991*. London: Associated University Presses, 1996.

Mayer, Geoff. *Roy Ward Baker*. Manchester, UK: Manchester University Press, 2004.

McArthur, Colin *The Big Heat*. London: British Film Institute, 1992.

McCarthy, Todd, and Charles Flynn, eds. *Kings of the Bs: Working within the Hollywood System*. New York: E. P. Dutton, 1975.

Muller, Eddie. *Dark City: The Lost World of Film Noir*. London: Titan Books, 1998.

———. *Dark City Dames: The Wicked Women of Film Noir*. New York: Regan Books, 2001.

Murphy, Robert. *Realism and Tinsel: Cinema and Society in Britain, 1939–1948*. London: Routledge, 1989.

Naremore, James. *More Than Night: Film Noir in Its Contexts*. Los Angeles: University of California Press, 1998.

Neale, Steve. *Genre and Hollywood*. London: Routledge, 2000.

Neve, Brian. *Film and Politics in America: A Social Tradition*. London: Routledge, 1992.

Nevins, Francis M., Jr. *Cornell Woolrich: First You Dream, Then You Die*. New York: Mysterious Press, 1988.

O'Brien, Geoffrey. *Hardboiled America: Lurid Paperbacks and the Masters of Noir*. New York: Da Capo Press, 1997.

Palmer, R. Barton. *Hollywood's Dark Cinema: The American Film Noir*. New York: Twayne, 1994.

———, ed. *Perspectives on Film Noir*. New York: G. K. Hall, 1996.

Phillips, Gene D. *Creatures of Darkness: Raymond Chandler, Detective Fiction, and Film Noir*. Lexington: University Press of Kentucky, 2000.

Polan, Dana. *In a Lonely Place*. London: British Film Institute, 1993.

Porfirio, Robert, A. Silver, and J. Ursini, eds. *Film Noir Reader 3*. New York: Limelight Editions, 2002.

Rabinowitz, Paula. *Black and White and Noir: America's Pulp Modernism*. New York: Columbia University Press, 2002.

Richardson, Carl. *Autopsy: An Element of Realism in Film Noir*. Metuchen, NJ: Scarecrow Press, 1992.

Schatz, Thomas. *Boom and Bust: The American Cinema in the 1940s*. New York: Charles Scribner's Sons, 1997.

Schickel, Richard. *Double Indemnity*. London: British Film Institute, 1992.

Schwartz, Ronald. *Neo-Noir: The New Film Noir Style from Psycho to Collateral*. Lanham, MD: Scarecrow Press, 2005.

Selby, Spencer. *Dark City: The Film Noir*. Jefferson, NC: McFarland, 1997.

Server, Lee. *Encyclopedia of Pulp Fiction Writers*. New York: Checkmark Books, 2002.

Siegel, Joel. E. *Val Lewton: The Reality of Terror*. London: Secker and Warburg, 1972.

Silver, Alain, and James Ursini, eds. *Film Noir Reader*. New York: Limelight Editions, 1996.

———, eds. *Film Noir Reader 2*. New York: Limelight Editions, 1999.

———. *The Noir Style*. London: Aurum Press, 1999.

———. *Film Noir*. Cologne, Germany: Taeschen, 2004.

———, eds. *Film Noir Reader 4*. New York: Limelight Editions, 2004.

———. *L.A. Noir: The City As Character*. Santa Monica, CA: Santa Monica Press, 2005.

Silver, Alain, and Elizabeth Ward. *Film Noir: An Encyclopedic Reference to the American Style*. New York: Overlook Press, 1992.

Smith, R. J. *The Great Black Way: L.A. in the 1940s and the Lost African American Renaissance*. New York: Public Affairs/Perseus, 2006.

Spicer, Andrew. *Film Noir*. Harlow, UK: Longman, 2002.

Taubin, Amy. *Taxi Driver*. London: British Film Institute, 2000.

Telotte, J. P. *Dreams of Darkness: Fantasy and the Films of Val Lewton*. Chicago: University of Illinois Press, 1985.

Thomson, David. *The Big Sleep*. London: British Film Institute, 1997.

Tuska, Jon. *Dark Cinema: American "Film Noir" in a Cultural Perspective*. Westport, CT: Greenwood Press, 1984.

Wager, Jans. B. *Dames in the Driver's Seat: Rereading Film Noir*. Austin: University of Texas Press, 2005.

Williams, Tony. *Structures of Desire: British Cinema, 1939–1955*. Albany: State University of New York Press, 2000.

Wilt, David. *Hardboiled in Hollywood*. Bowling Green, OH: Bowling Green State University Popular Press, 1991.

# Index

Note: Page numbers in *italic* type refer to illustrations.

**About the Authors**

GEOFF MAYER is a Reader and Associate Professor in Cinema Studies at La Trobe University. He is Head of the School of Communication, Arts and Critical Enquiry. His previous books include: *Roy Ward Baker* (2004), *Guide to British Cinema* (Greenwood, 2003), *The Oxford Companion to Australian Film* (1999), and *New Australian Cinema* (1992). His most recent book is the co-edited volume, *The Cinema of Australia and New Zealand* (2007).

BRIAN MCDONNELL is an experienced film teacher and researcher with a PhD from the University of Auckland. He is currently a Senior Lecturer in Film Studies and Program Coordinator in Media Studies at the Auckland campus of Massey University in New Zealand. His previous publications include the book *Fresh Approaches to Film* (1998) and chapters in the Italian encyclopaedias *Storia del Cinema Mondiale* and *Dizionario del registi del cinema mondiale*.